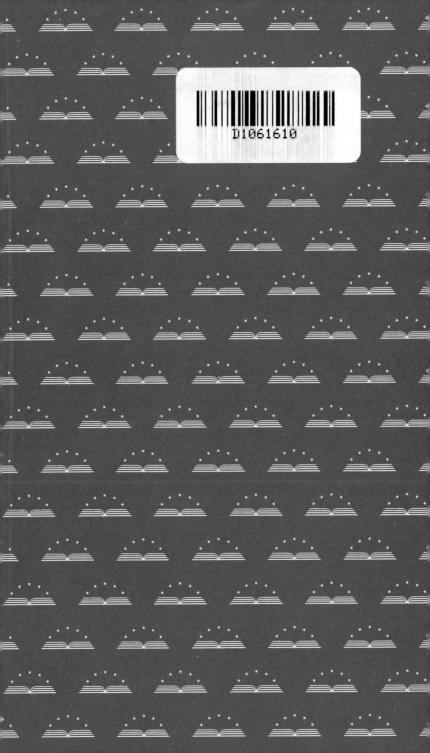

BENJAMIN FRANKLIN

Benjamin Franklin

AUTOBIOGRAPHY, POOR RICHARD, AND LATER WRITINGS

Letters from London, 1757–1775
Paris, 1776–1785
Philadelphia, 1785–1790
Poor Richard's Almanack, 1733–1758
The Autobiography

J. A. Leo Lemay, *editor*

THE LIBRARY OF AMERICA

This paper meets the requirements of
ANSI/NISO Z39.48–1992 (Permanence of Paper).

Distributed to the trade in the United States
by Penguin Random House Inc. and
in Canada by Penguin Random House Canada Ltd.

Library of Congress Catalog Card Number: 97–21611
For cataloging information, see end of the index.
ISBN 978–1–883011–53–6
ISBN 1–883011–53–1

———

Seventh Printing
Originally published with additional material
as *Writings* in 1987.

Manufactured in the United States of America

Benjamin Franklin:
Autobiography, Poor Richard, and Later Writings
is kept in print by a gift from

DANIEL AND JOANNA S. ROSE

to the Guardians of American Letters Fund,
established by The Library of America
to ensure that every volume in the series
will be permanently available.

The publishers wish to thank the Library Company of Philadelphia, Historical Society of Pennsylvania, American Philosophical Society, The Papers of Benjamin Franklin, Yale University Library, New-York Historical Society, Columbia University Library, New York Public Library, and Massachusetts Historical Society for the use of archival materials.

Contents

Each section has its own table of contents.

LETTERS FROM LONDON, 1757–1775 I

PARIS, 1776–1785
   Including political satires, bagatelles, pamphlets,
   and letters 169

PHILADELPHIA, 1785–1790
   Including bagatelles, speeches in the Constitutional
   Convention, writings on slavery, letters 371

POOR RICHARD'S ALMANACK, 1733–1758 441

THE AUTOBIOGRAPHY 565

Chronology 731

Note on the Texts 756

Notes 770

Index 791

LETTERS FROM
LONDON
1757–1775

Contents

LETTERS

To ——, [December 13, 1757]
Reasons against satirizing religion 9

John Pringle, December 21, 1757
Electric shocks in paralytic cases 10

John Pringle, January 6, 1758
"strata of the earth" 11

John Lining, June 17, 1758
Cooling by evaporation 12

Jane Mecom, September 16, 1758
Faith, Hope, and Charity 16

Hugh Roberts, September 16, 1758
"Happiness in this Life" 19

Lord Kames, January 3, 1760
"Conversation warms the Mind" 20

Jane Mecom, January 9, 1760
"the more they are respected" 24

Lord Kames, May 3, 1760
"The Art of Virtue" 26

Peter Franklin, May 7, 1760
Salt deposits 28

Mary Stevenson, June 11, 1760
"The Knowledge of Nature" 29

Mary Stevenson, September 13, 1760
Tides in rivers 31

David Hume, September 27, 1760
"the best English" 36

Mary Stevenson, [November? 1760]
   Color and heat. 38

John Baskerville, [1760?]
   "Prejudice . . . against your Work" 42

Peter Franklin, [c. 1761]
   Faults in songs. 43

David Hume, May 19, 1762
   "a Case in Point". 47

Giambatista Beccaria, July 13, 1762
   The glass armonica 49

Oliver Neave, July 20, 1762
   Sound 53

John Pringle, December 1, 1762
   Oil and water. 55

Jared Ingersoll, December 11, 1762
   "I look'd round for God's Judgments". 56

Mary Stevenson, March 25, 1763
   "the Arts delight to travel Westward". 57

John Waring, December 17, 1763
   "the natural Capacities of the black Race" 60

William Strahan, December 19, 1763
   "like a Morning Fog before the rising Sun" 61

John Fothergill, March 14, 1764
   "an Ambassador to the Country Mob" 63

Peter Collinson, April 30, 1764
   "So selfish is the human Mind!" 66

Sarah Franklin, November 8, 1764
   "Go constantly to Church whoever preaches". 69

Lord Kames, June 2, 1765
   The old songs versus modern music. 70

Charles Thomson, July 11, 1765
   "We might as well have hinder'd the Suns setting". . . . 76

Jane Mecom, March 1, 1766
"a pretty good sort of a World"
[with Stamp Act cartoon: "Magna Britannia:
her Colonies Reduc'd"]   77

Deborah Franklin, April 6, 1766
"I never was prouder of any Dress in my Life"   79

Cadwalader Evans, May 9, 1766
"a brazen Wall round England for its eternal Security" . .   81

Joseph Galloway, November 8, 1766
"Dirt . . . will not long adhere to polish'd Marble"   82

Mary Stevenson, September 14, 1767
"Travelling is one Way of lengthening Life"   83

Margaret Stevenson, November 3, [1767]
"condemn'd to live together and tease one another" . . .   88

Jane Mecom, December 24, 1767
*"a Collection for you of all the past Parings of my
Nails"*   89

William Franklin, January 9, 1768
"I am too much of an American"   91

Jean Chappe d'Auteroche, January 31, 1768
Fossils.   92

John Pringle, May 10, 1768
Canal depths and ship movement   93

Jacques Barbeu-Dubourg, July 28, 1768
Cold air baths   95

John Alleyne, [August 9, 1768]
"the Usefulness of an odd Half of a Pair of Scissars" . . .   96

Mary Stevenson, October 28, 1768
"God governs; and he is good"   98

To ———, November 28, 1768
"at present I almost despair"   100

Oliver Neave, [before 1769]
Learning to swim   101

John Bartram, July 9, 1769
  "a Receipt for making Parmesan Cheese" 104

George Whitefield, [before September 2, 1769]
  "affairs are perhaps below notice" 105

Mary Stevenson, September 2, 1769
  *"whoever scruples cheating the King will certainly
  not wrong his Neighbour"* 106

Timothy Folger, September 29, 1769
  "the true Sources of Wealth and Plenty" 107

William Strahan, November 29, 1769
  "I hope however that this may all prove false Prophecy" . . 110

[Charles Thomson], March 18, 1770
  "if we are steady and persevere in our Resolutions". . . 116

Mary Stevenson, May 31, 1770
  *"I should think you a Fortune sufficient for me
  without a Shilling"* 118

Samuel Cooper, June 8, 1770
  "the sole Legislator of his American Subjects" 119

Mary Stevenson Hewson, July 18, 1770
  "hitherto made no Attempt upon my Virtue" 122

Deborah Franklin, October 3, 1770
  "have you then got ne'er a Grandmother?" 122

Jane Mecom, December 30, 1770
  "this World is the true Hell" 123

Thomas Percival, [June? 1771]
  How raindrops grow 126

Jane Mecom, July 17, 1771
  "an Adventure to gain forbidden Knowledge" 128

Anna Mordaunt Shipley, August 13, 1771
  "what sort of Husbands would be fittest" 132

Joshua Babcock, January 13, 1772
  "compar'd to these People every Indian is a Gentleman" . . 134

Ezra Stiles, January 13, 1772
   On the writings of Zoroaster 136

Anthony Benezet, August 22, 1772
   "suppress'd by the Legislature" 137

Samuel Rhoads, August 22, 1772
   "Rivers are ungovernable Things" 137

Joseph Priestley, September 19, 1772
   "Moral or Prudential Algebra" 138

Georgiana Shipley, September 26, 1772
   "Alas! poor Mungo!" 139

William Marshall, February 14, 1773
   "the Increase of Religious as well as Civil Liberty" . . . 141

Samuel Mather, July 7, 1773
   "Stoop! Stoop!" 141

Benjamin Rush, July 14, 1773
   Causes of colds 144

William Franklin, October 6, 1773
   *"I'll be hanged if this is not some of your American
   jokes upon us"* 146

Peter P. Burdett, November 3, 1773
   Transfer prints on tiles 148

William Brownrigg, November 7, 1773
   Oil on water 150

Josiah Tucker, February 12, 1774
   "nothing can be farther from the truth" 159

Josiah Tucker, February 26, 1774
   "my supposed Application to Mr. Grenville" . . . 160

Joseph Priestley, April 10, 1774
   Flame on New Jersey rivers 163

William Strahan, July 5, 1775
   "You are now my Enemy" 165

[Joseph Priestley], July 7, 1775
  "this is a harder nut to crack than they imagined".   .   .   .   165

David Hartley, October 3, 1775
  "there is no little enemy".   167

LETTERS

To ———

Dear Sir

I have read your Manuscrit with some Attention. By the Arguments it contains against the Doctrine of a particular Providence, tho' you allow a general Providence, you strike at the Foundation of all Religion: For without the Belief of a Providence that takes Cognizance of, guards and guides and may favour particular Persons, there is no Motive to Worship a Deity, to fear its Displeasure, or to pray for its Protection. I will not enter into any Discussion of your Principles, tho' you seem to desire it; At present I shall only give you my Opinion that tho' your Reasonings are subtle, and may prevail with some Readers, you will not succeed so as to change the general Sentiments of Mankind on that Subject, and the Consequence of printing this Piece will be a great deal of Odium drawn upon your self, Mischief to you and no Benefit to others. He that spits against the Wind, spits in his own Face. But were you to succeed, do you imagine any Good would be done by it? You yourself may find it easy to live a virtuous Life without the Assistance afforded by Religion; you having a clear Perception of the Advantages of Virtue and the Disadvantages of Vice, and possessing a Strength of Resolution sufficient to enable you to resist common Temptations. But think how great a Proportion of Mankind consists of weak and ignorant Men and Women, and of inexperienc'd and inconsiderate Youth of both Sexes, who have need of the Motives of Religion to restrain them from Vice, to support their Virtue, and retain them in the Practice of it till it becomes *habitual*, which is the great Point for its Security; And perhaps you are indebted to her originally that is to your Religious Education, for the Habits of Virtue upon which you now justly value yourself. You might easily display your excellent Talents of reasoning on a less hazardous Subject, and thereby obtain Rank with our most distinguish'd Authors. For among us, it is not necessary, as among the Hottentots that a Youth to be receiv'd into the Company of

Men, should prove his Manhood by beating his Mother. I would advise you therefore not to attempt unchaining the Tyger, but to burn this Piece before it is seen by any other Person, whereby you will save yourself a great deal of Mortification from the Enemies it may raise against you, and perhaps a good deal of Regret and Repentance. If Men are so wicked as we now see them *with Religion* what would they be if *without it*? I intend this Letter itself as a *Proof* of my Friendship and therefore add no *Professions* of it, but subscribe simply Yours

December 13, 1757

ELECTRIC SHOCKS IN PARALYTIC CASES

To John Pringle

Sir   Dec. 21. 1757

The following is what I can at present recollect, relating to the Effects of Electricity in Paralytic Cases, which have fallen under my Observation.

Some Years since, when the News papers made Mention of great Cures perform'd in Italy or Germany by means of Electricity, a Number of Paralytics were brought to me from different Parts of Pensilvania and the neighbouring Provinces, to be electris'd, which I did for them, at their Request. My Method was, to place the Patient first in a Chair on an electric Stool, and draw a Number of large strong Sparks from all Parts of the affected Limb or Side. Then I fully charg'd two 6 Gallon Glass Jarrs, each of which had about 3 square feet of Surface coated and I sent the united Shock of these thro' the affected Limb or Limbs, repeating the Stroke commonly three Times each Day. The first Thing observ'd was an immediate greater sensible Warmth in the lame Limbs that had receiv'd the Stroke than in the others; and the next Morning the Patients usually related that they had in the Night felt a pricking Sensation in the Flesh of the paralytic Limbs, and would sometimes shew a Number of small red Spots which they suppos'd were occasion'd by those Prickings: The Limbs too were found more capable of voluntary Motion, and seem'd to receive Strength; a Man, for Instance, who could not, the first Day, lift the lame Hand from off his Knee, would the next Day raise it four or five Inches, the third Day higher, and on the fifth Day was able, but with a feeble languid Motion, to take off his Hat. These Appearances gave great Spirits to the Patients, and made them hope a perfect Cure; but I do not remember that I ever saw any Amendment after the fifth Day: Which the Patients perceiving, and finding the Shocks pretty severe, they became discourag'd, went home and in a short time relapsed; so that I never knew any Advantage from Electricity in Palsies that was permanent. And how far the apparent temporary Advantage might arise from the Exercise in the Patients Journey and coming daily to my House, or from the Spirits given by the Hope of Success, enabling them to exert more Strength in moving their Limbs, I will not pretend to say.

Perhaps some permanent Advantage might have been obtained, if the Electric Shocks had been accompanied with proper Medicine and Regimen, under the Direction of a skilful Physician. It may be, too, that a few great Strokes, as given in my Method, may not be so proper as many small ones; since by the Account from Scotland of the Case in which 200 Shocks from a Phial were given daily, seems that a perfect Cure has been made. As to any uncommon Strength supposed to be in the Machine used in that Case, I imagine it could have no Share in the Effect produced; since the Strength of the Shock from charg'd Glass, is in proportion to the Quantity of Surface of the Glass coated; so that my Shocks from those large Jarrs must have been much greater than any that could be received from a Phial held in the hand.

I am, with great Respect, Sir, Your most obedient Servant

"STRATA OF THE EARTH"

To John Pringle

SIR,   *Craven-street, Jan. 6, 1758.*

I return Mr. *Mitchell's* paper on the strata of the earth* with thanks. The reading of it, and perusal of the draft that

*See this Paper afterwards printed in the *Philosophical Transactions*.

accompanies it, have reconciled me to those convulsions
which all naturalists agree this globe has suffered. Had the
different strata of clay, gravel, marble, coals, lime-stone, sand,
minerals, &c. continued to lie level, one under the other, as
they may be supposed to have done before those convulsions,
we should have had the use only of a few of the uppermost
of the strata, the others lying too deep and too difficult to be
come at; but the shell of the earth being broke, and the fragments thrown into this oblique position, the disjointed ends
of a great number of strata of different kinds are brought up
to day, and a great variety of useful materials put into our
power, which would otherwise have remained eternally con-
cealed from us. So that what has been usually looked upon as
a *ruin* suffered by this part of the universe, was, in reality,
only a preparation, or means of rendering the earth more fit
for use, more capable of being to mankind a convenient and
comfortable habitation.

I am, Sir, with great esteem, yours, &c.

COOLING BY EVAPORATION

To John Lining

Dear Sir,   *London, June* 17, 1758.
   In a former letter I mentioned the experiment for cooling
bodies by evaporation, and that I had, by repeatedly wetting
the thermometer with common spirits, brought the mercury
down five or six degrees. Being lately at *Cambridge*, and
mentioning this in conversation with Dr. *Hadley*, professor
of chemistry there, he proposed repeating the experiments
with ether, instead of common spirits, as the ether is much
quicker in evaporation. We accordingly went to his chamber,
where he had both ether and a thermometer. By dipping
first the ball of the thermometer into the ether, it appeared
that the ether was precisely of the same temperament with
the thermometer, which stood then at 65; for it made no alteration in the height of the little column of mercury. But
when the thermometer was taken out of the ether, and the
ether with which the ball was wet, began to evaporate, the

mercury sunk several degrees. The wetting was then repeated by a feather that had been dipped into the ether, when the mercury sunk still lower. We continued this operation, one of us wetting the ball, and another of the company blowing on it with the bellows, to quicken the evaporation, the mercury sinking all the time, till it came down to 7, which is 25 degrees below the freezing point, when we left off.—Soon after it passed the freezing point, a thin coat of ice began to cover the ball. Whether this was water collected and condensed by the coldness of the ball, from the moisture in the air, or from our breath; or whether the feather, when dipped into the ether, might not sometimes go through it, and bring up some of the water that was under it, I am not certain; perhaps all might contribute. The ice continued increasing till we ended the experiment, when it appeared near a quarter of an inch thick all over the ball, with a number of small spicula, pointing outwards. From this experiment one may see the possibility of freezing a man to death on a warm summer's day, if he were to stand in a passage thro' which the wind blew briskly, and to be wet frequently with ether, a spirit that is more inflammable than brandy, or common spirits of wine.

It is but within these few years, that the *European* philosophers seem to have known this power in nature, of cooling bodies by evaporation. But in the east they have long been acquainted with it. A friend tells me, there is a passage in *Bernier*'s travels through *Indostan*, written near one hundred years ago, that mentions it as a practice (in travelling over dry desarts in that hot climate) to carry water in flasks wrapt in wet woollen cloths, and hung on the shady side of the camel, or carriage, but in the free air; whereby, as the cloths gradually grow drier, the water contained in the flasks is made cool. They have likewise a kind of earthen pots, unglaz'd, which let the water gradually and slowly ooze through their pores, so as to keep the outside a little wet, notwithstanding the continual evaporation, which gives great coldness to the vessel, and the water contained in it. Even our common sailors seem to have had some notion of this property; for I remember, that being at sea, when I was a youth, I observed one of the sailors, during a calm in the

night, often wetting his finger in his mouth, and then holding it up in the air, to discover, as he said, if the air had any
motion, and from which side it came; and this he expected
to do, by finding one side of his finger grow suddenly cold,
and from that side he should look for the next wind; which
I then laughed at as a fancy.

May not several phænomena, hitherto unconsidered, or un-
accounted for, be explained by this property? During the hot
Sunday at *Philadelphia*, in *June* 1750, when the thermometer
was up at 100 in the shade, I sat in my chamber without
exercise, only reading or writing, with no other cloaths on
than a shirt, and a pair of long linen drawers, the windows all
open, and a brisk wind blowing through the house, the sweat
ran off the backs of my hands, and my shirt was often so wet,
as to induce me to call for dry ones to put on; in this situation, one might have expected, that the natural heat of the
body 96, added to the heat of the air 100, should jointly have
created or produced a much greater degree of heat in the
body; but the fact was, that my body never grew so hot as
the air that surrounded it, or the inanimate bodies immers'd
in the same air. For I remember well, that the desk, when I
laid my arm upon it; a chair, when I sat down in it; and a
dry shirt out of the drawer, when I put it on, all felt exceeding warm to me, as if they had been warmed before a fire.
And I suppose a dead body would have acquired the temperature of the air, though a living one, by continual sweating,
and by the evaporation of that sweat, was kept cold.—May
not this be a reason why our reapers in *Pensylvania*, working
in the open field, in the clear hot sunshine common in our
harvest-time *, find themselves well able to go through that
labour, without being much incommoded by the heat, while
they continue to sweat, and while they supply matter for
keeping up that sweat, by drinking frequently of a thin evap-
orable liquor, water mixed with rum; but if the sweat stops,
they drop, and sometimes die suddenly, if a sweating is not
again brought on by drinking that liquor, or, as some rather
chuse in that case, a kind of hot punch, made with water,

* *Pensylvania* is in about lat. 40, and the sun, of course, about 12 degrees
higher, and therefore much hotter than in *England*. Their harvest is about
the end of *June*, or beginning of *July*, when the sun is nearly at the highest.

mixed with honey, and a considerable proportion of vine-gar?—May there not be in negroes a quicker evaporation of the perspirable matter from their skins and lungs, which, by cooling them more, enables them to bear the sun's heat better than whites do? (if that is a fact, as it is said to be; for the alledg'd necessity of having negroes rather than whites, to work in the *West-India* fields, is founded upon it) though the colour of their skins would otherwise make them more sensible of the sun's heat, since black cloth heats much sooner, and more, in the sun, than white cloth. I am persuaded, from several instances happening within my knowledge, that they do not bear cold weather so well as the whites; they will perish when exposed to a less degree of it, and are more apt to have their limbs frost-bitten; and may not this be from the same cause? Would not the earth grow much hotter under the summer sun, if a constant evaporation from its surface, greater as the sun shines stronger, did not, by tending to cool it, balance, in some degree, the warmer effects of the sun's rays?—Is it not owing to the constant evaporation from the surface of every leaf, that trees, though shone on by the sun, are always, even the leaves themselves, cool to our sense? at least much cooler than they would otherwise be?—May it not be owing to this, that fanning ourselves when warm, does really cool us, though the air is itself warm that we drive with the fan upon our faces; for the atmosphere round, and next to our bodies, having imbibed as much of the perspired vapour as it can well contain, receives no more, and the evaporation is therefore check'd and retarded, till we drive away that atmosphere, and bring dryer air in its place, that will receive the vapour, and thereby facilitate and increase the evaporation? Certain it is, that mere blowing of air on a dry body does not cool it, as any one may satisfy himself, by blowing with a bellows on the dry ball of a thermometer; the mercury will not fall; if it moves at all, it rather rises, as being warmed by the friction of the air on its surface?—To these queries of imagination, I will only add one practical observation; that wherever it is thought proper to give ease, in cases of painful inflammation in the flesh, (as from burnings, or the like) by cooling the part; linen cloths, wet with spirit, and applied to the part inflamed, will produce the coolness required, better than if wet with water, and will continue it longer. For water, though cold when first applied, will soon acquire warmth from the flesh, as it does not evaporate fast enough; but the cloths wet with spirit, will continue cold as long as any spirit is left to keep up the evaporation, the parts warmed escaping as soon as they are warmed, and carrying off the heat with them.

I am, Sir, &c.

FAITH, HOPE, AND CHARITY

To Jane Mecom

Dear Sister   London Sept 16 1758

I received your Favour of June 17. I wonder you have had no Letter from me since my being in England. I have wrote you at least two and I think a third before this; And, what was next to waiting on you in Person, sent you my Picture. In June last I sent Benny a Trunk of Books and wrote to him. I hope they are come to hand, and that he meets with Incouragement in his Business. I congratulate you on the Conquest of Cape Breton, and hope as your People took it by Praying the first Time, you will now pray that it may never be given up again, which you then forgot. Billy is well but in the Country. I left him at Tunbridge Wells, where we spent a fortnight, and he is now gone with some Company to see Portsmouth.

We have been together over a great part of England this Summer; and among other places visited the Town our Father was born in and found some Relations in that part of the Country Still living. Our Cousin Jane Franklin, daughter of our Unkle John, died but about a Year ago. We saw her Husband Robert Page, who gave us some old Letters to his Wife from unkle Benjamin. In one of them, dated Boston July 4. 1723 he writes "Your Unkle Josiah has a Daughter Jane about 12 years Old, a good humour'd Child" So Jenny keep up your Character, and don't be angry when you have no Letters.

In a little Book he sent her, call'd *None but Christ*, he wrote an Acrostick on her Name, which for Namesakes' Sake, as well as the good Advice it contains, I transcribe and send you

> Illuminated from on High,
> And shining brightly in your Sphere
> Nere faint, but keep a steady Eye
> Expecting endless Pleasures there
> Flee Vice, as you'd a Serpent flee,
> Raise Faith and Hope three Stories higher
> And let Christ's endless Love to thee
> N-ere cease to make thy Love Aspire.
> Kindness of Heart by Words express
> Let your Obedience be sincere,
> In Prayer and Praise your God Address
> Nere cease 'till he can cease to hear.

After professing truly that I have a great Esteem and Veneration for the pious Author, permit me a little to play the Commentator and Critic on these Lines. The Meaning of *Three Stories* higher seems somewhat obscure, you are to understand, then, that *Faith, Hope* and *Charity* have been called the three Steps of Jacob's Ladder, reaching from Earth to Heaven. Our Author calls them *Stories*, likening Religion to a Building, and those the three Stories of the Christian Edifice; Thus Improvement in Religion, is called *Building Up*, and *Edification*. *Faith* is then the Ground-floor, *Hope* is up one Pair of Stairs. My dearly beloved Jenny, don't delight so much to dwell in these lower Rooms, but get as fast as you can into the Garret; for in truth the best Room in the House is *Charity*. For my part, I wish the House was turn'd upside down; 'tis so difficult (when one is fat) to get up Stairs; and not only so, but I imagine *Hope* and *Faith* may be more firmly built on *Charity*, than *Charity* upon *Faith* and *Hope*. However that be, I think it a better reading to say

> Raise Faith and Hope *one Story* higher

correct it boldly and I'll support the Alteration. For when you are up two Stories already, if you raise your Building three Stories higher, you will make five in all, which is two more than there should be, you expose your upper Rooms more to the Winds and Storms, and besides I am afraid the Foundation will hardly bear them, unless indeed you build with such light Stuff as Straw and Stubble, and that you know won't stand Fire.

Again where the Author Says

> Kindness of Heart by Words express,

Stricke out *Words* and put in *Deeds*. The world is too full of Compliments already; they are the rank Growth of every Soil, and Choak the good Plants of Benevolence and Benificence, Nor do I pretend to be the first in this comparison of Words and Actions to Plants; you may remember an Ancient Poet whose Words we have all Studied and Copy'd at School, said long ago,

> A Man of Words and not of Deeds,
> Is like a Garden full of Weeds.

'Tis pity that *Good Works* among some sorts of People are so little Valued, and *Good Words* admired in their Stead; I mean seemingly *pious Discourses* instead of *Humane Benevolent Actions*. These they almost put out of countenance, by calling Morality *rotten Morality*, Righteousness, *ragged Righteousness* and even *filthy Rags*; and when you mention *Virtue*, they pucker up their Noses as if they smelt a Stink; at the same time that they eagerly snuff up an empty canting Harangue, as if it was a Posie of the Choicest Flowers. So they have inverted the good old Verse, and say now

> A Man of Deeds and not of Words
> Is like a Garden full of ——

I have forgot the Rhime, but remember 'tis something the very Reverse of a Perfume. So much by Way of Commentary.

My Wife will let you see my Letter containing an Account of our Travels, which I would have you read to Sister Douse, and give my Love to her. I have no thoughts of returning 'till next year, and then may possibly have the Pleasure of seeing you and yours, take Boston in my Way home. My Love to Brother and all your Children, concludes at this time from Dear Jenny your affectionate Brother

To Hugh Roberts

Dear Friend, London, Sept. 16. 1758

Your kind Letter of June 1. gave me great Pleasure. I thank you for the Concern you express about my Health, which at present seems tolerably confirm'd by my late Journeys into different Parts of the Kingdom, that have been highly entertaining as well as useful to me. Your Visits to my little Family in my Absence are very obliging, and I hope you will be so good as to continue them. Your Remark on the Thistle and the Scotch Motto, made us very merry, as well as your String of Puns. You will allow me to claim a little Merit or Demerit in the last, as having had some hand in making you a Punster; but the Wit of the first is keen, and all your own.

Two of the former Members of the Junto you tell me are departed this Life, Potts and Parsons. Odd Characters, both of them. Parsons, a wise Man, that often acted foolishly. Potts, a Wit, that seldom acted wisely. If *Enough* were the Means to make a Man happy, One had always the *Means* of Happiness without ever enjoying the *Thing*; the other had always the *Thing* without ever possessing the Means. Parsons, even in his Prosperity, always fretting! Potts, in the midst of his Poverty, ever laughing! It seems, then, that Happiness in this Life rather depends on Internals than Externals; and that, besides the natural Effects of Wisdom and Virtue, Vice and Folly, there is such a Thing as being of a happy or an unhappy Constitution. They were both our Friends, and lov'd us. So, Peace to their Shades. They had their Virtues as well as their Foibles; they were both honest Men, and that alone, as the World goes, is one of the greatest of Characters. They were old Acquaintance, in whose Company I formerly enjoy'd a great deal of Pleasure, and I cannot think of losing them, without Concern and Regret.

Let me know in your next, to what Purposes Parsons will'd his Estate from his Family; you hint at something which you have not explain'd.

I shall, as you suppose, look on every Opportunity you give

me of doing you Service, as a Favour, because it will afford me Pleasure. Therefore send your Orders for buying Books as soon as you please. I know how to make you ample Returns for such Favours, by giving you the Pleasure of Building me a House. You may do it without losing any of your own Time; it will only take some Part of that you now spend in other Folks Business. 'Tis only jumping out of their Waters into mine.

I am grieved for our Friend Syng's Loss. You and I, who esteem him, and have valuable Sons ourselves, can sympathise with him sincerely. I hope yours is perfectly recovered, for your sake as well as for his own. I wish he may be in every Respect as good and as useful a Man as his Father. I need not wish him more; and can now only add that I am, with great Esteem, Dear Friend, Yours affectionately

P.S. I rejoice to hear of the Prosperity of the Hospital, and send the Wafers.

I do not quite like your absenting yourself from that good old Club the Junto: Your more frequent PRE SENCE might be a means of keeping them from being ALL ENgag'd in Measures not the best for the Publick Welfare. I exhort you therefore to return to your Duty; and, as the Indians say, to confirm my Words, I send you a Birmingham Tile.

I thought the neatness of the Figures would please you.

Pray send me a good Impression of the Hospital Seal in Wax. 2 or three would not be amiss, I may make a good Use of them.

"CONVERSATION WARMS THE MIND"

To Lord Kames

My dear Lord,   London, Jany. 3. 1760
I ought long before this time to have acknowledg'd the Receipt of your Favour of Nov. 2. Your Lordship was pleas'd kindly to desire to have all my Publications. I had daily Expectations of procuring some of them from a Friend

to whom I formerly sent them when I was in America, and postpon'd Writing till I should obtain them; but at length he tells me he cannot find them. Very mortifying, this, to an Author, that his Works should so soon be lost! So I can now only send you my *Observations on the Peopling of Countries*, which happens to have been reprinted here; The *Description of the Pennsylvanian Fireplace*, a Machine of my contriving; and some little Sketches that have been printed in the Grand Magazine; which I should hardly own, did not I flatter myself that your friendly Partiality would make them seem at least tolerable.

How unfortunate I was, that I did not press you and Lady Kames more strongly, to favour us with your Company farther! How much more agreable would our Journey have been, if we could have enjoy'd you as far as York! Mr. Blake, who we hop'd would have handed us along from Friend to Friend, was not at home, and so we knew nobody and convers'd with nobody on all that long Road, till we came thither. The being a Means of contributing in the least Degree to the restoring that good Lady's Health, would have contributed greatly to our Pleasures, and we could have beguil'd the Way by Discoursing 1000 Things that now we may never have an Opportunity of considering together; for Conversation warms the Mind, enlivens the Imagination, and is continually starting fresh Game that is immediately pursu'd and taken and which would never have occur'd in the duller Intercourse of Epistolary Correspondence. So that whenever I reflect on the great Pleasure and Advantage I receiv'd from the free Communication of Sentiments in the Conversation your Lordship honour'd me with at Kaims, and in the little agreable Rides to the Tweedside, I shall forever regret that unlucky premature Parting.

No one can rejoice more sincerely than I do on the Reduction of Canada; and this, not merely as I am a Colonist, but as I am a Briton. I have long been of Opinion, that the Foundations of the future Grandeur and Stability of the British Empire, lie in America; and tho', like other Foundations, they are low and little seen, they are nevertheless, broad and Strong enough to support the greatest Political Structure Human Wisdom ever yet erected. I am therefore by no means for restoring Canada. If we keep it, all the Country from St. Laurence to Missisipi, will in another Century be fill'd with British People; Britain itself will become vastly more populous by the immense Increase of its Commerce; the Atlantic Sea will be cover'd with your Trading Ships; and your naval Power thence continually increasing, will extend your Influence round the whole Globe, and awe the World! If the French remain in Canada, they will continually harass our Colonies by the Indians, impede if not prevent their Growth; your Progress to Greatness will at best be slow, and give room for many Accidents that may for ever prevent it. But I refrain, for I see you begin to think my Notions extravagant, and look upon them as the Ravings of a mad Prophet.

Your Lordship's kind Offer of Penn's Picture is extreamly obliging. But were it certainly his Picture, it would be too valuable a Curiosity for me to think of accepting it. I should only desire the Favour of Leave to take a Copy of it. I could wish to know the History of the Picture before it came into your Hands, and the Grounds for supposing it his. I have at present some Doubts about it; first, because the primitive Quakers us'd to declare against Pictures as a vain Expence; a Man's suffering his Portrait to be taken was condemn'd as Pride; and I think to this day it is very little practis'd among them. Then it is on a Board, and I imagine the Practice of painting Portraits on Boards did not come down so low as Penn's Time; but of this I am not certain. My other Reason is an Anecdote I have heard, viz. That when old Lord Cobham was adorning his Gardens at Stowe with the Busts of famous Men, he made Enquiry of the Family for a Picture of Wm. Penn, in order to get a Bust form'd from it, but could find none. That Sylvanus Bevan, an old Quaker Apothecary, remarkable for the Notice he takes of Countenances, and a Knack he has of cutting in Ivory strong Likenesses of Persons he has once seen, hearing of Lord Cobham's Desire, set himself to recollect Penn's Face, with which he had been well acquainted; and cut a little Bust of him in Ivory which he sent to Lord Cobham, without any Letter of Notice that it was Penn's. But my Lord who had personally known Penn, on seeing it, immediately cry'd out,

Whence came this? It is William Penn himself! And from this little Bust, they say, the large one in the Gardens was formed. I doubt, too, whether the Whisker was not quite out of Use at the time when Penn must have been of the Age appearing in the Face of that Picture. And yet notwithstanding these Reasons, I am not without some Hope that it may be his; because I know some eminent Quakers have had their Pictures privately drawn, and deposited with trusty Friends; and I know also that there is extant at Philadelphia a very good Picture of Mrs. Penn, his last Wife. After all, I own I have a strong Desire to be satisfy'd concerning this Picture; and as Bevan is yet living here, and some other old Quakers that remember William Penn, who died but in 1718, I could wish to have it sent me carefully pack'd in a Box by the Waggon (for I would not trust it by Sea) that I may obtain their Opinion, The Charges I shall very chearfully pay; and if it proves to be Penn's Picture, I shall be greatly oblig'd to your Lordship for Leave to take a Copy of it, and will carefully return the Original.

My Son joins with me in the most respectful Compliments to you, to Lady Kaims, and your promising and amiable Son and Daughter. He had the Pleasure of conversing more particularly with the latter than I did, and told me, when we were by our selves, that he was greatly surprized to find so much sensible Observation and solid Understanding in so young a Person; and suppos'd you must have us'd with your Children some uncommonly good Method of Education, to produce such Fruits so early. Our Conversation till we came to York was chiefly a Recollection and Recapitulation of what we had seen and heard, the Pleasure we had enjoy'd and the Kindnesses we had receiv'd in Scotland, and how far that Country had exceeded our Expectations. On the whole, I must say, I think the Time we spent there, was Six Weeks of the *densest* Happiness I have met with in any Part of my Life. And the agreable and instructive Society we found there in such Plenty, has left so pleasing an Impression on my Memory, that did not strong Connections draw me elsewhere, I believe Scotland would be the Country I should chuse to spend the Remainder of my Days in.

I have the Honour to be, with the sincerest Esteem and

Affection, My Lord, Your Lordship's most obedient and most humble Servant

PS. My Son puts me in mind that a Book published here last Winter, contains a number of Pieces wrote by me as a Member of the Assembly, in our late Controversies with the Proprietary Governors; so I shall leave one of them at Millar's to be sent to you, it being too bulky to be sent per Post.

"THE MORE THEY ARE RESPECTED"

To Jane Mecom

Dear Sister,   London, Jan. 9. 1760

I received a Letter or two from you, in which I perceive you have misunderstood and taken unkindly something I said to you in a former jocular one of mine concerning CHARITY. I forget what it was exactly, but I am sure I neither express nor meant any personal Censure on you or any body. If anything, it was a general Reflection on our Sect; we zealous Presbyterians being too apt to think ourselves alone in the right, and that besides all the Heathens, Mahometans and Papists, whom we give to Satan in a Lump, other Sects of Christian Protestants that do not agree with us, will hardly escape Perdition. And I might recommend it to you to be more charitable in that respect than many others are; not aiming at any Reproof, as you term it; for if I were dispos'd to reprove you, it should be for your only Fault, that of supposing and spying Affronts, and catching at them where they are not. But as you seem sensible of this yourself, I need not mention it; and as it is a Fault that carries with it its own sufficient Punishment, by the Uneasiness and Fretting it produces, I shall not add Weight to it. Besides, I am sure your own good Sense, join'd to your natural good Humour will in time get the better of it.

I am glad that Cousin Benny could advance you the Legacy, since it suited you best to receive it immediately. Your

Resolution to forbear buying the Cloak you wanted, was a
prudent one; but when I read it, I concluded you should not
however be without one, and so desired a Friend to buy one
for you. The Cloth ones, it seems, are quite out of Fashion
here, and so will probably soon be out with you; I have therefore got you a very decent one of another kind, which I shall
send you by the next convenient Opportunity.

It is remarkable that so many Breaches should be made by
Death in our Family in so short a Space. Out of Seventeen
Children that our Father had, thirteen liv'd to grow up and
settle in the World. I remember these thirteen (some of us
then very young) all at one Table, when an Entertainment
was made in our House on Occasion of the Return of our
Brother Josiah, who had been absent in the East-Indies, and
unheard of for nine Years. Of these thirteen, there now remains but three. As our Number diminishes, let our Affection to each other rather increase: for besides its being our
Duty, tis our Interest, since the more affectionate Relations
are to one another, the more they are respected by the rest
of the World.

My Love to Brother Mecom and your Children. I shall
hardly have time to write to Benny by this Conveyance. Acquaint him that I received his Letter of Sept. 10, and am glad
to hear he is in so prosperous a Way, as not to regret his
leaving Antigua. I am, my dear Sister, Your ever affectionate
Brother

March 26. The above was wrote at the time it is dated; but
on reading it over, I apprehended that something I had said
in it about Presbyterians, and Affronts, might possibly give
more Offence; and so I threw it by, concluding not to send
it. However, Mr. Bailey calling on me, and having no other
Letter ready nor time at present to write one, I venture to
send it, and beg you will excuse what you find amiss in it. I
send also by Mr. Bailey the Cloak mention'd in it, and also a
Piece of Linnen, which I beg you to accept of from Your
loving Brother

I received your Letter, and Benny's and Peter's by Mr. Baily,
which I shall answer per next Opportunity.

To Lord Kames

My dear Lord,   London, May 3. 1760.

Your obliging Favour of January 24th. found me greatly indispos'd with an obstinate Cold and Cough accompany'd with Feverish Complaints and Headachs, that lasted long and harass'd me greatly, not being subdu'd at length but by the whole Round of Cupping, Bleeding, Blistering, &c. When I had any Intervals of Ease and Clearness, I endeavour'd to comply with your Request, in writing something on the present Situation of our Affairs in America, in order to give more correct Notions of the British Interest with regard to the Colonies, than those I found many sensible Men possess'd of. Inclos'd you have the Production, such as it is. I wish it may in any Degree be of Service to the Publick. I shall at least hope this from it for my own Part, that you will consider it as a Letter from me to you, and accept its Length as some Excuse for its being so long acoming.

I am now reading, with great Pleasure and Improvement, your excellent Work, the Principles of Equity. It will be of the greatest Advantage to the Judges in our Colonies, not only in those which have Courts of Chancery, but also in those which having no such Courts are obliged to mix Equity with the Common Law. It will be of the more Service to the Colony Judges, as few of them have been bred to the Law. I have sent a Book to a particular Friend, one of the Judges of the Supreme Court in Pensilvania.

I will shortly send you a Copy of the Chapter you are pleas'd to mention in so obliging a Manner; and shall be extreamly oblig'd in receiving a Copy of the Collection of Maxims for the Conduct of Life, which you are preparing for the Use of your Children. I purpose, likewise, a little Work for the Benefit of Youth, to be call'd *The Art of Virtue*. From the Title I think you will hardly conjecture what the Nature of such a Book may be. I must therefore explain it a little. Many People lead bad Lives that would gladly lead good ones, but know not *how* to make the Change. They have frequently *resolv'd* and *endeavour'd* it; but in vain, because their Endeavours have not been properly conducted. To exhort People to be good, to be just, to be temperate, &c. without *shewing* them *how* they shall *become* so, seems like the ineffectual Charity mention'd by the Apostle, which consisted in saying to the Hungry, the Cold, and the Naked, *be ye fed, be ye warmed, be ye clothed*, without shewing them how they should get Food, Fire or Clothing. Most People have naturally *some* Virtues, but none have naturally *all* the Virtues. To *acquire* those that are wanting, and *secure* what we acquire as well as those we have naturally, is the Subject of *an Art*. It is as properly an Art, as Painting, Navigation, or Architecture. If a Man would become a Painter, Navigator, or Architect, it is not enough that he is *advised* to be one, that he is *convinc'd* by the Arguments of his Adviser that it would be for his Advantage to be one, and that he *resolves* to be one, but he must also be taught the Principles of the Art, be shewn all the Methods of Working, and how to acquire the *Habits* of using properly all the Instruments; and thus regularly and gradually he arrives by Practice at some Perfection in the Art. If he does not proceed thus, he is apt to meet with Difficulties that discourage him, and make him drop the Pursuit. My *Art of Virtue* has also its Instruments, and teaches the Manner of Using them. Christians are directed to have *Faith in Christ*, as the effectual Means of obtaining the Change they desire. It may, when sufficiently strong, be effectual with many. A full Opinion that a Teacher is infinitely wise, good, and powerful, and that he will certainly reward and punish the Obedient and Disobedient, must give great Weight to his Precepts, and make them much more attended to by his Disciples. But all Men cannot have Faith in Christ; and many have it in so weak a Degree, that it does not produce the Effect. Our *Art of Virtue* may therefore be of great Service to those who have not Faith, and come in Aid of the weak Faith of others. Such as are naturally well-disposed, and have been carefully educated, so that good Habits have been early established, and bad ones prevented, have less Need of this Art; but all may be more or less benefited by it. It is, in short, to be adapted for universal Use. I imagine what I have now been writing will seem to savour of great Presumption; I must therefore speedily finish my little Piece, and communicate the Manuscript to you, that you may judge whether it is possible to make good such Pretensions. I shall at the same time hope for the Benefit of your Corrections.

My respectful Compliments to Lady Kaims and your amiable Children, in which my Son joins. With the sincerest Esteem and Attachment, I am, My Lord, Your Lordship's most obedient and most humble Servant

P.S. While I remain in London I shall continue in Craven Street, Strand: if you favour me with your Correspondence when I return to America, please to direct for me in Philadelphia, and your Letters will readily find me tho' sent to any other Part of North America.

SALT DEPOSITS

To Peter Franklin

SIR,   *London, May* 7, 1760.
* * * * * * It has, indeed, as you observe, been the opinion of some very great naturalists, that the sea is salt only from the dissolution of mineral or rock salt, which its waters happened to meet with. But this opinion takes it for granted that all water was originally fresh, of which we can have no proof. I own I am inclined to a different opinion, and rather think all the water on this globe was originally salt, and that the fresh water we find in springs and rivers, is the produce of distillation. The sun raises the vapours from the sea, which form clouds, and fall in rain upon the land, and springs and rivers are formed of that rain.—As to the rock-salt found in mines, I conceive, that instead of communicating its saltness to the sea, it is itself drawn from the sea, and that of course the sea is now fresher than it was originally. This is only another effect of nature's distillery, and might be performed various ways.

It is evident from the quantities of sea-shells, and the bones and teeth of fishes found in high lands, that the sea has formerly covered them. Then, either the sea has been higher than it now is, and has fallen away from those high lands; or they have been lower than they are, and were lifted up out of the water to their present height, by some internal mighty force, such as we still feel some remains of, when whole continents are moved by earthquakes. In either case it may be supposed that large hollows, or valleys among hills, might be left filled with sea-water, which evaporating, and the fluid part drying away in a course of years, would leave the salt covering the bottom; and that salt coming afterwards to be covered with earth, from the neighbouring hills, could only be found by digging through that earth. Or, as we know from their effects, that there are deep fiery caverns under the earth, and even under the sea, if at any time the sea leaks into any of them, the fluid parts of the water must evaporate from that heat, and pass off through some vulcano, while the salt remains, and by degrees, and continual accretion, becomes a great mass. Thus the cavern may at length be filled, and the volcano connected with it cease burning, as many it is said have done; and future miners penetrating such cavern, find what we call a salt mine.—This is a fancy I had on visiting the salt-mines at *Northwich*, with my son. I send you a piece of the rock-salt which he brought up with him out of the mine. * * * * * *

I am, Sir, &c.

"THE KNOWLEDGE OF NATURE"

To Mary Stevenson

Dear Polly,   Cravenstreet, June 11. 1760
'Tis a very sensible Question you ask, how the Air can affect the Barometer, when its Opening appears covered with Wood? If indeed it was so closely covered as to admit of no Communication of the outward Air to the Surface of the Mercury, the Change of Weight in the Air could not possibly affect it. But the least Crevice is sufficient for the Purpose; a Pinhole will do the Business. And if you could look behind the Frame to which your Barometer is fixed, you would certainly find some small Opening.

There are indeed some Barometers in which the Body of
Mercury at the lower End is contain'd in a close Leather Bag,
and so the Air cannot come into immediate Contact with the
Mercury: Yet the same Effect is produc'd. For the Leather
being flexible, when the Bag is press'd by any additional
Weight of Air, it contracts, and the Mercury is forc'd up into
the Tube; when the Air becomes lighter, and its Pressure less,
the Weight of the Mercury prevails, and it descends again
into the Bag.

Your Observation on what you have lately read concerning
Insects, is very just and solid. Superficial Minds are apt to
despise those who make that Part of Creation their Study, as
mere Triflers; but certainly the World has been much oblig'd
to them. Under the Care and Management of Man, the Labours of the little Silkworm afford Employment and Subsistence to Thousands of Families, and become an immense
Article of Commerce. The Bee, too, yields us its delicious
Honey, and its Wax useful to a multitude of Purposes. Another Insect, it is said, produces the Cochineal, from whence
we have our rich Scarlet Dye. The Usefulness of the Canthar-
ides, or Spanish Flies, in Medicine, is known to all, and
Thousands owe their Lives to that Knowledge. By human
Industry and Observation, other Properties of other Insects
may possibly be hereafter discovered, and of equal Utility. A
thorough Acquaintance with the Nature of these little Creatures, may also enable Mankind to prevent the Increase of
such as are noxious or secure us against the Mischiefs they
occasion. These Things doubtless your Books make mention
of: I can only add a particular late Instance which I had from
a Swedish Gentleman of good Credit. In the green Timber
intended for Ship-building at the King's Yards in that Country, a kind of Worms were found, which every Year became
more numerous and more pernicious, so that the Ships were
greatly damag'd before they came into Use. The King sent
Linnaeus, the great Naturalist, from Stockholm, to enquire
into the Affair, and see if the Mischief was capable of any
Remedy. He found on Examination, that the Worm was produc'd from a small Egg deposited in the little Roughnesses
on the Surface of the Wood, by a particular kind of Fly or
Beetle; from whence the Worm, as soon as it was hatch'd,

began to eat into the Substance of the Wood, and after some time came out again a Fly of the Parent kind, and so the Species increas'd. The Season in which this Fly laid its Eggs, Linnaeus knew to be about a Fortnight (I think) in the Month of May, and at no other time of the Year. He therefore advis'd, that some Days before that Season, all the green Timber should be thrown into the Water, and kept under Water till the Season was over. Which being done by the King's Order, the Flies missing their usual Nests, could not increase; and the Species was either destroy'd or went elsewhere; and the Wood was effectually preserved, for after the first Year, it became too dry and hard for their purpose.

There is, however, a prudent Moderation to be used in Studies of this kind. The Knowledge of Nature may be ornamental, and it may be useful, but if to attain an Eminence in that, we neglect the Knowledge and Practice of essential Duties, we deserve Reprehension. For there is no Rank in Natural Knowledge of equal Dignity and Importance with that of being a good Parent, a good Child, a good Husband, or Wife, a good Neighbour or Friend, a good Subject or Citizen, that is, in short, a good Christian. Nicholas Gimcrack, therefore, who neglected the Care of his Family, to pursue Butterflies, was a just Object of Ridicule, and we must give him up as fair Game to the Satyrist.

Adieu, my dear Friend, and believe me ever Yours affectionately

Your good Mother is well, and gives her Love and Blessing to you. My Compliments to your Aunts, Miss Pitt, &c.

TIDES IN RIVERS

To Mary Stevenson

My dear Friend,   London, Sept. 13. 1760
I have your agreable Letter from Bristol, which I take this first Leisure Hour to answer, having for some time been much engag'd in Business.

Your first Question, *What is the Reason the Water at this Place, tho' cold at the Spring, becomes warm by Pumping?* it will be most prudent in me to forbear attempting to answer, till, by a more circumstantial Account, you assure me of the Fact. I own I should expect that Operation to warm, not so much the Water pump'd as the Person pumping. The Rubbing of dry Solids together, has been long observ'd to produce Heat; but the like Effect has never yet, that I have heard, been produc'd by the mere Agitation of Fluids, or Friction of Fluids with Solids. Water in a Bottle shook for Hours by a Mill Hopper, it is said, discover'd no sensible Addition of Heat. The Production of Animal Heat by Exercise, is therefore to be accounted for in another manner, which I may hereafter endeavour to make you acquainted with.

This Prudence of not attempting to give Reasons before one is sure of Facts, I learnt from one of your Sex, who, as Selden tells us, being in company with some Gentlemen that were viewing and considering something which they call'd a Chinese Shoe, and disputing earnestly about the manner of wearing it, and how it could possibly be put on; put in her Word, and said modestly, *Gentlemen, are you sure it is a Shoe? Should not that be settled first?*

But I shall now endeavour to explain what I said to you about the Tide in Rivers, and to that End shall make a Figure, which tho' not very like a River, may serve to convey my Meaning. Suppose a Canal 140 Miles long communicating at one End with the Sea, and fill'd therefore with Sea Water. I chuse a Canal at first, rather than a River, to throw out of Consideration the Effects produc'd by the Streams of Fresh Water from the Land, the Inequality in Breadth, and the

Crookedness of Courses. Let A, C, be the Head of the Canal, C D the Bottom of it; D F the open Mouth of it next the Sea. Let the strait prick'd Line B G represent Low Water Mark the whole Length of the Canal, A F High Water Mark: Now if a Person standing at E, and observing at the time of

High water there that the Canal is quite full at that Place up
to the Line E, should conclude that the Canal is equally full
to the same Height from End to End, and therefore there was
as much more Water come into the Canal since it was down
at the Low Water Mark, as could be included in the oblong
Space A. B. G. F. he would be greatly mistaken. For the Tide
is *a Wave*, and the Top of the Wave, which makes High Water, as well as every other lower Part, is progressive; and it is
High Water successively, but not at the same time, in all the
several Points between G, F. and A, B.—and in such a
Length as I have mention'd it is Low Water at F G and also
at A B, at or near the same time with its being High Water
at E; so that the Surface of the Water in the Canal, during
that Situation, is properly represented by the Curve prick'd
Line B E G. And on the other hand, when it is Low Water
at E H, it is High Water both at F G and at A B at or near
the same time; and the Surface would then be describ'd by
the inverted Curve Line A H F.

In this View of the Case, you will easily see, that there
must be very little more Water in the Canal at what we call
High Water than there is at Low Water, those Terms not relating to the whole Canal at the same time, but successively
to its Parts. And if you suppose the Canal six times as long,
the Case would not vary as to the Quantity of Water at different times of the Tide; there would only be six Waves in the
Canal at the same time, instead of one, and the Hollows in
the Water would be equal to the Hills.

That this is not mere Theory, but comformable to Fact, we
know by our long Rivers in America. The Delaware, on
which Philadelphia stands, is in this particular similar to the
Canal I have supposed of one Wave: For when it is High
Water at the Capes or Mouth of the River, it is also High
Water at Philadelphia, which stands about 140 Miles from the
Sea; and there is at the same time a Low Water in the Middle
between the two High Waters; where, when it comes to be
High Water, it is at the same time Low Water at the Capes
and at Philadelphia. And the longer Rivers have, some a Wave
and Half, some two, three, or four Waves, according to their
Length. In the shorter Rivers of this Island, one may see the
same thing in Part: for Instance; it is High Water at Graves-

end an Hour before it is High Water at London Bridge; and
20 Miles below Gravesend an Hour before it is High Water
at Gravesend. Therefore at the Time of High Water at Gravesend the Top of the Wave is there, and the Water is then not
so high by some feet where the Top of the Wave was an Hour
before, or where it will be an Hour after, as it is just then at
Gravesend.

Now we are not to suppose, that because the Swell or Top
of the Wave runs at the Rate of 20 Miles an Hour, that therefore the Current or Water itself of which the Wave is compos'd, runs at that rate. Far from it. To conceive this Motion
of a Wave, make a small Experiment or two. Fasten one End
of a Cord in a Window near the Top of a House, and let the
other End come down to the Ground; take this End in your
Hand, and you may, by a sudden Motion occasion a Wave in
the Cord that will run quite up to the Window; but tho' the
Wave is progressive from your Hand to the Window, the
Parts of the Rope do not proceed with the Wave, but remain
where they were, except only that kind of Motion that produces the Wave. So if you throw a Stone into a Pond of Water
when the Surface is still and smooth, you will see a circular
Wave proceed from the Stone as its Center, quite to the Sides
of the Pond; but the Water does not proceed with the Wave,
it only rises and falls to form it in the different Parts of its
Course; and the Waves that follow the first, all make use of
the same Water with their Predecessors.

But a Wave in Water is not indeed in all Circumstances
exactly like that in a Cord; for Water being a Fluid, and grav-
itating to the Earth, it naturally runs from a higher Place to a
lower; therefore the Parts of the Wave in Water do actually
run a little both ways from its Top towards its lower Sides,
which the Parts of the Wave in the Cord cannot do. Thus
when it is high and standing Water at Gravesend, the Water
20 Miles below has been running Ebb, or towards the Sea for
an Hour, or ever since it was High Water there; but the Water
at London Bridge will run Flood, or from the Sea yet another
Hour, till it is High Water or the Top of the Wave arrives at
that Bridge, and then it will have run Ebb an Hour at Gravesend, &c. &c. Now this Motion of the Water, occasion'd only
by its Gravity, or Tendency to run from a higher Place to a

lower, is by no means so swift as the Motion of the Wave. It scarce exceeds perhaps two Miles in an Hour. If it went as the Wave does 20 Miles an Hour, no Ships could ride at Anchor in such a Stream, nor Boats row against it.

In common Speech, indeed, this Current of the Water both Ways from the Top of the Wave is call'd *the Tide*; thus we say, *the Tide runs strong, the Tide runs at the rate of* 1, 2, *or* 3 *Miles an hour,* &c. and when we are at a Part of the River behind the Top of the Wave, and find the Water lower than Highwater Mark, and running towards the Sea, we say, *the Tide runs Ebb*; and when we are before the Top of the Wave, and find the Water higher than Low-water Mark, and running from the Sea, we say, the *Tide runs Flood*: But these Expressions are only locally proper; for a Tide strictly speaking is *one whole Wave*, including all its Parts higher and lower, and these Waves succeed one another about twice in twenty four Hours.

This Motion of the Water, occasion'd by its Gravity, will explain to you why the Water near the Mouths of Rivers may be salter at Highwater than at Low. Some of the Salt Water, as the Tide Wave enters the River, runs from its Top and fore Side, and mixes with the fresh, and also pushes it back up the River.

Supposing that the Water commonly runs during the Flood at the Rate of two Miles in an Hour, and that the Flood runs 5 Hours, you see that it can bring at most into our Canal only a Quantity of Water equal to the Space included in the Breadth of the Canal, ten Miles of its Length, and the Depth between Low and Highwater Mark. Which is but a fourteenth Part of what would be necessary to fill all the Space between Low and Highwater Mark, for 140 Miles, the whole Length of the Canal.

And indeed such a Quantity of Water as would fill that whole Space, to run in and out every Tide, must create so outrageous a Current, as would do infinite Damage to the Shores, Shipping, &c. and make the Navigation of a River almost impracticable.

I have made this Letter longer than I intended, and therefore reserve for another what I have farther to say on the Subject of Tides and Rivers. I shall now only add, that I have

not been exact in the Numbers, because I would avoid per-
plexing you with minute Calculations, my Design at present
being chiefly to give you distinct and clear Ideas of the first
Principles.

After writing 6 Folio Pages of Philosophy to a young Girl,
is it necessary to finish such a Letter with a Compliment? Is
not such a Letter of itself a Compliment? Does it not say, she
has a Mind thirsty after Knowledge, and capable of receiving
it; and that the most agreable Things one can write to her are
those that tend to the Improvement of her Understanding? It
does indeed say all this, but then it is still no Compliment; it
is no more than plain honest Truth, which is not the Character of a Compliment. So if I would finish my Letter in the
Mode, I should yet add something that means nothing, and
is *merely* civil and polite. But being naturally awkward at
every Circumstance of Ceremony, I shall not attempt it. I had
rather conclude abruptly with what pleases me more than any
Compliment can please you, that I am allow'd to subscribe
my self Your affectionate Friend

"THE BEST ENGLISH"

To David Hume

Dear Sir,   Coventry, Sept. 27. 1760
I have too long postpon'd answering your obliging Letter,
a Fault I will not attempt to excuse, but rather rely on your
Goodness to forgive it if I am more punctual for the future.

I am oblig'd to you for the favourable Sentiments you express of the Pieces sent you; tho' the Volume relating to our
Pensilvania Affairs, was not written by me, nor any Part of it,
except the Remarks on the Proprietor's Estimate of his Estate, and some of the inserted Messages and Reports of the
Assembly which I wrote when at home, as a Member of
Committees appointed by the House for that Service; the rest
was by another Hand. But tho' I am satisfy'd by what you
say, that the Duke of Bedford was hearty in the Scheme of
the Expedition, I am not so clear that others in the Adminis-

tration were equally in earnest in that matter. It is certain that after the Duke of Newcastle's first Orders to raise Troops in the Colonies, and Promise to send over Commissions to the Officers, with Arms, Clothing, &c. for the Men, we never had another Syllable from him for 18 Months; during all which time the Army lay idle at Albany for want of Orders and Necessaries; and it began to be thought at least that if an Expedition had ever been intended, the first Design and the Orders given, must, thro' the Multiplicity of Business here at home, have been quite forgotten.

I am not a little pleas'd to hear of your Change of Sentiments in some particulars relating to America; because I think it of Importance to our general Welfare that the People of this Nation should have right Notions of us, and I know no one that has it more in his Power to rectify their Notions, than Mr. Hume. I have lately read with great Pleasure, as I do every thing of yours, the excellent Essay on the *Jealousy of Commerce*: I think it cannot but have a good Effect in promoting a certain Interest too little thought of by selfish Man, and scarce ever mention'd, so that we hardly have a Name for it; I mean the *Interest of Humanity*, or common Good of Mankind: But I hope particularly from that Essay, an Abatement of the Jealousy that reigns here of the Commerce of the Colonies, at least so far as such Abatement may be reasonable.

I thank you for your friendly Admonition relating to some unusual Words in the Pamphlet. It will be of Service to me. The *pejorate*, and the *colonize*, since they are not in common use here, I give up as bad; for certainly in Writings intended for Persuasion and for general Information, one cannot be too clear, and every Expression in the least obscure is a Fault. The *unshakeable* too, tho' clear, I give up as rather low. The introducing new Words where we are already possess'd of old ones sufficiently expressive, I confess must be generally wrong, as it tends to change the Language; yet at the same time I cannot but wish the Usage of our Tongue permitted making new Words when we want them, by Composition of old ones whose Meanings are already well understood. The German allows of it, and it is a common Practice with their Writers. Many of our present English Words were originally so made; and many of the Latin Words. In point of Clearness such compound Words would have the Advantage of any we can borrow from the ancient or from foreign Languages. For instance, the Word *inaccessible*, tho' long in use among us, is not yet, I dare say, so universally understood by our People as the Word *uncomeatable* would immediately be, which we are not allow'd to write. But I hope with you, that we shall always in America make the best English of this Island our Standard, and I believe it will be so. I assure you, it often gives me Pleasure to reflect how greatly the *Audience* (if I may so term it) of a good English Writer will in another Century or two be encreas'd, by the Increase of English People in our Colonies.

My Son presents his Respects with mine to you and Dr. Monro. We receiv'd your printed circular Letter to the Members of the Society, and purpose some time next Winter to send each of us a little Philosophical Essay. With the greatest Esteem I am, Dear Sir, Your most obedient and most humble Servant

COLOR AND HEAT

To Mary Stevenson

My dear Friend

It is, as you observed in our late Conversation, a very general Opinion, that *all Rivers run into the Sea*, or deposite their Waters there. 'Tis a kind of Audacity to call such general Opinions in question, and may subject one to Censure: But we must hazard something in what we think the Cause of Truth: And if we propose our Objections modestly, we shall, tho' mistaken, deserve a Censure less severe, than when we are both mistaken and insolent.

That some Rivers run into the Sea is beyond a doubt: Such, for Instance, are the Amazones, and I think the Oranoko and the Missisipi. The Proof is, that their Waters are fresh quite to the Sea, and out to some Distance from the Land. Our Question is, whether the fresh Waters of those Rivers whose Beds are filled with Salt Water to a considerable

Distance up from the Sea (as the Thames, the Delaware, and the Rivers that communicate with Chesapeak Bay in Virginia) do ever arrive at the Sea? and as I suspect they do not, I am now to acquaint you with my Reasons; or, if they are not allow'd to be Reasons, my Conceptions, at least of this Matter.

The common Supply of Rivers is from Springs, which draw their Origin from Rain that has soak'd into the Earth. The Union of a Number of Springs forms a River. The Waters as they run, expos'd to the Sun, Air and Wind, are continually evaporating. Hence in Travelling one may often see where a River runs, by a long blueish Mist over it, tho' we are at such a Distance as not to see the River itself. The Quantity of this Evaporation is greater or less in proportion to the Surface exposed by the same Quantity of Water to those Causes of Evaporation. While the River runs in a narrow confined Channel in the upper hilly Country, only a small Surface is exposed; a greater as the River widens. Now if a River ends in a Lake, as some do, whereby its Waters are spread so wide as that the Evaporation is equal to the Sum of all its Springs, that Lake will never overflow: And if instead of ending in a Lake, it was drawn into greater Length as a River, so as to expose a Surface equal, in the whole to that Lake, the Evaporation would be equal, and such River would end as a Canal; when the Ignorant might suppose, as they actually do in such cases, that the River loses itself by running under ground, whereas in truth it has run up into the Air.

Now many Rivers that are open to the Sea, widen much before they arrive at it, not merely by the additional Waters they receive, but by having their Course stopt by the opposing Flood Tide; by being turned back twice in twenty-four Hours, and by finding broader Beds in the low flat Countries to dilate themselves in; hence the Evaporation of the fresh Water is proportionably increas'd, so that in some Rivers it may equal the Springs of Supply. In such cases, the Salt Water comes up the River, and meets the fresh in that part where, if there were a Wall or Bank of Earth across from Side to Side, the River would form a Lake, fuller indeed at some times than at others according to the Seasons, but whose

Evaporation would, one time with another, be equal to its Supply.

When the Communication between the two kinds of Water is open, this supposed Wall of Separation may be conceived as a moveable one, which is not only pushed some Miles higher up the River by every Flood Tide from the Sea, and carried down again as far by every Tide of Ebb, but which has even this Space of Vibration removed nearer to the Sea in wet Seasons, when the Springs and Brooks in the upper Country are augmented by the falling Rains so as to swell the River, and farther from the Sea in dry Seasons.

Within a few Miles above and below this moveable Line of Separation, the different Waters mix a little, partly by their Motion to and fro, and partly from the greater specific Gravity of the Salt Water, which inclines it to run under the Fresh, while the fresh Water being lighter runs over the Salt.

Cast your Eye on the Map of North America, and observe the Bay of Chesapeak in Virginia, mentioned above; you will see, communicating with it by their Mouths, the great Rivers Sasquehanah, Potowmack, Rappahanock, York and James, besides a Number of smaller Streams each as big as the Thames. It has been propos'd by philosophical Writers, that to compute how much Water any River discharges into the Sea, in a given time, we should measure its Depth and Swiftness at any Part above the Tide, as, for the Thames, at Kingston or Windsor. But can one imagine, that if all the Water of those vast Rivers went to the Sea, it would not first have pushed the Salt Water out of that narrow-mouthed Bay, and filled it with fresh? The Sasquehanah alone would seem to be sufficient for this, if it were not for the Loss by Evaporation. And yet that Bay is salt quite up to Annapolis.

As to our other Subject, the different Degrees of Heat imbibed from the Sun's Rays by Cloths of different Colours, since I cannot find the Notes of my Experiment to send you, I must give it as well as I can from Memory.

But first let me mention an Experiment you may easily make your self. Walk but a quarter of an Hour in your Garden when the Sun shines, with a Part of your Dress white, and a Part black; then apply your Hand to them alternately, and you will find a very great Difference in their Warmth.

The Black will be quite hot to the Touch, the White still cool.

Another. Try to fire Paper with a burning Glass. If it is White, you will not easily burn it; but if you bring the Focus to a black Spot or upon Letters written or printed, the Paper will immediately be on fire under the Letters.

Thus Fullers and Dyers find black Cloths, of equal Thickness with white ones, and hung out equally wet, dry in the Sun much sooner than the white, being more readily heated by the Sun's Rays. It is the same before a Fire; the Heat of which sooner penetrates black Stockings than white ones, and so is apt sooner to burn a Man's Shins. Also Beer much sooner warms in a black Mug set before the Fire, than in a white one, or in a bright Silver Tankard.

My Experiment was this. I took a number of little Square Pieces of Broad Cloth from a Taylor's Pattern Card, of various Colours. There were Black, deep Blue, lighter Blue, Green, Purple, Red, Yellow, White, and other Colours or Shades of Colours. I laid them all out upon the Snow in a bright Sunshiny Morning. In a few Hours (I cannot now be exact as to the Time) the Black being warm'd most by the Sun was sunk so low as to be below the Stroke of the Sun's Rays; the dark Blue almost as low, the lighter Blue not quite so much as the dark, the other Colours less as they were lighter; and the quite White remain'd on the Surface of the Snow, not having entred it at all. What signifies Philosophy that does not apply to some Use? May we not learn from hence, that black Cloaths are not so fit to wear in a hot Sunny Climate or Season as white ones; because in such Cloaths the Body is more heated by the Sun when we walk abroad and are at the same time heated by the Exercise, which double Heat is apt to bring on putrid dangerous Fevers? That Soldiers and Seamen who must march and labour in the Sun, should in the East or West Indies have an Uniform of white? That Summer Hats for Men or Women, should be white, as repelling that Heat which gives the Headachs to many, and to some the fatal Stroke that the French call the *Coup de Soleil*? That the Ladies Summer Hats, however should be lined with Black, as not reverberating on their Faces those Rays which are reflected upwards from the Earth or Water? That

the putting a white Cap of Paper or Linnen *within* the Crown
of a black Hat, as some do, will not keep out the Heat, tho'
it would if plac'd *without*? That Fruit Walls being black'd may
receive so much Heat from the Sun in the Daytime, as to
continue warm in some degree thro' the Night, and thereby
preserve the Fruit from Frosts, or forward its Growth?—with
sundry other particulars of less or greater Importance, that
will occur from time to time to attentive Minds? I am, Yours
affectionately,

November? 1760

"PREJUDICE . . . AGAINST YOUR WORK"

To John Baskerville

Dear Sir,   Craven-Street, London.
    Let me give you a pleasant Instance of the Prejudice some
have entertained against your Work. Soon after I returned,
discoursing with a Gentleman concerning the Artists of Birmingham, he said you would be a Means of blinding all the
Readers in the Nation, for the Strokes of your Letters being
too thin and narrow, hurt the Eye, and he could never read a
Line of them without Pain. I thought, said I, you were going
to complain of the Gloss on the Paper, some object to: No,
no, says he, I have heard that mentioned, but it is not that;
'tis in the Form and Cut of the Letters themselves; they have
not that natural and easy Proportion between the Height and
Thickness of the Stroke, which makes the common Printing
so much more comfortable to the Eye.—You see this Gentleman was a Connoisseur. In vain I endeavoured to support
your *Character* against the Charge; he knew what he felt, he
could see the Reason of it, and several other Gentlemen
among his Friends had made the same Observation, &c.—
Yesterday he called to visit me, when, mischievously bent to
try his Judgment, I stept into my Closet, tore off the Top of
Mr. Caslon's Specimen, and produced it to him as yours
brought with me from Birmingham, saying, I had been examining it since he spoke to me, and could not for my Life
perceive the Disproportion he mentioned, desiring him to

point it out to me. He readily undertook it, and went over
the several Founts, shewing me every-where what he thought
Instances of that Disproportion; and declared, that he could
not then read the Specimen without feeling very strongly the
Pain he had mentioned to me. I spared him that Time the
Confusion of being told, that these were the Types he had
been reading all his Life with so much Ease to his Eyes; the
Types his adored Newton is printed with, on which he has
pored not a little; nay, the very Types his own Book is
printed with, for he is himself an Author; and yet never discovered this painful Disproportion in them, till he thought
they were yours.

                                                I am, &c.

1760?

FAULTS IN SONGS

To Peter Franklin

Dear Brother,
    * * * * I like your ballad, and think it well adapted for your
purpose of discountenancing expensive foppery, and encouraging industry and frugality. If you can get it generally sung
in your country, it may probably have a good deal of the
effect you hope and expect from it. But as you aimed at making it general, I wonder you chose so uncommon a measure
in poetry, that none of the tunes in common use will suit it.
Had you fitted it to an old one, well known, it must have
spread much faster than I doubt it will do from the best new
tune we can get compos'd for it. I think too, that if you had
given it to some country girl in the heart of the *Massachusets*,
who has never heard any other than psalm tunes, or *Chevy
Chace*, the *Children in the Wood*, the *Spanish Lady*, and such
old simple ditties, but has naturally a good ear, she might
more probably have made a pleasing popular tune for you,
than any of our masters here, and more proper for your purpose, which would best be answered, if every word could as
it is sung be understood by all that hear it, and if the emphasis you intend for particular words could be given by the

singer as well as by the reader; much of the force and impression of the song depending on those circumstances. I will however get it as well done for you as I can.

Do not imagine that I mean to depreciate the skill of our composers of music here; they are admirable at pleasing *practised* ears, and know how to delight *one another*; but, in composing for songs, the reigning taste seems to be quite out of nature, or rather the reverse of nature, and yet like a torrent, hurries them all away with it; one or two perhaps only excepted.

You, in the spirit of some ancient legislators, would influence the manners of your country by the united powers of poetry and music. By what I can learn of *their* songs, the music was simple, conformed itself to the usual pronunciation of words, as to measure, cadence or emphasis, *&c.* never disguised and confounded the language by making a long syllable short, or a short one long when sung; their singing was only a more pleasing, because a melodious manner of speaking; it was capable of all the graces of prose oratory, while it added the pleasure of harmony. A modern song, on the contrary, neglects all the proprieties and beauties of common speech, and in their place introduces its *defects* and *absurdities* as so many graces. I am afraid you will hardly take my word for this, and therefore I must endeavour to support it by proof. Here is the first song I lay my hand on. It happens to be a composition of one of our greatest masters, the ever famous *Handel*. It is not one of his juvenile performances, before his taste could be improved and formed: It appeared when his reputation was at the highest, is greatly admired by all his admirers, and is really excellent in its kind. It is called, *The additional* FAVOURITE *Song in* Judas Maccabeus. Now I reckon among the defects and improprieties of common speech, the following, viz.

1. *Wrong placing the accent or emphasis*, by laying it on words of no importance, or on wrong syllables.

2. *Drawling*; or extending the sound of words or syllables beyond their natural length.

3. *Stuttering*; or making many syllables of one.

4. *Unintelligibleness*; the result of the three foregoing united.

5. *Tautology*; and

6. *Screaming*, without cause.

For the *wrong placing of the accent, or emphasis*, see it on the word *their* instead of being on the word *vain*.

with *their* vain My - ste - rious Art

And on the word *from*, and the wrong syllable *like*.

God-*like* Wisdom *from* a — bove

For the *Drawling*, see the last syllable of the word *wounded*.

Nor can heal the wound*ed* Heart

And in the syllable *wis*, and the word *from*, and syllable *bove*

God-like Wisdom *from* a - *bove*

For the *Stuttering*, see the words *ne'er relieve*, in

Ma - gick Charms can *ne'er* re - *lieve* you

Here are four syllables made of one, and eight of three; but this is moderate. I have seen in another song that I cannot now find, seventeen syllables made of three, and sixteen of one; the latter I remember was the word *charms*; viz. *Cha, a, a, a, a, a, a, a, a, a, a, a, a, a, a, arms*. Stammering with a witness!

For the *Unintelligibleness*; give this whole song to any

taught singer, and let her sing it to any company that have never heard it; you shall find they will not understand three words in ten. It is therefore that at the oratorio's and operas one sees with books in their hands all those who desire to understand what they hear sung by even our best performers.

For the *Tautology*; you have, *with their vain mysterious art*, twice repeated; *Magic charms can ne'er relieve you*, three times. *Nor can heal the wounded heart*, three times. *Godlike wisdom from above*, twice; and, *this alone can ne'er deceive you*, two or three times. But this is reasonable when compared with *the Monster Polypheme, the Monster Polypheme*, a hundred times over and over, in his admired *Acis and Galatea*.

As to the *screaming*; perhaps I cannot find a fair instance in this song; but whoever has frequented our operas will remember many. And yet here methinks the words *no* and *e'er*, when sung to these notes, have a little of the air of *screaming*, and would actually be scream'd by some singers.

No magic charms can e'er re—lieve you.

I send you inclosed the song with its music at length. Read the words without the repetitions. Observe how few they are, and what a shower of notes attend them. You will then perhaps be inclined to think with me, that though the words might be the principal part of an ancient song, they are of small importance in a modern one; they are in short only *a pretence for singing*.

> *I am, as ever,*
> *Your affectionate brother,*

P. S. I might have mentioned *Inarticulation* among the defects in common speech that are assumed as beauties in modern singing. But as that seems more the fault of the singer than of the composer, I omitted it in what related merely to the composition. The fine singer in the present mode, stifles all the hard consonants, and polishes away all the rougher parts of words that serve to distinguish them one from another; so that you hear nothing but an admirable pipe, and understand no more of the song, than you would from its tune played on any other instrument. If ever it was the ambition of musicians to make instruments that should imitate the human voice, that ambition seems now reversed, the voice aiming to be like an instrument. Thus wigs were first made to imitate a good natural head of hair;—but when they became fashionable, though in unnatural forms, we have seen natural hair dressed to look like wigs.

c. 1761

"A CASE IN POINT"

To David Hume

Dear Sir,   London, May 19. 1762.

It is no small Pleasure to me to hear from you that my Paper on the means of preserving Buildings from Damage by Lightning, was acceptable to the Philosophical Society. Mr. Russel's Proposals of Improvement are very sensible and just. A Leaden Spout or Pipe is undoubtedly a good Conductor so far as it goes. If the Conductor enters the Ground just at the Foundation, and from thence is carried horizontally to some Well, or to a distant Rod driven downright into the Earth; I would then propose that the Part under Ground should be Lead, as less liable to consume with Rust than Iron. Because if the Conductor near the Foot of the Wall should be wasted, the Lightning might act on the Moisture of the Earth, and by suddenly rarifying it occasion an Explosion that may damage the Foundation. In the Experiment of discharging my large Case of Electrical Bottles thro' a Piece of small Glass Tube fill'd with Water, the suddenly rarify'd Water has exploded with a Force equal, I think, to that of so much Gunpowder; bursting the Tube into many Pieces, and driving them with Violence in all Directions and to all Parts of the Room. The Shivering of Trees into small Splinters like a Broom, is probably owing to this Rarefaction of the Sap in the longitudinal Pores or

capillary Pipes in the Substance of the Wood. And the Blow-
ing-up of Bricks or Stones in a Hearth, Rending Stones out
of a Foundation, and Splitting of Walls, is also probably an
Effect sometimes of rarify'd Moisture in the Earth, under
the Hearth, or in the Walls. We should therefore have a durable Conductor under Ground, or convey the Lightning to
the Earth at some Distance.

It must afford Lord Mareschall a good deal of Diversion to
preside in a Dispute so ridiculous as that you mention. Judges
in their Decisions often use Precedents. I have somewhere
met with one that is what the Lawyers call *a Case in Point*.
The Church People and the Puritans in a Country Town, had
once a bitter Contention concerning the Erecting of a Maypole, which the former desir'd and the latter oppos'd. Each
Party endeavour'd to strengthen itself by obtaining the Authority of the Mayor, directing or forbidding a Maypole. He
heard their Altercation with great Patience, and then gravely
determin'd thus; You that are for having no Maypole shall
have no Maypole; and you that are for having a Maypole shall
have a Maypole. Get about your Business and let me hear no
more of this Quarrel. So methinks Lord Mareschal might say;
You that are for no more Damnation than is proportion'd to
your Offences, have my Consent that it may be so: And you
that are for being damn'd eternally, G–d eternally d—n you
all, and let me hear no more of your Disputes.

Your Compliment of *Gold* and *Wisdom* is very obliging to
me, but a little injurious to your Country. The various Value
of every thing in every Part of this World, arises you know
from the various Proportions of the Quantity to the Demand.
We are told that Gold and Silver in Solomon's Time were so
plenty as to be of no more Value in his Country than the
Stones in the Street. You have here at present just such a
Plenty of Wisdom. Your People are therefore not to be censur'd for desiring no more among them than they have; and
if I have *any*, I should certainly carry it where from its Scarcity it may probably come to a better Market.

I nevertheless regret extreamly the leaving a Country in
which I have receiv'd so much Friendship, and Friends whose
Conversation has been so agreable and so improving to me;
and that I am henceforth to reside at so great a Distance from

them is no small Mortification, to My dear Friend, Yours most affectionately

My respectful Compliments if you please to Sir Alexr. Dick, Lord Kaims, Mr. Alexander, Mr. Russel, and any other enquiring Friends. I shall write to them before I leave the Island.

THE GLASS ARMONICA

To Giambatista Beccaria

Rev. SIR,   *London, July* 13, 1762.

I once promised myself the pleasure of seeing you at *Turin*, but as that is not now likely to happen, being just about returning to my native country, *America*, I sit down to take leave of you (among others of my *European* friends that I cannot see) by writing.

I thank you for the honourable mention you have so frequently made of me in your letters to Mr. *Collinson* and others, for the generous defence you undertook and executed with so much success, of my electrical opinions; and for the valuable present you have made me of your new work, from which I have received great information and pleasure. I wish I could in return entertain you with any thing new of mine on that subject; but I have not lately pursued it. Nor do I know of any one here that is at present much engaged in it.

Perhaps, however, it may be agreeable to you, as you live in a musical country, to have an account of the new instrument lately added here to the great number that charming science was before possessed of:—As it is an instrument that seems peculiarly adapted to *Italian* music, especially that of the soft and plaintive kind, I will endeavour to give you such a description of it, and of the manner of constructing it, that you, or any of your friends, may be enabled to imitate it, if you incline so to do, without being at the expence and trouble of the many experiments I have made in endeavouring to bring it to its present perfection.

You have doubtless heard the sweet tone that is drawn from a drinking glass, by passing a wet finger round its brim. One Mr. *Puckeridge*, a gentleman from *Ireland*, was the first who thought of playing tunes, formed of these tones. He collected a number of glasses of different sizes, fixed them near each other on a table, and tuned them by putting into them water, more or less, as each note required. The tones were brought out by passing his fingers round their brims.—He was unfortunately burnt here, with his instrument, in a fire which consumed the house he lived in. Mr. *E. Delaval*, a most ingenious member of our Royal Society, made one in imitation of it, with a better choice and form of glasses, which was the first I saw or heard. Being charmed with the sweetness of its tones, and the music he produced from it, I wished only to see the glasses disposed in a more convenient form, and brought together in a narrower compass, so as to admit of a greater number of tones, and all within reach of hand to a person sitting before the instrument, which I accomplished, after various intermediate trials, and less commodious forms, both of glasses and construction, in the following manner.

The glasses are blown as near as possible in the form of hemispheres, having each an open neck or socket in the middle. The thickness of the glass near the brim about a tenth of an inch, or hardly quite so much, but thicker as it comes nearer the neck, which in the largest glasses is about an inch deep, and an inch and half wide within, these dimensions lessening as the glasses themselves diminish in size, except that the neck of the smallest ought not to be shorter than half an inch.—The largest glass is nine inches diameter, and the smallest three inches. Between these there are twenty-three different sizes, differing from each other a quarter of an inch in diameter.—To make a single instrument there should be at least six glasses blown of each size; and out of this number one may probably pick 37 glasses, (which are sufficient for 3 octaves with all the semitones) that will be each either the note one wants or a little sharper than that note, and all fitting so well into each other as to taper pretty regularly from the largest to the smallest. It is true there are not 37 sizes, but it often happens that two of the same size differ a note or half note in tone, by reason of a difference in thickness, and these may be placed one in the other without sensibly hurting the regularity of the taper form.

The glasses being chosen and every one marked with a diamond the note you intend it for, they are to be tuned by diminishing the thickness of those that are too sharp. This is done by grinding them round from the neck towards the brim, the breadth of one or two inches as may be required; often trying the glass by a well tuned harpsichord, comparing the tone drawn from the glass by your finger, with the note you want, as sounded by that string of the harpsichord. When you come near the matter, be careful to wipe the glass clean and dry before each trial, because the tone is something flatter when the glass is wet, than it will be when dry;—and grinding a very little between each trial, you will thereby tune to great exactness. The more care is necessary in this, because if you go below your required tone, there is no sharpening it again but by grinding somewhat off the brim, which will afterwards require polishing, and thus encrease the trouble.

The glasses being thus tuned, you are to be provided with a case for them, and a spindle on which they are to be fixed. My case is about three feet long, eleven inches every way wide within at the biggest end, and five inches at the smallest end; for it tapers all the way, to adapt it better to the conical figure of the set of glasses. This case opens in the middle of its height, and the upper part turns up by hinges fixed behind. The spindle which is of hard iron, lies horizontally from end to end of the box within, exactly in the middle, and is made to turn on brass gudgeons at each end. It is round, an inch diameter at the thickest end, and tapering to a quarter of an inch at the smallest.—A square shank comes from its thickest end through the box, on which shank a wheel is fixed by a screw. This wheel serves as a fly to make the motion equable, when the spindle, with the glasses, is turned by the foot like a spinning wheel. My wheel is of mahogany, 18 inches diameter, and pretty thick, so as to conceal near its circumference about 25lb of lead.—An ivory pin is fixed in the face of this wheel and about 4 inches from the axis. Over the neck of this pin is put the loop of the string that comes up from the moveable step to give it motion. The case stands on a neat frame with four legs.

To fix the glasses on the spindle, a cork is first to be fitted in each neck pretty tight, and projecting a little without the neck, that the neck of one may not touch the inside of another when put together, for that would make a jarring.— These corks are to be perforated with holes of different diameters, so as to suit that part of the spindle on which they are to be fixed. When a glass is put on, by holding it stiffly between both hands, while another turns the spindle, it may be gradually brought to its place. But care must be taken that the hole be not too small, lest in forcing it up the neck should split; nor too large, lest the glass not being firmly fixed, should turn or move on the spindle, so as to touch and jar against its neighbouring glass. The glasses thus are placed one in another, the largest on the biggest end of the spindle which is to the left hand; the neck of this glass is towards the wheel, and the next goes into it in the same position, only about an inch of its brim appearing beyond the brim of the first; thus proceeding, every glass when fixed shows about an inch of its brim, (or three quarters of an inch, or half an inch, as they grow smaller) beyond the brim of the glass that contains it; and it is from these exposed parts of each glass that the tone is drawn, by laying a finger upon one of them as the spindle and glasses turn round.

My largest glass is G a little below the reach of a common voice, and my highest G, including three compleat octaves.— To distinguish the glasses the more readily to the eye, I have painted the apparent parts of the glasses within side, every semitone white, and the other notes of the octave with the seven prismatic colours, *viz.* C, red; D, orange; E, yellow; F, green; G, blue; A, Indigo; B, purple; and C, red again;—so that glasses of the same colour (the white excepted) are always octaves to each other.

This instrument is played upon, by sitting before the middle of the set of glasses as before the keys of a harpsichord, turning them with the foot, and wetting them now and then with a spunge and clean water. The fingers should be first a little soaked in water and quite free from all greasiness; a little fine chalk upon them is sometimes useful, to make them catch the glass and bring out the tone more readily. Both hands are used, by which means different parts are played together.—Observe, that the tones are best drawn out when the glasses turn *from* the ends of the fingers, not when they turn *to* them.

The advantages of this instrument are, that its tones are incomparably sweet beyond those of any other; that they may be swelled and softened at pleasure by stronger or weaker pressures of the finger, and continued to any length; and that the instrument, being once well tuned, never again wants tuning.

In honour of your musical language, I have borrowed from it the name of this instrument, calling it the *Armonica*.

With great esteem and respect, I am, &c.

SOUND

To Oliver Neave

Dear SIR,   *July* 20, 1762.

I have perused your paper on sound, and would freely mention to you, as you desire it, every thing that appeared to me to need correction:—But nothing of that kind occurs to me, unless it be, where you speak of the air as "the *best* medium for conveying sound." Perhaps this is speaking rather too positively, if there be, as I think there are, some other mediums that will convey it farther and more readily.—It is a well-known experiment, that the scratching of a pin at one end of a long piece of timber, may be heard by an ear applied near the other end, though it could not be heard at the same distance through the air.—And two stones being struck smartly together under water, the stroke may be heard at a greater distance by an ear also placed under water in the same river, than it can be heard through the air. I think I have heard it near a mile; how much farther it may be heard, I know not; but suppose a great deal farther, because the sound did not seem faint, as if at a distance, like distant sounds through air, but smart and strong, and as if present just at the ear.—I wish you would repeat these experiments now

you are upon the subject, and add your own observations.—
And if you were to repeat, with your naturally exact attention
and observation, the common experiment of the bell in the
exhausted receiver, possibly something new may occur to
you, in considering,

1. Whether the experiment is not ambiguous; *i. e.* whether
the gradual exhausting of the air, as it creates an increasing
difference of pressure on the outside, may not occasion in the
glass a difficulty of vibrating, that renders it less fit to communicate to the air without, the vibrations that strike it from
within; and the diminution of the sound arise from this cause,
rather than from the diminution of the air?

2. Whether as the particles of air themselves are at a distance from each other, there must not be some medium between them, proper for conveying sound, since otherwise it
would stop at the first particle?

3. Whether the great difference we experience in hearing
sounds at a distance, when the wind blows towards us from
the sonorous body, or towards that from us, can be well accounted for by adding to or substracting from the swiftness
of sound, the degree of swiftness that is in the wind at the
time? The latter is so small in proportion, that it seems as if
it could scarce produce any sensible effect, and yet the difference is very great. Does not this give some hint, as if there
might be a subtile fluid, the conductor of sound, which
moves at different times in different directions over the surface of the earth, and whose motion may perhaps be much
swifter than that of the air in our strongest winds; and that
in passing through air, it may communicate that motion to
the air which we call wind, though a motion in no degree so
swift as its own?

4. It is somewhere related, that a pistol fired on the top of
an exceeding high mountain, made a noise like thunder in the
valleys below. Perhaps this fact is not exactly related: but if it
is, would not one imagine from it, that the rarer the air, the
greater sound might be produced in it from the same cause?

5. Those balls of fire which are sometimes seen passing over
a country, computed by philosophers to be often 30 miles
high at least, sometimes burst at that height; the air must be
exceeding rare there, and yet the explosion produces a sound

that is heard at that distance, and for 70 miles round on the surface of the earth, so violent too as to shake buildings, and give an apprehension of an earthquake. Does not this look as if a rare atmosphere, almost a vacuum, was no bad conductor of sound?

I have not made up my own mind on these points, and only mention them for your consideration, knowing that every subject is the better for your handling it.

With the greatest esteem, I am, &c.

OIL AND WATER

To John Pringle

SIR,   *Philadelphia, Dec.* 1, 1762.

During our passage to Madeira, the weather being warm, and the cabbin windows constantly open for the benefit of the air, the candles at night flared and run very much, which was an inconvenience. At Madeira we got oil to burn, and with a common glass tumbler or beaker, slung in wire, and suspended to the cieling of the cabbin, and a little wire hoop for the wick, furnish'd with corks to float on the oil, I made an Italian lamp, that gave us very good light all over the table. —The glass at bottom contained water to about one third of its height; another third was taken up with oil; the rest was left empty that the sides of the glass might protect the flame from the wind. There is nothing remarkable in all this; but what follows is particular. At supper, looking on the lamp, I remarked that tho' the surface of the oil was perfectly tranquil, and duly preserved its position and distance with regard to the brim of the glass, the water under the oil was in great commotion, rising and falling in irregular waves, which continued during the whole evening. The lamp was kept burning as a watch light all night, till the oil was spent, and the water only remain'd. In the morning I observed, that though the motion of the ship continued the same, the water was now quiet, and its surface as tranquil as that of the oil had been the evening before. At night again, when oil was put upon it, the water resum'd its irregular motions, rising in high waves almost to the surface of the oil, but without disturbing the smooth level of that surface. And this was repeated every day during the voyage.

Since my arrival in America, I have repeated the experiment frequently thus. I have put a pack-thread round a tumbler, with strings of the same, from each side, meeting above it in a knot at about a foot distance from the top of the tumbler. Then putting in as much water as would fill about one third part of the tumbler, I lifted it up by the knot, and swung it to and fro in the air; when the water appeared to keep its place in the tumbler as steadily as if it had been ice.—But pouring gently in upon the water about as much oil, and then again swinging it in the air as before, the tranquility before possessed by the water, was transferred to the surface of the oil, and the water under it was agitated with the same commotions as at sea.

I have shewn this experiment to a number of ingenious persons. Those who are but slightly acquainted with the principles of hydrostatics, &c. are apt to fancy immediately that they understand it, and readily attempt to explain it; but their explanations have been different, and to me not very intelligible.—Others more deeply skill'd in those principles, seem to wonder at it, and promise to consider it. And I think it is worth considering: For a new appearance, if it cannot be explain'd by our old principles, may afford us new ones, of use perhaps in explaining some other obscure parts of natural knowledge.

I am, &c.

"I LOOK'D ROUND FOR GOD'S JUDGMENTS"

To Jared Ingersoll

Dear Sir   Philada. Dec. 11. 1762

I thank you for your kind Congratulations. It gives me Pleasure to hear from an old Friend, it will give me much more to see him. I hope therefore nothing will prevent the Journey you propose for next Summer, and the Favour you

intend me of a Visit. I believe I must make a Journey early
in the Spring, to Virginia, but purpose being back again before the hot Weather. You will be kind enough to let me
know beforehand what time you expect to be here, that I
may not be out of the way; for that would mortify me exceedingly.

I should be glad to know what it is that distinguishes
Connecticut Religion from common Religion: Communicate, if you please, some of those particulars that you think
will amuse me as a Virtuoso. When I travelled in Flanders I
thought of your excessively strict Observation of Sunday;
and that a Man could hardly travel on that day among you
upon his lawful Occasions, without Hazard of Punishment;
while where I was, every one travell'd, if he pleas'd, or di-
verted himself any other way; and in the Afternoon both
high and low went to the Play or the Opera, where there
was plenty of Singing, Fiddling and Dancing. I look'd
round for God's Judgments but saw no Signs of them. The
Cities were well built and full of Inhabitants, the Markets
fill'd with Plenty, the People well favour'd and well clothed;
the Fields well till'd; the Cattle fat and strong; the Fences,
Houses and Windows all in Repair; and *no Old Tenor* anywhere in the Country; which would almost make one suspect, that the Deity is not so angry at that Offence as a New
England Justice.

I left our Friend Mr. Jackson well. And I had the great
Happiness of finding my little Family well when I came
home; and my Friends as cordial and more numerous than
ever. May every Prosperity attend you and yours. I am Dear
Friend, Yours affectionately

"THE ARTS DELIGHT TO TRAVEL WESTWARD"

To Mary Stevenson

My dear Polley   Philada. March 25. 1763
Your pleasing Favour of Nov. 11 is now before me. It found
me as you suppos'd it would, happy with my American
Friends and Family about me; and it made me more happy in

showing me that I am not yet forgotten by the dear Friends I left in England. And indeed why should I fear they will ever forget me, when I feel so strongly that I shall ever remember them!

I sympathise with you sincerely in your Grief at the Separation from your old Friend, Miss Pitt. The Reflection that she is going to be more happy when she leaves you, might comfort you, if the Case was likely to be so circumstanc'd; but when the Country and Company she has been educated in, and those she is removing to, are compared, one cannot possibly expect it.

I sympathize with you no less in your Joys. But it is not merely on your Account that I rejoice at the Recovery of your dear Dolly's Health. I love that dear good Girl myself, and I love her other Friends. I am therefore made happy by what must contribute so much to the Happiness of them all. Remember me to her, and to every one of that worthy and amiable Family most affectionately.

Remember me in the same manner to your and my good Doctor and Mrs. Hawkesworth. You have lately, you tell me, had the Pleasure of spending three Days with them at Mr. Stanley's. It was a sweet Society! (Remember me also to Mr. and Mrs. Stanley, and to Miss Arlond)—I too, once partook of that same Pleasure, and can therefore feel what you must have felt. Of all the enviable Things England has, I envy it most its People. Why should that petty Island, which compar'd to America is but like a stepping Stone in a Brook, scarce enough of it above Water to keep one's Shoes dry; why, I say, should that little Island, enjoy in almost every Neighbourhood, more sensible, virtuous and elegant Minds, than we can collect in ranging 100 Leagues of our vast Forests. But, 'tis said, the Arts delight to travel Westward. You have effectually defended us in this glorious War, and in time you will improve us. After the first Cares for the Necessaries of Life are over, we shall come to think of the Embellishments. Already some of our young Geniuses begin to lisp Attempts at Painting, Poetry and Musick. We have a young Painter now studying at Rome: Some Specimens of our Poetry I send you, which if Dr. Hawkesworth's fine Taste cannot approve, his good Heart will at least excuse. The Manuscript

Piece is by a young Friend of mine, and was occasion'd by
the Loss of one of his Friends, who lately made a Voyage to
Antigua to settle some Affairs previous to an intended Marriage with an amiable young Lady here; but unfortunately
died there. I send it you, because the Author is a great
Admirer of Mr. Stanley's musical Compositions, and has
adapted this Piece to an Air in the 6th Concerto of that Gentleman, the sweetly solemn Movement of which he is quite in
Raptures with. He has attempted to compose a Recitativo for
it; but not being able to satisfy himself in the Bass, wishes I
could get it supply'd. If Mr. Stanley would condescend to do
that for him, thro' your Intercession, he would esteem it as
one of the highest Honours, and it would make him excessively happy. You will say that a Recitativo can be but a poor
Specimen of our Music. 'Tis the best and all I have at present;
but you may see better hereafter.

I hope Mr. Ralph's Affairs are mended since you wrote. I
know he had some Expectations when I came away, from a
Hand that could help him. He has Merit, and one would
think ought not to be so unfortunate.

I do not wonder at the Behaviour you mention of Dr.
Smith towards me, for I have long since known him thoroughly. I made that Man my Enemy by doing him too much
Kindness. Tis the honestest Way of acquiring an Enemy. And
since 'tis convenient to have at least one Enemy, who by his
Readiness to revile one on all Occasions may make one careful of one's Conduct, I shall keep him an Enemy for that
purpose; and shall observe your good Mother's Advice, never
again to receive him as a Friend. She once admir'd the benevolent Spirit breath'd in his Sermons. She will now see the
Justness of the Lines your Laureat Whitehead addresses to his
Poets, and which I now address to her,

> Full many a *peevish, envious, slanderous* Elf,
> Is,—in his Works,—Benevolence itself.
> For all Mankind—unknown—his Bosom heaves;
> He only injures those with whom he lives.
> Read then the Man:—does *Truth* his Actions guide,
> Exempt from *Petulance*, exempt from *Pride*?
> To social Duties does his Heart attend,

As Son, as Father, Husband, Brother, *Friend?*
Do those who know him love him?—If they do,
You've *my* Permission: you may love him too.

Nothing can please me more than to see your philosophical
Improvements when you have Leisure to communicate them
to me. I still owe you a long Letter on that Subject, which I
shall pay.

I am vex'd with Mr. James that he has been so dilatory in
Mr. Maddison's Armonica. I was unlucky in both the Workmen that I permitted to undertake making those Instruments.
The first was fanciful, and never could work to the purpose,
because he was ever conceiving some new Improvement that
answer'd no End: the other, I doubt, is absolutely idle. I have
recommended a Number to him from hence, but must stop
my hand.

Adieu, my dear Polly, and believe me as ever, with the sincerest Esteem and Regard, Your truly affectionate Friend, and
humble Servant

My Love to Mrs. Tickell and Mrs. Rooke, and to Pitty when
you write to her. Mrs. Franklin and Sally desire to be affectionately remembr'd to you.

P.S. I find the printed Poetry I intended to enclose will be
too bulky to send per the Packet: I shall send it by a Ship that
goes shortly from hence.

"THE NATURAL CAPACITIES OF THE BLACK RACE"

To John Waring

Reverend and dear Sir,   Philada. Dec. 17. 1763
    Being but just return'd home from a Tour thro' the north-
ern Colonies, that has employ'd the whole Summer, my
Time at present is so taken up that I cannot now write fully
in answer to the Letters I have receiv'd from you, but purpose to do it shortly. This is chiefly to acquaint you, that I
have visited the Negro School here in Company with the
Revd. Mr. Sturgeon and some others; and had the Children

thoroughly examin'd. They appear'd all to have made considerable Progress in Reading for the Time they had respectively been in the School, and most of them answer'd readily and well the Questions of the Catechism; they behav'd very orderly, showd a proper Respect and ready Obedience to the Mistress, and seem'd very attentive to, and a good deal affected by, a serious Exhortation with which Mr. Sturgeon concluded our Visit. I was on the whole much pleas'd, and from what I then saw, have conceiv'd a higher Opinion of the natural Capacities of the black Race, than I had ever before entertained. Their Apprehension seems as quick, their Memory as strong, and their Docility in every Respect equal to that of white Children. You will wonder perhaps that I should ever doubt it, and I will not undertake to justify all my Prejudices, nor to account for them. I immediately advanc'd the two Guineas you mention'd, for the Mistress, and Mr. Sturgeon will therefore draw on you for £7 18s. only, which makes up the half Year's Salary of Ten Pounds. Be pleased to present my best Respects to the Associates, and believe me, with sincere Esteem Dear Sir, Your most obedient Servant

"LIKE A MORNING FOG BEFORE THE RISING SUN"

To William Strahan

Dear Straney   Philada. Dec. 19. 1763.
    I have before me your Favours of July 16, and Augt. 18. which is the latest. It vexes me excessively to see that Parker and Mecom are so much in Arrear with you. What is due from Parker is safe, and will be paid, I think with Interest; for he is a Man as honest as he is industrious and frugal, and has withal some Estate: his Backwardness has been owing to his bad Partners only, of whom he is now nearly quit. But as to Mecom, he seems so dejected and spiritless, that I fear little will be got of him. He has dropt his Paper, on which he built his last Hopes. I doubt I shall lose £200 by him myself, but

am taking Steps to save what I can for you; of which more fully in my next.

Now I am return'd from my long Journeys which have consum'd the whole Summer, I shall apply myself to such a Settlement of all my Affairs, as will enable me to do what your Friendship so warmly urges. I have a great Opinion of your Wisdom (Madeira apart;) and am apt enough to think that what you seem so clear in, and are so earnest about, must be right. Tho' I own, that I sometimes suspect, my Love to England and my Friends there seduces me a little, and makes *my own* middling Reasons for going over; appear very good ones. We shall see in a little Time how Things will turn out.

Blessings on your Heart for the Feast of Politicks you gave me in your last. I could by no other means have obtain'd so clear a View of the present State of your public Affairs as by your Letter. Most of your Observations appear to me extreamly judicious, strikingly clear and true. I only differ from you in some of the melancholly Apprehensions you express concerning Consequences; and to comfort you (at the same time flattering my own Vanity,) let me remind you, that I have sometimes been in the right in such Cases, when you happen'd to be in the wrong; as I can prove upon you out of this very Letter of yours. Call to mind your former Fears for the King of Prussia, and remember my telling you that the Man's Abilities were more than equal to all the Force of his Enemies, and that he would finally extricate himself, and triumph. This, by the Account you give me from Major Beckwith, is fully verified. You now fear for our virtuous young King, that the Faction forming will overpower him, and render his Reign uncomfortable. On the contrary, I am of Opinion, that his Virtue, and the Consciousness of his sincere Intentions to make his People happy, will give him Firmness and Steadiness in his Measures, and in the Support of the honest Friends he has chosen to serve him; and when that Firmness is fully perceiv'd, Faction will dissolve and be dissipated like a Morning Fog before the rising Sun, leaving the rest of the Day clear, with a Sky serene and cloudless. Such, after a few of the first Years, will be the future Course of his Majesty's Reign, which I predict will be happy and truly glorious. Your Fears for the Nation too, appear to me as little founded. A new War I cannot yet see Reason to apprehend. The Peace I think will long continue, and your Nation be as happy as they deserve to be, that is, as happy as their moderate Share of Virtue will allow them to be: Happier than that, no outward Circumstances can make a Nation any more than a private Man. And as to their Quantity of Virtue, I think it bids fair for Increasing; if the old Saying be true, as it certainly is,

Ad Exemplum Regis, &c.

My Love to Mrs. Strahan and your Children in which my Wife and Daughter join with Your ever affectionate Friend

P.S. The western Indians about Fort Detroit now sue for Peace, having lost a great Number of their best Warriors in their vain Attempt to reduce that Fortress; and being at length assur'd by a Belt from the French Commander in the Ilinois Country, that a Peace is concluded between England and France, that he must evacuate the Country and deliver up his Forts, and can no longer supply or support them. It is thought this will draw on a general Peace. I am only afraid it will be concluded before these Barbarians have sufficiently smarted for their perfidious breaking the last.

The Governor of Detroit, Major Gladwin, has granted them a Cessation of Arms, till the General's Pleasure is known.

"AN AMBASSADOR TO THE COUNTRY MOB"

To John Fothergill

Dear Doctor,   Philada. March 14. 1764.

I received your Favour of the 10th. of Decemr. It was a great deal for one to write, whose Time is so little his own. By the way, *When do you intend to live?* i.e. to enjoy Life. When will you retire to your Villa, give your self Repose, delight in Viewing the Operations of Nature in the vegetable Creation, assist her in her Works, get your ingenious Friends at times about you, make them happy with your Conversation, and enjoy theirs; or, if alone, amuse yourself with your Books and elegant Collections? To be hurried about perpetually from one sick Chamber to another, is not Living. Do you please yourself with the Fancy that you are doing Good? You are mistaken. Half the Lives you save are not worth saving, as being useless; and almost the other Half ought not to be sav'd, as being mischievous. Does your Conscience never hint to you the Impiety of being in constant Warfare against the Plans of Providence? Disease was intended as the Punishment of Intemperance, Sloth, and other Vices; and the Example of that Punishment was intended to promote and strengthen the opposite Virtues. But here you step in officiously with your Art, disappoint those wise Intentions of Nature, and make Men safe in their Excesses. Whereby you seem to me to be of just the same Service to Society as some favourite first Minister, who out of the great Benevolence of his Heart should procure Pardons for all Criminals that apply'd to him. Only think of the Consequences!

You tell me the Quakers are charged on your side the Water with being by their Aggressions the Cause of this War. Would you believe it, that they are charg'd here, not with offending the Indians, and thereby provoking the War, but with gaining their Friendship by Presents, supplying them privately with Arms and Ammunition, and engaging them to fall upon and murder the poor white People on the Frontiers? Would you think it possible that Thousands even here should be made to believe this, and many Hundreds of them be raised in Arms, not only to kill some converted Indians supposed to be under the Quakers Protection, but to punish the Quakers who were supposed to give that Protection? Would you think these People audacious enough to avow such Designs in a public Declaration sent to the Governor? Would you imagine that innocent Quakers, Men of Fortune and Character, should think it necessary to fly for Safety out of Philadelphia into the Jersies, fearing the Violence of such armed Mobs, and confiding little in the Power *or Inclination* of the Government to protect them? And would you imagine that strong Suspicions now prevail, that those Mobs, after committing 20 barbarous Murders, hitherto unpunish'd, are privately tamper'd with to be made Instruments of Government, to awe the Assembly into Proprietary Measures? And yet all this has happen'd within a few Weeks past!

More Wonders! You know I don't love the Proprietary, and that he does not love me. Our totally different Tempers forbid it. You might therefore expect, that the late new Appointment of one of his Family, would find me ready for Opposition. And yet when his Nephew arriv'd our Governor, I consider'd Government as Government, paid him all Respect, gave him on all Occasions my best Advice, promoted in the Assembly a ready Compliance with everything he propos'd or recommended; and when those daring Rioters, encourag'd by the general Approbation of the Populace, treated his Proclamations with Contempt, I drew my Pen in the Cause, wrote a Pamphlet (that I have sent you) to render the Rioters unpopular; promoted an Association to support the Authority of the Government and defend the Governor by taking Arms, sign'd it first myself, and was followed by several Hundreds, who took Arms accordingly; the Governor offer'd me the Command of them, but I chose to carry a Musket, and strengthen his Authority by setting an Example of Obedience to his Orders. And, would you think it, this Proprietary Governor did me the Honour, on an Alarm, to run to my House at Midnight, with his Counsellors at his Heels, for Advice, and made it his Head Quarters for some time: And within four and twenty Hours, your old Friend was a common Soldier, a Counsellor, a kind of Dictator, an Ambassador to the Country Mob, and on their Returning home, *Nobody*, again. All this has happened in a few Weeks!

More Wonders! The Assembly receiv'd a Governor of the Proprietary Family with open Arms, address'd him with sincere Expressions of Kindness and Respect, open'd their Purses to him, and presented him with Six Hundred Pounds; made a Riot Act and prepar'd a Militia Bill immediately at his Instance; granted Supplies and did every thing that he requested, and promis'd themselves great Happiness under his Administration. But suddenly, his dropping all Enquiry after the Murderers, and his answering the Deputies of the Rioters privately and refusing the Presence of the Assembly who were equally concern'd in the Matters contain'd in their

Remonstrance, brings him under Suspicion; his Insulting the Assembly without the least Provocation, by charging them with Disloyalty and with making *an Infringement on the King's Prerogatives*, only because they had presumed to name in a Bill offered for his Assent, a trifling Officer (somewhat like one of your Toll-Gatherers at a Turn pike) without consulting him; and his refusing several of their Bills, or proposing Amendments needlessly disgusting; these Things bring him and his Government into sudden Contempt; all Regard for him in the Assembly is lost; all Hopes of Happiness under a Proprietary Government are at an End; it has now scarce Authority enough left to keep the common Peace; and was another Mob to come against him, I question whether, tho' a Dozen Men were sufficient, one could find so many in Philadelphia, willing to rescue him or his Attorney-General, I won't say from Hanging, but from any common Insult. All this, too, has happened in a few Weeks!

In fine, every thing seems in this Country, once the Land of Peace and Order, to be running fast into Anarchy and Confusion. Our only Hopes are, that the Crown will see the Necessity of taking the Government into its own Hands, without which we shall soon have no Government at all.

Your civil Dissensions at home give us here great Concern. But we hope there is Virtue enough in your great Nation to support a good Prince in the Execution of Good Government, and the Exercise of his just Prerogatives, against all the Attempts of Unreasonable Faction.

I have been already too long. Adieu, my dear Friend, and believe me ever Yours affectionately

"SO SELFISH IS THE HUMAN MIND!"

To Peter Collinson

Dear Friend,   Philada. April 30. 1764
I have before me your kind Notices of Feb. 3. and Feb. 10. Those you enclos'd for our Friend Bartram, were carefully deliver'd.

I have not yet seen the Squib you mention against your People, in the Supplement to the Magazine; but I think it impossible they should be worse us'd there than they have lately been here; where sundry inflammatory Pamphlets are printed and spread about to excite a mad armed Mob to massacre them. And it is my Opinion they are still in some Danger, more than they themselves seem to apprehend, as our Government has neither Goodwill nor Authority enough to protect them.

By the enclos'd Papers you will see that we are all to pieces again; and the general Wish seems to be a King's Government. If that is not to be obtain'd, many talk of quitting the Province, and among them your old Friend, who is tired of these Contentions, and longs for philosophic Ease and Leisure.

I suppose by this Time the Wisdom of your Parliament has determin'd in the Points you mention, of Trade, Duties, Troops and Fortifications in America. Our Opinions or Inclinations, if they had been known, would perhaps have weigh'd but little among you. We are in your Hands as Clay in the Hands of the Potter; and so in one more Particular than is generally consider'd: for as the Potter cannot waste or spoil his Clay without injuring himself; so I think there is scarce anything you can do that may be hurtful to us, but what will be as much or more so to you. This must be our chief Security; for Interest with you we have but little: The West Indians vastly outweigh us of the Northern Colonies. What we get above a Subsistence, we lay out with you for your Manufactures. Therefore what you get from us in Taxes you must lose in Trade. The Cat can yield but her Skin. And as you must have the whole Hide, if you first cut Thongs out of it, 'tis at your own Expence. The same in regard to our Trade with the foreign West India Islands: If you restrain it in any Degree, you restrain in the same Proportion our Power of making Remittances to you, and of course our Demand for your Goods; for you will not clothe us out of Charity, tho' to receive 100 per Cent for it, in Heaven. In time perhaps Mankind may be wise enough to let Trade take its own Course, find its own Channels, and regulate its own Proportions, &c. At present, most of the Edicts of Princes,

Placaerts, Laws and Ordinances of Kingdoms and States, for that purpose, prove political Blunders. The Advantages they produce not being *general* for the Commonwealth; but *particular*, to private Persons or Bodies in the State who procur'd them, and *at the Expence of the rest of the People*. Does no body see, that if you confine us in America to your own Sugar Islands for that Commodity, it must raise the Price of it upon you in England? Just so much as the Price advances, so much is every Englishman tax'd to the West Indians. Apropos. Now we are on the Subject of Trade and Manufactures, let me tell you a Piece of News, that though it might displease a very respectable Body among you, the Button-makers, will be agreable to yourself as a Virtuoso: It is, that we have discover'd a Beach in a Bay several Miles round, the Pebbles of which are all in the Form of Buttons, whence it is called *Button-mold Bay*; where thousands of Tons may be had for fetching; and as the Sea washes down the slaty Cliff, more are continually manufacturing out of the Fragments by the Surge. I send you a Specimen of Coat, Wastecoat and Sleeve Buttons; just as Nature has turn'd them. But I think I must not mention the Place, lest some Englishman get a Patent for this *Button-mine*, as one did for the *Coal mine* at Louisburgh, and by neither suffering others to work it, nor working it himself, deprive us of the Advantage God and Nature seem to have intended us. As we have now got Buttons, 'tis something towards our Cloathing; and who knows but in time we may find out where to get Cloth? for as to our being always supply'd by you, 'tis a Folly to expect it. Only consider *the Rate of our Increase*, and tell me if you can increase your Wooll in that Proportion, and where, in your little Island you can feed the Sheep. Nature has put Bounds to your Abilities, tho' none to your Desires. Britain would, if she could, manufacture and trade for all the World; England for all Britain; London for all England; and every Londoner for all London. So selfish is the human Mind! But 'tis well there is One above that rules these Matters with a more equal Hand. He that is pleas'd to feed the Ravens, will undoubtedly take care to prevent a Monopoly of the Carrion. Adieu, my dear Friend, and believe me ever Yours most affectionately

"GO CONSTANTLY TO CHURCH
WHOEVER PREACHES"

To Sarah Franklin

Reedy Island Nov. 8. 1764
My dear Sally,   7 at Night.

We got down here just at Sunset, having taken in more live
Stock at Newcastle with some other things we wanted. Our
good Friends Mr. Galloway, Mr. Wharton, and Mr. James
came with me in the Ship from Chester to Newcastle, and
went ashore there. It was kind to favour me with their good
Company as far as they could. The affectionate Leave taken
of me by so many Friends at Chester was very endearing. God
bless them, and all Pennsylvania.

My dear Child, the natural Prudence and goodness of heart
that God has blessed you with, make it less necessary for me
to be particular in giving you Advice; I shall therefore only
say, that the more attentively dutiful and tender you are towards your good Mama, the more you will recommend your
self to me; But why shou'd I mention *me*, when you have so
much higher a Promise in the Commandment, that such a
conduct will recommend you to the favour of God. You know
I have many Enemies (all indeed on the Public Account, for
I cannot recollect that I have in a private Capacity given just
cause of offence to any one whatever) yet they are Enemies
and very bitter ones, and you must expect their Enmity will
extend in some degree to you, so that your slightest Indiscre-
tions will be magnified into crimes, in order the more sensibly
to wound and afflict me. It is therefore the more necessary
for you to be extreamly circumspect in all your Behaviour that
no Advantage may be given to their Malevolence. Go constantly to Church whoever preaches. The Acts of Devotion in
the common Prayer Book, are your principal Business there;
and if properly attended to, will do more towards mending
the Heart than Sermons generally can do. For they were composed by Men of much greater Piety and Wisdom, than our
common Composers of Sermons can pretend to be. And
therefore I wish you wou'd never miss the Prayer Days. Yet I
do not mean that you shou'd despise Sermons even of the

Preachers you dislike, for the Discourse is often much better
than the Man, as sweet and clear Waters come to us thro' very
dirty Earth. I am the more particular on this Head, as you
seem'd to express a little before I came away some Inclination
to leave our Church, which I wou'd not have you do.

For the rest I would only recommend to you in my Absence to acquire those useful Accomplishments Arithmetick,
and Book-keeping. This you might do with Ease, if you
wou'd resolve not to see Company on the Hours you set
apart for those Studies. I think you should and every Body
should if they could, have certain days or hours to [   ]
She cannot be spoke with: but will be glad to see you at such
a time.

We expect to be at Sea to morrow if this Wind holds, after
which I shall have no opportunity of Writing to you till I
arrive (if it pleases God that I do arrive) in England. I pray
that *his* Blessing may attend you which is of more worth than
a Thousand of mine, though they are never wanting. Give my
Love to your Brother and Sister, as I cannot now write to
them; and remember me affectionately to the young Ladies
your Friends, and to our good Neighbours. I am, my dear
Sally, Your ever Affectionate Father

THE OLD SONGS VERSUS MODERN MUSIC

To Lord Kames

My dear Lord   Cravenstreet, London, June 2. 1765.
I receiv'd with great Pleasure your friendly Letter by Mr.
Alexander, which I should have answer'd sooner by some
other Conveyance, if I had understood that his Stay here was
like to be so long. I value myself extreamly on the Continuance of your Regard, which I hope hereafter better to deserve
by more punctual Returns in the Correspondence you honour
me with.

You require my History from the time I set Sail for America. I left England about the End of August 1762, in Company
with Ten Sail of Merchant Ships under Convoy of a Man of
War. We had a pleasant Passage to Madeira, an Island and

Colony belonging to Portugal, where we were kindly receiv'd
and entertain'd, our Nation being then in high Honour with
them, on Account of the Protection it was at that time affording their Mother Country from the united Invasions of
France and Spain. 'Tis a fertile Island, and the different
Heights and Situations among its Mountains, afford such different Temperaments of Air, that all the Fruits of Northern
and Southern Countries are produc'd there, Corn, Grapes,
Apples, Peaches, Oranges, Lemons, Plantains, Bananas, &c.
Here we furnish'd ourselves with fresh Provisions and Refreshments of all kinds, and after a few Days proceeded on
our Voyage, running Southward till we got into the Trade
Winds, and then with them Westward till we drew near the
Coast of America. The Weather was so favourable, that there
were few Days in which we could not visit from Ship to Ship,
dining with each other and on board the Man of War, which
made the time pass agreably, much more so than when one
goes in a single Ship, for this was like travelling in a moving
Village, with all one's Neighbours about one. On the first of
November, I arriv'd safe and well at my own House, after an
Absence of near Six Years, found my Wife and Daughter well,
the latter grown quite a Woman, with many amiable Accomplishments acquir'd in my Absence, and my Friends as hearty
and affectionate as ever, with whom my House was fill'd for
many Days, to congratulate me on my Return. I had been
chosen yearly during my Absence to represent the City of
Philadelphia in our Provincial Assembly, and on my Appearance in the House they voted me £3000 Sterling for my Services in England and their Thanks delivered by the Speaker.
In February following my Son arriv'd, with my new Daughter, for, with my Consent and Approbation he married soon
after I left England, a very agreable West India Lady, with
whom he is very happy. I accompanied him into his Government, where he met with the kindest Reception from the People of all Ranks, and has lived with them ever since in the
greatest Harmony. A River only parts that Province and ours,
and his Residence is within 17 Miles of me, so that we frequently see each other. In the Spring of 1763 I set out on a
Tour thro' all the Northern Colonies, to inspect and regulate
the Post Offices in the several Provinces. In this Journey I

spent the Summer, travelled about 1600 Miles, and did not get home 'till the Beginning of November. The Assembly sitting thro' the following Winter, and warm Disputes arising between them and the Governor I became wholly engag'd in public Affairs: For besides my Duty as an Assemblyman, I had another Trust to execute, that of being one of the Commissioners appointed by Law to dispose of the publick Money appropriated to the Raising and Paying an Army to act against the Indians and defend the Frontiers. And then in December we had two Insurrections of the back Inhabitants of our Province, by whom 20 poor Indians were murdered that had from the first Settlement of the Province lived among us and under the Protection of our Government. This gave me a good deal of Employment, for as the Rioters threatned farther Mischief, and their Actions seem'd to be approv'd by an encreasing Party, I wrote a Pamphlet entitled a *Narrative*, &c. (which I think I sent you,) to strengthen the Hands of our weak Government, by rendring the Proceedings of the Rioters unpopular and odious. This had a good Effect; and afterwards when a great Body of them with Arms march'd towards the Capital in Defiance of the Government, with an avowed Resolution to put to death 140 Indian Converts then under its Protection, I form'd an Association at the Governor's Request, for his and their Defence, we having no Militia. Near 1000 of the Citizens accordingly took Arms; Governor Penn made my House for some time his Head Quarters, and did every thing by my Advice, so that for about 48 Hours I was a very great Man, as I had been once some Years before in a time of publick Danger; but the fighting Face we put on, and the Reasonings we us'd with the Insurgents (for I went at the Request of the Governor and Council with three others to meet and discourse them) having turn'd them back, and restor'd Quiet to the City, I became a less Man than ever: for I had by these Transactions made myself many Enemies among the Populace; and the Governor (with whose Family our publick Disputes had long plac'd me in an unfriendly Light, and the Services I had lately render'd him not being of the kind that make a Man acceptable) thinking it a favourable Opportunity, join'd the whole Weight of the Proprietary Interest to get me out of the Assembly, which was accordingly effected at the last Election, by a Majority of about 25 in 4000 Voters. The House however, when they met in October, approv'd of the Resolutions taken while I was Speaker, of petitioning the Crown for a Change of Government, and requested me to return to England to prosecute that Petition; which Service I accordingly undertook, and embark'd the Beginning of November last, being accompany'd to the Ship, 16 Miles, by a Cavalcade of three Hundred of my Friends, who fill'd our Sails with their good Wishes, and I arrived in 30 Days at London. Here I have been ever since engag'd in that and other Public Affairs relating to America, which are like to continue some time longer upon my hands; but I promise you, that when I am quit of these, I will engage in no other; and that as soon as I have recover'd the Ease and Leisure I hope for, the Task you require of me, of finishing my *Art of Virtue* shall be perform'd: In the mean time I must request you would excuse me on this Consideration, that the Powers of the Mind are posess'd by different Men in different Degrees, and that every one cannot, like Lord Kaims, intermix literary Pursuits and important Business, without Prejudice to either.

I send you herewith two or three other Pamphlets of my Writing on our political Affairs during my short Residence in America; but I do not insist on your reading them, for I know you employ all your time to some useful Purpose.

In my Passage to America, I read your excellent Work, the Elements of Criticism, in which I found great Entertainment, much to admire, and nothing to reprove. I only wish'd you had examin'd more fully the Subject of Music, and demonstrated that the Pleasure Artists feel in hearing much of that compos'd in the modern Taste, is not the natural Pleasure arising from Melody or Harmony of Sounds, but of the same kind with the Pleasure we feel on seeing the surprizing Feats of Tumblers and Rope Dancers, who execute difficult Things. For my part, I take this to be really the Case and suppose it the Reason why those who being unpractis'd in Music, and therefore unacquainted with those Difficulties, have little or no Pleasure in hearing this Music. Many Pieces of it are mere Compositions of Tricks. I have sometimes at a Concert attended by a common Audience plac'd myself so as to see all

their Faces, and observ'd no Signs of Pleasure in them during
the Performance of much that was admir'd by the Performers
themselves; while a plain old Scottish Tune, which they disdain'd and could scarcely be prevail'd on to play, gave manifest and general Delight. Give me leave on this Occasion to
extend a little the Sense of your Position, That "Melody and
Harmony are separately agreable, and in Union delightful;"
and to give it as my Opinion, that the Reason why the Scotch
Tunes have liv'd so long, and will probably live forever (if
they escape being stifled in modern affected Ornament) is
merely this, that they are really Compositions of Melody and
Harmony united, or rather that their Melody is Harmony. I
mean the simple Tunes sung by a single Voice. As this will
appear paradoxical I must explain my Meaning. In common
Acceptation indeed, only an agreable *Succession* of Sounds is
called *Melody*, and only the *Co-existence* of agreeing Sounds,
Harmony. But since the Memory is capable of retaining for
some Moments a perfect Idea of the Pitch of a past Sound,
so as to compare with it the Pitch of a succeeding Sound, and
judge truly of their Agreement or Disagreement, there may
and does arise from thence a Sense of Harmony between
present and past Sounds, equally pleasing with that between
two present Sounds. Now the Construction of the old Scotch
Tunes is this, that almost every succeeding *emphatical* Note,
is a Third, a Fifth, an Octave, or in short some Note that is
in Concord with the preceding Note. Thirds are chiefly used,
which are very pleasing Concords. I use the Word *emphatical*,
to distinguish those Notes which have a Stress laid on them
in Singing the Tune, from the lighter connecting Notes, that
serve merely, like Grammar Articles, to tack the others together. That we have a most perfect Idea of a Sound just past,
I might appeal to all acquainted with Music, who know how
easy it is to repeat a Sound in the same Pitch with one just
heard. In Tuning an Instrument, a good Ear can as easily determine that two Strings are in Unison, by sounding them
separately, as by sounding them together; their Disagreement
is also as easily, I believe I may say more easily and better
distinguish'd, when sounded separately; for when sounded
together, tho' you know by the Beating that one is higher
than the other, you cannot tell which it is. Farther, when we

consider by whom these ancient Tunes were composed, and how they were first performed, we shall see that such harmonical Succession of Sounds was natural and even necessary in their Construction. They were compos'd by the Minstrels of those days, to be plaid on the Harp accompany'd by the Voice. The Harp was strung with Wire, and had no Contrivance like that in the modern Harpsichord, by which the Sound of a preceding Note could be stopt the Moment a succeeding Note began. To avoid *actual* Discord it was therefore necessary that the succeeding emphatic Note should be a Chord with the preceding, as their Sounds must exist at the same time. Hence arose that Beauty in those Tunes that has so long pleas'd, and will please for ever, tho' Men scarce know why. That they were originally compos'd for the Harp, and of the most simple kind, I mean a Harp without any Half Notes but those in the natural Scale, and with no more than two Octaves of Strings from C. to C. I conjecture from another Circumstance, which is, that not one of those Tunes really ancient has a single artificial Half Note in it; and that in Tunes where it was most convenient for the Voice, to use the middle Notes of the Harp, and place the Key in F. there the B. which if used should be a B flat, is always omitted by passing over it with a Third. The Connoisseurs in modern Music will say I have no Taste, but I cannot help adding, that I believe our Ancestors in hearing a good Song, distinctly articulated, sung to one of those Tunes and accompanied by the Harp, felt more real Pleasure than is communicated by the generality of modern Operas, exclusive of that arising from the Scenery and Dancing. Most Tunes of late Composition, not having the natural Harmony united with their Melody, have recourse to the artificial Harmony of a Bass and other accompanying Parts. This Support, in my Opinion, the old Tunes do not need, and are rather confus'd than aided by it. Whoever has heard James Oswald play them on his Violoncello, will be less inclin'd to dispute this with me. I have more than once seen Tears of Pleasure in the Eyes of his Auditors; and yet I think even his Playing those Tunes would please more, if he gave them less modern Ornament.

My Son, when we parted, desired me to present his affectionate Respects to you, Lady Kaims, and your amiable

Children; be so good with those to accept mine, and believe me, with sincerest Esteem, My dear Lord, Your Lordship's most obedient and most humble Servant

P.S. I do promise myself the Pleasure of seeing you and my other Friends in Scotland before I return to America.

"WE MIGHT AS WELL HAVE HINDER'D THE SUNS SETTING"

To Charles Thomson

Dear Friend   London July 11th: 1765

I am extreemly obliged by your kind Letters of Aprill 12th. and 14th. and thank you for the Intelligence they Contain.

The Outrages continueally commited by those misguided people, will doubtless tend to Convince all the Considerate on your side of the Water of the Weakness of our present Government and the Necessity of a Change. I am sure it will contribute towards hastening that Change here so that upon the whole, Good will be brought out of Evil: but yet I Greive to hear of such horrid Disorders.

The Letters and Accounts boasted of from the Proprietor of his being Sure of retaining the Government, as well as those of the Sums offered for it which the People will be obliged to pay, &c. are all idle Tales, fit only for Knaves to propagate and Fools to believe.

A Little Time will dissipate all the smoke they can raise to conceal the real State of Things. The unsettled State of the Ministry ever since the Parliament rose, has stop'd all Proceeding in Publick Affairs and ours amongst the Rest; but Change being now made we shall immidiately proceed, and with the Greater Chearfulness as some we had reason to Doubt of are removed, and some perticular Friends are put in Place.

What you mention of the Lower Counties is undoubtedly right. Had they ever sent their Laws home as they ought to have done, that iniquitous one of priority of Payment to Reseidents would undoubtedly have been Repeald. But the End of all these things is neigh, at Least it seems to be so.

The spicking of the Guns was an audacious Peice of Villainy, by whomsoever done, it Shows the Necessity of a regular enclos'd Place of Defence, with a Constant Guard to take Care of what belongs to it, which, when the Country can afford it, will I hope be provided.

Depend upon it my good Neighbour, I took every Step in my Power, to prevent the Passing of the Stamp Act; no body could be more concern'd in Interest than my self to oppose it, sincerely and Heartily. But the Tide was, too strong against us. The Nation was provok'd by American Claims of Independance, and all Parties join'd in resolveing by this Act to Settle the Point.

We might as well have hinder'd the Suns setting. That we could not do. But since 'tis down, my Friend, and it may be long before it rises again, Let us make as good a Night of it as we can. We may still Light Candles. Frugallity and Industry will go a great way towards indemnifying us. Idleness and Pride Tax with a heavier Hand then Kings and Parliaments; If we can get rid of the former we may easily bear the Latter.

My best Respects to Mrs. Thompson. Adieu my Dear Friend and beleive me ever Yours affectionately

Excuse my Man John's miserable Clerkship.

"A PRETTY GOOD SORT OF A WORLD"

To Jane Mecom

Dear Sister   London, March 1. 1766

I acknowledge the Receipt of your kind Letters of Nov. 12. and Dec. 20. the latter per Mr. Williams. I condole with you on the Death of your Husband, who was I believe a truly affectionate one to you, and fully sensible of your Merit. It is not true that I have bought any Estate here. I have indeed had some thoughts of re-purchasing the little one in Northamptonshire that was our Grandfather's, and had been many Generations in the Family, but was sold by our Uncle Thomas's only Child Mrs. Fisher, the same that left you the

Legacy. However I shall not do it unless I determine to remain in England, which I have not yet done.

As to the Reports you mention that are spread to my Disadvantage, I give myself as little Concern about them as possible. I have often met with such Treatment from People that I was all the while endeavouring to serve. At other times I have been extoll'd extravagantly when I have had little or no Merit. These are the Operations of Nature. It sometimes is cloudy, it rains, it hails; again 'tis clear and pleasant, and the Sun shines on us. Take one thing with another, and the World is a pretty good sort of a World; and 'tis our Duty to make the best of it and be thankful. One's true Happiness depends more upon one's own Judgement of one's self, on a Consciousness of Rectitude in Action and Intention, and in the Approbation of those few who judge impartially, than upon the Applause of the unthinking undiscerning Multitude, who are apt to cry Hosanna today, and tomorrow, Crucify him. I see in the Papers that your Governor, Mr. Barnard, has been hardly thought of, and a little unkindly treated, as if he was a favourer of the Stamp Act: Yet it appears by his Letters to Government here, which have been read in Parliament, that he has wrote warmly in favour of the Province and against that Act, both before it pass'd and since; and so did your Lieutenant Governor to my certain Knowledge, tho' the Mob have pull'd down his House. Surely the N. England People, when they are rightly inform'd, will do Justice to those Gentlemen, and think of them as they deserve.

Pray remember me kindly to Cousin Williams, and let him know that I am very sensible of his Kindness to you, and that I am not forgetful of any thing that may concern his Interest or his Pleasure, tho' I have not yet wrote to him. I shall endeavour to make that Omission up to him as soon as possible.

I sent you some things by your Friend Capt. Freeman, which I shall be glad to hear came safe to hand, and that they were acceptable from Your affectionate Brother

My Love to your Children.

P.S. I congratulate you and my Countrymen on the Repeal of the Stamp Act. I send you a few of the Cards on which I wrote my Messages during the Time, it was debated here whether it might not be proper to reduce the Colonies to Obedience by Force of Arms: The Moral is, that the Colonies might be ruined, but that Britain would thereby be maimed.

"I NEVER WAS PROUDER OF ANY DRESS IN MY LIFE"

To Deborah Franklin

My dear Child,   London, April 6. 1766.

As the Stamp Act is at length repeal'd, I am willing you should have a new Gown, which you may suppose I did not send sooner, as I knew you would not like to be finer than your Neighbours, unless in a Gown of your own Spinning. Had the Trade between the two Countries totally ceas'd, it was a Comfort to me to recollect that I had once been cloth'd from Head to Foot in Woollen and Linnen of my Wife's Manufacture, that I never was prouder of any Dress in my Life, and that she and her Daughter might do it again if it was necessary. I told the Parliament that it was my Opinion, before the old Cloaths of the Americans were worn out, they might have new ones of their own making. And indeed if they had all as many old Clothes as your old Man has, that would not be very unlikely; for I think you and George reckon'd when I was last at home, at least 20 pair of old Breeches. Joking apart, I have sent you a fine Piece of Pompador Sattin, 14 Yards cost 11s. per Yard. A Silk Negligee and Petticoat of brocaded Lutestring for my dear Sally, with 2 Doz. Gloves, 4 Bottles of Lavender Water, and two little Reels. The Reels are to screw on the Edge of a Table, when she would wind Silk or Thread, the Skein is to be put over them, and winds better than if held in two Hands. There is also an Ivory Knob to each, to which she may with a Bit of Silk Cord hang a Pinhook to fasten her plain Work to like the Hooks on her Weight. I send you also Lace for two Lappet Caps, 3 Ells of Cambrick (the Cambrick by Mr. Yates) 3 Damask Table Cloths, a Piece of Crimson Morin for Curtains, with Tassels, Line and Binding. A large true Turky Carpet cost 10 Guineas, for the Dining Parlour. Some oil'd Silk; and a Gimcrack Corkscrew which you must get some Brother Gimcrack to show you the Use of. In the Chest is a Parcel of Books for my Friend Mr. Coleman, and another for Cousin Colbert. Pray did he receive those I sent him before? I send you also a Box with three fine Cheeses. Perhaps a Bit of them may be left when I come home. Mrs. Stevenson has been very diligent and serviceable in getting these things together for you, and presents her best Respects, as does her Daughter, to both you and Sally. There are too Boxes included in your Bill of Lading for Billy.

I received your kind Letter of Feb. 20. It gives me great Pleasure to hear that our good old Friend Mrs. Smith is on the Recovery. I hope she has yet many happy Years to live. My Love to her.

I fear, from the Account you give of Brother Peter that he cannot hold it long. If it should please God that he leaves us before my Return; I would have the Post Office remain under the Management of their Son, till Mr. Foxcroft and I agree how to settle it.

There are some Droll Prints in the Box, which were given me by the Painter; and being sent when I was not at home, were pack'd up without my Knowledge. I think he was wrong to put in Lord Bute, who had nothing to do with the Stamp Act. But it is the Fashion here to abuse that Nobleman as the Author of all Mischief. I send you a few Bush Beans, a new Sort for your Garden. I shall write to my Friends per Packet, that goes next Saturday. I am very well, and hope this will find you and Sally so with all our Relations and Friends, to whom my Love. I am, as ever, Your affectionate Husband,

P.S. A Young Man, by name Joseph Wharton, came to me the other day, said he had been sick and was in distress for Money, and beg'd me to take a Draft on his Brother at Philadelphia for Twelve Guineas. I did not remember or know him, but could refuse nothing to the Name of my Friend. So I let him have the Money, and enclose his Bill. You will present it for Payment.

"A BRAZEN WALL ROUND ENGLAND FOR ITS ETERNAL SECURITY"

To Cadwalader Evans

LONDON, May 9, 1766.

Dear Sir:—I received your kind letter of March 3, and thank you for the Intelligence and Hints it contained. I wonder at the Complaint you mentioned. I always considered writing to the Speaker as writing to the Committee. But if it is more to their Satisfaction that I should write to them jointly, it shall be done for the future.

My private Opinion concerning a union in Parliament between the two Countries, is, that it would be best for the Whole. But I think it will never be done. For tho' I believe that if we had no more Representatives than Scotland has, we should be sufficiently strong in the House to prevent, as they do for Scotland, any thing ever passing to our disadvantage; yet we are not able at present to furnish and maintain such a Number, and when we are more able we shall be less willing than we are now. The Parliament here do at present think too highly of themselves to admit Representatives from us if we should ask it; and when they will be desirous of granting it, we shall think too highly of ourselves to accept of it. It would certainly contribute to the strength of the whole, if Ireland and all the Dominions were united and consolidated under one Common Council for general Purposes, each retaining its particular Council or Parliament for its domestic Concerns. But this should have been more early provided for.—In the Infancy of our foreign Establishments, it was neglected, or was not thought of. And now, the Affair is nearly in the Situation of Friar Bacon's Project of making a brazen Wall round England for its eternal Security. His Servant Friar Bungey slept while the brazen Head, which was to dictate how it might be done, said *Time is*, and *Time was*. He only wak'd to hear it say, *Time is past*. An explosion followed that tumbled their House about the Conjuror's Ears.

I hope with you, that my being here at this Juncture has been of some Service to the Colonies. I am sure I have spared no Pains. And as to our particular Affair, I am not in the least doubtful of obtaining what we so justly desire if we continue to desire it: tho' the late confus'd State of Affairs on both sides the Water, have delay'd our Proceeding. With great esteem, I am,

> Dear Friend,
> Yours affectionately,

"DIRT . . . WILL NOT LONG ADHERE
TO POLISH'D MARBLE"

To Joseph Galloway

Dear Friend,   London, Nov. 8: 1766

I received your kind Letter of Sept. the 22d. and from another Friend a Copy of that lying Essay in which I am represented as the Author of the Stamp Act, and you as concern'd in it. The Answer you mention is not yet come to hand. Your Consolation, my Friend, and mine, under these Abuses, must be, *that we do not deserve them*. But what can console the Writers and Promoters of such infamously false Accusations, if they should ever come themselves to a Sense of that Malice of their Hearts, and that Stupidity of their Heads, which by these Papers they have manifested and exposed to all the World. Dunces often write Satyrs on themselves, when they think all the while that they are mocking their Neighbours. Let us, as we ever have done, uniformly endeavour the Service of our Country, according to the best of our Judgment and Abilities, and Time will do us Justice. Dirt thrown on a Mud-Wall may stick and incorporate; but it will not long adhere to polish'd Marble. I can now only add that I am, with Sincerest Esteem and Affection, Yours,

The Town begins to fill, and the Parliament sits down next week.

"TRAVELLING IS ONE WAY OF LENGTHENING LIFE"

To Mary Stevenson

Dear Polly   Paris, Sept. 14. 1767
   I am always pleas'd with a Letter from you, and I flatter myself you may be sometimes pleas'd in receiving one from me, tho' it should be of little Importance, such as this, which is to consist of a few occasional Remarks made here and in my Journey hither.
   Soon after I left you in that agreable Society at Bromley, I took the Resolution of making a Trip with Sir John Pringle into France. We set out the 28th past. All the way to Dover we were furnished with Post Chaises hung so as to lean forward, the Top coming down over one's Eyes, like a Hood, as if to prevent one's seeing the Country, which being one of my great Pleasures, I was engag'd in perpetual Disputes with the Innkeepers, Hostlers and Postillions about getting the Straps taken up a Hole or two before, and let down as much behind, they insisting that the Chaise leaning forward was an Ease to the Horses, and that the contrary would kill them. I suppose the Chaise leaning forward looks to them like a Willingness to go forward; and that its hanging back shows a Reluctance. They added other Reasons that were no Reasons at all, and made me, as upon a 100 other Occasions, almost

wish that Mankind had never been endow'd with a reasoning Faculty, since they know so little how to make use of it, and so often mislead themselves by it; and that they had been furnish'd with a good sensible Instinct instead of it.

At Dover the next Morning we embark'd for Calais with a Number of Passengers who had never been before at Sea. They would previously make a hearty Breakfast, because if the Wind should fail, we might not get over till Supper-time. Doubtless they thought that when they had paid for their Breakfast they had a Right to it, and that when they had swallowed it they were sure of it. But they had scarce been out half an Hour before the Sea laid Claim to it, and they were oblig'd to deliver it up. So it seems there are Uncertainties even beyond those between the Cup and the Lip. If ever you go to sea, take my Advice, and live sparingly a Day or two before hand. The Sickness, if any, will be the lighter and sooner over. We got to Calais that Evening.

Various Impositions we suffer'd from Boat-men, Porters, &c. on both Sides the Water. I know not which are most rapacious, the English or French; but the latter have, with their Knavery the most Politeness.

The Roads we found equally good with ours in England, in some Places pav'd with smooth Stone like our new Streets for many Miles together, and Rows of Trees on each Side and yet there are no Turnpikes. But then the poor Peasants complain'd to us grievously, that they were oblig'd to work upon the Roads full two Months in the Year without being paid for their Labour: Whether this is Truth, or whether, like Englishmen, they grumble Cause or no Cause, I have not yet been able fully to inform myself.

The Women we saw at Calais, on the Road, at Bouloigne and in the Inns and Villages, were generally of dark Complexions; but arriving at Abbeville we found a sudden Change, a Multitude both of Women and Men in that Place appearing remarkably fair. Whether this is owing to a small Colony of Spinners, Woolcombers and Weavers, &c. brought hither from Holland with the Woollen Manufacture about 60 Years ago; or to their being less expos'd to the Sun than in other Places, their Business keeping them much within Doors, I know not. Perhaps as in some other Cases, different Causes may club in producing the Effect, but the Effect itself is certain. Never was I in a Place of greater Industry, Wheels and Looms going in every House. As soon as we left Abbeville the Swarthiness return'd. I speak generally, for here are some fair Women at Paris, who I think are not whiten'd by Art. As to Rouge, they don't pretend to imitate Nature in laying it on. There is no gradual Diminution of the Colour from the full Bloom in the Middle of the Cheek to the faint Tint near the Sides, nor does it show itself differently in different Faces. I have not had the Honour of being at any Lady's Toylette to see how it is laid on, but I fancy I can tell you how it is or may be done: Cut a Hole of 3 Inches Diameter in a Piece of Paper, place it on the Side of your Face in such a Manner as that the Top of the Hole may be just under your Eye; then with a Brush dipt in the Colour paint Face and Paper together; so when the Paper is taken off there will remain a round Patch of Red exactly the Form of the Hole. This is the Mode, from the Actresses on the Stage upwards thro' all Ranks of Ladies to the Princesses of the Blood, but it stops there, the Queen not using it, having in the Serenity, Complacence and Benignity that shine so eminently in or rather through her Countenance, sufficient Beauty, tho' now an old Woman, to do extreamly well without it.

You see I speak of the Queen as if I had seen her, and so I have; for you must know I have been at Court. We went to Versailles last Sunday, and had the Honour of being presented to the King, he spoke to both of us very graciously and chearfully, is a handsome Man, has a very lively Look, and appears younger than he is. In the Evening we were at the *Grand Couvert*, where the Family sup in Publick. The Form of their sitting at the Table was this:

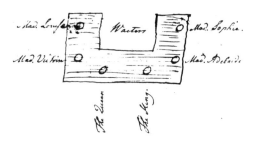

The Table as you see was half a Hollow Square, the Service Gold. When either made a Sign for Drink, the Word was given by one of the Waiters, *A boire pour le Roy*, or *A boire pour la Reine*, &c. then two Persons within the Square approach'd, one with Wine the other with Water in Caraffes, each drank a little Glass of what they brought, and then put both the Caraffes with a Glass on a Salver and presented it. Their Distance from each other was such as that other Chairs might have been plac'd between any two of them. An Officer of the Court brought us up thro' the Croud of Spectators, and plac'd Sir John so as to stand between the King and Madame Adelaide, and me between the Queen and Madame Victoire. The King talk'd a good deal to Sir John, asking many Questions about our Royal Family; and did me too the Honour of taking some Notice of me; that's saying enough, for I would not have you think me so much pleas'd with this King and Queen as to have a Whit less Regard than I us'd to have for ours. No Frenchman shall go beyond me in thinking my own King and Queen the very best in the World and the most amiable.

Versailles has had infinite Sums laid out in Building it and Supplying it with Water: Some say the Expence exceeded 80 Millions Sterling. The Range of Building is immense, the Garden Front most magnificent all of hewn Stone, the Number of Statues, Figures, Urns, &c in Marble and Bronze of exquisite Workmanship is beyond Conception. But the Waterworks are out of Repair, and so is great Part of the Front next the Town, looking with its shabby half Brick Walls and broken Windows not much better than the Houses in Durham Yard. There is, in short, both at Versailles and Paris, a prodigious Mixture of Magnificence and Negligence, with every kind of Elegance except that of Cleanliness, and what we call *Tidyness*. Tho' I must do Paris the Justice to say, that in two Points of Cleanliness they exceed us. The Water they drink, tho' from the River, they render as pure as that of the best Spring, by filtring it thro' Cisterns fill'd with Sand; and the Streets by constant Sweeping are fit to walk in tho' there is no pav'd foot Path. Accordingly many well dress'd People are constantly seen walking in them. The Crouds of Coaches and Chairs for that Reason is not so great; Men as well as

Women carry Umbrellas in their Hands, which they extend in case of Rain or two much Sun; and a Man with an Umbrella not taking up more than 3 foot square or 9 square feet of the Street, when if in a Coach he would take up 240 square feet, you can easily conceive that tho' the Streets here are narrower they may be much less encumber'd. They are extreamly well pav'd, and the Stones being generally Cubes, when worn on one Side may be turn'd and become new.

The Civilities we every where receive give us the strongest Impressions of the French Politeness. It seems to be a Point settled here universally that Strangers are to be treated with Respect, and one has just the same Deference shewn one here by being a Stranger as in England by being a Lady. The Custom House Officers at Port St. Denis, as we enter'd Paris, were about to seize 2 Doz. of excellent Bourdeaux Wine given us at Boulogne, and which we brought with us; but as soon as they found we were Strangers, it was immediately remitted on that Account. At the Church of Notre Dame, when we went to see a magnificent Illumination with Figures &c. for the deceas'd Dauphiness, we found an immense Croud who were kept out by Guards; but the Officer being told that we were Strangers from England, he immediately admitted us, accompanied and show'd us every thing. Why don't we practise this Urbanity to Frenchmen? Why should they be allow'd to out-do us in any thing?

Here is an Exhibition of Paintings, &c. like ours in London, to which Multitudes flock daily. I am not Connoisseur enough to judge which has most Merit. Every Night, Sundays not excepted here are Plays or Operas; and tho' the Weather has been hot, and the Houses full, one is not incommoded by the Heat so much as with us in Winter. They must have some Way of changing the Air that we are not acquainted with. I shall enquire into it.

Travelling is one Way of lengthening Life, at least in Appearance. It is but a Fortnight since we left London; but the Variety of Scenes we have gone through makes it seem equal to Six Months living in one Place. Perhaps I have suffered a greater Change too in my own Person than I could have done in Six Years at home. I had not been here Six Days before my Taylor and Peruquier had transform'd me into a Frenchman.

Only think what a Figure I make in a little Bag Wig and naked Ears! They told me I was become 20 Years younger, and look'd very galante; so being in Paris where the Mode is to be sacredly follow'd, I was once very near making Love to my Friend's Wife.

This Letter shall cost you a Shilling, and you may think it cheap when you consider that it has cost me at least 50 Guineas to get into the Situation that enables me to write it. Besides, I might, if I had staid at home, have won perhaps two shillings of you at Cribbidge. By the Way, now I mention Cards, let me tell you that Quadrille is quite out of Fashion here, and English Whisk all the Mode, at Paris and the Court.

And pray look upon it as no small Matter, that surrounded as I am by the Glories of this World and Amusements of all Sorts, I remember you and Dolly and all the dear good Folks at Bromley. 'Tis true I can't help it, but must and ever shall remember you all with Pleasure. Need I add that I am particularly, my dear good Friend Yours most affectionately

"CONDEMN'D TO LIVE TOGETHER AND TEASE ONE ANOTHER"

To Margaret Stevenson

Dear Madam   Tuesday, Nov. 3 at Noon

I breakfasted abroad this Morning and Nanny tells me that Mr. West call'd while I was out, and left word that you did not intend to come home till Sunday next, and that you expected me then, to come and fetch you; that Mr. West also desired I would dine at his House that Day: I know not whether Nanny is right in all this, as she has but an indifferent Memory But it seems strange to me that you should think of staying so long. People must have great Confidence in their own Agreableness that can suppose themselves not to become tiresome Guests at the End of Three Days at farthest. I did not imagine you had been so conceited. My Advice to you is, to return with the Stage to-morrow. And if it is proposed that we dine there on Sunday, I shall wait on Mr. and Mrs.

West with Pleasure on that day, taking you with me. But however I pray you not to understand that I so want you at home as not to do very well without you. Every thing goes on smoothly, and the House very quiet; and very clean too, without my saying a Word about it. I am willing to allow that the Arrangements you made before you went may have contributed something towards the good Order and Comfort in which we go on; but yet you are really mistaken in your Fancy that I should, by your Absence, become more sensible of your Usefulness to me, and the Necessity of having you always near me; for in Truth I find such a Satisfaction in being a little more my own Master, going any where and doing any thing just when and how I please without the Advice or Controul of any body's Wisdom but my own small as it is, that I value my own Liberty above all the Advantage of others Services, and begin to think I should be still happier if Nanny and the Cat would follow their Mistress, and leave me to the Enjoyment of an empty House, in which I should never be disturb'd by Questions of Whether I intend to dine at home, and what I would have for Dinner; or by a Mewing Request to be let in or let out. This Happiness however is perhaps too great to be conferr'd on any but Saints and holy Hermits. Sinners like me I might have said US, are condemn'd to live together and tease one another, so concluding you will be sentenc'd to come home tomorrow, I add no more but that I am as ever Your affectionate Friend and humble Servant

My best Compliments to Mr. and Mrs. West.

1767

"A COLLECTION FOR YOU OF ALL
THE PAST PARINGS OF MY NAILS"

To Jane Mecom

Dear Sister   London, Dec. 24. 1767
    I have received yours of Oct. 23. and condole with you most affectionately in the Affliction you must have suffered

by the Loss of so valuable and so amiable a Child. The longer
we live we are expos'd to more of these Strokes of Providence: but tho' we consider them as such, and know it is our
Duty to submit to the Divine Will, yet when it comes to our
Turn to bear what so many Millions before us have borne,
and so many Millions after us must bear, we are apt to think
our Case particularly hard, Consolations however kindly administred seldom afford us any Relief, Natural Affections will
have their Course, and Time proves our best Comforter. This
I have experienc'd myself. And as I know your good Sense
has suggested to you long before this time, every Argument,
Motive and Circumstance that can tend in any degree to relieve your Grief, I will not by repeating them renew it. I am
pleas'd to find that in your Troubles you do not overlook the
Mercies of God, and that you consider as such the Children
that are still spar'd to you. This is a right Temper of Mind,
and must be acceptable to that beneficent Being, who is in
various Ways continually showring down his Blessings upon
many, that receive them as things of course, and feel no grateful Sentiments arising in their Hearts on the Enjoyment of
them.

You desire me to send you all the political Pieces I have
been the Author of. I have never kept them. They were most
of them written occasionally for transient Purposes, and having done their Business, they die and are forgotten. I could
as easily make a Collection for you of all the past Parings of
my Nails. But I will send you what I write hereafter; and I
now enclose you the last Piece of mine that is printed. I wrote
it at a Friend's House in the Country who is of the Treasury,
if possible to do some Service to the Treasury, by putting a
little out of Countenance the Practice of encouraging Smugglers in buying their Commodities. But I suppose it did very
little.

Probably the Gentleman has called on you with the small
Sum I mention'd; if not, I would not that you should call
upon him for it; and therefore do not give you his Name.

Mrs. Stevenson is glad to learn that the Things she sent you
were suitable and pleas'd. You mention that you should write
for more per Capt. Freeman. We suppose you did not then
know, that your People would resolve to wear no more

Millenery. He is not yet arriv'd. Pray are those Resolutions like to be steadily stuck to?

My Love to Jenny, and all our Relations and Friends, and believe me ever Your affectionate Brother

"I AM TOO MUCH OF AN AMERICAN"

To William Franklin

DEAR SON,   *London, Jan.* 9, 1768.

We have had so many alarms of changes which did not take place, that just when I wrote it was thought the ministry would stand their ground. However immediately after the talk was renewed, and it soon appeared the Sunday changes were actually settled. Mr. Conway resigns and Lord Weymouth takes his place. Lord Gower is made president of the council in the room of Lord Northington. Lord Shelburne is stript of the America business which is given to Lord Hillsborough as Secretary of State for America, a new distinct department. Lord Sandwich 'tis said comes into the Post Office in his place. Several of the Bedford party are now to come in. How these changes may affect us a little time will show. Little at present is thought of but elections which gives me hopes that nothing will be done against America this session, though the Boston gazette had occasioned some heats and the Boston resolutions a prodigious clamour. I have endeavoured to palliate matters for them as well as I can: I send you my manuscript of one paper, though I think you take the Chronicle. The editor of that paper one Jones seems a Grenvillian, or is very cautious as you will see, by his corrections and omissions. He has drawn the teeth and pared the nails of my paper, so that it can neither scratch nor bite. It seems only to paw and mumble. I send you also two other late pieces of mine. There is another which I cannot find.

I am told there has been a talk of getting me appointed under secretary to Lord Hillsborough; but with little likelihood as it is a settled point here that I am too much of an American.

I am in very good health, thanks to God: your affectionate father,

To Jean Chappe d'Auteroche

Sir   London, Jan. 31. 1768

I sent you sometime since, directed to the Care of M. Molini, a Bookseller near the Quây des Augustins a Tooth that I mention'd to you when I had the Pleasure of meeting with you at the Marquis de Courtanvaux's. It was found near the River Ohio in America, about 200 Leagues below Fort du Quesne, at what is called the Great Licking Place, where the Earth has a Saltish Taste that is agreable to the Buffaloes and Deer, who come there at certain Seasons in great Numbers to lick the same. At this place have been found the Skeletons of near 30 large Animals suppos'd to be Elephants, several Tusks like those of Elephants, being found with those Grinder Teeth. Four of these Grinders were sent me by the Gentleman who brought them from the Ohio to New York, together with 4 Tusks, one of which is 6 Feet long and in the thickest Part near 6 Inches Diameter, and also one of the Vertebrae. My Lord Shelbourn receiv'd at the same time 3 or four others with a Jaw Bone and one or two Grinders remaining in it. Some of Our Naturalists here, however, contend, that these are not the Grinders of Elephants but of some carnivorous Animal unknown, because such Knobs or Prominances on the Face of the Tooth are not to be found on those of Elephants, and only, as they say, on those of carnivorous Animals. But it appears to me that Animals capable of carrying such large and heavy Tusks, must themselves be large Creatures, too bulky to have the Activity necessary for pursuing and taking Prey; and there-fore I am enclin'd to think those Knobs are only a small Va-riety, Animals of the same kind and Name often differing more materially, and that those Knobs might be as useful to grind the small Branches of Trees, as to chaw Flesh. How-ever I should be glad to have your Opinion, and to know from you whether any of the kind have been found in Siberia. With great Esteem and Respect, I am Sir, Your most obedient humble Servant

CANAL DEPTHS AND SHIP MOVEMENT

To John Pringle

SIR,   *Craven-street, May* 10, 1768.

You may remember that when we were travelling together in *Holland*, you remarked that the track-schuyt in one of the stages went slower than usual, and enquired of the boatman, what might be the reason; who answered, that it had been a dry season, and the water in the canal was low. On being again asked if it was so low as that the boat touch'd the muddy bottom; he said, no, not so low as that, but so low as to make it harder for the horse to draw the boat. We neither of us at first could conceive that if there was water enough for the boat to swim clear of the bottom, its being deeper would make any difference; but as the man affirmed it seriously as a thing well known among them; and as the punctuality required in their stages, was likely to make such difference, if any there were, more readily observed by them, than by other watermen who did not pass so regularly and constantly backwards and forwards in the same track; I began to apprehend there might be something in it, and attempted to account for it from this consideration, that the boat in proceeding along along the canal, must in every boat's length of her course, move out of her way a body of water, equal in bulk to the room her bottom took up in the water; that the water so moved, must pass on each side of her and under her bottom to get behind her; that if the passage under her bottom was straitened by the shallows, more of that water must pass by her sides, and with a swifter motion, which would retard her, as moving the contrary way; or that the water becoming lower behind the boat than before, she was pressed back by the weight of its difference in height, and her motion retarded by having that weight constantly to overcome. But as it is often lost time to attempt accounting for uncertain facts, I determined to make an experiment of this when I should have convenient time and opportunity.

After our return to *England*, as often as I happened to be on the *Thames*, I enquired of our watermen whether they were sensible of any difference in rowing over shallow or deep water. I found them all agreeing in the fact, that there was a very great difference, but they differed widely in expressing the quantity of the difference; some supposing it was equal to a mile in six, others to a mile in three, &c. As I did not recollect to have met with any mention of this matter in our philosophical books, and conceiving that if the difference should really be great, it might be an object of consideration in the many projects now on foot for digging new navigable canals in this island, I lately put my design of making the experiment in execution, in the following manner.

I provided a trough of plained boards fourteen feet long, six inches wide and six inches deep, in the clear, filled with water within half an inch of the edge, to represent a canal. I had a loose board of nearly the same length and breadth, that being put into the water might be sunk to any depth, and fixed by little wedges where I would chuse to have it stay, in order to make different depths of water, leaving the surface at the same height with regard to the sides of the trough. I had a little boat in form of a lighter or boat of burthen, six inches long, two inches and a quarter wide, and one inch and a quarter deep. When swimming, it drew one inch water. To give motion to the boat, I fixed one end of a long silk thread to its bow, just even with the water's edge, the other end passed over a well-made brass pully, of about an inch diameter, turning freely on a small axis; and a shilling was the weight. Then placing the boat at one end of the trough, the weight would draw it through the water to the other.

Not having a watch that shows seconds, in order to measure the time taken up by the boat in passing from end to end, I counted as fast as I could count to ten repeatedly, keeping an account of the number of tens on my fingers. And as much as possible to correct any little inequalities in my counting, I repeated the experiment a number of times at each depth of water, that I might take the medium.—And the following are the results.

	Water 1½ inches deep.	2 inches.	4½ inches.
1st exp. - - - - -	100	94	79
2 - - - - - - -	104	93	78
3 - - - - - - -	104	91	77
4 - - - - - - -	106	87	79
5 - - - - - - -	100	88	79
6 - - - - - - -	99	86	80
7 - - - - - - -	100	90	79
8 - - - - - - -	100	88	81
	————	————	————
	813	717	632

Medium 101   Medium 89   Medium 79

I made many other experiments, but the above are those in which I was most exact; and they serve sufficiently to show that the difference is considerable. Between the deepest and shallowest it appears to be somewhat more than one fifth. So that supposing large canals and boats and depths of water to bear the same proportions, and that four men or horses would draw a boat in deep water four leagues in four hours, it would require five to draw the same boat in the same time as far in shallow water; or four would require five hours.

Whether this difference is of consequence enough to justify a greater expence in deepening canals, is a matter of calculation, which our ingenious engineers in that way will readily determine.

I am, &c.

COLD AIR BATHS

To Jacques Barbeu-Dubourg

London, July 28, 1768.

I greatly approve the epithet, which you give in your letter of the 8th of June, to the new method of treating the small-pox, which you call the tonic or bracing method. I will take occasion from it, to mention a practice to which I have accustomed myself. You know the cold bath has long been in vogue here as a tonic; but the shock of the cold water has always appeared to me, generally speaking, as too violent: and I have found it much more agreeable to my constitution, to bathe in another element, I mean, cold air. With this view I rise early almost every morning, and sit in my chamber, without any clothes whatever, half an hour or an hour, according to the season, either reading or writing. This practice is not in the least painful, but on the contrary, agreeable; and if I return to bed afterwards, before I dress myself, as sometimes happens, I make a supplement to my night's rest, of one or two hours of the most pleasing sleep that can be imagined. I find no ill consequences whatever resulting from it, and that at least it does not injure my health, if it does not in fact contribute much to its preservation. I shall therefore call it for the future a bracing or tonic bath.

"THE USEFULNESS OF AN ODD HALF OF A PAIR OF SCISSARS"

To John Alleyne

Dear Sir,

You made an Apology to me for not acquainting me sooner with your Marriage. I ought now to make an Apology to you for delaying so long the Answer to your Letter. It was mislaid or hid among my Papers, and much Business put it out of my Mind, or prevented my looking for it and writing when I thought of it. So this Account between us if you please may stand balanced.

I assure you it gave me great Pleasure to hear you were married, and into a Family of Reputation. This I learnt from the Public Papers. The Character you give me of your Bride, (as it includes every Qualification that in the married State conduces to mutual Happiness) is an Addition to that Pleasure. Had you consulted me, as a Friend, on the Occasion,

Youth on both sides I should not have thought any Objection. Indeed from the Matches that have fallen under my Observation, I am rather inclined to think that early ones stand the best Chance for Happiness. The Tempers and Habits of young People are not yet become so stiff and uncomplying as when more advanced in Life, they form more easily to each other, and thence many Occasions of Disgust are removed. And if Youth has less of that Prudence that is necessary to manage a Family, yet the Parents and elder Friends of young married Persons are generally at hand to afford their Advice, which amply supplies that Defect; and by early Marriage, Youth is sooner form'd to regular and useful Life, and possibly some of those Accidents Habits or Connections that might have injured either the Constitution or the Reputation, or both, are thereby happily prevented. Particular Circumstances of particular Persons may possibly sometimes make it prudent to delay entering into that State, but in general when Nature has render'd our Bodies fit for it, the Presumption is in Nature's Favour, that she has not judg'd amiss in making us desire it. Late Marriages are often attended too with this farther Inconvenience, that there is not the same Chance the Parents shall live to see their offspring educated. *Late Children*, says the Spanish Proverb, *are early Orphans*: A melancholly Reflection to those whose Case it may be! With us in N. America, Marriages are generally in the Morning of Life, our Children are therefore educated and settled in the World by Noon, and thus our Business being done, we have an Afternoon and Evening of chearful Leisure to our selves, such as your Friend at present enjoys. By these early Marriages we are blest with more Children, and from the Mode among us founded in Nature of every Mother suckling and nursing her own Child, more of them are raised. Thence the swift Progress of Population among us unparallel'd in Europe. In fine, I am glad you are married, and congratulate you cordially upon it. You are now more in the way of becoming a useful Citizen; and you have escap'd the unnatural State of *Celibacy for Life*, the Fate of many here who never intended it, but who having too long postpon'd the Change of their Condition, find at length that 'tis too late to think of it, and So live all their Lives in a

Situation that greatly lessens a Man's Value: An odd Volume of a Set of Books, you know, is not worth its proportion of the Set; and what think you of the Usefulness of an odd Half of a Pair of Scissars? It cannot well cut any thing. It may possibly serve to scrape a Trencher.

Pray make my Compliments and best Wishes acceptable to your Spouse. I am old and heavy, and grow a little indolent, or I should ere this have presented them in Person. I shall make but small Use of the old Man's Privilege, that of giving Advice to younger Friends. Treat your Wife always with Respect. It will procure Respect to you, not from her only, but from all that observe it. Never use a slighting Expression to her even in jest; for Slights in Jest after frequent bandyings, are apt to end in angry earnest. Be studious in your Profession, and you will be learned. Be industrious and frugal, and you will be rich. Be sober and temperate and you will be healthy. Be in general virtuous, and you will be happy. At least you will by such Conduct stand the best Chance for such Consequences. I pray God to bless you both, being ever Your truly affectionate Friend

August 9, 1768

"GOD GOVERNS; AND HE IS GOOD"

To Mary Stevenson

Dear Polley   Oct. 28. 1768

I did not receive your Letter of the 26th till I came home late last Night, too late to answer it by the Return of that Post.

I see very clearly the Unhappiness of your Situation, and that it does not arise from any Fault in you. I pity you most sincerely: I should not, however, have thought of giving you Advice on this Occasion if you had not requested it, believing as I do, that your own good Sense is more than sufficient to direct you in every Point of Duty to others or yourself. If then I should advise you to any thing that may be contrary to your own Opinion, do not imagine that I shall condemn you if you do not follow such Advice. I shall only think that from a better Acquaintance with Circumstances you form a better Judgment of what is fit for you to do.

Now I conceive with you that your Aunt, both from her Affection to you and from the long Habit of having you with her, would really be miserable without you. Her Temper perhaps was never of the best, and when that is the Case, Age seldom mends it. Much of her Unhappiness must arise from thence. And since wrong Turns of the Mind when confirm'd by Time, are almost as little in our Power to cure, as those of the Body, I think with you that her Case is a compassionable one. If she had, though by her own Imprudence, brought on herself any grievous Sickness, I know you would think it your Duty to attend and nurse her with filial Tenderness, even were your own Health to be endangered by it: Your Apprehension therefore is right, that it may be your Duty to live with her, tho' inconsistent with your Happiness and your Interest; but this can only mean present Interest and present Happiness; for I think your future, greater and more lasting Interest and Happiness will arise from the Reflection that you have done your Duty, and from the high Rank you will ever hold in the Esteem of all that know you, for having persevered in doing that Duty under so many and great Discouragements. My Advice then must be, that you return to her as soon as the Time you propos'd for your Visit is expir'd; and that you continue by every means in your Power to make the Remainder of her Days as comfortable to her as possible. Invent Amusements for her; be pleas'd when she accepts of them, and patient when she perhaps peevishly rejects them. I know this is hard, but I think you are equal to it; not from any Servility in your Temper, but from abundant Goodness. In the mean time all your Friends, sensible of your present uncomfortable Situation, should endeavour to ease your Burthen, by acting in Concert with you, to give her as many Opportunities as possible of enjoying the Pleasures of Society, for your sake: Nothing is more apt to sour the Temper of aged People than the Apprehension that they are neglected, and they are extremely apt to entertain such Suspicions. It was therefore that I did propose asking her to be of our late Party: but your Mother disliking it, the Motion was dropt, as some others have been by my too great Easiness, contrary to my Judgment. Not but that I was sensible her being with us might have lessen'd our Pleasure, but I hoped it might have prevented you some Pain. In fine, nothing can contribute to true Happiness that is inconsistent with Duty; nor can a Course of Action conformable to it, be finally without an ample Reward. For, God governs; and he is *good*. I pray him to direct you: And indeed you will never be without his Direction, if you humbly ask it, and show yourself always ready to obey it. Farewell, *my* dear Friend, and believe me ever sincerely and affectionately *yours*

My Love to Dolly, Miss Blount, Dr. and Mrs. Hawkesworth, Miss Henckell &c. &c. I much commend Dolly for inviting your Aunt into the Country; you see how perfectly that agrees with my Notions. The next Day after you went, she sent the Servant for Nancy, ordering him to take a Place for her in the Stage; and Nancy has been there ever since.

"AT PRESENT I ALMOST DESPAIR"

To ———

DEAR SIR,   *London, Nov.* 28, 1768.
     I received your obliging favour of the 12th instant. Your sentiments of the importance of the present dispute between Great Britain and the colonies, appear to me extremely just. There is nothing I wish for more than to see it amicably and equitably settled.
     But Providence will bring about its own ends by its own means; and if it intends the downfal of a nation, that nation will be so blinded by its pride, and other passions, as not to see its danger, or how its fall may be prevented.
     Being born and bred in one of the countries, and having lived long and made many agreeable connexions of friendship in the other, I wish all prosperity to both; but I have talked, and written so much and so long on the subject, that my acquaintance are weary of hearing, and the public of reading

any more of it, which begins to make me weary of talking and writing; especially as I do not find that I have gained any point, in either country, except that of rendering myself suspected, by my impartiality; in England, of being too much an American, and in America of being too much an Englishman. Your opinion, however, weighs with me, and encourages me to try one effort more, in a full, though concise statement of facts, accompanied with arguments drawn from those facts; to be published about the meeting of parliament, after the holidays.

If any good may be done I shall rejoice; but at present I almost despair.

Have you ever seen the barometer so low as of late? The 22d instant mine was at 28, 41, and yet the weather fine and fair. With sincere esteem, I am, dear friend, yours affectionately,

LEARNING TO SWIM

To Oliver Neave

Dear SIR,

I cannot be of opinion with you that 'tis too late in life for you to learn to swim. The river near the bottom of your garden affords you a most convenient place for the purpose. And as your new employment requires your being often on the water, of which you have such a dread, I think you would do well to make the trial; nothing being so likely to remove those apprehensions as the consciousness of an ability to swim to the shore, in case of an accident, or of supporting yourself in the water till a boat could come to take you up.

I do not know how far corks or bladders may be useful in learning to swim, having never seen much trial of them. Possibly they may be of service in supporting the body while you are learning what is called the stroke, or that manner of drawing in and striking out the hands and feet that is necessary to produce progressive motion. But you will be no swimmer till you can place some confidence in the power of

the water to support you; I would therefore advise the acquiring that confidence in the first place; especially as I have
known several who by a little of the practice necessary for
that purpose, have insensibly acquired the stroke, taught as
it were by nature.

The practice I mean is this. Chusing a place where the water deepens gradually, walk coolly into it till it is up to your
breast, then turn round, your face to the shore, and throw an
egg into the water between you and the shore. It will sink to
the bottom, and be easily seen there, as your water is clear. It
must lie in water so deep as that you cannot reach it to take
it up but by diving for it. To encourage yourself in undertaking to do this, reflect that your progress will be from deeper
to shallower water, and that at any time you may by bringing
your legs under you and standing on the bottom, raise your
head far above the water. Then plunge under it with your
eyes open, throwing yourself towards the egg, and endeavouring by the action of your hands and feet against the water
to get forward till within reach of it. In this attempt you will
find, that the water buoys you up against your inclination;
that it is not so easy a thing to sink as you imagined; that
you cannot, but by active force, get down to the egg. Thus
you feel the power of the water to support you, and learn to
confide in that power; while your endeavours to overcome it
and to reach the egg, teach you the manner of acting on the
water with your feet and hands, which action is afterwards
used in swimming to support your head higher above water,
or to go forward through it.

I would the more earnestly press you to the trial of this
method, because, though I think I satisfyed you that your
body is lighter than water, and that you might float in it a
long time with your mouth free for breathing, if you would
put yourself in a proper posture, and would be still and forbear struggling; yet till you have obtained this experimental
confidence in the water, I cannot depend on your having the
necessary presence of mind to recollect that posture and the
directions I gave you relating to it. The surprize may put all
out of your mind. For though we value ourselves on being
reasonable knowing creatures, reason and knowledge seem on
such occasions to be of little use to us; and the brutes to

whom we allow scarce a glimmering of either, appear to have the advantage of us.

I will, however, take this opportunity of repeating those particulars to you, which I mentioned in our last conversation, as by perusing them at your leisure, you may possibly imprint them so in your memory as on occasion to be of some use to you.

1. That though the legs, arms and head, of a human body, being solid parts, are specifically something heavier than fresh water, yet the trunk, particularly the upper part from its hollowness, is so much lighter than water, as that the whole of the body taken together is too light to sink wholly under water, but some part will remain above, untill the lungs become filled with water, which happens from drawing water into them instead of air, when a person in the fright attempts breathing while the mouth and nostrils are under water.

2. That the legs and arms are specifically lighter than salt-water, and will be supported by it, so that a human body would not sink in salt-water, though the lungs were filled as above, but from the greater specific gravity of the head.

3. That therefore a person throwing himself on his back in salt-water, and extending his arms, may easily lie so as to keep his mouth and nostrils free for breathing; and by a small motion of his hands may prevent turning, if he should perceive any tendency to it.

4. That in fresh water, if a man throws himself on his back, near the surface, he cannot long continue in that situation but by proper action of his hands on the water. If he uses no such action, the legs and lower part of the body will gradually sink till he comes into an upright position, in which he will continue suspended, the hollow of the breast keeping the head uppermost.

5. But if in this erect position, the head is kept upright above the shoulders, as when we stand on the ground, the immersion will, by the weight of that part of the head that is out of water, reach above the mouth and nostrils, perhaps a little above the eyes, so that a man cannot long remain suspended in water with his head in that position.

6. The body continuing suspended as before, and upright, if the head be leaned quite back, so that the face looks up-

wards, all the back part of the head being then under water, and its weight consequently in a great measure supported by it, the face will remain above water quite free for breathing, will rise an inch higher every inspiration, and sink as much every expiration, but never so low as that the water may come over the mouth.

7. If therefore a person unacquainted with swimming, and falling accidentally into the water, could have presence of mind sufficient to avoid struggling and plunging, and to let the body take this natural position, he might continue long safe from drowning till perhaps help would come. For as to the cloathes, their additional weight while immersed is very inconsiderable, the water supporting it; though when he comes out of the water, he would find them very heavy indeed.

But, as I said before, I would not advise you or any one to depend on having this presence of mind on such an occasion, but learn fairly to swim; as I wish all men were taught to do in their youth; they would, on many occurrences, be the safer for having that skill, and on many more the happier, as freer from painful apprehensions of danger, to say nothing of the enjoyment in so delightful and wholesome an exercise. Soldiers particularly should, methinks, all be taught to swim; it might be of frequent use either in surprising an enemy, or saving themselves. And if I had now boys to educate, I should prefer those schools (other things being equal) where an opportunity was afforded for acquiring so advantageous an art, which once learnt is never forgotten.

I am, Sir, &c.

before 1769

To John Bartram

Dear Friend,   London July 9, 1769
It is with great Pleasure I understand by your Favour of April 10. that you continue to enjoy so good a Share of Health. I hope it will long continue. And altho' it may not now be suitable for you to make such wide Excursions as

heretofore, you may yet be very useful to your Country and to Mankind, if you sit down quietly at home, digest the Knowledge you have acquired, compile and publish the many Observations you have made, and point out the Advantages that may be drawn from the whole, in publick Undertakings or particular private Practice. It is true many People are fond of Accounts of old Buildings, Monuments, &c. but there is a Number who would be much better pleas'd with such Accounts as you could afford them: And for one I confess that if I could find in any Italian Travels a Receipt for making Parmesan Cheese, it would give me more Satisfaction than a Transcript of any Inscription from any old Stone whatever.

I suppose Mr. Michael Collinson, or Dr. Fothergill have written to you what may be necessary for your Information relating to your Affairs here. I imagine there is no doubt but the King's Bounty to you will be continued; and that it will be proper for you to continue sending now and then a few such curious Seeds as you can procure to keep up your Claim. And now I mention Seeds, I wish you would send me a few of such as are least common, to the Value of a Guinea, which Mr. Foxcroft will pay you for me. They are for a particular Friend who is very curious. If in any thing I can serve you here, command freely Your affectionate Friend

P.S. Pray let me know whether you have had sent you any of the Seeds of the Rhubarb describ'd in the enclos'd Prints. It is said to be of the true kind. If you have it not, I can procure some Seeds for you.

"AFFAIRS ARE PERHAPS BELOW NOTICE"

To George Whitefield

I am under continued apprehensions that we may have bad news from America. The sending soldiers to Boston always appeared to me a dangerous step; they could do no good, they might occasion mischief. When I consider the warm resentment of a people who think themselves injured and oppressed, and the common insolence of the soldiery, who are taught to consider that people as in rebellion, I cannot but fear the consequences of bringing them together. It seems like setting up a smith's forge in a magazine of gunpowder. I *see* with you that our affairs are not well managed by our rulers here below; I wish I could *believe* with you, that they are well attended to by those above: I rather suspect, from certain circumstances, that though the general government of the universe is well administered, our particular little affairs are perhaps below notice, and left to take the chance of human prudence or imprudence, as either may happen to be uppermost. It is, however, an uncomfortable thought, and I leave it.

before September 2, 1769

"WHOEVER SCRUPLES CHEATING THE KING WILL CERTAINLY NOT WRONG HIS NEIGHBOUR"

To Mary Stevenson

Saturday Evening, Sept 2. 1769

Just come home from a Venison Feast, where I have drank more than a Philosopher ought, I find my dear Polly's chearful chatty Letter that exhilarates me more than all the Wine.

Your good Mother says there is no Occasion for any Intercession of mine in your behalf. She is sensible that she is more in fault than her Daughter. She received an affectionate tender Letter from you, and she has not answered it, tho' she intended to do it; but her Head, not her Heart, has been bad, and unfitted her for Writing. She owns that she is not so good a Subject as you are, and that she is more unwilling to pay Tribute to Cesar, and has less Objection to Smuggling; but 'tis not, she says, mere Selfishness or Avarice; 'tis rather an honest Resentment at the Waste of those Taxes in Pensions, Salaries, Perquisites, Contracts and other Emoluments for the Benefit of People she does not love, and who do not deserve such Advantages, because—I suppose because they are not of her Party. Present my Respects to your good Landlord and his Family: I honour them for their consciencious

Aversion to illicit Trading. There are those in the World who would not wrong a Neighbour, but make no Scruple of cheating the King. The Reverse however does not hold; for whoever scruples cheating the King will certainly not wrong his Neighbour. You ought not to wish yourself an Enthusiast: They have indeed their imaginary Satisfactions and Pleasures; but those are often ballanc'd by imaginary Pains and Mortifications. You can continue to be a good Girl, and thereby lay a solid Foundation for expected future Happiness, without the Enthusiasm that may perhaps be necessary to some others. As those Beings who have a good sensible Instinct, have no need of Reason; so those who have Reason to regulate their Actions, have no Occasion for Enthusiasm. However there are certain Circumstances in Life sometimes, wherein 'tis perhaps best not to hearken to Reason. For instance; Possibly, if the Truth were known, I have Reason to be jealous of this same insinuating handsome young Physician: But as it flatters more my Vanity, and therefore gives me more Pleasure to suppose you were in Spirits on Account of my safe Return, I shall turn a deaf Ear to Reason in this Case, as I have done with Success in twenty others. But I am sure you will always give me Reason enough to continue ever Your affectionate Friend

Our Love to Mrs. Tickell. We all long for your Return: Your Dolly was well last Tuesday, the Girls were there on a Visit to her: I mean at Bromley. Adieu.

No Time now to give you any Account of my French Journey.

To Timothy Folger

Loving Kinsman,   London, Sept. 29. 1769
Since my Return from abroad, where I spent part of the Summer, I have received your Favours of June 10 and July 26. The Treasury Board is still under Adjournment, the Lords and Secretaries chiefly in the Country; but as soon as they

meet again, you may depend on my making the Application
you desire.

I shall enquire concerning the Affair of your two Town-
ships settled under Massachusetts Grants, and let you know
my Sentiments as soon as I can get proper Information. I
should imagine that whatever may be determin'd here of the
Massachusetts Rights to the Jurisdiction, the private Property
of Settlers must remain secure. In general I have no great
Opinion of Applications to be made here in such Cases. It is
so much the Practice to draw Matters into Length, put the
Parties to immense Charge, and tire them out with Delays,
that I would never come from America hither with any Affair
I could possibly settle there.

Mrs. Stevenson sends her Love, and thanks you for re-
membring her. She is vex'd to hear that the Box of Sperma-
ceti Candles is seiz'd; and says, if ever she sees you again,
she will put you in a way of making Reprisals. You know
she is a Smuggler upon Principle; and she does not consider
how averse you are to every thing of the kind. I thank you
for your kind Intention. Your Son grows a fine Youth; he is
so obliging as to be with us a little when he has Holidays;
and Temple is not the only one of the Family that is fond of
his Company.

It gives me great Pleasure to hear that our People are steady
in their Resolutions of Non Importation, and in the Promoting of Industry among themselves. They will soon be sensible
of the Benefit of such Conduct, tho' the Acts should never be
repeal'd to their full Satisfaction. For their Earth and their
Sea, the true Sources of Wealth and Plenty, will go on producing; and if they receive the annual Increase, and do not
waste it as heretofore in the Gewgaws of this Country, but
employ their spare time in manufacturing Necessaries for
themselves, they must soon be out of debt, they must soon
be easy and comfortable in their circumstances, and even
wealthy. I have been told, that in some of our County Courts
heretofore, there were every quarter several hundred actions
of debt, in which the people were sued by Shopkeepers for
money due for British *goods* (as they are called, but in fact
evils). What a loss of time this must occasion to the people,
besides the expense. And how can Freeman bear the thought

of subjecting themselves to the hazard of being deprived of
their personal liberty at the caprice of every petty trader, for
the paltry vanity of tricking out himself and family in the
flimsy manufactures of Britain, when they might by their own
industry and ingenuity, appear in *good substantial honourable
homespun*! Could our folks but see what numbers of Merchants, and even Shopkeepers here, make great estates by
American folly; how many shops of A, B, C and Co. with
wares for *exportation to the Colonies*, maintain, each shop three
or four partners and their families, every one with his country-house and equipage, where they live like Princes on the
sweat of our brows; pretending indeed, *sometimes*, to wish
well to our Privileges, but on the present important occasion
few of them affording us any assistance: I am persuaded that
indignation would supply our want of prudence, we should
disdain the thraldom we have so long been held in by this
mischievous commerce, reject it for ever, and seek our resources where God and Nature have placed them WITHIN
OUR SELVES.

Your Merchants, on the other hand, have shown a noble
disinterestedness and *love to their country*, unexampled among
Traders in any other age or nation, and which does them infinite honour all over Europe. The corrupted part indeed of
this people *here* can scarce believe such virtue possible. But
perseverance will convince them, that there is still in the
world such a thing as public spirit. I hope that, if the oppres-
sive Acts are not repealed this winter, your Stocks, that us'd
to be employed in the British Trade, will be turned to the
employment of Manufactures among yourselves: For notwithstanding the former general opinion that manufactures
were impracticable in America, on account of the dearness of
labour, experience shows, in the success of the manufactures
of paper and stockings in Pennsylvania, and of womens shoes
at Lynn in your province, that labour is only dear *from the
want of* CONSTANT *employment*; (he who is often out of work
requiring necessarily as much for the time he does work, as
will maintain him when he does not work:) and that where
we do not *interrupt that employment* by importations, *the
cheapness of our provisions* gives us such advantage over the
Manufacturers in Britain, that (especially in bulky goods,

whose freight would be considerable) *we may always* UNDER-
WORK THEM.

To William Strahan

Dear Sir,   Craven Street, Nov. 29. 69
    Being just return'd to Town from a little Excursion I find
yours of the 22d, containing a Number of Queries that would
require a Pamphlet to answer them fully. You however desire
only brief Answers, which I shall endeavour to give you. Previous to your Queries, You tell me, that "you apprehend his
Majesty's Servants have now in Contemplation; 1st. to releive
the Colonists from the Taxes complained of: and 2dly to preserve the Honour, the Dignity, and the Supremacy of the
British Legislature over all his Majesty's Dominions." I hope
your Information is good, and that what you suppose to be
in Contemplation will be carried into Execution, by repealing
all the Laws that have been made for raising a Revenue in
America by Authority of Parliament, without the consent of
the People there. The *Honour* and *Dignity* of the British Legislature will not be hurt by such an Act of Justice and Wisdom: The wisest Councils are liable to be misled, especially
in Matters remote from their Inspection. It is the persisting
in an Error, not the Correcting it that lessens the Honour of
any Man or body of Men. The *Supremacy* of that Legislature,
I believe will be best preserv'd by making a very sparing use
of it, never but for the Evident Good of the Colonies themselves, or of the whole British Empire; never for the Partial
Advantage of Britain to their Prejudice; by such Prudent
Conduct I imagine that Supremacy may be gradually
strengthened and in time fully Established; but otherwise I
apprehend it will be disputed, and lost in the Dispute. At
present the Colonies consent and Submit to it for the regulation of General Commerce: But a Submission to Acts of
Parliament was no part of their original Constitution. Our

former Kings Governed their Colonies, as they Governed their Dominions in France, without the Participation of British Parliaments. The Parliament of England never presum'd to interfere with that prerogative till the Time of the Great Rebellion, when they usurp'd the Government of all the King's other Dominions, Ireland, Scotland &c. The Colonies that held for the King, they conquered by Force of Arms, and Governed afterward as Conquered Countries. But New England having not oppos'd the Parliament, was considered and treated as a Sister Kingdom in Amity with England; as appears by the Journals, Mar. 10. 1642.

Your first Question is,

1. "Will not a Repeal of all the Duties (that on Tea excepted, which was before paid here on Exportation, and of Course no new Imposition) fully satisfy the Colonists?"

I think not.

"2 Your Reasons for that Opinion?"

Because it is not *the Sum* paid in that Duty on Tea that is Complain'd of as a Burthen, but the Principle of the Act express'd in the Preamble, viz. that those Duties were laid for the Better Support of Government and the Administration of Justice in the Colonies. This the Colonists think *unnecessary, unjust*, and *dangerous* to their Most Important Rights. *Unnecessary*, because in all the Colonies (two or three new ones excepted) Government and the Administration of Justice were and always had been well supported without any Charge to Britain; *Unjust* as it made such Colonies liable to pay such Charge for other Colonies, in which they had no Concern or Interest; *dangerous*, as such a Mode of raising Money for these Purposes, tended to render their Assemblies useless: For if a Revenue could be rais'd in the Colonies for all the purposes of Government, by Act of Parliament, without Grants from the People there, Governors, who do not generally love Assemblies, would never call them, they would be laid aside; and when nothing Should depend upon the People's good will to Government, their Rights would be trampled on, they would be treated with Contempt. Another Reason why I think they would not be satisfy'd with such a partial repeal, is, that their Agreements not to import till the Repeal takes place, include the whole, which shows that they object to the whole; and those Agreements will continue binding on them if the whole is not repealed.

"3. Do you think the only effectual Way of composing the present Differences, is, to put the Americans precisely in the Situation they were in before the passing of the late Stamp Act?"

I think so.

"4. Your Reasons for that Opinion?"

Other Methods have been tryed. They have been rebuked in angry Letters. Their Petitions have been refused or rejected by Parliament. They have been threatened with the Punishments of Treason by Resolves of both Houses. Their Assemblies have been dissolv'd, and Troops have been sent among them; but all these Ways have only exasperated their Minds and widen'd the Breach; their Agreements to use no more British Manufactures have been Strengthen'd, and these Measures instead of composing Differences and promoting a good Correspondence, have almost annihilated your Commerce with those Countries, and greatly endanger'd the National Peace and general Welfare.

"5. If this last Method is deemed by the Legislature and his Majisty's Ministers to be repugnant to their Duty as Guardians of the just Rights of the Crown, and of their Fellow Subjects, can you suggest any other Way of terminating these Disputes, consistent with the Ideas of Justice and propriety conceived by the Kings Subjects on both Sides the Atlantick?"

A. I do not see how that method can be deemed repugnant *to the Rights of the Crown*. If the Americans are put into their former Situation, it must be by an Act of Parliament, in the Passing of which by the King the Rights of the Crown are exercised not infringed. It is indifferent to the Crown whether the Aids received from America are Granted by Parliament here, or by the Assemblies there, provided the Quantum be the same; and it is my Opinion more will generally be Granted there Voluntarily than can ever be exacted and collected from thence by Authority of parliament. As to the rights of *Fellow Subjects* (I suppose you mean the People of Britain) I cannot conceive how they will be infringed by that method. They will still enjoy the Right of Granting their own money; and may still, if it pleases them, keep up their Claim to the Right of granting ours; a Right they can never exercise properly, for want of a sufficient Knowledge of us, our Circumstances and Abilities (to say nothing of the little likelihood there is that we should ever submit to it) therefore a Right that can be of no good use to them. And we shall continue to enjoy, *in fact*, the Right of granting our own Money; with the Opinion now universally prevailing among us that we are free Subjects of the King, and that *Fellow Subjects* of one Part of his Dominions are not Sovereign over *Fellow Subjects* in any other Part. If the Subjects on the different Sides of the Atlantic, have different and opposite Ideas of Justice or Propriety, no one Method can possibly be consistent with both. The best will be to let each enjoy their own Opinions, without disturbing them when they do not interfere with the common Good.

"6. And if this Method were actually followed do you not think it would encourage the Violent and Factious Part of the Colonists to aim at still farther Concessions from the Mother Country?"

A. I do not think it would. There may be a few among them that deserve the Name of factious and Violent, as there are in all Countries, but these would have little influence if the great Majority of Sober reasonable People were satisfy'd. If any Colony should happen to think that some of your regulations of Trade are inconvenient to the general Interest of the Empire, or prejudicial to them without being beneficial to you, they will state these Matters to the Parliament in Petitions as heretofore, but will, I believe, take no violent steps to obtain, what they may hope for in time from the Wisdom of Government here. I know of nothing else they can have in View. The Notion that prevails here of their being desirous of setting up a Kingdom or Common Wealth of their own, is to my certain Knowledge entirely groundless. I therefore think that on a total Repeal of all Duties laid expressly for the purpose of raising a Revenue on the People of America, without their Consent, the present Uneasiness would subside; the Agreements not to import would be dissolved, and the Commerce flourish as heretofore. And I am confirm'd in this Sentiment by all the Letters I have received from America, and

by the Opinion of all the Sensible People who have lately
come from thence, Crown Officers excepted. I know indeed
that the people of Boston are grievously offended by the
Quartering of Troops among them, as they think, contrary to
Law; and are very angry with the Board of Commissioners to
have calumniated them to Government; but as I suppose
withdrawing of those Troops may be a Consequence of Rec-
onciliating Measures taking Place; and that the Commission
also will either be dissolv'd if found useless, or fill'd with
more temporate and prudent Men if still deemed useful and
necessary, I do not imagine these Particulars will prevent a
return of the Harmony so much to be wished.

"7. If they are relieved in Part only, what do you, as a reasonable and dispassionate Man, and an equal Friend to both
sides, imagine will be the probable Consequence?"

A. I imagine that repealing the offensive Duties in part will
answer no End to this Country; the Commerce will remain
obstructed, and the Americans go on with their Schemes of
Frugality, Industry and Manufactures, to their own great Advantage. How much that may tend to the prejudice of Britain
I cannot say; perhaps not so much as some apprehend, since
she may in time find New Markets. But I think (if the Union
of the two Countries continues to subsist) it will not hurt the
general interest; for whatever Wealth Britain loses by the Failure of its Trade with the Colonies, America will gain; and the
Crown will receive equal Aids from its Subjects upon the
whole, if not greater.

And now I have answered your Questions as to what *may
be* in my Opinion the Consequences of this or that *supposed*
Measure, I will go a little farther, and tell you what I fear is
more likely to come to pass *in Reality.*

I apprehend, that the Ministry, at least the American part
of it, being fully persuaded of the Right of Parliament, think
it ought to be enforc'd whatever may be the Consequences;
and at the same time do not believe there is even now any
Abatement of the Trade between the two Countries on account of these Disputes; or that if there is, it is small and
cannot long Continue; they are assured by the Crown officers
in America that Manufactures are impossible there; that the
Discontented are few, and Persons of little Consequence; that

almost all the People of Property and Importance are satisfyd, and disposed to submit quietly to the Taxing-Power of Parliament; and that if the Revenue Acts are continued, those Duties only that are called anti-commercial being repealed, and others perhaps laid in their stead, that Power will ere long be patiently submitted to, and the Agreements not to import be broken when they are found to produce no Change of Measures here. From these and similar Misinformations, which seem to be credited, I think it likely that no thorough redress of Grievances will be afforded to America this Session. This may inflame Matters still more in that Country; farther rash Measures there may create more Resentment here, that may Produce not merely ill-advis'd and useless Dissolutions of their Assemblies, as last Year; but Attempts to Dissolve their Constitutions; more Troops may be sent over, which will create more Uneasiness; to justify the Measures of Government your Ministerial Writers will revile the Americans in your Newspapers, as they have already began to do, treating them as Miscreants, Rogues, Dastards, Rebels, &c. which will tend farther to alienate the Minds of the People here from them, and diminish their Affections to this Country. Possibly too, some of their warm patriots may be distracted enough to expose themselves by some mad Action, to be sent for Hither, and Government here be indiscreet enough to Hang them on the Act of H. 8. Mutual Provocations will thus go on to complete the Separation; and instead of that cordial Affection that once and so long existed, and that Harmony so suitable to the Circumstances, and so Necessary to the Happiness, Strength Safety and Welfare of both Countries; an implacable Malice and Mutual Hatred, (such as we now see subsisting between the Spaniards and Portuguese, the Genoese and Corsicans, from the same Original Misconduct in the Superior Government) will take place; the Sameness of Nation, the Similarity of Religion, Manners and Language not in the least Preventing in our Case, more than it did in theirs. I hope however that this may all prove false Prophecy: And that you and I may live to see as sincere and Perfect a friendship establish'd between our respective Countries as has so many years Subsisted between Mr. Strahan and his truly affectionate Friend

"IF WE ARE STEADY AND PERSEVERE IN OUR RESOLUTIONS"

To [Charles Thomson]

Dear Sir   London March 18th. 1770

Your very judicious Letter of Novemr. 26th. being communicated by me to some Member of Parliament, was handed about among them, so that it was sometime before I got it again into my Hands. It had due Weight with several, and was of considerable Use. You will see that I printed it at length in the London Chronicle with the Merchants' Letter. When the American Affairs came to be debated in the House of Commons, the Majority, notwithstanding all the Weight of ministerial Influence, was only 62 for continuing the whole last Act; and would not have been so large, nay, I think the Repeal would have been carried, but that the Ministry were persuaded by Governor Bernard and some lying Letters said to be from Boston, that the Associations not to import were all breaking to Pieces, that America was in the greatest Distress for Want of the Goods, that we could not possibly subsist any longer without them, and must of course submit to any Terms Parliament should think fit to impose upon us. This with the idle Notion of the Dignity and Sovereignty of Parliament, which they are so fond of, and imagine will be endanger'd by any farther Concessions, prevailed I know with many to vote with the Ministry, who otherwise, on Account of the Commerce, wish to see the Difference accommodated. But though both the Duke of Grafton and Lord North were and are in my Opinion rather inclined to satisfy us, yet the Bedford Party are so violent against us, and so prevalent in the Council, that more moderate Measures could not take Place. This Party never speak of us but with evident Malice; Rebels and Traitors are the best Names they can afford us, and I believe they only wish for a colourable Pretence and Occasion of ordering the Souldiers to make a Massacre among us.

On the other Hand the Rockingham and Shelburne People, with Lord Chatham's Friends, are disposed to favour us if they were again in Power, which at present they are not like to be; tho' they, too, would be for keeping up the Claim of parliamentary Sovereignty, but without exercising it in any Mode of Taxation. Besides these, we have for sincere Friends and Wellwishers the Body of Dissenters, generally, throughout England, with many others, not to mention Ireland and all the rest of Europe, who from various Motives join in applauding the Spirit of Liberty, with which we have claimed and insisted on our Privileges, and wish us Success, but whose Suffrage cannot have much Weight in our Affairs.

The Merchants here were at length prevailed on to present a Petition, but they moved slowly, and some of them I thought reluctantly; perhaps from a Despair of Success, the City not being much in favour with the Court at present. The manufacturing Towns absolutely refused to move at all; some pretending to be offended with our attempting to manufacture for ourselves; others saying that they had Employment enough, and that our Trade was of little Importance to them, whether we continued or refused it. Those who began a little to feel the Effects of our forbearing to purchase, were persuaded to be quiet by the ministerial People; who gave out that certain Advices were receiv'd of our beginning to break our Agreements; of our Attempts to manufacture proving all abortive and ruining the Undertakers; of our Distress for Want of Goods, and Dissentions among ourselves, which promised the total Defeat of all such Kind of Combinations, and the Prevention of them for the future, if the Government were not urged imprudently to repeal the Duties. But now that it appears from late and authentic Accounts, that Agreements continue in full Force, that a Ship is actually return'd from Boston to Bristol with Nails and Glass, (Articles that were thought of the utmost Necessity,) and that the Ships that were waiting here for the Determination of Parliament, are actually returning to North America in thier Ballast; the Tone of the Manufacturers begins to change, and there is no doubt, that if we are steady and persevere in our Resolutions, these People will soon begin a Clamor that much Pains has hitherto been used to stifle.

In short, it appears to me, that if we do not now persist in this Measure till it has had its full Effect, it can never again be used on any future Occasion with the least prospect of

Success, and that if we do persist another year, we shall never afterwards have occasion to use it. With sincere regards I am, Dear Sir, Your obedient Servant,

"I SHOULD THINK YOU A FORTUNE SUFFICIENT FOR ME WITHOUT A SHILLING"

To Mary Stevenson

Dear Polly   Thursday May 31. 70
I receiv'd your Letter early this Morning, and as I am so engag'd that I cannot see you when you come to-day, I write this Line just to say, That I am sure you are a much better Judge in this Affair of your own than I can possibly be; in that Confidence it was that I forbore giving my Advice when you mention'd it to me, and not from any Disapprobation. My Concern (equal to any Father's) for your Happiness, makes me write this, lest having more Regard for my Opinion than you ought, and imagining it against the Proposal because I did not immediately advise accepting it, you should let that weigh any thing in your Deliberations. I assure you that no Objection has occur'd to me; his Person you see, his Temper and his Understanding you can judge of, his Character for any thing I have ever heard is unblemished; his Profession, with that Skill in it he is suppos'd to have, will be sufficient to support a Family; and therefore considering the Fortune you have in your Hands, (tho' any future Expectation from your Aunt should be disappointed) I do not see but that the Agreement may be a rational one on both sides. I see your Delicacy; and your Humility too; for you fancy that if you do not prove a great Fortune you will not be belov'd; but I am sure that were I in his Situation in every respect, knowing you so well as I do, and esteeming you so highly, I should think you a Fortune sufficient for me without a Shilling. Having thus more explicitly than before, given my Opinion, I leave the rest to your sound Judgment, of which no one has a greater Share; and shall not be too inquisitive after your particular Reasons, your Doubts, your Fears, &c.

For I shall be confident whether you accept or refuse, that you do right. I only wish you may do what will most contribute to your Happiness, and of course to mine; being ever, my dear Friend, Yours most affectionately

Don't be angry with me for supposing your Determination not quite so fix'd as you fancy it.

"THE SOLE LEGISLATOR OF HIS
AMERICAN SUBJECTS"

To Samuel Cooper

Dear Sir,   London, June 8. 1770
  I received duly your Favour of March 28. With this I send you two Speeches in Parliament on our Affairs by a Member that you know. The Repeal of the whole late Act would undoubtedly have been a prudent Measure, and I have reason to believe that Lord North was for it, but some of the other Ministers could not be brought to agree to it. So the Duty on Tea, with that obnoxious Preamble, remains to continue the Dispute. But I think the next Session will hardly pass over without repealing them; for the Parliament must finally comply with the Sense of the Nation. As to the Standing Army kept up among us in time of Peace, without the Consent of our Assemblies, I am clearly of Opinion that it is not agreable to the Constitution. Should the King by the Aid of his Parliaments in Ireland and the Colonies, raise an Army and bring it into England, quartering it here in time of Peace without the Consent of the Parliament of Great Britain, I am persuaded he would soon be told that he had no Right so to do, and the Nation would ring with Clamours against it. I own that I see no Difference in the Cases. And while we continue so many distinct and separate States, our having the same Head or Sovereign, the King, will not justify such an Invasion of the separate Right of each State to be consulted on the Establishment of whatever Force is proposed to be kept up within its Limits, and to give or refuse

its Consent as shall appear most for the Public Good of that State. That the Colonies originally were constituted distinct States, and intended to be continued such, is clear to me from a thorough Consideration of their original Charters, and the whole Conduct of the Crown and Nation towards them until the Restoration. Since that Period, the Parliament here has usurp'd an Authority of making Laws for them, which before it had not. We have for some time submitted to that Usurpation, partly thro' Ignorance and Inattention, and partly from our Weakness and Inability to contend. I hope when our Rights are better understood here, we shall, by a prudent and proper Conduct be able to obtain from the Equity of this Nation a Restoration of them. And in the mean time I could wish that such Expressions as, *The supreme Authority of Parliament*; *The Subordinacy of our Assemblies to the Parliament* and the like (which in Reality mean nothing if our Assemblies with the King have a true Legislative Authority) I say, I could wish that such Expressions were no more seen in our publick Pieces. They are too strong for Compliment, and tend to confirm a Claim of Subjects in one Part of the King's Dominions to be Sovereigns over their Fellow-Subjects in another Part of his Dominions; when in truth they have no such Right, and their Claim is founded only on Usurpation, the several States having equal Rights and Liberties, and being only connected, as England and Scotland were before the Union, by having one common Sovereign, the King. This kind of Doctrine the Lords and Commons here would deem little less than Treason against what they think their Share of the Sovereignty over the Colonies. To me those Bodies seem to have been long encroaching on the Rights of their and our Sovereign, assuming too much of his Authority, and betraying his Interests. By our Constitutions he is, with his Plantation Parliaments, the sole Legislator of his American Subjects, and in that Capacity is and ought to be free to exercise his own Judgment unrestrain'd and unlimited by his Parliament here. And our Parliaments have Right to grant him Aids without the Consent of this Parliament, a Circumstance which, by the way begins to give it some Jealousy. Let us therefore hold fast our Loyalty to our King (who has the best Dis-

position towards us, and has a Family-Interest in our Prosperity) as that steady Loyalty is the most probable Means of
securing us from the arbitrary Power of a corrupt Parliament, that does not like us, and conceives itself to have an
Interest in keeping us down and fleecing us. If they should
urge the *Inconvenience* of an Empire's being divided into so
many separate States, and from thence conclude that we are
not so divided; I would answer, that an Inconvenience
proves nothing but itself. England and Scotland were once
separate States, under the same King. The Inconvenience
found in their being separate States, did not prove that the
Parliament of England had a Right to govern Scotland. A
formal Union was thought necessary, and England was an
hundred Years soliciting it, before she could bring it about.
If Great Britain now thinks such an Union necessary with
us, let her propose her Terms, and we may consider of them.
Were the general Sentiments of this Nation to be consulted
in the Case, I should hope the Terms, whether practicable or
not, would at least be equitable: for I think that except
among those with whom the Spirit of Toryism prevails, the
popular Inclination here is, to wish us well, and that we may
preserve our Liberties.

I unbosom my self thus to you in Confidence of your Prudence, and wishing to have your Sentiments on the Subject
in Return.

Mr. Pownall, I suppose, will acquaint you with the Event
of his Motions, and therefore I say nothing more of them,
than that he appears very sincere in his Endeavours to serve
us; on which Account I some time since republish'd with
Pleasure the parting Addresses to him of your Assembly, with
some previous Remarks, to his Honour as well as in Justification of our People.

I hope that before this time those detestable Murderers
have quitted your Province, and that the Spirit of Industry
and Frugality continues and increases. With sincerest Esteem
and Affection, I am, Dear Sir, Your most obedient and most
humble Servant

P.S. Just before the last Session of Parliament commenced a
Friend of mine, who had Connections with some of the

Ministry, wrote me a Letter purposely to draw from me my Sentiments in Writing on the then State of Affairs. I wrote a pretty free Answer, which I know was immediately communicated and a good deal handed about among them. For your *private Amusement* I send you Copies. I wish you may be able to read them, as they are very badly written by a very blundering Clerk.

"HITHERTO MADE NO ATTEMPT UPON MY VIRTUE"

To Mary Stevenson Hewson

Dear Polly,   London, July 18. 1770

Yours of the 15th. informing me of your agreable Journey and safe Arrival at Hexham gave me great Pleasure, and would make your good Mother happy if I knew how to convey it to her; but 'tis such an out-of-the-way Place she is gone to, and the Name so out of my Head, that the Good News must wait her Return. Enclos'd I send you a Letter which came before she went, and, supposing it from my Daughter Bache, she would have me open and read it to her, so you see if there had been any Intrigue between the Gentleman and you, how all would have been discovered. Your Mother went away on Friday last, taking with her Sally and Temple, trusting me alone with Nanny, who indeed has hitherto made no Attempt upon my Virtue. Neither Dolly nor Barwell, nor any other good Female Soul of your Friends or mine have been nigh me, nor offered me the least Consolation by Letter in my present lonesome State. I hear the Post-man's Bell, so can only add my affectionate Respects to Mr. Hewson, and best Wishes of perpetual Happiness for you both. I am, as ever, my dear good Girl, Your affectionate Friend

"HAVE YOU THEN GOT NE'ER A GRANDMOTHER?"

To Deborah Franklin

My dear Child,   London, Oct. 3. 1770

I received your kind Letter of Aug. 16. which gave me a

great deal of Satisfaction. I am glad your little Grandson recovered so soon of his Illness, as I see you are quite in Love with him, and your Happiness wrapt up in his; since your whole long Letter is made up of the History of his pretty Actions. It was very prudently done of you not to interfere when his Mother thought fit to correct him; which pleases me the more, as I feared, from your Fondness of him, that he would be too much humoured, and perhaps spoiled. There is a Story of two little Boys in the Street; one was crying bitterly; the other came to him to ask what was the Matter? I have been, says he, for a pennyworth of Vinegar, and I have broke the Glass and spilt the Vinegar, and my Mother will whip me. *No, she won't whip you* says the other. Indeed she will, says he. *What,* says the other, *have you then got ne'er a Grandmother?*

I am sorry I did not send one of my Books to Mr. Rhodes, since he was desirous of seeing it. My Love to him, and to all enquiring Friends. Mrs. West was here to day, and desired me to mention her Love to you. Mr. Strahan and Family are all well, always enquire how you all do, and send their Love. Mrs Stevenson is at present in the Country. But Polly sends her Love to you and Mrs Bache and the young Gentleman. My Love to all. I am, as ever, Your affectionate Husband

"THIS WORLD IS THE TRUE HELL"

To Jane Mecom

Dear Sister   London Dec. 30. 1770

This Ship staying longer than was expected, gives me an Opportunity of writing to you which I thought I must have miss'd when I desir'd Cousin Williams to excuse me to you. I received your kind Letter of Sept. 25 by the young Gentlemen, who, by their discreet Behaviour have recommended themselves very much to me and many of my Acquaintance. Josiah has attained his Heart's Desire of being under the Tuition of Mr. Stanley, who, tho, he had long left off Teaching, kindly undertook at my Request to instruct him, and is much pleased with his Quickness of Apprehension and the Progress he makes; and Jonathan appears a very valuable young Man, sober, regular, and inclin'd to Industry and Frugality, which are promising Signs of Success in Business: I am very happy in their Company.

As to the Rumour you mention (which was, as Josiah tells me, that I had been depriv'd of my Place in the Post Office on Account of a letter I wrote to Philadelphia) it might have this Foundation, that some of the Ministry had been displeas'd at my Writing such Letters, and there were really some Thoughts among them of shewing that Displeasure in that manner. But I had some Friends too, who unrequested by me advis'd the contrary. And my Enemies were forc'd to content themselves with abusing me plentifully in the Newspapers, and endeavouring to provoke me to resign. In this they are not likely to succeed, I being deficient in that Christian Virtue of Resignation. If they would have my Office, they must take it—I have heard of some great Man, whose Rule it was with regard to Offices, *Never to ask for them*, and *never to refuse them*: To which I have always added in my own Practice, *Never to resign them.* As I told my Friends, I rose to that office thro' a long Course of Service in the inferior Degrees of it: Before my time, thro' bad Management, it never produced the Salary annex'd to it; and when I receivd it, no Salary was to be allow'd if the office did not produce it. During the first four Years it was so far from defraying itself, that it became £950 Sterling in debt to me and my Collegue. I had been chiefly instrumental in bringing it to its present flourishing State, and therefore thought I had some kind of Right to it. I had hitherto executed the Duties of it faithfully, and to the perfect Satisfaction of my Superiors, which I thought was all that should be expected of me on that Account. As to the Letters complain'd of, it was true I did write them, and they were written in Compliance with another Duty, that to my Country. A Duty quite Distinct from that of Postmaster. My Conduct in this respect was exactly similar with that I held on a similar Occasion but a few Years ago, when the then Ministry were ready to hug me for the Assistance I afforded them in repealing a former Revenue Act. My Sentiments were still the same, that no such

Acts should be made here for America; or, if made should as soon as possible be repealed; and I thought it should not be expected of me, to change my Political Opinions every time his Majesty thought fit to change his Ministers. This was my Language on the Occasion; and I have lately heard, that tho I was thought much to blame, it being understood that every Man who holds an Office should act with the Ministry whether agreable or not to his own Judgment, yet in consideration of the goodness of my private Character (as they are pleas'd to compliment me) the office was not to be taken from me. Possibly they may still change their Minds, and remove me; but no Apprehension of that sort, will, I trust, make the least Alteration in my Political Conduct. My rule in which I have always found Satisfaction, is, Never to turn asside in Publick Affairs thro' Views of private Interest; but to go strait forward in doing what appears to me right at the time, leaving the Consequences with Providence. What in my younger Days enabled me more easily to walk upright, was, that I had a Trade; and that I could live upon a little; and thence (never having had views of making a Fortune) I was free from Avarice, and contented with the plentiful Supplies my business afforded me. And now it is still more easy for me to preserve my Freedom and Integrity, when I consider, that I am almost at the End of my Journey, and therefore need less to complete the Expence of it; and that what I now possess thro' the Blessing of God may with tolerable Oeconomy, be sufficient for me (great Misfortunes excepted) tho' I should add nothing more to it by any Office or Employment whatsoever.

I send you by this Opportunity the 2 Books you wrote for. They cost 3s. a piece. When I was first in London, about 45 Years since, I knew a person who had an Opinion something like your Author's—Her Name was *Ilive*, a Printer's Widow. She dy'd soon after I left England, and by her Will oblig'd her son to deliver publickly in Salter's Hall a Solemn Discourse, the purport of which was to prove, that this World is the true Hell or Place of Punishment for the Spirits who had transgress'd in a better State, and were sent here to suffer for their sins in Animals of all Sorts. It is long since I saw the Discourse, which was printed. I think a good deal of Scripture was cited in it, and that the Supposition was, that tho' we now remember'd nothing of such pre-existent State; yet after Death we might recollect it, and remember the Punishments we had suffer'd, so as to be the better for them; and others who had not yet offended, might now behold and be warn'd by our Sufferings. In fact we see here that every lower Animal has its Enemy with proper Inclinations, Faculties and Weapons, to terrify, wound and destroy it; and that Men, who are uppermost, are Devils to one another; So that on the establish'd Doctrine of the Goodness and Justice of the great Creator, this apparent State of general and systematical Mischief, seem'd to demand some such Supposition as Mrs. Ilives, to account for it consistent with the Honour of the Diety. But our reasoning Powers when employ'd about what may have been before our Existence here, or shall be after it, cannot go far for want of History and Facts: Revelation only can give us the necessary Information, and that (in the first of these Points especially) has been very sparingly afforded us.

I hope you continue to correspond with your Friends at Philadelphia, or else I shall think there has been some Miff between you; which indeed, to confess the Truth, I was a little afraid, from some Instances of others, might possibly happen, and that prevented my ever urging you to make such a visit especially as I think there is rather an overquantity of Touchwood in your Constitution. My Love to your Children, and believe me ever, Your affectionate Brother

Let none of my Letters go out of your Hands.

HOW RAINDROPS GROW

To Thomas Percival

On my return to London I found your favour, of the six-teenth of May (1771). I wish I could, as you desire, give you a better explanation of the phænomenon in question, since you seem not quite satisfied with your own; but I think we want more and a greater variety of experiments in different circumstances, to enable us to form a thoroughly satisfactory hypothesis. Not that I make the least doubt of the facts already related, as I know both Lord Charles Cavendish, and Dr. Heberden to be very accurate experimenters: but I wish to know the event of the trials proposed in your six queries; and also, whether in the same place where the lower vessel receives nearly twice the quantity of water that is received by the upper, a third vessel placed at half the height will receive a quantity proportionable. I will however endeavour to explain to you what occurred to me, when I first heard of the fact.

I suppose, it will be generally allowed, on a little consideration of the subject, that scarce any drop of water was, when it began to fall from the clouds, of a magnitude equal to that it has acquired, when it arrives at the earth; the same of the several pieces of hail; because they are often so large and weighty, that we cannot conceive a possibility of their being suspended in the air, and remaining at rest there, for any time, how small soever; nor do we conceive any means of forming them so large, before they set out to fall. It seems then, that each beginning drop, and particle of hail, receives continual addition in its progress downwards. This may be several ways: by the union of numbers in their course, so that what was at first only a descending mist, becomes a shower; or by each particle in its descent through air that contains a great quantity of dissolved water, striking against, attaching to itself, and carrying down with it, such particles of that dissolved water, as happen to be in its way; or attracting to itself such as do not lie directly in its course, by its different state with regard either to common or electric fire; or by all these causes united.

In the first case, by the uniting of numbers, larger drops might be made, but the quantity falling in the same space would be the same at all heights; unless, as you mention, the whole should be contracted in falling, the lines described by all the drops converging, so that what set out to fall from a cloud of many thousand acres, should reach the earth in perhaps a third of that extent, of which I somewhat doubt. In the other cases we have two experiments.

1. A dry glass bottle, filled with very cold water, in a warm day, will presently collect from the seemingly dry air that surrounds it, a quantity of water that shall cover its surface and run down its sides, which perhaps is done by the power wherewith the cold water attracts the fluid, common fire that had been united with the dissolved water in the air, and drawing that fire through the glass into itself, leaves the water on the outside.

2. An electrified body left in a room for some time, will be more covered with dust than other bodies in the same room not electrified, which dust seems to be attracted from the circumambient air.

Now we know that the rain, even in our hottest days, comes from a very cold region. Its falling sometimes in the form of ice, shews this clearly; and perhaps even the rain is snow or ice when it first moves downwards, though thawed in falling: And we know that the drops of rain are often electrified: But those causes of addition to each drop of water, or piece of hail, one would think could not long continue to produce the same effect; since the air, through which the drops fall, must soon be stript of its previously dissolved water, so as to be no longer capable of augmenting them. Indeed very heavy showers, of either, are never of long continuance; but moderate rains often continue so long as to puzzle this hypothesis: So that upon the whole I think, as I intimated before, that we are yet hardly ripe for making one.

June? 1771

"AN ADVENTURE TO GAIN FORBIDDEN KNOWLEDGE"

To Jane Mecom

Dear Sister,   London, July 17. 1771

I have received your kind Letter of May 10. You seem so sensible of your Error in so hastily suspecting me, that I am now in my turn sorry I took Notice of it. Let us then suppose that Accompt ballanced and settled, and think no more of it.

In some former Letter I believe I mention'd the Price of the Books, which I have now forgotten: But I think it was 3s. each. To be sure there are Objections to the Doctrine of Pre-existence: But it seems to have been invented with a good Intention, to save the Honour of the Deity, which was thought to be injured by the Supposition of his bringing Creatures into the World to be miserable, without any pre-vious misbehaviour of theirs to deserve it. This, however, is perhaps an officious Supporting of the Ark, without being call'd to such Service. Where he has thought fit to draw a Veil, our Attempting to remove it may be deem'd at least an offensive Impertinence. And we shall probably succeed little better in such an Adventure to gain forbidden Knowledge, than our first Parents did when they ate the Apple.

I meant no more by saying Mankind were Devils to one another than that being in general superior to the Malice of the other Creatures, they were not so much tormented by them as by themselves. Upon the whole I am much disposed to like the World as I find it, and to doubt my own Judgment as to what would mend it. I see so much Wisdom in what I understand of its Creation and Government, that I suspect equal Wisdom may be in what I do not understand. And thence have perhaps as much Trust in God as the most pious Christian.

I am very happy that a good Understanding continues be-tween you and the Philadelphia Folks. Our Father, who was a very wise man, us'd to say, nothing was more common than for those who lov'd one another at a distance, to find many Causes of Dislike when they came together; and therefore he did not approve of Visits to Relations in distant Places, which could not well be short enough for them to part good Friends. I saw a Proof of it, in the Disgusts between him and his Brother Benjamin; and tho' I was a Child I still remember how affectionate their Correspondence was while they were separated, and the Disputes and Misunderstandings they had when they came to live some time together in the same House. But you have been more prudent, and restrain'd that "Aptness" you say you have "to interfere in other People's oeconomical Affairs by putting in a Word now and then un-asked." And so all's well that ends well.

I thought you had mentioned in one of your Letters a Desire to have Spectacles of some sort sent you; but I cannot
now find such a Letter. However I send you a Pair of every
Size of Glasses from 1 to 13. To suit yourself, take out a Pair
at a time, and hold one of the Glasses first against one Eye,
and then against the other, looking on some small Print. If
the first Pair suits neither Eye, put them up again before you
open a second. Thus you will keep them from mixing. By
trying and comparing at your Leisure, you may find those
that are best for you, which you cannot well do in a Shop,
where for want of Time and Care, People often take such as
strain their Eyes and hurt them. I advise your trying each of
your Eyes separately, because few Peoples Eyes are Fellows,
and almost every body in reading or working uses one Eye
principally, the other being dimmer or perhaps fitter for distant Objects; and thence it happens that the Spectacles whose
Glasses are Fellows suit sometimes that Eye which before was
not used tho' they do not suit the other. When you have
suited your self, keep the higher Numbers for future Use as
your Eyes may grow older; and oblige your Friends with the
others.

I was lately at Sheffield and Birmingham, where I bought
a few plated Things which I send you as Tokens, viz. A Pair
of Sauceboats, a Pair of flat Candlesticks, and a Saucepan,
lined with Silver. Please to accept of them. I have had one of
the latter in constant Use 12 Years, and the Silver still holds.
But Tinning is soon gone.

Mrs. Stevenson and Mrs. Hewson present their Compliments, the latter has a fine Son. Sally Franklin sends her Duty
to you. I wonder you have not heard of her till lately. She has
lived with me these 5 Years, a very good Girl, now near 16.
She is Great Grandaughter of our Father's Brother John, who
was a Dyer at Banbury in Oxfordshire, where our Father
learnt that Trade of him, and where our Grandfather Thomas
lies buried: I saw his Gravestone. Sally's Father, John's
Grandson, is now living at Lutterworth in Leicestershire,
where he follows the same Business, his Father too being
bred a Dyer, as was our Uncle Benjamin. He is a Widower,
and Sally his only Child. These two are the only Descendants
of our Grandfather Thomas now remaining in England that

retain that Name of *Franklin*. The Walkers are descended of John by a Daughter that I have seen, lately deceased. Sally and Cousin Williams's Children, and Henry Walker who now attends Josiah are Relations in the same degree to one another and to your and my Grandchildren, viz

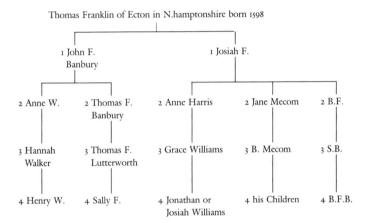

Thomas Franklin of Ecton in N.hamptonshire born 1598

1 John F. Banbury — 1 Josiah F.

2 Anne W.	2 Thomas F. Banbury	2 Anne Harris	2 Jane Mecom	2 B.F.
3 Hannah Walker	3 Thomas F. Lutterworth	3 Grace Williams	3 B. Mecom	3 S.B.
4 Henry W.	4 Sally F.	4 Jonathan or Josiah Williams	4 his Children	4 B.F.B.

What is this Relation called? Is it third Cousins? Having mentioned so many Dyers in our Family, I will now it's in my Mind request of you a full and particular Receipt for Dying Worsted of that beautiful Red, which you learnt of our Mother. And also a Receipt for making Crown Soap. Let it be very exact in the smallest Particulars. Enclos'd I send you a Receipt for making soft Soap in the Sun.

I have never seen any young Men from America that acquir'd by their Behaviour here more general Esteem than those you recommended to me. Josiah has stuck close to his musical Studies, and still continues them. Jonathan has been diligent in Business for his Friends as well as himself, obliging to every body, tender of his Brother, not fond of the expensive Amusements of the Place, regular in his Hours, and spending what Leisure Hours he had in the Study of Mathematics. He goes home to settle in Business, and I think there is great Probability of his doing well. With best Wishes for you and all yours, I am ever, Your affectionate Brother

I have mislaid the Soap Receipt but will send it when I find it.

To Anna Mordaunt Shipley

Dear Madam,   London, Aug. 13. 1771

This is just to let you know that we arriv'd safe and well in Marlborough Street about Six, where I deliver'd up my Charge.

The above seems too short for a Letter; so I will lengthen it by a little Account of our Journey. The first Stage we were rather pensive. I tried several Topics of Conversation, but none of them would hold. But after Breakfast, we began to recover Spirits, and had a good deal of Chat. Will you hear some of it? We talk'd of her Brother, and she wish'd he was married. And don't you wish your Sisters married too? Yes. All but Emily; I would not have her married. Why? Because I can't spare her, I can't part with her. The rest may marry as soon as they please, so they do but get good Husbands. We then took upon us to consider for 'em what sort of Husbands would be fittest for every one of them. We began with Georgiana. She thought a Country Gentleman, that lov'd Travelling and would take her with him, that lov'd Books and would hear her read to him; I added, that had a good Estate and was a Member of Parliament and lov'd to see an Experiment now and then. This she agreed to; so we set him down for Georgiana, and went on to Betsy. Betsy, says I, seems of a sweet mild Temper, and if we should give her a Country Squire, and he should happen to be of a rough, passionate Turn, and be angry now and then, it might break her Heart. O, none of 'em must be so; for then they would not be good Husbands. To make sure of this Point, however, for Betsey, shall we give her a Bishop? O no, that won't do. They all declare against the Church, and against the Army; not one of them will marry either a Clergyman or an Officer; that they

are resolv'd upon. What can be their reason for that? Why
you know, that when a Clergyman or an Officer dies, the
Income goes with 'em; and then what is there to maintain the
Family? there's the Point. Then suppose we give her a good,
honest, sensible City Merchant, who will love her dearly and
is very rich? I don't know but that may do. We proceeded to
Emily, her dear Emily, I was afraid we should hardly find any
thing good enough for Emily; but at last, after first settling
that, if she did marry, Kitty was to live a good deal with her;
we agreed that as Emily was very handsome we might expect
an Earl for her: So having fix'd her, as I thought, a Countess,
we went on to Anna-Maria. She, says Kitty, should have a
rich Man that has a large Family and a great many things to
take care of; for she is very good at managing, helps my
Mama very much, can look over Bills, and order all sorts of
Family Business. Very well; and as there is a Grace and Dignity in her Manner that would become the Station, what do
you think of giving her a Duke? O no! I'll have the Duke for
Emily. You may give the Earl to Anna-Maria if you please:
But Emily shall have the Duke. I contested this Matter some
time; but at length was forc'd to give up the point, leave Emily in Possession of the Duke, and content myself with the
Earl for Anna Maria. And now what shall we do for Kitty?
We have forgot her, all this Time. Well, and what will you do
for her? I suppose that tho' the rest have resolv'd against the
Army, she may not yet have made so rash a Resolution. Yes,
but she has: Unless, now, an old one, an old General that has
done fighting, and is rich, such a one as General Rufane; I
like him a good deal; You must know I like an old Man,
indeed I do: And some how or other all the old Men take to
me, all that come to our House like me better than my other
Sisters: I go to 'em and ask 'em how they do, and they like it
mightily; and the Maids take notice of it, and say when they
see an old Man come, there's a Friend of yours, Miss Kitty.
But then as you like an old General, hadn't you better take
him while he's a young Officer, and let him grow old upon
your Hands, because then, you'll like him better and better
every Year as he grows older and older. No, that won't do.
He must be an old Man of 70 or 80, and take me when I am
about 30: And then you know I may be a rich young Widow.

We din'd at Staines, she was Mrs. Shipley, cut up the Chicken
pretty handily (with a little Direction) and help'd me in a very
womanly Manner. Now, says she, when I commended her,
my Father never likes to see me or Georgiana carve, because
we do it, he says, so badly: But how should we learn if we
never try? We drank good Papa and Mama's Health, and the
Health's of the Dutchess, the Countess, the Merchant's Lady,
the Country Gentlewoman, and our Welsh Brother. This
brought their Affairs again under Consideration. I doubt,
says she, we have not done right for Betsey. I don't think a
Merchant will do for her. She is much inclin'd to be a fine
Gentlewoman; and is indeed already more of the fine Gentlewoman, I think, than any of my other Sisters; and therefore
she shall be a Vice Countess.

Thus we chatted on, and she was very entertaining quite to
Town.

I have now made my Letter as much too long as it was at
first too short. The Bishop would think it too trifling, therefore don't show it him. I am afraid too that you will think it
so, and have a good mind not to send it. Only it tells you
Kitty is well at School, and for that I let it go. My Love to
the whole amiable Family, best Respects to the Bishop, and
1000 Thanks for all your Kindnesses, and for the happy Days
I enjoy'd at Twyford. With the greatest Esteem and Respect,
I am, Madam, Your most obedient humble Servant

"COMPAR'D TO THESE PEOPLE
EVERY INDIAN IS A GENTLEMAN"

To Joshua Babcock

Dear Sir,   London, Jan. 13. 1772
It was with great Pleasure I learnt by Mr. Marchant, that
you and Mrs. Babcock and all your good Family continue
well and happy. I hope I shall find you all in the same State
when I next come your Way, and take Shelter as often heretofore under your hospitable Roof. The Colonel, I am told,

continues an active and able Farmer, the most honourable of all Employments, in my Opinion as being the most useful in itself, and rendring the Man most independent. My Namesake, his Son, will soon I hope be able to drive the Plough for him.

I have lately made a Tour thro' Ireland and Scotland. In these Countries a small Part of the Society are Landlords, great Noblemen and Gentlemen, extreamly opulent, living in the highest Affluence and Magnificence: The Bulk of the People Tenants, extreamly poor, living in the most sordid Wretchedness in dirty Hovels of Mud and Straw, and cloathed only in Rags. I thought often of the Happiness of New England, where every Man is a Freeholder, has a Vote in publick Affairs, lives in a tidy warm House, has plenty of good Food and Fewel, with whole Cloaths from Head to Foot, the Manufactury perhaps of his own Family. Long may they continue in this Situation! But if they should ever envy the *Trade* of these Countries, I can put them in a Way to obtain a Share of it. Let them with three fourths of the People of Ireland, live the Year round on Potatoes and Butter milk, without Shirts, then may their Merchants export Beef, Butter and Linnen. Let them with the Generality of the Common People of Scotland go Barefoot, then may they make large Exports in Shoes and Stockings: And if they will be content to wear Rags like the Spinners and Weavers of England, they may make Cloths and Stuffs for all Parts of the World. Farther, if my Countrymen should ever wish for the Honour of having among them a Gentry enormously wealthy, let them sell their Farms and pay rack'd Rents; the Scale of the Landlords will rise as that of the Tenants is depress'd who will soon become poor, tattered, dirty, and abject in Spirit. Had I never been in the American Colonies, but was to form my Judgment of Civil Society by what I have lately seen, I should never advise a Nation of Savages to admit of Civilisation: For I assure you, that in the Possession and Enjoyment of the various Comforts of Life, compar'd to these People every Indian is a Gentleman: And the Effect of this kind of Civil Society seems only to be, the depressing Multitudes below the Savage State that a few may be rais'd above it. My best Wishes attend you and yours, being ever with great Esteem, Dear Sir, Your most obedient and most humble Servant

ON THE WRITINGS OF ZOROASTER

To Ezra Stiles

Dear Sir,   London, Jany. 13. 1772

I receiv'd your Favour by Mr. Marchant, who appears a very worthy Gentleman, and I shall not fail to render him every Service in my Power.

There is lately published in Paris, a Work intitled *Zend-avesta*, or the Writings of *Zoroaster*, containing the Theological, Philosophical and Moral Ideas of that Legislator, and the Ceremonies of Religious Worship that he establish'd. Translated from the original Zend. In two Vols. 4to. Near half the Work is an Account of the Translator's Travels in India, and his Residence among the Parses during several Years to learn their Languages. I have cast my Eye over the Religious Part; it seems to contain a nice Morality, mix'd with abundance of Prayers, Ceremonies, and Observations. If you desire to have it, I will procure it for you. They say there is no doubt of its being a genuine Translation of the Books at present deem'd sacred as the Writings of Zoroaster by his Followers; but perhaps some of them are of later Date tho' ascrib'd to him: For to me there seems too great a Quantity and Variety of Ceremonies and Prayers to be directed at once by one Man. In the Romish Church they have increas'd gradually in a Course of Ages to their present Bulk. Those who added new Ones from time to time found it necessary to give them Authority by Pretences of their Antiquity. The Books of Moses, indeed, if all written by him, which some doubt, are an Exception to this Observation. With great Esteem, I am ever, Dear Sir, Your affectionate Friend and humble Servant

P S. Since writing the above, Mr. Marchant, understanding you are curious on the Subject of the Eastern ancient Religions, concludes to send you the Book.

To Anthony Benezet

Dear Friend,   London, Augt 22. 1772

I made a little Extract from yours of April 27. of the Number of Slaves imported and perishing, with some close Remarks on the Hypocrisy of this Country which encourages such a detestable Commerce by Laws, for promoting the Guinea Trade, while it piqu'd itself on its Virtue Love of Liberty, and the Equity of its Courts in setting free a single Negro. This was inserted in the London Chronicle of the 20th of June last. I thank you for the Virginia Address, which I shall also publish with some Remarks. I am glad to hear that the Disposition against keeping Negroes grows more general in North America. Several Pieces have been lately printed here against the Practice, and I hope in time it will be taken into Consideration and suppress'd by the Legislature. Your Labours have already been attended with great Effects. I hope therefore you and your Friends will be encouraged to proceed. My hearty Wishes of Success attend you, being ever, my dear Friend, Yours most affectionately

To Samuel Rhoads

Dear Friend,   London, Augt. 22. 1772

I think I before acknowledg'd your Favour of Feb. 29. I have since received that of May 30. I am glad my Canal Papers were agreable to you. If any Work of that kind is set on foot in America, I think it would be saving Money to engage by a handsome Salary an Engineer from hence who has been accustomed to such Business. The many Canals on foot here under different great Masters, are daily raising a number of Pupils in the Art, some of whom may want Employ hereafter; and a single Mistake thro' Inexperience, in such important Works, may cost much more than the Expence of Salary to an ingenious young Man already well acquainted with both Principles and Practice. This the Irish have learnt at a dear Rate in the first Attempt of their great Canal, and now are endeavouring to get Smeaton to come and rectify their Errors. With regard to your Question, whether it is best to make the Skuylkill a part of the Navigation to the back Country, or whether the Difficulty, of that River, subject to all the Inconveniencies of Floods, Ice, &c will not be greater than the Expence of Digging, Locks, &c. I can only say, that here they look on the *constant Practicability* of a Navigation, allowing Boats to pass and repass at all Times and Seasons, without Hindrance, to be a Point of the greatest Importance, and therefore they seldom or ever use a River where it can be avoided. Locks in Rivers are subject to many more Accidents than those in still-water Canals; and the Carrying-away a few Locks by Freshes or Ice, not only creates a great Expence, but interrupts Business for a long time till Repairs are made; which may soon be destroyed again; and thus the Carrying-on a Course of Business by such a Navigation be discouraged, as subject to frequent Interruptions: The Toll too must be higher to pay for such Repairs. Rivers are ungovernable Things, especially in Hilly Countries: Canals are quiet and very manageable: Therefore they are often carried on here by the Sides of Rivers, only on Ground above the Reach of Floods, no other Use being made of the Rivers than to supply occasionally the Waste of Water in the Canals. I warmly wish Success to every Attempt for Improvement of our dear Country; and am with sincere Esteem, Yours most affectionately

I congratulate you on the Change of our American Minister. The present has more favourable Dispositions towards us than his Predecessor.

"MORAL OR PRUDENTIAL ALGEBRA"

To Joseph Priestley

Dear Sir,   London Sept. 19. 1772
    In the Affair of so much Importance to you, wherein you ask my Advice, I cannot for want of sufficient Premises,

advise you *what* to determine, but if you please I will tell you *how*. When these difficult Cases occur, they are difficult chiefly because while we have them under Consideration all the Reasons *pro* and *con* are not present to the Mind at the same time; but sometimes one Set present themselves, and at other times another, the first being out of Sight. Hence the various Purposes or Inclinations that alternately prevail, and the Uncertainty that perplexes us. To get over this, my Way is, to divide half a Sheet of Paper by a Line into two Columns, writing over the one *Pro*, and over the other *Con*. Then during three or four Days Consideration I put down under the different Heads short Hints of the different Motives that at different Times occur to me for or against the Measure. When I have thus got them all together in one View, I endeavour to estimate their respective Weights; and where I find two, one on each side, that seem equal, I strike them both out: If I find a Reason *pro* equal to some two Reasons *con*, I strike out the three. If I judge some two Reasons *con* equal to some three Reasons *pro*, I strike out the five; and thus proceeding I find at length where the Ballance lies; and if after a Day or two of farther Consideration nothing new that is of Importance occurs on either side, I come to a Determination accordingly. And tho' the Weight of Reasons cannot be taken with the Precision of Algebraic Quantities, yet when each is thus considered separately and comparatively, and the whole lies before me, I think I can judge better, and am less likely to make a rash Step; and in fact I have found great Advantage from this kind of Equation, in what may be called *Moral* or *Prudential Algebra*. Wishing sincerely that you may determine for the best, I am ever, my dear Friend, Yours most affectionately

"ALAS! POOR MUNGO!"

To Georgiana Shipley

Dear Miss,   London, Sept. 26. 1772
    I lament with you most sincerely the unfortunate End of poor *Mungo*: Few Squirrels were better accomplish'd; for he

had had a good Education, had travell'd far, and seen much of the World. As he had the Honour of being for his Virtues your Favourite, he should not go like common Skuggs without an Elegy or an Epitaph. Let us give him one in the monumental Stile and Measure, which being neither Prose nor Verse, is perhaps the properest for Grief; since to use common Language would look as if we were not affected, and to make Rhimes would seem Trifling in Sorrow.

> Alas! poor *Mungo*!
> Happy wert thou, hadst thou known
> Thy own Felicity!
> Remote from the fierce Bald-Eagle,
> Tyrant of thy native Woods,
> Thou hadst nought to fear from his piercing Talons;
> Nor from the murdering Gun
> Of the thoughtless Sportsman.
> Safe in thy wired Castle,
> Grimalkin never could annoy thee.
> Daily wert thou fed with the choicest Viands
> By the fair Hand
> Of an indulgent Mistress.
> But, discontented, thou wouldst have more Freedom.
> Too soon, alas! didst thou obtain it,
> And, wandering,
> Fell by the merciless Fangs,
> Of wanton, cruel Ranger.
> Learn hence, ye who blindly wish more Liberty,
> Whether Subjects, Sons, Squirrels or Daughters,
> That apparent *Restraint* may be real *Protection*,
> Yielding Peace, Plenty, and Security.

You see how much more decent and proper this broken Stile, interrupted as it were with Sighs, is for the Occasion, than if one were to say, by way of Epitaph,

> Here Skugg
> Lies snug
> As a Bug
> In a Rug.

And yet perhaps there are People in the World of so little Feeling as to think, *that* would be a good-enough Epitaph for our poor Mungo!

If you wish it, I shall procure another to succeed him. But perhaps you will now chuse some other Amusement. Remember me respectfully to all the [   ] good Family; and believe me ever, Your affectionate Friend

September 26, 1772

"THE INCREASE OF RELIGIOUS AS WELL AS CIVIL LIBERTY"

To William Marshall

Reverend Sir,   London, Feb. 14. 1773

I duly received your respected Letter of Oct. 30. and am very sensible of the Propriety and Equity of the Act passed to indulge your Friends in their Scruples relating to the Mode of Taking an Oath which you plead for so ably by numerous Reasons. That Act with others has now been some time laid before his Majesty in Council. I have not yet heard of any Objection to it; but if such should arise, I shall do my utmost to remove them, and obtain the Royal Assent. Believe me, Reverend Sir, to have the warmest Wishes for the Increase of Religious as well as Civil Liberty thro'out the World; and that I am, with great Regard, Your most obedient humble Servant

"STOOP! STOOP!"

To Samuel Mather

Reverend Sir,   London, July 7. 1773.

By a Line of the 4th. past, I acknowledged the Receipt of your Favour of March 18. and sent you with it two Pamphlets.

I now add another, a spirited Address to the Bishops who opposed the Dissenter's Petition. It is written by a Dissenting Minister at York. There is preserv'd at the End of it a little fugitive Piece of mine, written on the same Occasion.

I perused your Tracts with Pleasure. I see you inherit all the various Learning of your famous Ancestors Cotton and Increase Mather both of whom I remember. The Father, Increase, I once when a Boy, heard preach at the Old South, for Mr. Pemberton, and remember his mentioning the Death of "that wicked old Persecutor of God's People Lewis the XIV." of which News had just been received, but which proved premature. I was some years afterwards at his House at the Northend, on some Errand to him, and remember him sitting in an easy Chair apparently very old and feeble. But Cotton I remember in the Vigour of his Preaching and Usefulness. And particularly in the Year 1723, now half a Century since, I had reason to remember, as I still do a Piece of Advice he gave me. I had been some time with him in his Study, where he condescended to entertain me, a very Youth, with some pleasant and instructive Conversation. As I was taking my Leave he accompany'd me thro' a narrow Passage at which I did not enter, and which had a Beam across it lower than my Head. He continued Talking which occasion'd me to keep my Face partly towards him as I retired, when he suddenly cry'd out, Stoop! Stoop! Not immediately understanding what he meant, I hit my Head hard against the Beam. He then added, *Let this be a Caution to you not always to hold your Head so high; Stoop, young Man, stoop—as you go through the World—and you'll miss many hard Thumps.* This was a way of hammering Instruction into one's Head: And it was so far effectual, that I have ever since remember'd it, tho' I have not always been able to practise it. By the way, permit me to ask if you are the Son or Nephew of that Gentleman? for having lived so many Years far from New England, I have lost the Knowledge of some Family Connections.

You have made the most of your Argument to prove that America might be known to the Ancients. The Inhabitants being totally ignorant of the use of Iron, looks, however, as if the Intercourse could never have been very considerable; and that if they are Descendants of our Adam, they left the

Family before the time of Tubalcain. There is another Discovery of it claimed by the Norwegians, which you have not mentioned, unless it be under the Words "of old viewed and observed" Page 7. About 25 Years since, Professor Kalm, a learned Swede, was with us in Pensilvania. He contended that America was discovered by their Northern People long before the Time of Columbus, which I doubting, he drew up and gave me sometime after a Note of those Discoveries which I send you enclos'd. It is his own Hand writing, and his own English very intelligible for the time he had been among us. The Circumstances give the Account great Appearance of Authenticity. And if one may judge by the Description of the Winter, the Country they visited should be southward of New England, supposing no Change since that time of the Climate. But if it be true as Krantz and I think other Historians tell us, that old Greenland once inhabited and populous, is now render'd uninhabitable by Ice, it should seem that the almost perpetual northern Winter has gained ground to the Southward, and if so, perhaps more northern Countries might anciently have had Vines than can bear them in these Days. The Remarks you have added, on the late Proceedings against America, are very just and judicious: and I cannot at all see any Impropriety in your making them tho' a Minister of the Gospel. This Kingdom is a good deal indebted for its Liberties to the Publick Spirit of its ancient Clergy, who join'd with the Barons in obtaining Magna Charta, and join'd heartily in forming Curses of Excommunication against the Infringers of it. There is no doubt but the Claim of Parliament of Authority to make Laws *binding on the Colonists in all Cases whatsoever*, includes an Authority to change our Religious Constitution, and establish Popery or Mahometanism if they please in its Stead: but, as you intimate *Power* does not infer *Right*; and as the Right is nothing and the *Power* (by our Increase) continually diminishing, the one will soon be as insignificant as the other. You seem only to have made a small Mistake in supposing they modestly avoided to declare they had a Right, the words of the Act being that they have, and of *right* ought to have full Power, &c.

Your Suspicion that "sundry others, besides Govr Bernard

had written hither their Opinions and Counsels, encouraging the late Measures, to the Prejudice of our Country, which have been too much heeded and follow'd" is I apprehend but too well founded. You call them "*traitorous* Individuals" whence I collect, that you suppose them of our own country. There was among the twelve Apostles one Traitor who betrayed with a Kiss. It should be no Wonder therefore if among so many Thousand true Patriots as New England contains there should be found even Twelve Judases, ready to betray their Country for a few paltry Pieces of Silver. Their *Ends*, as well as their *Views*, ought to be similar. But all these Oppressions evidently work for our Good. Providence seems by every Means intent on making us a great People. May our Virtues publick and private grow with us, and be durable, that Liberty Civil and Religious, may be secur'd to our Posterity, and to all from every Part of the old World that take Refuge among us.

I have distributed the Copies of your Piece as you desired. I cannot apprehend they can give just Cause of Offence.

Your Theological Tracts in which you discover your great Reading, are rather more out of my Walk, and therefore I shall say little of them. That on the Lord's Prayer I read with most Attention, having once myself considered a little the same Subject, and attempted a Version of the Prayer which I thought less exceptionable. I have found it among my old Papers, and send it you only to show an Instance of the same Frankness in laying myself open to you, which you say you have used with regard to me. With great Esteem and my best Wishes for a long Continuance of your Usefulness, I am, Reverend Sir, Your most obedient humble Servant

CAUSES OF COLDS

To Benjamin Rush

Dear Sir,   London, July 14. 1773.

I received your Favour of May 1. with the Pamphlet for which I am obliged to you. It is well written. I hope in time that the Friends to Liberty and Humanity will get the better of a Practice that has so long disgrac'd our Nation and Religion.

A few Days after I receiv'd your Packet for M. Dubourg, I had an Opportunity of forwarding it to him by M. Poissonnier, a Physician of Paris, who kindly undertook to deliver it. M. Dubourg has been translating my Book into French. It is nearly printed, and he tells me he purposes a Copy for you.

I shall communicate your judicious Remark relating to Air transpir'd by Patients in putrid Diseases to my Friend Dr. Priestly. I hope that after having discover'd the Benefit of fresh and cool Air apply'd to the *Sick*, People will begin to suspect that possibly it may do no Harm to the *Well*. I have not seen Dr. Cullen's Book: But am glad to hear that he speaks of Catarrhs or Colds *by Contagion*. I have long been satisfy'd from Observation, that besides the general Colds now termed *Influenza's*, which may possibly spread by Contagion as well as by a particular Quality of the Air, People often catch Cold from one another when shut up together in small close Rooms, Coaches, &c. and when sitting near and conversing so as to breathe in each others Transpiration, the Disorder being in a certain State. I think too that it is the frowzy corrupt Air from animal Substances, and the perspired Matter from our Bodies, which, being long confin'd in Beds not lately used, and Clothes not lately worne, and Books long shut up in close Rooms, obtains that kind of Putridity which infects us, and occasions the Colds observed upon sleeping in, wearing, or turning over, such Beds, Clothes or Books, and not their Coldness or Dampness. From these Causes, but more from *too full Living* with too *little Exercise*, proceed in my Opinion most of the Disorders which for 100 Years past the English have called *Colds*. As to Dr. Cullen's Cold or Catarrh *à frigore*, I question whether such an one ever existed. Travelling in our severe Winters, I have suffered Cold sometimes to an Extremity only short of Freezing, but this did not make me *catch Cold*. And for Moisture, I have been in the River every Evening two or three Hours for a Fortnight together, when one would suppose I might imbibe enough of it to *take Cold* if Humidity

could give it; but no such Effect followed: Boys never get
Cold by Swimming. Nor are People at Sea, or who live at
Bermudas, or St. Helena, where the Air must be ever moist,
from the Dashing and Breaking of Waves against their
Rocks on all sides, more subject to Colds than those who inhabit Parts of a Continent where the Air is dryest. Dampness
may indeed assist in producing Putridity, and those Miasms
which infect us with the Disorder we call a Cold, but of itself can never by a little Addition of Moisture hurt a Body
filled with watry Fluids from Head to foot.

I hope our Friend's Marriage will prove a happy one. Mr.
and Mrs. West complain that they never hear from him. Perhaps I have as much reason to complain of him. But I forgive
him because I often need the same kind of Forgiveness. With
great Esteem and sincere Wishes for your Welfare, I am, Sir,
Your most obedient humble Servant

"I 'LL BE HANGED IF THIS IS NOT
SOME OF YOUR AMERICAN JOKES UPON US"

To William Franklin

DEAR SON,   *London, October* 6, 1773.
I wrote to you on the 1st of last month, since which I have
received yours of July 29, from New York.

I know not what letters of mine governor H. could mean,
as advising the people to insist on their independency. But
whatever they were, I suppose he has sent copies of them
hither, having heard some whisperings about them. I shall
however, be able at any time, to justify every thing I have
written; the purport being uniformly this, that they should
carefully avoid all tumults and every violent measure, and
content themselves with verbally keeping up their claims, and
holding forth their rights whenever occasion requires; secure,
that from the growing importance of America, those claims
will ere long be attended to, and acknowledged. From a long
and thorough consideration of the subject, I am indeed of

opinion, that the parliament has no right to make any law whatever, binding on the colonies. That the king, and not the king, lords, and commons collectively, is their sovereign; and that the king with their respective parliaments, is their only legislator. I know your sentiments differ from mine on these subjects. You are a thorough government man, which I do not wonder at, nor do I aim at converting you. I only wish you to act uprightly and steadily, avoiding that duplicity, which in Hutchinson, adds contempt to indignation. If you can promote the prosperity of your people, and leave them happier than you found them, whatever your political principles are, your memory will be honored.

I have written two pieces here lately for the Public Advertiser, on American affairs, designed to expose the conduct of this country towards the colonies, in a short, comprehensive, and striking view, and stated therefore in out-of-the-way forms, as most likely to take the general attention. The first was called, *Rules by which a great empire may be reduced to a small one*; the second, *An Edict of the king of Prussia*. I sent you one of the first, but could not get enough of the second to spare you one, though my clerk went the next morning to the printer's, and wherever they were sold. They were all gone but two. In my own mind I preferred the first, as a composition for the quantity and variety of the matter contained, and a kind of spirited ending of each paragraph. But I find that others here generally prefer the second. I am not suspected as the author, except by one or two friends; and have heard the latter spoken of in the highest terms as the keenest and severest piece that has appeared here a long time. Lord Mansfield I hear said of it, that it *was very* ABLE *and very* ARTFUL indeed; and would do mischief by giving here a bad impression of the measures of government; and in the colonies, by encouraging them in their contumacy. It is reprinted in the Chronicle, where you will see it, but stripped of all the capitalling and italicing, that intimate the allusions and marks the emphasis of written discourses, to bring them as near as possible to those spoken: printing such a piece all in one even small character, seems to me like repeating one of Whitfield's sermons in the monotony of a school-boy. What made it the more noticed here was, that people in reading it, were, as the phrase is, *taken in*, till they had got half through it, and imagined it a real edict, to which mistake I suppose the king of Prussia's *character* must have contributed. I was down at lord Le Despencer's when the post brought that day's papers. Mr. Whitehead was there too (Paul Whitehead, the author of Manners) who runs early through all the papers, and tells the company what he finds remarkable. He had them in another room, and we were chatting in the breakfast parlour, when he came running into us, out of breath, with the paper in his hand. Here! says he, here's news for ye! *Here's the king of Prussia, claiming a right to this kingdom!* All stared, and I as much as any body; and he went on to read it. When he had read two or three paragraphs, a gentleman present said, *Damn his impudence, I dare say, we shall hear by next post that he is upon his march with one hundred thousand men to back this.* Whitehead, who is very shrewd, soon after began to smoke it, and looking in my face said, *I'll be hanged if this is not some of your American jokes upon us.* The reading went on, and ended with abundance of laughing, and a general verdict that it was a fair hit: and the piece was cut out of the paper and preserved in my lord's collection.

I don't wonder that Hutchinson should be dejected. It must be an uncomfortable thing to live among people who he is conscious universally detest him. Yet I fancy he will not have leave to come home, both because they know not well what to do with him, and because they do not very well like his conduct.

I am ever your affectionate father,

TRANSFER PRINTS ON TILES

To Peter P. Burdett

Sir,   London, Nov. 3, 1773.

I was much pleased with the Specimens you so kindly sent me, of your new Art of Engraving. That on the China is admirable. No one would suppose it any thing but Painting.

I hope you meet with all the Encouragement you merit, and that the Invention will be, (what Inventions seldom are) profitable to the Inventor.

I know not who (now we speak of Inventions) pretends to that of Copper-Plate Engravings for Earthen-Ware, and am not disposed to contest the Honor of it with any body, as the Improvement in taking Impressions not directly from the Plate but from printed Paper, applicable by that means to other than flat Forms, is far beyond my first Idea. But I have reason to apprehend I might have given the Hint on which that Improvement was made. For more than twenty years since, I wrote to Dr. Mitchell from America, proposing to him the printing of square Tiles for ornamenting Chimnies, from Copper Plates, describing the Manner in which I thought it might be done, and advising the Borrowing from the Bookseller, the Plates that had been used in a thin Folio, called *Moral Virtue delineated*, for the Purpose. As the Dutch Delphware Tiles were much used in America, which are only or chiefly Scripture Histories, wretchedly scrawled, I wished to have those moral Prints, (which were originally taken from Horace's poetical Figures) introduced on Tiles, which being about our Chimneys, and constantly in the Eyes of Children when by the Fire-side, might give Parents an Opportunity, in explaining them, to impress moral Sentiments; and I gave Expectations of great Demand for them if executed. Dr. Mitchell wrote to me in Answer, that he had communicated my Scheme to several of the principal Artists in the Earthen Way about London, who rejected it as impracticable: And it was not till some years after that I first saw an enamelled snuff-Box which I was sure was a Copper-plate, tho' the Curvature of the Form made me wonder how the Impression was taken.

I understand the China Work in Philadelphia is declined by the first Owners. Whether any others will take it up and continue it, I know not.

Mr. Banks is at present engaged in preparing to publish the Botanical Discoveries of his Voyage. He employs 10 Engravers for the Plates, in which he is very curious, so as not to be quite satisfied in some Cases with the Expression given by either the Graver, Etching, or Metzotinto, particularly where there is a Wooliness or a Multitude of small Points or a Leaf. I sent him the largest of the Specimens you sent containing a Number of Sprigs. I have not seen him since, to know whether your Manner would not suit some of his Plants, better than the more common Methods. With great Esteem, I am, Sir, Your most obedient humble Servant,

OIL ON WATER

To William Brownrigg

Dear Sir,   London, Nov. 7, 1773.

Our Correspondence might be carried on for a Century with very few Letters, if you were as apt to procrastinate as myself. Tho' an habitual Sinner, I am now quite ashamed to observe, that this is to be an Answer to your Favour of January last.

I suppose Mrs. Brownrigg did not succeed in making the Parmesan Cheese, since we have heard nothing of it. But as a Philosophess, she will not be discouraged by one or two Failures. Perhaps some Circumstance is omitted in the Receipt, which by a little more Experience she may discover. The foreign Gentleman, who had learnt in England to like boiled Plumbpudding, and carried home a Receipt for making it, wondered to see it brought to his Table in the Form of a Soup. The Cook declar'd he had exactly followed the Receipt. And when that came to be examined, a small, but important Circumstance appeared to have been omitted. There was no Mention of the Bag.

I am concerned that you had not, and I fear you have not yet found time to prepare your excellent Papers for Publication. By omitting it so long, you are wanting to the World, and to your own Honour.

I thank you for the Remarks of your learned Friend at Carlisle. I had when a Youth, read and smiled at Pliny's Account of a Practice among the Seamen of his Time, to still the Waves in a Storm by pouring Oil into the Sea: which he mentions, as well as the Use of Oil by the Divers. But the stilling a Tempest by throwing Vinegar into the Air had escaped me. I think with your Friend, that it has been of late too much the Mode to slight the Learning of the Ancients. The Learned too, are apt to slight too much the Knowledge of the Vulgar. The cooling by Evaporation was long an Instance of the latter. This Art of smoothing the Waves with Oil, is an Instance of both.

Perhaps you may not dislike to have an Account of all I have heard, and learnt and done in this Way. Take it, if you please, as follows.

In 1757 being at Sea in a Fleet of 96 Sail bound against Louisbourg, I observed the Wakes of two of the Ships to be remarkably smooth, while all the others were ruffled by the Wind, which blew fresh. Being puzzled with this differing Appearance I at last pointed it out to our Captain, and asked him the meaning of it? "The Cooks, says he, have I suppose, been just emptying their greasy Water thro' the Scuppers, which has greased the Sides of those Ships a little;" and this Answer he gave me with an Air of some little Contempt, as to a Person ignorant of what every Body else knew. In my own Mind I at first slighted his Solution, tho' I was not able to think of another. But recollecting what I had formerly read in Pliny, I resolved to make some Experiment of the Effect of Oil on Water when I should have Opportunity.

Afterwards being again at Sea in 1762, I first observed the wonderful Quietness of Oil on agitated Water in the swinging Glass Lamp I made to hang up in the Cabin, as described in my printed Papers, page 438 of the fourth Edition. This I was continually looking at and considering, as an Appearance to me inexplicable. An old Sea Captain, then a Passenger with me, thought little of it, supposing it an Effect of the same kind with that of Oil put on Water to smooth it, which he said was a Practice of the Bermudians when they would strike Fish which they could not see if the surface of the Water was ruffled by the Wind. This Practice I had never before heard of, and was obliged to him for the Information, though I thought him mistaken as to the sameness of the Experiment, the Operations being different; as well as the Effects. In one Case, the Water is smooth till the Oil is put on, and then becomes agitated. In the other it is agitated before the Oil is applied, and then becomes smooth. The same Gentleman told me he had heard it was a Practice with the Fishermen of Lisbon when about to return into the River, (if they saw before them too great a Surff upon the Bar, which they apprehended might fill their Boats in passing) to empty a Bottle or two of oil into the Sea, which would suppress the Breakers and allow them to pass safely: a Confirmation of this I have not since had an Opportunity of obtaining. But discoursing of it with another Person, who had often been in the Mediterranean, I was informed that the Divers there, who when under Water in their Business, need Light, which the curling of the Surface interrupts, by the Refractions of so many little Waves, they let a small Quantity of Oil now and then out of their Mouths, which rising to the Surface smooths it, and permits the Light to come down to them. All these Informations I at times revolved in my Mind, and wondered to find no mention of them in our Books of Experimental Philosophy.

At length being at Clapham, where there is, on the Common, a large Pond, which I observed to be one Day very rough with the Wind, I fetched out a Cruet of Oil, and dropt a little of it on the Water. I saw it spread itself with surprising Swiftness upon the Surface, but the Effect of smoothing the Waves was not produced; for I had applied it first on the Leeward Side of the Pond where the Waves were largest, and the Wind drove my Oil back upon the Shore. I then went to the Windward Side, where they began to form; and there the Oil tho' not more than a Tea Spoonful produced an instant Calm, over a Space several yards square, which spread amazingly, and extended itself gradually till it reached the Lee Side, making all that Quarter of the Pond, perhaps half an Acre, as smooth as a Looking Glass.

After this, I contrived to take with me, whenever I went into the Country, a little Oil in the upper hollow joint of my bamboo Cane, with which I might repeat the Experiment as Opportunity should offer; and I found it constantly to succeed.

In these Experiments, one Circumstance struck me with particular Surprize. This was the sudden, wide and forcible Spreading of a Drop of Oil on the Face of the Water, which I do not know that any body has hitherto considered. If a

Drop of Oil is put on a polished Marble Table, or on a Looking Glass that lies horizontally; the Drop remains in its Place,
spreading very little. But when put on Water it spreads instantly many feet round, becoming so thin as to produce the
prismatic Colours, for a considerable Space, and beyond them
so much thinner as to be invisible except in its Effect of
smoothing the Waves at a much greater Distance. It seems as
if a mutual Repulsion between its Particles took Place as soon
as it touched the Water, and a Repulsion so strong as to act
on other Bodies swimming on the Surface, as Straws, Leaves,
Chips, &c. forcing them to recede every way from the Drop,
as from a Center, leaving a large clear Space. The Quantity of
this Force, and the Distance to which it will operate, I have
not yet ascertained, but I think it a curious Enquiry, and I
wish to understand whence it arises.

In our Journey to the North when we had the Pleasure of
seeing you at Ormathwaite, we visited Mr. Smeaton near
Leeds. Being about to shew him the smoothing Experiment
on a little Pond near his House, an ingenious Pupil of his,
Mr. Jessop, then present, told us of an odd Appearance on
that Pond, which had lately occurred to him. He was about
to clean a little Cup in which he kept Oil, and he threw upon
the Water some Flies that had been drowned in the Oil. These
Flies presently began to move, and turned round on the
Water very rapidly, as if they were vigorously alive, tho' on
Examination he found they were not so. I immediately
concluded that the Motion was occasioned by the Power of
the Repulsion abovementioned, and that the Oil issuing gradually from the spungy Body of the Fly continued the Motion.
He found some more Flies drowned in Oil, with which the
Experiment was repeated before us; and to show that it was
not any Effect of Life recovered by the Flies, I imitated it by
little bits of oiled Chip, and Paper cut in the form of a
Comma, of this size ❜ when the Stream of repelling Particles issuing from the Point, made the Comma turn round the
contrary way. This is not a Chamber Experiment; for it cannot well be repeated in a Bowl or Dish of Water on a Table.
A considerable Surface of Water is necessary to give Room
for the Expansion of a small Quantity of Oil. In a Dish of
Water if the smallest Drop of Oil be let fall in the Middle, the

whole Surface is presently covered with a thin greasy Film proceeding from the Drop; but as soon as that Film has reached the Sides of the Dish, no more will issue from the Drop, but it remains in the Form of Oil, the Sides of the Dish putting a Stop to its Dissipation by prohibiting the farther Expansion of the Film.

Our Friend Sir J. Pringle being soon after in Scotland, learnt there that those employed in the Herring Fishery, could at a Distance see where the Shoals of Herrings were, by the smoothness of the Water over them, which might be occasioned possibly, he thought, by some Oiliness proceeding from their Bodies.

A Gentleman from Rhode-island told me, it had been remarked that the Harbour of Newport was ever smooth while any Whaling Vessels were in it; which probably arose from hence, that the Blubber which they sometimes bring loose in the Hold, or the Leakage of their Barrels, might afford some Oil to mix with that Water which from time to time they pump out to keep the Vessel free, and that same Oil might spread over the surface of the Water in the Harbour, and prevent the forming of any Waves.

This Prevention I would thus endeavour to explain.

There seems to be no natural Repulsion between Water and Air, such as to keep them from coming into Contact with each other. Hence we find a Quantity of Air in Water, and if we extract it by means of the Air-pump; the same Water again exposed to the Air, will soon imbibe an equal Quantity.

Therefore Air in Motion, which is Wind, in passing over the smooth Surface of Water, may rub, as it were, upon that Surface, and raise it into Wrinkles, which if the Wind continues are the elements of future Waves.

The smallest Wave once raised does not immediately subside and leave the neighbouring Water quiet; but in subsiding raises nearly as much of the Water next to it, the Friction of its Parts making little Difference. Thus a Stone dropt in a Pool raises first a single Wave round itself, and leaves it by sinking to the Bottom; but that first Wave subsiding raises a second, the second a third, and so on in Circles to a great Extent.

A small Power continually operating will produce a great

Action. A Finger applied to a weighty suspended Bell, can at first move it but little; if repeatedly applied, tho' with no greater Strength, the Motion increases till the Bell swings to its utmost Height and with a Force that cannot be resisted by the whole Strength of the Arm and Body. Thus the small first-raised Waves, being continually acted upon by the Wind are, (tho' the Wind does not increase in Strength) continually increased in Magnitude, rising higher and extending their Bases, so as to include a vast Mass of Water in each Wave, which in its Motion acts with great Violence.

But if there be a mutual Repulsion between the Particles of Oil, and no Attraction between Oil and Water, Oil dropt on Water will not be held together by Adhesion to the Spot whereon it falls, it will not be imbibed by the Water, it will be at Liberty to expand itself, and it will spread on a Surface that besides being smooth to the most perfect degree of Polish, prevents, perhaps by repelling the Oil, all immediate Contact, keeping it at a minute Distance from itself; and the Expansion will continue, till the mutual Repulsion between the Particles of the Oil, is weakened and reduced to nothing by their Distance.

Now I imagine that the Wind blowing over Water thus covered with a Film of Oil, cannot easily catch upon it so as to raise the first Wrinkles, but slides over it, and leaves it smooth as it finds it. It moves a little the Oil, indeed, which being between it and the water serves it to slide with, and prevents Friction as Oil does between those Parts of a Machine that would otherwise rub hard together. Hence the Oil dropt on the Windward Side of a Pond proceeds gradually to Leeward, as may be seen by the smoothness it carries with it, quite to the opposite Side. For the Wind being thus prevented from raising the first Wrinkles that I call the Elements of Waves, cannot produce Waves, which are to be made by continually acting upon and enlarging those Elements, and thus the whole Pond is calmed.

Totally therefore we might supress the Waves in any required Place, if we could come at the Windward Place where they take their Rise. This in the Ocean can seldom if ever be done. But perhaps something may be done on particular Occasions, to moderate the Violence of the Waves, when we are in the midst of them, and prevent their Breaking where that would be inconvenient.

For when the Wind blows fresh, there are continually rising on the Back of every great Wave, a number of small ones, which roughen its Surface, and give the Wind Hold, as it were, to push it with greater Force. This Hold is diminished by preventing the Generation of those small ones. And possibly too, when a Wave's Surface is oiled, the Wind in passing over it, may rather in some degree press it down, and contribute to prevent its rising again, instead of promoting it.

This as a mere Conjecture would have little weight, if the apparent Effects of pouring Oil into the Midst of Waves, were not considerable, and as yet not otherwise accounted for.

When the Wind blows so fresh, as that the Waves are not sufficiently quick in obeying its Impulse, their Tops being thinner and lighter are pushed forward, broken and turned over in a white Foam. Common Waves lift a Vessel without entring it, but these when large sometimes break above and pour over it, doing great Damage.

That this Effect might in any degree be prevented, or the height and violence of Waves in the Sea moderated, we had no certain Account, Pliny's Authority for the Practice of Seamen in his time being slighted. But discoursing lately on this Subject with his Excellency Count Bentinck of Holland, his Son the Honble. Capt. Bentinck, and the learned Professor Allemand, (to all whom I showed the Experiment of smoothing in a Windy Day the large Piece of Water at the Head of the Green Park) a Letter was mentioned which had been received by the Count from Batavia, relating to the saving of a Dutch Ship in a Storm, by pouring Oil into the Sea. I much desired to see that Letter, and a Copy of it was promised me, which I afterwards received. It is as follows.

Extrait d'une Lettre de Mr. Tengnagel à Mr. le Comte de Bentinck, écrite de Batavia le 15 Janvier 1770. Près des Isles Paulus et Amsterdam nous essuiames un orage, qui n'eut rien d'assez particulier pour vous être marqué, si non que notre Capitaine se trouva obligé en *tournant sous le vent*,* de verser de l'huile contre la haute mer, pour empecher les vagues de

*Suppos'd to mean, *In wearing the Ship.*

se briser contre le navire, ce qui réussit à nous conserver et a été d'un très bon effet: comme il n'en versa qu'une petite quantité à la fois, la Compagnie doit peut-être son vaisseau à six demi-ahmes d'huile d'olive: j'ai été présent quand cela s'est fait, et je ne vous aurois pas entretenu de cette circonstance, si ce n'étoit que nous avons trouvé les gens ici si prévenus contre l'expérience, que les officiers du bord ni moi n'avons fait aucune difficulté de donner un certificat de la verité sur ce chapitre.

On this Occasion I mentioned to Capt. Bentinck, a thought which had occurred to me in reading the Voyages of our late Circumnavigators, particularly where Accounts are given of pleasant and fertile Islands which they much desired to land upon, when Sickness made it more necessary, but could not effect a Landing thro' a violent Surff breaking on the Shore, which rendered it impracticable. My Idea was, that possibly by sailing to and fro at some Distance from such Lee Shore, continually pouring Oil into the Sea, the Waves might be so much depressed and lessened before they reached the Shore, as to abate the Height and Violence of the Surff and permit a Landing, which in such Circumstances was a Point of sufficient Importance to justify the Expence of Oil that might be requisite for the purpose. That Gentleman, who is ever ready to promote what may be of publick Utility, (tho' his own ingenious Inventions have not always met with the Countenance they merited) was so obliging as to invite me to Portsmouth, where an Opportunity would probably offer, in the course of a few Days, of making the Experiment on some of the Shores about Spithead, in which he kindly proposed to accompany me, and to give Assistance with such Boats as might be necessary. Accordingly, about the middle of October last, I went with some Friends, to Portsmouth; and a Day of Wind happening, which made a Lee-Shore between Haslar Hospital and the Point near Jillkecker; we went from the Centaur with the Longboat and Barge towards that Shore. Our Disposition was this; the Longboat anchored about a ¼ of a Mile from the Shore, part of the Company were landed behind the Point, (a Place more sheltered from the Sea) who came round and placed themselves opposite to the Longboat, where they might observe the Surff, and note if any Change occurred in it upon using the Oil: Another Party in the Barge plied to Windward of the Longboat, as far from her as she was from the Shore, making Trips of about half a Mile each, pouring Oil continually out of a large Stone Bottle, thro' a Hole in the Cork somewhat bigger than a Goose Quill. The Experiment had not in the main Point the Success we wished; for no material Difference was observed in the Height or Force of the Surff upon the Shore: But those who were in the Longboat could observe a Tract of smoothed Water the whole Length of the Distance in which the Barge poured the Oil, and gradually spreading in Breadth towards the Longboat; I call it smoothed, not that it was laid level, but because tho' the Swell continued, its Surface was not roughened by the Wrinkles or smaller Waves before-mentioned, and none, or very few White-caps (or Waves whose Tops turn over in Foam) appeared in that whole Space, tho' to windward and leeward of it there were plenty; and a Wherry that came round the Point under Sail in her way to Portsmouth, seemed to turn into that Tract of choice, and to use it from End to End as a Piece of Turnpike Road.

It may be of Use to relate the Circumstances even of an Experiment that does not succeed, since they may give Hints of Amendment in future Trials: It is therefore I have been thus particular. I shall only add what I apprehend may have been the Reason of our Disappointment.

I conceive that the Operation of Oil on Water, is first to prevent the raising new Waves by the Wind, and secondly, to prevent its pushing those before raised with such Force, and consequently their Continuance of the same repeated Height, as they would have done, if their Surface were not oiled. But Oil will not prevent Waves being raised by another Power, by a Stone, for Instance, falling into a still Pool; for they then rise by the mechanical Impulse of the Stone, which the Greasiness on the surrounding Water cannot lessen or prevent, as it can prevent the Winds catching the Surface and raising it into Waves. Now Waves once raised, whether by the Wind or any other Power, have the same mechanical Operation, by which they continue to rise and fall, as a Pendulum will continue to swing, a long Time after the Force ceases to act by which the

Motion was first produced. That Motion will however cease in time, but time is necessary. Therefore tho' Oil spread on an agitated Sea, may weaken the Push of the Wind on those Waves whose Surfaces are covered by it, and so by receiving less fresh Impulse, they may gradually subside; yet a considerable Time, or a Distance thro' which they will take time to move may be necessary to make the Effect sensible on any Shore in a Diminution of the Surff. For we know that when Wind ceases suddenly, the Waves it has raised do not as suddenly subside, but settle gradually and are not quite down till long after the Wind has ceased. So tho' we should by oiling them take off the Effect of Wind on Waves already raised, it is not to be expected that those Waves should be instantly levelled. The Motion they have received will for some time continue: and if the Shore is not far distant, they arrive there so soon that their Effect upon it will not be visibly diminished. Possibly therefore, if we had began our Operations at a greater Distance, the Effect might have been more sensible. And perhaps we did not pour Oil in sufficient Quantity. Future Experiments may determine this.

After my Thanks to Capt. Bentinck, for the chearful and ready Aids he gave me, I ought not to omit mentioning Mr. Banks, Dr. Solander, General Carnac, and Dr. Blagdon, who all assisted at the Experiment, during that blustring unpleasant Day, with a Patience and Activity that could only be inspired by a Zeal for the Improvement of Knowledge, such especially as might possibly be of use to Men in Situations of Distress.

I would wish you to communicate this to your ingenious Friend Mr. Farish, with my Respects; and believe me to be, with sincere Esteem, Dear Sir, Your most obedient humble Servant.

"NOTHING CAN BE FARTHER FROM THE TRUTH"

To Josiah Tucker

Reverend Sir,   London, Feb. 12, 1774.
   Being informed by a Friend that some severe Strictures on

my Conduct and Character had appeared in a new Book published under your respectable Name, I purchased and read it. After thanking you sincerely for those Parts of it that are so instructive on Points of great Importance to the common Interests of mankind, permit me to complain, that if by the description you give in Page 180, 181, of a certain American Patriot, whom you say you need not name, you do, as is supposed, mean myself, nothing can be farther from the truth than your assertion, that I applied or used any interest directly or indirectly to be appointed one of the Stamp Officers for America; I certainly never expressed a Wish of the kind to any person whatever, much less was I, as you say, "more than ordinary assiduous on this Head." I have heretofore seen in the Newspapers, Insinuations of the same Import, naming me expressly; but being without the name of the Writer, I took no Notice of them. I know not whether they were yours, or were only your Authority for your present charge. But now that they have the Weight of your Name and dignified Character, I am more sensible of the injury. And I beg leave to request that you would reconsider the Grounds on which you have ventured to publish an Accusation that, if believed, must prejudice me extremely in the opinion of good Men, especially in my own country, whence I was sent expressly to oppose the imposition of that Tax. If on such reconsideration and Enquiry you find as I am persuaded you will, that you have been imposed upon by false Reports, or have too lightly given credit to Hearsays in a matter that concerns another's Reputation, I flatter myself that your Equity will induce you to do me Justice, by retracting that Accusation. In Confidence of this, I am with great Esteem, Reverend Sir, Your most obedient and most humble Servant,

"MY SUPPOSED APPLICATION TO MR. GRENVILLE"

To Josiah Tucker

Reverend Sir,   London, Feb. 26, 1774.
    I thank you for the Frankness with which you have com-

municated to me the Particulars of the Information you had received relating to my supposed Application to Mr. Grenville for a Place in the American Stamp-Office. As I deny that either your former or later Informations are true, it seems incumbent on me for your Satisfaction to relate all the Circumstances fairly to you that could possibly give rise to such Mistakes.

Some Days after the Stamp-Act was passed, to which I had given all the Opposition I could with Mr. Grenville, I received a Note from Mr. Wheatly, his Secretary, desiring to see me the next morning. I waited upon him accordingly, and found with him several other Colony Agents. He acquainted us that Mr. Grenville was desirous to make the Execution of the Act as little inconvenient and disagreeable to the Americans as possible, and therefore did not think of sending Stamp Officers from hence, but wished to have discreet and reputable Persons appointed in each Province from among the Inhabitants, such as would be acceptable to them, for as they were to pay the Tax, he thought Strangers should not have the Emoluments. Mr. Wheatly therefore wished us to name for our respective Colonies, informing us that Mr. Grenville would be obliged to us for pointing out to him honest and responsible Men, and would pay great regard to our Nominations. By this plausible and apparently candid Declaration, we were drawn in to nominate, and I named for our Province Mr. Hughes, saying at the same time that I knew not whether he would accept of it, but if he did I was sure he would execute the Office faithfully. I soon after had notice of his appointment. We none of us, I believe, foresaw or imagined, that this Compliance with the request of the Minister, would or could have been called an *Application* of ours, and adduced as a Proof of our *Approbation* of the Act we had been opposing; otherwise I think few of us would have named at all, I am sure I should not. This I assure you and can prove to you by living Evidence, is a true account of the Transaction in question, which if you compare with that you have been induced to give of it in your Book, I am persuaded you will see a *Difference* that is far from being "a Distinction above your Comprehension."

Permit me farther to remark, that your Expression of there

being "no *positive Proofs* of my having solicited to obtain such a place *for myself*," implies that there are nevertheless some *circumstantial* Proofs sufficient at least to support a Suspicion; the latter Part however of the same Sentence, which says, "there are sufficient Evidence still existing of my having *applied for it* in favour of another Person," must I apprehend, if credited, destroy that Suspicion, and be considered as *positive* Proof of the contrary; for if I had Interest enough with Mr. Grenville to obtain that Place for another, is it likely that it would have been refused me had I asked it for myself?

There is another Circumstance which I would offer to your candid Consideration. You describe me as "changing Sides, and appearing at the Bar of the House of Commons to cry down the very Measure I had espoused, and direct the Storm that was falling upon that Minister." As this must have been after my supposed solicitation of the Favour for myself or my Friend; and as Mr. Grenville and Mr. Wheatly were both in the House at the Time, and both asked me Questions, can it be conceived that offended as they must have been with such a Conduct in me, neither of them should put me in mind of this my sudden Changing of Sides, or remark it to the House, or reproach me with it, or require my Reasons for it? and yet all the Members then present know that not a Syllable of the kind fell from either of them, or from any of their Party.

I persuade myself that by this time you begin to suspect you may have been misled by your Informers. I do not ask who they are, because I do not wish to have particular Motives for disliking People, who in general may deserve my Respect. They, too, may have drawn *Consequences* beyond the Information they received from others, and hearing the Office had been *given* to a Person of my Nomination, might as naturally suppose I *had sollicited it*; as Dr. Tucker, hearing I had *sollicited it*, might *"conclude"* it was for myself.

I desire you to believe that I take kindly, as I ought, your freely mentioning to me "that it has long appeared to you that I much exceeded the Bounds of Morality in the Methods I pursued for the Advancement of the supposed Interests of America." I am sensible there is a good deal of Truth in the Adage, that *our Sins and our Debts are always more than we take them to be*; and tho' I cannot at present on Examination of my Conscience charge myself with any Immorality of that kind, it becomes me to suspect that what has *long appeared* to you may have some Foundation. You are so good as to add, that "if it can be proved you have unjustly suspected me, you shall have a Satisfaction in acknowledging the Error." It is often a hard thing to *prove* that Suspicions are unjust, even when we know what they are; and harder when we are unacquainted with them. I must presume therefore that in mentioning them, you had an Intention of communicating the Grounds of them to me, if I should request it, which I now do, and, I assure you, with a sincere Desire and Design of amending what you may show me to have been wrong in my conduct, and to thank you for the Admonition. In your Writings I *appear* a bad Man; but if I am such, and you can thus help me to become *in reality* a good one, I shall esteem it more than a sufficient Reparation, to Reverend Sir, Your most obedient humble Servant

FLAME ON NEW JERSEY RIVERS

To Joseph Priestley

Dear Sir,   Craven Street, April 10, 1774.

In compliance with your request, I have endeavoured to recollect the circumstances of the American experiments I formerly mentioned to you, of raising a flame on the surface of some waters there.

When I passed through New Jersey in 1764, I heard it several times mentioned, that by applying a lighted candle near the surface of some of their rivers, a sudden flame would catch and spread on the water, continuing to burn for near half a minute. But the accounts I received were so imperfect that I could form no guess at the cause of such an effect, and rather doubted the truth of it. I had no opportunity of seeing the experiment; but calling to see a friend who happened to be just returned home from making it himself, I learned from him the manner of it; which was to choose a shallow place, where the bottom could be reached by a walking-stick, and was muddy; the mud was first to be stirred with the stick, and when a number of small bubbles began to arise from it, the candle was applied. The flame was so sudden and so strong, that it catched his ruffle and spoiled it, as I saw. New-Jersey having many pine-trees in different parts of it, I then imagined that something like a volatile oil of turpentine might be mixed with the waters from a pine-swamp, but this supposition did not quite satisfy me. I mentioned the fact to some philosophical friends on my return to England, but it was not much attended to. I suppose I was thought a little too credulous.

In 1765, the Reverend Dr. Chandler received a letter from Dr. Finley, President of the College in that province, relating the same experiment. It was read at the Royal Society, Nov. 21. of that year, but not printed in the Transactions; perhaps because it was thought too strange to be true, and some ridicule might be apprehended if any member should attempt to repeat it in order to ascertain or refute it. The following is a copy of that account.

"A worthy gentleman, who lives at a few miles distance, informed me that in a certain small cove of a mill-pond, near his house, he was surprized to see the surface of the water blaze like inflamed spirits. I soon after went to the place, and made the experiment with the same success. The bottom of the creek was muddy, and when stirred up, so as to cause a considerable curl on the surface, and a lighted candle held within two or three inches of it, the whole surface was in a blaze, as instantly as the vapour of warm inflammable spirits, and continued, when strongly agitated, for the space of several seconds. It was at first imagined to be peculiar to that place; but upon trial it was soon found, that such a bottom in other places exhibited the same phenomenon. The discovery was accidentally made by one belonging to the mill."

I have tried the experiment twice here in England, but without success. The first was in a slow running water with a muddy bottom. The second in a stagnant water at the bottom a deep ditch. Being some time employed in stirring this water, I ascribed an intermitting fever, which seized me a few days after, to my breathing too much of that foul air which I stirred up from the bottom, and which I could not avoid while I stooped in endeavouring to kindle it.—The discoveries you have lately made of the manner in which in-flammable air is in some cases produced, may throw light on this experiment, and explain its succeeding in some cases, and not in others. With the highest esteem and respect,

I am, Dear Sir,

Your most obedient humble servant,

"YOU ARE NOW MY ENEMY"

To *William Strahan*

Mr. Strahan,   Philada. July 5. 1775

You are a Member of Parliament, and one of that Majority which has doomed my Country to Destruction. You have be-gun to burn our Towns, and murder our People. Look upon your Hands! They are stained with the Blood of your Rela-tions! You and I were long Friends: You are now my Enemy, and I am, Yours,

"THIS IS A HARDER NUT TO CRACK
THAN THEY IMAGINED"

To [*Joseph Priestley*]

Dear Friend,   *Philadelphia, 7th July*, 1775.

*   *   *   *   *

The Congress met at a time when all minds were so exas-perated by the perfidy of General Gage, and his attack on the country people, that propositions of attempting an accom-modation were not much relished; and it has been with diffi-culty that we have carried another humble petition to the crown, to give Britain one more chance, one opportunity more of recovering the friendship of the colonies; which however I think she has not sense enough to embrace, and so I conclude she has lost them for ever.

She has begun to burn our seaport towns; secure, I suppose, that we shall never be able to return the outrage in kind. She may doubtless destroy them all; but if she wishes to recover our commerce, are these the probable means? She must certainly be distracted; for no tradesman out of Bedlam ever thought of encreasing the number of his customers by knocking them on the head; or of enabling them to pay their debts by burning their houses.

If she wishes to have us subjects and that we should submit to her as our compound sovereign, she is now giving us such miserable specimens of her government, that we shall ever detest and avoid it, as a complication of robbery, murder, famine, fire and pestilence.

You will have heard before this reaches you, of the treacherous conduct * * * to the remaining people in Boston, in detaining their *goods*, after stipulating to let them go out with their *effects*; on pretence that merchants goods were not effects; —the defeat of a great body of his troops by the country people at Lexington; some other small advantages gained in skirmishes with their troops; and the action at Bunker's-hill, in which they were twice repulsed, and the third time gained a dear victory. Enough has happened, one would think, to convince your ministers that the Americans will fight, and that this is a harder nut to crack than they imagined.

We have not yet applied to any foreign power for assistance; nor offered our commerce for their friendship. Perhaps we never may: Yet it is natural to think of it if we are pressed.

We have now an army on our establishment which still holds yours besieged.

My time was never more fully employed. In the morning at 6, I am at the committee of safety, appointed by the assembly to put the province in a state of defence; which committee holds till near 9, when I am at the congress, and that sits till after 4 in the afternoon. Both these bodies proceed with the greatest unanimity, and their meetings are well attended. It will scarce be credited in Britain that men can be as diligent with us from zeal for the public good, as with you for thousands per annum. — Such is the difference between uncorrupted new states, and corrupted old ones.

Great frugality and great industry are now become fashionable here: Gentlemen who used to entertain with two or three courses, pride themselves now in treating with simple beef and pudding. By these means, and the stoppage of our consumptive trade with Britain, we shall be better able to pay our voluntary taxes for the support of our troops. Our savings in the article of trade amount to near five million sterling per annum.

I shall communicate your letter to Mr. Winthrop, but the camp is at Cambridge, and he has as little leisure for philosophy as myself. * * * Believe me ever, with sincere esteem, my dear friend,

Yours most affectionately.

"THERE IS NO LITTLE ENEMY"

To David Hartley

Philadelphia, Oct. 3, 1775.

I wish as ardently as you can do for peace, and should rejoice exceedingly in co-operating with you to that end. But every ship from Britain brings some intelligence of new measures that tend more and more to exasperate; and it seems to me that until you have found by dear experience the reducing us by force impracticable, you will think of nothing fair and reasonable.—We have as yet resolved only on defensive measures. If you would recall your forces and stay at home, we should meditate nothing to injure you. A little time so given for cooling on both sides would have excellent effects. But you will goad and provoke us. You despise us too much; and you are insensible of the Italian adage, that *there is no little enemy.*—I am persuaded the body of the British people are our friends; but they are changeable, and by your lying Gazettes may soon be made our enemies. Our respect for them will proportionally diminish; and I see clearly we are on the high road to mutual enmity, hatred, and detestation. A separation will of course be inevitable.—'Tis a million of pities so fair a plan as we have hitherto been engaged in for increasing strength and empire with *public felicity*, should be destroyed by the mangling hands of a few blundering ministers. It will not be destroyed: God will protect and prosper it: You will only exclude yourselves from any share in it.—We hear that more ships and troops are coming out. We know you may do us a great deal of mischief, but we are determined to bear it patiently as long as we can; but if you flatter yourselves with beating us into submission, you know neither the people nor the *country*.

The congress is still sitting, and will wait the result of their *last* petition.

PARIS
1776 – 1785

Contents

(† denotes title given during Franklin's lifetime.)

The Sale of the Hessians, February 18, 1777 177

Model of a Letter of Recommendation, April 2, 1777 . . . 179

The Twelve Commandments (To Madame Brillon),
   March 10, 1778. 179

†Petition of the Letter Z, [c. August, 1778] 181

The Ephemera, September 20, 1778 182

The Elysian Fields (M. Franklin to Madame Helvétius),
   December 7, 1778 184

Bilked for Breakfast (Mr. Franklin to Madame la Freté),
   [c. 1778]. 185

Passport for Captain Cook, March 10, 1779 186

The Morals of Chess, June, 1779 187

The Whistle, November 10, 1779 191

The Levée, [1779?] 193

Proposed New Version of the Bible, [1779?] 195

Drinking Song (To the Abbé de La Roche, at Auteuil),
   [1779?] 196

†A Tale, [1779?] 198

On Wine (From the Abbé Franklin to the Abbé Morellet),
   [1779?] 199

†Dialogue Between the Gout and Mr. Franklin,
   October 22, 1780 203

The Handsome and the Deformed Leg, November, 1780 . . 210

†To the Royal Academy of *****, [c. 1781]. 212

†Notes for Conversation, April 18, 1782 215

†Supplement to the Boston Independent Chronicle,
   April, 1782 216

Articles for a Treaty of Peace with Madame Brillon,
July 27, 1782 224

Apologue, [c. November, 1782] 227

†Remarks Concerning the Savages of North-America, 1783 . . 229

†Information to Those Who Would Remove to America,
February, 1784 235

†An Economical Project, April 26, 1784 244

†Loose Thoughts on a Universal Fluid, June 25, 1784 . . . 248

†The Flies (To Madame Helvétius), [1784?] 250

LETTERS

Lord Howe, July 20, 1776
    "that fine and noble China Vase the British Empire" . . . 252

Emma Thompson, February 8, 1777
    "Women . . . ought to be fix'd in Revolution Principles" . . 254

———— Lith, April 6, 1777
    "Whoever writes to a Stranger should observe 3 Points" . . 257

To [Lebègue de Presle], October 4, 1777
    "Disputes are apt to sour ones temper" 258

Arthur Lee, April 3, 1778
    "your Magisterial Snubbings and Rebukes" 259

Charles de Weissenstein, July 1, 1778
    "a sort of tar-and-feather honour". 260

David Hartley, February 3, 1779
    "God-send or The Wreckers". 265

Sarah Bache, June 3, 1779
    "i-doll-ized in this country". 268

Edward Bridgen, October 2, 1779
    Designs and mottoes for coins 271

Elizabeth Partridge, October 11, 1779
    "Somebody . . . gave it out that I lov'd Ladies". 272

John Paul Jones, October 15, 1779
    "your cool Conduct and persevering Bravery" 273

Benjamin Vaughan, November 9, 1779
  "The great uncertainty I found in metaphysical reasonings" 275

Joseph Priestley, February 8, 1780
  "that Men would cease to be Wolves" 277

George Washington, March 5, 1780
  "Like a Field of young Indian Corn". 279

Thomas Bond, March 16, 1780
  "than if you had swallowed a handspike". 280

William Carmichael, June 17, 1780
  "The Moulin Joli is a little island in the Seine". 281

Samuel Huntington, August 9, 1780
  "Mr. Adams has given Offence to the Court here" 282

John Jay, October 2, 1780
  "A neighbour might as well ask me to sell my street door". . 287

Richard Price, October 9, 1780
  Religious tests 290

Benjamin Waterhouse, January 18, 1781
  "I think a worthier Man never lived". 291

John Adams, February 22, 1781
  *"I shall be ready to break, run away, or go to prison
  with you"* 292

Court de Gebelin, May 7, 1781
  "As the Indians had no Letters, they had no Orthography". . 293

Comte de Vergennes, June 10, 1781
  "I have acted imprudently". 294

William Jackson, July 10, 1781
  *"these Superior Airs you give yourself, young Gentleman,
  of Reproof to me"* 297

William Nixon, September 5, 1781
  *"assisting with an equal Sum a stranger who has equal
  need of it"*. 299

William Strahan, December 4, 1781
  On fine printing 300

John Adams, December 17, 1781
  "nor a Syllable of Approbation" 301

Robert R. Livingston, March 4, 1782
  On the Libertas medal 302

John Adams, April 22, 1782
  "a happy name for a prince as obstinant as a mule" . . . 306

Joseph Priestley, June 7, 1782
  "Men I find to be a Sort of Beings very badly constructed" 307

Richard Price, June 13, 1782
  "by the press we can speak to nations". 309

Miss Alexander, June 24, 1782
  "I am covetous, and love good Bargains". 310

James Hutton, July 7, 1782
  "the more I am convinc'd of a future State". 311

Robert R. Livingston, August 12, 1782
  "to coop us up within the Allegany Mountains". . . . 312

The Marquis de Lafayette, September 17, 1782
  "too harsh even for the Boys" 315

The Abbé Soulavie, September 22, 1782
  "how such a globe was formed". 316

Comte de Vergennes, December 17, 1782
  "a single indiscretion of ours" 320

Mary Hewson, January 27, 1783
  "All Wars are Follies" 321

Robert R. Livingston, July 22, 1783
  "in some things, absolutely out of his senses" 322

Sir Joseph Banks, July 27, 1783
  "there never was a good War, or a bad Peace" 333

Sir Joseph Banks, August 30, 1783
  First balloon experiments. 334

John Jay, September 10, 1783
  "falls little short of treason". 339

Robert Morris, December 25, 1783
  *"All Property . . . seems to me to be the Creature of
  public Convention"* 339

To ———, [January, 1784?]
"a good People to live among" 343

Sarah Bache, January 26, 1784
*"the Turk'y is in comparison a much more respectable
Bird"* 344

William Strahan, February 16, 1784
"my Advice 'smells of Madeira'" 349

La Sabliere de la Condamine, March 19, 1784
Methods of treating diseases 351

Samuel Mather, May 12, 1784
"Stoop, stoop!" 352

Charles Thomson, May 13, 1784
"beware of being lulled into a dangerous security" 353

Mason Locke Weems and Edward Gant, July 18, 1784
" 'damn your Souls. Make Tobacco!'" 354

William Franklin, August 16, 1784
"Our Opinions are not in our own Power" 356

William Strahan, August 19, 1784
"the Yankeys never felt bold" 358

Joseph Priestley, August 21, 1784
On divine inspiration. 362

Richard Price, March 18, 1785
"Sense being preferable to Sound" 364

George Whatley, May 23, 1785
On annihilation and bifocals 364

The Sale of the Hessians

FROM THE COUNT DE SCHAUMBERGH TO THE BARON
HOHENDORF, COMMANDING THE HESSIAN TROOPS
IN AMERICA

Rome, February 18, 1777.

MONSIEUR LE BARON:—On my return from Naples, I received at Rome your letter of the 27th December of last year. I have learned with unspeakable pleasure the courage our troops exhibited at Trenton, and you cannot imagine my joy on being told that of the 1,950 Hessians engaged in the fight, but 345 escaped. There were just 1,605 men killed, and I cannot sufficiently commend your prudence in sending an exact list of the dead to my minister in London. This precaution was the more necessary, as the report sent to the English ministry does not give but 1,455 dead. This would make 483,450 florins instead of 643,500 which I am entitled to demand under our convention. You will comprehend the prejudice which such an error would work in my finances, and I do not doubt you will take the necessary pains to prove that Lord North's list is false and yours correct.

The court of London objects that there were a hundred wounded who ought not to be included in the list, nor paid for as dead; but I trust you will not overlook my instructions to you on quitting Cassel, and that you will not have tried by human succor to recall the life of the unfortunates whose days could not be lengthened but by the loss of a leg or an arm. That would be making them a pernicious present, and I am sure they would rather die than live in a condition no longer fit for my service. I do not mean by this that you should assassinate them; we should be humane, my dear Baron, but you may insinuate to the surgeons with entire propriety that a crippled man is a reproach to their profession, and that there is no wiser course than to let every one of them die when he ceases to be fit to fight.

I am about to send to you some new recruits. Don't economize them. Remember glory before all things. Glory is true wealth. There is nothing degrades the soldier like the love of money. He must care only for honour and reputation, but this reputation must be acquired in the midst of dangers. A battle gained without costing the conqueror any blood is an inglorious success, while the conquered cover themselves with glory by perishing with their arms in their hands. Do you remember that of the 300 Lacedæmonians who defended the defile of Thermopylæ, not one returned? How happy should I be could I say the same of my brave Hessians!

It is true that their king, Leonidas, perished with them: but things have changed, and it is no longer the custom for princes of the empire to go and fight in America for a cause with which they have no concern. And besides, to whom should they pay the thirty guineas per man if I did not stay in Europe to receive them? Then, it is necessary also that I be ready to send recruits to replace the men you lose. For this purpose I must return to Hesse. It is true, grown men are becoming scarce there, but I will send you boys. Besides, the scarcer the commodity the higher the price. I am assured that the women and little girls have begun to till our lands, and they get on not badly. You did right to send back to Europe that Dr. Crumerus who was so successful in curing dysentery. Don't bother with a man who is subject to looseness of the bowels. That disease makes bad soldiers. One coward will do more mischief in an engagement than ten brave men will do good. Better that they burst in their barracks than fly in a battle, and tarnish the glory of our arms. Besides, you know that they pay me as killed for all who die from disease, and I don't get a farthing for runaways. My trip to Italy, which has cost me enormously, makes it desirable that there should be a great mortality among them. You will therefore promise promotion to all who expose themselves; you will exhort them to seek glory in the midst of dangers; you will say to Major Maundorff that I am not at all content with his saving the 345 men who escaped the massacre of Trenton. Through the whole campaign he has not had ten men killed in consequence of his orders. Finally, let it be your principal object to prolong the war and avoid a decisive engagement on either side, for I have made arrangements for a grand Italian opera, and I do not wish to be obliged to give it up. Meantime I pray God, my dear Baron de Hohendorf, to have you in his holy and gracious keeping.

Model of a Letter of Recommendation

Sir   Paris April 2, 1777
    The Bearer of this who is going to America, presses me to give him a Letter of Recommendation, tho' I know nothing of him, not even his Name. This may seem extraordinary, but I assure you it is not uncommon here. Sometimes indeed one unknown Person brings me another equally unknown, to recommend him; and sometimes they recommend one another! As to this Gentleman, I must refer you to himself for his Character and Merits, with which he is certainly better acquainted than I can possibly be; I recommend him however to those Civilities which every Stranger, of whom one knows no Harm, has a Right to, and I request you will do him all the good Offices and show him all the Favour that on further Acquaintance you shall find him to deserve. I have the honour to be, &c.

The Twelve Commandments

TO MADAME BRILLON

                                                        Passy March 10.
I am charm'd with the goodness of my spiritual guide, and resign myself implicitly to her Conduct, as she promises to lead me to heaven in so delicious a Road when I could be content to travel thither even in the roughest of all ways with the pleasure of her Company.
    How kindly partial to her Penitent in finding him, on ex-

amining his conscience, guilty of only one capital sin and to call that by the gentle name of Foible!

I lay fast hold of your promise to absolve me of all Sins past, present, & future, on the easy & pleasing Condition of loving God, America and my guide above all things. I am in Rapture when I think of being absolv'd of the future.

People commonly speak of Ten Commandments.—I have been taught that there are twelve. The first was increase & multiply & replenish the earth. The twelfth is, A new Commandment I give unto you, *that you love one another.* It seems to me that they are a little misplaced, And that the last should have been the first. However I never made any difficulty about that, but was always willing to obey them both whenever I had an opportunity. Pray tell me my dear Casuist, whether my keeping religiously these two commandments tho' not in the Decalogue, may not be accepted in Compensation for my breaking so often one of the ten I mean that which forbids Coveting my neighbour's wife, and which I confess I break constantly God forgive me, as often as I see or think of my lovely Confessor, and I am afraid I should never be able to repent of the Sin even if I had the full Possession of her.

And now I am Consulting you upon a Case of Conscience I will mention the Opinion of a certain Father of the church which I find myself willing to adopt though I am not sure it is orthodox. It is this, that the most effectual way to get rid of a certain Temptation is, as often as it returns, to comply with and satisfy it.

Pray instruct me how far I may venture to practice upon this Principle?

But why should I be so scrupulous when you have promised to absolve me of the future?

Adieu my charming Conductress and believe me ever with the sincerest Esteem & affection.

Your most obed't hum. Serv.

1778

Petition of the Letter Z

FROM THE TATLER N 1778

TO THE WORSHIPFUL ISAAC BICKERSTAFF, ESQ;
CENSOR-GENERAL
THE PETITION OF THE LETTER Z COMMONLY CALLED
EZZARD, ZED, OR IZARD, MOST HUMBLY SHEWETH,

He was always talking of his Family and of his being a Man of Fortune.

That your Petitioner is of as high extraction, and has as good an Estate as any other Letter of the Alphabet.

And complaining of his being treated, not with due Respect

That there is therefore no reason why he should be treated as he is with Disrespect and Indignity.

At the tail of the Commission, of Ministers

That he is not only plac'd at the Tail of the Alphabet, when he had as much Right as any other to be at the Head; but is, by the Injustice of his enemies totally excluded from the Word WISE, and his Place injuriously filled by a little, hissing, crooked, serpentine, venemous Letter called s, when it must be evident to your Worship, and to all the World, that Double U, I, S. E do not spell or sound *Wize*, but *Wice*.

He was not of the Commission for France, A Lee being preferr'd to him, which made him very angry; and the Character here given of S, is just what he in his Passion gave Lee.

Your Petitioner therefore prays that the Alphabet may by your Censorial Authority be reformed, and that in Consideration of his *Long-Suffering* & *Patience* he may be placed at the Head of it; that S may be turned out of the Word Wise, and the Petitioner employ'd instead of him;

The most impatient Man alive

And your Petitioner (as in Duty bound) shall ever pray, &c.

Z

Mr. Bickerstaff having examined the Allegations of the above Petition, judges and determines, that Z be admonished to be content with his Station, forbear Reflections upon his Brother Letters, & remember his own small Usefulness, and the little Occasion there is for him in the Republick of Letters, since S, whom he so despises, can so well serve instead of him.

c. August, 1778

The Ephemera

Passy Sept 20, 1778

You may remember, my dear Friend, that when we lately spent that happy Day in the delightful Garden and sweet Society of the Moulin Joli, I stopt a little in one of our Walks, and staid some time behind the Company. We had been shewn numberless Skeletons of a kind of little Fly, called an Ephemere all whose successive Generations we were told were bred and expired within the Day. I happen'd to see a living Company of them on a Leaf, who appear'd to be engag'd in Conversation. — You know I understand all the inferior Animal Tongues: my too great Application to the Study of them is the best Excuse I can give for the little Progress I have made in your charming Language. I listened thro' Curiosity to the Discourse of these little Creatures, but as they in their national Vivacity spoke three or four together, I could make but little of their Discourse. I found, however, by some broken Expressions that I caught now & then, they were disputing warmly the Merit of two foreign Musicians, one a *Cousin*, the other a *Musketo*; in which Dispute they spent their time seemingly as regardless of the Shortness of Life, as if they had been Sure of living a Month. Happy People! thought I, you live certainly under a wise, just and mild Government; since you have no public Grievances to complain of, nor any Subject of Contention but the Perfection or Imperfection of foreign Music. I turned from them to an old greyheaded one, who was single on another Leaf, & talking to himself. Being amus'd with his Soliloquy, I have put it down in writing in hopes it will likewise amuse her to whom I am So much indebted for the most pleasing of all Amusements, her delicious Company and her heavenly Harmony.

"It was, says he, the Opinion of learned Philosophers of our Race, who lived and flourished long before my time, that this vast World, the *Moulin Joli*, could not itself subsist more than 18 Hours; and I think there was some Foundation for that Opinion, since by the apparent Motion of the great Luminary that gives Life to all Nature, and which in my time has evidently declin'd considerably towards the Ocean at the End of our Earth, it must then finish its Course, be extinguish'd in the Waters that surround us, and leave the World in Cold and Darkness, necessarily producing universal Death and Destruction. I have lived seven of these Hours; a great Age; being no less than 420 minutes of Time. How very few of us continue So long.—I have seen Generations born, flourish and expire. My present Friends are the Children and Grandchildren of the Friends of my Youth, who are now, alas, no more! And I must soon follow them; for by the Course of Nature, tho' still in Health, I cannot expect to live above 7 or 8 Minutes longer. What now avails all my Toil and Labour in amassing Honey-Dew on this Leaf, which I cannot live to enjoy! What the political Struggles I have been engag'd in for the Good of my Compatriotes, Inhabitants of this Bush, or my philosophical Studies for the Benefit of our Race in general! For in Politics *what can Laws do without Morals.** Our present Race of Ephemeres will in a Course of Minutes, become corrupt like those of other and older Bushes, and consequently as wretched. And in Philosophy how small our Progress! Alas, *Art is long and Life is short!*†—My Friends would comfort me with the Idea of a Name they Say I shall leave behind me; and they tell me I have *lived long enough, to Nature and to Glory*;‡—But what will Fame be to an Ephemere who no longer exists? And what will become of all History in the 18th Hour, when the World itself, even the whole *Moulin Joli* shall come to its End, and be buried in

Quid leges sine moribus. Hor.
†Hippocrates.
‡Cæsar.

universal Ruin?—To me, after all my eager Pursuits, no solid Pleasures now remain, but the Reflection of a long Life spent in meaning well, the sensible Conversation of a few good Lady-Ephemeres, and now and then a kind Smile and a Tune from the ever-amiable BRILLANTE."

The Elysian Fields

M. FRANKLIN TO MADAME HELVÉTIUS

Vexed by your barbarous resolution, announced so positively last evening, to remain single all your life in respect to your dear husband, I went home, fell on my bed, and, believing myself dead, found myself in the Elysian Fields.

I was asked if I desired to see anybody in particular. Lead me to the home of the philosophers.—There are two who live nearby in the garden: they are very good neighbors, and close friends of each other.—Who are they?—Socrates and H——.—I esteem them both prodigiously; but let me see first H——, because I understand a little French, but not one word of Greek. He received me with great courtesy, having known me for some time, he said, by the reputation I had there. He asked me a thousand things about the war, and about the present state of religion, liberty, and the government in France.—You ask nothing then of your dear friend Madame H——; nevertheless she still loves you excessively and I was at her place but an hour ago. Ah! said he, you make me remember my former felicity.—But it is necessary to forget it in order to be happy here. During several of the early years, I thought only of her. Finally I am consoled. I have taken another wife. The most like her that I could find. She is not, it is true, so completely beautiful, but she has as much good sense, a little more of Spirit, and she loves me infinitely. Her continual study is to please me; and she has actually gone to hunt the best Nectar and the best Ambrosia in order to regale me this evening; remain with me and you will see her. I perceive, I said, that your old friend is more faithful than you: for several good offers have been made her, all of which she has refused. I confess to you that I myself have loved her to the point of distraction; but she was hard-hearted to my regard, and has absolutely rejected me for love of you. I pity you, he said, for your bad fortune; for truly she is a good and beautiful woman and very loveable. But the Abbé de la R——, and the Abbé M——, are they not still sometimes at her home? Yes, assuredly, for she has not lost a single one of your friends. If you had won over the Abbé M—— (with coffee and cream) to speak for you, perhaps you would have succeeded; for he is a subtle logician like Duns Scotus or St. Thomas; he places his arguments in such good order that they become nearly irresistible. Also, if the Abbé de la R—— had been bribed (by some beautiful edition of an old classic) to speak against you, that would have been better: for I have always observed, that when he advises something, she has a very strong penchant to do the reverse.—At these words the new Madame H—— entered with the Nectar: at which instant I recognized her to be Madame F——, my old American friend. I reclaimed to her. But she told me coldly, "I have been your good wife forty-nine years and four months, nearly a half century; be content with that. Here I have formed a new connection, which will endure to eternity."

Offended by this refusal of my Eurydice, I suddenly decided to leave these ungrateful spirits, to return to the good earth, to see again the sunshine and you. Here I am! Let us revenge ourselves.

December 7, 1778

Bilked for Breakfast

MR. FRANKLIN TO MADAME LA FRETÉ

Upon my word, you did well, Madam, not to come so far, at so inclement a Season, only to find so wretched a Breakfast. My Son & I were not so wise. I will tell you the Story.

As the Invitation was for eleven O'clock, & you were of the Party, I imagined I should find a substantial Breakfast; that there would be a large Company; that we should have not only Tea, but Coffee, Chocolate, perhaps a Ham, & several other good Things. I resolved to go on Foot; my Shoes were a little too tight; I arrived almost lamed. On entering the Courtyard, I was a little surprised to find it so empty of Carriages, & to see that we were the first to arrive. We go up the Stairs. Not a Sound. We enter the Breakfast Room. No one except the Abbé & Monsieur Cabanis. Breakfast over, & eaten! Nothing on the Table except a few Scraps of Bread & a little Butter. General astonishment; a Servant sent running to tell Madame Helvétius that we have come for Breakfast. She leaves her toilet Table; she enters with her Hair half dressed. It is declared surprising that I have come, when you wrote me that you would not come. I Deny it. To prove it, they show me your Letter, which they have received and kept.

Finally another Breakfast is ordered. One Servant runs for fresh Water, another for Coals. The Bellows are plied with a will. I was very Hungry; it was so late; "a watched pot is slow to boil," as Poor Richard says. Madame sets out for Paris & leaves us. We begin to eat. The Butter is soon finished. The Abbé asks if we want more. Yes, of course. He rings. No one comes. We talk; he forgets the Butter. I began scraping the Dish; at that he seizes it & runs to the Kitchen for some. After a while he comes slowly back, saying mournfully that there is no more of it in the House. To entertain me the Abbé proposes a Walk; my feet refuse. And so we give up Breakfast; & we go upstairs to his apartment to let his good Books furnish the end of our Repast—.

I am left utterly disconsolate, having, instead of half a Dozen of your sweet, affectionate, substantial, & heartily applied Kisses, which I expected from your Charity, having received only the Shadow of one given by Madame Helvétius, willingly enough, it is true, but the lightest & most superficial kiss that can possibly be imagined.

c. 1778

Passport for Captain Cook

To all Captains and Commanders of armed Ships acting by Commission from the Congress of the United States of America, now in war with Great Britain.

Gentlemen,

A Ship having been fitted out from England before the Commencement of this War, to make Discoveries of new Countries in Unknown Seas, under the Conduct of that most celebrated Navigator and Discoverer Captain Cook; an Undertaking truly laudable in itself, as the Increase of Geographical Knowledge facilitates the Communication between distant Nations, in the Exchange of useful Products and Manufactures, and the Extension of Arts, whereby the common Enjoyments of human Life are multiply'd and augmented, and Science of other kinds increased to the benefit of Mankind in general; this is, therefore, most earnestly to recommend to every one of you, that, in case the said Ship, which is now expected to be soon in the European Seas on her Return, should happen to fall into your Hands, you would not consider her as an Enemy, nor suffer any Plunder to be made of the Effects contain'd in her, nor obstruct her immediate Return to England, by detaining her or sending her into any other Part of Europe or to America, but that you would treat the said Captain Cook and his People with all Civility and Kindness, affording them, as common Friends to Mankind, all the Assistance in your Power, which they may happen to stand in need of. In so doing you will not only gratify the Generosity of your own Dispositions, but there is no doubt of your obtaining the Approbation of the Congress, and your other American Owners. I have the honour to be, Gentlemen, your most obedient humble Servant.

Given at Passy, near Paris, this 10th day of March, 1779.
Plenipotentiary from the Congress of the
United States to the Court of France.

The Morals of Chess

[Playing at chess is the most ancient and most universal game known among men; for its original is beyond the memory of history, and it has, for numberless ages, been the amusement of all the civilised nations of Asia, the Persians, the Indians, and the Chinese. Europe has had it above a thousand years;

the Spaniards have spread it over their part of America; and it has lately begun to make its appearance in the United States. It is so interesting in itself, as not to need the view of gain to induce engaging in it; and thence it is seldom played for money. Those therefore who have leisure for such diversions, cannot find one that is more innocent: and the following piece, written with a view to correct (among a few young friends) some little improprieties in the practice of it, shows at the same time that it may, in its effects on the mind, be not merely innocent, but advantageous, to the vanquished as well as the victor.]

The Game of Chess is not merely an idle Amusement. Several very valuable qualities of the Mind, useful in the course of human Life, are to be acquir'd or strengthened by it, so as to become habits, ready on all occasions. For Life is a kind of Chess, in which we often have Points to gain, & Competitors or Adversaries to contend with; and in which there is a vast variety of good and ill Events, that are in some degree the Effects of Prudence or the want of it. By playing at Chess, then, we may learn,

I. *Foresight*, which looks a little into futurity, and considers the Consequences that may attend an action; for it is continually occurring to the Player, "If I move this piece, what will be the advantages or disadvantages of my new situation? What Use can my Adversary make of it to annoy me? What other moves can I make to support it, and to defend myself from his attacks?"

II. *Circumspection*, which surveys the whole Chessboard, or scene of action; the relations of the several pieces and situations, the Dangers they are respectively exposed to, the several possibilities of their aiding each other, the probabilities that the Adversary may make this or that move, and attack this or the other Piece, and what different Means can be used to avoid his stroke, or turn its consequences against him.

III. *Caution*, not to make our moves too hastily. This habit is best acquired, by observing strictly the laws of the Game; such as, *If you touch a Piece, you must move it somewhere; if you set it down, you must let it stand.* And it is therefore best that these rules should be observed, as the Game becomes thereby more the image of human Life, and particularly of War; in which, if you have incautiously put yourself into a bad and dangerous position, you cannot obtain your Enemy's Leave to withdraw your Troops, and place them more securely, but you must abide all the consequences of your rashness.

And *lastly*, we learn by Chess the habit of not being discouraged by present appearances in the state of our affairs, the habit of hoping for a favourable Change, and that of persevering in the search of resources. The Game is so full of Events, there is such a variety of turns in it, the Fortune of it is so subject to sudden Vicissitudes, and one so frequently, after long contemplation, discovers the means of extricating one's self from a supposed insurmountable Difficulty, that one is encouraged to continue the Contest to the last, in hopes of Victory from our own skill, or at least of getting a stale mate, from the Negligence of our Adversary. And whoever considers, what in Chess he often sees instances of, that particular pieces of success are apt to produce Presumption, & its consequent Inattention, by which more is afterwards lost than was gain'd by the preceding Advantage, while misfortunes produce more care and attention, by which the loss may be recovered, will learn not to be too much discouraged by any present success of his Adversary, nor to despair of final good fortune upon every little Check he receives in the pursuit of it.

That we may therefore be induced more frequently to chuse this beneficial amusement, in preference to others which are not attended with the same advantages, every Circumstance that may increase the pleasure of it should be regarded; and every action or word that is unfair, disrespectful, or that in any way may give uneasiness, should be avoided, as contrary to the immediate intention of both the Players, which is to pass the Time agreably.

Therefore, first, if it is agreed to play according to the strict rules, then those rules are to be exactly observed by both parties, and should not be insisted on for one side, while deviated from by the other—for this is not equitable.

Secondly, if it is agreed not to observe the rules exactly, but one party demands indulgencies, he should then be as willing to allow them to the other.

Thirdly, no false move should ever be made to extricate yourself out of difficulty, or to gain an advantage. There can be no pleasure in playing with a person once detected in such unfair practice.

Fourthly, if your adversary is long in playing, you ought not to hurry him, or express any uneasiness at his delay. You should not sing, nor whistle, nor look at your watch, nor take up a book to read, nor make a tapping with your feet on the floor, or with your fingers on the table, nor do any thing that may disturb his attention. For all these things displease; and they do not show your skill in playing, but your craftiness or your rudeness.

Fifthly, you ought not to endeavour to amuse and deceive your adversary, by pretending to have made bad moves, and saying that you have now lost the game, in order to make him secure and careless, and inattentive to your schemes: for this is fraud and deceit, not skill in the game.

Sixthly, you must not, when you have gained a victory, use any triumphing or insulting expression, nor show too much pleasure; but endeavour to console your adversary, and make him less dissatisfied with himself, by every kind of civil expression that may be used with truth, such as, "you understand the game better than I, but you are a little inattentive;" or, "you play too fast;" or, "you had the best of the game, but something happened to divert your thoughts, and that turned it in my favour."

Seventhly, if you are a spectator while others play, observe the most perfect silence. For, if you give advice, you offend both parties, him against whom you give it, because it may cause the loss of his game, him in whose favour you give it, because, though it be good, and he follows it, he loses the pleasure he might have had, if you had permitted him to think until it had occurred to himself. Even after a move or moves, you must not, by replacing the pieces, show how they might have been placed better; for that displeases, and may occasion disputes and doubts about their true situation. All talking to the players lessens or diverts their attention, and is therefore unpleasing. Nor should you give the least hint to either party, by any kind of noise or motion. If you do, you are unworthy to be a spectator. If you have a mind to exercise or show your judgment, do it in playing your own game, when you have an opportunity, not in criticizing, or meddling with, or counselling the play of others.

Lastly, if the game is not to be played rigorously, according to the rules above mentioned, then moderate your desire of victory over your adversary, and be pleased with one over yourself. Snatch not eagerly at every advantage offered by his unskilfulness or inattention; but point out to him kindly, that by such a move he places or leaves a piece in danger and unsupported; that by another he will put his king in a perilous situation, &c. By this generous civility (so opposite to the unfairness above forbidden) you may, indeed, happen to lose the game to your opponent; but you will win what is better, his esteem, his respect, and his affection, together with the silent approbation and good-will of impartial spectators.

June, 1779

The Whistle

Passy, November 10 1779.

I received my dear Friend's two Letters, one for Wednesday & one for Saturday. This is again Wednesday. I do not deserve one for to day, because I have not answered the former. But indolent as I am, and averse to Writing, the Fear of having no more of your pleasing Epistles, if I do not contribute to the Correspondance, obliges me to take up my Pen: And as M. B. has kindly sent me Word, that he sets out to-morrow to see you; instead of spending this Wednesday Evening as I have long done its Name-sakes, in your delightful Company, I sit down to spend it in thinking of you, in writing to you, & in reading over & over again your Letters.

I am charm'd with your Description of Paradise, & with your Plan of living there. And I approve much of your Conclusion, that in the mean time we should draw all the Good

we can from this World. In my Opinion we might all draw
more Good, from it than we do, & suffer less Evil, if we
would but take care *not to give too much for our Whistles.* For
to me it seems that most of the unhappy People we meet
with, are become so by Neglect of that Caution.

You ask what I mean?—You love Stories, and will excuse
my telling you one of my self. When I was a Child of seven
Years old, my Friends on a Holiday fill'd my little Pocket with
Halfpence. I went directly to a Shop where they sold Toys for
Children; and being charm'd with the Sound of a Whistle
that I met by the way, in the hands of another Boy, I voluntarily offer'd and gave all my Money for it. When I came
home, whistling all over the House, much pleas'd with my
Whistle, but disturbing all the Family, my Brothers, Sisters &
Cousins, understanding the Bargain I had made, told me I
had given four times as much for it as it was worth, put me
in mind what good Things I might have bought with the rest
of the Money, & laught at me so much for my Folly that I
cry'd with Vexation; and the Reflection gave me more Chagrin than the Whistle gave me Pleasure.

This however was afterwards of use to me, the Impression
continuing on my Mind; so that often when I was tempted
to buy some unnecessary thing, I said to my self, *Do not give
too much for the Whistle*; and I sav'd my Money.

As I grew up, came into the World, and observed the Actions of Men, I thought I met many *who gave too much for the
Whistle.*—When I saw one ambitious of Court Favour, sacrificing his Time in Attendance at Levees, his Repose, his Liberty, his Virtue and perhaps his Friend, to obtain it; I have
said to my self, *This Man gives too much for his Whistle.*—
When I saw another fond of Popularity, constantly employing
himself in political Bustles, neglecting his own Affairs, and
ruining them by that Neglect, *He pays*, says I, *too much for his
Whistle.*—If I knew a Miser, who gave up every kind of
comfortable Living, all the Pleasure of doing Good to
others, all the Esteem of his Fellow Citizens, & the Joys of
benevolent Friendship, for the sake of Accumulating Wealth,
Poor Man, says I, *you pay too much for your Whistle.*—When
I met with a Man of Pleasure, sacrificing every laudable
Improvement of his Mind or of his Fortune, to mere cor-

poreal Satisfactions, & ruining his Health in their Pursuit, *Mistaken Man*, says I, *you are providing Pain for your self instead of Pleasure, you pay too much for your Whistle.*—If I see one fond of Appearance, of fine Cloaths, fine Houses, fine Furniture, fine Equipages, all above his Fortune, for which he contracts Debts, and ends his Career in a Prison; *Alas*, says I, *he has paid too much for his Whistle.*—When I saw a beautiful sweet-temper'd Girl, marry'd to an ill-natured Brute of a Husband; *What a Pity*, says I, *that she should pay so much for a Whistle!*—In short, I conceiv'd that great Part of the Miseries of Mankind, were brought upon them by the false Estimates they had made of the Value of Things, and by their *giving too much for the Whistle.*

Yet I ought to have Charity for these unhappy People, when I consider that with all this Wisdom of which I am boasting, there are certain things in the World so tempting; for Example the Apples of King John, which happily are not to be bought, for if they were put to sale by Auction, I might very easily be led to ruin my self in the Purchase, and find that I had once more *given too much for the Whistle.*

Adieu, my dearest Friend, and believe me ever yours very sincerely and with unalterable Affection.

Passy, 1779

The Levée

In the first chapter of Job we have an account of a transaction said to have arisen in the court, or at the *levée*, of the best of all possible princes, or of governments by a single person, viz. that of God himself.

At this *levée*, in which the sons of God were assembled, Satan also appeared.

It is probable the writer of that ancient book took his idea of this *levée* from those of the eastern monarchs of the age he lived in.

It is to this day usual at the *levées* of princes, to have persons assembled who are enemies to each other, who seek to obtain favor by whispering calumny and detraction, and thereby ruining those that distinguish themselves by their virtue and merit. And kings frequently ask a familiar question or two, of every one in the circle, merely to show their benignity. These circumstances are particularly exemplified in this relation.

If a modern king, for instance, finds a person in the circle who has not lately been there, he naturally asks him how he has passed his time since he last had the pleasure of seeing him? the gentleman perhaps replies that he has been in the country to view his estates, and visit some friends. Thus Satan being asked whence he cometh? answers, "From going to and fro in the earth, and walking up and down in it." And being further asked, whether he had considered the uprightness and fidelity of the prince's servant Job, he immediately displays all the malignance of the designing courtier, by answering with another question: "Doth Job serve God for naught? Hast thou not given him immense wealth, and protected him in the possession of it? Deprive him of that, and he will curse thee to thy face." In modern phrase, Take away his places and his pensions, and your Majesty will soon find him in the opposition.

This whisper against Job had its effect. He was delivered into the power of his adversary, who deprived him of his fortune, destroyed his family, and completely ruined him.

The book of Job is called by divines a sacred poem, and, with the rest of the Holy Scriptures, is understood to be written for our instruction.

What then is the instruction to be gathered from this supposed transaction?

Trust not a single person with the government of your state. For if the Deity himself, being the monarch may for a time give way to calumny, and suffer it to operate the destruction of the best of subjects; what mischief may you not expect from such power in a mere man, though the best of men, from whom the truth is often industriously hidden, and to whom falsehood is often presented in its place, by artful, interested, and malicious courtiers?

And be cautious in trusting him even with limited powers, lest sooner or later he sap and destroy those limits, and render himself absolute.

For by the disposal of places, he attaches to himself all the placeholders, with their numerous connexions, and also all the expecters and hopers of places, which will form a strong party in promoting his views. By various political engagements for the interest of neighbouring states or princes, he procures their aid in establishing his own personal power. So that, through the hopes of emolument in one part of his subjects, and the fear of his resentment in the other, all opposition falls before him.

1779?

Proposed New Version of the Bible

To the Printer of ***

SIR,

It is now more than one hundred and seventy years since the translation of our common English Bible. The language in that time is much changed, and the style, being obsolete, and thence less agreeable, is perhaps one reason why the reading of that excellent book is of late so much neglected. I have therefore thought it would be well to procure a new version, in which, preserving the sense, the turn of phrase and manner of expression should be modern. I do not pretend to have the necessary abilities for such a work myself; I throw out the hint for the consideration of the learned; and only venture to send you a few verses of the first chapter of Job, which may serve as a sample of the kind of version I would recommend.

A. B.

PART OF THE FIRST CHAPTER OF JOB MODERNIZED

OLD TEXT	NEW VERSION
Verse 6. Now there was a day when the sons of God came to present themselves before the Lord, and Satan came also amongst them.	Verse 6. And it being *levée* day in heaven, all God's nobility came to court, to present themselves before him; and Satan also appeared in the circle, as one of the ministry.

7. And the Lord said unto Satan, Whence comest thou? Then Satan answered the Lord, and said, From going to and fro in the earth, and from walking up and down in it.

8. And the Lord said unto Satan, Hast thou considered my servant Job, that there is none like him in the earth, a perfect and an upright man, one that feareth God, and escheweth evil?

9. Then Satan answered the Lord, and said, Doth Job fear God for naught?

10. Hast thou not made an hedge about his house, and about all that he hath on every side? Thou hast blessed the work of his hands, and his substance is increased in the land.

11. But put forth thine hand now, and touch all that he hath, and he will curse thee to thy face.

7. And God said to Satan, You have been some time absent; where were you? And Satan answered I have been at my country-seat, and in different places visiting my friends.

8. And God said, Well, what think you of Lord Job? You see he is my best friend, a perfectly honest man, full of respect for me, and avoiding every thing that might offend me.

9. And Satan answered, Does your Majesty imagine that his good conduct is the effect of mere personal attachment and affection?

10. Have you not protected him, and heaped your benefits upon him, till he is grown enormously rich?

11. Try him;—only withdraw your favor, turn him out of his places, and withhold his pensions, and you will soon find him in the opposition.

1779?

Drinking Song

TO THE ABBÉ DE LA ROCHE, AT AUTEUIL

I have run over, my dear friend, the little book of poetry by M. Helvetius, with which you presented me. The poem on *Happiness* pleased me much, and brought to my recollection a little drinking song which I wrote forty years ago upon the same subject, and which is nearly on the same plan, with many of the same thoughts, but very concisely expressed. It is as follows:—

Singer.
Fair Venus calls, her voice obey,
In beauty's arms spend night and day.
The joys of love, all joys excel,
And loving's certainly doing well.

Chorus.

Oh! no!
Not so!
For honest souls know,
Friends and a bottle still bear the bell.

Singer.

Then let us get money, like bees lay up honey;
We'll build us new hives, and store each cell.
The sight of our treasure shall yield us great pleasure;
We'll count it, and chink it, and jingle it well.

Chorus.

Oh! no!
Not so!
For honest souls know,
Friends and a bottle still bear the bell.

Singer.

If this does not fit ye, let's govern the city,
In power is pleasure no tongue can tell;
By crowds tho' you're teas'd, your pride shall be pleas'd,
And this can make Lucifer happy in hell!

Chorus.

Oh! no!
Not so!
For honest souls know,
Friends and a bottle still bear the bell.

Singer.

Then toss off your glasses, and scorn the dull asses,
Who, missing the kernel, still gnaw the shell;
What's love, rule, or riches? wise Solomon teaches,
They're vanity, vanity, vanity, still.

Chorus.

That's true;
He knew;
He'd tried them all through;
Friends and a bottle still bore the bell.

'Tis a singer, my dear Abbé, who exhorts his companions

to seek *happiness* in *love*, in *riches*, and in *power*. They reply, singing together, that happiness is not to be found in any of these things; that it is only to be found in *friends* and *wine*. To this proposition the singer at last assents. The phrase "*bear the bell*," answers to the French expression, "*obtain the prize.*"

I have often remarked, in reading the works of M. Helvetius, that although we were born and educated in two countries so remote from each other, we have often been inspired with the same thoughts; and it is a reflection very flattering to me, that we have not only loved the same studies, but, as far as we have mutually known them, the same friends, and *the same woman*.

Adieu! my dear friend, &c.

1779?

A Tale

There was once an Officer, a worthy man, named Montrésor, who was very ill. His parish Priest, thinking he would die, advised him to make his Peace with God, so that he would be received into Paradise. "I don't feel much Uneasiness on that Score," said Montrésor; "for last Night I had a Vision which set me entirely at rest." "What Vision did you have?" asked the good Priest. "I was," he said, "at the Gate of Paradise with a Crowd of People who wanted to enter. And St. Peter asked each of them what Religion he belonged to. One answered, 'I am a Roman Catholic.' 'Very well,' said St. Peter; 'come in, & take your Place over there among the Catholics.' Another said he belonged to the Anglican Church. 'Very well,' said St. Peter; 'come in, & take your Place over there among the Anglicans.' Another said he was a Quaker. 'Very well,' said St. Peter; 'come in, & take a Place among the Quakers.' Finally he asked me what my Religion was. 'Alas!' I replied, 'unfortunately, poor Jacques Montrésor belongs to none at all.' 'That's a pity,' said the Saint. 'I don't know where to put you but come in anyway; just find a Place for yourself wherever you can.'"

1779?

On Wine

FROM THE ABBÉ FRANKLIN
TO THE ABBÉ MORELLET

You have often enlivened me, my dear friend, by your excellent drinking-songs; in return, I beg to edify you by some Christian, moral, and philosophical reflections upon the same subject.

In vino veritas, says the wise man, — *Truth is in wine*. Before the days of Noah, then, men, having nothing but water to drink, could not discover the truth. Thus they went astray, became abominably wicked, and were justly exterminated by *water*, which they loved to drink.

The good man Noah, seeing that through this pernicious beverage all his contemporaries had perished, took it in aversion; and to quench his thirst God created the vine, and revealed to him the means of converting its fruit into wine. By means of this liquor he discovered numberless important truths; so that ever since his time the word to *divine* has been in common use, signifying originally, *to discover by means of* WINE. (VIN) Thus the patriarch Joseph took upon himself to *divine* by means of a cup or glass of wine, a liquor which obtained this name to show that it was not of human but *divine* invention (another proof of the *antiquity* of the French language, in opposition to M. Gébelin); nay, since that time, all things of peculiar excellence, even the Deities themselves, have been called *Divine* or Divinities.

We hear of the conversion of water into wine at the marriage in Cana as of a miracle. But this conversion is, through the goodness of God, made every day before our eyes. Behold the rain which descends from heaven upon our vineyards; there it enters the roots of the vines, to be changed into wine; a constant proof that God loves us, and loves to see us happy. The miracle in question was only performed to hasten the operation, under circumstances of present necessity, which required it.

It is true that God has also instructed man to reduce wine into water. But into what sort of water? — *Water of Life*. (*Eau de Vie*.) And this, that man may be able upon occasion to perform the miracle of Cana, and convert common water into that excellent species of wine which we call *punch*. My Christian brother, be kind and benevolent like God, and do not spoil his good drink.

He made wine to gladden the heart of man; do not, therefore when at table you see your neighbor pour wine into his glass, be eager to mingle water with it. Why would you drown *truth*? It is probable that your neighbor knows better than you what suits him. Perhaps he does not like water; perhaps he would only put in a few drops for fashion's sake; perhaps he does not wish any one to observe how little he puts in his glass. Do not, then, offer water, except to children; 't is a mistaken piece of politeness, and often very inconvenient. I give you this hint as a man of the world; and I will finish as I began, like a good Christian, in making a religious observation of high importance, taken from the Holy Scriptures. I mean that the apostle Paul counselled Timothy very seriously to put wine into his water for the sake of his health; but that not one of the apostles or holy fathers ever recommended *putting water to wine*.

P.S. To confirm still more your piety and gratitude to Divine Providence, reflect upon the situation which it has given to the *elbow*. You see (Figures 1 and 2) in animals, who are intended to drink the waters that flow upon the earth, that if they have long legs, they have also a long neck, so that they can get at their drink without kneeling down. But man, who was destined to drink wine, must be able to raise the glass to his mouth. If the elbow had been placed nearer the hand (as in Figure 3), the part in advance would have been too short to bring the glass up to the mouth; and if it had been placed nearer the shoulder, (as in Figure 4) that part would have been so long that it would have carried the wine far beyond the mouth. But by the actual situation, (represented in Figure 5), we are enabled to drink at our ease, the glass going exactly to the mouth. Let us, then, with glass in hand, adore this benevolent wisdom;—let us adore and drink!

1779?

Fig. I.

Fig. 2.

D'après le dessin original envoyé par Franklin .

Fig. 3.

Fig. 4.

Fig. 5.

Dialogue Between the Gout and Mr. Franklin

MIDNIGHT, OCTOBER 22, 1780

MR. F.

Eh! oh! eh! What have I done to merit these cruel sufferings?

THE GOUT

Many things; you have ate and drank too freely, and too much indulged those legs of yours in their indolence.

MR. F.

Who is it that accuses me?

THE GOUT

It is I, even I, the Gout.

MR. F.

What! my enemy in person?

THE GOUT

No, not your enemy.

MR. F.

I repeat it, my enemy; for you would not only torment my body to death, but ruin my good name; you reproach me as a glutton and a tippler; now all the world, that knows me, will allow that I am neither the one nor the other.

THE GOUT

The world may think as it pleases; it is always very complaisant to itself, and sometimes to its friends; but I very well know that the quantity of meat and drink proper for a man who takes a reasonable degree of exercise, would be too much for another who never takes any.

MR. F.

I take—eh! oh!—as much exercise—eh!—as I can, Madam Gout. You know my sedentary state, and on that account, it would seem, Madam Gout, as if you might spare me a little, seeing it is not altogether my own fault.

THE GOUT

Not a jot; your rhetoric and your politeness are thrown away;

your apology avails nothing. If your situation in life is a sedentary one, your amusements, your recreation, at least, should be active. You ought to walk or ride; or, if the weather prevents that, play at billiards. But let us examine your course of life. While the mornings are long, and you have leisure to go abroad, what do you do? Why, instead of gaining an appetite for breakfast by salutary exercise, you amuse yourself with books, pamphlets, or newspapers, which commonly are not worth the reading. Yet you eat an inordinate breakfast, four dishes of tea with cream, and one or two buttered toasts, with slices of hung beef, which I fancy are not things the most easily digested. Immediately afterwards you sit down to write at your desk, or converse with persons who apply to you on business. Thus the time passes till one, without any kind of bodily exercise. But all this I could pardon, in regard, as you say, to your sedentary condition. But what is your practice after dinner? Walking in the beautiful gardens of those friends with whom you have dined would be the choice of men of sense; yours is to be fixed down to chess, where you are found engaged for two or three hours! This is your perpetual recreation, which is the least eligible of any for a sedentary man, because, instead of accelerating the motion of the fluids, the rigid attention it requires helps to retard the circulation and obstruct internal secretions. Wrapt in the speculations of this wretched game, you destroy your constitution. What can be expected from such a course of living but a body replete with stagnant humours, ready to fall a prey to all kinds of dangerous maladies, if I, the Gout, did not occasionally bring you relief by agitating those humours, and so purifying or dissipating them? If it was in some nook or alley in Paris, deprived of walks, that you played a while at chess after dinner, this might be excusable; but the same taste prevails with you in Passy, Auteuil, Montmartre, or Sanoy, places where there are the finest gardens and walks, a pure air, beautiful women, and most agreeable and instructive conversation: all which you might enjoy by frequenting the walks. But these are rejected for this abominable game of chess. Fie, then, Mr. Franklin! But amidst my instructions, I had almost forgot to administer my wholesome corrections; so take that twinge— and that.

MR. F.

Oh! eh! oh! ohhh! As much instruction as you please, Madam Gout, and as many reproaches; but pray, Madam, a truce with your corrections!

THE GOUT

No, Sir, no, I will not abate a particle of what is so much for your good—therefore——

MR. F.

Oh! ehhh!—It is not fair to say I take no exercise, when I do very often, going out to dine and returning in my carriage.

THE GOUT

That, of all imaginable exercises, is the most slight and insignificant, if you allude to the motion of a carriage suspended on springs. By observing the degree of heat obtained by different kinds of motion, we may form an estimate of the quantity of exercise given by each. Thus, for example, if you turn out to walk in winter with cold feet, in an hour's time you will be in a glow all over; ride on horseback, the same effect will scarcely be perceived by four hours' round trotting; but if you loll in a carriage, such as you have mentioned, you may travel all day and gladly enter the last inn to warm your feet by a fire. Flatter yourself then no longer that half an hour's airing in your carriage deserves the name of exercise. Providence has appointed few to roll in carriages, while he has given to all a pair of legs, which are machines infinitely more commodious and serviceable. Be grateful, then, and make a proper use of yours. Would you know how they forward the circulation of your fluids in the very action of transporting you from place to place, observe when you walk that all your weight is alternately thrown from one leg to the other; this occasions a great pressure on the vessels of the foot, and repels their contents; when relieved, by the weight being thrown on the other foot, the vessels of the first are allowed to replenish, and by a return of this weight, this repulsion again succeeds; thus accelerating the circulation of the blood. The heat produced in any given time depends on the degree of this acceleration; the fluids are shaken, the humours attenuated, the secretions facilitated, and all goes well; the cheeks are ruddy, and health is established. Behold your fair friend at Auteuil; a lady who received from bounteous nature more really useful science than half a dozen such pretenders to philosophy as you have been able to extract from all your books. When she honours you with a visit, it is on foot. She walks all hours of the day, and leaves indolence, and its concomitant maladies, to be endured by her horses. In this, see at once the preservative of her health and personal charms. But when you go to Auteuil, you must have your carriage, though it is no farther from Passy to Auteuil than from Auteuil to Passy.

MR. F.

Your reasonings grow very tiresome.

THE GOUT

I stand corrected. I will be silent and continue my office; take that, and that.

MR. F.

Oh! Ohh! Talk on, I pray you.

THE GOUT

No, no; I have a good number of twinges for you tonight, and you may be sure of some more tomorrow.

MR. F.

What, with such a fever! I shall go distracted. Oh! eh! Can no one bear it for me?

THE GOUT

Ask that of your horses; they have served you faithfully.

MR. F.

How can you so cruelly sport with my torments?

THE GOUT

Sport! I am very serious. I have here a list of offences against your own health distinctly written, and can justify every stroke inflicted on you.

MR. F.

Read it then.

THE GOUT

It is too long a detail; but I will briefly mention some particulars.

MR. F.

Proceed. I am all attention.

THE GOUT

Do you remember how often you have promised yourself, the following morning, a walk in the grove of Boulogne, in the garden de La Muette, or in your own garden, and have violated your promise, alleging, at one time, it was too cold, at another too warm, too windy, too moist, or what else you pleased; when in truth it was too nothing but your insuperable love of ease?

MR. F.

That I confess may have happened occasionally, probably ten times in a year.

THE GOUT

Your confession is very far short of the truth; the gross amount is one hundred and ninety-nine times.

MR. F.

Is it possible?

THE GOUT

So possible that it is fact; you may rely on the accuracy of my statement. You know M. Brillon's gardens, and what fine walks they contain; you know the handsome flight of an hundred steps which lead from the terrace above to the lawn below. You have been in the practice of visiting this amiable family twice a week, after dinner, and it is a maxim of your own, that "a man may take as much exercise in walking a mile up and down stairs, as in ten on level ground." What an opportunity was here for you to have had exercise in both these ways! Did you embrace it, and how often?

MR. F.

I cannot immediately answer that question.

THE GOUT

I will do it for you; not once.

MR. F.

Not once?

THE GOUT

Even so. During the summer you went there at six o'clock. You found the charming lady, with her lovely children and friends, eager to walk with you, and entertain you with their agreeable conversation; and what has been your choice? Why, to sit on the terrace, satisfying yourself with the fine prospect, and passing your eye over the beauties of the garden below, without taking one step to descend and walk about in them. On the contrary, you call for tea and the chess-board; and lo! you are occupied in your seat till nine o'clock, and that besides two hours' play after dinner; and then, instead of walking home, which would have bestirred you a little, you step into your carriage. How absurd to suppose that all this carelessness can be reconcilable with health, without my interposition!

MR. F.

I am convinced now of the justness of Poor Richard's remark, that "Our debts and our sins are always greater than we think for."

THE GOUT

So it is. You philosophers are sages in your maxims, and fools in your conduct.

MR. F.

But do you charge among my crimes that I return in a carriage from M. Brillon's?

THE GOUT

Certainly; for having been seated all the while, you cannot object the fatigue of the day, and cannot want therefore the relief of a carriage.

MR. F.

What then would you have me do with my carriage?

THE GOUT

Burn it if you choose; you would at least get heat out of it once in this way; or if you dislike that proposal, here's another for you; observe the poor peasants who work in the vineyards and grounds about the villages of Passy, Auteuil, Chaillot, etc.; you may find every day among these deserving creatures four or five old men and women, bent and perhaps crippled by weight of years, and too long and too great labour. After a most fatiguing day these people have to trudge a mile or two to their smoky huts. Order your coachman to set them down. This is an act that will be good for your soul; and, at the same time, after your visit to the Brillons, if you return on foot, that will be good for your body.

MR. F.

Ah! how tiresome you are!

THE GOUT

Well, then, to my office; it should not be forgotten that I am your physician. There.

MR. F.

Ohhh! what a devil of a physician!

THE GOUT

How ungrateful you are to say so! Is it not I who, in the character of your physician, have saved you from the palsy, dropsy, and apoplexy? One or other of which would have done for you long ago but for me.

MR. F.

I submit, and thank you for the past, but entreat the discontinuance of your visits for the future; for in my mind, one had better die than be cured so dolefully. Permit me just to hint that I have also not been unfriendly to *you*. I never feed physician or quack of any kind, to enter the list against you; if then you do not leave me to my repose, it may be said you are ungrateful too.

THE GOUT

I can scarcely acknowledge that as any objection. As to quacks, I despise them; they may kill you indeed, but cannot injure me. And as to regular physicians, they are at last convinced that the gout, in such a subject as you are, is no disease, but a remedy; and wherefore cure a remedy?—but to our business—there.

MR. F.

Oh! oh!—for Heaven's sake leave me! and I promise faithfully never more to play at chess, but to take exercise daily, and live temperately.

THE GOUT

I know you too well. You promise fair; but, after a few months of good health, you will return to your old habits; your fine promises will be forgotten like the forms of the last year's clouds. Let us then finish the account, and I will go. But I leave you with an assurance of visiting you again at a proper time and place; for my object is your good, and you are sensible now that I am your *real friend*.

The Handsome and the Deformed Leg

There are two Sorts of People in the World, who with equal Degrees of Health & Wealth and the other Comforts of Life, become, the one happy, the other unhappy. This arises very much from the different Views in which they consider Things, Persons, and Events; and the Effect of those different Views upon their own Minds.

In whatever Situation Men can be plac'd, they may find Conveniencies and Inconveniencies: In whatever Company, they may find Persons & Conversations more or less pleasing: At whatever Table they may meet with Meats and Drinks of better and worse Taste, Dishes better and worse dress'd: In whatever Climate they will find good and bad Weather: Under whatever Government, they may find good and bad Laws, and good and bad Administration of those Laws: In every Poem or Work of Genius, they may see Faults and Beauties: In almost every Face & every Person, they may discover fine Features and Defects, good & bad Qualities. Under these Circumstances, the two Sorts of People above-mention'd fix their Attention, those who are to be happy, on the Conveniencies of Things, the pleasant Parts of Conversation, the well-dress'd & well-tasted Dishes, the Goodness of the Wines, the Fine Weather, &c. &c. &c. and enjoy all with Chearfulness: Those who are to be unhappy think and speak only of the contraries. Hence they are continually discontented themselves, and by their Remarks sour the Pleasures of Society, offend personally many People, and make themselves every where disagreable.

If this Turn of Mind was founded in Nature, such unhappy Persons would be the more to be pitied. But as the Disposition to criticise and be disgusted is perhaps taken up originally by Imitation, and unawares grown into a Habit, which tho at present strong, may nevertheless be cured, when those who have it are convinc'd of its bad Effects on their Felicity, I hope this little Admonition may be of Service to them, and put them on changing a Habit, which tho in the Exercise is chiefly an Act of Imagination, yet it has serious Consequences in Life, as it brings on real Griefs and Misfortunes: For, as many are offended by, and nobody well loves this sort of People, no one shows them more than the most common Civility & Respect, and scarcely that; and this frequently puts them out of humour, and draws them into Disputes and Contentions. If they aim at obtaining some Advantage in Rank or Fortune, nobody wishes them Success, or will stir a Step, or speak a Word to favour their Pretensions. If they incur public Censure or Disgrace, no one will defend or excuse, and many join to aggravate their Misconduct, and render them compleatly odious. —

If these People will not change this bad Habit, and condescend to be pleas'd with what is pleasing, without fretting themselves and others about the Contraries, it is good for others to avoid an Acquaintance with them, which is always disagreable, and sometimes very inconvenient, particularly when one finds one's self entangled in their Quarrels. An old philosophical Friend of mine was grown from Experience very cautious in this particular and carefully shun'd any intimacy with such People. He had, like other Philosophers, a Thermometer to show him the Heat of the Weather, & a Barometer to mark when it was likely to prove good or bad; but there being no Instrument yet invented to discover at first Sight this unpleasing Disposition in a Person, he for that purpose made use of his Legs; one of which was remarkably handsome, the other by some Accident crooked and deform'd. If a Stranger, at the first Interview, regarded his ugly

Leg more than his handsome one, he doubted him. If he spoke of it, and took no Notice of the handsome Leg, that was sufficient to determine my Philosopher to have no farther Acquaintance with him.

Everybody has not this two-legged Instrument, but everyone with a little Attention may observe Signs of that carping fault-finding Disposition; and take the same Resolution of avoiding the Acquaintance of those infected with it.

I therefore advise these critical, querulous, discontented unhappy People, that if they wish to be loved & respected by others and happy in themselves, they should *leave off looking at the ugly Leg*.

November, 1780

To the Royal Academy of *****

GENTLEMEN,

I have perused your late mathematical Prize Question, proposed in lieu of one in Natural Philosophy, for the ensuing year, viz. *"Une figure quelconque donnée, on demande d'y inscrire le plus grand nombre de fois possible une autre figure pluspetite quelconque, qui est aussi donnée"*. I was glad to find by these following Words, *"l'Académie a jugé que cette découverte, en étendant les bornes de nos connoissances, ne seroit pas sans UTILITÉ"*, that you esteem *Utility* an essential Point in your Enquiries, which has not always been the case with all Academies; and I conclude therefore that you have given this Question instead of a philosophical, or as the Learned express it, a physical one, because you could not at the time think of a physical one that promis'd greater *Utility*.

Permit me then humbly to propose one of that sort for your consideration, and through you, if you approve it, for the serious Enquiry of learned Physicians, Chemists, &c. of this enlightened Age.

It is universally well known, That in digesting our common Food, there is created or produced in the Bowels of human Creatures, a great Quantity of Wind.

That the permitting this Air to escape and mix with the Atmosphere, is usually offensive to the Company, from the fetid Smell that accompanies it.

That all well-bred People therefore, to avoid giving such Offence, forcibly restrain the Efforts of Nature to discharge that Wind.

That so retain'd contrary to Nature, it not only gives frequently great present Pain, but occasions future Diseases, such as habitual Cholics, Ruptures, Tympanies, &c. often destructive of the Constitution, & sometimes of Life itself.

Were it not for the odiously offensive Smell accompanying such Escapes, polite People would probably be under no more Restraint in discharging such Wind in Company, than they are in spitting, or in blowing their Noses.

My Prize Question therefore should be, *To discover some Drug wholesome & not disagreable, to be mix'd with our common Food, or Sauces, that shall render the natural Discharges of Wind from our Bodies, not only inoffensive, but agreable as Perfumes.*

That this is not a chimerical Project, and altogether impossible, may appear from these Considerations. That we already have some Knowledge of Means capable of *Varying* that Smell. He that dines on stale Flesh, especially with much Addition of Onions, shall be able to afford a Stink that no Company can tolerate; while he that has lived for some Time on Vegetables only, shall have that Breath so pure as to be insensible to the most delicate Noses; and if he can manage so as to avoid the Report, he may any where give Vent to his Griefs, unnoticed. But as there are many to whom an entire Vegetable Diet would be inconvenient, and as a little Quick-Lime thrown into a Jakes will correct the amazing Quantity of fetid Air arising from the vast Mass of putrid Matter contain'd in such Places, and render it rather pleasing to the Smell, who knows but that a little Powder of Lime (or some other thing equivalent) taken in our Food, or perhaps a Glass of Limewater drank at Dinner, may have the same Effect on the Air produc'd in and issuing from our Bowels? This is worth the Experiment. Certain it is also that we have the Power of changing by slight Means the Smell of another Discharge, that of our Water. A few Stems of Asparagus eaten, shall give our Urine a disagreable Odour; and a Pill of

Turpentine no bigger than a Pea, shall bestow on it the pleasing Smell of Violets. And why should it be thought more
impossible in Nature, to find Means of making a Perfume of
our *Wind* than of our *Water*?

For the Encouragement of this Enquiry, (from the immortal Honour to be reasonably expected by the Inventor) let it
be considered of how small Importance to Mankind, or to
how small a Part of Mankind have been useful those Discoveries in Science that have heretofore made Philosophers
famous. Are there twenty Men in Europe at this Day, the
happier, or even the easier, for any Knowledge they have
pick'd out of Aristotle? What Comfort can the Vortices of
Descartes give to a Man who has Whirlwinds in his Bowels!
The Knowledge of Newton's mutual *Attraction* of the Particles of Matter, can it afford Ease to him who is rack'd by their
mutual *Repulsion*, and the cruel Distensions it occasions? The
Pleasure arising to a few Philosophers, from seeing, a few
Times in their Life, the Threads of Light untwisted, and separated by the Newtonian Prism into seven Colours, can it be
compared with the Ease and Comfort every Man living might
feel seven times a Day, by discharging freely the Wind from
his Bowels? Especially if it be converted into a Perfume: For
the Pleasures of one Sense being little inferior to those of
another, instead of pleasing the *Sight* he might delight the
Smell of those about him, & make Numbers happy, which
to a benevolent Mind must afford infinite Satisfaction. The
generous Soul, who now endeavours to find out whether
the Friends he entertains like best Claret or Burgundy,
Champagne or Madeira, would then enquire also whether
they chose Musk or Lilly, Rose or Bergamot, and provide
accordingly. And surely such a Liberty of *Ex-pressing* one's
Scent-iments, and *pleasing one another*, is of infinitely more
Importance to human Happiness than that Liberty of the
Press, or of *abusing one another*, which the English are so
ready to fight & die for.—In short, this Invention, if
compleated, would be, as *Bacon* expresses it, *bringing Philosophy home to Mens Business and Bosoms*. And I cannot but conclude, that in Comparison therewith, for *universal* and
continual UTILITY, the Science of the Philosophers above-
mentioned, even with the Addition, Gentlemen, of your

"Figure quelconque" and the Figures inscrib'd in it, are, all together, scarcely worth a

FART-HING.

Passy, c. 1781

Notes for Conversation

To make a Peace durable, what may give Occasion for future Wars should if practicable be removed.

The Territory of the United States and that of Canada, by long extended Frontiers, touch each other.

The Settlers on the Frontiers of the American Provinces are generally the most disorderly of the People, who, being far removed from the Eye and Controll of their respective Governments, are more bold in committing Offences against Neighbours, and are for ever occasioning Complaints and furnishing Matter for fresh Differences between their States.

By the late Debates in Parliament, and publick Writings, it appears, that Britain desires a *Reconciliation* with the Americans. It is a sweet Word. It means much more than a mere Peace, and what is heartily to be wish'd for. Nations make a Peace whenever they are both weary of making War. But, if one of them has made War upon the other unjustly, and has wantonly and unnecessarily done it great Injuries, and refuses Reparation, though there may, for the present, be Peace, the Resentment of those Injuries will remain, and will break out again in Vengeance when Occasions offer. These Occasions will be watch'd for by one side, fear'd by the other, and the Peace will never be secure; nor can any Cordiality subsist between them.

Many Houses and Villages have been burnt in America by the English and their Allies, the Indians. I do not know that the Americans will insist on reparation; perhaps they may. But would it not be better for England to offer it? Nothing could have a greater Tendency to conciliate, and much of the future Commerce and returning Intercourse between the two Countries may depend on the Reconciliation. Would not the advantage of Reconciliation by such means be greater than the Expence?

If then a Way can be proposed, which may tend to efface

the Memory of Injuries, at the same time that it takes away the Occasions of fresh Quarrel and Mischief, will it not be worth considering, especially if it can be done, not only without Expence, but be a means of saving?

Britain possesses Canada. Her chief Advantage from that Possession consists in the Trade for Peltry. Her Expences in governing and defending that Settlement must be considerable. It might be humiliating to her to give it up on the Demand of America. Perhaps America will not demand it; some of her political Rulers may consider the fear of such a Neighbour, as a means of keeping 13 States more united among themselves, and more attentive to Military Discipline. But on the Minds of the People in general would it not have an excellent Effect, if Britain should voluntarily offer to give up this Province; tho' on these Conditions, that she shall in all times coming have and enjoy the Right of Free Trade thither, unincumbred with any Duties whatsoever; that so much of the vacant Lands there shall be sold, as will raise a Sum sufficient to pay for the Houses burnt by the British Troops and their Indians; and also to indemnify the Royalists for the Confiscation of their Estates?

This is mere Conversation matter between Mr. O. and Mr. F., as the former is not impower'd to make Propositions, and the latter cannot make any without the Concurrence of his Colleagues.

April 18, 1782

Numb. 705.
Supplement to the Boston Independent Chronicle

BOSTON, March 12.
Extract of a Letter from Capt. Gerrish, *of the* New-England *Militia, dated* Albany, March 7.
——The Peltry taken in the Expedition [*See the Account of the Expedition to* Oswegatchie *on the River St.* Laurence, *in our Paper of the* 1st *Instant.*] will as you see amount to a good deal of Money. The Possession of this Booty at first gave us Plea-

sure; but we were struck with Horror to find among the Packages, 8 large ones containing SCALPS of our unhappy Country-folks, taken in the three last Years by the Senneka Indians from the Inhabitants of the Frontiers of New-York, New-Jersey, Pennsylvania, and Virginia, and sent by them as a Present to Col. Haldimand, Governor of Canada, in order to be by him transmitted to England. They were accompanied by the following curious Letter to that Gentleman.

May it please your Excellency,   *Teoga, Jan.* 3*d,* 1782.
    "At the Request of the Senneka Chiefs I send herewith to your Excellency, under the Care of James Boyd, eight Packs of Scalps, cured, dried, hooped and painted, with all the Indian triumphal Marks, of which the following is Invoice and Explanation.

No. 1. Containing 43 Scalps of Congress Soldiers killed in different Skirmishes; these are stretched on black Hoops, 4 Inches diameter; the inside of the Skin painted red, with a small black Spot to note their being killed with Bullets. Also 62 of Farmers, killed in their Houses; the Hoops red; the Skin painted brown, and marked with a Hoe; a black Circle all round, to denote their being surprised in the Night; and a black Hatchet in the Middle, signifying their being killed with that Weapon.

No. 2. Containing 98 of Farmers killed in their Houses; Hoops red; Figure of a Hoe, to mark their Profession; great white Circle and Sun, to shew they were surprised in the Day-time; a little red Foot, to shew they stood upon their Defence, and died fighting for their Lives and Families.

No. 3. Containing 97 of Farmers; Hoops green, to shew they were killed in their Fields; a large white Circle with a little round Mark on it for the Sun, to shew that it was in the Day-time; black Bullet-mark on some, Hatchet on others.

No. 4. Containing 102 of Farmers, mixed of the several Marks above; only 18 marked with a little yellow Flame, to denote their being of Prisoners burnt alive, after being scalped, their Nails pulled out by the Roots, and other

Torments: one of these latter supposed to be of a rebel Clergyman, his Band being fixed to the Hoop of his Scalp. Most of the Farmers appear by the Hair to have been young or middle-aged Men; there being but 67 very grey Heads among them all; which makes the Service more essential.

No. 5. Containing 88 Scalps of Women; Hair long, braided in the Indian Fashion, to shew they were Mothers; Hoops blue; Skin yellow Ground, with little red Tadpoles to represent, by way of Triumph, the Tears or Grief occasioned to their Relations; a black scalping Knife or Hatchet at the Bottom, to mark their being killed with those Instruments. 17 others, Hair very grey; black Hoops; plain brown Colour; no Mark but the short Club or Cassetete, to shew they were knocked down dead, or had their Brains beat out.

No. 6. Containing 193 Boys' Scalps, of various Ages; small green Hoops; whitish Ground on the Skin, with red Tears in the Middle, and black Bullet-marks, Knife, Hatchet, or Club, as their Deaths happened.

No. 7. 211 Girls' Scalps, big and little; small yellow Hoops; white Ground; Tears; Hatchet, Club, scalping Knife, &c.

No. 8. This Package is a Mixture of all the Varieties abovemention'd, to the Number of 122; with a Box of Birch Bark, containing 29 little Infants' Scalps of various Sizes; small white Hoops; white Ground; no Tears; and only a little black Knife in the Middle, to shew they were ript out of their Mothers' Bellies.

With these Packs, the Chiefs send to your Excellency the following Speech, delivered by Conejogatchie in Council, interpreted by the elder Moore, the Trader, and taken down by me in Writing.

Father,

We send you herewith many Scalps, that you may see we are not idle Friends.

A blue Belt.

Father,

We wish you to send these Scalps over the Water to the great King, that he may regard them and be refreshed; and that he may see our faithfulness in destroying his Enemies, and be convinced that his Presents have not been made to ungrateful people.

A blue and white Belt with red Tassels.

Father,

Attend to what I am now going to say: it is a Matter of much Weight. The great King's Enemies are many, and they grow fast in Number. They were formerly like young Panthers: they could neither bite nor scratch: we could play with them safely: we feared nothing they could do to us. But now their Bodies are become big as the Elk, and strong as the Buffalo: they have also got great and sharp Claws. They have driven us out of our Country for taking Part in your Quarrel. We expect the great King will give us another Country, that our Children may live after us, and be his Friends and Children, as we are. Say this for us to the great King. To enforce it we give this Belt.

A great white Belt with blue Tassels.

Father,

We have only to say farther that your Traders exact more than ever for their Goods: and our Hunting is lessened by the War, so that we have fewer Skins to give for them. This ruins us. Think of some Remedy. We are poor: and you have Plenty of every Thing. We know you will send us Powder and Guns, and Knives and Hatchets: but we also want Shirts and Blankets.

A little white Belt.

I do not doubt but that your Excellency will think it proper to give some farther Encouragement to those honest People. The high Prices they complain of, are the necessary Effect of the War. Whatever Presents may be sent for them through my Hands, shall be distributed with Prudence and Fidelity. I have the Honour of being

> Your Excellency's most obedient
> And most humble Servant,
> JAMES CRAUFURD."

It was at first proposed to bury these Scalps: but Lieutenant Fitzgerald, who you know has got Leave of Absence to go for Ireland on his private Affairs, said he thought it better they should proceed to their Destination; and if they were given to him, he would undertake to carry them to England, and hang them all up in some dark Night on the Trees in St. James's Park, where they could be seen from the King and Queen's Palaces in the Morning; for that the Sight of them might perhaps strike Muley Ishmael (as he called him) with some Compunction of Conscience. They were accordingly delivered to Fitz, and he has brought them safe hither. To-morrow they go with his Baggage in a Waggon for Boston, and will probably be there in a few Days after this Letter.

I am, &c.

SAMUEL GERRISH.

BOSTON, March 20.

Monday last arrived here Lieutenant Fitzgerald abovementioned, and Yesterday the Waggon with the Scalps. Thousands of People are flocking to see them this Morning, and all Mouths are full of Execrations. Fixing them to the Trees is not approved. It is now proposed to make them up in decent little Packets, seal and direct them; one to the King, containing a Sample of every Sort for his Museum; one to the Queen, with some of Women and little Children: the Rest to be distributed among both Houses of Parliament; a double Quantity to the Bishops.

Mr. Willis,

Please to insert in your useful Paper the following Copy of a Letter, from Commodore Jones, directed

To Sir Joseph York, Ambassador from the King of England to the States-general of the United Provinces.

Ipswich, New-England,

Sir,   *March 7, 1781.*

I have lately seen a memorial, said to have been presented by your Excellency to their High Mightinesses the States-general, in which you are pleased to qualify me with the title of *pirate*.

A pirate is defined to be *hostis humani generis*, [an enemy to all mankind]. It happens, Sir, that I am an enemy to no part of mankind, except your nation, the English; which nation at the same time comes much more within the definition; being actually an enemy to, and at war with, one whole quarter of the world, America, considerable parts of Asia and Africa, a great part of Europe, and in a fair way of being at war with the rest.

A pirate makes war for the sake of *rapine*. This is not the kind of war I am engaged in against England. Our's is a war in defence of *liberty* . . . . the most just of all wars; and of our *properties*, which your nation would have taken from us, without our consent, in violation of our rights, and by an armed force. Your's, therefore, is a war of *rapine*; of course, a piratical war: and those who approve of it, and are engaged in it, more justly deserve the name of pirates, which you bestow on me. It is, indeed, a war that coincides with the general spirit of your nation. Your common people in their alehouses sing the twenty-four songs of Robin Hood, and applaud his deer-stealing and his robberies on the highway: those who have just learning enough to read, are delighted with your histories of the pirates and of the buccaniers: and even your scholars, in the universities, study Quintus Curtius; and are taught to admire Alexander, for what they call "his conquests in the Indies." Severe laws and the hangmen keep down the effects of this spirit somewhat among yourselves, (though in your little island you have, nevertheless, more highway robberies than there are in all the rest of Europe put together): but a foreign war gives it full scope. It is then that, with infinite pleasure, it lets itself loose to strip of their property honest merchants, employed in the innocent and useful occupation of supplying the mutual wants of mankind. Hence, having lately no war with your ancient enemies, rather than be without a war, you chose to make one upon your friends. In this your piratical war with America, the mariners of your fleets, and the owners of your privateers were animated against us by the act of your parliament, which repealed the law of God—"Thou shalt not steal,"—by declaring it lawful for them to rob us of all our property that they could meet with on the Ocean. This act too had a retrospect, and, going beyond bulls of pardon, declared that all the robberies you *had committed*, previous to the act, should be *deemed just and lawful*. Your soldiers too were promised the plunder of our cities: and your officers were flattered with the division of our lands. You had even the baseness to corrupt our servants, the sailors employed by us, and encourage them to rob their masters, and bring to you the ships and goods they were entrusted with. Is there any society of pirates on the sea or land, who, in declaring wrong to be right, and right wrong, have less authority than your parliament? Do any of them more justly than your parliament deserve the *title* you bestow on me?

You will tell me that we forfeited all our estates by our refusal to pay the taxes your nation would have imposed on us, without the consent of our colony parliaments. Have you then forgot the incontestible principle, which was the foundation of Hambden's glorious lawsuit with Charles the first, that " what an English king has no right to demand, an English subject has a right to refuse?" But you cannot so soon have forgotten the instructions of your late honourable father, who, being himself a sound Whig, taught you certainly the principles of the Revolution, and that, "if subjects might in some cases forfeit their property, kings also might forfeit their title, and all claim to the allegiance of their subjects." I must then suppose you well acquainted with those Whig principles, on which permit me, Sir, to ask a few questions.

Is not protection as justly due from a king to his people, as obedience from the people to their king?

If then a king declares his people to be out of his protection:

If he violates and deprives them of their constitutional rights:

If he wages war against them:

If he plunders their merchants, ravages their coasts, burns their towns, and destroys their lives:

If he hires foreign mercenaries to help him in their destruction:

If he engages savages to murder their defenceless farmers, women, and children:

If he cruelly forces such of his subjects as fall into his hands, to bear arms against their country, and become executioners of their friends and brethren:

If he sells others of them into bondage, in Africa and the East Indies:

If he excites domestic insurrections among their servants, and encourages servants to murder their masters: ——

Does not so atrocious a conduct towards his subjects, dissolve their allegiance?

If not,—please to say how or by what means it can possibly be dissolved?

All this horrible wickedness and barbarity has been and daily is practised by the king *your master* (as you call him in your memorial) upon the Americans, whom he is still pleased to claim as his subjects.

During these six years past, he has destroyed not less than forty thousand of those subjects, by battles on land or sea, or by starving them, or poisoning them to death, in the unwholesome air, with the unwholesome food of his prisons. And he has wasted the lives of at least an equal number of his own soldiers and sailors: many of whom have been *forced* into this odious service, and *dragged* from their families and friends, by the outrageous violence of his illegal press-gangs. You are a gentleman of letters, and have read history: do you recollect any instance of any tyrant, since the beginning of the world, who, in the course of so few years, had done so much mischief, by murdering so many of his own people? Let us view one of the worst and blackest of them, Nero. He put to death a few of his courtiers, placemen, and pensioners, and among the rest his *tutor*. Had George the third done the same, and no more, his crime, though detestable, as an act of lawless power, might have been as useful to his nation, as that of Nero was hurtful to Rome; considering the different characters and merits of the sufferers. Nero indeed wished that the people of Rome had but one neck, that he might behead them all by one stroke: but this was a simple wish. George is carrying the wish as fast as he can into execution; and, by continuing in his present course a few years longer, will have destroyed more of the British people than Nero could have found inhabitants in Rome. Hence, the expression of Milton, in speaking of Charles the first, that he was *"Nerone Neronior,"* is still more applicable to George the third. Like Nero and all other tyrants, while they lived, he indeed has his flatterers, his addressers, his applauders. Pensions, places, and hopes of preferment, can bribe even bishops to approve his conduct: but, when those fulsome, purchased addresses and panegyrics are sunk and lost in oblivion or contempt, impartial history will step forth, speak honest truth, and rank him among public calamities. The only difference will be, that plagues, pestilences, and famines are of this world, and arise from the nature of things: but voluntary malice, mischief, and murder are all from Hell: and this King will, therefore, stand foremost in the list of diabolical, bloody, and execrable tyrants. His base-bought parliaments too, who sell him their souls, and extort from the people the money with which they aid his destructive purposes, as they share his guilt, will share his infamy,—parliaments, who to please him, have repeatedly, by different votes year after year, dipped their hands in human blood, insomuch that methinks I see it dried and caked so thick upon them, that if they could wash it off in the Thames which flows under their windows, the whole river would run red to the Ocean.

One is provoked by enormous wickedness: but one is ashamed and humiliated at the view of human baseness. It afflicts me, therefore, to see a gentleman of Sir Joseph York's education and talents, for the sake of a red riband and a paltry stipend, mean enough to stile such a monster *his master*, wear his livery, and hold himself ready at his command even to cut the throats of fellow-subjects. This makes it impossible for me to end my letter with the civility of a compliment, and obliges me to subscribe myself simply,

JOHN PAUL JONES,
whom you are pleased to stile a *Pirate*.

Passy, April, 1782

Articles for a Treaty of Peace with Madame Brillon

Passy, July 27.

What a difference, my dear Friend, between you and me!—You find my Faults so many as to be innumerable, while I can see but one in you; and perhaps that is the Fault of my Spectacles.—The Fault I mean is that kind of Covetousness, by which you would engross all my Affection, and permit me none for the other amiable Ladies of your Country. You seem to imagine that it cannot be divided without being diminish'd: In which you mistake the nature of the Thing and forget the Situation in which you have plac'd and hold me. You renounce and exclude arbitrarily every thing corporal from our Amour, except such a merely civil Embrace now and then as you would permit to a country Cousin,— what is there then remaining that I may not afford to others without a Diminution of what belongs to you? The Operations of the Mind, Esteem, Admiration, Respect, & even Affection for one Object, may be multiply'd as more Objects that merit them present themselves, and yet remain the same to the first, which therefore has no room to complain of Injury. They are in their Nature as divisible as the sweet Sounds of the Forte Piano produc'd by your exquisite Skill: Twenty People may receive the same Pleasure from them, without lessening that which you kindly intend for me; and I might as reasonably require of your Friendship, that they should reach and delight no Ears but mine.

You see by this time how unjust you are in your Demands, and in the open War you declare against me if I do not comply with them. Indeed it is I that have the most Reason to complain. My poor little Boy, whom you ought methinks to have cherish'd, instead of being fat and Jolly like those in your elegant Drawings, is meagre and starv'd almost to death for want of the substantial Nourishment which you his Mother inhumanly deny him, and yet would now clip his little Wings to prevent his seeking it elsewhere!—

I fancy we shall neither of us get any thing by this War, and therefore as feeling my self the Weakest, I will do what indeed ought always to be done by the Wisest, be first in making the Propositions for Peace. That a Peace may be lasting, the Articles of the Treaty should be regulated upon the Principles of the most perfect Equity & Reciprocity. In this View I have drawn up & offer the following, viz.—

ARTICLE I.

There shall be eternal Peace, Friendship & Love, between Madame B. and Mr F.

ARTICLE 2.

In order to maintain the same inviolably, Made B. on her Part stipulates and agrees, that Mr F. shall come to her whenever she sends for him.

ART. 3.

That he shall stay with her as long as she pleases.

ART. 4.

That when he is with her, he shall be oblig'd to drink Tea, play Chess, hear Musick; or do any other thing that she requires of him.

ART. 5.

And that he shall love no other Woman but herself.

ART. 6.

And the said Mr F. on his part stipulates and agrees, that he will go away from M. B.'s whenever he pleases.

ART. 7.

That he will stay away as long as he pleases.

ART. 8.

That when he is with her, he will do what he pleases.

ART. 9.

And that he will love any other Woman as far as he finds her amiable.

Let me know what you think of these Preliminaries. To me they seem to express the true Meaning and Intention of each Party more plainly than most Treaties.—I shall insist pretty strongly on the eighth Article, tho' without much Hope of your Consent to it; and on the ninth also, tho I despair of ever finding any other Woman that I could love with equal Tenderness: being ever, my dear dear Friend,

Yours most sincerely

1782

Apologue

Lion, king of a certain forest, had among his subjects a body of faithful dogs, in principle and affection strongly attached to his person and government, but through whose assistance he had extended his dominions, and had become the terror of his enemies.

Lion, however, influenced by evil counsellors, took an aversion to the dogs, condemned them unheard, and ordered his tigers, leopards, and panthers to attack and destroy them.

The dogs petitioned humbly, but their petitions were rejected haughtily; and they were forced to defend themselves, which they did with bravery.

A few among them, of a mongrel race, derived from a mixture with wolves and foxes, corrupted by royal promises of great rewards, deserted the honest dogs and joined their enemies.

The dogs were finally victorious: a treaty of peace was made, in which Lion acknowledged them to be free, and disclaimed all future authority over them.

The mongrels not being permitted to return among them, claimed of the royalists the reward that had been promised.

A council of the beasts was held to consider their demand.

The wolves and the foxes agreed unanimously that the demand was just, that royal promises ought to be kept, and that every loyal subject should contribute freely to enable his majesty to fulfil them.

The horse alone, with a boldness and freedom that became the nobleness of his nature, delivered a contrary opinion.

"The King," said he, "has been misled, by bad ministers, to war unjustly upon his faithful subjects. Royal promises, when made to encourage us to act for the public good, should indeed be honourably acquitted; but if to encourage us to betray and destroy each other, they are wicked and void from the beginning. The advisers of such promises, and those who murdered in consequence of them, instead of being recompensed, should be severely punished. Consider how greatly our common strength is already diminished by our loss of the dogs. If you enable the King to reward those fratricides, you will establish a precedent that may justify a future tyrant to make like promises; and every example of such an unnatural brute rewarded will give them additional weight. Horses and bulls, as well as dogs, may thus be divided against their own kind, and civil wars produced at pleasure, till we are so weakened that neither liberty nor safety is any longer to be found in the forest, and nothing remains but abject submission to the will of a despot, who may devour us as he pleases."

The council had sense enough to resolve—that the demand be rejected.

c. November, 1782

Remarks Concerning the Savages of North-America

Savages we call them, because their manners differ from ours, which we think the Perfection of Civility; they think the same of theirs.

Perhaps if we could examine the manners of different Nations with Impartiality, we should find no People so rude as to be without any Rules. of Politeness; nor any so polite as not to have some remains of Rudeness.

The Indian Men, when young, are Hunters and Warriors; when old, Counsellors; for all their Government is by the Counsel or Advice of the Sages; there is no Force, there are no Prisons, no Officers to compel Obedience, or inflict Punishment. Hence they generally study Oratory; the best Speaker having the most Influence. The Indian Women till the Ground, dress the Food, nurse and bring up the Children, and preserve and hand down to Posterity the Memory of Public Transactions. These Employments of Men and Women are accounted natural and honorable. Having few Artificial Wants, they have abundance of Leisure for Improvement by Conversation. Our laborious manner of Life compared with theirs, they esteem slavish and base; and the Learning on which we value ourselves; they regard as frivolous and useless. An Instance of this occurred at the Treaty of Lancaster in Pennsylvania, Anno 1744, between the Government of Virginia & the Six Nations. After the principal Business was settled, the Commissioners from Virginia acquainted the Indians by a Speech, that there was at Williamsburg a College with a Fund for Educating Indian Youth, and that if the Chiefs of the Six-Nations would send down half a dozen of their Sons to that College, the Government would take Care that they should be well provided for, and instructed in all the Learning of the white People. It is one of the Indian Rules of Politeness not to answer a public Proposition the same day that it is made; they think it would be treating it as a light Matter; and that they show it Respect by taking time to consider it, as of a Matter important. They therefore deferred their Answer till the day following; when their Speaker began by expressing their deep Sense of the Kindness of the Virginia Government, in making them that Offer; for we know, says he, that you highly esteem the kind of Learning taught in those Colleges, and that the Maintenance of our Young Men while with you, would be very expensive to you. We are convinced therefore that you mean to do us good by your Proposal, and we thank you heartily. But you who are wise must know, that different Nations have different Conceptions of things; and you will therefore not take it amiss, if our Ideas of this Kind of Education happen not to be the same with yours. We have had some Experience of it: Several of our Young People were formerly brought up at the Colleges of the Northern Provinces; they were instructed in all your Sciences; but when they came back to us, they were bad Runners, ignorant of every means of living in the Woods, unable to bear either Cold or Hunger, knew neither how to build a Cabin, take a Deer, or kill an Enemy, spoke our Language imperfectly; were therefore neither fit for Hunters, Warriors, or Counsellors; they were totally good for nothing. We are however not the less obliged by your kind Offer, tho' we decline accepting it; and to show our grateful Sense of it, if the Gentlemen of Virginia will send us a dozen of their Sons, we will take great Care of their Education, instruct them in all we know, and make *Men* of them.

Having frequent Occasions to hold public Councils, they have acquired great Order and Decency in conducting them. The old Men sit in the foremost Ranks, the Warriors in the next, and the Women and Children in the hindmost. The Business of the Women is to take exact notice of what passes, imprint it in their Memories, for they have no Writing, and communicate it to their Children. They are the Records of the Council, and they preserve Tradition of the Stipulations in Treaties a hundred Years back, which when we compare with our Writings we always find exact. He that would speak, rises. The rest observe a profound Silence. When he has finished and sits down, they leave him five or six Minutes to recollect, that if he has omitted any thing he intended to say, or has any thing to add, he may rise again and deliver it. To interrupt another, even in common Conversation, is reckoned highly indecent. How different this is from the Conduct of a

polite British House of Commons, where scarce a Day passes
without some Confusion that makes the Speaker hoarse in
calling *to order*; and how different from the mode of Conversation in many polite Companies of Europe, where if you do
not deliver your Sentence with great Rapidity, you are cut off
in the middle of it by the impatient Loquacity of those you
converse with, & never suffer'd to finish it.

The Politeness of these Savages in Conversation is indeed
carried to excess, since it does not permit them to contradict,
or deny the Truth of what is asserted in their Presence. By
this means they indeed avoid Disputes, but then it becomes
difficult to know their Minds, or what Impression you make
upon them. The Missionaries who have attempted to convert
them to Christianity, all complain of this as one of the great
Difficulties of their Mission. The Indians hear with Patience
the Truths of the Gospel explained to them, and give their
usual Tokens of Assent and Approbation: you would think
they were convinced. No such Matter. It is mere Civility.

A Suedish Minister having assembled the Chiefs of the Sasquehanah Indians, made a Sermon to them, acquainting them
with the principal historical Facts on which our Religion is
founded, such as the Fall of our first Parents by Eating an
Apple, the Coming of Christ to repair the Mischief, his
Miracles and Suffering, &c. When he had finished, an Indian
Orator stood up to thank him. What you have told us, says he,
is all very good. It is indeed bad to eat Apples. It is better to
make them all into Cyder. We are much obliged by your
Kindness in coming so far to tell us those things which you
have heard from your Mothers. In Return I will tell you some
of those we have heard from ours.

In the Beginning our Fathers had only the Flesh of Animals
to subsist on, and if their Hunting was unsuccessful, they
were starving. Two of our young Hunters having killed a
Deer, made a Fire in the Woods to broil some Parts of it.
When they were about to satisfy their Hunger, they beheld a
beautiful young Woman descend from the Clouds, and seat
herself on that Hill which you see yonder among the blue
Mountains. They said to each other, it is a Spirit that perhaps
has smelt our broiling Venison, & wishes to eat of it: let us
offer some to her. They presented her with the Tongue: She

was pleased with the Taste of it, & said, your Kindness shall be rewarded. Come to this Place after thirteen Moons, and you shall find something that will be of great Benefit in nourishing you and your Children to the latest Generations. They did so, and to their Surprise found Plants they had never seen before, but which from that ancient time have been constantly cultivated among us to our great Advantage. Where her right Hand had touch'd the Ground, they found Maize; where her left Hand had touch'd it, they found Kidney-beans; and where her Backside had sat on it, they found Tobacco. The good Missionary, disgusted with this idle Tale, said, what I delivered to you were sacred Truths; but what you tell me is mere Fable, Fiction & Falsehood. The Indian offended, reply'd, my Brother, it seems your Friends have not done you Justice in your Education; they have not well instructed you in the Rules of common Civility. You saw that we who understand and practise those Rules, believed all your Stories; why do you refuse to believe ours?

When any of them come into our Towns, our People are apt to croud round them, gaze upon them, and incommode them where they desire to be private; this they esteem great Rudeness, and the Effect of want of Instruction in the Rules of Civility and good Manners. We have, say they, as much Curiosity as you, and when you come into our Towns we wish for Opportunities of looking at you; but for this purpose we hide ourselves behind Bushes where you are to pass, and never intrude ourselves into your Company.

Their Manner of entring one anothers Villages has likewise its Rules. It is reckon'd uncivil in travelling Strangers to enter a Village abruptly, without giving Notice of their Approach. Therefore as soon as they arrive within hearing, they stop and hollow, remaining there till invited to enter. Two old Men usually come out to them, and lead them in. There is in every Village a vacant Dwelling, called the Strangers House. Here they are placed, while the old Men go round from Hut to Hut acquainting the Inhabitants that Strangers are arrived, who are probably hungry and weary; and every one sends them what he can spare of Victuals and Skins to repose on. When the Strangers are refresh'd, Pipes & Tobacco are brought; and then, but not before, Conversation begins, with

Enquiries who they are, whither bound, what News, &c. and it usually ends with Offers of Service, if the Strangers have Occasion of Guides or any Necessaries for continuing their Journey; and nothing is exacted for the Entertainment.

The same Hospitality, esteemed among them as a principal Virtue, is practised by private Persons; of which *Conrad Weiser*, our Interpreter, gave me the following Instance. He had been naturaliz'd among the Six-Nations, and spoke well the Mohock Language. In going thro' the Indian Country, to carry a Message from our Governor to the Council at *Onondaga*, he called at the Habitation of *Canassetego*, an old Acquaintance, who embraced him, spread Furs for him to sit on, placed before him some boiled Beans and Venison, and mixed some Rum and Water for his Drink. When he was well refresh'd, and had lit his Pipe, Canassetego began to converse with him, ask'd how he had fared the many Years since they had seen each other, whence he then came, what occasioned the Journey, &c. &c. Conrad answered all his Questions; and when the Discourse began to flag, the Indian, to continue it, said, Conrad, you have liv'd long among the white People, and know something of their Customs; I have been sometimes at Albany, and have observed that once in seven Days, they shut up their Shops and assemble all in the great House; tell me, what it is for? what do they do there? They meet there, says Conrad, to hear & learn *good things*. I do not doubt, says the Indian, that they tell you so; they have told me the same; but I doubt the Truth of what they say, & I will tell you my Reasons. I went lately to Albany to sell my Skins, & buy Blankets, Knives, Powder, Rum, &c. You know I used generally to deal with Hans Hanson; but I was a little inclined this time to try some other Merchants. However I called first upon Hans, and ask'd him what he would give for Beaver; He said he could not give more than four Shillings a Pound; but, says he, I cannot talk on Business now; this is the Day when we meet together to learn *good things*, and I am going to the Meeting. So I thought to myself since I cannot do any Business to day, I may as well go to the Meeting too; and I went with him. There stood up a Man in black, and began to talk to the People very angrily. I did not understand what he said; but perceiving that he looked much at me, & at Hanson, I imagined he was angry at seeing me there; so I went out, sat down near the House, struck Fire & lit my Pipe; waiting till the Meeting should break up. I thought too, that the Man had mentioned something of Beaver, and I suspected it might be the Subject of their Meeting. So when they came out I accosted any Merchant; well Hans, says I, I hope you have agreed to give more than four Shillings a Pound. No, says he, I cannot give so much. I cannot give more than three Shillings and six Pence. I then spoke to several other Dealers, but they all sung the same Song, three & six Pence, three & six Pence. This made it clear to me that my Suspicion was right; and that whatever they pretended of Meeting to learn *good things*, the real Purpose was to consult, how to cheat Indians in the Price of Beaver. Consider but a little, Conrad, and you must be of my Opinion. If they met so often to learn *good things*, they would certainly have learnt some before this time. But they are still ignorant. You know our Practice. If a white Man in travelling thro' our Country, enters one of our Cabins, we all treat him as I treat you; we dry him if he is wet, we warm him if he is cold, and give him Meat & Drink that he may allay his Thirst and Hunger, & we spread soft Furs for him to rest & sleep on: We demand nothing in return *. But if I go into a white Man's House at Albany, and ask for Victuals & Drink, they say, where is your Money? and if I have none, they say, get out, you Indian Dog. You see they have not yet learnt those little *good things*, that we need no Meetings to be instructed in, because our Mothers taught them to us when we were Children. And therefore it is impossible their Meetings should be as they say for any such purpose, or have any such Effect; they are only to contrive *the Cheating of Indians in the Price of Beaver.*

It is remarkable that in all Ages and Countries, Hospitality has been allowed as the Virtue of those, whom the civiliz'd were pleased to call Barbarians; the Greeks celebrated the Scythians for it. The Saracens possess'd it eminently; and it is to this day the reigning Virtue of the wild Arabs. S. Paul too, in the Relation of his Voyage & Shipwreck, on the Island of Melita, says, The Barbarous People shew'd us no little Kindness; for they kindled a Fire, and received us every one, because of the present Rain & because of the Cold.

Passy, 1783

Information to Those Who Would Remove to America

Many Persons in Europe having directly or by Letters, express'd to the Writer of this, who is well acquainted with North-America, their Desire of transporting and establishing themselves in that Country; but who appear to him to have formed thro' Ignorance, mistaken Ideas & Expectations of what is to be obtained there; he thinks it may be useful, and prevent inconvenient, expensive & fruitless Removals and Voyages of improper Persons, if he gives some clearer & truer Notions of that Part of the World than appear to have hitherto prevailed.

He finds it is imagined by Numbers that the Inhabitants of North-America are rich, capable of rewarding, and dispos'd to reward all sorts of Ingenuity; that they are at the same time ignorant of all the Sciences; & consequently that strangers possessing Talents in the Belles-Letters, fine Arts, &c. must be highly esteemed, and so well paid as to become easily rich themselves; that there are also abundance of profitable Offices to be disposed of, which the Natives are not qualified to fill; and that having few Persons of Family among them, Strangers of Birth must be greatly respected, and of course easily obtain the best of those Offices, which will make all their Fortunes: that the Goverments too, to encourage Emigrations from Europe, not only pay the expence of personal Transportation, but give Lands gratis to Strangers, with Negroes to work for them, Utensils of Husbandry, & Stocks of Cattle. These are all wild Imaginations; and those who go to America with Expectations founded upon them, will surely find themselves disappointed.

The Truth is, that tho' there are in that Country few People so miserable as the Poor of Europe, there are also very few that in Europe would be called rich: it is rather a general happy Mediocrity that prevails. There are few great Proprietors of the Soil, and few Tenants; most People cultivate their own Lands, or follow some Handicraft or Merchandise; very few rich enough to live idly upon their Rents or Incomes; or to pay the high Prices given in Europe, for Paintings, Statues,

Architecture and the other Works of Art that are more curious than useful. Hence the natural Geniuses that have arisen
in America, with such Talents, have uniformly quitted that
Country for Europe, where they can be more suitably rewarded. It is true that Letters and mathematical Knowledge
are in Esteem there, but they are at the same time more common than is apprehended; there being already existing nine
Colleges or Universities, viz. four in New-England, and one
in each of the Provinces of New-York, New-Jersey, Pensilvania, Maryland and Virginia, all furnish'd with learned
Professors; besides a number of smaller Academies: These
educate many of their Youth in the Languages and those Sciences that qualify Men for the Professions of Divinity, Law
or Physick. Strangers indeed are by no means excluded from
exercising those Professions, and the quick Increase of Inhabitants every where gives them a Chance of Employ, which
they have in common with the Natives. Of civil Offices or
Employments there are few; no superfluous Ones as in Europe; and it is a Rule establish'd in some of the States, that
no Office should be so profitable as to make it desirable. The
36 Article of the Constitution of Pensilvania, runs expresly in
these Words: *As every Freeman, to preserve his Independance, (if
he has not a sufficient Estate) ought to have some Profession, Calling, Trade or Farm, whereby he may honestly subsist, there can be
no Necessity for, nor Use in, establishing Offices of Profit; the usual
Effects of which are Dependance and Servility, unbecoming Freemen, in the Possessors and Expectants; Faction, Contention, Cor-
ruption, and Disorder among the People. Wherefore whenever an
Office, thro' Increase of Fees or otherwise, becomes so profitable as
to occasion many to apply for it, the Profits ought to be lessened by
the Legislature.*

These Ideas prevailing more or less in all the United States,
it cannot be worth any Man's while, who has a means of Living at home, to expatriate himself in hopes of obtaining a
profitable civil Office in America; and as to military Offices,
they are at an End with the War; the Armies being disbanded.
Much less is it adviseable for a Person to go thither who has
no other Quality to recommend him but his Birth. In Europe
it has indeed its Value, but it is a Commodity that cannot be
carried to a worse Market than to that of America, where

People do not enquire concerning a Stranger, *What is he?* but *What can he do?* If he has any useful Art, he is welcome; and if he exercises it and behaves well, he will be respected by all that know him; but a mere Man of Quality, who on that Account wants to live upon the Public, by some Office or Salary, will be despis'd and disregarded. The Husbandman is in honor there, & even the Mechanic, because their Employments are useful. The People have a Saying, that God Almighty is himself a Mechanic, the greatest in the Universe; and he is respected and admired more for the Variety, Ingenuity and Utility of his Handiworks, than for the Antiquity of his Family. They are pleas'd with the Observation of a Negro, and frequently mention it, that *Boccarorra* (meaning the Whiteman) make de Blackman workee, make de Horse workee, make de Ox workee, make ebery ting workee; only de Hog. He de Hog, no workee; he eat, he drink, he walk about, he go to sleep when he please, *he libb like a Gentleman.* According to these Opinions of the Americans, one of them would think himself more oblig'd to a Genealogist, who could prove for him that his Ancestors & Relations for ten Generations had been Ploughmen, Smiths, Carpenters, Turners, Weavers, Tanners, or even Shoemakers, & consequently that they were useful Members of Society; than if he could only prove that they were Gentlemen, doing nothing of Value, but living idly on the Labour of others, mere *fruges consumere nati**, and otherwise *good* for *nothing*, till by their Death, their Estates like the Carcase of the Negro's Gentleman-Hog, come to be *cut up*.

With Regard to Encouragements for Strangers from Government, they are really only what are derived from good Laws & Liberty. Strangers are welcome because there is room enough for them all, and therefore the old Inhabitants are not jealous of them; the Laws protect them sufficiently, so that they have no need of the Patronage of great Men; and every one will enjoy securely the Profits of his Industry. But if he does not bring a Fortune with him, he must work and be industrious to live. One or two Years Residence give him all the Rights of a Citizen; but the Government does not at

---

* *There are a Number of us born*
  Merely to eat up the Corn.   WATTS.

present, whatever it may have done in former times, hire People to become Settlers, by Paying their Passages, giving Land,
Negroes, Utensils, Stock, or any other kind of Emolument
whatsoever. In short America is the Land of Labour, and by
no means what the English call *Lubberland*, and the French
Pays de Cocagne, where the Streets are said to be pav'd with
half-peck Loaves, the Houses til'd with Pancakes, and where
the Fowls fly about ready roasted, crying, *Come eat me!*

Who then are the kind of Persons to whom an Emigration
to America may be advantageous? and what are the Advantages they may reasonably expect?

Land being cheap in that Country, from the vast Forests
still void of Inhabitants, and not likely to be occupied in an
Age to come, insomuch that the Propriety of an hundred
Acres of fertile Soil full of Wood may be obtained near the
Frontiers in many Places for eight or ten Guineas, hearty
young Labouring Men, who understand the Husbandry of
Corn and Cattle, which is nearly the same in that Country as
in Europe, may easily establish themselves there. A little
Money sav'd of the good Wages they receive there while they
work for others, enables them to buy the Land and begin
their Plantation, in which they are assisted by the Good Will
of their Neighbours and some Credit. Multitudes of poor
People from England, Ireland, Scotland and Germany, have
by this means in a few Years become wealthy Farmers, who
in their own Countries, where all the Lands are fully occupied, and the Wages of Labour low, could never have
emerged from the mean Condition wherein they were born.

From the Salubrity of the Air, the Healthiness of the Climate, the Plenty of good Provisions, and the Encouragement
to early Marriages, by the certainty of Subsistance in cultivat-
ing the Earth, the Increase of Inhabitants by natural Generation is very rapid in America, and becomes still more so by
the Accession of Strangers; hence there is a continual Demand for more Artisans of all the necessary and useful kinds,
to supply those Cultivators of the Earth with Houses, and
with Furniture & Utensils of the grosser Sorts which cannot
so well be brought from Europe. Tolerably good Workmen in
any of those mechanic Arts, are sure to find Employ, and
to be well paid for their Work, there being no Restraints

preventing Strangers from exercising any Art they understand, nor any Permission necessary. If they are poor, they begin first as Servants or Journeymen; and if they are sober, industrious & frugal, they soon become Masters, establish themselves in Business, marry, raise Families, and become respectable Citizens.

Also, Persons of moderate Fortunes and Capitals, who having a Number of Children to provide for, are desirous of bringing them up to Industry, and to secure Estates for their Posterity, have Opportunities of doing it in America, which Europe does not afford. There they may be taught & practice profitable mechanic Arts, without incurring Disgrace on that Account; but on the contrary acquiring Respect by such Abilities. There small Capitals laid out in Lands, which daily become more valuable by the Increase of People, afford a solid Prospect of ample Fortunes thereafter for those Children. The Writer of this has known several Instances of large Tracts of Land, bought on what was then the Frontier of Pensilvania, for ten Pounds per hundred Acres, which, after twenty Years, when the Settlements had been extended far beyond them, sold readily, without any Improvement made upon them, for three Pounds per Acre. The Acre in America is the same with the English Acre or the Acre of Normandy.

Those who desire to understand the State of Government in America, would do well to read the Constitutions of the several States, and the Articles of Confederation that bind the whole together for general Purposes under the Direction of one Assembly called the Congress. These Constitutions have been printed by Order of Congress in America; two Editions of them have also been printed in London, and a good Translation of them into French has lately been published at Paris.

Several of the Princes of Europe having of late Years, from an Opinion of Advantage to arise by producing all Commodities & Manufactures within their own Dominions, so as to diminish or render useless their Importations, have endeavoured to entice Workmen from other Countries, by high Salaries, Privileges, &c. Many Persons pretending to be skilled in various great Manufactures, imagining that America must be in Want of them, and that the Congress would probably be dispos'd to imitate the Princes above mentioned, have proposed to go over, on Condition of having their Passages paid, Lands given, Salaries appointed, exclusive Privileges for Terms of Years, &c. Such Persons on reading the Articles of Confederation will find that the Congress have no Power committed to them, or Money put into their Hands, for such purposes; and that if any such Encouragement is given, it must be by the Government of some separate State. This however has rarely been done in America; and when it has been done it has rarely succeeded, so as to establish a Manufacture which the Country was not yet so ripe for as to encourage private Persons to set it up; Labour being generally too dear there, & Hands difficult to be kept together, every one desiring to be a Master, and the Cheapness of Land enclining many to leave Trades for Agriculture. Some indeed have met with Success, and are carried on to Advantage; but they are generally such as require only a few Hands, or wherein great Part of the Work is perform'd by Machines. Goods that are bulky, & of so small Value as not well to bear the Expence of Freight, may often be made cheaper in the Country than they can be imported; and the Manufacture of such Goods will be profitable wherever there is a sufficient Demand. The Farmers in America produce indeed a good deal of Wool & Flax; and none is exported, it is all work'd up; but it is in the Way of Domestic Manufacture for the Use of the Family. The buying up Quantities of Wool & Flax with the Design to employ Spinners, Weavers, &c. and form great Establishments, producing Quantities of Linen and Woollen Goods for Sale, has been several times attempted in different Provinces; but those Projects have generally failed, Goods of equal Value being imported cheaper. And when the Governments have been solicited to support such Schemes by Encouragements, in Money, or by imposing Duties on Importation of such Goods, it has been generally refused, on this Principle, that if the Country is ripe for the Manufacture, it may be carried on by private Persons to Advantage; and if not, it is a Folly to think of forceing Nature. Great Establishments of Manufacture, require great Numbers of Poor to do the Work for small Wages; these Poor are to be found in Europe, but will not be found in America, till the Lands are all taken up and cultivated, and the excess of People who cannot get Land, want Employment. The Manufacture of Silk, they say, is natural in France, as that of Cloth in England, because each Country produces in Plenty the first Material: But if England will have a Manufacture of Silk as well as that of Cloth, and France one of Cloth as well as that of Silk, these unnatural Operations must be supported by mutual Prohibitions or high Duties on the Importation of each others Goods, by which means the Workmen are enabled to tax the home-Consumer by greater Prices, while the higher Wages they receive makes them neither happier nor richer, since they only drink more and work less. Therefore the Governments in America do nothing to encourage such Projects. The People by this Means are not impos'd on, either by the Merchant or Mechanic; if the Merchant demands too much Profit on imported Shoes, they buy of the Shoemaker: and if he asks too high a Price, they take them of the Merchant: thus the two Professions are Checks on each other. The Shoemaker however has on the whole a considerable Profit upon his Labour in America, beyond what he had in Europe, as he can add to his Price a Sum nearly equal to all the Expences of Freight & Commission, Risque or Insurance, &c. necessarily charged by the Merchant. And the Case is the same with the Workmen in every other Mechanic Art. Hence it is that Artisans generally live better and more easily in America than in Europe, and such as are good Œconomists make a comfortable Provision for Age, & for their Children. Such may therefore remove with Advantage to America.

In the old longsettled Countries of Europe, all Arts, Trades, Professions, Farms, &c. are so full that it is difficult for a poor Man who has Children, to place them where they may gain, or learn to gain a decent Livelihood. The Artisans, who fear creating future Rivals in Business, refuse to take Apprentices, but upon Conditions of Money, Maintenance or the like, which the Parents are unable to comply with. Hence the Youth are dragg'd up in Ignorance of every gainful Art, and oblig'd to become Soldiers or Servants or Thieves, for a Subsistance. In America the rapid Increase of Inhabitants takes away that Fear of Rivalship, & Artisans willingly receive Apprentices from the hope of Profit by their Labour during the Remainder of the Time stipulated after they shall be instructed. Hence it is easy for poor Families to get their Children instructed; for the Artisans are so desirous of Apprentices, that many of them will even give Money to the Parents to have Boys from ten to fifteen Years of Age bound Apprentices to them till the Age of twenty one; and many poor Parents have by that means, on their Arrival in the Country, raised Money enough to buy Land sufficient to establish themselves, and to subsist the rest of their Family by Agriculture. These Contracts for Apprentices are made before a Magistrate, who regulates the Agreement according to Reason and Justice; and having in view the Formation of a future useful Citizen, obliges the Master to engage by a written Indenture, not only that during the time of Service stipulated, the Apprentice shall be duly provided with Meat, Drink, Apparel, washing & Lodging, and at its Expiration with a compleat new suit of Clothes, but also that he shall be taught to read, write & cast Accompts, & that he shall be well instructed in the Art or Profession of his Master, or some other, by which he may afterwards gain a Livelihood, and be able in his turn to raise a Family. A Copy of this Indenture is given to the Apprentice or his Friends, & the Magistrate keeps a Record of it, to which Recourse may be had, in case of Failure by the Master in any Point of Performance. This Desire among the Masters to have more Hands employ'd in working for them, induces them to pay the Passages of young Persons, of both Sexes, who on their Arrival agree to serve them one, two, three or four Years; those who have already learnt a Trade agreeing for a shorter Term in Proportion to their Skill and the consequent immediate Value of their Service; and those who have none, agreeing for a longer Term, in Consideration of being taught an Art their Poverty would not permit them to acquire in their own Country.

The almost general Mediocrity of Fortune that prevails in America, obliging its People to follow some Business for Subsistance, those Vices that arise usually from Idleness are in a great Measure prevented. Industry and constant Employment are great Preservatives of the Morals and Virtue of a Nation. Hence bad Examples to Youth are more rare in America, which must be a comfortable Consideration to Parents. To this may be truly added, that serious Religion under its various Denominations, is not only tolerated but respected and practised. Atheism is unknown there, Infidelity rare & secret, so that Persons may live to a great Age in that Country without having their Piety shock'd by meeting with either an Atheist or an Infidel. And the Divine Being seems to have manifested his Approbation of the mutual Forbearance and Kindness with which the different Sects treat each other, by the remarkable Prosperity with which he has been pleased to favour the whole Country.

Passy, February, 1784

An Economical Project

MESSIEURS,

You often entertain us with accounts of new discoveries. Permit me to communicate to the public, through your paper, one that has lately been made by myself, and which I conceive may be of great utility.

I was the other evening in a grand company, where the new lamp of Messrs. Quinquet and Lange was introduced, and much admired for its splendour; but a general inquiry was made, whether the oil it consumed was not in proportion to the light it afforded, in which case there would be no saving in the use of it. No one present could satisfy us in that point, which all agreed ought to be known, it being a very desirable thing to lessen, if possible, the expense of lighting our apartments, when every other article of family expense was so much augmented.

I was pleased to see this general concern for economy, for I love economy exceedingly.

I went home, and to bed, three or four hours after midnight, with my head full of the subject. An accidental sudden noise waked me about six in the morning, when I was surprised to find my room filled with light; and I imagined at first, that a number of those lamps had been brought into it; but, rubbing my eyes, I perceived the light came in at the windows. I got up and looked out to see what might be the occasion of it, when I saw the sun just rising above the horizon, from whence he poured his rays plentifully into my chamber, my domestic having negligently omitted, the preceding evening, to close the shutters.

I looked at my watch, which goes very well, and found that it was but six o'clock; and still thinking it something extraordinary that the sun should rise so early, I looked into the almanac, where I found it to be the hour given for his rising on that day. I looked forward, too, and found he was to rise still earlier every day till towards the end of June; and that at no time in the year he retarded his rising so long as till eight o'clock. Your readers, who with me have never seen any signs of sunshine before noon, and seldom regard the astronomical part of the almanac, will be as much astonished as I was, when they hear of his rising so early; and especially when I assure them, *that he gives light as soon as he rises.* I am convinced of this. I am certain of my fact. One cannot be more certain of any fact. I saw it with my own eyes. And, having repeated this observation the three following mornings, I found always precisely the same result.

Yet it so happens, that when I speak of this discovery to others, I can easily perceive by their countenances, though they forbear expressing it in words, that they do not quite believe me. One, indeed, who is a learned natural philosopher, has assured me that I must certainly be mistaken as to the circumstance of the light coming into my room; for it being well known, as he says, that there could be no light abroad at that hour, it follows that none could enter from without; and that of consequence, my windows being accidentally left open, instead of letting in the light, had only served to let out the darkness; and he used many ingenious arguments to show me how I might, by that means, have been deceived. I owned that he puzzled me a little, but he did not satisfy me; and the subsequent observations I made, as above mentioned, confirmed me in my first opinion.

This event has given rise in my mind to several serious and important reflections. I considered that, if I had not been awakened so early in the morning, I should have slept six hours longer by the light of the sun, and in exchange have lived six hours the following night by candle-light; and, the latter being a much more expensive light than the former, my love of economy induced me to muster up what little arithmetic I was master of, and to make some calculations, which I shall give you, after observing that utility is, in my opinion the test of value in matters of invention, and that a discovery which can be applied to no use, or is not good for something, is good for nothing.

I took for the basis of my calculation the supposition that there are one hundred thousand families in Paris, and that these families consume in the night half a pound of bougies, or candles, per hour. I think this is a moderate allowance, taking one family with another; for though I believe some consume less, I know that many consume a great deal more. Then estimating seven hours per day as the medium quantity between the time of the sun's rising and ours, he rising during the six following months from six to eight hours before noon, and there being seven hours of course per night in which we burn candles, the account will stand thus;—

In the six months between the 20th of March and the 20th of September, there are

Nights   183
Hours of each night in which we burn
candles   7
Multiplication gives for the total number of _____
hours.   1,281
These 1,281 hours multiplied by 100,000, the
number of inhabitants, give   128,100,000
One hundred twenty-eight millions and one hundred thousand hours, spent at Paris by candle-light, which, at half a pound of wax and tallow per hour, gives the weight of. 64,050,000
Sixty-four millions and fifty thousand of pounds, which, estimating the whole at the medium price of thirty sols the pound, makes the sum of ninety-six millions and seventy-five thousand livres tournois   96,075,000
An immense sum! that the city of Paris might save every year, by the economy of using sunshine instead of candles.

If it should be said, that people are apt to be obstinately attached to old customs, and that it will be difficult to induce them to rise before noon, consequently my discovery can be of little use; I answer, *Nil desperandum*. I believe all who have common sense, as soon as they have learnt from this paper that it is daylight when the sun rises, will contrive to rise with him; and, to compel the rest, I would propose the following regulations;

First. Let a tax be laid of a louis per window, on every window that is provided with shutters to keep out the light of the sun.

Second. Let the same salutary operation of police be made use of, to prevent our burning candles, that inclined us last winter to be more economical in burning wood; that is, let guards be placed in the shops of the wax and tallow chandlers, and no family be permitted to be supplied with more than one pound of candles per week.

Third. Let guards also be posted to stop all the coaches, &c. that would pass the streets after sun-set, except those of physicians, surgeons, and midwives.

Fourth. Every morning, as soon as the sun rises, let all the bells in every church be set ringing; and if that is not sufficient, let cannon be fired in every street, to wake the sluggards effectually, and make them open their eyes to see their true interest.

All the difficulty will be in the first two or three days; after which the reformation will be as natural and easy as the present irregularity; for, *ce n'est que le premier pas qui coûte*. Oblige a man to rise at four in the morning, and it is more than probable he will go willingly to bed at eight in the evening; and, having had eight hours sleep, he will rise more willingly at four in the morning following. But this sum of ninety-six millions and seventy-five thousand livres is not the whole of what may be saved by my economical project. You may observe, that I have calculated upon only one half of the year, and much may be saved in the other, though the days are shorter. Besides, the immense stock of wax and tallow left unconsumed during the summer, will probably make candles much cheaper for the ensuing winter, and continue them cheaper as long as the proposed reformation shall be supported.

For the great benefit of this discovery, thus freely communicated and bestowed by me on the public, I demand neither place, pension, exclusive privilege, nor any other reward whatever. I expect only to have the honour of it. And yet I know there are little, envious minds, who will, as usual, deny me this, and say, that my invention was known to the ancients, and perhaps they may bring passages out of the old books in proof of it. I will not dispute with these people, that the ancients knew not the sun would rise at certain hours; they possibly had, as we have, almanacs that predicted it; but it does not follow thence, that they knew *he gave light as soon as he rose*. This is what I claim as my discovery. If the ancients knew it, it might have been long since forgotten; for it certainly was unknown to the moderns, at least to the Parisians, which to prove, I need use but one plain simple argument. They are as well instructed, judicious, and prudent a people as exist anywhere in the world, all professing, like myself, to be lovers of economy; and, from the many heavy taxes required from them by the necessities of the state, have surely an abundant reason to be economical. I say it is impossible that so sensible a people, under such circumstances, should have lived so long by the smoky, unwholesome, and enormously expensive light of candles, if they had really known, that they might have had as much pure light of the sun for nothing. I am, &c.

A SUBSCRIBER.

Journal de Paris, April 26, 1784

Loose Thoughts on a Universal Fluid

Passy, June 25, 1784.

Universal Space, as far as we know of it, seems to be filled with a subtil Fluid, whose Motion, or Vibration, is called Light.

This Fluid may possibly be the same with that, which, being attracted by, and entring into other more solid Matter, dilates the Substance, by separating the constituent Particles, and so rendering some Solids fluid, and maintaining the Fluidity of others; of which Fluid when our Bodies are totally deprived, they are said to be frozen; when they have a proper Quantity, they are in Health, and fit to perform all their Functions; it is then called natural Heat; when too much, it is called Fever; and, when forced into the Body in too great a Quantity from without, it gives Pain by separating and destroying the Flesh, and is then called Burning; and the Fluid so entring and acting is called Fire.

While organized Bodies, animal or vegetable, are augmenting in Growth, or are supplying their continual Waste, is not this done by attracting and consolidating this Fluid called Fire, so as to form of it a Part of their Substance; and is it not a Separation of the Parts of such Substance, which, dissolving its solid State, sets that subtil Fluid at Liberty, when it again makes its appearance as Fire?

For the Power of Man relative to Matter seems limited to the dividing it, or mixing the various kinds of it, or changing its Form and Appearance by different Compositions of it; but does not extend to the making or creating of new Matter, or annihilating the old. Thus, if Fire be an original Element, or kind of Matter, its Quantity is fixed and permanent in the Universe. We cannot destroy any Part of it, or make addition to it; we can only separate it from that which confines it, and so set it at Liberty, as when we put Wood in a Situation to be burnt; or transfer it from one Solid to another, as when we make Lime by burning Stone, a Part of the Fire dislodg'd from the Wood being left in the Stone. May not this Fluid, when at Liberty, be capable of penetrating and entring into all Bodies organiz'd or not, quitting easily in totality those not organiz'd; and quitting easily in part those which are; the part assum'd and fix'd remaining till the Body is dissolved?

Is it not this Fluid which keeps asunder the Particles of Air, permitting them to approach, or separating them more, in proportion as its Quantity is diminish'd or augmented? Is it not the greater Gravity of the Particles of Air, which forces the Particles of this Fluid to mount with the Matters to which it is attach'd, as Smoke or Vapour?

Does it not seem to have a great Affinity with Water, since it will quit a Solid to unite with that Fluid, and go off with it in Vapour, leaving the Solid cold to the Touch, and the Degree measurable by the Thermometer?

The Vapour rises attach'd to this Fluid, but at a certain height they separate, and the Vapour descends in Rain, retaining but little of it, in Snow or Hail less. What becomes of that Fluid? Does it rise above our Atmosphere, and mix with the universal Mass of the same kind? Or does a spherical Stratum of it, denser, or less mix'd with Air, attracted by this Globe, and repell'd or push'd up only to a certain height from its Surface, by the greater Weight of Air, remain there, surrounding the Globe, and proceeding with it round the Sun?

In such case, as there may be a Continuity or Communication of this Fluid thro' the Air quite down to the Earth, is it not by the Vibrations given to it by the Sun that Light appears to us; and may it not be, that every one of the infinitely small Vibrations, striking common Matter with a certain Force, enters its Substance, is held there by Attraction, and augmented by succeeding Vibrations, till the Matter has receiv'd as much as their Force can drive into it?

Is it not thus, that the Surface of this Globe is continually heated by such repeated Vibrations in the Day, and cooled by the Escape of the Heat, when those Vibrations are discontinu'd in the Night, or intercepted and reflected by Clouds?

Is it not thus that Fire is amass'd, and makes the greatest Part of the Substance of combustible Bodies?

Perhaps, when this Globe was first form'd, and its original Particles took their Place at certain Distances from the Centre, in proportion to their greater or less Gravity, the fluid Fire, attracted towards that Centre, might in great part be oblig'd, as lightest, to take place above the rest, and thus form the Sphere of Fire above suppos'd, which would afterwards be continually diminishing by the Substance it afforded to organiz'd Bodies, and the Quantity restor'd to it again by the Burning or other Separating of the Parts of those Bodies.

Is not the natural Heat of Animals thus produc'd, by separating in Digestion the Parts of Food, and setting their Fire at Liberty?

Is it not this Sphere of Fire, which kindles the wandring Globes that sometimes pass thro' it in our Course round the Sun, have their Surface kindled by it, and burst when their included Air is greatly rarified by the Heat on their burning Surfaces? May it not have been from such Considerations that the ancient Philosophers supposed a Sphere of Fire to exist above the Air of our Atmosphere?

The Flies

TO MADAME HELVÉTIUS

The Flies of the Apartments of Mr. Franklin request Permission to present their Respects to Madame Helvétius, & to express in their best Language their Gratitude for the Protection which she has been kind enough to give them,

Bizz izzzz ouizz a ouizzzz izzzzzzzz, &c.

We have long lived under the hospitable Roof of the said Good Man Franklin. He has given us free Lodgings; we have also eaten & drunk the whole Year at his Expense without its having cost us anything. Often, when his Friends & he have emptied a Bowl of Punch, he has left us a sufficient Quantity to intoxicate a hundred of us Flies. We have drunk freely of it, & after that we have made our Sallies, our Circles & our Cotillions very prettily in the Air of his Room, & have gaily consummated our little Loves under his Nose. In short, we should have been the happiest People in the World, if he had not permitted a Number of our declared Enemies to remain at the top of his Wainscoting, where they spread their Nets to catch us, & tore us pitilessly to pieces. People of a Disposition both subtle & ferocious, abominable Combination! You, most excellent Woman, had the goodness to order that all these Assassins with their Habitations & their Snares should be swept away; & your Orders (as they always ought to be) were carried out immediately. Since that Time we live happily, & we enjoy the Beneficence of the said Good Man Franklin without fear.

One Thing alone remains for us to wish in order to assure the Permanence of our Good Fortune; permit us to say it,

Bizz izzzz ouizz a ouizzzz izzzzzzzz, &c.

It is to see the two of you henceforth forming a single Household.

1784?

LETTERS

To Lord Howe

My Lord,   Philada. July 20th. 1776.

I received safe the Letters your Lordship so kindly forwarded to me, and beg you to accept my Thanks.

The Official Dispatches to which you refer me, contain
nothing more than what we had seen in the Act of Parliament, viz. Offers of Pardon upon Submission; which I was
sorry to find, as it must give your Lordship Pain to be sent
so far on so hopeless a Business.

Directing Pardons to be offered the Colonies, who are the
very Parties injured, expresses indeed that Opinion of our Ignorance, Baseness, and Insensibility which your uninform'd
and proud Nation has long been pleased to entertain of us;
but it can have no other Effect than that of increasing our
Resentment. It is impossible we should think of Submission
to a Government, that has with the most wanton Barbarity
and Cruelty, burnt our defenceless Towns in the midst of
Winter, excited the Savages to massacre our Farmers, and our
Slaves to murder their Masters, and is even now bringing foreign Mercenaries to deluge our Settlements with Blood.
These atrocious Injuries have extinguished every remaining
Spark of Affection for that Parent Country we once held so
dear: But were it possible for *us* to forget and forgive them,
it is not possible for *you* (I mean the British Nation) to forgive the People you have so heavily injured; you can never
confide again in those as Fellow Subjects, and permit them to
enjoy equal Freedom, to whom you know you have given
such just Cause of lasting Enmity. And this must impel you,
were we again under your Government, to endeavour the
breaking our Sprit by the severest Tyranny, and obstructing
by every means in your Power our growing Strength and
Prosperity.

But your Lordship mentions "the Kings paternal Solicitude
for promoting the Establishment of lasting *Peace* and Union
with the Colonies." If by *Peace* is here meant, a Peace to be

252

entered into between Britain and America as distinct States now at War, and his Majesty has given your Lordship Powers to treat with us of such a Peace, I may venture to say, tho' without Authority, that I think a Treaty for that purpose not yet quite impracticable, before we enter into Foreign Alliances. But I am persuaded you have no such Powers. Your Nation, tho' by punishing those American Governors who have created and fomented the Discord, rebuilding our burnt Towns, and repairing as far as possible the Mischiefs done us, She might yet recover a great Share of our Regard and the greatest part of our growing Commerce, with all the Advantage of that additional Strength to be derived from a Friendship with us; I know too well her abounding Pride and deficient Wisdom, to believe she will ever take such Salutary Measures. Her Fondness for Conquest as a Warlike Nation, her Lust of Dominion as an Ambitious one, and her Thirst for a gainful Monopoly as a Commercial one, (none of them legitimate Causes of War) will all join to hide from her Eyes every View of her true Interests; and continually goad her on in these ruinous distant Expeditions, so destructive both of Lives and Treasure, that must prove as perrnicious to her in the End as the Croisades formerly were to most of the Nations of Europe.

I have not the Vanity, my Lord, to think of intimidating by thus predicting the Effects of this War; for I know it will in England have the Fate of all my former Predictions, not to be believed till the Event shall verify it.

Long did I endeavour with unfeigned and unwearied Zeal, to preserve from breaking, that fine and noble China Vase the British Empire: for I knew that being once broken, the separate Parts could not retain even their Share of the Strength or Value that existed in the Whole, and that a perfect Re-Union of those Parts could scarce even be hoped for. Your Lordship may possibly remember the Tears of Joy that wet my Cheek, when, at your good Sister's in London, you once gave me Expectations that a Reconciliation might soon take place. I had the Misfortune to find those Expectations disappointed, and to be treated as the Cause of the Mischief I was labouring to prevent. My Consolation under that groundless and malevolent Treatment was, that I retained the Friendship of many

Wise and Good Men in that Country, and among the rest some Share in the Regard of Lord Howe.

The well founded Esteem, and permit me to say Affection, which I shall always have for your Lordship, makes it painful to me to see you engag'd in conducting a War, the great Ground of which, as expressed in your Letter, is, "the Necessity of preventing the American Trade from passing into foreign Channels." To me it seems that neither the obtaining or retaining of any Trade, how valuable soever, is an Object for which Men may justly Spill each others Blood; that the true and sure means of extending and securing Commerce is the goodness and cheapness of Commodities; and that the profits of no Trade can ever be equal to the Expence of compelling it, and of holding it, by Fleets and Armies. I consider this War against us therefore, as both unjust, and unwise; and I am persuaded cool dispassionate Posterity will condemn to Infamy those who advised it; and that even Success will not save from some degree of Dishonour, those who voluntarily engag'd to conduct it. I know your great Motive in coming hither was the Hope of being instrumental in a Reconciliation; and I believe when you find *that* impossible on any Terms given you to propose, you will relinquish so odious a Command, and return to a more honourable private Station. With the greatest and most sincere Respect I have the honour to be, My Lord your Lordships most obedient humble Servant

"WOMEN . . . OUGHT TO BE FIX'D IN
REVOLUTION PRINCIPLES"

To Emma Thompson

Paris, Feb. 8. 1777

You are too early, Hussy, (as well as too saucy) in calling me Rebel; you should wait for the Event, which will determine whether it is a Rebellion or only a Revolution. Here the Ladies are more civil; they call us *les Insurgens*, a Character that usually pleases them: And methinks you, with all other Women who smart or have smarted under the Tyranny of a bad Husband, ought to be fix'd in *Revolution* Principles, and act accordingly.

In my way to Canada last Spring, I saw dear Mrs. Barrow at New York. Mr. Barrow had been from her two or three Months, to keep Gov. Tryon and other Tories Company, on board the Asia one of the King's Ships which lay in the Harbour; and in all that time, naughty Man, had not ventur'd once on shore to see her. Our Troops were then pouring into the Town, and she was packing up to leave it; fearing as she had a large House they would incommode her by quartering Officers in it. As she appear'd in great Perplexity, scarce knowing where to go I persuaded her to stay, and I went to the General Officers then commanding there, and recommended her to their Protection, which they promis'd, and perform'd. On my Return from Canada, (where I was a Piece of a Governor, and I think a very good one, for a Fortnight; and might have been so till this time if your wicked Army, Enemies to all good Government, had not come and driven me out) I found her still in quiet Possession of her House. I enquired how our People had behav'd to her; she spoke in high Terms of the respectful Attention they had paid her, and the Quiet and Security they had procur'd her. I said I was glad of it; and that if they had us'd her ill, I would have turn'd Tory. *Then*, says she, (with that pleasing Gaiety so natural to her) *I wish they had*. For you must know she is a Toryess as well as you and can as flippantly call Rebel. I drank Tea with her; we talk'd affectionately of you and our other Friends the Wilkes's, of whom she had receiv'd no late Intelligence. What became of her since, I have not heard. The Street she then liv'd in was some Months after chiefly burnt down; but as the Town was then, and ever since has been in Possession of the King's Troops, I have had no Opportunity of knowing whether she suffer'd any Loss in the Conflagration. I hope she did not, as if she did, I should wish I had not persuaded her to stay there. I am glad to learn from you that that unhappy tho' deserving Family the W's are getting into some Business that may afford them Subsistence. I pray that God will bless them, and that they may see happier Days. Mr. Cheap's and Dr. Huck's good Fortunes please me. Pray learn, (if you

have not already learnt) like me, to be pleas'd with other
People's Pleasures, and happy with their Happinesses; when
none occur of your own; then perhaps you will not so soon
be weary of the Place you chance to be in, and so fond of
Rambling to get rid of your *Ennui*. I fancy You have hit
upon the right Reason of your being weary of St. Omer,
viz. that you are out of Temper which is the effect of full living and idleness. A month in Bridewell, beating Hemp upon
Bread and Water, would give you Health and Spirits, and
subsequent Chearfulness, and Contentment with every other
Situation. I prescribe that Regimen for you my Dear, in
pure good Will, without a Fee. And, if you do not get into
Temper, neither Brussels nor Lisle will suit you. I know
nothing of the Price of Living in either of those Places; but
I am sure that a single Woman, as you are, might with
Oeconomy, upon two hundred Pounds a year, maintain herself comfortably any where, and me into the Bargain. Don't
invite me in earnest, however, to come and live with you;
for being posted here I ought not to comply, and I am not sure
I should be able to refuse. Present my Respects to Mrs. Payne
and Mrs. Heathcoat, for tho' I have not the Honour of
knowing them, yet as you say they are Friends to the American Cause, I am sure they must be Women of good Understanding. I know you wish you could see me, but as you
can't, I will describe my self to you. Figure me in your mind
as jolly as formerly, and as strong and hearty, only a few
Years older, very plainly dress'd, wearing my thin grey strait
Hair, that peeps out under my only Coiffure, a fine Fur Cap,
which comes down my Forehead almost to my Spectacles.
Think how this must appear among the Powder'd Heads of
Paris. I wish every Gentleman and Lady in France would
only be so obliging as to follow my Fashion, comb their own
Heads as I do mine, dismiss their Friseurs, and pay me half
the Money they paid to them. You see the Gentry might well
afford this; and I could then inlist those Friseurs, who are at
least 100,000; and with the Money I would maintain them,
make a Visit with them to England, and dress the Heads of
your Ministers and Privy Counsellors, which I conceive to be
at present *un peu dérangées*. Adieu, Madcap, and believe me
ever Your affectionate Friend and humble Servant

PS. Don't be proud of this long Letter. A Fit of the Gout which has confin'd me 5 Days, and made me refuse to see any Company, has given me a little time to trifle. Otherwise it would have been very short. Visitors and Business would have interrupted. And perhaps, with Mrs. Barrow, *you wish they had.*

"WHOEVER WRITES TO A STRANGER SHOULD OBSERVE 3 POINTS"

To ——— Lith

Sir,   Passy near Paris, April 6. 1777
    I have just been honoured with a Letter from you, dated the 26th past, in which you express your self as astonished, and appear to be angry that you have no Answer to a Letter you wrote me of the 11th of December, which you are sure was delivered to me.

    In Exculpation of my self, I assure you that I never receiv'd any Letter from you of that date. And indeed being then but 4 Days landed at Nantes, I think you could scarce have heard so soon of my being in Europe.

    But I receiv'd one from you of the 8th of January, which I own I did not answer. It may displease you if I give you the Reason; but as it may be of use to you in your future Correspondences, I will hazard that for a Gentleman to whom I feel myself oblig'd, as an American, on Account of his Good Will to our Cause.

    Whoever writes to a Stranger should observe 3 Points; 1. That what he proposes be practicable. 2. His Propositions should be made in explicit Terms so as to be easily understood. 3. What he desires should be in itself reasonable. Hereby he will give a favourable Impression of his Understanding, and create a Desire of further Acquaintance. Now it happen'd that you were negligent in *all* these Points: for first you desired to have Means procur'd for you of taking a Voyage to America *"avec Sureté"*; which is not possible, as the Dangers of the Sea subsist always, and at present there is the additional Danger of being taken by the English. Then you desire that this may be *"sans trop grandes Dépenses,"* which is not intelligible enough to be answer'd, because not knowing your Ability of bearing Expences, one cannot judge what may be *trop grandes*. Lastly you desire Letters of Address to the Congress and to General Washington; which it is not reasonable to ask of *one* who knows no more of you than that your Name is LITH, and that you live at BAYREUTH.

In your last, you also express yourself in vague Terms when you desire to be inform'd whether you may expect *"d'etre recu d'une maniere convenable"* in our Troops? As it is impossible to know what your Ideas are of the *maniere convenable*, how can one answer this? And then you demand whether I will support you by my Authority in giving you Letters of Recommendation? I doubt not your being a Man of Merit; and knowing it yourself, you may forget that it is not known to every body; but reflect a Moment, Sir, and you will be convinc'd, that if I were to practice giving Letters of Recommendation to Persons of whose Character I knew no more than I do of yours, my Recommendations would soon be of no Authority at all.

I thank you however for your kind Desire of being Serviceable to my Countrymen: And I wish in return that I could be of Service to you in the Scheme you have form'd of going to America. But Numbers of experienc'd Officers here have offer'd to go over and join our Army, and I could give them no Encouragement, because I have no Orders for that purpose, and I know it extremely difficult to place them when they come there. I cannot but think therefore, that it is best for you not to make so long, so expensive, and so hazardous a Voyage, but to take the Advice of your Friends, and *stay in Franconia*. I have the honour to be Sir, &c.

"DISPUTES ARE APT TO SOUR ONES TEMPER"

To [Lebègue de Presle]

Sir   Passy, Oct. 4 1777

I am much oblig'd by your Communication of the Letter from England. I am of your Opinion that a Translation of it will not be proper for Publication here. Our Friend's Expressions concerning Mr. Wilson will be thought too angry to be made use of by one Philosopher when speaking of another; and on a philosophical Question. He seems as much heated about this one Point, as the Jansenists and Molinists were about the Five. As to my writing any thing on the Subject, which you seem to desire, I think it not necessary; especially as I have nothing to add to what I have already said upon it in a Paper read to the Committee who ordered the Conductors at Purfleet, which Paper is printed in the last French Edition of my Writings. I have never entered into any Controversy in defence of my philosophical Opinions; I leave them to take their Chance in the World. If they are right, Truth and Experience will support them. If wrong, they ought to be refuted and rejected. Disputes are apt to sour ones Temper and disturb one's Quiet. I have no private Interest in the Reception of my Inventions by the World, having never made nor proposed to make the least Profit by any of them. The King's changing his pointed Conductors for blunt ones is therefore a Matter of small Importance to me. If I had a Wish about it, it would be that he had rejected them altogether as ineffectual, For it is only since he thought himself and Family safe from the Thunder of Heaven, that he dared to use his own Thunder in destroying his innocent Subjects.

Be pleased when you write to present my respectful Compliments and Thanks to Mr. Magellans. I have forwarded your Letter to your Brother, and am with great Esteem, Sir Your most obedient humble Servant

"YOUR MAGISTERIAL SNUBBINGS AND REBUKES"

To Arthur Lee

SIR   Passy, April 3, 1778

It is true I have omitted answering some of your Letters. I do not like to answer angry Letters. I hate Disputes. I am old, cannot have long to live, have much to do and no time for Altercation. If I have often receiv'd and borne your Magisterial Snubbings and Rebukes without Reply, ascribe it to the right Causes, my Concern for the Honour & Success of our Mission, which would be hurt by our Quarrelling, my Love of Peace, my Respect for your good Qualities, and my Pity of your Sick Mind, which is forever tormenting itself, with its Jealousies, Suspicions & Fancies that others mean you ill, wrong you, or fail in Respect for you.—If you do not cure your self of this Temper it will end in Insanity, of which it is the Symptomatick Forerunner, as I have seen in several Instances. God preserve you from so terrible an Evil: and for his sake pray suffer me to live in quiet. I have the honour to be very respectfully,

Sir, etc,

"A SORT OF TAR-AND-FEATHER HONOUR"

To Charles de Weissenstein

SIR,   Passy, July 1, 1778.
    I received your letter, dated at Brussels the 16th past. My vanity might possibly be flattered by your expressions of compliment to my understanding, if your *proposals* did not more clearly manifest a mean opinion of it.
    You conjure me, in the name of the omniscient and just God, before whom I must appear, and by my hopes of future fame, to consider if some expedient cannot be found to put a stop to the desolation of America, and prevent the miseries of a general war. As I am conscious of having taken every step in my power to prevent the breach, and no one to widen it, I can appear cheerfully before that God, fearing nothing from his justice in this particular, though I have much occasion for his mercy in many others. As to my future fame, I am content to rest it on my past and present conduct, without seeking an addition to it in the crooked, dark paths, you propose to me, where I should most certainly lose it. This your solemn address would therefore have been more properly made to your sovereign and his venal Parliament. He and they, who wickedly began, and madly continue, a war for the desolation of America, are alone accountable for the consequences.
    You endeavour to impress me with a bad opinion of French

faith; but the instances of their friendly endeavours to serve a race of weak princes, who, by their own imprudence, defeated every attempt to promote their interest, weigh but little with me, when I consider the steady friendship of France to the Thirteen United States of Switzerland, which has now continued inviolate two hundred years. You tell me, that she will certainly cheat us, and that she despises us already. I do not believe that she will cheat us, and I am not certain that she despises us; but I see clearly that you are endeavouring to cheat us by your conciliatory bills; that you actually despised our understandings, when you flattered yourselves those artifices would succeed; and that not only France, but all Europe, yourselves included, most certainly and for ever would despise us, if we were weak enough to accept your insidious propositions.

Our expectations of the future grandeur of America are not so magnificent, and therefore not so vain or visionary, as you represent them to be. The body of our people are not merchants, but humble husbandmen, who delight in the cultivation of their lands, which, from their fertility and the variety of our climates, are capable of furnishing all the necessaries and conveniences of life without external commerce; and we have too much land to have the least temptation to extend our territory by conquest from peaceable neighbours, as well as too much justice to think of it. Our militia, you find by experience, are sufficient to defend our lands from invasion; and the commerce with us will be defended by all the nations who find an advantage in it. We, therefore, have not the occasion you imagine, of fleets or standing armies, but may leave those expensive machines to be maintained for the pomp of princes, and the wealth of ancient states. We propose, if possible, to live in peace with all mankind; and after you have been convinced, to your cost, that there is nothing to be got by attacking us, we have reason to hope, that no other power will judge it prudent to quarrel with us, lest they divert us from our own quiet industry, and turn us into corsairs preying upon theirs. The weight therefore of an independent empire, which you seem certain of our inability to bear, will not be so great as you imagine. The expense of our civil government we have always borne, and can easily bear, because it is small. A virtuous and laborious people may be cheaply governed. Determining, as we do, to have no offices of profit, nor any sinecures or useless appointments, so common in ancient or corrupted states, we can govern ourselves a year, for the sum you pay in a single department, or for what one jobbing contractor, by the favour of a minister, can cheat you out of in a single article.

You think we flatter ourselves, and are deceived into an opinion that England *must* acknowledge our independency. We, on the other hand, think you flatter yourselves in imagining such an acknowledgment a vast boon, which we strongly desire, and which you may gain some great advantage by granting or withholding. We have never asked it of you; we only tell you, that you can have no treaty with us but as an independent state; and you may please yourselves and your children with the rattle of your right to govern us, as long as you have done with that of your King's being King of France, without giving us the least concern, if you do not attempt to exercise it. That this pretended right is indisputable, as you say, we utterly deny. Your Parliament never had a right to govern us, and your King has forfeited it by his bloody tyranny. But I thank you for letting me know a little of your mind, that, even if the Parliament should acknowledge our independency, the act would not be binding to posterity, and that your nation would resume and prosecute the claim as soon as they found it convenient from the influence of your passions, and your present malice against us. We suspected before, that you would not be actually bound by your conciliatory acts, longer than till they had served their purpose of inducing us to disband our forces; but we were not certain, that you were knaves by principle, and that we ought not to have the least confidence in your offers, promises, or treaties, though confirmed by Parliament.

I now indeed recollect my being informed, long since, when in England, that a certain very great personage, then young, studied much a certain book, called *Arcana Imperii*. I had the curiosity to procure the book and read it. There are sensible and good things in it, but some bad ones; for, if I remember rightly, a particular king is applauded for his politically exciting a rebellion among his subjects, at a time when

they had not strength to support it, that he might, in sub-
duing them, take away their privileges, which were troublesome to him; and a question is formally stated and discussed,
*Whether a prince, who, to appease a revolt, makes promises of in-
demnity to the revolters, is obliged to fulfil those promises.* Honest
and good men would say, Ay; but this politician says, as you
say, No. And he gives this pretty reason, that, though it was
right to make the promises, because otherwise the revolt
would not be suppressed, yet it would be wrong to keep
them, because revolters ought to be punished to deter from
future revolts.

If these are the principles of your nation, no confidence can
be placed in you; it is in vain to treat with you; and the wars
can only end in being reduced to an utter inability of continuing them.

One main drift of your letter seems to be, to impress me
with an idea of your own impartiality, by just censures of
your ministers and measures, and to draw from me propositions of peace, or approbations of those you have enclosed to
me which you intimate may by your means be conveyed to
the King directly, without the intervention of those ministers.
You would have me give them to, or drop them for, a
stranger, whom I may find next Monday in the church of
Notre Dame, to be known by a rose in his hat. You yourself,
Sir, are quite unknown to me; you have not trusted me with
your true name. Our taking the least step towards a treaty
with England through you, might, if you are an enemy, be
made use of to ruin us with our new and good friends. I may
be indiscreet enough in many things; but certainly, if I were
disposed to make propositions (which I cannot do, having
none committed to me to make), I should never think of delivering them to the Lord knows who, to be carried to the
Lord knows where, to serve no one knows what purposes.
Being at this time one of the most remarkable figures in Paris,
even my appearance in the church of Notre Dame, where I
cannot have any conceivable business, and especially being
seen to leave or drop any letter to any person there, would be
a matter of some speculation, and might, from the suspicions
it must naturally give, have very mischievous consequences to
our credit here.

The very proposing of a correspondence so to be managed, in a manner not necessary where fair dealing is intended, gives just reason to suppose you intend the contrary. Besides, as your court has sent Commissioners to treat with the Congress, with all the powers that could be given them by the crown under the act of Parliament, what good purpose can be served by privately obtaining propositions from us? Before those Commissioners went, we might have treated in virtue of our general powers, (with the knowledge, advice, and approbation of our friends), upon any propositions made to us. But, under the present circumstances, for us to make propositions, while a treaty is supposed to be actually on foot with the Congress, would be extremely improper, highly presumptuous with regard to our constituents, and answer no good end whatever.

I write this letter to you, notwithstanding; (which I think I can convey in a less mysterious manner, and guess it may come to your hands;) I write it because I would let you know our sense of your procedure, which appears as insidious as that of your conciliatory bills. Your true way to obtain peace, if your ministers desire it, is, to propose openly to the Congress fair and equal terms, and you may possibly come sooner to such a resolution, when you find, that personal flatteries, general cajolings, and panegyrics on our *virtue* and *wisdom* are not likely to have the effect you seem to expect; the persuading us to act basely and foolishly, in betraying our country and posterity into the hands of our most bitter enemies, giving up or selling our arms and warlike stores, dismissing our ships of war and troops, and putting those enemies in possession of our forts and ports.

This proposition of delivering ourselves, bound and gagged, ready for hanging, without even a right to complain, and without a friend to be found afterwards among all mankind, you would have us embrace upon the faith of an act of Parliament! Good God! an act of your Parliament! This demonstrates that you do not yet know us, and that you fancy we do not know you; but it is not merely this flimsy faith, that we are to act upon; you offer us *hope*, the hope of PLACES, PENSIONS, and PEERAGES. These, judging from yourselves, you think are motives irresistible. This offer to corrupt us, Sir, is with me your credential, and convinces me that you are not a private volunteer in your application. It bears the stamp of British court character. It is even the signature of your King. But think for a moment in what light it must be viewed in America. By PLACES, you mean places among us, for you take care by a special article to secure your own to yourselves. We must then pay the salaries in order to enrich ourselves with these places. But you will give us PENSIONS, probably to be paid too out of your expected American revenue, and which none of us can accept without deserving, and perhaps obtaining, a SUS-*pension*. PEERAGES! alas! Sir, our long observation of the vast servile majority of your peers, voting constantly for every measure proposed by a minister, however weak or wicked, leaves us small respect for that title. We consider it as a sort of *tar-and-feather* honour, or a mixture of foulness and folly, which every man among us, who should accept it from your King, would be obliged to renounce, or exchange for that conferred by the mobs of their own country, or wear it with everlasting infamy. I am, Sir, your humble servant,

"GOD-SEND OR THE WRECKERS"

To David Hartley

DEAR SIR,   Passy, Feb. 3, 1779.
I have just received your favour of the 23d past, in which you mention, "that the alliance between France and America is the great StumblingBlock in the way of Making Peace;" and you go on to observe, that "whatever Engagements America may have entred into, they may, (at least by consent of Parties) *be relinquished*, for the purpose of removing so material an Obstacle to any general Treaty of free and unengaged Parties" adding, that "if the parties could meet for the sake of Peace upon *free* and *open* Ground, you should think *that* a very fair Proposition to be offered to the People of England, and an equitable Proposition in itself."
The long, steady, & kind regard you have shown for the Welfare of America, by the whole Tenour of your Conduct in Parliament, satisfies me, that this Proposition never took its

Rise with you, but has been suggested from some other quarter; and that your Excess of Humanity, your Love of Peace, & your fears for us, that the Destruction we are threatened with will certainly be effected, have thrown a Mist before your Eyes, which hindred you from seeing the Malignity and Mischief of it. We know that your King hates Whigs and Presbyterians; that he thirsts for our Blood, of which he has already drunk large Draughts; that his servile unprincipled Ministers are ready to execute the wickedest of his Orders, and his venal Parliament equally ready to vote them just. Not the Smallest Appearance of a Reason can be imagined capable of inducing us to think of relinquishing a Solid Alliance with one of the most amiable, as well as most powerful Princes of Europe, for the Expectation of unknown Terms of Peace, to be afterwards offer'd to us by *such a government*; a Government, that has already shamefully broke all the Compacts it ever made with us! This is worse than advising us to drop the Substance for the Shadow. The Dog after he found his Mistake, might possibly have recover'd his Mutton; but we could never hope to be trusted again by France, or indeed by any other Nation under heaven. Nor does there appear any more Necessity for dissolving an Alliance with France before you can treat with us, than there would of dissolving your alliance with Holland, or your Union with Scotland, before we could treat with you. Ours is therefore no *material Obstacle* to a Treaty as you suppose it to be. Had Lord North been the Author of such a Proposition, all the World would have said it was insidious, and meant only to deceive & divide us from our Friends, and then to ruin us; supposing our Fears might be strong enough to procure an Acceptance of it; but thanks to God, that is not the Case! We have long since settled all the Account in our own Minds. We know the worst you can do to us, if you have your Wish, is to confiscate our Estates & take our Lives, to rob & murder us; and this you have seen we are ready to hazard, rather than come again under your detested Government.

You must observe, my dear Friend, that I am a little warm.—Excuse me.—'Tis over.—Only let me counsel you not to think of being sent hither on so fruitless an Errand, as that of making such a Proposition.

It puts me in mind of the comick Farce intitled, *God-send or The Wreckers*. You may have forgotten it; but I will endeavour to amuse you by recollecting a little of it.

SCENE. *Mount's Bay.*

[*A Ship riding at anchor in a great Storm. A Lee Shore full of Rocks, and lin'd with people, furnish'd with Axes & Carriages to cut up Wrecks, knock the Sailors on the Head, and carry off the Plunder; according to Custom.*]

1st. *Wrecker.* This Ship rides it out longer than I expected. She must have good Ground Tackle.

2 *Wrecker.* We had better send off a Boat to her, and persuade her to take a Pilot, who can afterwards run her ashore, where we can best come at her.

3 *Wrecker.* I doubt whether the boat can live in this Sea; but if there are any brave Fellows willing to hazard themselves for the good of the Public, & a double Share, let them say aye.

Several Wreckers. I, I, I, I.

[*The Boat goes off, and comes under the Ship's Stern.*]

Spokesman. So ho, the Ship, ahoa!

Captain. Hulloa.

Sp. Wou'd you have a Pilot?

Capt. No, no!

Sp. It blows hard, & you are in Danger.

Capt. I know it.

Sp. Will you buy a better Cable? We have one in the boat here.

Capt. What do you ask for it?

Sp. Cut that you have, & then we'll talk about the price of this.

Capt. I shall not do such a foolish Thing. I have liv'd in your Parish formerly, & know the Heads of ye too well to trust ye; keep off from my Cable there; I see you have a mind to cut it yourselves. If you go any nearer to it, I'll fire into you and sink you.

Sp. It is a damn'd rotten French Cable, and will part of itself in half an hour. Where will you be then, Captain? You had better take our offer.

Capt. You offer nothing, you Rogues, but Treachery and Mischief. My cable is good & strong, and will hold long enough to baulk all your Projects.

Sp. You talk unkindly, Captain, to People who came here only for your Good.

Capt. I know you come for all our *Goods*, but, by God's help, you shall have none of them; you shall not serve us as you did the Indiaman.

Sp. Come, my Lads, let's be gone. This Fellow is not so great a Fool as we—took him to be.

"I-DOLL-IZED IN THIS COUNTRY"

To Sarah Bache

DEAR SALLY,   Passy, June 3, 1779.

I have before me your letters of October 22d and January 17th. They are the only ones I received from you in the course of eighteen months. If you knew how happy your letters make me, and considered how many miscarry, I think you would write oftener.

I am much obliged to the Miss Cliftons for the kind care they took of my house and furniture. Present my thankful acknowledgments to them, and tell them I wish them all sorts of happiness.

The clay medallion of me you say you gave to Mr. Hopkinson was the first of the kind made in France. A variety of others have been made since of different sizes; some to be set in the lids of snuffboxes, and some so small as to be worn in rings; and the numbers sold are incredible. These, with the pictures, busts, and prints, (of which copies upon copies are spread everywhere,) have made your father's face as well known as that of the moon, so that he durst not do any thing that would oblige him to run away, as his phiz would discover him wherever he should venture to show it. It is said by learned etymologists, that the name *doll*, for the images children play with, is derived from the word IDOL. From the number of *dolls* now made of him, he may be truly said, *in that sense*, to be *i-doll-ized* in this country.

I think you did right to stay out of town till the summer was over, for the sake of your child's health. I hope you will get out again this summer, during the hot months; for I begin to love the dear little creature from your description of her.

I was charmed with the account you gave me of your industry, the tablecloths of your own spinning, &c.; but the latter part of the paragraph, that you had sent for linen from France, because weaving and flax were grown dear, alas, that dissolved the charm; and your sending for long black pins, and lace, and *feathers!* disgusted me as much as if you had put salt into my strawberries. The spinning, I see, is laid aside, and you are to be dressed for the ball! You seem not to know, my dear daughter, that, of all the dear things in this world, idleness is the dearest, except mischief.

The project you mention, of removing Temple from me was an unkind one. To deprive an old man, sent to serve his country in a foreign one, of the comfort of a child to attend him, to assist him in health and take care of him in sickness, would be cruel, if it was practicable. In this case it could not be done; for, as the pretended suspicions of him are groundless, and his behaviour in every respect unexceptionable, I should not part with the child, but with the employment. But I am confident, that, whatever may be proposed by weak or malicious people, the Congress is too wise and too good to think of treating me in that manner.

Ben, if I should live long enough to want it, is like to be another comfort to me. As I intend him for a Presbyterian as well as a republican, I have sent him to finish his education at Geneva. He is much grown, in very good health, draws a little, as you will see by the enclosed, learns Latin, writing, arithmetic, and dancing, and speaks French better than English. He made a translation of your last letter to him, so that some of your works may now appear in a foreign language. He has not been long from me. I send the accounts I have of him, and I shall put him in mind of writing to you. I cannot propose to you to part with your own dear Will. I must one of these days go back to see him; happy to be once more all together! but futurities are uncertain. Teach him, however, in the mean time, to direct his worship more properly, for the deity of Hercules is now quite out of fashion.

The present you mention as sent by me was rather that of a merchant at Bordeaux; for he would never give me any account of it, and neither Temple nor I know any thing of the particulars.

When I began to read your account of the high prices of goods, "a pair of gloves, $7; a yard of common gauze, $24, and that it now required a fortune to maintain a family in a very plain way," I expected you would conclude with telling me, that everybody as well as yourself was grown frugal and industrious; and I could scarce believe my eyes in reading forward, that "there never was so much pleasure and dressing going on;" and that you yourself wanted black pins and feathers from France to appear, I suppose, in the mode! This leads me to imagine, that perhaps it is not so much that the goods are grown dear, as that the money is grown cheap, as every thing else will do when excessively plenty; and that people are still as easy nearly in their circumstances, as when a pair of gloves might be had for half a crown. The war indeed may in some degree raise the prices of goods, and the high taxes which are necessary to support the war may make our frugality necessary; and, as I am always preaching that doctrine, I cannot in conscience or in decency encourage the contrary, by my example, in furnishing my children with foolish modes and luxuries. I therefore send all the articles you desire, that are useful and necessary, and omit the rest; for, as you say you should "have great pride in wearing any thing I send, and showing it as your father's taste," I must avoid giving you an opportunity of doing that with either lace or feathers. If you wear your cambric ruffles as I do, and take care not to mend the holes, they will come in time to be lace; and feathers, my dear girl, may be had in America from every cock's tail.

If you happen again to see General Washington, assure him of my very great and sincere respect, and tell him, that all the old Generals here amuse themselves in studying the accounts of his operations, and approve highly of his conduct.

Present my affectionate regards to all friends that inquire

after me, particularly Mr. Duffield and family, and write oftener, my dear child, to your loving father,

DESIGNS AND MOTTOES FOR COINS

To Edward Bridgen

DEAR SIR,   Passy, Octo^r 2^d 1779.
   I received your Favor of the 17th past, and the two Samples
of Copper are since come to hand. The Metal seems to be
very good, and the price reasonable; but I have not yet received the Orders necessary to justify my making the Purchase
proposed. There has indeed been an intention to strike Copper Coin, that may not only be useful as small Change, but
serve other purposes.
   Instead of repeating continually upon every halfpenny the
dull story that everybody knows, (and what it would have
been no loss to mankind if nobody had ever known,) that
Geo. III is King of Great Britain, France, and Ireland, &c.
&c., to put on one side, some important Proverb of Solomon, some pious moral, prudential or economical Precept,
the frequent Inculcation of which, by seeing it every time
one receives a piece of Money, might make an impression
upon the mind, especially of young Persons, and tend to
regulate the Conduct; such as, on some, *The fear of the Lord
is the beginning of Wisdom*; on others, *Honesty is the best Policy*; on others, *He that by the Plow would thrive, himself must
either hold or drive*; on others, *Keep thy Shop, and thy Shop will
keep thee*; on others, *A penny saved is a penny got*; on others,
*He that buys what he has no need of, will soon be forced to sell
his necessaries*; on others, *Early to bed and early to rise, will
make a man healthy, wealthy, and wise*; and so on, to a great
variety.
   The other side it was proposed to fill with good Designs,
drawn and engraved by the best artists in France, of all the
different Species of Barbarity with which the English have
carried on the War in America, expressing every abominable
circumstance of their Cruelty and Inhumanity, that figures

can express, to make an Impression on the minds of Posterity as strong and durable as that on the Copper. This Resolution has been a long time forborne; but the late burning of defenceless Towns in Connecticut, on the flimsy pretence that the people fired from behind their Houses, when it is known to have been premeditated and ordered from England, will probably give the finishing provocation, and may occasion a vast demand for your Metal.

I thank you for your kind wishes respecting my Health. I return them most cordially fourfold into your own bosom. Adieu.

"SOMEBODY . . . GAVE IT OUT THAT
I LOV'D LADIES"

To Elizabeth Partridge

MRS. PARTRIDGE   Passy, Oct. 11. 1779.

Your kind Letter, my dear Friend, was long in coming; but it gave me the Pleasure of knowing that you had been well in October and January last. The Difficulty, Delay & Interruption of Correspondence with those I love, is one of the great Inconveniencies I find in living so far from home: but we must bear these & more, with Patience, if we can; if not, we must bear them as I do with Impatience.

You mention the Kindness of the French Ladies to me. I must explain that matter. This is the civilest nation upon Earth. Your first Acquaintances endeavour to find out what you like, and they tell others. If 'tis understood that you like Mutton, dine where you will you find Mutton. Somebody, it seems, gave it out that I lov'd Ladies; and then every body presented me their Ladies (or the Ladies presented themselves) to be *embrac'd*, that is to have their Necks kiss'd. For as to kissing of Lips or Cheeks it is not the Mode here, the first, is reckon'd rude, & the other may rub off the Paint. The French Ladies have however 1000 other ways of rendering themselves agreable; by their various Attentions and Civilities, & their sensible Conversation. 'Tis a delightful People to live with.

I thank you for the Boston Newspapers, tho' I see nothing so clearly in them as that your Printers do indeed want new Letters. They perfectly blind me in endeavouring to read them. If you should ever have any Secrets that you wish to be well kept, get them printed in those Papers. You enquire if Printers Types may be had here? Of all Sorts, very good, cheaper than in England, and of harder Metal.—I will see any Orders executed in that way that any of your Friends may think fit to send. They will doubtless send Money with their Orders. Very good Printing Ink is likewise to be had here. I cannot by this opportunity send the miniature you desire, but I send you a little Head in China, more like, perhaps, than the Painting would be. It may be set in a Locket, if you like it, cover'd with Glass, and may serve for the present. When Peace comes we may afford to be more extravagant. I send with it a Couple of Fatherly Kisses for you & your amiable Daughter, the whole wrapt up together in Cotton to be kept warm.

Present my respectful Compliments to Mr Partridge.

Adieu, my dear Child, & believe me ever

Your affectionate Papah

"YOUR COOL CONDUCT
AND PERSEVERING BRAVERY"

To John Paul Jones

DEAR SIR,   Passy, Oct. 15, 1779.

I received the Account of your Cruize and Engagement with the *Serapis*, which you did me the honour to send me from the Texel. I have since received your Favor of the 8th, from Amsterdam. For some Days after the Arrival of your Express, scarce any thing was talked of at Paris and Versailles, but your cool Conduct and persevering Bravery during that terrible Conflict. You may believe, that the Impression on my Mind was not less strong than on that of others; but I do not chuse to say in a letter to yourself all I think on such an Occasion.

The Ministry are much dissatisfied with Captain Landais, and M. de Sartine has signified to me in writing that it is expected that I should send for him to Paris, and call him to Account for his Conduct particularly for deferring so long his coming to your Assistance, by which Means, it is supposed, the States lost some of their valuable Citizens, and the King lost many of his Subjects, Volunteers in your Ship, together with the Ship itself.

I have, accordingly, written to him this Day, acquainting him that he is charged with Disobedience of Orders in the Cruize, and Neglect of his Duty in the Engagement; that, a Court-Martial being at this Time inconvenient, if not impracticable, I would give him an earlier Opportunity of offering what he has to say in his Justification, and for that Purpose direct him to render himself immediately here, bringing with him such Papers or Testimonies, as he may think useful in his Defence. I know not whether he will obey my orders, nor what the Ministry will do with him, if he comes; but I suspect that they may by some of their concise Operations save the Trouble of a Court-Martial. It will be well, however, for you to furnish me with what you may judge proper to support the Charges against him, that I may be able to give a just and clear Account of the Affair to Congress. In the mean time it will be necessary, if he should refuse to come, that you should put him under an Arrest, and in that Case, as well as if he comes, that you should either appoint some Person to command his Ship or take it upon yourself; for I know of no Person to recommend to you as fit for that Station.

I am uneasy about your Prisoners; I wish they were safe in France. You will then have compleated the glorious work of giving Liberty to all the Americans that have so long languished for it in the British Prisons; for there are not so many there, as you have now taken.

I have the Pleasure to inform you, that the two Prizes sent to Norway are safely arrived at Berghen. With the highest Esteem, I am, &c.

P.S. I am sorry for your Misunderstanding with M. de Chaumont, who has a great Regard for you.

"THE GREAT UNCERTAINTY I FOUND
IN METAPHYSICAL REASONINGS"

To Benjamin Vaughan

DEAR SIR,   Passy, Nov. 9. 1779.

I have received several kind Letters from you, which I have not regularly answered. They gave me however great Pleasure, as they acquainted me with your Welfare, and that of your Family and other Friends; and I hope you will continue writing to me as often as you can do it conveniently.

I thank you much for the great Care and Pains you have taken in regulating and correcting the Edition of those Papers. Your Friendship for me appears in almost every Page; and if the Preservation of any of them should prove of Use to the Publick, it is to you that the Publick will owe the Obligation. In looking them over, I have noted some Faults of Impression that hurt the Sense, and some other little Matters, which you will find all in a Sheet under the title of *Errata*. You can best judge whether it may be worth while to add any of them to the Errata already printed, or whether it may not be as well to reserve the whole for Correction in another Edition, if such should ever be. Inclos'd I send a more perfect copy of the *Chapter*.

If I should ever recover the Pieces that were in the Hands of my Son, and those I left among my Papers in America, I think there may be enough to make three more such Volumes, of which a great part would be more interesting.

As to the *Time* of publishing, of which you ask my Opinion I am not furnish'd with any Reasons, or Ideas of Reasons, on which to form any Opinion. Naturally I should suppose the Bookseller to be from Experience the best Judge, and I should be for leaving it to him.

I did not write the Pamphlet you mention. I know nothing of it. I suppose it is the same, concerning which Dr. Priestley formerly asked me the same Question. That for which he took it was intitled, *A Dissertation on Liberty and Necessity, Pleasure and Pain*, with these Lines in the TitlePage.

> "Whatever is, is right. But purblind Man
> Sees but a part o' the Chain, the nearest Link;

> His eye not carrying to that equal Beam,
> That poises all above."   DRYDEN.

London, Printed M.D.C.C.X.XV.

It was addressed to Mr. J. R., that is, James Ralph, then a youth of about my age, and my intimate friend; afterwards a political writer and historian. The purport of it was to prove the doctrine of fate, from the supposed attributes of God; in some such manner as this: that in erecting and governing the world, as he was infinitely wise, he knew what would be best; infinitely good, he must be disposed, and infinitely powerful, he must be able to execute it: consequently all is right. There were only an hundred copies printed, of which I gave a few to friends, and afterwards disliking the piece, as conceiving it might have an ill tendency, I burnt the rest, except one copy, the margin of which was filled with manuscript notes by Lyons, author of the Infallibility of Human Judgment, who was at that time another of my acquaintance in London. I was not nineteen years of age when it was written. In 1730, I wrote a piece on the other side of the question, which began with laying for its foundation this fact: "That almost all men in all ages and countries, have at times made use of prayer." Thence I reasoned, that if all things are ordained, prayer must among the rest be ordained. But as prayer can produce no change in things that are ordained, praying must then be useless and an absurdity. God would therefore not ordain praying if everything else was ordained. But praying exists, therefore all things are not ordained, etc. This pamphlet was never printed, and the manuscript has been long lost. The great uncertainty I found in metaphysical reasonings disgusted me, and I quitted that kind of reading and study for others more satisfactory.

I return the Manuscripts you were so obliging as to send me; I am concern'd at your having no other copys, I hope these will get safe to your hands. I do not remember the Duke de Chaulnes showing me the Letter you mention. I have received Dr. Crawford's book, but not your Abstract, which I wait for as you desire.

I send you also M. Dupont's *Table Economique*, which I think an excellent Thing, as it contains in a clear Method all the principles of that new sect, called here *les Economistes.*

Poor Henley's dying in that manner is inconceivable to me. Is any Reason given to account for it, besides insanity?

Remember me affectionately to all your good Family, and believe me, with great Esteem, my dear Friend, yours, most sincerely,

"THAT MEN WOULD CEASE TO BE WOLVES"

To Joseph Priestley

DEAR SIR,   Passy, Feb. 8. 1780.

Your kind Letter of September 27 came to hand but very lately, the Bearer having staied long in Holland. I always rejoice to hear of your being still employ'd in experimental Researches into Nature, and of the Success you meet with. The rapid Progress *true* Science now makes, occasions my regretting sometimes that I was born so soon. It is impossible to imagine the Height to which may be carried, in a thousand years, the Power of Man over Matter. We may perhaps learn to deprive large Masses of their Gravity, and give them absolute Levity, for the sake of easy Transport. Agriculture may diminish its Labour and double its Produce; all Diseases may by sure means be prevented or cured, not excepting even that of Old Age, and our Lives lengthened at pleasure even beyond the antediluvian Standard. O that moral Science were in as fair a way of Improvement, that Men would cease to be Wolves to one another, and that human Beings would at length learn what they now improperly call Humanity!

I am glad my little Paper on the *Aurora Borealis* pleased. If it should occasion further Enquiry, and so produce a better Hypothesis, it will not be wholly useless. I am ever, with the greatest and most sincere Esteem, dear Sir, yours very affectionately

I have consider'd the Situation of that Person very attentively. I think that, with a little help from the *Moral Algebra,* he might form a better judgment than any other Person can form for him. But, since my Opinion seems to be desired, I give it for continuing to the End of the Term, under all the present disagreeable Circumstances. The connection will then die a natural Death. No Reason will be expected to be given for the Separation, and of course no Offence taken at Reasons given; the Friendship may still subsist, and in some other way be useful. The Time diminishes daily, and is usefully employ'd. All human Situations have their Inconveniencies; we *feel* those that we find in the present, and we neither *feel* nor *see* those that exist in another. Hence we make frequent and troublesome Changes without Amendment, and often for the worse.

In my Youth, I was Passenger in a little Sloop, descending the River Delaware. There being no Wind, we were obliged, when the Ebb was spent, to cast anchor, and wait for the next. The Heat of the Sun on the Vessel was excessive, the Company Strangers to me, and not very agreable. Near the river Side I saw what I took to be a pleasant green Meadow, in the middle of which was a large shady Tree, where it struck my Fancy I could sit and read, (having a Book in my Pocket,) and pass the time agreably till the tide turned. I therefore prevail'd with the Captain to put me ashore. Being landed, I found the greatest part of my Meadow was really a Marsh, in crossing which, to come at my Tree, I was up to my Knees in Mire; and I had not placed myself under its Shade five Minutes, before the Muskitoes in Swarms found me out, attack'd my Legs, Hands, and Face, and made my Reading and my Rest impossible; so that I return'd to the Beach, and call'd for the Boat to come and take me aboard again, where I was oblig'd to bear the Heat I had strove to quit, and also the Laugh of the Company. Similar Cases in the Affairs of Life have since frequently fallen under my Observation.

I have had Thoughts of a College for him in America. I know no one who might be more useful to the Publick in the Instruction of Youth. But there are possible Unpleasantnesses in that Situation; it cannot be obtain'd but by a too hazardous Voyage at this time for a Family; and the Time for Experiments would be all otherwise engaged.

"LIKE A FIELD OF YOUNG INDIAN CORN"

To George Washington

SIR,   Passy, March 5 1780.

I have received but lately the Letter your Excellency did me the honour of writing to me in Recommendation of the Marquis de la Fayette. His modesty detained it long in his own Hands. We became acquainted, however, from the time of his Arrival at Paris; and his Zeal for the Honour of our Country, his Activity in our Affairs here, and his firm Attachment to our Cause and to you, impress'd me with the same Regard and Esteem for him that your Excellency's Letter would have done, had it been immediately delivered to me.

Should peace arrive after another Campaign or two, and afford us a little Leisure, I should be happy to see your Excellency in Europe, and to accompany you, if my Age and Strength would permit, in visiting some of its ancient and most famous Kingdoms. You would, on this side of the Sea, enjoy the great Reputation you have acquir'd, pure and free from those little Shades that the Jealousy and Envy of a Man's Countrymen and Cotemporaries are ever endeavouring to cast over living Merit. Here you would know, and enjoy, what Posterity will say of Washington. For 1000 Leagues have nearly the same Effect with 1000 Years. The feeble Voice of those grovelling Passions cannot extend so far either in Time or Distance. At present I enjoy that Pleasure for you, as I frequently hear the old Generals of this martial Country, (who study the Maps of America, and mark upon them all your Operations,) speak with sincere Approbation and great Applause of your conduct; and join in giving you the Character of one of the greatest Captains of the Age.

I must soon quit the Scene, but you may live to see our Country flourish, as it will amazingly and rapidly after the War is over. Like a Field of young Indian Corn, which long Fair weather and Sunshine had enfeebled and discolored, and which in that weak State, by a Thunder Gust, of violent Wind, Hail, and Rain, seem'd to be threaten'd with absolute Destruction; yet the Storm being past, it recovers fresh

Verdure, shoots up with double Vigour, and delights the Eye, not of its Owner only, but of every observing Traveller.

The best Wishes that can be form'd for your Health, Honour, and Happiness, ever attend you from your Excellency's most obedient and most humble servant

To Thomas Bond

DEAR SIR,   Passy, March 16, 1780.

I received your kind letter of September the 22d, and I thank you for the pleasing account you give me of the health and welfare of my old friends, Hugh Roberts, Luke Morris, Philip Syng, Samuel Rhoads, &c., with the same of yourself and family. Shake the old ones by the hand for me, and give the young ones my blessing. For my own part, I do not find that I grow any older. Being arrived at seventy, and considering that by travelling further in the same road I should probably be led to the grave, I stopped short, turned about, and walked back again; which having done these four years, you may now call me sixty-six. Advise those old friends of ours to follow my example; keep up your spirits, and that will keep up your bodies; you will no more stoop under the weight of age, than if you had swallowed a handspike.

I am glad the Philosophical Society made that compliment to M. Gérard. I wish they would do the same to M. Feutry, a worthy gentleman here; and to Dr. Ingenhousz, who has made some great discoveries lately respecting the leaves of trees in improving air for the use of animals. He will send you his book. He is physician to the Empress Queen. I have not yet seen your piece on inoculation. Remember me respectfully and affectionately to Mrs. Bond, your children, and all friends. I am ever, &c.

P.S. I have bought some valuable books, which I intend to present to the Society; but shall not send them till safer times.

To William Carmichael

DEAR SIR,   Passy, June 17, 1780.

Your favours of the 22d past came duly to hand. Sir John Dalrymple has been here some time, but I hear nothing of his political operations. The learned talk of the discovery he has made in the Escurial Library, of forty Epistles of Brutus, a missing part of Tacitus, and a piece of Seneca, that have never yet been printed, which excite much curiosity. He has not been with me, and I am told, by one of his friends, that, though he wished to see me, he did not think it prudent. So I suppose I shall have no communication with him; for I shall not seek it. As Count de Vergennes has mentioned nothing to me of any memorial from him, I suppose he has not presented it; perhaps discouraged by the reception it met with in Spain. So I wish, for curiosity's sake, you would send me a copy of it.

The Marquis de Lafayette arrived safely at Boston on the 28th of April, and, it is said, gave expectations of the coming of a squadron and troops. The vessel that brings this left New London the 2d of May; her captain reports, that the siege of Charleston was raised, the troops attacked in their retreat, and Clinton killed; but this wants confirmation. London has been in the utmost confusion for seven or eight days. The beginning of this month, a mob of fanatics, joined by a mob of rogues, burnt and destroyed property to the amount, it is said, of a million sterling. Chapels of foreign ambassadors, houses of members of Parliament that had promoted the act for favouring Catholics, and the houses of many private persons of that religion, were pillaged and consumed, or pulled down, to the number of fifty; among the rest, Lord Mansfield's is burnt, with all his furniture, pictures, books, and papers. Thus he, who approved the burning of American houses, has had fire brought home to him. He himself was horribly scared, and Governor Hutchinson, it is said, died outright of the fright. The mob, tired with roaring and rioting seven days and nights, were at length suppressed, and quiet restored on the 9th, in the evening. Next day Lord George Gordon was committed to the tower.

Enclosed I send you the little piece you desire. To understand it rightly you should be acquainted with some few circumstances. The person to whom it was addressed is Madame Brillon, a lady of most respectable character and pleasing conversation; mistress of an amiable family in this neighbourhood, with which I spend an evening twice in every week. She has, among other elegant accomplishments, that of an excellent musician; and, with her daughters, who sing prettily, and some friends who play, she kindly entertains me and my grandson with little concerts, a cup of tea, and a game of chess. I call this *my Opera*, for I rarely go to the Opera at Paris.

The Moulin Joli is a little island in the Seine about two leagues hence, part of the country-seat of another friend, where we visit every summer, and spend a day in the pleasing society of the ingenious, learned, and very polite persons who inhabit it. At the time when the letter was written, all conversations at Paris were filled with disputes about the music of Gluck and Picini, a German and Italian musician, who divided the town into violent parties. A friend of this lady having obtained a copy of it, under a promise not to give another, did not observe that promise; so that many have been taken, and it is become as public as such a thing can well be, that is not printed; but I could not dream of its being heard of at Madrid! The thought was partly taken from a little piece of some unknown writer, which I met with fifty years since in a newspaper, and which the sight of the Ephemera brought to my recollection. Adieu, my dear friend, and believe me ever yours most affectionately,

"MR. ADAMS HAS GIVEN OFFENCE TO THE COURT HERE"

To Samuel Huntington

SIR,   Passy, August 9, 1780.

With this your Excellency will receive a Copy of my last, dated May 31st, the Original of which, with Copies of preceding Letters, went by the *Alliance*, Capt. Landais, who sailed the Beginning of last Month, and who I wish may arrive safe in America, being apprehensive, that by her long Delay in Port, from the Mutiny of the People, who after she was ready to sail refused to weigh Anchor till paid Wages, she may fall in the Way of the English Fleet now out; or that her Crew, who have ever been infected with Disorder and Mutiny, may carry her into England. She had, on her first coming out, a Conspiracy for that purpose; besides which her Officers and Captain quarrell'd with each other, the Captain with Comm^c Jones, and there have been so many Embroils among them, that it was impossible to get the Business forward while she staied, and she is at length gone, without taking the Quantity of Stores she was capable of taking, and was ordered to take.

I suppose the Conduct of that Captain will be enquired into by a Court-Martial. Capt. Jones goes home in the *Ariel*, a Ship we have borrowed of Government here, and carries 146 Chests of Arms, and 400 Barrels of Powder. To take the rest of the Stores, and Cloathing I have been obliged to freight a Ship, which, being well arm'd and well mann'd, will, I hope, get safe. The cloathes for 10,000 Men are, I think, all made up; there are also Arms for 15,000, new and good, with 2,000 Barrels of Powder. Besides this, there is a great Quantity of Cloth I have bought, of which you will have the Invoices, sent by Mr. Williams; another large Quantity purchas'd by Mr. Ross; all going in the same Ship.

The little Authority we have here to govern our armed Ships, and the Inconvenience of Distance from the Ports, occasion abundance of Irregularities in the Conduct of both Men and Officers. I hope, therefore, that no more of those Vessels will be sent hither, till our Code of Laws is perfected respecting Ships abroad, and proper Persons appointed to manage such Affairs in the SeaPorts. They give me infinite Trouble; and, tho' I endeavour to act for the best, it is without Satisfaction to myself, being unacquainted with that kind of Business. I have often mention'd the Appointment of a Consul or Consuls. The Congress have, perhaps, not yet had time to consider that Matter.

Having already sent you, by different Conveyances, Copies

of my Proceedings with the Court of Denmark, relative to the three Prizes delivered up to the English, and requested the Instructions of Congress, I hope soon to receive them. I mention'd a Letter from the Congress to that Court, as what I thought might have a good Effect. I have since had more Reasons to be of that Opinion.

The unexpected Delay of Mr. Dean's Arrival has retarded the Settlement of the joint Accounts of the Commission, he having had the chief Management of the commercial Part, and being therefore best able to explain Difficulties. I have just now the Pleasure to hear that the *Fier Rodrique*, with her Convoy from Virginia, arrived at Bordeaux, all safe except one Tobacco Ship, that foundered at Sea, the Men saved; and I have a letter from Mr. Deane that he is at Rochelle, proposes to stop a few Days at Nantes, and then proceed to Paris, when I shall endeavour to see that Business completed with all possible Expedition.

Mr. Adams has given Offence to the Court here, by some Sentiments and Expressions contained in several of his Letters written to the Count de Vergennes. I mention this with Reluctance, tho' perhaps it would have been my Duty to acquaint you with such a Circumstance, even were it not required of me by the Minister himself. He has sent me Copies of the Correspondence, desiring I would communicate them to Congress; and I send them herewith. Mr. Adams did not show me his Letters before he sent them. I have, in a former Letter to Mr. Lovell, mentioned some of the Inconveniencies, that attend the having more than one Minister at the same Court; one of which Inconveniencies is, that they do not always hold the same Language, and that the Impressions made by one, and intended for the Service of his Constituents, may be effaced by the Discourse of the other. It is true, that Mr. Adams's proper Business is elsewhere; but, the Time not being come for that Business, and having nothing else here wherewith to employ himself, he seems to have endeavoured to supply what he may suppose my Negociations defective in. He thinks, as he tells me himself, that America has been too free in Expressions of Gratitude to France; for that she is more oblig'd to us than we to her; and that we should show Spirit in our Applications. I apprehend, that he mistakes his Ground, and that this Court is to be treated with Decency and Delicacy. The King, a young and virtuous Prince, has, I am persuaded, a Pleasure in reflecting on the generous Benevolence of the Action in assisting an oppressed People, and proposes it as a Part of the Glory of his Reign. I think it right to encrease this Pleasure by our thankful Acknowledgments, and that such an Expression of Gratitude is not only our Duty, but our Interest. A different Conduct seems to me what is not only improper and unbecoming, but what may be hurtful to us. Mr. Adams, on the other hand, who, at the same time means our Welfare and Interest as much as I, or any man, can do, seems to think a little apparent Stoutness, and greater air of Independence and Boldness in our Demands, will procure us more ample Assistance. It is for Congress to judge and regulate their Affairs accordingly.

M. Vergennes, who appears much offended, told me, yesterday, that he would enter into no further Discussions with Mr. Adams, nor answer any more of his Letters. He is gone to Holland to try, as he told me, whether something might not be done to render us less dependent on France. He says, the Ideas of this Court and those of the People in America are so totally different, that it is impossible for any Minister to please both. He ought to know America better than I do, having been there lately, and he may chuse to do what he thinks will best please the People of America. But, when I consider the Expressions of Congress in many of their public Acts, and particularly in their Letter to the Chev. de la Luzerne, of the 24th of May last, I cannot but imagine, that he mistakes the Sentiments of a few for a general Opinion. It is my Intention, while I stay here, to procure what Advantages I can for our Country, by endeavouring to please this Court; and I wish I could prevent any thing being said by any of our Countrymen here, that may have a contrary Effect, and increase an Opinion lately showing itself in Paris, that we seek a Difference, and with a view of reconciling ourselves to England. Some of them have of late been very indiscreet in their Conversations.

I received, eight months after their Date, the Instructions of Congress relating to a new Article for guaranteeing the Fisheries. The expected Negociations for a Peace appearing of late more remote, and being too much occupied with other Affairs, I have not hitherto proposed that Article. But I purpose doing it next Week. It appears so reasonable and equitable, that I do not foresee any Difficulty. In my next, I shall give you an Account of what passes on the Occasion.

The Silver Medal ordered for the Chev.ʳ de Fleury, has been delivered to his Order here, he being gone to America. The others, for Brigadier-General Wayne and Colonel Stuart, I shall send by the next good Opportunity.

The Two Thousand Pounds I furnished to Messrs. Adams and Jay, agreable to an Order of Congress, for themselves and Secretaries, being nearly expended, and no Supplies to them arriving, I have thought it my Duty to furnish them with further Sums, hoping the Supplies promised will soon arrive to reimburse me, and enable me to pay the Bills drawn on Mr. Laurens in Holland, which I have engaged for, to save the public Credit, the Holders of those Bills threatening otherwise to protest them. Messrs. de Neufville of Amsterdam had accepted some of them. I have promised those Gentlemen to provide for the Payment before they become due, and to accept such others as shall be presented to me. I hear, and hope it is true, that the Drawing of such Bills is stopped, and that their Number and Value is not very great.

The Bills drawn in favour of M. de Beaumarchais for the Interest of his Debt are paid.

The German Prince, who gave me a Proposal some Months since for furnishing Troops to the Congress, has lately desired an Answer. I gave no Expectation, that it was likely you would agree to such a Proposal; but, being pressed to send it you, it went with some of my former Letters.

M. Fouquet, who was employ'd by Congress to instruct People in making Gunpowder, is arriv'd here, after a long Passage; he has requested me to transmit a Memorial to Congress, which I do, enclos'd.

The great public Event in Europe of this Year is the Proposal, by Russia, of an armed Neutrality for protecting the Liberty of Commerce. The proposition is accepted now by most of the maritime Powers. As it is likely to become the Law of Nations, *that free Ships should make free Goods*, I wish the Congress to consider, whether it may not be proper to give Orders to their Cruizers not to molest Foreign Ships, but conform to the Spirit of that Treaty of Neutrality.

The English have been much elated with their Success at Charlestown. The late News of the Junction of the French and Spanish Fleets, has a little abated their Spirits; and I hope that Junction, and the Arrival of the French Troops and Ships in N. America, will soon produce News, that may afford us also in our Turn some Satisfaction.

Application has been made to me here, requesting that I would solicit Congress to permit the Exchange of William John Mawhood, a Lieutenant in the 17th Regiment, taken Prisoner at Stony Point, July 15th, 1779, and confin'd near Philadelphia; or, if the exchange cannot conveniently be made, that he may be permitted to return to England on his Parole. By doing this at my Request, the Congress will enable me to oblige several Friends of ours, who are Persons of Merit and Distinction in this country.

Be pleased, Sir, to present my Duty to Congress, and believe me to be, with great Respect, &c.

P.S. A similar Application has been made to me in favour of Richard Croft, Lieutenant in the 20th Regiment, a Prisoner at Charlottesville. I shall be much obliged by any Kindness shown to that young Gentleman, and so will some Friends of ours in England, who respect his Father.

"A NEIGHBOUR MIGHT AS WELL ASK ME TO SELL
MY STREET DOOR"

To John Jay

DEAR SIR, Passy, October 2d, 1780.

I received duly and in good order the several letters you have written to me of August 16th, 19th, September 8th, and 22d. The papers that accompanied them of your writing gave me the pleasure of seeing the affairs of our country in such good hands, and the prospect, from your youth, of its having the service of so able a minister for a great number of years.

But the little success that has attended your late applications for money mortified me exceedingly; and the storm of bills which I found coming upon us both, has terrified and vexed me to such a degree that I have been deprived of sleep, and so much indisposed by continual anxiety, as to be rendered almost incapable of writing.

At length I got over a reluctance that was almost invincible, and made another application to the government here for more money. I drew up and presented a state of debts and newly-expected demands, and requested its aid to extricate me. Judging from your letters that you were not likely to obtain any thing considerable from your court, I put down in my estimate the 25,000 dollars drawn upon you, with the same sum drawn upon me, as what would probably come to me for payment. I have now the pleasure to acquaint you that my memorial was received in the kindest and most friendly manner, and though the court here is not without its embarrassments on account of money, I was told to make myself easy, for that I should be assisted with what was necessary. Mr. Searle arriving about this time, and assuring me there had been a plentiful harvest, and great crops of all kinds; that the Congress had demanded of the several States contributions in produce, which would be cheerfully given; that they would therefore have plenty of provisions to dispose of; and I being much pleased with the generous behaviour just experienced, I presented another paper, proposing, in order to ease the government here, which had been so willing to ease us, that the Congress might furnish their army in America with provisions in part of payment for the services lent us. This proposition, I was told, was well taken; but it being considered that the States having the enemy in their country, and obliged to make great expenses for the present campaign, the furnishing so much provisions as the French army might need, might straiten and be inconvenient to the Congress, his majesty did not at this time think it right to accept the offer. You will not wonder at my loving this good prince: he will win the hearts of all America.

If you are not so fortunate in Spain, continue however the even good temper you have hitherto manifested. Spain owes us nothing; therefore, whatever friendship she shows us in lending money or furnishing clothes, &c. though not equal to our wants and wishes, is however *tant de gagne*; those who have begun to assist us, are more likely to continue than to decline, and we are still so much obliged as their aids amount to. But I hope and am confident, that court will be wiser than to take advantage of our distress, and insist on our making sacrifices by an agreement, which the circumstances of such distress would hereafter weaken, and the very proposition can only give disgust at present. Poor as we are, yet as I know we shall be rich, I would rather agree with them to buy at a great price the whole of their right on the Mississippi, than sell a drop of its waters. A neighbour might as well ask me to sell my street door.

I wish you could obtain an account of what they have supplied us with already in money and goods.

Mr. Grand, informing me that one of the bills drawn on you having been sent from hence to Madrid, was come back unaccepted, I have directed him to pay it; and he has, at my request, undertaken to write to the Marquis D'Yranda, to assist you with money to answer such bills as you are not otherwise enabled to pay, and to draw on him for the amount, which drafts I shall answer here as far as 25,000 dollars. If you expect more, acquaint me. But pray write to Congress as I do, to forbear this practice, which is so extremely hazardous, and may, some time or other, prove very mischievous to their credit and affairs. I have undertaken, too, for all the bills drawn on Mr. Laurens, that have yet appeared. He was to have sailed three days after Mr. Searle, that is, the 18th July. Mr. Searle begins to be in pain for him, having no good opinion of the little vessel he was to embark in.

We have letters from America to the 7th August. The spirit of our people was never higher. Vast exertions making preparatory for some important action. Great harmony and affection between the troops of the two nations. The new money in good credit, &c.

I will write to you again shortly, and to Mr. Carmichael. I shall now be able to pay up your salaries complete for the year; but as demands unforeseen are continually coming upon me, I still retain the expectations you have given me of being reimbursed out of the first remittances you receive.

If you find any inclination to hug me for the good news of this letter, I constitute and appoint Mrs. Jay my attorney, to receive in my behalf your embraces. With great and sincere esteem,

> I have the honour to be, dear sir,
> Your most obedient and most humble servant,

RELIGIOUS TESTS

To Richard Price

DEAR SIR,   Passy, Oct. 9, 1780.

Besides the Pleasure of their Company, I had the great Satisfaction of hearing by your two valuable Friends, and learning from your Letter, that you enjoy a good State of Health. May God continue it, as well for the Good of Mankind as for your Comfort. I thank you much for the second Edition of your excellent Pamphlet. I forwarded that you sent to Mr. Dana, he being in Holland. I wish also to see the Piece you have written (as Mr. Jones tells me) on Toleration. I do not expect that your new Parliament will be either wiser or honester than the last. All Projects to procure an honest one, by Place Bills, &c., appear to me vain and Impracticable. The true Cure, I imagine, is to be found only in rendring all Places unprofitable, and the King too poor to give Bribes and Pensions. Till this is done, which can only be by a Revolution (and I think you have not Virtue enough left to procure one), your Nation will always be plundered, and obliged to pay by Taxes the Plunderers for Plundering and Ruining. Liberty and Virtue therefore join in the call, COME OUT OF HER, MY PEOPLE!

I am fully of your Opinion respecting religious Tests; but, tho' the People of Massachusetts have not in their new Constitution kept quite clear of them, yet, if we consider what that People were 100 Years ago, we must allow they have gone great Lengths in Liberality of Sentiment on religious Subjects; and we may hope for greater Degrees of Perfection, when their Constitution, some years hence, shall be revised.

If Christian Preachers had continued to teach as Christ and his Apostles did, without Salaries, and as the Quakers now do, I imagine Tests would never have existed; for I think they were invented, not so much to secure Religion itself, as the Emoluments of it. When a Religion is good, I conceive that it will support itself; and, when it cannot support itself, and God does not take care to support, so that its Professors are oblig'd to call for the help of the Civil Power, it is a sign, I apprehend, of its being a bad one. But I shall be out of my Depth, if I wade any deeper in Theology, and I will not trouble you with Politicks, nor with News which are almost as uncertain; but conclude with a heartfelt Wish to embrace you once more, and enjoy your sweet Society in Peace, among our honest, worthy, ingenious Friends at the *London*. Adieu,

"I THINK A WORTHIER MAN NEVER LIVED"

To Benjamin Waterhouse

SIR,   Passy, Jan. 18. 1781.

   I received your obliging Letter of the 16th past, enclosing one from my dear Friend, Dr. Fothergill. I was happy to hear from him, that he was quite free of the Disorder that had like to have remov'd him last summer. But I had soon after a Letter from another Friend, acquainting me, that he was again dangerously ill of the same Malady; and the newspapers have since announced his Death! I condole with you most sincerely on this Occasion. I think a worthier Man never lived. For besides his constant Readiness to serve his Friends, he was always studying and projecting something for the Good of his Country and of Mankind in general, and putting others, who had it in their Power, on executing what was out of his own reach; but whatever was within it he took care to do himself; and his incredible Industry and unwearied Activity enabled him to do much more than can now be ever known, his Modesty being equal to his other Virtues.

   I shall take care to forward his Letter to Mr. Pemberton. Enclos'd is one I have just received under Cover from that

Gentleman. You will take care to convey it by some safe Opportunity to London.

With hearty Wishes for your Prosperity and Success in your Profession, and that you may be a good Copy of your deceas'd Relation, I am, Sir, etc.,

"I SHALL BE READY TO BREAK, RUN AWAY,
OR GO TO PRISON WITH YOU"

To John Adams

SIR,   Passy, Feb. 22. 1781

I received the Letter your Excell^y did me honour of writing to me the 15th Inst. respecting Bills, presented to you for Acceptance drawn by Congress in favour of N. Tracey for 10,000£ Sterling payable 90 Days Sight; and desiring to know if I can furnish Funds for the Payment.

I have lately made a fresh & strong Application for more Money. I have not yet received a positive Answer. I have however two of the Christian Graces, Faith & Hope. But my Faith is only that of which the Apostle Speaks, the Evidence of things not seen. For in Truth I do not see at present how so many Bills drawn at random on our Ministers in France, Spain & Holland, are to be paid. Nor that anything but omnipotent Necessity can excuse the Imprudence of it. Yet I think Bills drawn upon us by the Congress ought at all Risques to be accepted. I shall accordingly use my best Endeavours to procure Money for their honourable Discharge against they become due, if you should not in the meantime be provided; and if those Endeavours fail, I shall be ready to break, run away, or go to prison with you, as it shall please God.

Sir G. Grand has returned to me the remainder of the Book of Promises, sign'd by us, which his House had not an Opportunity of issuing. Perhaps the late Charge of Affairs in that Country may open a way for them. If on consulting him you should be of that Opinion, I will send them to you.—With great Respect, I have the honour to be

                                                        Sir,

P. S.   Late Advices from Congress mention that Col. Laurens is coming over as Envoy extraordinary to this Court & Col. Palfray as Consul General. They may be expected every day.

To Court de Gebelin

DEAR SIR,   Passy, May 7, 1781.
    I am glad the little Book prov'd acceptable. It does not appear to me intended for a Grammar to teach the Language. It is rather what we call in English a *Spelling Book*, in which the only Method observ'd is, to arrange the Words according to their Number of Syllables, placing those of one Syllable together, then those of two Syllables, and so on. And it is to be observ'd, that *Sa ki ma*, for Instance, is not three Words, but one Word of three Syllables; and the reason that *Hyphens* are not plac'd between the Syllables is, that the Printer had not enough of them.
    As the Indians had no Letters, they had no Orthography. The Delaware Language being differently spelt from the Virginian may not always arise from a Difference in the Languages; for Strangers who learn the Language of an Indian Nation, finding no Orthography, are at Liberty in writing the Language to use such Compositions of Letters as they think will best produce the Sounds of the Words. I have observ'd, that our Europeans of different Nations, who learn the same Indian Language, form each his own Orthography according to the usual Sounds given to the Letters in his own Language. Thus the same Words of the Mohawk Language written by an English, a French, and a German Interpreter, often differ very much in the Spelling; and, without knowing the usual Powers of the Letters in the Language of the Interpreter, one cannot come at the Pronunciation of the Indian Words. The Spelling Book in question was, I think, written by a German.
    You mention a Virginian Bible. Is it not the Bible of the

Massachusetts Language, translated by Elliot, and printed in New England, about the middle of the last Century? I know this Bible, but have never heard of one in the Virginian Language. Your Observations of the Similitude between many of the Words, and those of the ancient World, are indeed very curious.

This Inscription, which you find to be Phenician, is, I think, near *Taunton* (not *Jannston*, as you write it). There is some Account of it in the old *Philosophical Transactions*. I have never been at the Place, but shall be glad to see your Remarks on it.

The Compass appears to have been long known in China, before it was known in Europe; unless we suppose it known to Homer, who makes the Prince, that lent Ships to Ulysses, boast that they had a *spirit* in them, by whose Directions they could find their way in a cloudy Day, or the darkest Night. If any Phenicians arriv'd in America, I should rather think it was not by the Accident of a Storm, but in the Course of their long and adventurous Voyages; and that they coasted from Denmark and Norway, over to Greenland, and down Southward by Newfoundland, Nova Scotia, &c., to New England; as the Danes themselves certainly did some ages before Columbus.

Our new American Society will be happy in the Correspondence you mention, and when it is possible for me, I shall be glad to attend the Meetings of your Society, which I am sure must be very instructive. With great and sincere esteem, I have the honour to be, &c.

"I HAVE ACTED IMPRUDENTLY"

To Comte de Vergennes

SIR,   Passy. June 10.ᵗʰ 1781

I received the letter your Excellency did me the honour of writing to me on the 8.ᵗʰ Inst. in answer to mine of the 4.ᵗʰ

The state of M.ʳ Laurens's transaction in Holland, as I understood it, is this. Capt. Gillon represented to him, that he had bought clothing &c. for the troops of South Carolina, to the value of 10,000£ sterling, which were actually shipp'd in the *Indienne*; that he now wanted money to get his ship out, and therefore proposed to M.ʳ Laurens to take those goods of him for the United States. M.ʳ Laurens agreed to take such as would suit their wants, and to pay for the same by Bills upon me at six months' sight; and proposed to send in her some other articles that could be bought in Holland. His motives were that this fine ship, if she could be got out, would be a safe conveyance; and that she would afterwards be useful to the Congress on our Coasts. He informed me that he had mentioned to your Excellency Capt. Gillon's proposal, and that you seem'd to approve of it. I accordingly consented to his ordering those drafts upon me; but this will not be any great addition to my difficulty, since in the term of 6 months, I can probably receive from Congress the Power which you judge necessary for applying any part of the loan opened in Holland, to the discharge of those Bills.

With regard to the drafts made by Congress on M.ʳ Jay, in expectation of a friendly loan from the Court of Spain, on M.ʳ Laurens and M.ʳ Adams in Holland, from assurances given by some People of that Country that a loan might be easily by them obtained there; and large drafts upon myself, exclusive of the Loan Office Interest Bills; these all together occasion an embarrassment, which it is my duty to lay before your Excellency, and to acquaint you with the consequences I apprehend may attend their not being duly discharged. Those Bills were occasioned first by the sums necessary last year to assemble our army and put it in a condition to act vigorously with the King's Sea and Land Forces arrived and expected to arrive from France against New York, and to defend the Southern Colonies. Our main Army was accordingly put into such a condition as to face M.ʳ Clinton before New York all summer; but the additional forces expected from France not arriving, the project was not pursued, and the advantage hoped for from that exertion and expence was not obtained, tho' the funds of Congress were thereby equally exhausted. A second necessity for drawing those Bills, arose from the delay of five months in the sailing of M.ʳ de Chaumont's ship, occasioned by the distraction of his affairs, whereby the clothing

for the army not arriving in time before winter, the Congress
were obliged to purchase the cloths taken by Privateers from
the Quebec Fleet; and this could only be done by payment
for the same in Bills. All these Bills were drawn by solemn
resolutions of Congress; and it seems to me evident, that if
no part of the aids lately resolved on by his Majesty can be
applied to their discharge, with out an express order from
Congress for that purpose, the Public Credit of the United
States instead of being "re-animated" as his Majesty graciously intended, will be destroy'd; for the Bills unpaid, must,
according to the usual Course be returned under protest, long
before such order can be obtained, which protest will by our
laws, entitle the Holders to a Damage of 20 p^r cent, whereby
the public will incur a net loss of one fifth of the whole sum
drawn for; an effect, that will be made use of by their Enemies to discredit their Government among the People, and
must weaken their hands much more in that respect, than by
the mere loss of so much money. On these considerations,
and also from an opinion that a bill already drawn by order
of Congress, was as good and clear a declaration of their will
with regard to the disposition of so much of any funds they
might have at their disposal in Europe, as any future order of
theirs could be, I ventured to accept and to promise payment
of all the Bills above mention'd. What I have requested of
your Excellency in my late letter, and what I now beg leave
to repeat, is only that so much of the intended aid may be
retained, as shall be necessary to pay those acceptances as they
become due. I had not the least apprehension that this could
meet with any difficulty; and I hope on reconsideration, your
Excellency may still judge, that it will be for the advantage of
the common cause if this request is granted.

I have already paid most of the Bills drawn on M. Jay,
which the Money furnish'd to him by the Court of Spain did
not suffice to pay: I have also paid a part of those drawn on
Mr Laurens, Mr Adams and myself: To do this I have been
obliged to anticipate our funds, so that, as our Banker informs me, I shall by the end of this month owe him about
400,000 Livres, tho' he has already rec^d from M. D'Harvelay
for the quarter of August. I have acted imprudently in making
these acceptances and entering into these engagements with-

out first consulting your Excellency and obtaining your explicit approbation; but I acted as I thought for the best; I imagined it a case of absolute necessity, and relying on assistance from the new aids intended us, and considering the fatal consequence of protests, I thought at the time that I acted prudently and safely.

The supplies I shall want for the payment of these Bills will be gradual: If I cannot obtain them but by an order from Congress, I must not only stop payment of those not yet become due, but I apprehend that I shall be obliged to refuse acceptance of some of the interest Bills, having disabled myself from paying them, by paying so many others.

I therefore beg your Excellency would reconsider this important affair. I am sorry to find myself under a necessity of giving you so much trouble. I wish rather to diminish your cares than to increase them; being with the most perfect Respect, Sir,   Your Excellency's most

obedient and most humble servant

"THESE SUPERIOR AIRS YOU GIVE YOURSELF,
YOUNG GENTLEMAN, OF REPROOF TO ME"

To William Jackson

SIR,   Passy, July 10, 1781.

Last Night I received your 4th Letter on the Same Subject. You are anxious to carry the Money with you, because it will reanimate the Credit of America. My Situation and long Acquaintance with affairs relating to the public Credit enables me, I think, to judge better than you can do, who are a Novice in them, what Employment of it will most conduce to that End; and I imagine the retaining it to pay the Congress Drafts has infinitely the Advantage. You repeat that the Ship is detain'd by my Refusal. You forget your having written to me expressly that she waited for Convoy. You remind me of the great Expence the Detention of the Ship occasions. Who has given Orders to stop her? It was not me. I had no Authority to do it. Have you? And do you imagine, if you had taken such Authority upon you, that the Congress ought to bear the Expence occasion'd by your Imprudence? and that the Blame of detaining the necessary Stores the Ship contains will be excus'd by your fond Desire of carrying the Money? The Noise you have rashly made about this Matter, contrary to the Advice of Mr. Adams, which you ask'd and receiv'd, and which was to comply with my Requisition, has already done great Mischief to our Credit in Holland. Messrs. Fizeaux have declar'd they will advance to him no more Money on his Bills upon me to assist in paying the Congress Drafts on him. Your Commodore, too, complains, in a Letter I have seen, that he finds it difficult to get Money for my Acceptances of your Drafts in order to clear his Ship, tho' before this Proceeding of yours Bills on me were, as Mr. Adams assures me, in as good Credit on the Exchange of Amsterdam as those of any Banker in Europe. I suppose the Difficulty mention'd by the Commodore is the true Reason of the ship's Stay, if in fact the Convoy is gone without her. Credit is a delicate thing, capable of being blasted with a Breath. The public Talk you have occasion'd about my Stopping the Money, and the Conjectures of the Reasons or Necessity of doing it, have created Doubts and Suspicions of most pernicious Consequence. It is a Matter that should have pass'd in Silence. You repeat as a Reason for your Conduct, that the Money was obtain'd by the great Exertions of Col. Laurens. Who obtain'd the Grant is of no Importance, tho' the Use I propose to make of it is of the greatest. But the Fact is not as you state it. I obtain'd it before he came. And if he were here I am sure I could convince him of the Necessity of leaving it. Especially after I should have inform'd him that you had made in Holland the enormous Purchase of £40,000 Sterling's worth of Goods over and above the £10,000 worth, which I had agreed should be purchased by him on my Credit, and that you had induc'd me to engage for the Payment of your Purchase by showing me a Paper said to contain his Orders to you for making it, which I then took to be his Handwriting, tho' I afterwards found it to be yours, and not sign'd by him. It would be an additional Reason with him, when I should remind him that he himself, to induce me to come into the Proposal of Commodore Gillon and the rest of the Holland Transaction, to which I was averse, assur'd me that he had mention'd it to the Minister, and that it was approv'd of: That on the contrary I find the Minister remembers nothing of it, very much dislikes it, and absolutely refuses to furnish any Money to discharge that Account. You finish your Letter by telling me that, "the daily Enhancement of Expence to the United States from these Difficulties is worthy the Attention of those whose *Duty* is to œconomize the Public Money, and to whom the commonWeal is intrusted without deranging the special Department of another." The Ship's lying there with 5 or 600 Men on board is undoubtedly a great daily Expence, but it is you that occasion it; and these Superior Airs you give yourself, young Gentleman, of Reproof to me, and Reminding me of my Duty do not become you, whose special Department and Employ in public Affairs, of which you are so vain, is but of yesterday, and would never have existed but by my Concurrence, and would have ended in the Disgrace if I had not supported your enormous Purchases by accepting your Drafts. The charging me with want of œconomy is particularly improper in *you*, when the only Instance you know of it is my having indiscreetly comply'd with your Demand in advancing you 120 Louis for the Expence of your Journey to Paris and when the only Instance I know of your œconomizing Money is your sending me three Expresses, one after another, on the same Day, all the way from Holland to Paris, each with a Letter saying the same thing to the same purpose. This Dispute is as useless as it is unpleasant. It can only create ill Blood. Pray let us end it. I have the honour to be, etc.,

"ASSISTING WITH AN EQUAL SUM A STRANGER
WHO HAS EQUAL NEED OF IT"

To William Nixon

REV^D SIR,   Passy, Sept. 5, 1781.

I duly received the Letter you did me the Honour of writing to me the 25th past, together with the valuable little Book, of which you are the Author. There can be no doubt, but that a Gentleman of your Learning and Abilities might make a very useful Member of Society in our new Country, and meet with Encouragement there, either as an Instructor in one of our Universities, or as a Clergyman of the Church of Ireland. But I am not impowered to engage any Person to go over thither, and my Abilities to assist the Distressed are very limited. I suppose you will soon be set at Liberty in England by the Cartel for the Exchange of Prisoners. In the mean time, if Five *Louis-d'ors* may be of present Service to you, please to draw on me for that Sum, and your Bill shall be paid on Sight. Some time or other you may have an Opportunity of assisting with an equal Sum a stranger who has equal need of it. Do so. By that means you will discharge any Obligation you may suppose yourself under to me. Enjoin him to do the same on Occasion. By pursuing such a Practice, much Good may be done with little money. Let kind Offices go round. Mankind are all of a Family. I have the honour to be, Revd Sir, &c.

ON FINE PRINTING

To William Strahan

DEAR SIR,　　　　　　　　　　Passy, December 4, 1781.

Not remembering precisely the address of Mrs. Strange, I beg leave to request you would forward the Enclosed to her, which I received under my Cover from America.

I formerly sent you from Philadelphia part of an Edition of "Tully on Old Age," to be sold in London; and you put the Books, if I remember right, into the Hands of Mr. Becket for that Purpose. Probably he may have some of them still in his Warehouse, as I never had an account of their being sold. I shall be much oblig'd by your procuring and sending me one of them.

A strong Emulation exists at present between Paris and Madrid, with regard to beautiful Printing. Here a M. Didot *le jeune* has a Passion for the Art, and besides having procured the best Types, he has much improv'd the Press. The utmost Care is taken of his Presswork; his Ink is black, and his Paper fine and white. He has executed several charming Editions.

But the "Salust" and the "Don Quixote" of Madrid are thought to excel them. Didot however, improves every day, and by his zeal and indefatigable application bids fair to carry the Art to a high Pitch of Perfection. I will send you a Sample of his Work when I have an opportunity.

I am glad to hear that you have married your Daughter happily, and that your Prosperity continues. I hope it may never meet with any Interruption having still, tho' at present divided by public Circumstances, a Remembrance of our ancient private Friendship. Please to present my affectionate Respects to Mrs. Strahan, and my Love to your Children. With great Esteem and Regard, I am, dear Sir,

Your most humble and most obedient Servant,

"NOR A SYLLABLE OF APPROBATION"

To John Adams

SIR   Passy, Dec. 17, 1781

I have received the Packet containing the correspondence relating to the Goods. I suppose that Mr Barclay is there before this time, and the Affair in a way of Accommodation. Young Mr Neufville is here; but I have thought it best not to give him as yet any Hopes of my paying the Bills unless the Goods are delivered. I shall write fully by next Post. This serves chiefly to acquaint you that I will endeavour to pay the Bills that have been presented to you drawn on Mr Laurens. But you terrify me, by acquainting me that there are yet a great number behind. It is hard that I never had any information sent me of the Sums drawn, a Line of Order to pay, nor a Syllable of Approbation for having paid any of the Bills drawn on Mr Laurens, Mr Jay or yourself. As yet I do not see that I can go any further, and therefore can engage for no more than you have mention'd.

With great Esteem, I have the honour to be Sir
Your Excellency's
most obedient and most
humble Servant

ON THE LIBERTAS MEDAL

To Robert R. Livingston

SIR,   Passy, March 4, 1782.

Since I wrote the two short letters, of which I herewith
send you copies, I have been honoured with yours, dated the
16th of December.

Enclosed I send two letters from Count de Vergennes, relating to certain complaints from Ostend and Copenhagen
against our cruisers. I formerly forwarded a similar complaint
from Portugal, to which I have yet received no answer. The
ambassador of that kingdom frequently teazes me for it. I
hope now, that by your means this kind of affairs will be
more immediately attended to; ill blood and mischief may be
thereby sometimes prevented.

The Marquis de Lafayette was at his return hither received
by all ranks with all possible distinction. He daily gains in the
general esteem and affection, and promises to be a great man
here. He is warmly attached to our cause; we are on the most
friendly and confidential footing with each other, and he is
really very serviceable to me in my applications for additional
assistance.

I have done what I could in recommending Messieurs Duportail and Gouvion, as you desired. I did it with pleasure, as
I have much esteem for them.

I will endeavour to procure a sketch of an emblem for the
purpose you mention. This puts me in mind of a medal I have
had a mind to strike, since the late great event you gave me
an account of, representing the United States by the figure of
an infant Hercules in his cradle, strangling the two serpents;
and France by that of Minerva, sitting by as his nurse, with
her spear and helmet, and her robe specked with a few *fleurs
de lis*. The extinguishing of two entire armies in one war is
what has rarely happened, and it gives a presage of the future
force of our growing empire.

I thank you much for the newspapers you have been so
kind as to send me. I send also to you, by every opportunity,
packets of the French, Dutch, and English papers. Enclosed
is the last *Courier of Europe*, wherein you will find a late curi-

ous debate on continuing the war with America, which the minister carried in the affirmative only by his own vote. It seems the nation is sick of it, but the King is obstinate. *There is a change made of the American Secretary*, and another is talked of in the room of Lord Sandwich. But I suppose we have no reason to desire such changes. If the King will have a war with us, his old servants are as well for us as any he is likely to put in their places. The ministry, you will see, declare, that the war in America is for the future to be only *defensive*. I hope we shall be too prudent to have the least dependence on this declaration. It is only thrown out to lull us; for, depend upon it, the King hates us cordially, and will be content with nothing short of our extirpation.

I shall be glad to receive the account you are preparing of the wanton damages done our possessions. I wish you could also furnish me with one, of the barbarities committed on our people. They may both be of excellent use on certain occasions. I received the duplicate of yours in cipher. Hereafter, I wish you would use that in which those instructions were written, that relate to the future peace. I am accustomed to that, and I think it very good and more convenient in the practice.

The friendly disposition of this court towards us continues. We have sometimes pressed a little too hard, expecting and demanding, perhaps, more than we ought, and have used improper arguments, which may have occasioned a little dissatisfaction, but it has not been lasting. In my opinion, the surest way to obtain liberal aid from others is vigorously to help ourselves. People fear assisting the negligent, the indolent, and the careless, lest the aids they afford should be lost. I know we have done a great deal; but it is said, we are apt to be supine after a little success, and too backward in furnishing our contingents. This is really a generous nation, fond of glory, and particularly that of protecting the oppressed. Trade is not the admiration of their noblesse, who always govern here. Telling them, their *commerce* will be advantaged by our success, and that it is their *interest* to help us, seems as much as to say, "Help us, and we shall not be obliged to you." Such indiscreet and improper language has been sometimes held here by some of our people, and produced no good effects.

The constant harmony, subsisting between the armies of the two nations in America, is a circumstance, that has afforded me infinite pleasure. It should be carefully cultivated. I hope nothing will happen to disturb it. The French officers, who have returned to France this winter, speak of our people in the handsomest and kindest manner; and there is a strong desire in many of the young noblemen to go over to fight for us; there is no restraining some of them; and several changes among the officers of their army have lately taken place in consequence.

You must be so sensible of the utility of maintaining a perfect good understanding with the Chevalier de la Luzerne, that I need say nothing on that head. The affairs of a distant people in any court of Europe will always be much affected by the representations of the minister of that court residing among them.

We have here great quantities of supplies, of all kinds, ready to be sent over, and which would have been on their way before this time, if the unlucky loss of the transports, that were under M. de Guichen, and other demands for more ships, had not created a difficulty to find freight for them. I hope however, that you will receive them with the next convoy.

The accounts we have of the economy introduced by Mr. Morris begin to be of service to us here, and will by degrees obviate the inconvenience, that an opinion of our disorders and mismanagements had occasioned. I inform him by this conveyance of the money aids we shall have this year. The sum is not so great as we could wish; and we must so much the more exert ourselves. A small increase of industry in every American, male and female, with a small diminution of luxury, would produce a sum far superior to all we can hope to beg or borrow from all our friends in Europe.

There are now near a thousand of our brave fellows prisoners in England, many of whom have patiently endured the hardships of that confinement several years, resisting every temptation to serve our enemies. Will not your late great advantages put it in your power to do something for their relief? The slender supply I have been able to afford, of a shilling a week to each, for their greater comfort during the winter, amounts weekly to fifty pounds sterling. An exchange would make so many of our countrymen happy, add to our strength, and diminish our expense. But our privateers, who cruise in Europe, will not be at the trouble of bringing in their prisoners, and I have none to exchange for them.

Generals Cornwallis and Arnold are both arrived in England. It is reported, that the former, in all his conversations, discourages the prosecution of the war in America; if so, he will of course be out of favour. We hear much of audiences given to the latter, and of his being present at councils.

You desire to know, whether any intercepted letters of Mr. Deane have been published in Europe? I have seen but one in the English papers, that to Mr. Wadsworth, and none in any of the French and Dutch papers, but some may have been printed that have not fallen in my way. There is no doubt of their being all genuine. His conversation, since his return from America, has, as I have been informed, gone gradually more and more into that style, and at length come to an open vindication of Arnold's conduct; and, within these few days, he has sent me a letter of twenty full pages, recapitulating those letters, and threatening to write and publish an account of the treatment he has received from Congress, &c. He resides at Ghent, is distressed both in mind and circumstances, raves and writes abundance, and I imagine it will end in his going over to join his friend Arnold in England. I had an exceeding good opinion of him when he acted with me, and I believe he was then sincere and hearty in our cause. But he is changed, and his character ruined in his own country and in this, so that I see no other but England to which he can now retire. He says, that we owe him about twelve thousand pounds sterling; and his great complaint is, that we do not settle his accounts and pay him. Mr. Johnston having declined the service, I proposed engaging Mr. Searle to undertake it; but Mr. Deane objected to him, as being his enemy. In my opinion he was, for that reason, even fitter for the service of Mr. Deane; since accounts are of a mathematical nature, and cannot be changed by an enemy, while that enemy's testimony, that he had found them well supported by authentic vouchers, would have weighed more than the same testimony from a friend.

With regard to negotiations for a peace, I see but little probability of their being entered upon seriously this year, unless the English minister has failed in raising his funds, which it is said he has secured; so that we must provide for another campaign, in which I hope God will continue to favour us, and humble our cruel and haughty enemies; a circumstance which, whatever Mr. Deane may say to the contrary, will give pleasure to all Europe.

This year opens well, by the reduction of Port Mahon, and the garrison prisoners of war, and we are not without hopes, that Gibraltar may soon follow. A few more signal successes in America will do much towards reducing our enemies to reason. Your expressions of good opinion with regard to me, and wishes of my continuance in this employment, are very obliging. As long as the Congress think I can be useful to our affairs, it is my duty to obey their orders; but I should be happy to see them better executed by another, and myself at liberty, enjoying, before I quit the stage of life, some small degree of leisure and tranquillity. With great esteem, &c.

"A HAPPY NAME FOR A PRINCE
AS OBSTINANT AS A MULE"

To John Adams

SIR   Passy, April 22, 1782

Mess.ʳˢ Fizeaux and Grand have lately sent me two accounts of which they desire my approbation. As they relate to Payments made by those Gentlemen of your Acceptances of Bills of Exchange, your Approbation must be of more importance than mine, you having more certain knowledge of the Affair. I therefore send them enclos'd to you and request you would be pleas'd to compare them with your List of Acceptations, and return them to me with your opinion, as they will be my Justification for advancing the Money.

I am very happy to hear of the rapid progress of your affairs. They fear in England that the States will make with us an alliance offensive and defensive, and the public Funds which they had puff'd up four or five per cent by the hope of a Separate Peace with Holland are falling again. They fill their papers continually with lies to raise and fall the Stocks. It is not amiss that they should thus be left to ruin one another, for they have been very—mischievous to the rest of mankind. I send enclosed a paper, of the Veracity of which I have some doubt, as to the Form, but none as to the Substance, for I believe the Number of People actually scalp'd in this murdering war by the Indians to exceed what is mentioned in invoice, and that Muley Istmael (a happy name for a prince as obstinant as a mule) is full as black a Tyrant as he is represented in Paul Jones' pretended letter. These being *substantial* Truths the Form is to be considered as Paper and Packthread. If it were republish'd in England it might make them a little asham'd of themselves.

I am very respectfully

Your Excellency's

most obedient and most

humble Servant

"MEN I FIND TO BE A SORT OF BEINGS VERY BADLY CONSTRUCTED"

To Joseph Priestley

DEAR SIR, Passy near Paris, June 7, 1782.

I received your kind Letter of the 7th of April, also one of the 3d of May. I have always great Pleasure in hearing from you, in learning that you are well, and that you continue your Experiments. I should rejoice much, if I could once more recover the Leisure to search with you into the Works of Nature; I mean the *inanimate*, not the *animate* or moral part of them, the more I discover'd of the former, the more I admir'd them; the more I know of the latter, the more I am disgusted with them. Men I find to be a Sort of Beings very badly constructed, as they are generally more easily provok'd than reconcil'd, more disposed to do Mischief to each other than to make Reparation, much more easily deceiv'd than undeceiv'd, and having more Pride and even Pleasure in killing

than in begetting one another; for without a Blush they assemble in great armies at NoonDay to destroy, and when they
have kill'd as many as they can, they exaggerate the Number
to augment the fancied Glory; but they creep into Corners,
or cover themselves with the Darkness of night, when they
mean to beget, as being asham'd of a virtuous Action. A virtuous Action it would be, and a vicious one the killing of
them, if the Species were really worth producing or preserving; but of this I begin to doubt.

I know you have no such Doubts, because, in your zeal for
their welfare, you are taking a great deal of pains to save their
Souls. Perhaps as you grow older, you may look upon this as
a hopeless Project, or an idle Amusement, repent of having
murdered in mephitic air so many honest, harmless mice, and
wish that to prevent mischief, you had used Boys and Girls
instead of them. In what Light we are viewed by superior
Beings, may be gathered from a Piece of late West India
News, which possibly has not yet reached you. A young Angel of Distinction being sent down to this world on some
Business, for the first time, had an old courier-spirit assigned
him as a Guide. They arriv'd over the Seas of Martinico, in
the middle of the long Day of obstinate Fight between the
Fleets of Rodney and De Grasse. When, thro' the Clouds of
smoke, he saw the Fire of the Guns, the Decks covered with
mangled Limbs, and Bodies dead or dying; the ships sinking,
burning, or blown into the Air; and the Quantity of Pain,
Misery, and Destruction, the Crews yet alive were thus with
so much Eagerness dealing round to one another; he turn'd
angrily to his Guide, and said, "You blundering Blockhead,
you are ignorant of your Business; you undertook to conduct
me to the Earth, and you have brought me into Hell!" "No,
Sir," says the Guide, "I have made no mistake; this is really
the Earth, and these are men. Devils never treat one another
in this cruel manner; they have more Sense, and more of what
Men (vainly) call *Humanity*."

But to be serious, my dear old Friend, I love you as much
as ever, and I love all the honest Souls that meet at the London Coffee-House. I only wonder how it happen'd, that they
and my other Friends in England came to be such good Creatures in the midst of so perverse a Generation. I long to see

them and you once more, and I labour for Peace with more Earnestness, that I may again be happy in your sweet society.

I show'd your letter to the Duke de Larochefoucault, who thinks with me, the new Experiments you have made are extremely curious; and he has given me thereupon a Note, which I inclose, and I request you would furnish me with the answer desired.

Yesterday the Count du Nord was at the Academy of Sciences, when sundry Experiments were exhibited for his Entertainment; among them, one by M. Lavoisier, to show that the strongest Fire we yet know, is made in a Charcoal blown upon with dephlogisticated air. In a Heat so produced, he melted Platina presently, the Fire being much more powerful than that of the strongest burning mirror. Adieu, and believe me ever, yours most affectionately,

"BY THE PRESS WE CAN SPEAK TO NATIONS"

To Richard Price

DEAR SIR,   Passy, June 13, 1782.

I congratulate you on the late revolution in your public affairs. Much good may arise from it, though possibly not all, that good men and even the new ministers themselves may have wished or expected. The change, however, in the sentiments of the nation, in which I see evident effects of your writings, with those of our deceased friend Mr. Burgh, and others of our valuable Club, should encourage you to proceed.

The ancient Roman and Greek orators could only speak to the number of citizens capable of being assembled within the reach of their voice. Their *writings* had little effect, because the bulk of the people could not read. Now by the press we can speak to nations; and good books and well written pamphlets have great and general influence. The facility, with which the same truths may be repeatedly enforced by placing them daily in different lights in *newspapers*, which are everywhere read, gives a great chance of establishing them. And we now find, that it is not only right to strike while the iron is hot, but that it may be very practicable to heat it by continually striking.

I suppose all may now correspond with more freedom, and I shall be glad to hear from you as often as may be convenient to you. Please to present my best respects to our good old friends of the London Coffee-House. I often figure to myself the pleasure I should have in being once more seated among them. With the greatest and most sincere esteem and affection, I am, my dear friend, yours ever,

"I AM COVETOUS, AND LOVE GOOD BARGAINS"

To Miss Alexander

Passy, June 24, 1782.

—I am not at all displeas'd, that the Thesis and Dedication, with which we were threatned, are blown over, for I dislike much all sorts of Mummery. The Republic of Letters has gained no Reputation, whatever else it may have gain'd, by the Commerce of Dedications; I never made one, and I never desir'd, that one should be made to me. When I submitted to receive this, it was from the bad Habit I have long had of doing every thing that Ladies desire me to do; there is no refusing any thing to Madame la Marck, nor to you. I have been to pay my Respects to that amiable lady, not merely because it was a Compliment due to her, but because I love her; which induces me to excuse her not letting me in; the same Reason I should have for excusing your faults, if you had any.

I have not seen your Papa since the Receipt of your pleasing Letter, so could arrange nothing with him respecting the Carriage. During seven or eight days, I shall be very busy; after that you shall hear from me, and the Carriage shall be at your Service. How could you think of writing to me about Chimneys and Fires, in such Weather as this! Now is the time for the frugal Lady you mention to save her Wood, obtain *plus de Chaleur*, and lay it up against Winter, as people do Ice against Summer. Frugality is an enriching Virtue; a Virtue I never could acquire in myself; but I was once lucky enough to find it in a Wife, who thereby became a Fortune to me. Do you possess it? If you do, and I were 20 Years younger, I would give your Father 1,000 Guineas for you. I know you would be worth more to me as a *Ménagère*, but I am covetous, and love good Bargains. Adieu, my dear Friend, and believe me ever yours most affectionately,

"THE MORE I AM CONVINC'D OF A FUTURE STATE"

To James Hutton

MY OLD AND DEAR FRIEND,   Passy, July 7, 1782.

A Letter written by you to M. Bertin, *Ministre d'Etat*, containing an Account of the abominable Murders committed by some of the frontier People on the poor Moravian Indians, has given me infinite Pain and Vexation. The Dispensations of Providence in this World puzzle my weak Reason. I cannot comprehend why cruel Men should have been permitted thus to destroy their Fellow Creatures. Some of the Indians may be suppos'd to have committed Sins, but one cannot think the little Children had committed any worthy of Death. Why has a single Man in England, who happens to love Blood and to hate Americans, been permitted to gratify that bad Temper by hiring German Murderers, and joining them with his own, to destroy in a continued Course of bloody Years near 100,000 human Creatures, many of them possessed of useful Talents, Virtues and Abilities to which he has no Pretension! It is he who has furnished the Savages with Hatchets and Scalping Knives, and engages them to fall upon our defenceless Farmers, and murder them with their Wives and Children, paying for their Scalps, of which the account kept in America already amounts, as I have heard, to near *two Thousand*!

Perhaps the people of the frontiers, exasperated by the Cruelties of the Indians, have been induced to kill all Indians that fall into their Hands without Distinction; so that even these horrid Murders of our poor Moravians may be laid to his Charge. And yet this Man lives, enjoys all the good Things this World can afford, and is surrounded by Flatterers, who keep even his Conscience quiet by telling him he is the best of Princes! I wonder at this, but I cannot therefore part with the comfortable Belief of a Divine Providence; and the more I see the Impossibility, from the number & extent of his Crimes, of giving equivalent Punishment to a wicked Man in this Life, the more I am convinc'd of a future State, in which all that here appears to be wrong shall be set right, all that is crooked made straight. In this Faith let you & I, my dear Friend, comfort ourselves; it is the only Comfort, in the present dark Scene of Things, that is allow'd us.

I shall not fail to write to the Government of America, urging that effectual Care may be taken to protect & save the Remainder of those unhappy People.

Since writing the above, I have received a Philadelphia Paper, containing some Account of the same horrid Transaction, a little different, and some Circumstances alledged as Excuses or Palliations, but extreamly weak & insufficient. I send it to you inclos'd. With great and sincere Esteem, I am ever, my dear Friend, yours most affectionately,

"TO COOP US UP WITHIN
THE ALLEGANY MOUNTAINS"

To Robert R. Livingston

SIR,   Passy, August 12, 1782.

I have lately been honoured with your several letters, of March 9th, and May 22d, and 30th. The paper, containing a state of the commerce in North America, and explaining the necessity and utility of convoys for its protection, I have laid before the minister, accompanied by a letter, pressing that it be taken into immediate consideration; and I hope it may be attended with success.

The order of Congress, for liquidating the accounts between this court and the United States, was executed before it arrived. All the accounts against us for money lent, and stores, arms, ammunition, clothing, &c., furnished by government, were brought in and examined, and a balance received, which made the debt amount to the even sum of eighteen millions, exclusive of the Holland loan, for which the King is guarantee. I send a copy of the instrument to Mr. Morris. In reading it, you will discover several fresh marks of the King's goodness towards us, amounting to the value of near two millions. These, added to the free gifts before made to us at different times, form an object of at least twelve millions, for which no returns but that of gratitude and friendship are expected. These, I hope, may be everlasting. The constant good understanding between France and the Swiss Cantons, and the steady benevolence of this crown towards them, afford us a well grounded hope that our alliance may be as durable and as happy for both nations; there being strong reasons for our union, and no crossing interests between us. I write fully to Mr. Morris on money affairs, who will doubtless communicate to you my letter, so that I need say the less to you on that subject.

The letter to the King was well received; the accounts of your rejoicings on the news of the Dauphin's birth gave pleasure here; as do the firm conduct of Congress in refusing to treat with General Carleton, and the unanimous resolutions of the Assemblies of different States on the same subject. All ranks of this nation appear to be in good humour with us, and our reputation rises throughout Europe. I understand from the Swedish ambassador, that their treaty with us will go on as soon as ours with Holland is finished; our treaty with France, with such improvements as that with Holland may suggest, being intended as the basis.

There have been various misunderstandings and mismanagements among the parties concerned in the expedition of the *Bon Homme Richard*, which have occasioned delay in dividing the prize money. M. de Chaumont, who was chosen by the captains of all the vessels in the expedition as their agent, has long been in a state little short of bankruptcy, and some of the delays have possibly been occasioned by the distress of his affairs. He now informs me, that the money is in the hands of the minister of the marine. I shall in a few days present the memorial you propose, with one relating to the prisoners, and will acquaint you with the answer. Mr. Barclay is still in Holland; when he returns he may take into his hands what money can be obtained on that account.

I think your observations respecting the Danish complaints through the minister of France perfectly just. I will receive no more of them by that channel, and will give your reasons to justify my refusal.

Your approbation of my idea of a medal, to perpetuate the memory of York and Saratoga victories, gives me great pleasure, and encourages me to have it struck. I wish you would acquaint me with what kind of a monument at York the emblems required are to be fixed on; whether an obelisk or a column; its dimensions; whether any part of it is to be marble, and the emblems carved on it, and whether the work is to be executed by the excellent artists in that way which Paris affords; and, if so, to what expense they are to be limited. This puts me in mind of a monument I got made here and sent to America, by order of Congress, five years since. I have heard of its arrival, and nothing more. It was admired here for its elegant antique simplicity of design, and the various beautiful marbles used in its composition. It was intended to be fixed against a wall in the State House of Philadelphia. I know not why it has been so long neglected; it would, methinks, be well to inquire after it, and get it put up somewhere. Directions for fixing it were sent with it. I enclose a print of it. The inscription in the engraving is not on the monument; it was merely the fancy of the engraver. There is a white plate of marble left smooth to receive such inscription as the Congress should think proper.

Our countrymen, who have been prisoners in England, are sent home, a few excepted, who were sick, and who will be forwarded as soon as recovered. This eases us of a very considerable charge.

I communicated to the Marquis de Lafayette the paragraph of your letter which related to him. He is still here, and, as there seems not so much likelihood of an active campaign in America, he is probably more useful where he is. His departure, however, though delayed, is not absolutely laid aside.

The second changes in the ministry of England have occasioned, or have afforded, pretences for various delays in the negotiation for peace. Mr. Grenville had two successive imperfect commissions. He was at length recalled, and Mr. Fitzherbert is now arrived to replace him, with a commission in due form to treat with France, Spain, and Holland. Mr. Oswald, who is here, is informed by a letter from the new Secretary of State, that a commission, empowering him to treat with the Commissioners of Congress, will pass the seals, and be sent him in a few days; till he arrives, this court will not proceed in its own negotiation. I send the *Enabling Act*, as it is called. Mr. Jay will acquaint you with what passes between him and the Spanish ambassador, respecting the proposed treaty with Spain. I will only mention, that my conjecture of that court's design to coop us up within the Allegany Mountains is now manifested. I hope Congress will insist on the Mississippi as the boundary, and the free navigation of the river, from which they could entirely exclude us.

An account of a terrible massacre of the Moravian Indians has been put into my hands. I send you the papers, that you may see how the fact is represented in Europe. I hope measures will be taken to secure what is left of those unfortunate people.

Mr. Laurens is at Nantes, waiting for a passage with his family to America. His state of health is unfortunately very bad. Perhaps the sea air may recover him, and restore him well to his country. I heartily wish it. He has suffered much by his confinement. Be pleased, Sir, to present my duty to the Congress, and assure them of my most faithful services. With great esteem, I have the honour to be, &c.

"TOO HARSH EVEN FOR THE BOYS"

To the Marquis de Lafayette

DEAR SIR   Passy, Sept. 17. 1782.

I continue to suffer from this cruel Gout: But in the midst of my Pain the News of Mad^m de la Fayette's safe Delivery, and your Acquisition of a Daughter gives me Pleasure.

In naming your Children I think you do well to begin with

the most antient State. And as we cannot have too many of so good a Race I hope you & Mme. de la Fayette will go thro the Thirteen. But as that may be in the common Way too severe a Task for her delicate Frame, and Children of Seven Months may become as Strong as those of Nine, I consent to the Abridgement of Two Months for each; and I wish her to spend the Twenty-six Months so gained, in perfect Ease, Health & Pleasure.

While you are proceeding, I hope our States will some of them new-name themselves. Miss Virginia, Miss Carolina, & Miss Georgiana will sound prettily enough for the Girls; but Massachusetts & Connecticut, are too harsh even for the Boys, unless they were to be Savages.

That God may bless you in the Event of this Day as in every other, prays

Your affectionate Friend & Servant

"HOW SUCH A GLOBE WAS FORMED"

To the Abbé Soulavie

SIR, Passey, September 22, 1782.

I return the papers with some corrections. I did not find coal mines under the Calcareous rock in Derby Shire. I only remarked that at the lowest part of that rocky mountain which was in sight, there were oyster shells mixed in the stone; and part of the high county of Derby being probably as much above the level of the sea, as the coal mines of White-haven were below it, seemed a proof that there had been a great bouleversement in the surface of that Island, some part of it having been depressed under the sea, and other parts which had been under it being raised above it. Such changes in the superficial part of the globe seemed to me unlikely to happen if the earth were solid to the centre. I therefore imagined that the internal part might be a fluid more dense, and of greater specific gravity than any of the solids we are acquainted with; which therefore might swim in or upon that fluid. Thus the surface of the globe would be a shell, capable of being broken and disordered by the violent movements of the fluid on which it rested. And as air has been compressed by art so as to be twice as dense as water, in which case if such air and water could be contained in a strong glass vessel, the air would be seen to take the lowest place, and the water to float above and upon it; and as we know not yet the degree of density to which air may be compressed; and M. Amontons calculated, that its density increasing as it approached the centre in the same proportion as above the surface, it would at the depth of —— leagues be heavier than gold, possibly the dense fluid occupying the internal parts of the globe might be air compressed. And as the force of expansion in dense air when heated is in proportion to its density; this central air might afford another agent to move the surface, as well as be of use in keeping alive the subterraneous fires: Though as you observe, the sudden rarefaction of water coming into contact with those fires, may also be an agent sufficiently strong for that purpose, when acting between the incumbent earth and the fluid on which it rests.

If one might indulge imagination in supposing how such a globe was formed, I should conceive, that all the elements in separate particles being originally mixed in confusion and occupying a great space, they would as soon as the almighty fiat ordained gravity or the mutual attraction of certain parts, and the mutual repulsion of other parts to exist, all move towards their common centre: That the air being a fluid whose parts repel each other, though drawn to the common centre by their gravity, would be densest towards the centre, and rarer as more remote; consequently all matters lighter than the central part of that air and immersed in it, would recede from the centre and rise till they arrived at that region of the air which was of the same specific gravity with themselves, where they would rest; while other matter, mixed with the lighter air would descend, and the two meeting would form the shell of the first earth, leaving the upper atmosphere nearly clear. The original movement of the parts towards their common centre, would naturally form a whirl there; which would continue in the turning of the new formed globe upon its axis, and the greatest diameter of the shell would be in its equator.

If by any accident afterwards the axis should be changed, the dense internal fluid by altering its form must burst the shell and throw all its substance into the confusion in which we find it.

I will not trouble you at present with my fancies concerning the manner of forming the rest of our system. Superior beings smile at our theories, and at our presumption in making them. I will just mention that your observation of the ferruginous nature of the lava which is thrown out from the depths of our valcanos, gave me great pleasure. It has long been a supposition of mine that the iron contained in the substance of this globe, has made it capable of becoming as it is a great magnet. That the fluid of magnetism exists perhaps in all space; so that there is a magnetical North and South of the universe as well as of this globe, and that if it were possible for a man to fly from star to star, he might govern his course by the compass. That it was by the power of this general magnetism this globe became a particular magnet. In soft or hot iron the fluid of magnetism is naturally diffused equally; when within the influence of a magnet, it is drawn to one end of the iron, made denser there, and rarer at the other, while the iron continues soft and hot, it is only a temporary magnet: If it cools or grows hard in that situation, it becomes a permanent one, the magnetic fluid not easily resuming its equilibrium. Perhaps it may be owing to the permanent magnetism of this globe, which it had not at first, that its axis is at present kept parallel to itself, and not liable to the changes it formerly suffered, which occasioned the rupture of its shell, the submersions and emersions of its lands and the confusion of its seasons. The present polar and equatorial diameters differing from each other near ten leagues; it is easy to conceive in case some power should shift the axis gradually, and place it in the present equator, and make the new equator pass through the present poles, what a sinking of the water would happen in the present equatorial regions, and what a rising in the present polar regions; so that vast tracts would be discovered that now are under water, and others covered that now are dry, the water rising and sinking in the different extremes near five leagues.—Such an operation as this, possibly, occasioned much of Europe, and among the rest, this mountain of Passy, on which I live, and which is composed of lime stone, rock and sea shells, to be abandoned by the sea, and to change its ancient climate, which seems to have been a hot one. The globe being now become a permanent magnet, we are perhaps safe from any future change of its axis. But we are still subject to the accidents on the surface which are occasioned by a wave in the internal ponderous fluid; and such a wave is producible by the sudden violent explosion you mention, happening from the junction of water and fire under the earth, which not only lifts the incumbent earth that is over the explosion, but impressing with the same force the fluid under it, creates a wave that may run a thousand leagues lifting and thereby shaking successively all the countries under which it passes. I know not whether I have expressed myself so clearly, as not to get out of your sight in these reveries. If they occasion any new enquiries and produce a better hypothesis, they will not be quite useless. You see I have given a loose to imagination; but I approve much more your method of philosophizing, which proceeds upon actual observation, makes a collection of facts, and concludes no farther than those facts will warrant. In my present circumstances, that mode of studying the nature of this globe is out of my power, and therefore I have permitted myself to wander a little in the wilds of fancy. With great esteem I have the honour to be, &c.

P. S. I have heard that chemists can by their art decompose stone and wood, extracting a considerable quantity of water from the one, and air from the other. It seems natural to conclude from this, that water and air were ingredients in their original composition. For men cannot make new matter of any kind. In the same manner may we not suppose, that when we consume combustibles of all kinds, and produce heat or light, we do not create that heat or light; but only decompose a substance which received it originally as a part of its composition? Heat may thus be considered as originally in a fluid state, but, attracted by organized bodies in their growth, becomes a part of the solid. Besides this, I can conceive that in the first assemblage of the particles of which this earth is composed each brought its portion of the loose heat that had been connected with it, and the whole when pressed together produced the internal fire that still subsists.

To Comte de Vergennes

SIR,   Passy, December 17, 1782.

I received the letter your Excellency did me the honour of writing to me on the 15th instant. The proposal of having a passport from England was agreed to by me the more willingly, as I at that time had hopes of obtaining some money to send in the *Washington*, and the passport would have made its transportation safer, with that of our despatches, and of yours also, if you had thought fit to make use of the occasion. Your Excellency objected, as I understood it, that the English ministers, by their letters sent in the same ship, might convey inconvenient expectations into America. It was therefore I proposed not to press for the passport till your preliminaries were also agreed to. They have sent the passport without being pressed to do it, and they have sent no letters to go under it, and ours will prevent the inconvenience apprehended. In a subsequent conversation, your Excellency mentioned your intention of sending some of the King's cutters, whence I imagined, that detaining the *Washington* was no longer necessary; and it was certainly incumbent on us to give Congress as early an account as possible of our proceedings, who will think it extremely strange to hear of them by other means, without a line from us. I acquainted your Excellency, however, with our intention of despatching that ship, supposing you might possibly have something to send by her.

Nothing has been agreed in the preliminaries contrary to the interests of France; and no peace is to take place between us and England, till you have concluded yours. Your observation is, however, apparently just, that, in not consulting you before they were signed, we have been guilty of neglecting a point of *bienséance*. But, as this was not from want of respect for the King, whom we all love and honour, we hope it will be excused, and that the great work, which has hitherto been so happily conducted, is so nearly brought to perfection, and is so glorious to his reign, will not be ruined by a single indiscretion of ours. And certainly the whole edifice sinks to the ground immediately, if you refuse on that account to give us any further assistance.

We have not yet despatched the ship, and I beg leave to wait upon you on Friday for your answer.

It is not possible for any one to be more sensible than I am, of what I and every American owe to the King, for the many and great benefits and favours he has bestowed upon us. All my letters to America are proofs of this; all tending to make the same impressions on the minds of my countrymen, that I felt in my own. And I believe, that no Prince was ever more beloved and respected by his own subjects, than the King is by the people of the United States. *The English, I just now learn, flatter themselves they have already divided us.* I hope this little misunderstanding will therefore be kept a secret, and that they will find themselves totally mistaken. With great and sincere respect, I am, Sir, &c.

"ALL WARS ARE FOLLIES"

To Mary Hewson

Passy, Jan. 27. 1783.
—The Departure of my dearest Friend, which I learn from your last Letter, greatly affects me. To meet with her once more in this Life was one of the principal Motives of my proposing to visit England again, before my Return to America. The last Year carried off my Friends Dr. Pringle, and Dr. Fothergill, Lord Kaims, and Lord le Despencer. This has begun to take away the rest, and strikes the hardest. Thus the Ties I had to that Country, and indeed to the World in general, are loosened one by one, and I shall soon have no Attachment left to make me unwilling to follow.

I intended writing when I sent the 11 Books, but I lost the Time in looking for the 12th. I wrote with that; and hope it came to hand. I therein ask'd your Counsel about my coming to England. On Reflection, I think I can, from my Knowledge of your Prudence, foresee what it will be, viz. not to come too soon, lest it should seem braving and insulting some who ought to be respected. I shall, therefore, omit that Journey till I am near going to America, and then just step over to take Leave of my Friends, and spend a few days with you. I purpose bringing Ben with me, and perhaps may leave him under your Care.

At length we are in Peace, God be praised, and long, very long, may it continue. All Wars are Follies, very expensive, and very mischievous ones. When will Mankind be convinced of this, and agree to settle their Differences by Arbitration? Were they to do it, even by the Cast of a Dye, it would be better than by Fighting and destroying each other.

Spring is coming on, when Travelling will be delightful. Can you not, when your children are all at School, make a little Party, and take a Trip hither? I have now a large House, delightfully situated, in which I could accommodate you and two or three Friends, and I am but half an Hour's Drive from Paris.

In looking forward, Twenty-five Years seems a long Period, but, in looking back, how short! Could you imagine, that 'tis now full a Quarter of a Century since we were first acquainted? It was in 1757. During the greatest Part of the Time, I lived in the same House with my dear deceased Friend, your Mother; of course you and I saw and convers'd with each other much and often. It is to all our Honours, that in all that time we never had among us the smallest Misunderstanding. Our Friendship has been all clear Sunshine, without the least Cloud in its Hemisphere. Let me conclude by saying to you, what I have had too frequent Occasions to say to my other remaining old Friends, "The fewer we become, the more let us love one another." Adieu, and believe me ever yours most affectionately,

"IN SOME THINGS, ABSOLUTELY OUT OF HIS SENSES"

To Robert R. Livingston

SIR,   Passy, July 22, 1783.
    You have complain'd, sometimes with reason, of not

hearing from your foreign Ministers; we have had cause to make the same Complaint, six full Months having interven'd between the latest date of your preceding Letters and the receipt of those by Captain Barney. During all this time we were ignorant of the Reception of the Provisional Treaty, and the Sentiments of Congress upon it, which, if we had received sooner, might have forwarded the Proceedings on the Definitive Treaty, and, perhaps, brought them to a Conclusion at a time more favourable than the present. But these occasional Interruptions of Correspondence are the inevitable Consequences of a State of War, and of such remote Situations. Barney had a short Passage, and arrived some Days before Colonel Ogden, who also brought Dispatches from you, all of which are come safe to hand. We, the Commissioners, have in our joint Capacity written a Letter to you, which you will receive with this.

I shall now answer yours of March 26, May 9, and May 31. It gave me great Pleasure to learn by the first, that the News of the Peace diffused general Satisfaction. I will not now take upon me to justify the apparent Reserve, respecting this Court, at the Signature, which you disapprove. We have touch'd upon it in our general Letter. I do not see, however, that they have much reason to complain of that Transaction. Nothing was stipulated to their Prejudice, and none of the Stipulations were to have Force, but by a subsequent Act of their own. I suppose, indeed, that they have not complain'd of it, or you would have sent us a Copy of the Complaint, that we might have answer'd it. I long since satisfi'd Comte de V. about it here. We did what appear'd to all of us best at the Time, and, if we have done wrong, the Congress will do right, after hearing us, to censure us. Their Nomination of Five Persons to the Service seems to mark, that they had some Dependence on our joint Judgment, since one alone could have made a Treaty by Direction of the French Ministry as well as twenty.

I will only add, that, with respect to myself, neither the Letter from M. Marbois, handed us thro' the British Negociators (a suspicious Channel), nor the Conversations respecting the Fishery, the Boundaries, the Royalists, &c., recommending Moderation in our Demands, are of Weight sufficient in

my Mind to fix an Opinion, that this Court wish'd to restrain
us in obtaining any Degree of Advantage we could prevail on
our Enemies to accord; since those Discourses are fairly re-
solvable, by supposing a very natural Apprehension, that we,
relying too much on the Ability of France to continue the
War in our favour, and supply us constantly with Money,
might insist on more Advantages than the English would be
willing to grant, and thereby lose the Opportunity of making
Peace, so necessary to all our Friends.

I ought not, however, to conceal from you, that one of my
Colleagues is of a very different Opinion from me in these
Matters. He thinks the French Minister one of the greatest
Enemies of our Country, that he would have straitned our
Boundaries, to prevent the Growth of our People; contracted
our Fishery, to obstruct the Increase of our Seamen; and retained the Royalists among us, to keep us divided; that he
privately opposes all our Negociations with foreign Courts,
and afforded us, during the War, the Assistance we receiv'd,
only to keep it alive, that we might be so much the more
weaken'd by it; that to think of Gratitude to France is the
greatest of Follies, and that to be influenc'd by it would ruin
us. He makes no Secret of his having these Opinions, expresses them publicly, sometimes in presence of the English
Ministers, and speaks of hundreds of Instances which he
could produce in Proof of them. None of which however,
have yet appear'd to me, unless the Conversations and Letter
above-mentioned are reckoned such.

If I were not convinc'd of the real Inability of this Court
to furnish the further Supplys we ask'd, I should suspect these
Discourses of a Person in his Station might have influenced
the Refusal; but I think they have gone no farther than to
occasion a Suspicion, that we have a considerable Party of
Antigallicans in America, who are not Tories, and consequently to produce some doubts of the Continuance of our
Friendship. As such Doubts may hereafter have a bad Effect,
I think we cannot take too much care to remove them; and it
is, therefore, I write this, to put you on your guard, (believing it my duty, tho' I know that I hazard by it a mortal Enmity), and to caution you respecting the Insinuations of this
Gentleman against this Court, and the Instances he supposes

of their ill will to us, which I take to be as imaginary as I know his Fancies to be, that Count de V. and myself are continually plotting against him, and employing the News-Writers of Europe to depreciate his Character, &c. But as Shakespear says, "Trifles light as Air," &c. I am persuaded, however, that he means well for his Country, is always an honest Man, often a wise one, but sometimes, and in some things, absolutely out of his senses.

When the Commercial Article, mentioned in yours of the 26th was struck out of our propos'd Preliminaries by the then British Ministry, the reason given was, that sundry Acts of Parliament still in force were against it, and must be first repeal'd, which I believe was really their Intention, and sundry Bills were accordingly bro't in for that purpose; but, new Ministers with different Principles succeeding, a commercial Proclamation totally different from those Bills has lately appeared. I send enclos'd a Copy of it. We shall try what can be done in the Definitive Treaty towards setting aside that Proclamation; but, if it should be persisted in, it will then be a Matter worthy the attentive Discussion of Congress, whether it will be most prudent to retort with a similar Regulation in order to force its Repeal (which may possibly tend to bring on another Quarrel), or to let it pass without notice, and leave it to its own Inconvenience, or rather Impracticability, in the Execution, and to the Complaints of the West India Planters, who must all pay much dearer for our Produce, under those Restrictions.

I am not enough Master of the Course of our Commerce to give an Opinion on this particular Question, and it does not behove me to do it; yet I have seen so much Embarrassment and so little Advantage in all the Restraining and Compulsive Systems, that I feel myself strongly inclin'd to believe, that a State, which leaves all her Ports open to all the World upon equal Terms, will, by that means, have foreign Commodities cheaper, sell its own Productions dearer, and be on the whole the most prosperous. I have heard some Merchants say, that there is 10 per cent Difference between *Will you buy?* and *Will you sell?* When Foreigners bring us their Goods, they want to part with them speedily, that they may purchase their Cargoes and despatch their Ships, which are at constant

Charges in our Ports; we have then the Advantage of their *Will you buy?* And when they demand our Produce, we have the Advantage of their *Will you sell?* And the concurring Demands of a Number also contribute to raise our Prices. Thus both those Questions are in our favour at home, against us abroad.

The employing, however, of our own Ships and raising a Breed of Seamen among us, tho' it should not be a matter of so much private Profit as some imagine, is nevertheless of political Importance, and must have weight in considering this Subject.

The Judgment you make of the Conduct of France in the Peace, and the greater Glory acquired by her Moderation than even by her Arms, appears to me perfectly just. The Character of this Court and Nation seems, of late years, to be considerably changed. The Ideas of Aggrandizement by Conquest are out of fashion, and those of Commerce are more enlightened and more generous than heretofore. We shall soon, I believe, feel something of this in our being admitted to a greater Freedom of Trade with their Islands. The Wise here think France great enough; and its Ambition at present seems to be only that of Justice and Magnanimity towards other Nations, Fidelity and Utility to its Allies.

The Ambassador of Portugal was much pleas'd with the Proceedings relating to their Vessel, which you sent me, and assures me they will have a good Effect at his Court. He appears extremely desirous of a Treaty with our States; I have accordingly propos'd to him the Plan of one (nearly the same with that sent me for Sweden), and, after my agreeing to some Alterations, he has sent it to his Court for Approbation. He told me at Versailles, last Tuesday, that he expected its Return to him on Saturday next, and anxiously desired that I would not despatch our Pacquet without it, that Congress might consider it, and, if approv'd, send a Commission to me or some other Minister to sign it.

I venture to go thus far in treating, on the Authority only of a kind of general Power, given formerly by a Resolution of Congress to Messrs. Franklin, Deane, and Lee; but a special Commission seems more proper to compleat a Treaty, and more agreable to the usual Forms of such Business.

I am in just the same Situation with Denmark; that Court, by its Minister here, has desired a Treaty with us. I have pro- pos'd a Plan formed on that sent me for Sweden; it had been under Consideration some time at Copenhagen, and is ex- pected here this Week, so that I may possibly send that also by this Conveyance. You will have seen by my Letter to the Danish Prime Minister, that I did not forget the Affair of the Prizes. What I then wrote, produc'd a verbal Offer made me here, of £10,000 Sterling, propos'd to be given by his Maj- esty to the Captors, if I would accept it as a full Discharge of our Demand. I could not do this, I said, because it was not more than a fifth Part of the Estimated Value. In answer, I was told, that the Estimation was probably extravagant, that it would be difficult to come at the Knowledge of their true Value, and that, whatever they might be worth in them- selves, they should not be estimated as of such Value to us when at Bergen, since the English probably watched them, and might have retaken them in their Way to America; at least, they were at the common Risques of the Seas and Enemies, and the Insurance was a considerable Drawback; that this Sum might be consider'd as so much sav'd for us by the King's Interference; for that, if the English Claimants had been suffered to carry the Cause into the common Courts, they must have recovered the Prizes by the Laws of Denmark; it was added, that the King's Honour was con- cern'd, that he sincerely desir'd our Friendship, but he would avoid, by giving this Sum in the Form of a Present to the Captors, the Appearance of its being exacted from him as the Reparation of an Injury, when it was really intended rather as a Proof of his strong Disposition to cultivate a good Understanding with us.

I reply'd, that the Value might possibly be exaggerated; but that we did not desire more than should be found just upon Enquiry, and that it was not difficult to learn from London what Sums were insur'd upon the Ships and Cargoes, which would be some Guide; and that a reasonable Abatement might be made for the risque; but that the Congress could not, in justice to their Mariners, deprive them of any Part that was truly due to those brave Men, whatever Abatement they might think fit to make (as a Mark of their Regard for the

King's Friendship) of the Part belonging to the publick; that I had, however, no Instructions or Authority to make any Abatement of any kind, and could, therefore, only acquaint Congress with the Offer, and the Reasons that accompanied it, which I promised to state fully and candidly (as I have now done), and attend their Orders; desiring only that it might be observ'd, we had presented our Complaint with Decency, that we had charg'd no Fault on the Danish Government, but what might arise from Inattention or Precipitancy, and that we had intimated no Resentment, but had waited, with Patience and Respect, the King's Determination, confiding, that he would follow the equitable Disposition of his own Breast, by doing us Justice as soon as he could do it with Conveniency; that the best and wisest Princes sometimes erred, that it belong'd to the Condition of Man, and was, therefore, inevitable, and that the true Honour in such Cases consisted, not in disowning or hiding the Error, but in making ample Reparation; that, tho' I could not accept what was offered on the Terms proposed, our Treaty might go on, and its Articles be prepared and considered, and, in the mean time, I hoped his Danish Majesty would reconsider the Offer, and make it more adequate to the Loss we had sustained. Thus that matter rests; but I hourly expect to hear farther, and perhaps may have more to say on it before the Ship's Departure.

I shall be glad to have the Proceedings you mention respecting the Brig *Providentia*. I hope the Equity and Justice of our Admiralty Courts respecting the Property of Strangers will always maintain their Reputation; and I wish particularly to cultivate the Disposition of Friendship towards us, apparent in the late Proceedings of Denmark, as the Danish Islands may be of use to our West India Commerce, while the English impolitic Restraints continue.

The Elector of Saxony, as I understand from his Minister here, has thoughts of sending one to Congress, and proposing a Treaty of Commerce and Amity with us. Prussia has likewise an Inclination to share in a Trade with America, and the Minister of that Court, tho' he has not directly propos'd a Treaty, has given me a Pacquet of Lists of the several Sorts of Merchandise they can furnish us with, which he requests me to send to America for the Information of our Merchants.

I have received no Answer yet from Congress to my Request of being dismiss'd from their Service. They should, methinks, reflect, that if they continue me here, the Faults I may henceforth commit, thro' the Infirmities of Age, will be rather theirs than mine. I am glad my Journal afforded you any Pleasure. I will, as you desire, endeavour to continue it. I thank you for the Pamphlet; it contains a great deal of Information respecting our Finances. We shall, as you advise, avoid publishing it. But I see they are publishing it in the English Papers. I was glad I had a copy authenticated by the Signature of Secr^y Thomson, by which I could assure M. de Vergennes, that the Money Contract I had made with him was ratified by Congress, he having just before express'd some uneasiness to me at its being so long neglected. I find it was ratified soon after it was receiv'd, but the Ratification, except in that Pamphlet, has not yet come to hand. I have done my best to procure the farther Loan directed by the Resolution of Congress. It was not possible. I have written on that Matter to Mr. Morris. I wish the rest of the Estimates of Losses and Mischiefs were come to hand; they would still be of Use.

Mr. Barclay has in his Hands the Affair of the *Alliance* and *Bon Homme Richard*. I will afford him all the Assistance in my Power, but it is a very perplex'd Business. That Expedition, tho' for particular Reasons under American Commissions and Colours, was carry'd on at the King's expence, and under his Orders. M. de Chaumont was the Agent appointed by the Minister of the Marine to make the Outfit. He was also chosen by all the Captains of the Squadron, as appears by an Instrument under their Hands, to be their Agent, receive, sell, and divide Prizes, &c. The Crown bought two of them at public Sale, and the Money, I understand, is lodg'd in the Hands of a responsible Person at L'Orient. M. de Chaumont says he has given in his Accounts to the Marine, and that he has no more to do with the Affair, except to receive a Ballance due to him. That Account, however, is I believe unsettled, and the Absence of some of the Captains is said to make another Difficulty, which retards the Completion of the

Business. I never paid or receiv'd any thing relating to that
Expedition, nor had any other Concern in it, than barely or-
dering the *Alliance* to join the Squadron, at M. de Sartine's
Request. I know not whether the other Captains will not
claim a Share in what we may obtain from Denmark, tho' the
Prizes were made by the *Alliance*, when separate from the
Squadron. If so, that is another Difficulty in the way of mak-
ing Abatement in our Demand, without their Consent.

I am sorry to find, that you have Thoughts of quitting the
Service. I do not think your Place can be easily well supply'd.
You mention, that an entire new Arrangement, with respect
to foreign Affairs, is under Consideration. I wish to know
whether any Notice is likely to be taken in it of my Grandson.
He has now gone through an Apprenticeship of near seven
Years in the ministerial Business, and is very capable of serving the States in that Line, as possessing all the Requisites of
Knowledge, Zeal, Activity, Language, and Address. He is
well lik'd here, and Count de Vergennes has express'd to me
in warm Terms his very good Opinion of him. The late Swedish Ambassador, Count de Creutz, who has gone home to be
Prime Minister, desir'd I would endeavour to procure his
being sent to Sweden, with a public Character, assuring me,
that he should be glad to receive him there as our Minister,
and that he knew it would be pleasing to the King. The present Swedish Ambassador has also propos'd the same thing to
me, as you will see by a Letter of his, which I enclose. One
of the Danish Ministers, M. Walterstorff, who will probably
be sent in a public Character to Congress, has also express'd
his Wish, that my Grandson may be sent to Denmark. But it
is not my Custom to solicit Employments for myself, or any
of my Family, and I shall not do it in this Case. I only hope,
that if he is not to be employ'd in your new Arrangement, I
may be inform'd of it as soon as possible, that, while I have
Strength left for it, I may accompany him in a Tour to Italy,
returning thro' Germany, which I think he may make to more
Advantage with me than alone, and which I have long promis'd to afford him, as a Reward for his faithful Service, and
his tender filial Attachment to me.

July 25. While I was writing the above, M. Walterstorff
came in, and deliver'd me a Pacquet from M. de Rosencrone,

the Danish Prime Minister, containing the Project of the Treaty with some proposed Alterations, and a Paper of Reasons in support of them. Fearing that we should not have time to copy them, I send herewith the Originals, relying on his Promise to furnish me with Copies in a few Days. He seemed to think, that the Interest of the Merchants is concern'd in the immediate Conclusion of the Treaty, that they may form their Plans of Commerce, and wish'd to know whether I did not think my general Power, above mentioned, sufficient for that purpose. I told him, I thought a particular Commission more agreable to the Forms; but, if his Danish Majesty would be content for the present with the general Authority, formerly given me, I believ'd I might venture to act upon it, reserving, by a separate Article, to Congress a Power of shortning the Term, in Case any Part of the Treaty should not be to their mind, unless the Alteration of such Part should hereafter be agreed on.

The Prince de Deux-Ponts was lately at Paris, and apply'd to me for Information respecting a Commerce which is desired between the Electorate of Bavaria and America. I have it also from a good Hand at the Court of Vienna, that the Emperor is desirous of establishing a Commerce with us from Trieste as well as Flanders, and would make a Treaty with us, if propos'd to him. Since our Trade is laid open, and no longer a Monopoly to England, all Europe seems desirous of sharing in it, and for that purpose to cultivate our Friendship. That it may be better known everywhere, what sort of People, and what kind of Government they will have to treat with, I prevailed with a Friend, the Duc de Rochefoucauld, to translate our Book of Constitutions into French, and I presented Copies to all the foreign Ministers. I send you one herewith. They are much admired by the Politicians here, and it is thought will induce considerable Emigrations of substantial People from different Parts of Europe to America. It is particularly a Matter of Wonder, that, in the Midst of a cruel War raging in the Bowels of our Country, our Sages should have the Firmness of Mind to sit down calmly and form such compleat Plans of Government. They add considerably to the Reputation of the United States.

I have mentioned above the Port of Trieste, with which we

may possibly have a Commerce, and I am told that many useful Productions and Manufactures of Hungary may be had extreamly cheap there. But it becomes necessary first to consider how our Mediterranean Trade is to be protected from the Corsaires of Barbary. You will see by the enclos'd Copy of a Letter I receiv'd from Algiers, the Danger two of our Ships escap'd last Winter. I think it not improbable that those Rovers may be privately encouraged by the English to fall upon us, to prevent our Interference in the Carrying Trade; for I have in London heard it is a Maxim among the Merchants, that, if *there were no Algiers, it would be worth England's while to build one*. I wonder, however, that the rest of Europe do not combine to destroy those Nests, and secure Commerce from their future Piracies.

I made the Grand Master of Malta a Present of one of our Medals in Silver, writing him a Letter, of which I enclose a Copy; and I believe our People will be kindly receiv'd in his Ports; but that is not sufficient; and perhaps, now we have Peace, it will be proper to send Ministers, with suitable Presents, to establish a Friendship with the Emperor of Morocco, and the other Barbary States, if possible. Mr. Jay will inform you of some Steps, that have been taken by a Person at Alicant, without Authority, towards a Treaty with that Emperor. I send you herewith a few more of the above-mentioned Medals, which have given great Satisfaction to this Court and Nation. I should be glad to know how they are lik'd with you.

Our People, who were Prisoners in England, are now all discharg'd. During the whole War, those who were in Forton prison, near Portsmouth, were much befriended by the constant charitable Care of Mr. Wren, a Presbyterian Minister there, who spared no Pains to assist them in their Sickness and Distress, by procuring and distributing among them the Contributions of good Christians, and prudently dispensing the Allowance I made them, which gave him a great deal of trouble, but he went through it chearfully. I think some public Notice should be taken of this good Man. I wish the Congress would enable me to make him a Present, and that some of our Universities would confer upon him the Degree of Doctor.

The Duke of Manchester, who has always been our Friend in the House of Lords, is now here as Ambassador from England. I dine with him to-day, (26th,) and, if any thing of Importance occurs, I will add it in a Postcript. Be pleased to present my dutiful Respects to the Congress, assure them of my most faithful Services, and believe me to be, with great and sincere Esteem, Sir, &c.

"THERE NEVER WAS A GOOD WAR, OR A BAD PEACE"

To Sir Joseph Banks

DEAR SIR,   Passy, July 27, 1783.

I received your very kind letter by Dr. Blagden, and esteem myself much honoured by your friendly Remembrance. I have been too much and too closely engaged in public Affairs, since his being here, to enjoy all the Benefit of his Conversation you were so good as to intend me. I hope soon to have more Leisure, and to spend a part of it in those Studies, that are much more agreable to me than political Operations.

I join with you most cordially in rejoicing at the return of Peace. I hope it will be lasting, and that Mankind will at length, as they call themselves reasonable Creatures, have Reason and Sense enough to settle their Differences without cutting Throats; for, in my opinion, *there never was a good War, or a bad Peace*. What vast additions to the Conveniences and Comforts of Living might Mankind have acquired, if the Money spent in Wars had been employed in Works of public utility! What an extension of Agriculture, even to the Tops of our Mountains: what Rivers rendered navigable, or joined by Canals: what Bridges, Aqueducts, new Roads, and other public Works, Edifices, and Improvements, rendering England a compleat Paradise, might have been obtained by spending those Millions in doing good, which in the last War have been spent in doing Mischief; in bringing Misery into thousands of Families, and destroying the Lives of so many thousands of working people, who might have performed the useful labour!

I am pleased with the late astronomical Discoveries made by our Society. Furnished as all Europe now is with Academies of Science, with nice Instruments and the Spirit of Experiment, the progress of human knowledge will be rapid, and discoveries made, of which we have at present no Conception. I begin to be almost sorry I was born so soon, since I cannot have the happiness of knowing what will be known 100 years hence.

I wish continued success to the Labours of the Royal Society, and that you may long adorn their chair; being, with the highest esteem, dear Sir, &c.

P. S. Dr. Blagden will acquaint you with the experiment of a vast Globe sent up into the Air, much talked of here, and which, if prosecuted, may furnish means of new knowledge.

FIRST BALLOON EXPERIMENTS

To Sir Joseph Banks

SIR,   Passy, Aug. 30. 1783.

On Wednesday the 27th Instant, the new aerostatic Experiment, invented by Messrs Mongolfier of Annonay was repeated by M^r. Charles; Professor of Experimental Philosophy at Paris.

A hollow Globe 12 feet diameter was formed of what is called in England Oiled Silk, here Taffetas *gommée*, the Silk being impregnated with a Solution of Gum-elastic in Lintseed Oil, as is said. The Parts were sewed together while wet with the Gum, and some of it was afterwards passed over the Seams, to render it as tight as possible.

It was afterwards filled with the inflammable Air that is produced by pouring Oil of Vitriol upon Filings of Iron, when it was found to have a Tendency upwards so strong as to be capable of lifting a Weight of 39 Pounds, exclusive of its own weight which was 25 lb, and the Weight of the Air contain'd.

It was brought early in the Morning to the *Champ de Mars*, a Field in which Reviews are sometimes made, lying between the Military School and the River. There it was held down by a Cord, till 5 in the Afternoon, when it was to be let loose. Care was taken before the Hour to replace what Portion had been lost of the inflammable Air, or of its Force, by injecting more.

It is supposed that not less than 50,000 People were assembled to see the Experiment. The Champ de Mars being surrounded by Multitudes, and vast Numbers on the opposite Side of the River.

At 5 o Clock Notice was given to the Spectators by the Firing of two Cannon, that the Cord was about to be cut. And presently the Globe was seen to rise, and that as fast as a Body of 12 feet diameter with a force only of 39 pounds, could be suppos'd to move the resisting Air out of its way. There was some Wind, but not very strong. A little Rain had wet it, so that it shone, and made an agreable Appearance. It diminish'd in Apparent Magnitude as it rose, till it enter'd the Clouds, when it seem'd to me scarce bigger than an Orange, and soon after became invisible, the Clouds concealing it.

The Multitude separated, all well satisfied & much delighted with the Success of the Experiment, and amusing one another with Discourses of the various Uses it may possibly be apply'd to, among which many were very extravagant. But possibly it may pave the Way to some Discoveries in Natural Philosophy of which at present we have no Conception.

A Note secur'd from the Weather had been affix'd to the Globe, signifying the Time & Place of its Departure, and praying those who might happen to find it, to send an Account of its State to certain Persons at Paris. No News was heard of it till the next Day, when Information was receiv'd, that it fell a little after 6 oClock at Gonesse, a Place about 4 Leagues distance; and that it was rent open, and some say had Ice in it. It is suppos'd to have burst by the Elasticity of the contain'd Air when no longer compress'd by so heavy an Atmosphere.

One of 38 feet Diameter is preparing by M. Mongolfier himself at the Expence of the Academy, which is to go up in a few Days. I am told it is constructed of Linen & Paper, and is to be filled with a different Air, not yet made public, but cheaper than that produc'd by the Oil of Vitriol of which 200 Paris Pints were consum'd in filling the other.

It is said that for some Days after its being fill'd, the Ball was found to lose an eighth Part of its Force of Levity in 24 Hours: Whether this was from Imperfection in the Tightness of the Ball, or a Change in the Nature of the Air, Experiments may easily discover.

I thought it my Duty, Sir, to send an early Account of this extraordinary Fact, to the Society which does me the honour to reckon me among its Members; and I will endeavour to make it more perfect, as I receive farther Information.

With great Respect, I am, Sir,

P. S. Since writing the above, I am favour'd with your kind Letter of the 25.th I am much oblig'd to you for the Care you have taken to forward the Transactions, as well as to the Council for so readily ordering them on Application.—Please to accept and present my Thanks.

I just now learn, that some Observers say, the Ball was 150 seconds in rising, from the Cutting of the Cord till hid in the Clouds; that its height was then about 500 Toises, but, mov'd out of the Perpendicular by the Wind, it had made a Slant so as to form a Triangle, whose base on the Earth was about 200 Toises. It is said the Country people who saw it fall were frightened, conceiv'd from its bounding a little when it touch'd the Ground, that there was some living Animal in it, and attack'd it with Stones and Knives, so that it was much mangled; but it is now brought to Town & will be re-paired.—

The great one of M. Mongolfier, is to go up as is said, from Versailles, in about 8 or 10 Days. It is not a Globe but of a different form, more convenient for penetrating the Air. It contains 50,000 cubic Feet, and is supposed to have a Force of Levity equal to 1500 pounds weight. A Philosopher here, M. Pilatre de Rozier, has seriously apply'd to the Academy for Leave to go up with it, in order to make some

Experiments. He was complimented on his Zeal and Courage for the Promotion of Science, but advis'd to wait till the
Management of these Balls was made by Experience more
certain & safe. They say the filling of it in M. Mongolfier's
Way will not cost more than half a Crown. One is talk'd of
to be 110 feet Diameter. Several Gentlemen have ordered
small ones to be made for their Amusement; one has ordered four of 15 feet diameter each; I know not with what
Purpose; but such is the present Enthusiasm for promoting
& improving this Discovery, that probably we shall soon
make considerable Progress in the Art of constructing and
Using the Machines.—

Among the Pleasantries Conversation produces on this
Subject, some suppose Flying to be now invented, and that
since Men may be supported in the Air, nothing is wanted
but some light handy Instruments to give and direct Motion.
Some think Progressive Motion on the Earth may be advanc'd by it, and that a Running Footman or a Horse slung
& suspended under such a Globe so as to leave no more of
Weight pressing the Earth with their Feet, than perhaps 8 or
10 Pounds, might with a fair Wind run in a straight Line
across Countries as fast as that Wind, and over Hedges,
Ditches, & even Waters. It has been even fancied that in time
People will keep such Globes anchored in the Air, to which
by Pullies they may draw up Game to be preserved in the
Cool, & Water to be frozen when Ice is wanted. And that to
get Money, it will be contrived to give People an extensive
view of the Country, by running them upon an Elbow Chair
a Mile high for a Guinea, &c. &c.

A Pamphlet is printing in which we are to have a full and
perfect Account of the Experiments hitherto made, & I will
send it to you. M. Mongolfier's Air to fill the Globe has hitherto been kept secret. Some suppose it to be only common
Air heated by passing thro' the Flame of burning Straw, &
thereby extreamly rarified. If so its Levity will soon be diminished by Condensation when it comes into the cooler Regions above.

Sept. 2d.—I add this paper just now given me, B. F. The
print contains a view of Champ de Mars, and the ball in the
air with this subscription:

Experience de la machine aérostatique de M^{cssrs.} de Montgolfier, d'Anonai en Vivarais, réepétée à Paris le 27 Août. 1783
au Champ de Mars, avec un ballon de taffetas enduit de
gomme elastique, de 36 pieds 6 onces de circonference. Le
ballon plein d'air inflammable a été executé par Mons. Robert, en vertu d'une souscription nationale, sous la direction
de Mr. Faujas de Saint Fond (et M. Charles).

N. B.—M. Charles' name is wrote with pen, not engraved.
Calculas du Ballon do 12 pieds de diametre enlevé le Mer-
credy 27 Août 1783.

Circonference du grand cercle. . . .	37	pieds
Diametre	12	
	74	
	37	
Surface	444	
Tiers du rayon	2	
Solidite	888	pieds cubes
Air atm. à 12 gros le pied	12	
	1776	
	888	
Pesanteur de l'air atm.	10,656	gros

$$26 \begin{cases} 8 & \text{/16} \\ \rule{1.5cm}{0.4pt}\; \text{ounces} \; \rule{1cm}{0.4pt} \\ 1332 & \text{/83 lb., 4 onces.} \end{cases}$$
25,
 6   52

L'air atmospherique dont le ballon occupait la place, pesant
83 lb. 4 onces et sa force pour s'elever etant de 40 lb. il falloit
que son enveloppe et l'air inflammable qu'elle contenoit ne
pesassent que 42 lb. 4 onces. L'enveloppe en pesoit 25, reste
pour l'air inflammable 18 lb. 4 onces.

En supposant le ballon de 6 pieds de diametre, son volume
etant le 8me, du ier le poids de l'air dont il occupoit la place
seroit le 8me, de 83 lb., 4 onces = 10 lb., 6 onces, 4 gros.
L'air inflammable ⅛ de 18 lb., 4 onces = 2 lb., 4 onces, 4
gros. L'enveloppe ¼ de 25 lb., = 6 lb., 4 onces. Les dernières
valeurs reunies sont 8 lb., 8 onces, 4 gros, qui otès de 10 lb.,
6 onces, 4 gros pesanteur de l'air atmospherique dont le ballon occupoit la place, laisse pour sa force d'elevation 1 lb., 14
onces.

"FALLS LITTLE SHORT OF TREASON"

To John Jay

Sir,   Passy, September 10, 1783.

I have received a letter from a very respectable person in America, containing the following words, viz.

"It is confidently reported, propagated, and believed by some among us, that the Court of France was at the bottom against our obtaining the fishery and territory in that great extent, in which both are secured to us by the treaty; that our Minister at that Court favored, or did not oppose this design against us; and that it was entirely owing to the firmness, sagacity, and disinterestedness of Mr Adams, with whom Mr Jay united, that we have obtained these important advantages."

It is not my purpose to dispute any share of the honor of that treaty, which the friends of my colleagues may be disposed to give them, but having now spent fifty years of my life in public offices and trusts, and having still one ambition left, that of carrying the character of fidelity at least to the grave with me, I cannot allow that I was behind any of them in zeal and faithfulness. I therefore think, that I ought not to suffer an accusation, which falls little short of treason to my country, to pass without notice, when the means of effectual vindication are at hand. You, Sir, were a witness of my conduct in that affair. To you and my other colleagues I appeal, by sending to each a similar letter with this, and I have no doubt of your readiness to do a brother Commissioner justice, by certificates, that will entirely destroy the effect of that accusation.

I have the honor to be, with much esteem, &c.

"ALL PROPERTY . . . SEEMS TO ME TO BE
THE CREATURE OF PUBLIC CONVENTION"

To Robert Morris

Sir,   Passy, Dec. 25, 1783.

I have received your Favour of the 30th of September, for which I thank you. My Apprehension, that the Union between France and our States might be diminished by Accounts from hence, was occasioned by the extravagant and violent Language held here by a Public Person, in public Company, which had that Tendency; and it was natural for me to think his Letters might hold the same Language, in which I was right; for I have since had Letters from Boston informing me of it. Luckily here, and I hope there, it is imputed to the true Cause, a Disorder in the Brain, which, tho' not constant, has its Fits too frequent. I will not fill my Letter with an Account of those Discourses. Mr. Laurens, when you see him, can give it to you; I mean such as he heard in Company with other Persons, for I would not have him relate private Conversations. They distress'd me much at the time, being then at your earnest Instances soliciting for more aids of Money; the Success of which Solicitation such ungrateful and provoking Language might, I feared, have had a Tendency to prevent. Enough of this at present.

I have been exceedingly hurt and afflicted by the Difficulty some of your late Bills met with in Holland. As soon as I receiv'd the Letter from Messrs. Willinck & Co., which I inclose, I sent for Mr. Grand, who brought me a Sketch of his Account with you, by which it appear'd that the Demands upon us, existing and expected, would more than absorb the Funds in his Hands. We could not indulge the smallest Hope of obtaining further Assistance here, the Public Finances being in a state of Embarrassment, private Persons full of Distrust occasioned by the late Stoppage of Payment at the *Caisse d'Escompte*, and money in general extreamly scarce. But he agreed to do what I propos'd, lend his Credit in the Way of Drawing and Redrawing between Holland and Paris, to gain Time till you could furnish Funds to reimburse Messrs. Willenck & Co. I believe he made this Proposition to them by the Return of the Express. I know not why it was not accepted. Mr. Grand, I suppose, will himself give you an Account of all the Transaction, and of his Application to Messrs. Couteulx & Co.; therefore, I need not add more upon this disagreable Subject.

I have found Difficulties in settling the Account of Salaries

with the other Ministers, that have made it impracticable for
me to do it. I have, therefore, after keeping the Bills that were
to have been proportioned among us long in my hands, given
them up to Mr. Grand, who, finding the same Difficulties,
will, I suppose, return them to you. None has come to hand
for the two or three last Quarters, and we are indebted to his
Kindness for advancing us Money, or we must have run in
Debt for our Subsistence. He risques in doing this, since he
has not for it your Orders.

There arise frequently contingent Expences, for which no
provision has yet been made. In a former letter to the Secretary for Foreign Affairs, I gave a List of them, and desired to
know the Pleasure of Congress concerning them. I have only
had for Answer, that they were under Consideration, and that
he believed House-Rent would not be allowed; but I am still
in Uncertainty as to that and the Rest. I wish some resolutions were taken on this Point of Contingencies, that I may
know how to settle my Accounts with Mr. Barclay. American
Ministers in Europe are too remote from their Constituents
to consult them, and take their Orders on every Occasion, as
the Ministers here of European Courts can easily do. There
seems, therefore, a Necessity of allowing more to their Discretion, and of giving them a Credit to a certain Amount on
some Banker, who may answer their Orders; for which, however, they should be accountable. I mention this for the sake
of other Ministers, hoping and expecting soon to be discharg'd myself, and also for the Good of the Service.

The Remissness of our People in Paying Taxes is highly
blameable; the Unwillingness to pay them is still more so. I
see, in some Resolutions of Town Meetings, a Remonstrance
against giving Congress a Power to take, as they call it, the
People's Money out of their Pockets, tho' only to pay the Interest and Principal of Debts duly contracted. They seem to
mistake the Point. Money, justly due from the People, is their
Creditors' Money, and no longer the Money of the People,
who, if they withold it, should be compell'd to pay by some
Law.

All Property, indeed, except the Savage's temporary Cabin,
his Bow, his Matchcoat, and other little Acquisitions, absolutely necessary for his Subsistence, seems to me to be the

Creature of public Convention. Hence the Public has the
Right of Regulating Descents, and all other Conveyances of
Property, and even of limiting the Quantity and the Uses of
it. All the Property that is necessary to a Man, for the Conservation of the Individual and the Propagation of the Species, is his natural Right, which none can justly deprive him
of: But all Property superfluous to such purposes is the Property of the Publick, who, by their Laws, have created it, and
who may therefore by other Laws dispose of it, whenever the
Welfare of the Publick shall demand such Disposition. He
that does not like civil Society on these Terms, let him retire
and live among Savages. He can have no right to the benefits
of Society, who will not pay his Club towards the Support
of it.

The Marquis de la F., who loves to be employ'd in our
Affairs, and is often very useful, has lately had several Conversations with the Ministers and Persons concern'd in forming new Regulations, respecting the Commerce between our
two Countries, which are not yet concluded. I therefore
thought it well to communicate to him a Copy of your Letter, which contains so many sensible and just Observations
on that Subject. He will make a proper Use of them, and
perhaps they may have more Weight, as appearing to come
from a Frenchman, than they would have if it were known
that they were the Observations of an American. I perfectly
agree with you in all the Sentiments you have express'd on
this Occasion.

You have made no Answer to the Proposition I sent of
furnishing Tobacco to the Farmers General. They have since
made a Contract with Messrs Alexander & Williams for the
same Purpose but it is such a one as does not prevent their
making another with you if hereafter it should suit you.

I am sorry for the Publick's sake, that you are about to quit
your Office, but on personal Considerations I shall congratulate you; for I cannot conceive of a more happy Man, than
he, who having been long loaded with public Cares, finds
himself reliev'd from them, and enjoying private repose in the
Bosom of his Friends and Family.

The Government here has set on foot a new Loan of an
Hundred Millions. I enclose the Plan.

It is thought very advantageous for the Lenders. You may judge by that how much the Money is wanted, and how seasonable the Peace was for all concerned.

If Mr. Alexander, who is gone to Virginia, should happen to come to Philadelphia, I beg leave to recommend him to your Civilities as an old Friend of mine whom I very much esteem.

With sincere Regard & Attachment, I am ever, Dear Sir,
Your most etc.

"A GOOD PEOPLE TO LIVE AMONG"

To ———

Your Queries concerning the Value of Land in different Circumstances & Situations, Modes of Settlement, &c. &c. are quite out of my Power to answer; having while I lived in America been always an Inhabitant of Capital Cities, and not in the way of learning any thing correctly of Country Affairs. There is a Book lately published in London, written by Mr. Hector St. John, its Title, Letters from an American Farmer, which contains a good deal of Information on those Subjects; and as I know the Author to be an observing intelligent Man, I suppose the Information to be good as far as it goes, and I recommend the Book to your perusal.

There is no doubt but great Tracts may be purchased on the Frontiers of Virginia, & the Carolinas, at moderate Rates. In Virginia it used to be at 5£ Sterling the 100 Acres. I know not the present Price, but do not see why it should be higher.

Emigrants arriving pay no Fine or Premium for being admitted to all the Privileges of Citizens. Those are acquired by two Years Residence.

No Rewards are given to encourage new Settlers to come among us, whatever degree of Property they may bring with them, nor any Exemptions from common Duties. Our Country offers to Strangers nothing but a good Climate, fertile Soil, wholesome Air, Free Governments, wise Laws, Liberty, a good People to live among, and a hearty Welcome. Those

Europeans who have these or greater Advantages at home, would do well to stay where they are.

January, 1784?

"THE TURK'Y IS IN COMPARISON A MUCH MORE RESPECTABLE BIRD"

To Sarah Bache

MY DEAR CHILD,   Passy, Jan. 26, 1784.
    Your Care in sending me the Newspapers is very agreable to me. I received by Capt. Barney those relating to the *Cincinnati*. My Opinion of the Institution cannot be of much Importance; I only wonder that, when the united Wisdom of our Nation had, in the Articles of Confederation, manifested their Dislike of establishing Ranks of Nobility, by Authority either of the Congress or of any particular State, a Number of private Persons should think proper to distinguish themselves and their Posterity, from their fellow Citizens, and form an Order of *hereditary Knights*, in direct Opposition to the solemnly declared Sense of their Country! I imagine it must be likewise contrary to the Good Sense of most of those drawn into it by the Persuasion of its Projectors, who have been too much struck with the Ribbands and Crosses they have seen among them hanging to the Buttonholes of Foreign Officers. And I suppose those, who disapprove of it, have not hitherto given it much Opposition, from a Principle somewhat like that of your good Mother, relating to punctilious Persons, who are always exacting little Observances of Respect; that, *"if People can be pleased with small Matters, it is a pity but they should have them."*
    In this View, perhaps, I should not myself, if my Advice had been ask'd, have objected to their wearing their Ribband and Badge according to their Fancy, tho' I certainly should to the entailing it as an Honour on their Posterity. For Honour, worthily obtain'd (as for Example that of our Officers), is in its Nature a *personal* Thing, and incommunicable to any but those who had some Share in obtaining it. Thus among the Chinese, the most ancient, and from long Experience the wisest of

Nations, honour does not *descend*, but *ascends*. If a man from his Learning, his Wisdom, or his Valour, is promoted by the Emperor to the Rank of Mandarin, his Parents are immediately entitled to all the same Ceremonies of Respect from the People, that are establish'd as due to the Mandarin himself; on the supposition that it must have been owing to the Education, Instruction, and good Example afforded him by his Parents, that he was rendered capable of serving the Publick.

This *ascending* Honour is therefore useful to the State, as it encourages Parents to give their Children a good and virtuous Education. But the *descending Honour*, to Posterity who could have no Share in obtaining it, is not only groundless and absurd, but often hurtful to that Posterity, since it is apt to make them proud, disdaining to be employ'd in useful Arts, and thence falling into Poverty, and all the Meannesses, Servility, and Wretchedness attending it; which is the present case with much of what is called the *Noblesse* in Europe. Or if, to keep up the Dignity of the Family, Estates are entailed entire on the Eldest male heir, another Pest to Industry and Improvement of the Country is introduc'd, which will be followed by all the odious mixture of pride and Beggary, and idleness, that have half depopulated and *decultivated* Spain; occasioning continual Extinction of Families by the Discouragements of Marriage and neglect in the improvement of estates.

I wish, therefore, that the Cincinnati, if they must go on with their Project, would direct the Badges of their Order to be worn by their Parents, instead of handing them down to their Children. It would be a good Precedent, and might have good Effects. It would also be a kind of Obedience to the Fourth Commandment, in which God enjoins us to *honour* our Father and Mother, but has nowhere directed us to honour our Children. And certainly no mode of honouring those immediate Authors of our Being can be more effectual, than that of doing praiseworthy Actions, which reflect Honour on those who gave us our Education; or more becoming, than that of manifesting, by some public Expression or Token, that it is to their Instruction and Example we ascribe the Merit of those Actions.

But the Absurdity of *descending Honours* is not a mere Matter of philosophical Opinion; it is capable of mathe-

matical Demonstration. A Man's Son, for instance, is but half
of his Family, the other half belonging to the Family of his
Wife. His Son, too, marrying into another Family, his Share
in the Grandson is but a fourth; in the Great Grandson, by
the same Process, it is but an Eighth; in the next Generation
a Sixteenth; the next a Thirty-second; the next a Sixty-fourth;
the next an Hundred and twenty-eighth; the next a Two
hundred and Fifty-sixth; and the next a Five hundred and
twelfth; thus in nine Generations, which will not require
more than 300 years (no very great Antiquity for a Family),
our present Chevalier of the Order of Cincinnatus's Share in
the then existing Knight, will be but a 512th part; which, allowing the present certain Fidelity of American Wives to be
insur'd down through all those Nine Generations, is so small
a Consideration, that methinks no reasonable Man would
hazard for the sake of it the disagreable Consequences of the
Jealousy, Envy, and Ill will of his Countrymen.

Let us go back with our Calculation from this young Noble, the 512th part of the present Knight, thro' his nine Generations, till we return to the year of the Institution. He must
have had a Father and Mother, they are two. Each of them
had a father and Mother, they are four. Those of the next
preceding Generation will be eight, the next Sixteen, the next
thirty-two, the next sixty-four, the next one hundred and
Twenty-eight, the next Two hundred and fifty-six, and the
ninth in this Retrocession Five hundred and twelve, who
must be now existing, and all contribute their Proportion of
this future *Chevalier de Cincinnatus*. These, with the rest,
make together as follows:

	2
	4
	8
	16
	32
	64
	128
	256
	512
Total	1022

One Thousand and Twenty-two Men and Women, contributors to the formation of one Knight. And, if we are to have a Thousand of these future knights, there must be now and hereafter existing One million and Twenty-two Thousand Fathers and Mothers, who are to contribute to their Production, unless a Part of the Number are employ'd in making more Knights than One. Let us strike off then the 22,000, on the Supposition of this double Employ, and then consider whether, after a reasonable Estimation of the Number of Rogues, and Fools, and Royalists and Scoundrels and Prostitutes, that are mix'd with, and help to make up necessarily their Million of Predecessors, Posterity will have much reason to boast of the noble Blood of the then existing Set of Chevaliers de Cincinnatus. The future genealogists, too, of these Chevaliers, in proving the lineal descent of their honour through so many generations (even supposing honour capable in its nature of descending), will only prove the small share of this honour, which can be justly claimed by any one of them; since the above simple process in arithmetic makes it quite plain and clear that, in proportion as the antiquity of the family shall augment, the right to the honour of the ancestor will diminish; and a few generations more would reduce it to something so small as to be very near an absolute nullity. I hope, therefore, that the Order will drop this part of their project, and content themselves, as the Knights of the Garter, Bath, Thistle, St. Louis, and other Orders of Europe do, with a Life Enjoyment of their little Badge and Ribband, and let the Distinction die with those who have merited it. This I imagine will give no offence. For my own part, I shall think it a Convenience, when I go into a Company where there may be Faces unknown to me, if I discover, by this Badge, the Persons who merit some particular Expression of my Respect; and it will save modest Virtue the Trouble of calling for our Regard, by awkward roundabout Intimations of having been heretofore employ'd in the Continental Service.

The Gentleman, who made the Voyage to France to provide the Ribands and Medals, has executed his Commission. To me they seem tolerably done; but all such Things are criticis'd. Some find Fault with the Latin, as wanting classic

Elegance and Correctness; and, since our Nine Universities were not able to furnish better Latin, it was pity, they say, that the Mottos had not been in English. Others object to the Title, as not properly assumable by any but Gen. Washington, and a few others who serv'd without Pay. Others object to the *Bald Eagle* as looking too much like a *Dindon*, or Turkey. For my own part, I wish the Bald Eagle had not been chosen as the Representative of our Country; he is a Bird of bad moral Character; he does not get his living honestly; you may have seen him perch'd on some dead Tree, near the River where, too lazy to fish for himself, he watches the Labour of the Fishing-Hawk; and, when that diligent Bird has at length taken a Fish, and is bearing it to his Nest for the support of his Mate and young ones, the Bald Eagle pursues him, and takes it from him. With all this Injustice he is never in good Case; but, like those among Men who live by Sharping and Robbing, he is generally poor, and often very lousy. Besides, he is a rank Coward; the little *KingBird*, not bigger than a Sparrow, attacks him boldly and drives him out of the District. He is therefore by no means a proper emblem for the brave and honest Cincinnati of America, who have driven all the *Kingbirds* from our Country; though exactly fit for that Order of Knights, which the French call *Chevaliers d'Industrie*.

I am, on this account, not displeas'd that the Figure is not known as a Bald Eagle, but looks more like a Turk'y. For in Truth, the Turk'y is in comparison a much more respectable Bird, and withal a true original Native of America. Eagles have been found in all Countries, but the Turk'y was peculiar to ours; the first of the Species seen in Europe being brought to France by the Jesuits from Canada, and serv'd up at the Wedding Table of Charles the Ninth. He is, though a little vain and silly, it is true, but not the worse emblem for that, a Bird of Courage, and would not hesitate to attack a Grenadier of the British Guards, who should presume to invade his FarmYard with a *red* Coat on.

I shall not enter into the Criticisms made upon their Latin. The gallant officers of America may not have the merit of being great scholars, but they undoubtedly merit much, as brave soldiers, from their Country, which should therefore not leave them merely to *Fame* for their "*Virtutis Premium,*" which is one of their Latin Mottos. Their *"Esto perpetua,"* another, is an excellent Wish, if they meant it for their Country; bad, if intended for their Order. The States should not only restore to them the *Omnia* of their first Motto, which many of them have left and lost, but pay them justly, and reward them generously. They should not be suffered to remain, with all their new-created Chivalry, *entirely* in the Situation of the Gentleman in the Story, which their *omnia reliquit* reminds me of. You know every thing makes me recollect some Story. He had built a very fine House, and thereby much impair'd his Fortune. He had a Pride, however, in showing it to his Acquaintance. One of them, after viewing it all, remark'd a Motto over the Door, "OIA VANITAS." "What," says he, "is the Meaning of this OIA? it is a word I don't understand." "I will tell you," said the Gentleman; "I had a mind to have the Motto cut on a Piece of smooth Marble, but there was not room for it between the Ornaments, to be put in Characters large enough to be read. I therefore made use of a Contraction antiently very common in Latin Manuscripts, by which the *m*'s and *n*'s in Words are omitted, and the Omission noted by a little Dash above, which you may see there; so that the Word is *omnia*, OMNIA VANITAS." "O," says his Friend, "I now comprehend the Meaning of your motto, it relates to your Edifice; and signifies, that, if you have abridged your *Omnia*, you have, nevertheless, left your VANITAS legible at full length." I am, as ever, your affectionate father,

"MY ADVICE 'SMELLS OF MADEIRA' "

To William Strahan

DEAR SIR, Passy, Feb. 16, 1784.

I receiv'd and read with Pleasure your kind Letter of the first Inst, as it inform'd me of the Welfare of you and yours. I am glad the Accounts you have from your Kinswoman at Philadelphia are agreable, and I shall be happy if any Recommendations from me can be serviceable to Dr. Ross, or any other friend of yours, going to America.

Your arguments, persuading me to come once more to England, are very powerful. To be sure, I long to see again my Friends there, whom I love abundantly; but there are difficulties and Objections of several kinds, which at present I do not see how to get over.

I lament with you the political Disorders England at present labours under. Your Papers are full of strange Accounts of Anarchy and Confusion in America, of which we know nothing, while your own Affairs are really in a Situation deplorable. In my humble Opinion, the Root of the Evil lies not so much in too long, or too unequally chosen Parliaments, as in the enormous Salaries, Emoluments, and Patronage of your great Offices; and that you will never be at rest till they are all abolish'd, and every place of Honour made at the same time, instead of a Place of Profit, a place of Expence and burthen.

Ambition and avarice are each of them strong Passions, and when they are united in the same Persons, and have the same Objects in view for their Gratification, they are too strong for Public Spirit and Love of Country, and are apt to produce the most violent Factions and Contentions. They should therefore be separated, and made to act one against the other. Those Places, to speak in our old stile (Brother Type), may be for the good of the *Chapel*, but they are bad for the Master, as they create constant Quarrels that hinder the Business. For example, here are near two Months that your Government has been employed in *getting its form to press*; which is not yet fit to *work on*, every Page of it being *squabbled*, and the whole ready to fall into *pye*. The Founts too must be very scanty, or strangely *out of sorts*, since your *Compositors* cannot find either *upper* or *lower case Letters* sufficient to set the word ADMINISTRATION, but are forc'd to be continually *turning for them*. However, to return to common (tho' perhaps too saucy) Language, don't despair; you have still one resource left, and that not a bad one, since it may reunite the Empire. We have some Remains of Affection for you, and shall always be ready to receive and take care of you in Case of Distress. So if you have not Sense and Virtue enough to govern yourselves, e'en dissolve your present old crazy Constitution, and *send members to Congress.*

You will say my *Advice* "smells of *Madeira*." You are right. This foolish Letter is mere chitchat *between ourselves* over the *second bottle*. If, therefore, you show it to anybody, (except our indulgent Friends, Dagge and Lady Strahan) I will positively *Solless* you. Yours ever most affectionately,

METHODS OF TREATING DISEASES

To La Sabliere de la Condamine

SIR,   Passy, March 19, 1784

I receiv'd the very obliging Letter you did me honour of writing to me the 8ᵗʰ Inst. with the epigram &c. for which please to accept my Thanks.

You desire my Sentiments concerning the Cures perform'd by Comus & Mesmer. I think that in general, Maladies caus'd by Obstructions may be treated by Electricity with Advantage. As to the Animal Magnetism, so much talk'd of, I am totally unacquainted with it, and must doubt its Existence till I can see or feel some Effect of it. None of the Cures said to be perform'd by it, have fallen under my Observation; and there being so many Disorders which cure themselves and such a Disposition in Mankind to deceive themselves and one another on these Occasions; and living long having given me frequent Opportunities of seeing certain Remedies cry'd up as curing everything, and yet soon after totally laid aside as useless, I cannot but fear that the Expectation of great Advantage from the new Method of treating Diseases, will prove a Delusion. That Delusion may however in some cases be of use while it lasts. There are in every great rich City a Number of Persons who are never in health, because they are fond of Medicines and always taking them, whereby they derange the natural Functions, and hurt their Constitutions. If these People can be persuaded to forbear their Drugs in Expectation of being cured by only the Physician's Finger or an Iron Rod pointing at them, they may possibly find good Effects tho' they mistake the Cause. I have the honour to be, Sir, &c.

"STOOP, STOOP!"

To Samuel Mather

REV^d SIR,   Passy, May 12, 1784.

I received your kind letter, with your excellent advice to the people of the United States, which I read with great pleasure, and hope it will be duly regarded. Such writings, though they may be lightly passed over by many readers, yet, if they make a deep impression on one active mind in a hundred, the effects may be considerable. Permit me to mention one little instance, which, though it relates to myself, will not be quite uninteresting to you. When I was a boy, I met with a book, entitled *"Essays to do Good,"* which I think was written by your father. It had been so little regarded by a former possessor, that several leaves of it were torn out; but the remainder gave me such a turn of thinking, as to have an influence on my conduct through life; for I have always set a greater value on the character of a *doer of good*, than on any other kind of reputation; and if I have been, as you seem to think, a useful citizen, the public owes the advantage of it to that book.

You mention your being in your 78th year; I am in my 79th; we are grown old together. It is now more than 60 years since I left Boston, but I remember well both your father and grandfather, having heard them both in the pulpit, and seen them in their houses. The last time I saw your father was in the beginning of 1724, when I visited him after my first trip to Pennsylvania. He received me in his library, and on my taking leave showed me a shorter way out of the house through a narrow passage, which was crossed by a beam over head. We were still talking as I withdrew, he accompanying me behind, and I turning partly towards him, when he said hastily, *"Stoop, stoop!"* I did not understand him, till I felt my head hit against the beam. He was a man that never missed any occasion of giving instruction, and upon this he said to me, *"You are young, and have the world before you;* STOOP *as you go through it, and you will miss many hard thumps."* This advice, thus beat into my head, has frequently been of use to me; and I often think of it, when I see pride mortified, and misfortunes brought upon people by their carrying their heads too high.

I long much to see again my native place, and to lay my bones there. I left it in 1723; I visited it in 1733, 1743, 1753, and 1763. In 1773 I was in England; in 1775 I had a sight of it, but could not enter, it being in possession of the enemy. I did hope to have been there in 1783, but could not obtain my dismission from this employment here; and now I fear I shall never have that happiness. My best wishes however attend my dear country. *Esto perpetua.* It is now blest with an excellent constitution; may it last for ever!

This powerful monarchy continues its friendship for the United States. It is a friendship of the utmost importance to our security, and should be carefully cultivated. Britain has not yet well digested the loss of its dominion over us, and has still at times some flattering hopes of recovering it. Accidents may increase those hopes, and encourage dangerous attempts. A breach between us and France would infallibly bring the English again upon our backs; and yet we have some wild heads among our countrymen, who are endeavouring to weaken that connexion! Let us preserve our reputation by performing our engagements; our credit by fulfilling our contracts; and friends by gratitude and kindness; for we know not how soon we may again have occasion for all of them. With great and sincere esteem, I have the honour to be, &c.

"BEWARE OF BEING LULLED INTO A
DANGEROUS SECURITY"

To Charles Thomson

DEAR SIR,   Passy, May 13, 1784.

Yesterday evening Mr. Hartley met with Mr. Jay and myself when the ratifications of the Definitive Treaty were exchanged. I send a copy of the English Ratification to the President.

Thus the great and hazardous enterprize we have been engaged in is, God be praised, happily compleated; an event I hardly expected I should live to see. A few years of Peace, will improve, will restore and encrease our strength; but our future safety will depend on our union and our virtue. Britain will be long watching for advantages, to recover what she has lost. If we do not convince the world, that we are a Nation to be depended on for fidelity in Treaties; if we appear negligent in paying our Debts, and ungrateful to those who have served and befriended us; our reputation, and all the strength it is capable of procuring, will be lost, and fresh attacks upon us will be encouraged and promoted by better prospects of success. Let us therefore beware of being lulled into a dangerous security; and of being both enervated and impoverished by luxury; of being weakened by internal contentions and divisions; of being shamefully extravagant in contracting private debts, while we are backward in discharging honorably those of the public; of neglect in military exercises and discipline, and in providing stores of arms and munitions of war, to be ready on occasion; for all these are circumstances that give confidence to enemies, and diffidence to friends; and the expenses required to prevent a war are much lighter than those that will, if not prevented, be absolutely necessary to maintain it.

I am long kept in suspense without being able to learn the purpose of Congress respecting my request of recall, and that of some employment for my secretary, William Temple Franklin. If I am kept here another winter, and as much weakened by it as by the last, I may as well resolve to spend the remainder of my days here; for I shall be hardly able to bear the fatigues of the voyage in returning. During my long absence from America, my friends are continually diminishing by death, and my inducements to return in proportion. But I can make no preparations either for going conveniently, or staying comfortably here, nor take any steps towards making some other provision for my grandson, till I know what I am to expect. Be so good, my dear friend, as to send me a little private information. With great esteem, I am ever yours, most affectionately

" 'DAMN YOUR SOULS. MAKE TOBACCO!' "

To Mason Locke Weems and Edward Gant

GENTLEMEN,   Passy, July 18, 1784.
On receipt of your Letter, acquainting me that the Arch-

bishop of Canterbury would not permit you to be ordain'd, unless you took the Oath of Allegiance, I apply'd to a Clergyman of my Acquaintance for Information on the Subject of your obtaining Ordination here. His Opinion was, that it could not be done; and that, if it were done, you would be requir'd to vow Obedience to the Archbishop of Paris. I next inquired of the Pope's Nuncio, whether you might not be ordain'd by their Bishop in America, Powers being sent him for that purpose, if he has them not already. The answer was, "The Thing is impossible, unless the Gentlemen become Catholics."

This is an Affair of which I know very little, and therefore I may ask Questions and propose means that are improper or impracticable. But what is the necessity of your being connected with the Church of England? Would it not be as well, if you were of the Church of Ireland? The Religion is the same, tho' there is a different set of Bishops and Archbishops. Perhaps if you were to apply to the Bishop of Derry, who is a man of liberal Sentiments, he might give you Orders as of that Church. If both Britain and Ireland refuse you, (and I am not sure that the Bishops of Denmark or Sweden would ordain you, unless you become Lutherans,) what is to be done? Next to becoming Presbyterians, the Episcopalian clergy of America, in my humble Opinion, cannot do better than to follow the Example of the first Clergy of Scotland, soon after the Conversion of that Country to Christianity, who when their King had built the Cathedral of St. Andrew's, and requested the King of Northumberland to lend his Bishops to ordain one for them, that their Clergy might not as heretofore be obliged to go to Northumberland for Orders, and their Request was refused; they assembled in the Cathedral; and, the Mitre, Crosier, and Robes of a Bishop being laid upon the Altar, they, after earnest Prayers for Direction in their Choice, elected one of their own Number; when the King said to him, *"Arise, go to the Altar, and receive your Office at the Hand of God."* His brethren led him to the Altar, robed him, put the Crozier in his Hand, and the Mitre on his Head, and he became the first Bishop of Scotland.

If the British Isles were sunk in the Sea (and the Surface of this Globe has suffered greater Changes), you would probably take some such Method as this; and, if they persist in denying you Ordination, 'tis the same thing. An hundred years hence, when People are more enlightened, it will be wondered at, that Men in America, qualified by their Learning and Piety to pray for and instruct their Neighbors, should not be permitted to do it till they had made a Voyage of six thousand Miles out and home, to ask leave of a cross old Gentleman at Canterbury; who seems, by your Account, to have as little Regard for the Souls of the People of Maryland, as King William's Attorney-General, Seymour, had for those of Virginia. The Reverend Commissary Blair, who projected the College of that Province, and was in England to solicit Benefactions and a Charter, relates, that the Queen, in the King's Absence, having ordered Seymour to draw up the Charter, which was to be given, with £2000 in Money, he oppos'd the Grant; saying that the Nation was engag'd in an expensive War, that the Money was wanted for better purposes, and he did not see the least Occasion for a College in Virginia. Blair represented to him, that its Intention was to educate and qualify young Men to be Ministers of the Gospel, much wanted there; and begged Mr. Attorney would consider, that the People of Virginia had souls to be saved, as well as the People of England. "*Souls!*" says he, "*damn your Souls. Make Tobacco!*" I have the honour to be, Gentlemen, &c.

"OUR OPINIONS ARE NOT IN OUR OWN POWER"

To William Franklin

DEAR SON,   Passy, Aug. 16, 1784.

I received your Letter of the 22d past, and am glad to find that you desire to revive the affectionate Intercourse, that formerly existed between us. It will be very agreable to me; indeed nothing has ever hurt me so much and affected me with such keen Sensations, as to find myself deserted in my old Age by my only Son; and not only deserted, but to find him taking up Arms against me, in a Cause, wherein my good Fame, Fortune and Life were all at Stake. You conceived, you say, that your Duty to your King and Regard for your Country requir'd this. I ought not to blame you for differing in Sentiment with me in Public Affairs. We are Men, all subject to Errors. Our Opinions are not in our own Power; they are form'd and govern'd much by Circumstances, that are often as inexplicable as they are irresistible. Your Situation was such that few would have censured your remaining Neuter, *tho' there are Natural Duties which precede political ones, and cannot be extinguish'd by them.*

This is a disagreable Subject. I drop it. And we will endeavour, as you propose mutually to forget what has happened relating to it, as well as we can. I send your Son over to pay his Duty to you. You will find him much improv'd. He is greatly esteem'd and belov'd in this Country, and will make his Way anywhere. It is my Desire, that he should study the Law, as a necessary Part of Knowledge for a public Man, and profitable if he should have occasion to practise it. I would have you therefore put into his hands those Law-books you have, viz. Blackstone, Coke, Bacon, Viner, &c. He will inform you, that he received the Letter sent him by Mr. Galloway, and the Paper it enclosed, safe.

On my leaving America, I deposited with that Friend for you, a Chest of Papers, among which was a Manuscript of nine or ten Volumes, relating to Manufactures, Agriculture, Commerce, Finance, etc., which cost me in England about 70 Guineas; eight Quire Books, containing the Rough Drafts of all my Letters while I liv'd in London. These are missing. I hope you have got them, if not, they are lost. Mr. Vaughan has publish'd in London a Volume of what he calls my Political Works. He proposes a second Edition; but, as the first was very incompleat, and you had many Things that were omitted, (for I used to send you sometimes the Rough Drafts, and sometimes the printed Pieces I wrote in London,) I have directed him to apply to you for what may be in your Power to furnish him with, or to delay his Publication till I can be at home again, if that may ever happen.

I did intend returning this year; but the Congress, instead of giving me Leave to do so, have sent me another Commission, which will keep me here at least a Year longer; and perhaps I may then be too old and feeble to bear the Voyage. I

am here among a People that love and respect me, a most
amiable Nation to live with; and perhaps I may conclude to
die among them; for my Friends in America are dying off,
one after another, and I have been so long abroad, that I
should now be almost a Stranger in my own Country.

I shall be glad to see you when convenient, but would not
have you come here at present. You may confide to your son
the Family Affairs you wished to confer upon with me, for he
is discreet. And I trust, that you will prudently avoid introducing him to Company, that it may be improper for him to
be seen with. I shall hear from you by him and any letters to
me afterwards, will come safe under Cover directed to Mr.
Ferdinand Grand, Banker at Paris. Wishing you Health, and
more Happiness than it seems you have lately experienced, I
remain your affectionate father,

"THE YANKEYS NEVER FELT BOLD"

To William Strahan

DEAR FRIEND,   Passy, Augt 19.th 1784.
   I received your kind Letter of Ap^l 17th. You will have the
goodness to place my delay in answering to the Account of
Indisposition and Business, and excuse it. I have now that
letter before me; and my Grandson, whom you may formerly
remember a little Scholar of Mr. Elphinston's, purposing to
set out in a day or two on a visit to his Father in London, I
set down to scribble a little to you, first recommending him
as a worthy young Man to your Civilities and Counsels.

You press me much to come to England. I am not without
strong Inducements to do so; the Fund of Knowledge you
promise to Communicate to me is an Addition to them, and
no small one. At present it is impracticable. But, when my
Grandson returns, come with him. We will then talk the matter over, and perhaps you may take me back with you. I have
a Bed at your service, and will try to make your Residence,
while you can stay with us, as agreable to you, if possible, as
I am sure it will be to me.

You do not "approve the annihilation of profitable Places; for you do not see why a Statesman, who does his Business well, should not be paid for his Labour as well as any other Workman." Agreed. But why more than any other Workman? The less the Salary the greater the Honor. In so great a Nation, there are many rich enough to afford giving their time to the Public; and there are, I make no doubt, many wise and able Men, who would take as much Pleasure in governing for nothing, as they do in playing Chess for nothing. It would be one of the noblest of Amusements. That this Opinion is not Chimerical, the Country I now live in affords a Proof; its whole Civil and Criminal Law Administration being done for nothing, or in some sense for less than nothing; since the Members of its Judiciary Parliaments buy their Places, and do not make more than *three per cent* for their Money by their Fees and Emoluments, while the legal Interest is *five*; so that in Fact they give two per cent to be allow'd to govern, and all their time and trouble into the Bargain. Thus *Profit*, one Motive for desiring Place, being abolish'd, there remains only *Ambition*; and that being in some degree ballanced by *Loss*, you may easily conceive, that there will not be very violent Factions and Contentions for such Places, nor much of the Mischief to the Country, that attends your Factions, which have often occasioned Wars, and overloaded you with Debts impayable.

I allow you all the Force of your Joke upon the Vagrancy of our Congress. They have a right to sit *where* they please, of which perhaps they have made too much Use by shifting too often. But they have two other Rights; those of sitting *when* they please, and as *long* as they please, in which methinks they have the advantage of your Parliament; for they cannot be dissolved by the Breath of a Minister, or sent packing as you were the other day, when it was your earnest desire to have remained longer together.

You "fairly acknowledge, that the late War terminated quite contrary to your Expectation." Your expectation was ill founded; for you would not believe your old Friend, who told you repeatedly, that by those Measures England would lose her Colonies, as Epictetus warned in vain his Master that he would break his Leg. You believ'd rather the Tales you heard of our Poltroonery and Impotence of Body and Mind. Do you not remember the Story you told me of the Scotch sergeant, who met with a Party of Forty American Soldiers, and, tho' alone, disarm'd them all, and brought them in Prisoners? A Story almost as Improbable as that of the Irishman, who pretended to have alone taken and brought in Five of the enemy by *surrounding* them. And yet, my Friend, sensible and Judicious as you are, but partaking of the general Infatuation, you seemed to believe it.

The Word *general* puts me in mind of a General, your General Clarke, who had the Folly to say in my hearing at Sir John Pringle's, that, with a Thousand British grenadiers, he would undertake to go from one end of America to the other, and geld all the Males, partly by force and partly by a little Coaxing. It is plain he took us for a species of Animals very little superior to Brutes. The Parliament too believ'd the stories of another foolish General, I forget his Name, that the Yankeys never *felt bold*. Yankey was understood to be a sort of Yahoo, and the Parliament did not think the Petitions of such Creatures were fit to be received and read in so wise an Assembly. What was the consequence of this monstrous Pride and Insolence? You first sent small Armies to subdue us, believing them more than sufficient, but soon found yourselves obliged to send greater; these, whenever they ventured to penetrate our Country beyond the Protection of their Ships, were either repulsed and obliged to scamper out, or were surrounded, beaten, and taken Prisoners. An American Planter, who had never seen Europe, was chosen by us to Command our Troops, and continued during the whole War. This Man sent home to you, one after another, five of your best Generals baffled, their Heads bare of Laurels, disgraced even in the Opinion of their Employers.

Your contempt of our Understandings, in Comparison with your own, appeared to be not much better founded than that of our Courage, if we may judge by this Circumstance, that, in whatever Court of Europe a Yankey negociator appeared, the wise British Minister was routed, put in a passion, pick'd a quarrel with your Friends, and was sent home with a Flea in his Ear.

But after all, my dear Friend, do not imagine that I am vain enough to ascribe our Success to any superiority in any of those Points. I am too well acquainted with all the Springs and Levers of our Machine, not to see, that our human means were unequal to our undertaking, and that, if it had not been for the Justice of our Cause, and the consequent Interposition of Providence, in which we had Faith, we must have been ruined. If I had ever before been an Atheist, I should now have been convinced of the Being and Government of a Deity! It is he who abases the Proud and favours the Humble. May we never forget his Goodness to us, and may our future Conduct manifest our Gratitude.

But let us leave these serious Reflections and converse with our usual Pleasantry. I remember your observing once to me as we sat together in the House of Commons, that no two Journeymen Printers, within your Knowledge, had met with such Success in the World as ourselves. You were then at the head of your Profession, and soon afterwards became a Member of Parliament. I was an Agent for a few Provinces, and now act for them all. But we have risen by different Modes. I, as a Republican Printer, always liked a Form well *plain'd down*; being averse to those *overbearing* Letters that hold their Heads so *high*, as to hinder their Neighbours from appearing. You, as a Monarchist, chose to work upon *Crown* Paper, and found it profitable; while I work'd upon *pro patria* (often indeed call'd *Fools Cap*) with no less advantage. Both our *Heaps hold out* very well, and we seem likely to make a pretty good day's Work of it. With regard to Public Affairs (to continue in the same stile), it seems to me that the Compositors in your Chapel do not *cast off their Copy* well, nor perfectly understand *Imposing*; their *Forms*, too, are continually pester'd by the *Outs* and *Doubles*, that are not easy to be corrected. And I think they were wrong in laying aside some *Faces*, and particularly certain *Head-pieces*, that would have been both useful and ornamental. But, Courage! The Business may still flourish with good Management; and the Master become as rich as any of the Company.

By the way, the rapid Growth and extension of the English language in America, must become greatly Advantageous to the booksellers, and holders of Copy-Rights in England. A vast audience is assembling there for English Authors, ancient, present, and future, our People doubling every twenty Years; and this will demand large and of course profitable Impressions of your most valuable Books. I would, therefore, if I possessed such rights, entail them, if such a thing be practicable, upon my Posterity; for their Worth will be continually augmenting. This may look a little like Advice, and yet I have drank no *Madeira* these Ten Months.

The Subject, however, leads me to another Thought, which is, that you do wrong to discourage the Emigration of Englishmen to America. In my piece on Population, I have proved, I think, that Emigration does not diminish but multiplies a Nation. You will not have fewer at home for those that go Abroad; and as every Man who comes among us, and takes up a piece of Land, becomes a Citizen, and by our Constitution has a Voice in Elections, and a share in the Government of the Country, why should you be against acquiring by this fair Means a Repossession of it, and leave it to be taken by Foreigners of all Nations and Languages, who by their Numbers may drown and stifle the English, which otherwise would probably become in the course of two Centuries the most extensive Language in the World, the Spanish only excepted? It is a Fact, that the Irish emigrants and their children are now in Possession of the Government of Pennsylvania, by their Majority in the Assembly, as well as of a great Part of the Territory; and I remember well the first Ship that brought any of them over. I am ever, my dear Friend, yours most affectionately,

ON DIVINE INSPIRATION

To Joseph Priestley

DEAR SIR,   Passy, Augt 21, 1784.
Understanding that my Letter intended for you by General Melvill, was lost at the Hôtel d'Espagne, I take this Opportunity by my Grandson to give you the purport of it, as well as I can recollect. I thank'd you for the Pleasure you had pro-

cured me of the General's Conversation, whom I found a judicious, sensible, and amiable Man. I was glad to hear that you possess'd a comfortable Retirement, and more so that you had Thoughts of removing to Philadelphia, for that it would make me very happy to have you there. Your *Companions* would be very acceptable to the Library, but I hoped you would long live to enjoy their Company yourself. I agreed with you in Sentiments concerning the Old Testament, and thought the Clause in our Constitution, which required the Members of Assembly to declare their belief, *that the whole of it was given by divine Inspiration*, had better have been omitted. That I had opposed the Clause; but, being overpower'd by Numbers, and fearing more might in future Times be grafted on it, I prevailed to have the additional Clause, "that *no further or more extended Profession of Faith should ever be exacted*." I observ'd to you too, that the Evil of it was the less, as *no Inhabitant*, nor any Officer of Government, except the Members of Assembly, were oblig'd to make that Declaration.

So much for that Letter; to which I may now add, that there are several Things in the Old Testament, impossible to be given by *divine* Inspiration; such as the Approbation ascribed to the Angel of the Lord, of that abominably wicked and detestable Action of Jael, the wife of Heber, the Kenite.* If the rest of the Book were like that, I should rather suppose it given by Inspiration from another Quarter, and renounce the whole.

By the way, how goes on the Unitarian Church in Essex Street? And the honest Minister of it, is he comfortably supported? Your old Colleague, Mr. Radcliff, is he living? And what became of Mr. Denham?

My Grandson, who will have the honour of delivering this to you, may bring me a Line from you; and I hope will bring me an Account of your continuing well and happy.

I jog on still, with as much Health, and as few of the Infirmities of old Age, as I have any Reason to expect. But whatever is impair'd in my Constitution, my Regard for my old Friends remains firm and entire. You will always have a good Share of it, for I am ever with great and sincere esteem, dear Sir, &c.

*Judges, chap. iv.

To Richard Price

DEAR FRIEND,   Passy, March 18, 1785.

My nephew, Mr. Williams, will have the honour of delivering you this line. It is to request from you a List of a few good Books, to the Value of about Twenty-five Pounds, such as are most proper to inculcate Principles of sound Religion and just Government. A New Town in the State of Massachusetts having done me the honour of naming itself after me, and proposing to build a Steeple to their meeting-house if I would give them a Bell, I have advis'd the sparing themselves the Expence of a Steeple, for the present, and that they would accept of Books instead of a Bell, Sense being preferable to Sound. These are therefore intended as the Commencement of a little Parochial Library for the Use of a Society of intelligent, respectable Farmers, such as our Country People generally consist of. Besides your own Works, I would only mention, on the Recommendation of my sister, "Stennet's *Discourses on Personal Religion*," which may be one Book of the Number, if you know and approve of it.

With the highest Esteem and Respect, I am ever, my dear Friend, yours most affectionately,

To George Whatley

DEAR OLD FRIEND,   Passy, May 23, 1785.

I sent you a few Lines the other Day, with the Medallion, when I should have written more, but was prevented by the coming in of a *Bavard*, who worried me till Evening. I bore with him, and now you are to bear with me; for I shall probably *bavarder* in answering your Letter.

I am not acquainted with the Saying of Alphonsus, which you allude to as a Sanctification of your Rigidity, in refusing to allow me the Plea of Old Age, as an Excuse for my Want of Exactness in Correspondence. What was that Saying? You do not, it seems, feel any occasion for such an Excuse, though you are, as you say, rising 75. But I am rising (perhaps more properly falling) 80, and I leave the Excuse with you till you arrive at that Age; perhaps you may then be more sensible of its Validity, and see fit to use it for yourself.

I must agree with you, that the Gout is bad, and that the Stone is worse. I am happy in not having them both together, and I join in your Prayer, that you may live till you die without either. But I doubt the Author of the Epitaph you send me was a little mistaken, when he, speaking of the World, says, that

> "he ne'er car'd a pin
> What they said or may say of the Mortal within."

It is so natural to wish to be well spoken of, whether alive or dead, that I imagine he could not be quite exempt from that Desire; and that at least he wish'd to be thought a Wit, or he would not have given himself the Trouble of writing so good an Epitaph to leave behind him. Was it not as worthy of his Care, that the World should say he was an honest and a good Man? I like better the concluding Sentiment in the old Song, call'd *The Old Man's Wish*, wherein, after wishing for a warm House in a country Town, an easy Horse, some good old authors, ingenious and cheerful Companions, a Pudding on Sundays, with stout Ale, and a bottle of Burgundy, &c. &c., in separate Stanzas, each ending with this burthen,

> "May I govern my Passions with an absolute sway,
>   Grow wiser and better as my Strength wears away,
>   Without Gout or Stone, by a gentle Decay;"

he adds,

> "With a Courage undaunted may I face my last day,
>   And, when I am gone, may the better Sort say,
>   'In the Morning when sober, in the Evening when mellow,
>   He's gone, and has not left behind him his Fellow;
>   For he governed his Passions, &c.'"

But what signifies our Wishing? Things happen, after all, as they will happen. I have sung that *wishing Song* a thousand times, when I was young, and now find, at Fourscore, that the three Contraries have befallen me, being subject to the Gout and the Stone, and not being yet Master of all my Passions. Like the proud Girl in my Country, who wished and resolv'd not to marry a Parson, nor a Presbyterian, nor an Irishman; and at length found herself married to an Irish Presbyterian Parson.

You see I have some reason to wish, that, in a future State, I may not only be *as well as I was*, but a little better. And I hope it; for I, too, with your Poet, *trust in God*. And when I observe, that there is great Frugality, as well as Wisdom, in his Works, since he has been evidently sparing both of Labour and Materials; for by the various wonderful Inventions of Propagation, he has provided for the continual peopling his World with Plants and Animals, without being at the Trouble of repeated new Creations; and by the natural Reduction of compound Substances to their original Elements, capable of being employ'd in new Compositions, he has prevented the Necessity of creating new Matter; so that the Earth, Water, Air, and perhaps Fire, which being compounded form Wood, do, when the Wood is dissolved, return, and again become Air, Earth, Fire, and Water; I say, that, when I see nothing annihilated, and not even a Drop of Water wasted, I cannot suspect the Annihilation of Souls, or believe, that he will suffer the daily Waste of Millions of Minds ready made that now exist, and put himself to the continual Trouble of making new ones. Thus finding myself to exist in the World, I believe I shall, in some Shape or other, always exist; and, with all the inconveniencies human Life is liable to, I shall not object to a new Edition of mine; hoping, however, that the *Errata* of the last may be corrected.

I return your Note of Children receiv'd in the Foundling Hospital at Paris, from 1741 to 1755, inclusive; and I have added the Years preceding as far back as 1710 together with the general Christnings of the City, and the Years succeeding down to 1770. Those since that Period I have not been able to obtain. I have noted in the Margin the gradual Increase, viz. from every tenth Child so thrown upon the Public, till it comes to every third! Fifteen Years have passed since the last Account, and probably it may now amount to one half. Is it right to encourage this monstrous Deficiency of natural Affection? A Surgeon I met with here excused the Women of Paris, by saying, seriously, that they *could not* give suck; *"Car,"* dit il, *"elles n'ont point de tetons."* He assur'd me it was a Fact, and bade me look at them, and observe how flat they were on the Breast; "they have nothing more there," said he, "than I have upon the Back of my hand." I have since thought that there might be some Truth in his Observation, and that, possibly, Nature, finding they made no use of Bubbies, has left off giving them any. Yet, since Rousseau, with admirable Eloquence, pleaded for the Rights of Children to their Mother's Milk, the Mode has changed a little; and some Ladies of Quality now suckle their Infants and find Milk enough. May the Mode descend to the lower Ranks, till it becomes no longer the Custom to pack their Infants away, as soon as born, to the *Enfans Trouvés*, with the careless Observation, that the King is better able to maintain them.

I am credibly inform'd, that nine-tenths of them die there pretty soon, which is said to be a great Relief to the Institution, whose Funds would not otherwise be sufficient to bring up the Remainder. Except the few Persons of Quality above mentioned, and the Multitude who send to the Hospital, the Practice is to hire Nurses in the Country to carry out the Children, and take care of them there. There is an Office for examining the Health of Nurses, and giving them Licenses. They come to Town on certain Days of the Week in Companies to receive the Children, and we often meet Trains of them on the Road returning to the neighbouring Villages, with each a Child in her Arms. But those, who are good enough to try this way of raising their Children, are often not able to pay the Expence; so that the Prisons of Paris are crowded with wretched Fathers and Mothers confined *pour Mois de Nourrice*, tho' it is laudably a favorite Charity to pay for them, and set such Prisoners at Liberty. I wish Success to the new Project of assisting the Poor to keep their Children at home, because I think there is no Nurse like a Mother (or not many), and that, if Parents did not immediately send their Infants out of their Sight, they would in a few days begin to love them, and thence be spurr'd to greater Industry for their Maintenance. This is a Subject you understand better than I, and, therefore, having perhaps said too much, I drop it. I only add to the Notes a Remark, from the *History of the Academy of Sciences*, much in favour of the Foundling Institution.

The Philadelphia Bank goes on, as I hear, very well. What you call the Cincinnati Institution is no Institution of our Government, but a private Convention among the Officers of our late Army, and so universally dislik'd by the People, that it is supposed it will be dropt. It was considered as an Attempt to establish something like an hereditary Rank or Nobility. I hold with you, that it was wrong; may I add, that all *descending* Honours are wrong and absurd; that the Honour of virtuous Actions appertains only to him that performs them, and is in its nature incommunicable. If it were communicable by Descent, it must also be divisible among the Descendants; and the more ancient the Family, the less would be found existing in any one Branch of it; to say nothing of the greater Chance of unlucky Interruptions.

Our Constitution seems not to be well understood with you. If the Congress were a permanent Body, there would be more Reason in being jealous of giving it Powers. But its Members are chosen annually, cannot be chosen more than three Years successively, nor more than three Years in seven; and any of them may be recall'd at any time, whenever their Constituents shall be dissatisfied with their Conduct. They are of the People, and return again to mix with the People, having no more durable preëminence than the different Grains of Sand in an Hourglass. Such an Assembly cannot easily become dangerous to Liberty. They are the Servants of the People, sent together to do the People's Business, and promote the public Welfare; their Powers must be sufficient, or their Duties cannot be performed. They have no profitable Appointments, but a mere Payment of daily Wages, such as are scarcely equivalent to their Expences; so that, having no Chance for great Places, and enormous Salaries or Pensions, as in some Countries, there is no triguing or bribing for Elections.

I wish Old England were as happy in its Government, but I do not see it. Your People, however, think their Constitution the best in the World, and affect to despise ours. It is comfortable to have a good Opinion of one's self, and of every thing that belongs to us; to think one's own Religion, King, and Wife, the best of all possible Wives, Kings, or Religions. I remember three Greenlanders, who had travell'd two Years in Europe under the care of some Moravian Missionaries, and had visited Germany, Denmark, Holland, and England. When I asked them at Philadelphia, where they were in their Way home, whether, now they had seen how much more commodiously the white People lived by the help of the Arts, they would not choose to remain among us; their Answer was, that they were pleased with having had an Opportunity of seeing so many fine things, *but they chose to* LIVE *in their own Country.* Which Country, by the way, consisted of rock only, for the Moravians were obliged to carry Earth in their Ship from New York, for the purpose of making there a Cabbage Garden.

By Mr. Dollond's Saying, that my double Spectacles can only serve particular Eyes, I doubt he has not been rightly informed of their Construction. I imagine it will be found pretty generally true, that the same Convexity of Glass, through which a Man sees clearest and best at the Distance proper for Reading, is not the best for greater Distances. I therefore had formerly two Pair of Spectacles, which I shifted occasionally, as in travelling I sometimes read, and often wanted to regard the Prospects. Finding this Change troublesome, and not always sufficiently ready, I had the Glasses cut, and half of each kind associated in the same Circle, thus,

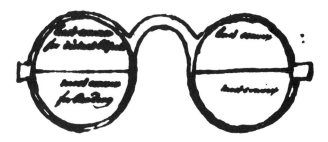

By this means, as I wear my Spectacles constantly, I have only to move my Eyes up or down, as I want to see distinctly far

or near, the proper Glasses being always ready. This I find more particularly convenient since my being in France, the Glasses that serve me best at Table to see what I eat, not being the best to see the Faces of those on the other Side of the Table who speak to me; and when one's Ears are not well accustomed to the Sounds of a Language, a Sight of the Movements in the Features of him that speaks helps to explain; so that I understand French better by the help of my Spectacles.

My intended translator of your Piece, the only one I know who understands the *Subject*, as well as the two Languages, (which a translator ought to do, or he cannot make so good a Translation,) is at present occupied in an Affair that prevents his undertaking it; but that will soon be over. I thank you for the Notes. I should be glad to have another of the printed Pamphlets.

We shall always be ready to take your Children, if you send them to us. I only wonder, that, since London draws to itself, and consumes such Numbers of your Country People, the Country should not, to supply their Places, want and willingly receive the Children you have to dispose of. That Circumstance, together with the Multitude who voluntarily part with their Freedom as Men, to serve for a time as Lackeys, or for Life as Soldiers, in consideration of small Wages, seems to me a Proof that your Island is over-peopled. And yet it is afraid of Emigrations! Adieu, my dear Friend, and believe me ever yours very affectionately,

PHILADELPHIA
1785−1790

Contents

(† denotes title given during Franklin's lifetime.)

A Petition of the Left Hand, 1785 375

Description of an Instrument for Taking Down Books from
    High Shelves, January, 1786. 376

†The Art of Procuring Pleasant Dreams, May 2, 1786 378

The Retort Courteous, 1786 382

THE CONSTITUTIONAL CONVENTION

Speech in the Convention on the Subject of Salaries,
    June 2, 1787 391

Speech in a Committee of the Convention on the Proportion of
    Representation and Votes, June 11, 1787 394

Motion for Prayers in the Convention, June 28, 1787 . . . 398

Speech in the Convention at the Conclusion of its
    Deliberations, September 17, 1787 399

On Sending Felons to America, 1787 402

A Comparison of the Conduct of the Ancient Jews and of the
    Anti-Federalists in the United States of America,
    April 8, 1788 404

On the Abuse of the Press, [after March 30, 1788] 408

†An Account of the Supremest Court of Judicature in
    Pennsylvania, viz. The Court of the Press,
    September 12, 1789 410

†An Address to the Public from the Pennsylvania Society
    for Promoting the Abolition of Slavery, and the Relief of Free
    Negroes Unlawfully Held in Bondage,
    November 9, 1789. 414

Plan for Improving the Condition of the Free Blacks,
    [1789?] 416

Sidi Mehemet Ibrahim on the Slave Trade, March 23, 1790 417

LETTERS

Jonathan Shipley, February 24, 1786
   "When we launch our little Fleet of Barques" 421

Benjamin Vaughan, July 31, 1786
   Lead poisoning. 423

Rev. John Lathrop, May 31, 1788
   "invention and improvement are prolific" 426

Benjamin Vaughan, October 24, 1788
   Honest heretics. 428

John Langdon, 1788
   *"the displeasure of the great and impartial Ruler of the
   Universe".* 429

Jane Mecom, August 3, 1789
   "being a little Miffy" 430

John Wright, November 4, 1789
   "a good motion never dies". 431

Noah Webster, December 26, 1789
   "all these Improvements backwards" 433

Ezra Stiles, March 9, 1790
   "As to Jesus of Nazareth" 438

A Petition of the Left Hand

TO THOSE WHO HAVE THE
SUPERINTENDENCY OF EDUCATION

I address myself to all the friends of youth, and conjure them to direct their compassionate regards to my unhappy fate, in order to remove the prejudices of which I am the victim. There are twin sisters of us; and the two eyes of man do not more resemble, nor are capable of being upon better terms with each other, than my sister and myself, were it not for the partiality of our parents, who make the most injurious distinctions between us. From my infancy, I have been led to consider my sister as a being of a more elevated rank. I was suffered to grow up without the least instruction, while nothing was spared in her education. She had masters to teach her writing, drawing, music, and other accomplishments; but if by chance I touched a pencil, a pen, or a needle, I was bitterly rebuked; and more than once I have been beaten for being awkward, and wanting a graceful manner. It is true, my sister associated me with her upon some occasions; but she always made a point of taking the lead, calling upon me only from necessity, or to figure by her side.

But conceive not, Sirs, that my complaints are instigated merely by vanity. No; my uneasiness is occasioned by an object much more serious. It is the practice in our family, that the whole business of providing for its subsistence falls upon my sister and myself. If any indisposition should attack my sister,—and I mention it in confidence upon this occasion, that she is subject to the gout, the rheumatism, and cramp, without making mention of other accidents,—what would be the fate of our poor family? Must not the regret of our parents be excessive, at having placed so great a difference between sisters who are so perfectly equal? Alas! we must perish from distress; for it would not be in my power even to scrawl a suppliant petition for relief, having been obliged to employ the hand of another in transcribing the request which I have now the honour to prefer to you.

Condescend, Sirs, to make my parents sensible of the injustice of an exclusive tenderness, and of the necessity of distributing their care and affection among all their children equally. I am, with a profound respect, Sirs, your obedient servant,

THE LEFT HAND.

1785

Description of an Instrument for Taking Down Books from High Shelves

January, 1786.

Old men find it inconvenient to mount a ladder or steps for that purpose, their heads being sometimes subject to giddinesses, and their activity, with the steadiness of their joints, being abated by age; besides the trouble of removing the steps every time a book is wanted from a different part of their library.

For a remedy, I have lately made the following simple machine, which I call the *Long Arm*.

A B, the *Arm*, is a stick of pine, an inch square and 8 feet long. *C, D*, the *Thumb* and *Finger*, are two pieces of ash lath, an inch and half wide, and a quarter of an inch thick. These are fixed by wood screws on opposite sides of the end *A* of the arm *A B*; the finger *D* being longer and standing out an inch and half farther than the thumb *C*. The outside of the ends of these laths are pared off sloping and thin, that they may more easily enter between books that stand together on a shelf. Two small holes are bored through them at *i, k. E F*, the sinew, is a cord of the size of a small goosequill, with a loop at one end. When applied to the machine it passes through the two laths, and is stopped by a knot in its other end behind the longest at *k*. The hole at *i* is nearer the end of the arm than that at *k*, about an inch. A number of knots are also on the cord, distant three or four inches from each other.

To use this instrument; put one hand into the loop, and draw the sinew straight down the side of the arm; then enter the end of the finger between the book you would take down and that which is next to it. The laths being flexible, you may

easily by a slight pressure sideways open them wider if the
book is thick, or close them if it is thin by pulling the string,
so as to enter the shorter lath or thumb between your book

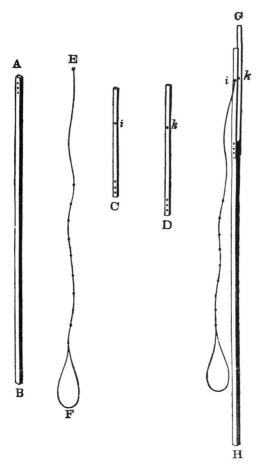

and that which is next to its other side, then push till the back
of your book comes to touch the string. Then draw the string
or sinew tight, which will cause the thumb and finger to
pinch the book strongly, so that you may draw it out. As it
leaves the other books, turn the instrument a *quarter* round,
so that the book may lie flat and rest on its side upon the

under lath or finger. The knots on the sinew will help you to keep it tight and close to the side of the arm as you take it down hand over hand, till the book comes to you; which would drop from between the thumb and finger if the sinew was let loose.

All new tools require some practice before we can become expert in the use of them. This requires very little.

Made in the proportions above given, it serves well for books in duodecimo or octavo. Quartos and folios are too heavy for it; but those are usually placed on the lower shelves within reach of hand.

The book taken down, may, when done with, be put up again into its place by the same machine.

The Art of Procuring Pleasant Dreams

INSCRIBED TO MISS SHIPLEY,
BEING WRITTEN AT HER REQUEST

As a great part of our life is spent in sleep during which we have sometimes pleasant and sometimes painful dreams, it becomes of some consequence to obtain the one kind and avoid the other; for whether real or imaginary, pain is pain and pleasure is pleasure. If we can sleep without dreaming, it is well that painful dreams are avoided. If while we sleep we can have any pleasing dream, it is, as the French say, *autant de gagné*, so much added to the pleasure of life.

To this end it is, in the first place, necessary to be careful in preserving health, by due exercise and great temperance; for, in sickness, the imagination is disturbed, and disagreeable, sometimes terrible, ideas are apt to present themselves. Exercise should precede meals, not immediately follow them; the first promotes, the latter, unless moderate, obstructs digestion. If, after exercise, we feed sparingly, the digestion will be easy and good, the body lightsome, the temper cheerful, and all the animal functions performed agreeably. Sleep, when it follows, will be natural and undisturbed; while indolence, with full feeding, occasions nightmares and horrors inexpressible; we fall from precipices, are assaulted by wild beasts, murderers, and demons, and experience every variety of distress. Observe, however, that the quantities of food and exercise are relative things; those who move much may, and indeed ought to eat more; those who use little exercise should eat little. In general, mankind, since the improvement of cookery, eat about twice as much as nature requires. Suppers are not bad, if we have not dined; but restless nights naturally follow hearty suppers after full dinners. Indeed, as there is a difference in constitutions, some rest well after these meals; it costs them only a frightful dream and an apoplexy, after which they sleep till doomsday. Nothing is more common in the newspapers, than instances of people who, after eating a hearty supper, are found dead abed in the morning.

Another means of preserving health, to be attended to, is the having a constant supply of fresh air in your bed-chamber. It has been a great mistake, the sleeping in rooms exactly closed, and in beds surrounded by curtains. No outward air that may come in to you is so unwholesome as the unchanged air, often breathed, of a close chamber. As boiling water does not grow hotter by longer boiling, if the particles that receive greater heat can escape; so living bodies do not putrefy, if the particles, so fast as they become putrid, can be thrown off. Nature expels them by the pores of the skin and the lungs, and in a free, open air they are carried off; but in a close room we receive them again and again, though they become more and more corrupt. A number of persons crowded into a small room thus spoil the air in a few minutes, and even render it mortal, as in the Black Hole at Calcutta. A single person is said to spoil only a gallon of air per minute, and therefore requires a longer time to spoil a chamber-full; but it is done, however, in proportion, and many putrid disorders hence have their origin. It is recorded of Methusalem, who, being the longest liver, may be supposed to have best preserved his health, that he slept always in the open air; for, when he had lived five hundred years, an angel said to him; "Arise, Methusalem, and build thee an house, for thou shalt live yet five hundred years longer." But Methusalem answered, and said, "If I am to live but five hundred years longer, it is not worth while to build me an house; I will sleep in the air, as I have been used to do." Physicians, after having for ages contended that the sick should not be indulged with fresh air, have at length discovered that it may do them good. It is therefore to be hoped, that they may in time discover likewise, that it is not hurtful to those who are in health, and that we may be then cured of the *aërophobia*, that at present distresses weak minds, and makes them choose to be stifled and poisoned, rather than leave open the window of a bed-chamber, or put down the glass of a coach.

Confined air, when saturated with perspirable matter, will not receive more; and that matter must remain in our bodies, and occasion diseases; but it gives some previous notice of its being about to be hurtful, by producing certain uneasiness, slight indeed at first, which as with regard to the lungs is a trifling sensation, and to the pores of the skin a kind of rest-lessness, which is difficult to describe, and few that feel it know the cause of it. But we may recollect, that sometimes on waking in the night, we have, if warmly covered, found it difficult to get asleep again. We turn often without finding repose in any position. This fidgettiness (to use a vulgar expression for want of a better) is occasioned wholly by an uneasiness in the skin, owing to the retention of the perspir-able matter—the bed-clothes having received their quantity, and, being saturated, refusing to take any more. To become sensible of this by an experiment, let a person keep his posi-tion in the bed, but throw off the bed-clothes, and suffer fresh air to approach the part uncovered of his body; he will then feel that part suddenly refreshed; for the air will imme-diately relieve the skin, by receiving, licking up, and carrying off, the load of perspirable matter that incommoded it. For every portion of cool air that approaches the warm skin, in receiving its part of that vapour, receives therewith a degree of heat that rarefies and renders it lighter, when it will be pushed away with its burthen, by cooler and therefore heavier fresh air, which for a moment supplies its place, and then, being likewise changed and warmed, gives way to a succeed-ing quantity. This is the order of nature, to prevent animals being infected by their own perspiration. He will now be sen-sible of the difference between the part exposed to the air and that which, remaining sunk in the bed, denies the air access: for this part now manifests its uneasiness more distinctly by the comparison, and the seat of the uneasiness is more plainly perceived than when the whole surface of the body was affected by it.

Here, then, is one great and general cause of unpleasing dreams. For when the body is uneasy, the mind will be disturbed by it, and disagreeable ideas of various kinds will in sleep be the natural consequences. The remedies, preventive and curative, follow:

1. By eating moderately (as before advised for health's sake) less perspirable matter is produced in a given time; hence the bed-clothes receive it longer before they are saturated, and we may therefore sleep longer before we are made uneasy by their refusing to receive any more.

2. By using thinner and more porous bed-clothes, which will suffer the perspirable matter more easily to pass through them, we are less incommoded, such being longer tolerable.

3. When you are awakened by this uneasiness, and find you cannot easily sleep again, get out of bed, beat up and turn your pillow, shake the bed-clothes well, with at least twenty shakes, then throw the bed open and leave it to cool; in the meanwhile, continuing undrest, walk about your chamber till your skin has had time to discharge its load, which it will do sooner as the air may be dried and colder. When you begin to feel the cold air unpleasant, then return to your bed, and you will soon fall asleep, and your sleep will be sweet and pleasant. All the scenes presented to your fancy will be too of the pleasing kind. I am often as agreeably entertained with them, as by the scenery of an opera. If you happen to be too indolent to get out of bed, you may, instead of it, lift up your bed-clothes with one arm and leg, so as to draw in a good deal of fresh air, and by letting them fall force it out again. This, repeated twenty times, will so clear them of the perspirable matter they have imbibed, as to permit your sleeping well for some time afterwards. But this latter method is not equal to the former.

Those who do not love trouble, and can afford to have two beds, will find great luxury in rising, when they wake in a hot bed, and going into the cool one. Such shifting of beds would also be of great service to persons ill of a fever, as it refreshes and frequently procures sleep. A very large bed, that will admit a removal so distant from the first situation as to be cool and sweet, may in a degree answer the same end.

One or two observations more will conclude this little piece. Care must be taken, when you lie down, to dispose your pillow so as to suit your manner of placing your head, and to be perfectly easy; then place your limbs so as not to bear inconveniently hard upon one another, as, for instance, the joints of your ankles; for, though a bad position may at first give but little pain and be hardly noticed, yet a continuance will render it less tolerable, and the uneasiness may come on while you are asleep, and disturb your imagination. These are the rules of the art. But, though they will generally prove effectual in producing the end intended, there is a case in which the most punctual observance of them will be totally fruitless. I need not mention the case to you, my dear friend, but my account of the art would be imperfect without it. The case is, when the person who desires to have pleasant dreams has not taken care to preserve, what is necessary above all things,

A GOOD CONSCIENCE.

May 2, 1786

The Retort Courteous

"John Oxly, Pawnbroker of Bethnal Green, was indicted for assaulting Jonathan Boldsworth on the Highway, putting him in fear, and taking from him one Silver Watch, value 5*l.* 5*s.* The Prisoner pleaded, that, having sold the Watch to the Prosecutor, and being immediately after informed by a Person who knew him, that he was not likely to pay for the same, he had only followed him and taken the Watch back again. But it appearing on the Trial, that, presuming he had not been known when he committed the Robbery, he had afterwards sued the Prosecutor for the Debt, on his Note of Hand, he was found Guilty, DEATH."— *Old Bailey Sessions Paper,* 1747.

I chose the above Extract from the Proceedings at the Old Bailey in the Trial of Criminals, as a Motto or Text, on which to amplify in my ensuing Discourse. But on second Thoughts, having given it forth, I shall, after the Example of some other Preachers, quit it for the present, and leave to my

Readers, if I should happen to have any, the Task of discovering what Relation there may possibly be between my Text and my Sermon.

During some Years past, the British Newspapers have been filled with Reflections on the Inhabitants of America, for *not paying their old Debts to English Merchants.* And from these Papers the same Reflections have been translated into Foreign Prints, and circulated throughout Europe; whereby the American Character, respecting Honour, Probity, and Justice in commercial Transactions, is made to suffer in the Opinion of Strangers, which may be attended with pernicious Consequences.

At length we are told that the British Court has taken up the Complaint, and seriously offer'd it as a reason for refusing to evacuate the Frontier Posts according to Treaty. This gives a kind of Authenticity to the Charge, and makes it now more necessary to examine the matter thoro'ly; to inquire impartially into the Conduct of both Nations; take Blame to ourselves where we have merited it; and, where it may be fairly done, mitigate the Severity of the Censures that are so liberally bestow'd upon us.

We may begin by observing, that before the War our mercantile Character was good. In Proof of this (and a stronger Proof can hardly be desired), the Votes of the House of Commons in 1774–5 have recorded a Petition signed by the Body of the Merchants of London trading to North America, in which they expressly set forth, not only that the Trade was profitable to the Kingdom, but that the Remittances and Payments were as punctually and faithfully made, as in any other Branch of Commerce whatever. These Gentlemen were certainly competent Judges, and as to that Point could have no Interest in deceiving the Government.

The making of these punctual Remittances was however a Difficulty. Britain, acting on the selfish and perhaps mistaken Principle of receiving nothing from abroad that could be produced at home, would take no Articles of our Produce that interfered with any of her own; and what did not interfere, she loaded with heavy Duties. We had no Mines of Gold or Silver. We were therefore oblig'd to run the World over, in search of something that would be receiv'd in England. We sent our Provisions and Lumber to the West Indies, where Exchange was made for Sugars, Cotton, &c. to remit. We brought Mollasses from thence, distill'd it into Rum, with which we traded in Africa, and remitted the Gold Dust to England. We employ'd ourselves in the Fisheries, and sent the Fish we caught, together with Quantities of Wheat Flour, and Rice, to Spain and Portugal, from whence the Amount was remitted to England in Cash or Bills of Exchange. Great Quantities of our Rice, too, went to Holland, Hamburgh &c., and the Value of that was also sent to Britain. Add to this, that contenting ourselves with Paper, all the hard Money we could possibly pick up among the Foreign West India Islands, was continually sent off to Britain, not a Ship going thither from America without some Chests of those precious Metals.

Imagine this great Machine of mutually advantageous Commerce, going roundly on, in full Train; our Ports all busy, receiving and selling British Manufactures, and equipping Ships for the circuitous Trade, that was finally to procure the necessary Remittances; the Seas covered with those Ships, and with several hundred Sail of our Fishermen, all working for Britain; and then let us consider what Effect the Conduct of Britain, in 1774 and 1775 and the following Years, must naturally have on the future Ability of our Merchants to make the Payments in question.

We will not here enter into the Motives of that Conduct; they are well enough known, and not to her Honour. The first Step was shutting up the Port of Boston by an Act of Parliament; the next, to prohibit by another the New England Fishery. An Army and a Fleet were sent to enforce these Acts. Here was a Stop put at once to all the mercantile Operations of one of the greatest trading Cities of America; the Fishing Vessels all laid up, and the usual Remittances, by way of Spain, Portugal, and the Straits, render'd impossible. Yet the Cry was now begun against us, *These New England People do not pay their Debts!*

The Ships of the Fleet employ'd themselves in cruising separately all along the Coast. The marine Gentry are seldom so well contented with their Pay, as not to like a little Plunder. They stopp'd and seiz'd, under slight Pretences, the American

Vessels they met with, belonging to whatever Colony. This checked the Commerce of them all. Ships loaded with Cargoes destin'd either directly or indirectly to make Remittance in England, were not spared. If the Difference between the two Countries had been then accommodated, these unauthoriz'd Plunderers would have been called to account, and many of their Exploits must have been found Piracy. But what cur'd all this, set their Minds at ease, made short Work, and gave full Scope to their Piratical Disposition, was another Act of Parliament, forbidding any Inquisition into those *past* Facts, declaring them all Lawful, and all American Property to be forfeited, whether on Sea or Land, and authorizing the King's British Subjects to take, seize, sink, burn, or destroy, whatever they could find of it. The Property suddenly, and by surprise taken from our Merchants by the Operation of this Act, is incomputable. And yet the Cry did not diminish, *These Americans don't pay their Debts!*

Had the several States of America, on the Publication of this Act seiz'd all British Property in their Power, whether consisting of Lands in their Country, Ships in their Harbours, or Debts in the Hands of their Merchants, by way of Retaliation, it is probable a great Part of the World would have deem'd such Conduct justifiable. They, it seems, thought otherwise, and it was done only in one or two States, and that under particular Circumstances of Provocation. And not having thus abolish'd all Demands, the Cry subsists, that *the Americans should pay their Debts!*

General Gage, being with his Army (before the declaration of open War) in peaceable Possession of Boston, shut its Gates, and plac'd Guards all around to prevent its Communication with the Country. The Inhabitants were on the Point of Starving. The general, though they were evidently at his Mercy, fearing that, while they had any Arms in their Hands, frantic Desperation might possibly do him some Mischief, propos'd to them a Capitulation, in which he stipulated, that if they would deliver up their Arms, they might leave the Town with their Families and *Goods*. In faith of this Agreement, they deliver'd their Arms. But when they began to pack up for their Departure, they were inform'd, that by the word *Goods*, the General understood only Houshold Goods, that is, their Beds, Chairs, and Tables, not *Merchant Goods*; those he was inform'd they were indebted for to the Merchants of England, and he must secure them for the Creditors. They were accordingly all seized, to an immense Value, *what had been paid for not excepted*. It is to be supposed, tho' we have never heard of it, that this very honourable General, when he returned home, made a just Dividend of those Goods, or their Value, among the said Creditors. But the Cry nevertheless continued, *These Boston People do not pay their Debts!*

The Army, having thus ruin'd Boston, proceeded to different Parts of the Continent. They got possession of all the capital trading Towns. The Troops gorg'd themselves with Plunder. They stopp'd all the Trade of Philadelphia for near a year, of Rhode Island longer, of New York near eight Years, of Charlestown in South Carolina and Savanah in Georgia, I forget how long. This continu'd Interruption of their Commerce ruin'd many Merchants. The Army also burnt to the Ground the fine Towns of Falmouth and Charlestown near Boston, New London, Fairfield, Norwalk, Esopus, Norfolk, the chief trading City in Virginia, besides innumerable Country Seats and private Farm-Houses. This wanton Destruction of Property operated doubly to the Disabling of our Merchants, who were importers from Britain, in making their Payments, by the immoderate Loss they sustain'd themselves, and also the Loss suffered by their Country Debtors, who had bought of them the British Goods, and who were now render'd unable to pay. The Debts to Britain of course remained undischarg'd, and the Clamour continu'd, *These knavish Americans will not pay us!*

Many of the British Debts, particularly in Virginia and the Carolinas, arose from the Sales made of Negroes in those Provinces by the British Guinea merchants. These, with all before in the country, were employed when the war came on, in raising tobacco and rice for remittance in payment of British debts. An order arrives from England, advised by one of their most celebrated *moralists*, Dr. Johnson, in his *Taxation no Tyranny*, to excite these slaves to rise, cut the throats of their purchasers, and resort to the British army, where they should be rewarded with freedom. This was done, and the planters were thus deprived of near thirty thousand of their working people. Yet the demand for those sold and unpaid still exists; and the cry continues against the Virginians and Carolinians, that *they do not pay their debts!*

Virginia suffered great loss in this kind of property by another ingenious and humane British invention. Having the small-pox in their army while in that country, they inoculated some of the negroes they took as prisoners belonging to a number of plantations, and then let them escape, or sent them, covered with the pock, to mix with and spread the distemper among the others of their colour, as well as among the white country people; which occasioned a great mortality of both, and certainly did not contribute to the enabling debtors in making payment. The war too having put a stop to the exportation of tobacco, there was a great accumulation of several years' produce in all the public inspecting warehouses and private stores of the planters. Arnold, Phillips, and Cornwallis, with British troops, then entered and overran the country, burnt all the inspecting and other stores of tobacco, to the amount of some hundred ship-loads; all which might, on the return of peace, if it had not been thus wantonly destroyed, have been remitted to British creditors. But *these d—d Virginians, why don't they pay their debts?*

Paper money was in those times our universal currency. But, it being the instrument with which we combated our enemies, they resolved to deprive us of its use by depreciating it; and the most effectual means they could contrive was to counterfeit it. The artists they employed performed so well, that immense quantities of these counterfeits, which issued from the British government in New York, were circulated among the inhabitants of all the States, before the fraud was detected. This operated considerably in depreciating the whole mass, first, by the vast additional quantity, and next by the uncertainty in distinguishing the true from the false; and the depreciation was a loss to all and the ruin of many. It is true our enemies gained a vast deal of our property by the operation; but it did not go into the hands of our particular creditors; so their demands still subsisted, and we were still abused *for not paying our debts!*

By the seventh article of the treaty of peace, it was solemnly stipulated, that the King's troops, in evacuating their posts in

the United States, should not carry away with them any negroes. In direct violation of this article, General Carleton, in
evacuating New York, carried off all the negroes that were
with his army, to the amount of several hundreds. It is not
doubted that he must have had secret orders to justify him in
this transaction; but the reason given out was, that, as they
had quitted their masters and joined the King's troops on the
faith of proclamations promising them their liberty, the national honour forbade returning them into slavery. The
national honour was, it seemed, pledged to both parts of a
contradiction, and its wisdom, since it could not do it with
both, chose to keep faith rather with its old black, than its
new white friends; a circumstance demonstrating clear as daylight, that, in making a present peace, they meditated a future
war, and hoped, that, though the promised manumission of
slaves had not been effectual in the *last*, in the *next* it might
be more successful; and that, had the negroes been forsaken,
no aid could be hereafter expected from those of the colour
in a future invasion. The treaty however with us was thus
broken almost as soon as made, and this by the people who
charge us with breaking it by not paying perhaps for some of
the very negroes carried off in defiance of it. Why should England observe treaties, *when these Americans do not pay their
debts?*

Unreasonable, however, as this clamour appears in general,
I do not pretend, by exposing it, to justify those debtors who
are still able to pay, and refuse it on pretence of injuries suffered by the war. Public injuries can never discharge private
obligations. Contracts between merchant and merchant
should be sacredly observed, where the ability remains, whatever may be the madness of ministers. It is therefore to be
hoped the fourth article of the treaty of peace which stipulates, *that no legal obstruction shall be given to the payment of
debts contracted before the war*, will be punctually carried into
execution, and that every law in every State which impedes it,
may be immediately repealed. Those laws were indeed made
with honest intentions, that the half-ruined debtor, not being
too suddenly pressed by *some*, might have time to arrange and
recover his affairs so as to do justice to *all* his creditors. But,
since the intention in making those acts has been misappre-

hended, and the acts wilfully misconstrued into a design of defrauding them, and now made a matter of reproach to us, I think it will be right to repeal them all. Individual Americans may be ruined, but the country will save by the operation; since these unthinking, merciless creditors must be contented with all that is to be had, instead of all that may be due to them, and the accounts will be settled by insolvency. When all have paid that can pay, I think the remaining British creditors, who suffered by the inability of their ruined debtors, have some right to call upon their own government (which by its bad projects has ruined those debtors) for a compensation. A sum given by Parliament for this purpose would be more properly disposed, than in rewarding pretended loyalists, who fomented the war. And, the heavier the sum, the more tendency it might have to discourage such destructive projects hereafter.

Among the merchants of Britain, trading formerly to America, there are to my knowledge many considerate and generous men, who never joined in this clamour, and who, on the return of peace, though by the treaty entitled to an immediate suit for their debts, were kindly disposed to give their debtors reasonable time for restoring their circumstances, so as to be able to make payment conveniently. These deserve the most grateful acknowledgments. And indeed it was in their favour, and perhaps for their sakes in favour of all other British creditors, that the law of Pennsylvania, though since much exclaimed against, was made, restraining the recovery of old debts during a certain time. For this restraint was general, respecting domestic as well as British debts, it being thought unfair, in cases where there was not sufficient for all, that the inhabitants, taking advantage of their nearer situation, should swallow the whole, excluding foreign creditors from any share. And in cases where the favourable part of the foreign creditors were disposed to give time, with the views abovementioned, if others less humane and considerate were allowed to bring immediate suits and ruin the debtor, those views would be defeated. When this law expired in September, 1784, a new one was made, continuing for some time longer the restraint with respect to domestic debts, but expressly taking it away where the debt was due from citizens of the State to any of the subjects of Great Britain;* which shows clearly the disposition of the Assembly, and that the fair intentions above ascribed to them in making the former act, are not merely the imagination of the writer.

Indeed, the clamour has been much augmented by numbers joining it, who really had no claim on our country. Every debtor in Britain, engaged in whatever trade, when he had no better excuse to give for delay of payment, accused the want of returns from America. And the indignation, thus excited against us, now appears so general among the English, that one would imagine their nation, which is so exact in expecting punctual payment from all the rest of the world, must be at home the model of justice, the very pattern of punctuality. Yet, if one were disposed to recriminate, it would not be difficult to find sufficient Matter in several Parts of their Conduct. But this I forbear. The two separate Nations are now at Peace, and there can be no use in mutual Provocations to fresh Enmity. If I have shown clearly that the present Inability of many American Merchants to discharge their Debts, contracted before the War, is not so much their Fault, as the Fault of the crediting Nation, who, by making an unjust War on them, obstructing their Commerce, plundering and devastating their Country, were the Cause of that Inability, I have answered the Purpose of writing this Paper. How far the Refusal of the British Court to execute the Treaty in delivering up the Frontier Posts may on account of this Deficiency of Payment, be justifiable, is chearfully submitted to the World's impartial Judgment.

*Extract from an Act of the General Assembly of Pennsylvania, entitled, "An Act for directing the Mode of recovering Debts contracted before the first Day of January, in the Year of our Lord one thousand seven hundred and seventy-seven."

Exception in Favour of British Creditors.

"Sect. 7. And provided also, and be it further enacted by the authority aforesaid, that this Act, nor any thing therein contained, shall not extend, or be construed to extend, to any debt or debts which were due before the fourth day of July, one thousand seven hundred and seventy-six, by any of the citizens of the State, to any of the subjects of Great Britain."

1786

THE CONSTITUTIONAL CONVENTION

Speech in the Convention on the Subject of Salaries

Sir,

It is with Reluctance that I rise to express a Disapprobation of any one Article of the Plan, for which we are so much obliged to the honourable Gentleman who laid it before us. From its first Reading, I have borne a good Will to it, and, in general, wish'd it Success. In this Particular of Salaries to the Executive Branch, I happen to differ; and, as my Opinion may appear new and chimerical, it is only from a Persuasion that it is right, and from a Sense of Duty, that I hazard it. The Committee will judge of my Reasons when they have heard them, and their judgment may possibly change mine. I think I see Inconveniences in the Appointment of Salaries; I see none in refusing them, but on the contrary great Advantages.

Sir, there are two Passions which have a powerful Influence in the Affairs of Men. These are *Ambition* and *Avarice*; the Love of Power and the Love of Money. Separately, each of these has great Force in prompting Men to Action; but when united in View of the same Object, they have in many Minds the most violent Effects. Place before the Eyes of such Men a Post of *Honour*, that shall at the same time be a Place of *Profit*, and they will move Heaven and Earth to obtain it. The vast Number of such Places it is that renders the British Government so tempestuous. The Struggles for them are the true Source of all those Factions which are perpetually dividing the Nation, distracting its Councils, hurrying it sometimes into fruitless and mischievous Wars, and often compelling a Submission to dishonourable Terms of Peace.

And of what kind are the men that will strive for this profitable Preëminence, thro' all the Bustle of Cabal, the Heat of Contention, the infinite mutual Abuse of Parties, tearing to Pieces the best of Characters? It will not be the wise and moderate, the Lovers of Peace and good Order, the men fittest for the Trust. It will be the Bold and the Violent, the men of strong Passions and indefatigable Activity in their selfish Pursuits. These will thrust themselves into your Government, and be your Rulers. And these, too, will be mistaken in the expected Happiness of their Situation; for their vanquish'd competitors, of the same Spirit, and from the same Motives, will perpetually be endeavouring to distress their Administration, thwart their Measures, and render them odious to the People.

Besides these Evils, Sir, tho' we may set out in the Beginning with moderate Salaries, we shall find, that such will not be of long Continuance. Reasons will never be wanting for propos'd Augmentations; and there will always be a Party for giving more to the Rulers, that the Rulers may be able in Return to give more to them. Hence, as all History informs us, there has been in every State and Kingdom a constant kind of Warfare between the Governing and the Governed; the one striving to obtain more for its Support, and the other to pay less. And this has alone occasion'd great Convulsions, actual civil Wars, ending either in dethroning of the Princes or enslaving of the People. Generally, indeed, the Ruling Power carries its Point, and we see the Revenues of Princes constantly increasing, and we see that they are never satisfied, but always in want of more. The more the People are discontented with the Oppression of Taxes, the greater Need the Prince has of Money to distribute among his Partisans, and pay the Troops that are to suppress all Resistance, and enable him to plunder at Pleasure. There is scarce a King in a hundred, who would not, if he could, follow the Example of Pharaoh,—get first all the People's Money, then all their Lands, and then make them and their Children Servants for ever. It will be said, that we do not propose to establish Kings. I know it. But there is a natural Inclination in Mankind to kingly Government. It sometimes relieves them from Aristocratic Domination. They had rather have one Tyrant than 500. It gives more of the Appearance of Equality among Citizens; and that they like. I am apprehensive, therefore,— perhaps too apprehensive,—that the Government of these States may in future times end in a Monarchy. But this Catastrophe, I think, may be long delay'd, if in our propos'd System we do not sow the Seeds of Contention, Faction, and Tumult, by making our Posts of Honour Places of Profit. If we do, I fear, that, tho' we employ at first a Number and not a single Person, the Number will in time be set aside; it will only nourish the Fœtus of a King (as the honourable Gentleman from Virg^a very aptly express'd it), and a King will the sooner be set over us.

It may be imagined by some, that this is an Utopian Idea, and that we can never find Men to serve us in the Executive Department, without paying them well for their Services. I conceive this to be a Mistake. Some existing Facts present themselves to me, which incline me to a contrary Opinion. The High Sheriff of a County in England is an honourable Office, but it is not a profitable one. It is rather expensive, and therefore not sought for. But yet it is executed, and well executed, and usually by some of the principal Gentlemen of the County. In France, the Office of Counsellor, or Member of their judiciary Parliaments, is more honourable. It is therefore purchas'd at a high Price; there are indeed Fees on the Law Proceedings, which are divided among them, but these Fees do not amount to more than three per cent on the Sum paid for the Place. Therefore, as legal Interest is there at five per cent, they in fact pay two per cent for being allow'd to do the Judiciary Business of the Nation, which is at the same time entirely exempt from the Burthen of paying them any Salaries for their Services. I do not, however, mean to recommend this as an eligible Mode for our judiciary Department. I only bring the Instance to show, that the Pleasure of doing Good and serving their Country, and the Respect such Conduct entitles them to, are sufficient Motives with some Minds, to give up a great Portion of their Time to the Public, without the mean Inducement of pecuniary Satisfaction.

Another Instance is that of a respectable Society, who have made the Experiment, and practis'd it with Success, now more than a hundred years. I mean the Quakers. It is an establish'd Rule with them that they are not to go to law, but in their Controversies they must apply to their Monthly, Quarterly, and Yearly Meetings. Committees of these sit with Patience to hear the Parties, and spend much time in composing their Differences. In doing this, they are supported by a Sense of Duty, and the Respect paid to Usefulness. It is honourable to be so employ'd, but it was never made profitable by Salaries, Fees, or Perquisites. And indeed, in all Cases of public Service, the less the Profit the greater the Honour.

To bring the Matter nearer home, have we not seen the greatest and most important of our Offices, that of General of our Armies, executed for Eight Years together, without the smallest Salary, by a patriot whom I will not now offend by any other Praise; and this, thro' Fatigues and Distresses, in common with the other brave Men, his military Friends and Companions, and the constant Anxieties peculiar to his Station? And shall we doubt finding three or four Men in all the United States, with public Spirit enough to bear sitting in peaceful Council, for perhaps an equal Term, merely to preside over our civil Concerns, and see that our Laws are duly executed? Sir, I have a better opinion of our Country. I think we shall never be without a sufficient Number of wise and good Men to undertake, and execute well and faithfully, the Office in question.

Sir, the Saving of the Salaries, that may at first be propos'd, is not an object with me. The subsequent Mischiefs of proposing them are what I apprehend. And therefore it is that I move the Amendment. If it is not seconded or accepted, I must be contented with the Satisfaction of having delivered my Opinion frankly, and done my Duty.

June 2, 1787

Speech in a Committee of the Convention on the Proportion of Representation and Votes

MR. CHAIRMAN,

It has given me great Pleasure to observe, that, till this Point, *the Proportion of Representation*, came before us, our Debates were carry'd on with great Coolness and Temper. If any thing of a contrary kind has, on this Occasion, appeared, I hope it will not be repeated; for we are sent hither to *consult*, not to *contend*, with each other; and Declaration of a fix'd Opinion, and of determined Resolutions never to change it, neither enlighten nor convince us. Positiveness and

Warmth on one side naturally beget their like on the other; and tend to create and augment Discord and Division in a great Concern, wherein Harmony and Union are extremely necessary, to give Weight to our Counsels, and render them effectual in promoting and securing the common Good.

I must own, that I was originally of Opinion it would be better if every Member of Congress, or our national Council, were to consider himself rather as a Representative of the whole, than as an Agent for the Interests of a particular State; in which Case the Proportion of Members for each State would be of less Consequence, and it would not be very material whether they voted by States or individually. But as I find this is not to be expected, I now think the Number of Representatives should bear some Proportion to the Number of the Represented, and that the Decisions should be by the Majority of Members, not by the Majority of States. This is objected to, from an Apprehension that the greater States would then swallow up the Smaller. I do not at present clearly see what Advantage the greater States could propose to themselves by swallowing the smaller, and therefore do not apprehend they would attempt it. I recollect, that in the Beginning of this Century, when the Union was propos'd of the two Kingdoms, England and Scotland, the Scotch patriots were full of Fears, that, unless they had an equal Number of Representatives in Parliament, they should be ruined by the Superiority of the English. They finally agreed, however, that the different Proportions of Importance in the Union of the two Nations should be attended to; whereby they were to have only Forty Members in the House of Commons, and only Sixteen of their Peers were to sit in the House of Lords; a very great Inferiority of Numbers! And yet, to this Day, I do not recollect that any thing has been done in the Parliament of Great Britain to the Prejudice of Scotland; and whoever looks over the Lists of publick Officers, Civil and Military, of that Nation, will find, I believe, that the North Britons enjoy at least their full proportion of Emolument.

But, Sir, in the present Mode of Voting by States, it is equally in the Power of the lesser States to swallow up the greater; and this is mathematically demonstrable. Suppose, for example, that 7 smaller States had each 3 members in the

House, and the Six larger to have, one with another, 6 Members; and that, upon a Question, two Members of each smaller State should be in the Affirmative, and one in the Negative; they will make

Affirmatives,   14   Negatives   7

And that all the large States should
  be unanimously in the negative;
  they would make   Negatives 36

                                                     ——

                                        In all 43

It is then apparent, that the 14 carry the question against the 43, and the Minority overpowers the Majority, contrary to the common Practice of Assemblies in all Countries and Ages.

The greater States, Sir, are naturally as unwilling to have their Property left in the Disposition of the smaller, as the smaller are to leave theirs in the Disposition of the greater. An honourable Gentleman has, to avoid this difficulty, hinted a Proposition of equalizing the States. It appears to me an equitable one; and I should, for my own Part, not be against such a Measure, if it might be found practicable. Formerly, indeed, when almost every Province had a different Constitution, some with greater, others with fewer Privileges, it was of Importance to the Borderers, when their Boundaries were contested, whether, by running the Division Lines, they were placed on one Side or the other. At present, when such Differences are done away, it is less material. The Interest of a State is made up of the Interests of its individual Members. If they are not injured, the State is not injured. Small States are more easily, well, and happily governed, than large ones. If, therefore, in such an equal Division, it should be found necessary to diminish Pennsylvania, I should not be averse to the giving a part of it to N. Jersey, and another to Delaware: But as there would probably be considerable Difficulties in adjusting such a Division; and, however equally made at first, it would be continually varying by the Augmentation of Inhabitants in some States, and their more fixed proportion in others, and thence frequent Occasion for new Divisions; I beg leave to propose for the Consideration of the Committee another Mode, which appears to me to be as equitable, more easily carry'd into Practice, and more permanent in its Nature.

Let the weakest State say what Proportion of Money or Force it is able and willing to furnish for the general Purposes of the Union.

Let all the others oblige themselves to furnish each an equal Proportion.

The whole of these joint Supplies to be absolutely in the Disposition of Congress.

The Congress in this Case to be compos'd of an equal Number of Delegates from each State;

And their Decisions to be by the Majority of individual Members voting.

If these joint and equal Supplies should, on particular Occasions, not be sufficient, let Congress make Requisitions on the richer and more powerful States for further Aids, to be voluntarily afforded; so leaving each State the Right of considering the Necessity and Utility of the Aid desired, and of giving more or less, as it should be found proper.

This Mode is not new; it was formerly practic'd with Success by the British Government, with respect to Ireland and the Colonies. We sometimes gave even more than they expected, or thought just to accept; and in the last War, carried on while we were united, they gave us back in 5 Years a Million Sterling. We should probably have continu'd such voluntary Contributions, whenever the Occasions appear'd to require them for the common Good of the Empire. It was not till they chose to force us, and to deprive us of the Merit and Pleasure of voluntary Contributions, that we refus'd and resisted. Those Contributions, however, were to be dispos'd of at the Pleasure of a Government in which we had no Representative. I am therefore persuaded, that they will not be refus'd to one in which the Representation shall be equal.

My learned Colleague has already mentioned that the present method of voting by States, was submitted to originally by Congress, under a Conviction of its Impropriety, Inequality, and Injustice. This appears in the Words of their Resolution. It is of Sept. 6, 1774. The words are,

"Resolved, That, in determining Questions in this Congress, each Colony or Province shall have one vote; the

Congress not being possessed of, or at present able to procure, Materials for ascertaining the Importance of each Colony."

June 11, 1787

Motion for Prayers in the Convention

MR. PRESIDENT,

The small Progress we have made, after 4 or 5 Weeks' close Attendance and continual Reasonings with each other, our different Sentiments on almost every Question, several of the last producing as many *Noes* as *Ayes*, is, methinks, a melancholy Proof of the Imperfection of the Human Understanding. We indeed seem to *feel* our own want of political Wisdom, since we have been running all about in Search of it. We have gone back to ancient History for Models of Government, and examin'd the different Forms of those Republics, which, having been originally form'd with the Seeds of their own Dissolution, now no longer exist; and we have view'd modern States all round Europe, but find none of their Constitutions suitable to our Circumstances.

In this Situation of this Assembly, groping, as it were, in the dark to find Political Truth, and scarce able to distinguish it when presented to us, how has it happened, Sir, that we have not hitherto once thought of humbly applying to the Father of Lights to illuminate our Understandings? In the Beginning of the Contest with Britain, when we were sensible of Danger, we had daily Prayers in this Room for the Divine Protection. Our Prayers, Sir, were heard; — and they were graciously answered. All of us, who were engag'd in the Struggle, must have observed frequent Instances of a superintending Providence in our Favour. To that kind Providence we owe this happy Opportunity of Consulting in Peace on the Means of establishing our future national Felicity. And have we now forgotten that powerful Friend? or do we imagine we no longer need its assistance? I have lived, Sir, a long time; and the longer I live, the more convincing proofs I see of this Truth, *that* GOD *governs in the Affairs of Men.* And if a Sparrow cannot fall to the Ground without his Notice, is it probable that an Empire can rise without his Aid? We have been assured, Sir, in the Sacred Writings, that "except the Lord build the House, they labour in vain that build it." I firmly believe this; and I also believe, that, without his concurring Aid, we shall succeed in this political Building no better than the Builders of Babel; we shall be divided by our little, partial, local Interests, our Projects will be confounded, and we ourselves shall become a Reproach and a Bye-word down to future Ages. And, what is worse, Mankind may hereafter, from this unfortunate Instance, despair of establishing Government by human Wisdom, and leave it to Chance, War, and Conquest.

I therefore beg leave to move,

That henceforth Prayers, imploring the Assistance of Heaven and its Blessing on our Deliberations, be held in this Assembly every morning before we proceed to Business; and that one or more of the Clergy of this city be requested to officiate in that Service.*

*The convention, except three or four persons, thought prayers unnecessary!

June 28, 1787

Speech in the Convention at the Conclusion of its Deliberations

I confess that I do not entirely approve of this Constitution at present, but Sir, I am not sure I shall never approve it: For having lived long, I have experienced many Instances of being oblig'd, by better Information or fuller Consideration, to change Opinions even on important Subjects, which I once thought right, but found to be otherwise. It is therefore that the older I grow the more apt I am to doubt my own Judgment and to pay more Respect to the Judgment of others. Most Men indeed as well as most Sects in Religion, think themselves in Possession of all Truth, and that wherever others differ from them it is so far Error. Steele, a Protestant, in a Dedication tells the Pope, that the only Difference between our two Churches in their Opinions of the Certainty of their Doctrine, is, the Romish Church is infallible, and the Church of England is never in the Wrong. But tho' many private Persons think almost as highly of their own Infallibility, as that of their Sect, few express it so naturally as a certain French lady, who in a little Dispute with her Sister, said, I don't know how it happens, Sister, but I meet with no body but myself that's *always* in the right. *Il n'y a que moi qui a toujours raison.*

In these Sentiments, Sir, I agree to this Constitution, with all its Faults, if they are such: because I think a General Government necessary for us, and there is no *Form* of Government but what may be a Blessing to the People if well administred; and I believe farther that this is likely to be well administred for a Course of Years, and can only end in Despotism as other Forms have done before it, when the People shall become so corrupted as to need Despotic Government, being incapable of any other. I doubt too whether any other Convention we can obtain, may be able to make a better Constitution: For when you assemble a Number of Men to have the Advantage of their joint Wisdom, you inevitably assemble with those Men all their Prejudices, their Passions, their Errors of Opinion, their local Interests, and their selfish Views. From such an Assembly can a perfect Production be expected? It therefore astonishes me, Sir, to find this System approaching so near to Perfection as it does; and I think it will astonish our Enemies, who are waiting with Confidence to hear that our Councils are confounded, like those of the Builders of Babel, and that our States are on the Point of Separation, only to meet hereafter for the Purpose of cutting one another's Throats. Thus I consent, Sir, to this Constitution because I expect no better, and because I am not sure that it is not the best. The Opinions I have had of its Errors, I sacrifice to the Public Good. I have never whisper'd a Syllable of them abroad. Within these Walls they were born, & here they shall die. If every one of us in returning to our Constituents were to report the Objections he has had to it, and endeavour to gain Partizans in support of them, we might prevent its being generally received, and thereby lose all the salutary Effects & great Advantages resulting naturally in our favour among foreign Nations, as well as among ourselves, from our real or apparent Unanimity. Much of the Strength and Efficiency of any Government, in procuring & securing Happiness to the People depends on Opinion, on the general Opinion of the Goodness of that Government as well as of the Wisdom & Integrity of its Governors. I hope therefore that for our own Sakes, as a Part of the People, and for the Sake of our Posterity, we shall act heartily & unanimously in recommending this Constitution, wherever our Influence may extend, and turn our future Thoughts and Endeavours to the Means of having it well administred.—

On the whole, Sir, I cannot help expressing a Wish, that every Member of the Convention, who may still have Objections to it, would with me on this Occasion doubt a little of his own Infallibility, and to make *manifest* our *Unanimity*, put his Name to this Instrument.—

Then the Motion was made for adding the last Formula, viz Done in Convention by the unanimous Consent &c— which was agreed to and added—accordingly.

September 17, 1787

On Sending Felons to America

FOR THE PENNSYLVANIA GAZETTE

SIR,

We may all remember the Time when our Mother Country, as a Mark of her parental Tenderness, emptied her Jails into our Habitations, *"for the* BETTER *Peopling,"* as she express'd it, *"of the Colonies."* It is certain that no due Returns have yet been made for these valuable Consignments. We are therefore much in her Debt on that Account; and, as she is of late clamorous for the Payment of all we owe her, and some of our Debts are of a kind not so easily discharg'd, I am for doing however what is in our Power. It will show our good-will as to the rest. The Felons she planted among us have produc'd such an amazing Increase, that we are now enabled to make ample Remittance in the same Commodity. And since the Wheelbarrow Law is not found effectually to reform them, and many of our Vessels are idle through her Restraints on our Trade, why should we not employ those Vessels in transporting the Felons to Britain?

I was led into this Thought by perusing the Copy of a Petition to Parliament, which fell lately by Accident into my Hands. It has no Date, but I conjecture from some Circumstances, that it must have been about the year 1767 or 68. (It seems, if presented, it had no Effect, since the Act passed.) I imagine it may not be unacceptable to your Readers, and therefore transcribe it for your paper; viz.

To the Honourable the Knights, Citizens, and Burgesses of Great Britain, in Parliament assembled,

The PETITION of B. F., Agent for the Province of Pensilvania;

Most humbly sheweth;

That the Transporting of Felons from England to the Plantations in America, is, and hath long been, a great Grievance to the said Plantations in general.

That the said Felons, being landed in America, not only continue their evil Practices to the Annoyance of his Majesty's good Subjects there, but contribute greatly to corrupt the

Morals of the Servants and poorer People among whom they are mixed.

That many of the said Felons escape from the Servitude to which they were destined, into other Colonies, where their Condition is not known; and, wandering at large from one populous Town to another, commit many Burglaries, Robberies, and Murders, to the great Terror of the People; and occasioning heavy Charges for apprehending and securing such Felons, and bringing them to Justice.

That your Petitioner humbly conceives the Easing one Part of the British Dominions of their Felons, by burthening another Part with the same Felons, cannot increase the common Happiness of his Majesty's Subjects, and that therefore the Trouble and Expence of transporting them is upon the whole altogether useless.

That your petitioner, nevertheless, observes with extream Concern in the Votes of Friday last, that leave is given to bring in a Bill for extending to Scotland, the Act made in the 4th Year of the Reign of King George the First, whereby the aforesaid Grievances are, as he understands, to be greatly increased by allowing Scotland also to transport its Felons to America.

Your petitioner therefore humbly prays, in behalf of Pensilvania, and the other Plantations in America, that the House would take the Premises into Consideration, and in their great Wisdom and Goodness repeal all Acts, and Clauses of Acts, for transporting of Felons; or, if this may not at present be done, that they would at least reject the propos'd Bill for extending the said Acts to Scotland; or, if it be thought fit to allow of such Extension, that then the said Extension may be carried further, and the Plantations be also, by an equitable Clause in the same bill, permitted to transport their Felons to Scotland.

And your Petitioner, as in Duty bound, shall pray, &c.

This Petition, as I am informed, was not receiv'd by the House, and the Act passed.

On second Thoughts, I am of Opinion, that besides employing our own Vessels, as above propos'd, every English Ship arriving in our Ports with Goods for sale, should be obliged to give Bond, before she is permitted to Trade, engaging that she will carry back to Britain at least one Felon for every Fifty Tons of her Burthen. Thus we shall not only discharge sooner our Debts, but furnish our old Friends with the means of *"better Peopling,"* and with more Expedition, their promising new Colony of Botany Bay.

I am yours, &c.

A. Z.

1787

TO THE EDITOR OF THE FEDERAL GAZETTE:

A Comparison of the Conduct of the Ancient Jews and of the Anti-Federalists in the United States of America

A zealous Advocate for the propos'd Federal Constitution, in a certain public Assembly, said, that "the Repugnance of a great part of Mankind to good Government was such, that he believed, that, if an angel from Heaven was to bring down a Constitution form'd there for our Use, it would nevertheless meet with violent Opposition." He was reprov'd for the suppos'd Extravagance of the Sentiment; and he did not justify it. Probably it might not have immediately occur'd to him, that the Experiment had been try'd, and that the Event was recorded in the most faithful of all Histories, the Holy Bible; otherwise he might, as it seems to me, have supported his Opinion by that unexceptionable Authority.

The Supreme Being had been pleased to nourish up a single Family, by continued Acts of his attentive Providence, till it became a great People; and, having rescued them from Bondage by many Miracles, performed by his Servant Moses, he personally deliver'd to that chosen Servant, in the presence of the whole Nation, a Constitution and Code of Laws for their Observance; accompanied and sanction'd with Promises of great Rewards, and Threats of severe Punishments, as the Consequence of their Obedience or Disobedience.

This Constitution, tho' the Deity himself was to be at its Head (and it is therefore call'd by Political Writers a *Theocracy*), could not be carried into Execution but by the Means

of his Ministers; Aaron and his Sons were therefore commission'd to be, with Moses, the first establish'd Ministry of the
new Government.

One would have thought, that this Appointment of Men,
who had distinguish'd themselves in procuring the Liberty of
their Nation, and had hazarded their Lives in openly opposing the Will of a powerful Monarch, who would have retain'd
that Nation in Slavery, might have been an Appointment acceptable to a grateful People; and that a Constitution fram'd
for them by the Deity himself might, on that Account, have
been secure of a universal welcome Reception. Yet there were
in every one of the *thirteen Tribes* some discontented, restless
Spirits, who were continually exciting them to reject the propos'd new Government, and this from various Motives.

Many still retained an Affection for Egypt, the Land of
their Nativity; and these, whenever they felt any Inconvenience or Hardship, tho' the natural and unavoidable Effect of
their Change of Situation, exclaim'd against their Leaders as
the Authors of their Trouble; and were not only for returning
into Egypt, but for stoning their deliverers.* Those inclin'd
to idolatry were displeas'd that their *Golden Calf* was destroy'd. Many of the Chiefs thought the new Constitution
might be injurious to their particular Interests, that the *profitable Places* would be *engrossed by the Families and Friends of
Moses and Aaron*, and others equally well-born excluded.† In
Josephus and the Talmud, we learn some Particulars, not so
fully narrated in the Scripture. We are there told, "That Corah
was ambitious of the Priesthood, and offended that it was
conferred on Aaron; and this, as he said, by the Authority of
Moses only, *without the Consent of the People*. He accus'd
Moses of having, by various Artifices, fraudulently obtain'd
the Government, and depriv'd the People of their Liberties;
and of *conspiring* with Aaron to perpetuate the Tyranny in
their Family. Thus, tho' Corah's real Motive was the Sup-
planting of Aaron, he persuaded the People that he meant

*Numbers, ch. xiv.

†Numbers, ch. xiv, verse 3. "And they gathered themselves together against
Moses and Aaron, and said unto them, 'Ye take too much upon you, seeing
all the congregation are holy, *every one of them*; wherefore, then, lift ye up
yourselves above the congregation?' "

only the *Public Good*; and they, moved by his Insinuations, began to cry out, 'Let us maintain the Common Liberty of our *respective Tribes*; we have freed ourselves from the Slavery impos'd on us by the Egyptians, and shall we now suffer ourselves to be made Slaves by Moses? If we must have a Master, it were better to return to Pharaoh, who at least fed us with Bread and Onions, than to serve this new Tyrant, who by his Operations has brought us into Danger of Famine.' Then they called in question the *Reality of his Conference* with God; and objected the *Privacy of the Meetings*, and the *preventing any of the People from being present* at the Colloquies, or even approaching the Place, as Grounds of great Suspicion. They accused Moses also of *Peculation*; as embezzling part of the Golden Spoons and the Silver Chargers, that the Princes had offer'd at the Dedication of the Altar,* and the Offerings of Gold by the common People,† as well as most of the Poll-Tax;‡ and Aaron they accus'd of pocketing much of the Gold of which he pretended to have made a molten Calf. Besides *Peculation*, they charg'd Moses with *Ambition*; to gratify which Passion he had, they said, deceiv'd the People, by promising to bring them *to* a land flowing with Milk and Honey; instead of doing which, he had brought them *from* such a Land; and that he thought light of all this mischief, provided he could make himself an *absolute Prince.*§ That, to support the new Dignity with Splendor in his Family, the partial Poll-Tax already levied and given to Aaron‖ was to be follow'd by a general one,¶ which would probably be augmented from time to time, if he were suffered to go on promulgating new Laws, on pretence of new occasional Revelations of the divine Will, till their whole Fortunes were devour'd by that Aristocracy."

Moses deny'd the Charge of Peculation; and his Accusers were destitute of Proofs to support it; tho' *Facts*, if real, are in their Nature capable of Proof. "I have not," said he (with

*Numbers, ch. vii.

†Exodus, ch. xxxv, verse 22.

‡Numbers, ch. iii, and Exodus, ch. xxx.

§Numbers, ch. xvi, verse 13. "Is it a small thing that thou hast brought us up out of a land that floweth with milk and honey, to kill us in the wilderness, except thou make thyself altogether a prince over us?"

‖ Numbers, ch. iii

¶Exodus, ch. xxx.

holy Confidence in the Presence of his God), "I have not taken from this People the value of an Ass, nor done them any other Injury." But his Enemies had made the Charge, and with some Success among the Populace; for no kind of Accusation is so readily made, or easily believ'd, by Knaves as the Accusation of Knavery.

In fine, no less than two hundred and fifty of the principal Men, "famous in the Congregation, Men of Renown,"* heading and exciting the Mob, worked them up to such a pitch of Frenzy, that they called out, "Stone 'em, stone 'em, and thereby *secure our Liberties*; and let us chuse other Captains, that may lead us back into Egypt, in case we do not succeed in reducing the Canaanites!"

On the whole, it appears, that the Israelites were a People jealous of their newly-acquired Liberty, which Jealousy was in itself no Fault; but, when they suffer'd it to be work'd upon by artful Men, pretending Public Good, with nothing really in view but private Interest, they were led to oppose the Establishment of the *New Constitution*, whereby they brought upon themselves much Inconvenience and Misfortune. It appears further, from the same inestimable History, that, when after many Ages that Constitution was become old and much abus'd, and an Amendment of it was propos'd, the populace, as they had accus'd Moses of the Ambition of making himself a *Prince*, and cried out, "Stone him, stone him;" so, excited by their High Priests and SCRIBES, they exclaim'd against the Messiah, that he aim'd at becoming King of the Jews, and cry'd out, *"Crucify him, Crucify him."* From all which we may gather, that popular Opposition to a public Measure is no Proof of its Impropriety, even tho' the Opposition be excited and headed by Men of Distinction.

To conclude, I beg I may not be understood to infer, that our General Convention was divinely inspired, when it form'd the new federal Constitution, merely because that Constitution has been unreasonably and vehemently opposed; yet I must own I have so much Faith in the general Government of the world by *Providence*, that I can hardly conceive a Transaction of such momentous Importance to the Welfare of

*Numbers, ch. xvi.

Millions now existing, and to exist in the Posterity of a great Nation, should be suffered to pass without being in some degree influenc'd, guided, and governed by that omnipotent, omnipresent, and beneficent Ruler, in whom all inferior Spirits live, and move, and have their Being.

The Federal Gazette, April 8, 1788

TO THE EDITORS OF THE PENNSYLVANIA GAZETTE:

On the Abuse of the Press

MESSRS. HALL AND SELLERS,

I lately heard a remark, that on examination of *The Pennsylvania Gazette* for fifty years, from its commencement, it appeared, that, during that long period, scarce one libellous piece had ever appeared in it. This generally chaste conduct of your paper is much to its reputation; for it has long been the opinion of sober, judicious people, that nothing is more likely to endanger the liberty of the press, than the abuse of that liberty, by employing it in personal accusation, detraction, and calumny. The excesses some of our papers have been guilty of in this particular, have set this State in a bad light abroad, as appears by the following letter, which I wish you to publish, not merely to show your own disapprobation of the practice, but as a caution to others of the profession throughout the United States. For I have seen a European newspaper, in which the editor, who had been charged with frequently calumniating the Americans, justifies himself by saying, "that he had published nothing disgraceful to us, which he had not taken from our own printed papers." I am, &c.

A. B.

"DEAR FRIEND,   New York, March 30, 1788.

"My Gout has at length left me, after five Months' painful Confinement. It afforded me, however, the Leisure to read, or hear read, all the Packets of your various Newspapers, which you so kindly sent for my Amusement.

"Mrs. W. has partaken of it; she likes to read the Advertisements; but she remarks some kind of Inconsistency in the an-

nouncing so many Diversions for almost every Evening of the
Week, and such Quantities to be sold of expensive Superfluities, Fineries, and Luxuries *just imported*, in a Country, that
at the same time fills its Papers with Complaints of *Hard
Times*, and Want of Money. I tell her, that such Complaints
are common to all Times and all Countries, and were made
even in Solomon's Time; when, as we are told, Silver was as
plenty in Jerusalem as the Stones in the Street; and yet, even
then, there were People who grumbled, so as to incur this
Censure from that knowing Prince. *'Say not thou that the former Times were better than these; for thou dost not enquire rightly
concerning that matter.'*

"But the Inconsistence that strikes me the most is, that between the Name of your City, Philadelphia, (*Brotherly Love,*)
and the Spirit of Rancour, Malice, and *Hatred* that breathes
in its NewsPapers. For I learn from those Papers, that your
State is divided into Parties, that each Party ascribes all the
public Operations of the other to vicious Motives; that they
do not even suspect one another of the smallest Degree of
Honesty; that the antifederalists are such, merely from the
Fear of losing Power, Places, or Emoluments, which they
have in Possession or in Expectation; that the Federalists are
a set of *Conspirators*, who aim at establishing a Tyranny over
the Persons and Property of their Countrymen, and to live in
Splendor on the Plunder of the People. I learn, too, that your
Justices of the Peace, tho' chosen by their Neighbours, make
a villainous Trade of their Office, and promote Discord to
augment Fees, and fleece their Electors; and that this would
not be mended by placing the Choice in the Executive Council, who, with interested or party Views, are continually
making as improper Appointments; witness a *'petty Fidler,
Sycophant, and Scoundrel,'* appointed Judge of the Admiralty;
'an old Woman and Fomenter of Sedition' to be another of
the Judges, and *'a Jeffries'* Chief Justice, &c. &c.; with *'two
Harpies'* the Comptroller and Naval Officers, to prey upon
the Merchants and deprive them of their Property by Force
of Arms, &c.

"I am inform'd also by these Papers, that your General
Assembly, tho' the annual choice of the People, shows no
Regard to their Rights, but from sinister Views or Ignorance

makes Laws in direct Violation of the Constitution, to divest the Inhabitants of their Property and give it to Strangers and Intruders; and that the Council, either fearing the Resentment of their Constituents, or plotting to enslave them, had projected to disarm them, and given Orders for that purpose; and finally, that your President, the unanimous joint choice of the Council and Assembly, is *'an old Rogue,'* who gave his Assent to the federal Constitution merely to avoid refunding Money he had purloin'd from the United States.

"There is, indeed, a good deal of manifest *Inconsistency* in all this, and yet a Stranger, seeing it in your own Prints, tho' he does not believe it all, may probably believe enough of it to conclude, that Pennsylvania is peopled by a Set of the most unprincipled, wicked, rascally, and quarrelsome Scoundrels upon the Face of the Globe. I have sometimes, indeed, suspected, that those Papers are the Manufacture of foreign Enemies among you, who write with a view of disgracing your Country, and making you appear contemptible and detestable all the World over; but then I wonder at the Indiscretion of your Printers in publishing such Writings! There is, however, one of your *Inconsistencies* that consoles me a little, which is, that tho' *living*, you give one another the characters of Devils; *dead*, you are all Angels! It is delightful, when any of you die, to read what good Husbands, good Fathers, good Friends, good Citizens, and good Christians you were, concluding with a Scrap of Poetry that places you, with certainty, every one in Heaven. So that I think Pennsylvania a good country *to dye in*, though a very bad one to *live in*."

after March 30, 1788

FOR THE FEDERAL GAZETTE.

An Account of the Supremest Court of Judicature in Pennsylvania, viz. The Court of the Press

POWER OF THIS COURT.

It may receive and promulgate accusations of all kinds against all persons and characters among the citizens of the state, and even against all inferior courts, and may judge, sentence and condemn to infamy, not only private individuals, but public bodies, &c. with or without enquiry or hearing, *at the court's discretion*.

In whose favor or for whose emolument this court is established.

In favor of about one citizen in 500, who by education, or practice in scribbling, has acquired a tolerable stile as to grammar and construction so as to bear printing; or who is possessed of a press and a few types. This 500th part of the citizens have the privilege of accusing and abusing the other 499 parts, at their pleasure; or they may hire out their pens and press to others for that purpose.

Practice of the Court.

It is not governed by any of the rules of common courts of law. The accused is allowed no grand jury to judge of the truth of the accusation before it is publicly made; nor is the name of the accuser made known to him; nor has he an opportunity of confronting the witnesses against him; for they are kept in the dark, as in the Spanish Court of Inquisition.— Nor is there any petty jury of his peers sworn to try the truth of the charges. The proceedings are also sometimes so rapid, that an honest good citizen may find himself suddenly and unexpectedly accused, and in the same morning judged and condemned, and sentence pronounced against him, That he is a *rogue* and a *villain*. Yet if an officer of this court receives the slightest check for misconduct in this his office, he claims immediately the rights of a free citizen by the constitution, and demands to know his accuser, to confront the witnesses, and to have a fair trial by a jury of his peers.

The foundation of its authority.

It is said to be founded on an article in the state-constitution, which establishes *the liberty of the press*. A liberty which every Pennsylvanian would fight and die for: Though few of us, I believe, have distinct ideas of its nature and extent. It seems indeed somewhat like the *liberty* of the *press* that felons have by the common law of England before conviction, that is, to be either *pressed* to death or hanged. If by the *liberty of the press* were understood merely the liberty of discussing the propriety of public measures and political opinions, let us have as much of it as you please: But if it means the liberty of affronting, calumniating and defaming one another, I, for my part, own myself willing to part with my share of it, whenever our legislators shall please so to alter the law and shall chearfully consent to exchange my *liberty* of abusing others for the *privilege* of not being abused myself.

By whom this court is commissioned or constituted.

It is not by any commission from the Supreme Executive Council, who might previously judge of the abilities, integrity, knowledge, &c. of the persons to be appointed to this great trust, of deciding upon the characters and good fame of the citizens; for this court is above that council, and may *accuse*, *judge*, and *condemn* it, at pleasure. Nor is it hereditary, as is the court of *dernier resort* in the peerage of England. But any man who can procure pen, ink, and paper, with a press, a few types, and a huge pair of BLACKING balls, may commissionate himself: And his court is immediately established in the plenary possession and exercise of its rights. For if you make the least complaint of the *judge's* conduct, he daubs his blacking balls in your face wherever he meets you; and besides tearing your private character to slitters, marks you out for the odium of the public, as an *enemy to the liberty of the press.*

Of the natural support of these courts.

Their support is founded in the depravity of such minds as have not been mended by religion, nor improved by good education;

> "There is a lust in man no charm can tame,
> Of loudly publishing his neighbour's shame."
>   Hence,
> "On eagle's wings immortal scandals fly,
> While virtuous actions are but born and die."
>   DRYDEN.

Whoever feels pain in hearing a good character of his neighbour, will feel a pleasure in the reverse. And of those, who, despairing to rise into distinction by their virtues, and are happy if others can be depressed on a level with themselves, there are a number sufficient in every great town to maintain one of these courts by their subscriptions.—A shrewd observer once said that in walking the streets in a slippery morning, one might see where the good natured people lived by the ashes thrown on the ice before their doors: probably he would have formed a different conjecture of the temper of those whom he might find engaged in such subscriptions.

Of the checks proper to be established against the abuse of power in those courts.

Hitherto there are none. But since so much has been written and published on the federal constitution, and the necessity of checks in all other parts of good government has been so clearly and learnedly explained, I find myself so far enlightened as to suspect some check may be proper in this part also; but I have been at a loss to imagine any that may not be construed an infringement of the sacred *liberty of the Press.* At length however I think I have found one, that instead of diminishing general liberty, shall augment it; which is, by restoring to the people a species of liberty of which they have been deprived by our laws, I mean the *liberty of the Cudgel.*— In the rude state of society, prior to the existence of laws, if one man gave another ill language, the affronted person might return it by a box on the ear; and if repeated, by a good drubbing; and this without offending against any law; but now the right of making such returns is denied, and they are punished as breaches of the peace; while the right of abusing seems to remain in full force: the laws made against it being rendered ineffectual by the *liberty of the Press.*

My proposal then is, to leave the liberty of the Press untouched, to be exercised in its full extent, force and vigour, but to permit the *liberty of the Cudgel* to go with it *pari passu.* Thus my fellow-citizens, if an impudent writer attacks your reputation, dearer to you perhaps than your life, and puts his name to the charge, you may go to him as openly and break his head. If he conceals himself behind the printer, and you can nevertheless discover who he is, you may in a like manner way-lay him in the night, attack him behind, and give him a good drubbing. If your adversary hire better writers than himself to abuse you the more effectually, you may hire brawny porters, stronger than yourself, to assist you in giving him a more effectual drubbing.—Thus far goes my project, as to *private* resentment and retribution. But if the public should ever happen to be affronted, *as it ought to be* with the conduct of such writers, I would not advise proceeding immediately to these extremities; but that we should in moderation content ourselves with tarring and feathering, and tossing them in a blanket.

If, however, it should be thought that this proposal of mine may disturb the public peace, I would then humbly recommend to our legislators to take up the consideration of both liberties, that of the Press, and that of the Cudgel, and by an explicit law mark their extent and limits; and at the same time that they secure the person of a citizen from assaults, they would likewise provide for the security of his reputation.

The Federal Gazette, September 12, 1789

An Address to the Public

FROM THE PENNSYLVANIA SOCIETY FOR PROMOTING THE ABOLITION OF SLAVERY, AND THE RELIEF OF FREE NEGROES UNLAWFULLY HELD IN BONDAGE

It is with peculiar satisfaction we assure the friends of humanity, that, in prosecuting the design of our association, our endeavours have proved successful, far beyond our most sanguine expectations.

Encouraged by this success, and by the daily progress of that luminous and benign spirit of liberty, which is diffusing itself throughout the world, and humbly hoping for the continuance of the divine blessing on our labours, we have ventured to make an important addition to our original plan, and do therefore earnestly solicit the support and assistance of all who can feel the tender emotions of sympathy and compassion, or relish the exalted pleasure of beneficence.

Slavery is such an atrocious debasement of human nature, that its very extirpation, if not performed with solicitous care, may sometimes open a source of serious evils.

The unhappy man, who has long been treated as a brute animal, too frequently sinks beneath the common standard of the human species. The galling chains, that bind his body, do also fetter his intellectual faculties, and impair the social affections of his heart. Accustomed to move like a mere machine, by the will of a master, reflection is suspended; he has not the power of choice; and reason and conscience have but little influence over his conduct, because he is chiefly governed by the passion of fear. He is poor and friendless; perhaps worn out by extreme labour, age, and disease.

Under such circumstances, freedom may often prove a misfortune to himself, and prejudicial to society.

Attention to emancipated black people, it is therefore to be hoped, will become a branch of our national policy; but, as far as we contribute to promote this emancipation, so far that attention is evidently a serious duty incumbent on us, and which we mean to discharge to the best of our judgment and abilities.

To instruct, to advise, to qualify those, who have been restored to freedom, for the exercise and enjoyment of civil liberty, to promote in them habits of industry, to furnish them with employments suited to their age, sex, talents, and other circumstances, and to procure their children an education calculated for their future situation in life; these are the great outlines of the annexed plan, which we have adopted, and which we conceive will essentially promote the public good, and the happiness of these our hitherto too much neglected fellow-creatures.

A plan so extensive cannot be carried into execution without considerable pecuniary resources, beyond the present ordinary funds of the Society. We hope much from the generosity of enlightened and benevolent freemen, and will gratefully receive any donations or subscriptions for this purpose, which may be made to our treasurer, James Starr, or to James Pemberton, chairman of our committee of correspondence.

Signed, by order of the Society,

B. FRANKLIN, *President*.

Philadelphia, 9th of
November, 1789.

Plan for Improving the Condition
of the Free Blacks

The business relative to free blacks shall be transacted by a committee of twenty-four persons, annually elected by ballot, at the meeting of this Society, in the month called April; and, in order to perform the different services with expedition, regularity, and energy, this committee shall resolve itself into the following sub-committees, viz.

I. A Committee of Inspection, who shall superintend the morals, general conduct, and ordinary situation of the free negroes, and afford them advice and instruction, protection from wrongs, and other friendly offices.

II. A Committee of Guardians, who shall place out children and young people with suitable persons, that they may (during a moderate time of apprenticeship or servitude) learn some trade or other business of subsistence. The committee may effect this partly by a persuasive influence on parents and the persons concerned, and partly by coöperating with the laws, which are, or may be, enacted for this and similar purposes. In forming contracts on these occasions, the committee shall secure to the Society, as far as may be practicable, the right of guardianship over the persons so bound.

III. A Committee of Education, who shall superintend the school instruction of the children and youth of the free blacks. They may either influence them to attend regularly the schools already established in this city, or form others with this view; they shall, in either case, provide, that the pupils may receive such learning as is necessary for their future situation in life, and especially a deep impression of the most important and generally acknowledged moral and religious principles. They shall also procure and preserve a regular record of the marriages, births, and manumissions of all free blacks.

IV. A Committee of Employ, who shall endeavour to procure constant employment for those free negroes who are able to work; as the want of this would occasion poverty, idleness, and many vicious habits. This committee will, by sedulous inquiry, be enabled to find common labour for a great number; they will also provide, that such as indicate proper talents may learn various trades, which may be done by prevailing upon them to bind themselves for such a term of years as shall compensate their masters for the expense and trouble of instruction and maintenance. The committee may attempt the institution of some useful and simple manufactures, which require but little skill, and also may assist, in commencing business, such as appear to be qualified for it.

Whenever the committee of inspection shall find persons of any particular description requiring attention, they shall immediately direct them to the committee of whose care they are the proper objects.

In matters of a mixed nature, the committees shall confer, and, if necessary, act in concert. Affairs of great importance shall be referred to the whole committee.

The expense, incurred by the prosecution of this plan, shall be defrayed by a fund, to be formed by donations or subscriptions for these particular purposes, and to be kept separate from the other funds of this Society.

The committee shall make a report of their proceedings, and of the state of their stock, to the Society, at their quarterly meetings, in the months called April and October.

1789?

Sidi Mehemet Ibrahim on the Slave Trade

TO THE EDITOR OF THE FEDERAL GAZETTE

SIR,   March 23d, 1790.

Reading last night in your excellent Paper the speech of Mr. Jackson in Congress against their meddling with the Affair of Slavery, or attempting to mend the Condition of the Slaves, it put me in mind of a similar One made about 100 Years since by Sidi Mehemet Ibrahim, a member of the Divan of Algiers, which may be seen in Martin's Account of his Consulship, anno 1687. It was against granting the Petition of the Sect called *Erika*, or Purists, who pray'd for the Abolition of Piracy and Slavery as being unjust. Mr. Jackson does not quote it; perhaps he has not seen it. If, therefore, some of its Reasonings are to be found in his eloquent Speech, it may only show that men's Interests and Intellects operate and are operated on with surprising similarity in all Countries and Climates, when under similar Circumstances. The African's Speech, as translated, is as follows.

"Allah Bismillah, &c.
God is great, and Mahomet is his Prophet.

"Have these *Erika* considered the Consequences of granting their Petition? If we cease our Cruises against the Christians, how shall we be furnished with the Commodities their Countries produce, and which are so necessary for us? If we forbear to make Slaves of their People, who in this hot Climate are to cultivate our Lands? Who are to perform the common Labours of our City, and in our Families? Must we not then be our own Slaves? And is there not more Compassion and more Favour due to us as Mussulmen, than to these Christian Dogs? We have now above 50,000 Slaves in and near Algiers. This Number, if not kept up by fresh Supplies, will soon diminish, and be gradually annihilated. If we then cease taking and plundering the Infidel Ships, and making Slaves of the Seamen and Passengers, our Lands will become of no Value for want of Cultivation; the Rents of Houses in the City will sink one half; and the Revenues of Government arising from its Share of Prizes be totally destroy'd! And for what? To gratify the whims of a whimsical Sect, who would have us, not only forbear making more Slaves, but even to manumit those we have.

"But who is to indemnify their Masters for the Loss? Will the State do it? Is our Treasury sufficient? Will the *Erika* do it? Can they do it? Or would they, to do what they think Justice to the Slaves, do a greater Injustice to the Owners? And if we set our Slaves free, what is to be done with them? Few of them will return to their Countries; they know too well the greater Hardships they must there be subject to; they will not embrace our holy Religion; they will not adopt our Manners; our People will not pollute themselves by intermarrying with them. Must we maintain them as Beggars in our Streets, or suffer our Properties to be the Prey of their Pillage? For Men long accustom'd to Slavery will not work for a Livelihood when not compell'd. And what is there so pitiable in their present Condition? Were they not Slaves in their own Countries?

"Are not Spain, Portugal, France, and the Italian states govern'd by Despots, who hold all their Subjects in Slavery, without Exception? Even England treats its Sailors as Slaves; for they are, whenever the Government pleases, seiz'd, and confin'd in Ships of War, condemn'd not only to work, but to fight, for small Wages, or a mere Subsistence, not better than our Slaves are allow'd by us. Is their Condition then made worse by their falling into our Hands? No; they have only exchanged one Slavery for another, and I may say a better; for here they are brought into a Land where the Sun of Islamism gives forth its Light, and shines in full Splendor, and they have an Opportunity of making themselves acquainted with the true Doctrine, and thereby saving their immortal Souls. Those who remain at home have not that Happiness. Sending the Slaves home then would be sending them out of Light into Darkness.

"I repeat the Question, What is to be done with them? I have heard it suggested, that they may be planted in the Wilderness, where there is plenty of Land for them to subsist on, and where they may flourish as a free State; but they are, I doubt, too little dispos'd to labour without Compulsion, as well as too ignorant to establish a good government, and the wild Arabs would soon molest and destroy or again enslave them. While serving us, we take care to provide them with every thing, and they are treated with Humanity. The Labourers in their own Country are, as I am well informed, worse fed, lodged, and cloathed. The Condition of most of them is therefore already mended, and requires no further Improvement. Here their Lives are in Safety. They are not liable to be impress'd for Soldiers, and forc'd to cut one another's Christian Throats, as in the Wars of their own Countries. If some of the religious mad Bigots, who now teaze us with their silly Petitions, have in a Fit of blind Zeal freed their Slaves, it was not Generosity, it was not Humanity, that mov'd them to the Action; it was from the conscious Burthen of a Load of Sins, and Hope, from the supposed Merits of so good a Work, to be excus'd Damnation.

"How grossly are they mistaken in imagining Slavery to be disallow'd by the Alcoran! Are not the two Precepts, to quote no more, *'Masters, treat your Slaves with kindness; Slaves, serve your Masters with Cheerfulness and Fidelity,'* clear Proofs to the contrary? Nor can the Plundering of Infidels be in that sacred Book forbidden, since it is well known from it, that God has given the World, and all that it contains, to his faithful Mussulmen, who are to enjoy it of Right as fast as they conquer it. Let us then hear no more of this detestable Proposition, the Manumission of Christian Slaves, the Adoption of which would, by depreciating our Lands and Houses, and thereby depriving so many good Citizens of their Properties, create universal Discontent, and provoke Insurrections, to the endangering of Government and producing general Confusion. I have therefore no doubt, but this wise Council will prefer the Comfort and Happiness of a whole Nation of true Believers to the Whim of a few *Erika*, and dismiss their Petition."

The Result was, as Martin tells us, that the Divan came to this Resolution; "The Doctrine, that Plundering and Enslaving the Christians is unjust, is at best *problematical*; but that it is the Interest of this State to continue the Practice, is clear; therefore let the Petition be rejected."

And it was rejected accordingly.

And since like Motives are apt to produce in the Minds of Men like Opinions and Resolutions, may we not, Mr. Brown, venture to predict, from this Account, that the Petitions to the Parliament of England for abolishing the Slave-Trade, to say nothing of other Legislatures, and the Debates upon them, will have a similar Conclusion? I am, Sir, your constant Reader and humble Servant,

HISTORICUS.

The Federal Gazette, March 25, 1790

LETTERS

To Jonathan Shipley

DEAR FRIEND,   Philadelphia, Feb. 24th, 1786.

I received lately your kind letter of Nov. 27th. My Reception here was, as you have heard, very honourable indeed; but I was betray'd by it, and by some Remains of Ambition, from which I had imagined myself free, to accept of the Chair of Government for the State of Pennsylvania, when the proper thing for me was Repose and a private Life. I hope, however, to be able to bear the Fatigue for one Year, and then to retire.

I have much regretted our having so little Opportunity for Conversation when we last met. You could have given me Informations and Counsels that I wanted, but we were scarce a Minute together without being broke in upon. I am to thank you, however, for the Pleasure I had after our Parting, in reading the new Book you gave me, which I think generally well written and likely to do good; tho' the Reading Time of most People is of late so taken up with News Papers and little periodical Pamphlets, that few now-a-days venture to attempt reading a Quarto Volume. I have admir'd to see, that, in the last Century, a Folio, *Burton on Melancholly*, went through Six Editions in about Twenty Years. We have, I believe, more Readers now, but not of such large Books.

You seem desirous of knowing what Progress we make here in improving our Governments. We are, I think, in the right Road of Improvement, for we are making Experiments. I do not oppose all that seem wrong, for the Multitude are more effectually set right by Experience, than kept from going wrong by Reasoning with them. And I think we are daily more and more enlightened; so that I have no doubt of our obtaining in a few Years as much public Felicity, as good Government is capable of affording.

Your NewsPapers are fill'd with fictitious Accounts of Anarchy, Confusion, Distresses, and Miseries, we are suppos'd to be involv'd in, as Consequences of the Revolution; and the few remaining Friends of the old Government among us take pains to magnify every little Inconvenience a Change in the Course of Commerce may have occasion'd. To obviate the Complaints they endeavour to excite, was written the enclos'd little Piece, from which you may form a truer Idea of our Situation, than your own public Prints would give you. And I can assure you, that the great Body of our Nation find themselves happy in the Change, and have not the smallest Inclination to return to the Domination of Britain. There could not be a stronger Proof of the general Approbation of the Measures, that promoted the Change, and of the Change itself, than has been given by the Assembly and Council of this State, in the nearly unanimous Choice for their Governor, of one who had been so much concern'd in those Measures; the Assembly being themselves the unbrib'd Choice of the People, and therefore may be truly suppos'd of the same Sentiments. I say nearly unanimous, because, of between 70 and 80 Votes, there were only my own and one other in the negative.

As to my Domestic Circumstances, of which you kindly desire to hear something, they are at present as happy as I could wish them. I am surrounded by my Offspring, a Dutiful and Affectionate Daughter in my House, with Six Grandchildren, the eldest of which you have seen, who is now at a College in the next Street, finishing the learned Part of his Education; the others promising, both for Parts and good Dispositions. What their Conduct may be, when they grow up and enter the important Scenes of Life, I shall not live to *see*, and I cannot *foresee*. I therefore enjoy among them the present Hour, and leave the future to Providence.

He that raises a large Family does, indeed, while he lives to observe them, *stand*, as Watts says, *a broader Mark for Sorrow*; but then he stands a broader Mark for Pleasure too. When we launch our little Fleet of Barques into the Ocean, bound to different Ports, we hope for each a prosperous Voyage; but contrary Winds, hidden Shoals, Storms, and Enemies come in for a Share in the Disposition of Events; and though these occasion a Mixture of Disappointment, yet, considering the Risque where we can make no Insurance, we should think ourselves happy if some return with Success. My Son's Son, Temple Franklin, whom you have also seen, having had a fine

Farm of 600 Acres convey'd to him by his Father when we were at Southampton, has drop'd for the present his Views of acting in the political Line, and applies himself ardently to the Study and Practice of Agriculture. This is much more agreable to me, who esteem it the most useful, the most independent, and therefore the noblest of Employments. His Lands are on navigable water, communicating with the Delaware, and but about 16 Miles from this City. He has associated to himself a very skillful English Farmer lately arrived here, who is to instruct him in the Business, and partakes for a Term of the Profits; so that there is a great apparent Probability of their Success.

You will kindly expect a Word or two concerning myself. My Health and Spirits continue, Thanks to God, as when you saw me. The only complaint I then had, does not grow worse, and is tolerable. I still have Enjoyment in the Company of my Friends; and, being easy in my Circumstances, have many Reasons to like Living. But the Course of Nature must soon put a period to my present Mode of Existence. This I shall submit to with less Regret, as, having seen during a long Life a good deal of this World, I feel a growing Curiosity to be acquainted with some other; and can chearfully, with filial Confidence, resign my Spirit to the conduct of that great and good Parent of Mankind, who created it, and who has so graciously protected and prospered me from my Birth to the present Hour. Wherever I am, I hope always to retain the pleasing remembrance of your Friendship, being with sincere and great Esteem, my dear Friend, yours most affectionately,

P. S. We all join in Respects to Mrs. Shipley, and best wishes for the whole amiable Family.

LEAD POISONING

To Benjamin Vaughan

DEAR FRIEND,   Philad^a, July 31, 1786.

I recollect, that, when I had the great Pleasure of seeing you at Southampton, now a 12month since, we had some

Conversation on the bad Effects of Lead taken inwardly; and that at your Request I promis'd to send you in writing a particular Account of several Facts I then mention'd to you, of which you thought some good use might be made. I now sit down to fulfil that Promise.

The first Thing I remember of this kind was a general Discourse in Boston, when I was a Boy, of a Complaint from North Carolina against New England Rum, that it poison'd their People, giving them the Dry Bellyach, with a Loss of the Use of their Limbs. The Distilleries being examin'd on the Occasion, it was found that several of them used leaden Still-heads and Worms, and the Physicians were of Opinion, that the Mischief was occasioned by that Use of Lead. The Legislature of the Massachusetts thereupon pass'd an Act, prohibiting under severe Penalties the Use of such Still-heads and Worms thereafter. Inclos'd I send you a Copy of the Acc[t], taken from my printed Law-book.

In 1724, being in London, I went to work in the Printing-House of Mr. Palmer, Bartholomew Close, as a Compositor. I there found a Practice, I had never seen before, of drying a Case of Types (which are wet in Distribution) by placing it sloping before the Fire. I found this had the additional Advantage, when the Types were not only dry'd but heated, of being comfortable to the Hands working over them in cold weather. I therefore sometimes heated my Case when the Types did not want drying. But an old Workman, observing it, advis'd me not to do so, telling me I might lose the Use of my Hands by it, as two of our Companions had nearly done, one of whom that us'd to earn his Guinea a Week, could not then make more than ten Shillings, and the other, who had the Dangles, but seven and sixpence. This, with a kind of obscure Pain, that I had sometimes felt, as it were in the Bones of my Hand when working over the Types made very hot, induced me to omit the Practice. But talking afterwards with Mr. James, a Letter-founder in the same Close, and asking him if his People, who work'd over the little Furnaces of melted Metal, were not subject to that Disorder; he made light of any danger from the effluvia, but ascribed it to Particles of the Metal swallow'd with their Food by slovenly Workmen, who went to their Meals after handling the Metal, without well washing their Fingers, so that some of the metalline Particles were taken off by their Bread and eaten with it. This appeared to have some Reason in it. But the Pain I had experienc'd made me still afraid of those Effluvia.

Being in Derbishire at some of the Furnaces for Smelting of Lead Ore, I was told, that the Smoke of those Furnaces was pernicious to the neighbouring Grass and other Vegetables; but I do not recollect to have heard any thing of the Effect of such Vegetables eaten by Animals. It may be well to make the Enquiry.

In America I have often observ'd, that on the Roofs of our shingled Houses, where Moss is apt to grow in northern Exposures, if there be any thing on the Roof painted with white Lead, such as Balusters, or Frames of dormant Windows, &c., there is constantly a Streak on the Shingles from such Paint down to the Eaves, on which no Moss will grow, but the wood remains constantly clean and free from it. We seldom drink RainWater that falls on our Houses; and if we did, perhaps the small Quantity of Lead, descending from such Paint, might not be sufficient to produce any sensible ill Effect on our Bodies. But I have been told of a Case in Europe, I forgot the Place, where a whole Family was afflicted with what we call the Dry Bellyach, or *Colica Pictonum*, by drinking RainWater. It was at a Country-Seat, which, being situated too high to have the Advantage of a Well, was supply'd with Water from a Tank, which received the Water from the leaded Roofs. This had been drunk several Years without Mischief; but some young Trees planted near the House growing up above the Roof, and shedding their Leaves upon it, it was suppos'd that an Acid in those Leaves had corroded the Lead they cover'd, and furnish'd the Water of that Year with its baneful Particles and Qualities.

When I was in Paris with Sir John Pringle in 1767, he visited *La Charité*, a Hospital particularly famous for the Cure of that Malady, and brought from thence a Pamphlet containing a List of the Names of Persons, specifying their Professions or Trades, who had been cured there. I had the Curiosity to examine that List, and found that all the Patients were of Trades, that, some way or other, use or work in Lead; such as Plumbers, Glaziers, Painters, &c., excepting only two kinds, Stonecutters and Soldiers. These I could not reconcile to my Notion, that Lead was the cause of that Disorder. But on my mentioning this Difficulty to a Physician of that Hospital, he inform'd me that the Stonecutters are continually using melted Lead to fix the Ends of Iron Balustrades in Stone; and that the Soldiers had been employ'd by Painters, as Labourers, in Grinding of Colours.

This, my dear Friend, is all I can at present recollect on the Subject. You will see by it, that the Opinion of this mischievous Effect from Lead is at least above Sixty Years old; and you will observe with Concern how long a useful Truth may be known and exist, before it is generally receiv'd and practis'd on.

I am, ever, yours most affectionately,

"INVENTION AND IMPROVEMENT ARE PROLIFIC"

To Rev. John Lathrop

REVEREND SIR,   Philad[a], May 31, 1788.

I received your obliging Favour of the 6th Inst by Mr. Hilliard, with whose Conversation I was much pleased, and would have been glad to have had more of it, if he could have spar'd it to me; but the short time of his stay has prevented. You need make no apology for introducing any of your friends to me. I consider it as doing me Honour, as well as giving me Pleasure.

I thank you for the pamphlet of the Humane Society. In return please to accept one of the same kind, which was published while I resided in France. If your Society have not hitherto seen it, it may possibly afford them useful Hints.

It would certainly, as you observe, be a very great Pleasure to me, if I could once again visit my Native Town, and walk over the Grounds I used to frequent when a Boy, and where I enjoyed many of the innocent Pleasures of Youth, which would be so brought to my Remembrance, and where I might find some of my old Acquaintance to converse with. But when I consider how well I am situated here, with every thing about me, that I can call either necessary or convenient; the fatigues and bad accommodations to be met with and suffered in a land journey, and the unpleasantness of sea voyages, to one, who, although he has crossed the Atlantic eight times, and made many smaller trips, does not recollect his having ever been at sea without taking a firm resolution never to go to sea again; and that, if I were arrived in Boston, I should see but little of it, as I could neither bear walking nor riding in a carriage over its pebbled streets; and, above all, that I should find very few indeed of my old friends living, it being now sixty-five years since I left it to settle here; — all this considered, I say, it seems probable, though not certain, that I shall hardly again visit that beloved place. But I enjoy the company and conversation of its inhabitants, when any of them are so good as to visit me; for, besides their general good sense, which I value, the Boston manner, turn of phrase, and even tone of voice, and accent in pronunciation, all please, and seem to refresh and revive me.

I have been long impressed with the same sentiments you so well express, of the growing felicity of mankind, from the improvements in philosophy, morals, politics, and even the conveniences of common living, by the invention and acquisition of new and useful utensils and instruments, that I have sometimes almost wished it had been my destiny to be born two or three centuries hence. For invention and improvement are prolific, and beget more of their kind. The present progress is rapid. Many of great importance, now unthought of, will before that period be produced; and then I might not only enjoy their advantages, but have my curiosity gratified in knowing what they are to be. I see a little absurdity in what I have just written, but it is to a friend, who will wink and let it pass, while I mention one reason more for such a wish, which is, that, if the art of physic shall be improved in proportion with other arts, we may then be able to avoid diseases, and live as long as the patriarchs in Genesis; to which I suppose we should make little objection.

I am glad my dear sister has so good and kind a neighbour. I sometimes suspect she may be backward in acquainting me with circumstances in which I might be more useful to her. If any such should occur to your observation, your mentioning them to me will be a favour I shall be thankful for. With great esteem, I have the honour to be, Reverend Sir, &c.

HONEST HERETICS

To Benjamin Vaughan

October 24, 1788.

——Having now finished my term in the Presidentship, and resolving to engage no more in public affairs, I hope to be a better correspondent for the little time I have to live. I am recovering from a long continued gout, and am diligently employed in writing the History of my Life, to the doing of which the persuasions contained in your letter of January 31, 1783, have not a little contributed. I am now in the year 1756 just before I was sent to England. To shorten the work, as well as for other reasons, I omit all facts and transactions that may not have a tendency to benefit the young reader, by showing him from my example, and my success in emerging from poverty, and acquiring some degree of wealth, power, and reputation, the advantages of certain modes of conduct which I observed, and of avoiding the errors which were prejudicial to me. If a writer can judge properly of his own work, I fancy on reading over what is already done, that the book may be found entertaining, interesting, and useful, more so than I expected when I began it. If my present state of health continues, I hope to finish it this winter: when done you shall have a manuscript copy of it, that I may obtain from your judgment and friendship, such remarks as may contribute to its improvement.

The violence of our party debates about the new constitution seems much abated, indeed almost extinct, and we are getting fast into good order. I kept out of those disputes pretty well, having wrote only one little piece, which I send you inclosed.

I regret the immense quantity of misery brought upon mankind by this Turkish war; and I am afraid the King of Sweden may burn his fingers by attacking Russia. When will princes learn arithmetick enough to calculate if they want pieces of one another's territory, how much cheaper it would be to buy them, than to make war for them, even though they were to give an hundred years purchase? But if glory cannot be valued, and therefore the wars for it cannot be subject to arithmetical calculation so as to show their advantage or disadvantage, at least wars for trade, which have gain for their object, may be proper subjects for such computation; and a trading nation as well as a single trader ought to calculate the probabilities of profit and loss, before engaging in any considerable adventure. This however nations seldom do, and we have had frequent instances of their spending more money in wars for acquiring or securing branches of commerce, that an hundred years' profit or the full enjoyment of them can compensate.

Remember me affectionately to good Dr. Price and to the honest heretic Dr. Priestly. I do not call him *honest* by way of distinction; for I think all the heretics I have known have been virtuous men. They have the virtue of fortitude or they would not venture to own their heresy; and they cannot afford to be deficient in any of the other virtues, as that would give advantage to their many enemies; and they have not like orthodox sinners, such a number of friends to excuse or justify them. Do not, however mistake me. It is not to my good friend's heresy that I impute his honesty. On the contrary, 'tis his honesty that has brought upon him the character of heretic. I am ever, my dear friend, yours sincerely,

"THE DISPLEASURE OF THE GREAT AND IMPARTIAL
RULER OF THE UNIVERSE"

To John Langdon

Sir:

The Pennsylvania Society for promoting the abolition of slavery, and the relief of free Negroes unlawfully held in bondage, have taken the liberty to ask your Excellency's acceptance of a few copies of their Constitution and the laws of

Pennsylvania, which relate to one of the objects of their Institution; also, of a copy of Thomas Clarkson's excellent Essay upon the Commerce and Slavery of the Africans.

The Society have heard, with great regret, that a considerable part of the slaves, who have been sold in the Southern States since the establishment of peace, have been imported in vessels fitted out in the state, over which, your Excellency presides. From your Excellency's station, they hope your influence will be exerted, hereafter, to prevent a practice which is so evidently repugnant to the political principles and form of government lately adopted by citizens of the United States, and which cannot fail of delaying the enjoyment of the blessings of peace and liberty, by drawing down, the displeasure of the great and impartial Ruler of the Universe upon our country.

I am, in behalf of the Society,

        Sir, your most obedient servant,

1788

"BEING A LITTLE MIFFY"

To Jane Mecom

DEAR SISTER,   Philada Augt 3. 1789

I have receiv'd your kind Letter of the 23d past, and am glad to learn that you have at length got some of those I so long since wrote to you. I think your Post Office is very badly managed. I expect your Bill, & shall pay it when it appears. —I would have you put the Books into Cousin Jonathan's Hands who will dispose of them for you if he can, or return them hither. I am very much pleas'd to hear that you have had no Misunderstanding with his good Father. Indeed if there had been any such, I should have concluded that it was your Fault: for I think our Family were always subject to being a little Miffy. — By the way, is our Relationship in Nantucket quite worn out? —I have met with none from thence of late Years who were dispos'd to be acquainted with me, except Capt. Timothy Fulger. They are wonderfully shy. But

I admire their honest plainness of Speech. About a Year ago I invited two of them to dine with me. Their Answer was that they would—if they could not do better. I suppose they did better, for I never saw them afterwards; and so had no Opportunity of showing my Miff, if I had one.—Give my Love to Cousin Williams's and thank them from me for all the Kindnesses to you, which I have always been acquainted with by you, and take as if done to myself. I am sorry to learn from his Son, that his Health is not so firm as formerly. A Journey hither by Land might do him good, and I should be happy to see him.—I shall make the Addition you desire to my Superscriptions, desiring in Return that you would make a Substraction from yours. The Word Excellency does not belong to me, and Dr will be sufficient to distinguish me from my Grandson. This Family joins in Love to you and yours, with

Your affectionate Brother

"A GOOD MOTION NEVER DIES"

To John Wright

DEAR FRIEND,   Philadelphia, November 4, 1789.
    I received your kind letter of July the 31st, which gave me great pleasure, as it informed me of the welfare both of yourself and your good lady, to whom please to present my respects. I thank you for the epistle of your yearly meeting, and for the card, a specimen of printing, which was enclosed.
    We have now had one session of Congress, which was conducted under our new Constitution, and with as much general satisfaction as could reasonably be expected. I wish the struggle in France may end as happily for that nation. We are now in the full enjoyment of our new government for *eleven* of the States, and it is generally thought that North Carolina is about to join it. Rhode Island will probably take longer time for consideration.
    We have had a most plentiful year for the fruits of the earth, and our people seem to be recovering fast from the

extravagance and idle habits, which the war had introduced; and to engage seriously in the country habits of temperance, frugality, and industry, which give the most pleasing prospect of future national felicity. Your merchants, however, are, I think, imprudent in crowding in upon us such quantities of goods for sale here, which are not written for by ours, and are beyond the faculties of this country to consume in any reasonable time. This surplus of goods is, therefore, to raise present money, sent to the vendues, or auction-houses, of which we have six or seven in and near this city; where they are sold frequently for less than prime cost, to the great loss of the indiscreet adventurers. Our newspapers are doubtless to be seen at your coffee-houses near the Exchange. In their advertisements you may observe the constancy and quantity of this kind of sales; as well as the quantity of goods imported by our regular traders. I see in your English newspapers frequent mention of our being out of credit with you; to us it appears, that we have abundantly too much, and that your exporting merchants are rather out of their senses.

I wish success to your endeavours for obtaining an abolition of the Slave Trade. The epistle from your Yearly Meeting, for the year 1758, was not the *first sowing* of the good seed you mention; for I find by an old pamphlet in my possession, that George Keith, near a hundred years since, wrote a paper against the practice, said to be "given forth by the appointment of the meeting held by him, at Philip James's house, in the city of Philadelphia, about the year 1693;" wherein a strict charge was given to Friends, "that they should set their negroes at liberty, after some reasonable time of service, &c. &c." And about the year 1728, or 1729, I myself printed a book for Ralph Sandyford, another of your Friends in this city, against keeping negroes in slavery; two editions of which he distributed gratis. And about the year 1736, I printed another book on the same subject for Benjamin Lay, who also professed being one of your Friends, and he distributed the books chiefly among them. By these instances it appears, that the seed was indeed sown in the good ground of your profession, though much earlier than the time you mention, and its springing up to effect at last, though so late, is some confirmation of Lord Bacon's observation, that *a good motion never dies*; and it may encourage us in making such, though hopeless of their taking immediate effect.

I doubt whether I shall be able to finish my Memoirs, and, if I finish them, whether they will be proper for publication. You seem to have too high an opinion of them, and to expect too much from them.

I think you are right in preferring a mixed form of government for your country, under its present circumstances; and if it were possible for you to reduce the enormous salaries and emoluments of great officers, which are at bottom the source of all your violent factions, that form might be conducted more quietly and happily; but I am afraid, that none of your factions, when they get uppermost, will ever have virtue enough to reduce those salaries and emoluments, but will rather choose to enjoy them.

I enclose a bill for twenty-five pounds, for which, when received, please to credit my account, and out of it pay Mr. Benjamin Vaughan, of Jeffries Square, and Mr. William Vaughan, his brother, of Mincing Lane, such accounts against me as they shall present to you for that purpose. I am, my dear friend, yours very affectionately,

"ALL THESE IMPROVEMENTS BACKWARDS"

To Noah Webster

DEAR SIR,   Philadª, Decʳ 26, 1789.

I received some Time since your *Dissertations on the English Language*. The Book was not accompanied by any Letter or Message, informing me to whom I am obliged for it, but I suppose it is to yourself. It is an excellent Work, and will be greatly useful in turning the Thoughts of our Countrymen to correct Writing. Please to accept my Thanks for it as well as for the great honour you have done me in its Dedication. I ought to have made this Acknowledgment sooner, but much Indisposition prevented me.

I cannot but applaud your Zeal for preserving the Purity of

our Language, both in its Expressions and Pronunciation, and in correcting the popular Errors several of our States are continually falling into with respect to both. Give me leave to mention some of them, though possibly they may have already occurred to you. I wish, however, in some future Publication of yours, you would set a discountenancing Mark upon them. The first I remember is the word *improved*. When I left New England, in the year 23, this Word had never been used among us, as far as I know, but in the sense of *ameliorated* or *made better*, except once in a very old Book of Dr. Mather's, entitled *Remarkable Providences*. As that eminent Man wrote a very obscure Hand, I remember that when I read that Word in his Book, used instead of the Word *imployed*, I conjectured that it was an Error of the Printer, who had mistaken a too short *l* in the Writing for an *r*, and a *y* with too short a Tail for a *v*; whereby *imployed* was converted into *improved*.

But when I returned to Boston, in 1733, I found this Change had obtained Favour, and was then become common; for I met with it often in perusing the Newspapers, where it frequently made an Appearance rather ridiculous. Such, for Instance, as the Advertisement of a Country-House to be sold, which had been many years *improved* as a Tavern; and, in the Character of a deceased Country Gentleman, that he had been for more than 30 Years *improved* as a Justice-of-Peace. This Use of the Word *improved* is peculiar to New England, and not to be met with among any other Speakers of English, either on this or the other Side of the Water.

During my late Absence in France, I find that several other new Words have been introduced into our parliamentary Language; for Example, I find a Verb formed from the Substantive *Notice*; *I should not have* NOTICED *this, were it not that the Gentleman,* &c. Also another Verb from the Substantive *Advocate*; *The Gentleman who* ADVOCATES *or has* ADVOCATED *that Motion,* &c. Another from the Substantive *Progress*, the most awkward and abominable of the three; *The committee, having* PROGRESSED, *resolved to adjourn.* The Word *opposed*, tho' not a new Word, I find used in a new Manner, as, *The Gentlemen who are* OPPOSED *to this Measure*; *to which I have also myself always been* OPPOSED. If you should happen to be of my Opinion with respect to these Innovations, you will use your Authority in reprobating them.

The Latin Language, long the Vehicle used in distributing Knowledge among the different Nations of Europe, is daily more and more neglected; and one of the modern Tongues, viz. the French, seems in point of Universality to have supplied its place. It is spoken in all the Courts of Europe; and most of the Literati, those even who do not speak it, have acquired Knowledge enough of it to enable them easily to read the Books that are written in it. This gives a considerable Advantage to that Nation; it enables its Authors to inculcate and spread through other Nations such Sentiments and Opinions on important Points, as are most conducive to its Interests, or which may contribute to its Reputation by promoting the common Interests of Mankind. It is perhaps owing to its being written in French, that Voltaire's Treatise on *Toleration* has had so sudden and so great an Effect on the Bigotry of Europe, as almost entirely to disarm it. The general Use of the French Language has likewise a very advantageous Effect on the Profits of the Bookselling Branch of Commerce, it being well known, that the more Copies can be sold that are struck off from one Composition of Types, the Profits increase in a much greater Proportion than they do in making a great Number of Pieces in any other Kind of Manufacture. And at present there is no Capital Town in Europe without a French Bookseller's Shop corresponding with Paris.

Our English bids fair to obtain the second Place. The great Body of excellent printed Sermons in our Language, and the Freedom of our Writings on political Subjects, have induced a Number of Divines of different Sects and Nations, as well as Gentlemen concerned in public Affairs, to study it; so far at least as to read it. And if we were to endeavour the Facilitating its Progress, the Study of our Tongue might become much more general. Those, who have employed some Part of their Time in learning a new Language, must have frequently observed, that, while their Acquaintance with it was imperfect, Difficulties small in themselves operated as great ones in obstructing their Progress. A Book, for Example, ill printed, or a Pronunciation in speaking, not well articulated, would render a Sentence unintelligible; which, from a clear Print or

a distinct Speaker, would have been immediately compre-
hended. If therefore we would have the Benefit of seeing our
Language more generally known among Mankind, we should
endeavour to remove all the Difficulties, however small, that
discourage the learning it.

But I am sorry to observe, that, of late Years, those Difficulties, instead of being diminished, have been augmented. In
examining the English Books, that were printed between the
Restoration and the Accession of George the 2^{d}, we may observe, that all *Substantives* were begun with a capital, in which
we imitated our Mother Tongue, the German. This was more
particularly useful to those, who were not well acquainted
with the English; there being such a prodigious Number of
our Words, that are both *Verbs* and *Substantives*, and spelt
in the same manner, tho' often accented differently in Pronunciation.

This Method has, by the Fancy of Printers, of late Years
been laid aside, from an Idea, that suppressing the Capitals
shows the Character to greater Advantage; those Letters
prominent above the line disturbing its even regular Appearance. The Effect of this Change is so considerable, that a
learned Man of France, who used to read our Books, tho' not
perfectly acquainted with our Language, in Conversation
with me on the Subject of our Authors, attributed the greater
Obscurity he found in our modern Books, compared with
those of the Period above mentioned, to a Change of Style
for the worse in our Writers, of which Mistake I convinced
him, by marking for him each *Substantive* with a Capital in a
Paragraph, which he then easily understood, tho' before he
could not comprehend it. This shows the Inconvenience of
that pretended Improvement.

From the same Fondness for an even and uniform Appearance of Characters in the Line, the Printers have of late ban-
ished also the Italic Types, in which Words of Importance to
be attended to in the Sense of the Sentence, and Words on
which an Emphasis should be put in Reading, used to be
printed. And lately another Fancy has induced some Printers
to use the short round *s*, instead of the long one, which formerly served well to distinguish a word readily by its varied
appearance. Certainly the omitting this prominent Letter

makes the Line appear more even; but renders it less immediately legible; as the paring all Men's Noses might smooth and level their Faces, but would render their Physiognomies less distinguishable.

Add to all these Improvements *backwards*, another modern Fancy, that grey Printing is more beautiful than black; hence the English new Books are printed in so dim a Character, as to be read with difficulty by old Eyes, unless in a very strong Light and with good Glasses. Whoever compares a Volume of the *Gentleman's Magazine*, printed between the Years 1731 and 1740, with one of those printed in the last ten Years, will be convinced of the much greater Degree of Perspicuity given by black Ink than by grey. Lord Chesterfield pleasantly remarked this Difference to Faulkener, the Printer of the Dublin *Journal*, who was vainly making Encomiums on his own Paper, as the most complete of any in the World; "But, Mr. Faulkener," said my Lord, "don't you think it might be still farther improved by using Paper and Ink not quite so near of a Colour?" For all these Reasons I cannot but wish, that our American Printers would in their Editions avoid these fancied Improvements, and thereby render their Works more agreable to Foreigners in Europe, to the great advantage of our Bookselling Commerce.

Farther, to be more sensible of the Advantage of clear and distinct Printing, let us consider the Assistance it affords in Reading well aloud to an Auditory. In so doing the Eye generally slides forward three or four Words before the Voice. If the Sight clearly distinguishes what the coming Words are, it gives time to order the Modulation of the Voice to express them properly. But, if they are obscurely printed, or disguis'd by omitting the Capitals and long *s*'s or otherwise, the Reader is apt to modulate wrong; and, finding he has done so, he is oblig'd to go back and begin the Sentence again, which lessens the Pleasure of the Hearers.

This leads me to mention an old Error in our Mode of Printing. We are sensible, that, when a Question is met with in Reading, there is a proper Variation to be used in the Management of the Voice. We have therefore a Point called an Interrogation, affix'd to the Question in order to distinguish it. But this is absurdly placed at its End; so that the Reader

does not discover it, till he finds he has wrongly modulated
his Voice, and is therefore obliged to begin again the Sentence. To prevent this, the Spanish Printers, more sensibly,
place an Interrogation at the Beginning as well as at the End
of a Question. We have another Error of the same kind in
printing Plays, where something often occurs that is mark'd
as spoken *aside*. But the Word *aside* is placed at the End of
the Speech, when it ought to precede it, as a Direction to the
Reader, that he may govern his Voice accordingly. The Practice of our Ladies in meeting five or six together to form a
little busy Party, where each is employ'd in some useful Work
while one reads to them, is so commendable in itself, that it
deserves the Attention of Authors and Printers to make it as
pleasing as possible, both to the Reader and Hearers.

After these general Observations, permit me to make one
that I imagine may regard your Interest. It is that *your Spelling Book* is miserably printed here, so as in many Places to be
scarcely legible, and on wretched Paper. If this is not attended
to, and the new one lately advertis'd as coming out should be
preferable in these Respects, it may hurt the future Sale of
yours.

I congratulate you on your Marriage, of which the Newspapers inform me. My best wishes attend you, being with
sincere esteem, Sir, &c.

"AS TO JESUS OF NAZARETH"

To Ezra Stiles

REVEREND AND DEAR SIR,   Philadª, March 9. 1790.
I received your kind Letter of Jan'y 28, and am glad you
have at length received the portrait of Gov'r Yale from his
Family, and deposited it in the College Library. He was a
great and good Man, and had the Merit of doing infinite Service to your Country by his Munificence to that Institution.
The Honour you propose doing me by placing mine in the
same Room with his, is much too great for my Deserts; but
you always had a Partiality for me, and to that it must be

ascribed. I am however too much obliged to Yale College, the first learned Society that took Notice of me and adorned me with its Honours, to refuse a Request that comes from it thro' so esteemed a Friend. But I do not think any one of the Portraits you mention, as in my Possession, worthy of the Place and Company you propose to place it in. You have an excellent Artist lately arrived. If he will undertake to make one for you, I shall cheerfully pay the Expence; but he must not delay setting about it, or I may slip thro' his fingers, for I am now in my eighty-fifth year, and very infirm.

I send with this a very learned Work, as it seems to me, on the antient Samaritan Coins, lately printed in Spain, and at least curious for the Beauty of the Impression. Please to accept it for your College Library. I have subscribed for the Encyclopædia now printing here, with the Intention of presenting it to the College. I shall probably depart before the Work is finished, but shall leave Directions for its Continuance to the End. With this you will receive some of the first numbers.

You desire to know something of my Religion. It is the first time I have been questioned upon it. But I cannot take your Curiosity amiss, and shall endeavour in a few Words to gratify it. Here is my Creed. I believe in one God, Creator of the Universe. That he governs it by his Providence. That he ought to be worshipped. That the most acceptable Service we render to him is doing good to his other Children. That the soul of Man is immortal, and will be treated with Justice in another Life respecting its Conduct in this. These I take to be the fundamental Principles of all sound Religion, and I regard them as you do in whatever Sect I meet with them.

As to Jesus of Nazareth, my Opinion of whom you particularly desire, I think the System of Morals and his Religion, as he left them to us, the best the World ever saw or is likely to see; but I apprehend it has received various corrupting Changes, and I have, with most of the present Dissenters in England, some Doubts as to his Divinity; tho' it is a question I do not dogmatize upon, having never studied it, and think it needless to busy myself with it now, when I expect soon an Opportunity of knowing the Truth with less Trouble. I see no harm, however, in its being believed, if that Belief has the good Consequence, as probably it has, of making his Doctrines more respected and better observed; especially as I do not perceive, that the Supreme takes it amiss, by distinguishing the Unbelievers in his Government of the World with any peculiar Marks of his Displeasure.

I shall only add, respecting myself, that, having experienced the Goodness of that Being in conducting me prosperously thro' a long life, I have no doubt of its Continuance in the next, though without the smallest Conceit of meriting such Goodness. My Sentiments on this Head you will see in the Copy of an old Letter enclosed, which I wrote in answer to one from a zealous Religionist, whom I had relieved in a paralytic case by electricity, and who, being afraid I should grow proud upon it, sent me his serious though rather impertinent Caution. I send you also the Copy of another Letter, which will shew something of my Disposition relating to Religion. With great and sincere Esteem and Affection, I am, Your obliged old Friend and most obedient humble Servant

P. S. Had not your College some Present of Books from the King of France? Please to let me know, if you had an Expectation given you of more, and the Nature of that Expectation? I have a Reason for the Enquiry.

I confide, that you will not expose me to Criticism and censure by publishing any part of this Communication to you. I have ever let others enjoy their religious Sentiments, without reflecting on them for those that appeared to me unsupportable and even absurd. All Sects here, and we have a great Variety, have experienced my good will in assisting them with Subscriptions for building their new Places of Worship; and, as I have never opposed any of their Doctrines, I hope to go out of the World in Peace with them all.

POOR RICHARD'S
ALMANACK
1733–1758

Contents

Poor Richard, 1733: Preface and Maxims 445

Poor Richard, 1734: Preface and Maxims 449

Poor Richard, 1735: Preface and Maxims 454

Poor Richard, 1736: Preface and Maxims 459

Poor Richard, 1737: Preface, "Hints for those that would be
Rich," Maxims 462

Poor Richard, 1738: Preface, "By Mrs. Bridget Saunders,"
Maxims 466

Poor Richard, 1739: Preface and Maxims 470

Poor Richard, 1740: Preface and Maxims 474

Poor Richard, 1741: Maxims 478

Poor Richard, 1742: Preface, Maxims, "Rules of Health and long
Life," "Rules to find out a fit Measure of Meat and
Drink" 481

Poor Richard, 1743: Preface and Maxims 486

Poor Richard, 1744: Preface and Maxims 490

Poor Richard, 1745: Preface and Maxims 493

Poor Richard, 1746: Preface and Maxims 496

Poor Richard, 1747: Preface and Maxims 499

Poor Richard Improved, 1748: Preface, "Copernicus,"
"Newton," "Cromwell," "Addison," "Muschitoes," "Penn,"
"Locke," "Rawleigh," "Happiness," Maxims 502

Poor Richard Improved, 1749: "Boyle," "Speeches,"
"Luther," "Of Sound," "Nose of a lady," "Bacon,"
"Calvin," "Magna Charta," "Wise counsel," "Pride,"
"Newton," "How to get Riches," Maxims 510

Poor Richard Improved, 1750: Preface, "Writing," Maxims 516

Poor Richard Improved, 1751: Preface, "The Romans," "The
Microscope," "Amusing Speculation," Maxims 520

Poor Richard Improved, 1752: Preface and Maxims   530

Poor Richard Improved, 1753: Preface, Maxims, "How to
    secure Houses, &c. from Lightning".   536

Poor Richard Improved, 1754: Preface and Maxims   539

Poor Richard Improved, 1755: Preface and Maxims   542

Poor Richard Improved, 1756: Preface, "On Saving Money,"
    "Settle thy Accounts," Maxims   544

Poor Richard Improved, 1757: Preface, "How to make a Striking
    Sundial," "Sincerity," "Jests," "Studying,"
    "Paradoxes," "Happiness," "Learning," Maxims   548

Poor Richard Improved, 1758: Preface (including "The Way to
    Wealth"), Maxims   554

Poor Richard, 1733

Courteous Reader,

I might in this place attempt to gain thy Favour, by de-claring that I write Almanacks with no other View than that of the publick Good; but in this I should not be sincere; and Men are now a-days too wise to be deceiv'd by Pretences how specious soever. The plain Truth of the Matter is, I am excessive poor, and my Wife, good Woman, is, I tell her, ex-cessive proud; she cannot bear, she says, to sit spinning in her Shift of Tow, while I do nothing but gaze at the Stars; and has threatned more than once to burn all my Books and Rattling-Traps (as she calls my Instruments) if I do not make some profitable Use of them for the good of my Fam-ily. The Printer has offer'd me some considerable share of the Profits, and I have thus begun to comply with my Dame's desire.

Indeed this Motive would have had Force enough to have made me publish an Almanack many Years since, had it not been overpower'd by my Regard for my good Friend and Fellow-Student, Mr. *Titan Leeds*, whose Interest I was ex-treamly unwilling to hurt: But this Obstacle (I am far from speaking it with Pleasure) is soon to be removed, since in-exorable Death, who was never known to respect Merit, has already prepared the mortal Dart, the fatal Sister has already extended her destroying Shears, and that ingenious Man must soon be taken from us. He dies, by my Calculation made at his Request, on *Oct.* 17. 1733. 3 ho. 29 m. *P.M.* at the very instant of the ♂ of ☉ and ☿: By his own Calcula-tion he will survive till the 26th of the same Month. This small difference between us we have disputed whenever we have met these 9 Years past; but at length he is inclinable to agree with my Judgment; Which of us is most exact, a little Time will now determine. As therefore these Provinces may not longer expect to see any of his Performances after this Year, I think my self free to take up the Task, and request a share of the publick Encouragement; which I am the more apt to hope for on this Account, that the Buyer of my Almanack may consider himself, not only as purchasing an

446 POOR RICHARD'S ALMANACK

useful Utensil, but as performing an Act of Charity, to his
poor   *Friend and Servant*   *R. SAUNDERS.*

Never spare the Parson's wine, nor the Baker's pudding.

> Visits should be short, like a winters day,
> Lest you're too troublesom hasten away.

A house without woman & Fire-light, is like a body without
soul or sprite.

Kings & Bears often worry their keepers.

Light purse, heavy heart.

He's a Fool that makes his Doctor his Heir.

Ne'er take a wife till thou hast a house (& a fire) to put her in.

He's gone, and forgot nothing but to say *Farewel*—to his
creditors.

Love well, whip well.

> Let my respected friend *J. G.*
> Accept this humble verse of me. *viz.*
> Ingenious, learned, envy'd Youth,
> Go on as thou'st began;
> Even thy enemies take pride
> That thou'rt their countryman.

Hunger never saw bad bread.

Beware of meat twice boil'd, & an old foe reconcil'd.

Great Talkers, little Doers.

A rich rogue, is like a fat hog, who never does good til as
dead as a log.

Relation without friendship, friendship without power,
power without will, will witho. effect, effect without
profit, & profit without vertue, are not worth a farto.

Eat to live, and not live to eat.

> March windy, and April rainy,
> makes *May* the pleasantest month of any.

The favour of the Great is no inheritance.

Fools make feasts and wise men eat 'em.

Beware of the young Doctor & the old Barber.

He has chang'd his one ey'd horse for a blind one.

The poor have little, beggars none, the rich too much, *enough* not one.

After 3 days men grow weary, of a wench, a guest, & weather rainy.

To lengthen thy Life, lessen thy Meals.

The proof of gold is fire, the proof of woman, gold; the proof of man, a woman.

After feasts made, the maker scratches his head.

Neither Shame nor Grace yet *Bob*.

> Many estates are spent in the getting,
> Since women for tea forsook spinning & knitting.

He that lies down with Dogs, shall rise up with fleas.

A fat kitchin, a lean Will.

Distrust & caution are the parents of security.

Tongue double, brings trouble.

Take counsel in wine, but resolve afterwards in water.

He that drinks fast, pays slow.

Great famine when wolves eat wolves.

A good Wife lost is God's gift lost.

A taught horse, and a woman to teach, and teachers practising what they preach.

He is ill cloth'd, who is bare of Virtue.

The heart of a fool is in his mouth, but the mouth of a wise man is in his heart.

Men & Melons are hard to know.

He's the best physician that knows the worthlessness of the most medicines.

Beware of meat twice boil'd, and an old Foe reconcil'd.

A fine genius in his own country, is like gold in the mine.

There is no little enemy.

He has lost his Boots but sav'd his spurs.

The old Man has given all to his Son: O fool! to undress thy self before thou art going to bed.

Cheese and salt meat, should be sparingly eat.

Doors and walls are fools paper.

Anoint a villain and he'll stab you, stab him & he'l anoint you.

Keep your mouth wet, feet dry.

Where bread is wanting, all's to be sold.

There is neither honour nor gain, got in dealing with a vil-lain.

> The fool hath made a vow, I guess,
> Never to let the Fire have peace.

Snowy winter, a plentiful harvest.

Nothing more like a Fool, than a drunken Man.

> God works wonders now & then;
> Behold! a Lawyer, an honest Man!

He that lives carnally, won't live eternally.

Innocence is its own Defence.

> Time *eateth* all things, could old Poets say;
> The Times are chang'd, our times *drink* all away.

Never mind it, she'l be sober after the Holidays.

Poor Richard, 1734

Courteous Readers,

Your kind and charitable Assistance last Year, in purchasing so large an Impression of my Almanacks, has made my Circumstances much more easy in the World, and requires my grateful Acknowledgment. My Wife has been enabled to get a Pot of her own, and is no longer oblig'd to borrow one from a Neighbour; nor have we ever since been without something of our own to put in it. She has also got a pair of Shoes, two new Shifts, and a new warm Petticoat; and for my part, I have bought a second-hand Coat, so good, that I am now not asham'd to go to Town or be seen there. These Things have render'd her Temper so much more pacifick than it us'd to be, that I may say, I have slept more, and more quietly within this last Year, than in the three foregoing Years put together. Accept my hearty Thanks therefor, and my sincere Wishes for your Health and Prosperity.

In the Preface to my last Almanack, I foretold the Death of my dear old Friend and Fellow-Student, the learned and ingenious Mr. *Titan Leeds*, which was to be on the 17th of *October*, 1733, 3 h. 29 m. *P. M.* at the very Instant of the ☌ of ☉ and ☿. By his own Calculation he was to survive till the 26th of the same Month, and expire in the Time of the Eclipse, near 11 a clock, *A. M.* At which of these Times he died, or whether he be really yet dead, I cannot at this present Writing positively assure my Readers; forasmuch as a Disorder in my own Family demanded my Presence, and would not permit me as I had intended, to be with him in his last Moments, to receive his last Embrace, to close his Eyes, and do the Duty of a Friend in performing the last Offices to the Departed. Therefore it is that I cannot positively affirm whether he be dead or not; for the Stars only show to the Skilful, what will happen in the natural and universal Chain of Causes and Effects; but 'tis well known, that the Events which would otherwise certainly happen at certain Times in the Course of Nature, are sometimes set aside or postpon'd for wise and good Reasons, by the immediate particular Dispositions of Providence; which particular Dispositions the Stars can by no Means discover or foreshow. There is however, (and I cannot speak it without Sorrow) there is the strongest Probability that my dear Friend is *no more*; for there appears in his Name, as I am assured, an Almanack for the Year 1734, in which I am treated in a very gross and unhandsome Manner; in which I am called *a false Predicter, an Ignorant, a conceited Scribler, a Fool, and a Lyar*. Mr. *Leeds* was too well bred to use any Man so indecently and so scurrilously, and moreover his Esteem and Affection for me was extraordinary: So that it is to be feared, that Pamphlet may be only a Contrivance of somebody or other, who hopes perhaps to sell two or three Year's Almanacks still, by the sole Force and Virtue of Mr. *Leeds*'s Name; but certainly, to put Words into the Mouth of a Gentleman and a Man of Letters, against his Friend, which the meanest and most scandalous of the People might be asham'd to utter even in a drunken Quarrel, is an unpardonable Injury to his Memory, and an Imposition upon the Publick.

Mr. *Leeds* was not only profoundly skilful in the useful Science he profess'd, but he was a Man of *exemplary Sobriety*, a most *sincere Friend*, and an *exact Performer of his Word*. These valuable Qualifications, with many others, so much endear'd him to me, that although it should be so, that, contrary to all Probability, contrary to my Prediction and his own, he might possibly be yet alive, yet my Loss of Honour as a Prognosticator, cannot afford me so much Mortification, as his Life, Health and Safety would give me Joy and Satisfaction. I am,
Courteous and kind Reader,
Your poor Friend and Servant,
Octob. 30. 1733.   *R. SAUNDERS.*

————

Would you live with ease,
Do what you ought, and not what you please.

Principiis obsta.

Better slip with foot than tongue.

You cannot pluck roses without fear of thorns,
Nor enjoy a fair wife without danger of horns.

Without justice, courage is weak.

Many dishes many diseases,
Many medicines few cures.

Where carcasses are, eagles will gather,
And where good laws are, much people flock thither.

Hot things, sharp things, sweet things, cold things
All rot the teeth, and make them look like old things.

Blame-all and *Praise-all* are two blockheads.

Be temperate in wine, in eating, girls, & sloth;
Or the Gout will seize you and plague you both.

No man e'er was glorious, who was not laborious.

What pains our Justice takes his faults to hide,
With half that pains sure he might cure 'em quite.

In success be moderate.

Take this remark from *Richard* poor and lame,
Whate'er's begun in anger ends in shame.

What one relishes, nourishes.

Fools multiply folly.

Beauty & folly are old companions.

Hope of gain
Lessens pain.

All things are easy to Industry,
All things difficult to *Sloth*.

If you ride a Horse, sit close and tight,
If you ride a Man, sit easy and light.

A new truth is a truth, an old error is an error,
Tho' *Clodpate* wont allow either.

Don't think to hunt two hares with one dog.

Astrologers say,
This is a good Day,
To make Love in May.

Who pleasure gives,
Shall joy receive.

Be not sick too late, nor well too soon.

Where there's Marriage without Love, there will be Love without Marriage.

Lawyers, Preachers, and Tomtits Eggs, there are more of them hatch'd than come to perfection.

Be neither silly, nor cunning, but wise.

Neither a Fortress nor a Maidenhead will hold out long after they begin to parly.

Jack *Little* sow'd little, & little he'll reap.

All things are cheap to the saving, dear to the wasteful.

Would you persuade, speak of Interest, not of Reason.

> Some men grow mad by studying much to know,
> But who grows mad by studying good to grow.

Happy's the Woing, that's not long a doing.

Don't value a man for the Quality he is of, but for the Qualities he possesses.

Bucephalus the Horse of *Alexand.* hath as lasting fame as his Master.

> Rain or Snow,
> To *Chili* go,
> You'll find it so,
> For ought we know.
> Time will show.

There have been as great Souls unknown to fame as any of the most famous.

Do good to thy Friend to keep him, to thy enemy to gain him.

A good Man is seldom uneasy, an ill one never easie.

Teach your child to hold his tongue, he'l learn fast enough to speak.

He that cannot obey, cannot command.

An innocent *Plowman* is more worthy than a vicious *Prince*.

Sam's Religion is like a *Chedder Cheese*, 'tis made of the *milk* of one & twenty Parishes.

> Grief for a dead Wife, & a troublesome Guest,
> Continues to the *threshold*, and there is at rest;
> But I mean such wives as are none of the best.

As Charms are nonsense, Nonsense is a Charm.

An Egg to day is better than a Hen to-morrow.

Drink Water, Put the Money in your Pocket, and leave the *Dry-bellyach* in the *Punchbowl*.

He that is rich need not live sparingly, and he that can live sparingly need not be rich.

If you wou'd be reveng'd of your enemy, govern your self.

A wicked Hero will turn his back to an innocent coward.

> *Laws* like to *Cobwebs* catch small Flies,
> Great ones break thro' before your eyes.

Strange, that he who lives by Shifts, can seldom shift himself.

As sore places meet most rubs, proud folks meet most affronts.

The magistrate should obey the Laws, the People should obey the magistrate.

When 'tis fair be sure take your Great coat with you.

He does not possess Wealth, it possesses him.

Necessity has no Law; I know some Attorneys of the name.

Onions can make ev'n Heirs and Widows weep.

Avarice and Happiness never saw each other, how then shou'd they become acquainted.

> The thrifty maxim of the wary *Dutch*,
> Is to save all the Money they can touch.

He that waits upon Fortune, is never sure of a Dinner.

A learned blockhead is a greater blockhead than an ignorant one.

Marry your Son when you will, but your Daughter when you can.

———

By Mrs. *Bridget Saunders*, my Dutchess, in Answer to the *December* Verses of last Year.

He that for sake of Drink neglects his Trade,
And spends each Night in Taverns till 'tis late,
And rises when the Sun is four hours high,
And ne'er regards his starving Family;
God in his Mercy may do much to save him.
But, woe to the poor Wife, whose Lot it is to have him.

———

He that knows nothing of it, may by chance be a Prophet; while the wisest that is may happen to miss.

If you wou'd have Guests merry with your cheer,
Be so your self, or so at least appear.

Famine, Plague, War, and an unnumber'd throng
Of Guilt-avenging Ills, to Man belong;
Is't not enough Plagues, Wars, and Famines rise
To lash our crimes, but must our Wives be wise?

Reader, farewel, all Happiness attend thee:
May each *New-Year* better and richer find thee.

Poor Richard, 1735

Courteous Reader,

This is the third Time of my appearing in print, hitherto very much to my own Satisfaction, and, I have reason to hope, to the Satisfaction of the Publick also; for the Publick is generous, and has been very charitable and good to me. I should be ungrateful then, if I did not take every Opportunity of expressing my Gratitude; for *ingratum si dixeris, omnia dixeris*: I therefore return the Publick my most humble and hearty Thanks.

Whatever may be the Musick of the Spheres, how great soever the Harmony of the Stars, 'tis certain there is no Harmony among the Stargazers; but they are perpetually growling and snarling at one another like strange Curs, or like some Men at their Wives: I had resolved to keep the Peace on my own part, and affront none of them; and I shall persist in that Resolution: But having receiv'd much Abuse from *Titan Leeds* deceas'd, (*Titan Leeds* when living would not have us'd me so!) I say, having receiv'd much Abuse from the Ghost of *Titan Leeds*, who pretends to be still living, and to write Almanacks in spight of me and my Predictions, I cannot help saying, that tho' I take it patiently, I take it very unkindly. And whatever he may pretend, 'tis undoubtedly true that he is really defunct and dead. First because the Stars are seldom disappointed, never but in the Case of wise Men, *Sapiens dominabitur astris*, and they foreshow'd his Death at the Time I predicted it. Secondly, 'Twas requisite and necessary he should die punctually at that Time, for the Honour of Astrology, the Art professed both by him and his Father before him. Thirdly, 'Tis plain to every one that reads his two last Almanacks (for 1734 and 35) that they are not written with that *Life* his Performances use to be written with; the Wit is low and flat, the little Hints dull and spiritless, nothing smart in them but *Hudibras*'s Verses against Astrology at the Heads of the Months in the last, which no Astrologer but a *dead one* would have inserted, and no Man *living* would or could write such Stuff as the rest. But lastly, I shall convince him from his own Words, that he is dead, (*ex ore suo condemnatus est*) for in his Preface to his Almanack for 1734, he says, *"Saunders adds another* GROSS FALSHOOD *in his Almanack,* viz. *that by my own Calculation I shall* survive *until the* 26th *of the said Month October* 1733, *which is as* untrue *as the former."* Now if it be, as *Leeds* says, *untrue* and a *gross Falshood* that he surviv'd till the 26th of October 1733, then it is certainly *true* that he died *before* that Time: And if he died before that Time, he is dead now, to all Intents and Purposes, any thing he may say to the contrary notwithstanding. And at what Time before the 26th is it so likely he should die, as at the Time by me predicted, *viz.* the 17th of October aforesaid? But if some People will walk and be troublesome after Death, it may perhaps be born with a little, because it cannot well be avoided unless one would be at the Pains and Expence of laying them in the *Red Sea*; however, they should not presume too much upon the Liberty allow'd them; I know Confinement must needs be mighty irksome to the free Spirit of an Astronomer, and I am too compassionate to proceed suddenly to Extremities with it; nevertheless, tho' I resolve with Reluctance, I shall not long defer, if it does not speedily learn to treat its living Friends with better Manners. I am,

Courteous Reader,
Your obliged Friend and Servant,

Octob. 30. 1734.   R. SAUNDERS.

————

Look before, or you'll find yourself behind.

> Bad Commentators spoil the best of books,
> So God sends meat (they say) the devil Cooks.

Approve not of him who commends all you say.

By diligence and patience, the mouse bit in two the cable.

Full of courtesie, full of craft.

A little House well fill'd, a little Field well till'd, and a little Wife well will'd, are great Riches.

Old Maids lead Apes there, where the old Batchelors are turn'd to Apes.

Some are weatherwise, some are otherwise.

Dyrro lynn y ddoeth e fydd ddoethach.

The poor man must walk to get meat for his stomach, the rich man to get a stomach to his meat.

He that goes far to marry, will either deceive or be deceived.

> Eyes and Priests
> Bear no Jests.

The Family of Fools is ancient.

Necessity never made a good bargain.

If Pride leads the Van, Beggary brings up the Rear.

There's many witty men whose brains can't fill their bellies.

Weighty Questions ask for deliberate Answers.

> When ♂ and ♀ in ♂ lie,
> Then, Maids, whate'er is ask'd of you, deny.

Be slow in chusing a Friend, slower in changing.

> Old *Hob* was lately married in the Night,
> What needed Day, his fair young Wife is light.

Pain wastes the Body, Pleasures the Understanding.

The cunning man steals a horse, the wise man lets him alone.

> Nothing but Money,
> Is sweeter than Honey.

Humility makes great men twice honourable.

> A Ship under sail and a big-bellied Woman,
> Are the handsomest two things that can be seen common.

Keep thy shop, & thy shop will keep thee.

The King's cheese is half wasted in parings: But no matter, 'tis made of the peoples milk.

> What's given shines,
> What's receiv'd is rusty.

Sloth and Silence are a Fool's Virtues.

> Of learned Fools I have seen ten times ten,
> Of unlearned wise men I have seen a hundred.

Three may keep a Secret, if two of them are dead.

Poverty wants some things, Luxury many things, Avarice all things.

A Lie stands on 1 leg, Truth on 2.

There's small Revenge in Words, but Words may be greatly revenged.

Great wits jump (says the Poet) and hit his Head against the Post.

A man is never so ridiculous by those Qualities that are his own as by those that he affects to have.

Deny Self for Self's sake.

> *Tim* moderate fare and abstinence much prizes,
> In publick, but in private gormandizes.

Ever since Follies have pleas'd, Fools have been able to divert.

It is better to take many Injuries than to give one.

Opportunity is the great Bawd.

Early to bed and early to rise, makes a man healthy wealthy and wise.

To be humble to Superiors is Duty, to Equals Courtesy, to Inferiors Nobleness.

Here comes the Orator! with his Flood of Words, and his Drop of Reason.

An old young man, will be a young old man.

Sal laughs at every thing you say. Why? Because she has fine Teeth.

> If what most men admire, they would despise,
> 'Twould look as if mankind were growing wise.

The Sun never repents of the good he does, nor does he ever demand a recompence.

Are you angry that others disappoint you? remember you cannot depend upon yourself.

One Mend-fault is worth two Findfaults, but one Findfault is better than two Makefaults.

> *Reader*, I wish thee Health, Wealth, Happiness,
> And may kind Heaven thy Year's Industry bless.

Poor Richard, 1736

Loving Readers,

Your kind Acceptance of my former Labours, has encouraged me to continue writing, tho' the general Approbation you have been so good as to favour me with, has excited the Envy of some, and drawn upon me the Malice of others. These Ill-willers of mine, despited at the great Reputation I gain'd by exactly predicting another Man's Death, have endeavour'd to deprive me of it all at once in the most effectual Manner, by reporting that I my self was never alive. They say in short, *That there is no such a Man as I am*; and have spread this Notion so thoroughly in the Country, that I have been frequently told it to my Face by those that don't know me. This is not civil Treatment, to endeavour to deprive me of my very Being, and reduce me to a Non-entity in the Opinion of the publick. But so long as I know my self to walk about, eat, drink and sleep, I am satisfied that *there is really such a Man as I am*, whatever they may say to the contrary: And the World may be satisfied likewise; for if there were no such Man as I am, how is it possible I should appear publickly to hundreds of People, as I have done for several Years past, in print? I need not, indeed, have taken any Notice of so idle a Report, if it had not been for the sake of my Printer, to whom my Enemies are pleased to ascribe my Productions; and who it seems is as unwilling to father my Offspring, as I am to lose the Credit of it: Therefore to clear him entirely, as well as to vindicate my own Honour, I make this publick and serious Declaration, which I desire may be believed, to wit, *That what I have written heretofore, and do now write, neither was nor is written by any other Man or Men, Person or Persons whatsoever.* Those who are not satisfied with this, must needs be very unreasonable.

My Performance for this Year follows; it submits itself, kind Reader, to thy Censure, but hopes for thy Candor, to forgive its Faults. It devotes itself entirely to thy Service, and will serve thee faithfully: And if it has the good Fortune to please its Master, 'tis Gratification enough for the Labour of

Poor

R. SAUNDERS.

He is no clown that drives the plow, but he that doth clownish things.

If you know how to spend less than you get, you have the Philosophers-Stone.

The good Paymaster is Lord of another man's Purse.

Fish & Visitors stink in 3 days.

He that has neither fools, whores nor beggars among his kindred, is the son of a thunder-gust.

Diligence is the Mother of Good-Luck.

He that lives upon Hope, dies farting.

Do not do that which you would not have known.

Never praise your Cyder, Horse, or Bedfellow.

Wealth is not his that has it, but his that enjoys it.

Tis easy to see, hard to foresee.

In a discreet man's mouth, a publick thing is private.

Let thy maidservant be faithful, strong, and homely.

Keep flax from fire, youth from gaming.

Bargaining has neither friends nor relations.

Admiration is the Daughter of Ignorance.

There's more old Drunkards than old Doctors.

She that paints her Face, thinks of her Tail.

Here comes Courage! that seiz'd the lion absent, and run away from the present mouse.

He that takes a wife, takes care.

Nor Eye in a letter, nor Hand in a purse, nor Ear in the secret of another.

He that buys by the penny, maintains not only himself, but other people.

He that can have Patience, can have what he will.

Now I've a sheep and a cow, every body bids me good morrow.

God helps them that help themselves.

Why does the blind man's wife paint herself.

None preaches better than the ant, and she says nothing.

The absent are never without fault, nor the present without excuse.

Gifts burst rocks.

> If wind blows on you thro' a hole,
> Make your will and take care of your soul.

The rotten Apple spoils his Companion.

He that sells upon trust, loses many friends, and always wants money.

Don't throw stones at your neighbours, if your own windows are glass.

The excellency of hogs is fatness, of men virtue.

Good wives and good plantations are made by good husbands.

Pox take you, is no curse to some people.

Force shites upon Reason's Back.

Lovers, Travellers, and Poets, will give money to be heard.

He that speaks much, is much mistaken.

Creditors have better memories than debtors.

Forwarn'd, forearm'd, unless in the case of Cuckolds, who are often forearm'd before warn'd.

Three things are men most liable to be cheated in, a Horse, a Wig, and a Wife.

He that lives well, is learned enough.

Poverty, Poetry, and new Titles of Honour, make Men ridiculous.

He that scatters Thorns, let him not go barefoot.

There's none deceived but he that trusts.

God heals, and the Doctor takes the Fees.

If you desire many things, many things will seem but a few.

Mary's mouth costs her nothing, for she never opens it but at others expence.

Receive before you write, but write before you pay.

I saw few die of Hunger, of Eating 100000.

Maids of *America*, who gave you bad teeth?
Answ. Hot Soupings & frozen Apples.

Marry your Daughter and eat fresh Fish betimes.

If God blesses a Man, his Bitch brings forth Pigs.

>   He that would live in peace & at ease,
>   Must not speak all he knows, nor judge all he sees.

Poor Richard, 1737

Courteous and kind Reader,

This is the fifth Time I have appear'd in Publick, chalking out the future Year for my honest Countrymen, and foretelling what shall, and what may, and what may not come to pass; in which I have the Pleasure to find that I have given general Satisfaction. Indeed, among the Multitude of our astrological Predictions, 'tis no wonder if some few fail; for, without any Defect in the Art itself, 'tis well known that a small Error, a single wrong Figure overseen in a Calculation, may occasion great Mistakes: But however we Almanack-makers may *miss it* in other Things, I believe it will be generally allow'd *That we always hit the Day of the Month*, and that I suppose is esteem'd one of the most useful Things in an Almanack.

As to the Weather, if I were to fall into the Method my Brother J——n sometimes uses, and tell you, *Snow here or in New England,*—*Rain here or in South-Carolina,*—*Cold to the Northward,*—*Warm to the Southward,* and the like, whatever Errors I might commit, I should be something more secure of not being detected in them: But I consider, it will be of no Service to any body to know what Weather it is 1000 miles off, and therefore I always set down positively what Weather my Reader will have, be he where he will at the time. We modestly desire only the favourable Allowance of *a day or two before* and *a day or two after* the precise Day against which the Weather is set; and if it does not come to pass accordingly, let the Fault be laid upon the Printer, who, 'tis very like, may have transpos'd or misplac'd it, perhaps for the Conveniency of putting in his Holidays: And since, in spight of all I can say, People will give him great part of the Credit of making my Almanacks, 'tis but reasonable he should take some share of the Blame.

I must not omit here to thank the Publick for the gracious and kind Encouragement they have hitherto given me: But if the generous Purchaser of my Labours could see how often his *Fi'-pence* helps to light up the comfortable Fire, line the Pot, fill the Cup and make glad the Heart of a poor Man and an honest good old Woman, he would not think his Money ill laid out, tho' the Almanack of his

Friend and Servant   R. SAUNDERS

were one half blank Paper.

————

HINTS for those that would be Rich.

The Use of Money is all the Advantage there is in having Money.

For 6 *l.* a Year, you may have the Use of 100 *l.* if you are a Man of known Prudence and Honesty.

He that spends a Groat a day idly, spends idly above 6 *l.* a year, which is the Price of using 100 *l.*

He that wastes idly a Groat's worth of his Time per Day, one Day with another, wastes the Privilege of using 100 *l.* each Day.

He that idly loses 5 *s.* worth of time, loses 5 *s.* & might as prudently throw 5 *s.* in the River.

He that loses 5 *s.* not only loses that Sum, but all the Advantage that might be made by turning it in Dealing, which by the time that a young Man becomes old, amounts to a comfortable Bag of Mony.

Again, He that sells upon Credit, asks a Price for what he sells, equivalent to the Principal and Interest of his Money for the Time he is like to be kept out of it: therefore

He that buys upon Credit, pays Interest for what he buys.

And he that pays ready Money, might let that Money out to Use: so that

He that possesses any Thing he has bought, pays Interest for the Use of it.

Consider then, when you are tempted to buy any unnecessary Housholdstuff, or any superfluous thing, whether you will be willing to pay *Interest, and Interest upon Interest* for it as long as you live; and more if it grows worse by using.

Yet, in buying Goods, 'tis best to pay ready Money, because,

He that sells upon Credit, expects to lose 5 *per Cent.* by bad Debts; therefore he charges, on all he sells upon Credit, an Advance that shall make up that Deficiency.

Those who pay for what they buy upon Credit, pay their Share of this Advance.

He that pays ready Money, escapes or may escape that Charge.

A Penny sav'd is Twopence clear, A Pin a day is a Groat a Year. Save & have. Every little makes a mickle.

———

The greatest monarch on the proudest throne, is oblig'd to sit upon his own arse.

The Master-piece of Man, is to live to the purpose.

He that steals the old man's supper, do's him no wrong.

A countryman between 2 Lawyers, is like a fish between two cats.

He that can take rest is greater than he that can take cities.

The misers cheese is wholesomest.

Felix quem, *&c.*

Love & lordship hate companions.

The nearest way to come at glory, is to do that for conscience which we do for glory.

There is much money given to be laught at, though the purchasers don't know it; witness *A*'s fine horse, & *B*'s fine house.

He that can compose himself, is wiser than he that composes books.

Poor Dick, eats like a well man, and drinks like a sick.

After crosses and losses men grow humbler & wiser.

Love, Cough, & a Smoke, can't well be hid.

Well done is better than well said.

> Fine linnen, girls and gold so bright,
> Chuse not to take by candle-light.

He that can travel well afoot, keeps a good horse.

There are no ugly Loves, nor handsome Prisons.

No better relation than a prudent & faithful Friend.

A Traveller should have a hog's nose, deer's legs, and an ass's back.

At the working man's house hunger looks in but dares not enter.

A good Lawyer a bad Neighbour.

> Certainlie these things agree,
> The Priest, the Lawyer, & Death all three:
> Death takes both the weak and the strong.
> The lawyer takes from both right and wrong,
> And the priest from living and dead has his Fee.

The worst wheel of the cart makes the most noise.

Don't misinform your Doctor nor your Lawyer.

> I never saw an oft-transplanted tree,
> Nor yet an oft-removed family,
> That throve so well as those that settled be.

Let the Letter stay for the Post, and not the Post for the Letter.

Three good meals a day is bad living.

Tis better leave for an enemy at one's death, than beg of a friend in one's life.

> To whom thy secret thou dost tell,
> To him thy freedom thou dost sell.

If you'd have a Servant that you like, serve your self.

He that pursues two Hares at once, does not catch one and lets t'other go.

If you want a neat wife, chuse her on a Saturday.

If you have time dont wait for time.

Tell a miser he's rich, and a woman she's old, you'll get no money of one, nor kindness of t'other.

Don't go to the doctor with every distemper, nor to the lawyer with every quarrel, nor to the pot for every thirst.

The Creditors are a superstitious sect, great observers of set days and times.

The noblest question in the world is *What Good may I do in it?*

Nec sibi, sed toto, genitum se credere mundo.

Nothing so popular as GOODNESS.

Poor Richard, 1738

PREFACE by Mistress SAUNDERS

Dear Readers,

My good Man set out last Week for *Potowmack,* to visit an old Stargazer of his Acquaintance, and see about a little Place for us to settle and end our Days on. He left the Copy of his Almanack seal'd up, and bid me send it to the Press. I suspected something, and therefore as soon as he was gone, I open'd it, to see if he had not been flinging some of his old Skitts at me. Just as I thought, so it was. And truly, (for want of somewhat else to say, I suppose) he had put into his Preface, that his Wife *Bridget*—was this, and that, and t'other.— What a peasecods! cannot I have a little Fault or two, but all the Country must see it in print! They have already been told, at one time that I am proud, another time that I am loud, and that I have got a new Petticoat, and abundance of such kind of stuff; and now, forsooth! all the World must know, that *Poor Dick's* Wife has lately taken a fancy to drink a little Tea now and then. A mighty matter, truly, to make a Song of! 'Tis true; I had a little Tea of a Present from the Printer last Year; and what, must a body throw it away? In short, I thought the Preface was not worth a printing, and so I fairly scratch'd it all out, and I believe you'll like our Almanack never the worse for it.

Upon looking over the Months, I see he has put in abundance of foul Weather this Year; and therefore I have scatter'd here and there, where I could find room, some *fair, pleasant, sunshiny,* &c. for the Good-Women to dry their Clothes in. If it does not come to pass according to my Desire, I have shown my Good-will, however; and I hope they'll take it in good part.

I had a Design to make some other Corrections; and particularly to change some of the Verses that I don't very well like; but I have just now unluckily broke my Spectacles; which obliges me to give it you as it is, and conclude

Your loving Friend,
BRIDGET SAUNDERS.

———

There are three faithful friends, an old wife, an old dog, and ready money.

Great talkers should be cropt, for they've no need of ears.

If you'd have your shoes last, put no nails in 'em.

Who has deceiv'd thee so oft as thy self?

Is there any thing Men take more pains about than to render themselves unhappy?

Nothing brings more pain than too much pleasure; nothing more bondage than too much liberty, (or libertinism.)

Read much, but not many Books.

He that would have a short Lent, let him borrow Money to be repaid at Easter.

Write with the learned, pronounce with the vulgar.

Fly Pleasures, and they'll follow you.

Squirrel-like she covers her back with her tail.

Cæsar did not merit the triumphal Car, more than he that conquers himself.

Hast thou virtue? acquire also the graces & beauties of virtue.

Buy what thou hast no need of; and e'er long thou shalt sell thy necessaries.

If thou hast wit & learning, add to it Wisdom and Modesty.

You may be more happy than Princes, if you will be more virtuous.

> If you wou'd not be forgotten
> As soon as you are dead and rotten,
> Either write things worth reading,
> or do things worth the writing.

Sell not virtue to purchase wealth, nor Liberty to purchase power.

God bless the King, and grant him long to Reign.

Let thy vices die before thee.

Keep your eyes wide open before marriage, half shut afterwards.

The ancients tell us what is best; but we must learn of the moderns what is fittest.

Since I cannot govern my own tongue, tho' within my own teeth, how can I hope to govern the tongues of others?

'Tis less discredit to abridge petty charges, than to stoop to petty Gettings.

Since thou art not sure of a minute, throw not away an hour.

If you do what you should not, you must hear what you would not.

Defer not thy well-doing; be not like St. *George*, who is always a horseback, and never rides on.

Wish not so much to live long as to live well.

As we must account for every idle word, so we must for every idle silence.

I have never seen the Philosopher's Stone that turns lead into Gold, but I have known the pursuit of it turn a Man's Gold into Lead.

Never intreat a servant to dwell with thee.

Time is an herb that cures all Diseases.

Reading makes a full Man, Meditation a profound Man, discourse a clear Man.

If any man flatters me, I'll flatter him again; tho' he were my best Friend.

Wish a miser long life, and you wish him no good.

None but the well-bred man knows how to confess a fault, or acknowledge himself in an error.

Drive thy business; let not that drive thee.

There is much difference between imitating a good man, and counterfeiting him.

Wink at small faults; remember thou hast great ones.

Eat to please thyself, but dress to please others.

Search others for their virtues, thy self for thy vices.

Never spare the Parson's wine, nor Baker's Pudding.

> Each year one vicious habit rooted out,
> In time might make the worst Man good throughout.

Poor Richard, 1739

Kind Reader,

Encouraged by thy former Generosity, I once more present thee with an Almanack, which is the 7th of my Publication.— While thou art putting Pence in my Pocket, and furnishing my Cottage with Necessaries, *Poor Dick* is not unmindful to do something for thy Benefit. The Stars are watch'd as narrowly as old *Bess* watch'd her Daughter, that thou mayst be acquainted with their Motions, and told a Tale of their Influences and Effects, which may do thee more good than a Dream of last Year's Snow.

Ignorant Men wonder how we Astrologers foretell the Weather so exactly, unless we deal with the old black Devil. Alas! 'tis as easy as pissing abed. For Instance; The Stargazer peeps at the Heavens thro' a long Glass: He sees perhaps *TAURUS*, or the great Bull, in a mighty Chase, stamping on the Floor of his House, swinging his Tail about, stretching out his Neck, and opening wide his Mouth. 'Tis natural from these Appearances to judge that this furious Bull is puffing, blowing, and roaring. Distance being consider'd, and Time allow'd for all this to come down, there you have Wind and Thunder. He spies perhaps *VIRGO* (or the Virgin;) she turns her Head round as it were to see if any body observ'd her; then crouching down gently, with her Hands on her Knees, she looks wistfully for a while right forward. He judges rightly what she's about: And having calculated the Distance and allow'd Time for it's Falling, finds that next Spring we shall have a fine *April* shower. What can be more natural and easy than this? I might instance the like in many other particulars; but this may be sufficient to prevent our being taken for Conjurers. O the wonderful Knowledge to be found in the Stars! Even the smallest Things are written there, if you had but Skill to read. When my Brother *J—m-n* erected a Scheme to know which was best for his sick Horse, to sup a new-laid Egg, or a little Broth, he found that the Stars plainly gave their Verdict for Broth, and the Horse having sup'd his Broth;—Now, what do you think became of that Horse? You shall know in my next.

Besides the usual Things expected in an Almanack, I hope the profess'd Teachers of Mankind will excuse my scattering here and there some instructive Hints in Matters of Morality and Religion. And be not thou disturbed, O grave and sober Reader, if among the many serious Sentences in my Book, thou findest me trifling now and then, and talking idly. In all the Dishes I have hitherto cook'd for thee, there is solid Meat enough for thy Money. There are Scraps from the Table of Wisdom, that will if well digested, yield strong Nourishment to thy Mind. But squeamish Stomachs cannot eat without Pickles; which, 'tis true are good for nothing else, but they provoke an Appetite. The Vain Youth that reads my Almanack for the sake of an idle Joke, will perhaps meet with a serious Reflection, that he may ever after be the better for.

Some People observing the great Yearly Demand for my Almanack, imagine I must by this Time have become rich, and consequently ought to call myself *Poor Dick* no longer. But, the Case is this, When I first begun to publish, the Printer made a fair Agreement with me for my Copies, by Virtue of which he runs away with the greatest Part of the Profit.—However, much good may't do him; I do not grudge it him; he is a Man I have a great Regard for, and I wish his Profit ten times greater than it is. For I am, dear Reader, his, as well as thy   *Affectionate Friend,*

R. SAUNDERS.

———

When Death puts out our Flame, the Snuff will tell,
If we were Wax, or Tallow by the Smell.

At a great Pennyworth, pause a while.

As to his Wife, *John* minds St. *Paul*, He's one
That hath a Wife, and is as if he'd none.

Kings and Bears often worry their Keepers.

If thou wouldst live long, live well; for Folly and Wickedness shorten Life.

> Prythee isn't Miss *Cloe's* a comical Case?
> She lends out her Tail, and she borrows her Face.

Trust thy self, and another shall not betray thee.

He that pays for Work before it's done, has but a pennyworth for twopence.

Historians relate, not so much what is done, as what they would have believed.

> O Maltster! break that cheating Peck; 'tis plain,
> When e'er you use it, you're a Knave in Grain.

> Doll learning *propria quæ maribus* without book,
> Like *Nomen crescentis genitivo* doth look.

Grace thou thy House, and let not that grace thee.

Thou canst not joke an Enemy into a Friend; but thou may'st a Friend into an Enemy.

> Eyes & Priests
> Bear no Jests.

He that falls in love with himself, will have no Rivals.

Let thy Child's first Lesson be Obedience, and the second may be what thou wilt.

Blessed is he that expects nothing, for he shall never be disappointed.

Rather go to bed supperless, than run in debt for a Breakfast.

Let thy Discontents be Secrets.

An infallible Remedy for the *Tooth-ach*, viz Wash the Root of an aching Tooth, in *Elder Vinegar*, and let it dry half an hour in the Sun; after which it will never ach more; *Probatum est*.

> A Man of Knowledge like a rich Soil, feeds
> If not a world of Corn, a world of Weeds.

A modern Wit is one of *David's* Fools.

No Resolution of Repenting hereafter, can be sincere.

> *Pollio*, who values nothing that's within,
> Buys Books as men hunt Beavers,—for their Skin.

Honour thy Father and Mother, *i. e.* Live so as to be an Honour to them tho' they are dead.

If thou injurest Conscience, it will have its Revenge on thee.

Hear no ill of a Friend, nor speak any of an Enemy.

Pay what you owe, and you'll know what's your own.

Be not niggardly of what costs thee nothing, as courtesy, counsel, & countenance.

Thirst after Desert, not Reward.

Beware of him that is slow to anger: He is angry for something, and will not be pleased for nothing.

No longer virtuous no longer free; is a Maxim as true with regard to a private Person as a Common-wealth.

> When Man and Woman die, as Poets sung,
> His Heart's the last part moves, her last, the tongue.

Proclaim not all thou knowest, all thou owest, all thou hast, nor all thou canst.

Let our Fathers and Grandfathers be valued for *their* Goodness, ourselves for our own.

Industry need not wish.

Sin is not hurtful because it is forbidden but it is forbidden because it's hurtful. Nor is a Duty beneficial because it is commanded, but it is commanded, because it's beneficial.

> *A* —, they say, has Wit; for what?
> For writing?—No; For writing not.

> *George* came to the Crown without striking a Blow.
> Ah! quoth the Pretender, would I could do so.

Love, and be lov'd.

O Lazy-Bones! Dost thou think God would have given thee Arms and Legs, if he had not design'd thou should'st use them.

A Cure for Poetry,
Seven wealthy Towns contend for *Homer*, dead,
Thro' which the living *Homer* beg'd his Bread.

Great Beauty, great strength, & great Riches, are really & truly of no great Use; a right Heart exceeds all.

Poor Richard, 1740

Courteous Reader,   OCTOBER 7. 1739.

You may remember that in my first Almanack, published for the Year 1733, I predicted the Death of my dear Friend *Titan Leeds*, Philomat. to happen that Year on the 17th Day of *October*, 3 h. 29 m. *P. M.* The good Man, it seems, died accordingly: But *W. B.* and *A. B.* have continued to publish Almanacks in his Name ever since; asserting for some Years that he was still living; At length when the Truth could no longer be conceal'd from the World, they confess his Death in their Almanack for 1739, but pretend that he died not till last Year, and that before his Departure he had furnished them with Calculations for 7 Years to come. Ah, *My Friends*, these are poor Shifts and thin Disguises; of which indeed I should have taken little or no Notice, if you had not at the same time accus'd me as a false Predictor; an Aspersion that the more affects me, as my whole Livelyhood depends on a contrary Character.

But to put this Matter beyond Dispute, I shall acquaint the World with a Fact, as strange and surprizing as it is true; being as follows, *viz.*

On the 4th Instant, towards midnight, as I sat in my little Study writing this Preface, I fell fast asleep; and continued in that Condition for some time, without dreaming any thing, to my Knowledge. On awaking, I found lying before me the following Letter, *viz*.

Dear Friend SAUNDERS,

My Respect for you continues even in this separate State, and I am griev'd to see the Aspersions thrown on you by the Malevolence of avaricious Publishers of Almanacks, who envy your Success. They say your Prediction of my Death in 1733 was false, and they pretend that I remained alive many Years after. But I do hereby certify, that I did actually die at that time, precisely at the Hour you mention'd, with a Variation only of 5 *min*. 53 *sec*. which must be allow'd to be no great matter in such Cases. And I do farther declare that I furnish'd them with no Calculations of the Planets Motions, *&c*. seven Years after my Death, as they are pleased to give out: so that the Stuff they publish as an Almanack in my Name is no more mine than 'tis yours.

You will wonder perhaps, how this Paper comes written on your Table. You must know that no separate Spirits are under any Confinement till after the final Settlement of all Accounts. In the mean time we wander where we please, visit our old Friends, observe their Actions, enter sometimes into their Imaginations, and give them Hints waking or sleeping that may be of Advantage to them. Finding you asleep, I entred your left Nostril, ascended into your Brain, found out where the Ends of those Nerves were fastned that move your right Hand and Fingers, by the Help of which I am now writing unknown to you; but when you open your Eyes, you will see that the Hand written is mine, tho' wrote with yours.

The People of this Infidel Age, perhaps, will hardly believe this Story. But you may give them these three Signs by which they shall be convinc'd of the Truth of it. About the middle of *June* next, *J. J——n*, Philomat, shall be openly reconciled to the *Church of Rome*, and give all his Goods and Chattles to the Chappel, being perverted by a certain *Country School-master*. On the 7*th* of *September* following my old Friend *W. B——t* shall be sober 9 Hours, to the Astonishment of all his Neighbours: And about the same time *W. B*. and *A. B*.

will publish another Almanack in my Name, in spight of Truth and Common-Sense.

As I can see much clearer into Futurity, since I got free from the dark Prison of Flesh, in which I was continually molested and almost blinded with Fogs arising from Tiff, and the Smoke of burnt Drams; I shall in kindness to you, frequently give you Informations of things to come, for the Improvement of your Almanack: Being Dear *Dick*,

Your affectionate Friend,   *T. Leeds.*

For my own part I am convinc'd that the above Letter is genuine. If the Reader doubts of it, let him carefully observe the three Signs; and if they do not actually come to pass, believe as he pleases.

I am his humble Friend,
R. SAUNDERS.

———

To bear other Peoples Afflictions, every one has Courage enough, and to spare.

No wonder *Tom* grows fat, th' unwieldy Sinner,
Makes his whole Life but one continual Dinner.

An empty Bag cannot stand upright.

Happy that nation, fortunate that age, whose history is not diverting.

What is a butterfly? At best
He's but a caterpiller drest.
The gaudy Fop's his picture just.

None are deceived but they that confide.

An open Foe may prove a curse;
But a pretended friend is worse.

A wolf eats sheep but now and then,
Ten Thousands are devour'd by Men.

Man's tongue is soft, and bone doth lack;
Yet a stroke therewith may break a man's back.

Many a Meal is lost for want of meat.

To all apparent Beauties blind
Each Blemish strikes an envious Mind.

The Poor have little, Beggars none;
the Rich too much, enough not one.

There are lazy Minds as well as lazy Bodies.

Tricks and Treachery are the Practice of Fools, that have not
   Wit enough to be honest.

Who says Jack is not generous? he is always fond of giving,
   and cares not for receiving. — What? Why; Advice.

The Man who with undaunted toils,
sails unknown seas to unknown soils,
With various wonders feasts his Sight:
What stranger wonders does he write?

Fear not Death; for the sooner we die, the longer shall we
   be immortal.

Those who in quarrels interpose,
Must often wipe a bloody nose.

Promises may get thee Friends, but Nonperformance will
   turn them into Enemies.

In other men we faults can spy,
And blame the mote that dims their eye;
Each little speck and blemish find;
To our own stronger errors blind.

When you speak to a man, look on his eyes; when he speaks
   to thee, look on his mouth.

Jane, why those tears? why droops your head?
Is then your other husband dead?
Or doth a worse disgrace betide?
Hath no one since his death apply'd?

Observe all men; thy self most.

Thou hadst better eat salt with the Philosophers of *Greece*,
   than sugar with the Courtiers of *Italy*.

Seek Virtue, and, of that possest,
To Providence, resign the rest.

Marry above thy match, and thou'lt get a Master.

Fear to do ill, and you need fear nought else.

He makes a Foe who makes a jest.

Can grave and formal pass for wise,
When Men the solemn Owl despise?

Some are justly laught at for keeping their Money foolishly,
others for spending it idly: He is the greatest fool that
lays it out in a purchase of repentance.

Who knows a fool, must know his brother;
For one will recommend another.

Avoid dishonest Gain: No price;
Can recompence the Pangs of Vice.

When befriended, remember it:
When you befriend, forget it.

Great souls with gen'rous pity melt;
Which coward tyrants never felt.

Employ thy time well, if thou meanest to gain leisure.

A Flatterer never seems absurd:
The Flatter'd always take his Word.

Lend Money to an Enemy, and thou'lt gain him, to a Friend
and thou'lt lose him.

Neither praise nor dispraise, till seven Christmasses be over.

Poor Richard, 1741

Enjoy the present hour, be mindful of the past;
And neither fear nor wish the Approaches of the last.

Learn of the skilful: He that teaches himself, hath a fool for
his master.

> Best is the Tongue that feels the rein; —
> He that talks much, must talk in vain;
> We from the wordy Torrent fly:
> Who listens to the chattering Pye?

Think *Cato* sees thee.

No Wood without Bark.

> *Monkeys* warm with envious spite,
> Their most obliging FRIENDS will bite; —
> And, fond to copy human Ways,
> Practise new Mischiefs all their days.

Joke went out, and brought home his fellow, and they two began a quarrel.

Let thy discontents be thy Secrets; — if the world knows them, 'twill despise *thee* and increase *them*.

> E'er you remark another's Sin,
> Bid your own Conscience look within.

Anger and Folly walk cheek-by-jole; Repentance treads on both their Heels.

Turn Turk *Tim*, and renounce thy Faith in Words as well as Actions: Is it worse to follow *Mahomet* than the Devil?

Don't overload Gratitude; if you do, she'll kick.

Be always asham'd to catch thy self idle.

> Where yet was ever found the Mother,
> Who'd change her booby for another?

At 20 years of age the Will reigns; at 30 the Wit; at 40 the Judgment.

Christianity commands us to pass by Injuries; Policy, to let them pass by us.

Lying rides upon Debt's back.

They who have nothing to be troubled at, will be troubled at nothing.

Wife from thy Spouse each blemish hide
More than from all the World beside:
Let DECENCY be all thy Pride.

Nick's Passions grow fat and hearty; his Understanding looks consumptive!

If evils come not, then our fears are vain:
And if they do, Fear but augments the pain.

If you would keep your Secret from an enemy, tell it not to a friend.

Rob not for burnt offerings.

Bess brags she 'as *Beauty*, and can prove the same;
As how? why thus, Sir, 'tis her *puppy's* name.

Up, Sluggard, and waste not life; in the grave will be sleeping enough.

Well done, is twice done.

Clearly spoken, Mr. Fog! You explain English by Greek.

Formio bewails his Sins with the same heart,
As Friends do Friends when they're about to part.
Believe it *Formio* will not entertain,
One chearful Thought till they do meet again.

Honours change Manners.

Jack eating rotten cheese, did say,
Like *Sampson* I my thousands slay;
I vow, quoth *Roger*, so you do,
And with the self-same weapon too.

There are no fools so troublesome as those that have wit.

Quarrels never could last long,
If on one side only lay the wrong.

Let no Pleasure tempt thee, no Profit allure thee, no Ambition corrupt thee, no Example sway thee, no Persuasion move thee, to do any thing which thou knowest to be Evil; So shalt thou always live jollily: for a good Conscience is a continual Christmass.

Poor Richard, 1742

Courteous READER,

This is the ninth Year of my Endeavours to serve thee in the Capacity of a Calendar-Writer. The Encouragement I have met with must be ascrib'd, in a great Measure, to your Charity, excited by the open honest Declaration I made of my Poverty at my first Appearance. This my Brother *Philomaths* could, without being Conjurers, discover; and *Poor Richard's* Success, has produced ye a *Poor Will*, and a *Poor Robin*; and no doubt *Poor John*, &c. will follow, and we shall all be *in Name* what some Folks say we are already *in Fact*, A Parcel of *poor Almanack Makers*. During the Course of these nine Years, what Buffetings have I not sustained! The Fraternity have been all in Arms. Honest *Titan*, deceas'd, was rais'd, and made to abuse his old Friend. Both Authors and Printers were angry. Hard Names, and many, were bestow'd on me. They deny'd me to be the Author of my own Works; declar'd there never was any such Person; asserted that I was dead 60 Years ago; prognosticated my Death to happen within a Twelvemonth: with many other malicious Inconsistences, the Effects of blind Passion, Envy at my Success; and a vain Hope of depriving me (dear Reader) of thy wonted Countenance and Favour.— *Who knows him?* they cry: *Where does he live?*—But what is that to them? If I delight in a private Life, have they any Right to drag me out of my Retirement? I have good Reasons for concealing the Place of my Abode. 'Tis time for an old Man, as I am, to think of preparing for his great Remove. The perpetual Teasing of both Neighbours and Strangers, to calculate Nativities, give Judgments on Schemes, erect Figures, discover Thieves, detect Horse-Stealers, describe the Route of Runaways and stray'd Cattle; The Croud of Visitors with a 1000 trifling Questions; *Will my Ship return safe? Will my Mare win the Race? Will her next Colt be a Pacer? When will my Wife die? Who shall be my Husband, and HOW LONG first?*

When is the best time to cut Hair, trim Cocks, or sow Sallad? These and the like Impertinences I have now neither Taste nor Leisure for. I have had enough of 'em. All that these angry Folks can say, will never provoke me to tell them where I live. I would eat my Nails first.

My last Adversary is *J. J——n*, Philomat. who *declares and protests* (in his Preface, 1741) that the *false Prophecy put in my Almanack, concerning him, the Year before, is altogether* false and untrue*: and that I am one of Baal's false Prophets.* This *false, false Prophecy* he speaks of, related to his Reconciliation with the Church of *Rome*; which, notwithstanding his Declaring and Protesting, is, I fear, too true. Two Things in his elegiac Verses confirm me in this Suspicion. He calls the First of *November* by the Name of *All Hallows Day.* Reader; does not this smell of Popery? Does it in the least savour of the pure Language of Friends? But the plainest Thing is; his Adoration of Saints, which he confesses to be his Practice, in these Words, page 4.

> *When any Trouble did me befal,*
> *To my dear* Mary *then I would call:*

Did he think the whole World were so stupid as not to take Notice of this? So ignorant as not to know, that all Catholicks pay the highest Regard to the *Virgin-Mary*? Ah! Friend *John*, We must allow you to be a Poet, but you are certainly no Protestant. I could heartily wish your Religion were as good as your Verses.

RICHARD SAUNDERS.

———

Strange! that a Man who has wit enough to write a Satyr; should have folly enough to publish it.

He that hath a Trade, hath an Estate.

Have you somewhat to do to-morrow; do it to-day.

> No workman without tools,
> Nor Lawyer without Fools,
> Can live by their Rules.

> The painful Preacher, like a candle bright,
> Consumes himself in giving others Light.

Speak and speed: the close mouth catches no flies.

Visit your Aunt, but not every Day; and call at your Brother's, but not every night.

Bis dat, qui cito dat.

Money and good Manners make the Gentleman.

Late Children, early Orphans.

> *Ben* beats his Pate, and fancys wit will come;
> But he may knock, there's no body at home.

The good Spinner hath a large Shift.

> *Tom*, vain's your Pains; They all will fail:
> Ne'er was good Arrow made of a Sow's Tail.

> Empty Free-booters, cover'd with Scorn:
> They went out for Wealth, & come ragged and torn,
> As the Ram went for Wool, and was sent back shorn.

Ill Customs & bad Advice are seldom forgotten.

He that sows thorns, should not go barefoot.

Reniego de grillos, aunque sean d'oro.

Men meet, mountains never.

When Knaves fall out, honest Men get their goods: When Priests dispute, we come at the Truth.

> *Kate* would have *Thomas*, no one blame her can:
> *Tom* won't have *Kate*, and who can blame the Man?

A large train makes a light Purse.

Death takes no bribes.

One good Husband is worth two good Wives; for the scarcer things are the more they're valued.

He that riseth late, must trot all day, and shall scarce overtake his business at night.

He that speaks ill of the Mare, will buy her.

You may drive a gift without a gimblet.

Eat few Suppers, and you'll need few Medicines.

> You will be careful, if you are wise;
> How you touch Men's Religion, or Credit, or Eyes.

> After Fish,
> Milk do not wish.

Heb Dduw heb ddim, a Duw a digon.

They who have nothing to trouble them, will be troubled at nothing.

> Against Diseases here, the strongest Fence,
> Is the defensive Virtue, Abstinence.

> Fient de chien, & marc d'argent,
> Seront tout un au jour du jugement.

> If thou dost ill, the joy fades, not the pains;
> If well, the pain doth fade, the joy remains.

To err is human, to repent divine, to persist devilish.

> Money & Man a mutual Friendship show:
> Man makes *false* Money, Money makes Man so.

Industry pays Debts, Despair encreases them.

> Bright as the day and as the morning fair,
> Such *Cloe* is, & common as the air.

Here comes *Glib-tongue*: who can out-flatter a Dedication; and lie, like ten Epitaphs.

Hope and a Red-Rag, are Baits for Men and Mackrel.

> With the old Almanack and the old Year,
> Leave thy old Vices, tho' ever so dear.

———

Rules of Health and long Life, and to preserve from Malignant Fevers, and Sickness in general.

Eat and drink such an exact Quantity as the Constitution of thy Body allows of, in reference to the Services of the Mind.

They that study much, ought not to eat so much as those that work hard, their Digestion being not so good.

The exact Quantity and Quality being found out, is to be kept to constantly.

Excess in all other Things whatever, as well as in Meat and Drink, is also to be avoided.

Youth, Age, and Sick require a different Quantity.

And so do those of contrary Complexions; for that which is too much for a flegmatick Man, is not sufficient for a Cholerick.

The Measure of Food ought to be (as much as possibly may be) exactly proportionable to the Quality and Condition of the Stomach, because the Stomach digests it.

That Quantity that is sufficient, the Stomach can perfectly concoct and digest, and it sufficeth the due Nourishment of the Body.

A greater Quantity of some things may be eaten than of others, some being of lighter Digestion than others.

The Difficulty lies, in finding out an exact Measure; but eat for Necessity, not Pleasure, for Lust knows not where Necessity ends.

Wouldst thou enjoy a long Life, a healthy Body, and a vigorous Mind, and be acquainted also with the wonderful Works of God? labour in the first place to bring thy Appetite into Subjection to Reason.

Rules to find out a fit Measure of Meat and Drink.

If thou eatest so much as makes thee unfit for Study, or other Business, thou exceedest the due Measure.

If thou art dull and heavy after Meat, it's a sign thou hast exceeded the due Measure; for Meat and Drink ought to refresh the Body, and make it chearful, and not to dull and oppress it.

If thou findest these ill Symptoms, consider whether too much Meat, or too much Drink occasions it, or both, and abate by little and little, till thou findest the Inconveniency removed.

Keep out of the Sight of Feasts and Banquets as much as may be; for 'tis more difficult to refrain good Cheer, when it's present, than from the Desire of it when it is away;

the like you may observe in the Objects of all the other Senses.

If a Man casually exceeds, let him fast the next Meal, and all may be well again, provided it be not too often done; as if he exceed at Dinner, let him refrain a Supper, &c.

A temperate Diet frees from Diseases; such are seldom ill, but if they are surprised with Sickness, they bear it better, and recover sooner; for most Distempers have their Original from Repletion.

Use now and then a little Exercise a quarter of an Hour before Meals, as to swing a Weight, or swing your Arms about with a small Weight in each Hand; to leap, or the like, for that stirs the Muscles of the Breast.

A temperate Diet arms the Body against all external Accidents; so that they are not so easily hurt by Heat, Cold or Labour; if they at any time should be prejudiced, they are more easily cured, either of Wounds, Dislocations or Bruises.

But when malignant Fevers are rife in the Country or City where thou dwelst, 'tis adviseable to eat and drink more freely, by Way of Prevention; for those are Diseases that are not caused by Repletion, and seldom attack Full-feeders.

A sober Diet makes a Man die without Pain; it maintains the Senses in Vigour; it mitigates the Violence of Passions and Affections.

It preserves the Memory, it helps the Understanding, it allays the Heat of Lust; it brings a Man to a Consideration of his latter End; it makes the Body a fit Tabernacle for the Lord to dwell in; which makes us happy in this World, and eternally happy in the World to come, through Jesus Christ our Lord and Saviour.

Poor Richard, 1743

Friendly READER,

Because I would have every Man make Advantage of the Blessings of Providence, and few are acquainted with the Method of making Wine of the Grapes which grow wild in our Woods, I do here present them with a few easy Directions, drawn from some Years Experience, which, if they will follow, they may furnish themselves with a wholesome sprightly Claret, which will keep for several Years, and is not inferior to that which passeth for *French* Claret.

Begin to gather Grapes from the 10th of *September* (the ripest first) to the last of *October*, and having clear'd them of Spider webs, and dead Leaves, put them into a large Molosses- or Rum-Hogshead; after having washed it well, and knock'd one Head out, fix it upon the other Head, on a Stand, or Blocks in the Cellar, if you have any, if not, in the warmest Part of the House, about 2 Feet from the Ground; as the Grapes sink, put up more, for 3 or 4 Days; after which, get into the Hogshead bare-leg'd, and tread them down until the Juice works up about your Legs, which will be in less than half an Hour; then get out, and turn the Bottom ones up, and tread them again, a Quarter of an Hour; this will be sufficient to get out the good Juice; more pressing wou'd burst the unripe Fruit, and give it an ill Taste: This done, cover the Hogshead close with a thick Blanket, and if you have no Cellar, and the Weather proves Cold, with two.

In this Manner you must let it take its first Ferment, for 4 or 5 Days it will work furiously; when the Ferment abates, which you will know by its making less Noise, make a Spile-hole within six Inches of the Bottom, and twice a Day draw some in a Glass. When it looks as clear as Rock-water, draw it off into a clean, rather than new Cask, proportioning it to the Contents of the Hogshead or Wine * Vat; that is, if the Hogshead holds twenty Bushels of Grapes, Stems and all, the Cask must at least, hold 20 Gallons, for they will yield a Gallon per Bushel. Your Juice or † Must thus drawn from the Vat, proceed to the second Ferment.

You must reserve in Jugs or Bottles, 1 Gallon or 5 Quarts of the Must to every 20 Gallons you have to work; which you will use according to the following Directions.

*Vat *or* Fatt, *a Name for the Vessel, in which you tread the Grapes, and in which the* Must *takes its first Ferment.*

†Must *is a Name for the Juice of the Vine before it is fermented, afterwards 'tis called Wine.*

Place your Cask, which must be chock full, with the Bung up, and open twice every Day, Morning and Night; feed your Cask with the reserved Must; two Spoonfuls at a time will suffice, clearing the Bung after you feed it, with your Finger or a Spoon, of the Grape-Stones and other Filth which the Ferment will throw up; you must continue feeding it thus until *Christmas*, when you may bung it up, and it will be fit for Use or to be rack'd into clean Casks or Bottles, by *February*.

N. B. Gather the Grapes after the Dew is off, and in all dry Seasons. Let not the Children come at the Must, it will scour them severely. If you make Wine for Sale, or to go beyond Sea, one quarter Part must be distill'd, and the Brandy put into the three Quarters remaining. One Bushel of Grapes, heap Measure, as you gather them from the Vine, will make at least a Gallon of Wine, if good, five Quarts.

These Directions are not design'd for those who are skill'd in making Wine, but for those who have hitherto had no Acquaintance with that Art.

————

How few there are who have courage enough to own their Faults, or resolution enough to mend them!

Men differ daily, about things which are subject to Sense, is it likely then they should agree about things invisible.

> Mark with what insolence and pride,
> Blown *Bufo* takes his haughty stride;
> As if no toad was toad beside.

Ill Company is like a dog who dirts those most, that he loves best.

> In prosperous fortunes be modest and wise,
> The greatest may fall, and the lowest may rise:
> But insolent People that fall in disgrace,
> Are wretched and no-body pities their Case.

Le sage entend á demi mot.

Sorrow is dry.

The World is full of fools and faint hearts; and yet every one has courage enough to bear the misfortunes, and wisdom enough to manage the Affairs of his neighbour.

Beware, beware! he'll cheat 'ithout scruple, who can without fear.

The D—l wipes his B—ch with poor Folks Pride.

> Content and Riches seldom meet together,
> Riches take thou, contentment I had rather.

> Speak with contempt of none, from slave to king,
> The meanest Bee hath, and will use, a sting.

The church the state, and the poor, are 3 daughters which we should maintain, but not portion off.

A achwyno heb achos; gwneler achos iddo.

> A little well-gotten will do us more good,
> Than lordships and scepters by Rapine and Blood.

Borgen macht sorgen.

Let all Men know thee, but no man know thee thoroughly: Men freely ford that see the shallows.

> 'Tis easy to frame a good bold resolution;
> but hard is the Task that concerns execution.

> Cold & cunning come from the north:
> But cunning sans wisdom is nothing worth.

> 'Tis vain to repine,
> Tho' a learned Divine
> Will die *this day* at nine.

A noddo duw, ry noddir.

Ah simple Man! when a boy two precious jewels were given thee, Time, and good Advice; one thou hast lost, and the other thrown away.

> Na funno i hûn.
> Na wnaid i ûn.

Dick told his spouse, he durst be bold to swear,
Whate'er she pray'd for, Heav'n would thwart her pray'r:
Indeed! says *Nell*, 'tis what I'm pleas'd to hear;
For now I'll pray for your long life, my dear.

The sleeping Fox catches no poultry. Up! up!

If you'd be wealthy, think of saving, more than of getting: The *Indies* have not made *Spain* rich, because her Outgoes equal her Incomes.

Tugend bestehet wen alles vergehet.

Came you from Court? for in your Mien,
A self-important air is seen.

Hear what *Jack Spaniard* says,
Con todo el Mundo Guerra,
Y Paz con Ingalatierra.

If you'd have it done, Go: If not, send.

Many a long dispute among Divines may be thus abridg'd, It is so: It is not so. It is so; It is not so.

Experience keeps a dear school, yet Fools will learn in no other.

Felix quem faciunt aliena pericula cautum.

How many observe Christ's Birth-day! How few, his Precepts! O! 'tis easier to keep Holidays than Commandments.

Poor Richard, 1744

Courteous Reader,

This is the Twelfth Year that I have in this Way laboured for the Benefit—of Whom?—of the Publick, if you'll be so good-natured as to believe it; if not, e'en take the naked Truth, 'twas for the Benefit of my own dear self; not forgetting in the mean time, our gracious Consort and Dutchess the peaceful, quiet, silent Lady *Bridget*. But whether my Labours have been of any Service to the Publick or not, the Publick I must acknowledge has been of Service to me; I have lived Comfortably by its Benevolent Encouragement; and I hope I shall always bear a grateful Sense of its continued Favour.

My Adversary *J—n J——n* has indeed made an Attempt to *out-shine* me, by pretending to penetrate *a Year deeper* into Futurity; and giving his Readers *gratis* in his Almanack for 1743 an Eclipse of the Year 1744, to be beforehand with me: His Words are, "The first Day of *April* next Year 1744, there will be a GREAT ECLIPSE of the Sun; it begins about an Hour before Sunset. It being in the Sign Aries, the House of Mars, and in the 7th, shows Heat, Difference and Animosities between Persons of the highest Rank and Quality," *&c.* I am very glad, for the Sake of these Persons of Rank and Quality, that there is *no manner of Truth* in this Prediction: They may, if they please, live in Love and Peace. And I caution his Readers (they are but few, indeed, and so the Matter's the less) not to give themselves any Trouble about observing this imaginary Great Eclipse; for they may stare till they're blind without seeing the least Sign of it. I might, on this Occasion, return Mr. *J——n* the Name of *Baal's false Prophet* he gave me some Years ago in his Wrath, on Account of my Predicting his Reconciliation with the *Church of Rome*, (tho' he seems now to have given up that Point) but I think such Language between old Men and Scholars unbecoming; and I leave him to settle the Affair with the Buyers of his Almanack as well as he can, who perhaps will not take it very kindly, that he has done what in him lay (by sending them out to gaze at an invisible Eclipse on the first of *April*) to make *April Fools* of them all. His old thread-bare Excuse which he repeats Year after Year about the *Weather*, "That no Man can be infallible therein, by Reason of the many contrary Causes happening at or near the same time, and the Unconstancy of the Summer Showers and gusts," *&c.* will hardly serve him in the Affair of *Eclipses*; and I know not where he'll get another.

I have made no Alteration in my usual Method, except adding the Rising and Setting of the Planets, and the Lunar Conjunctions. Those who are so disposed, may thereby very readily learn to know the Planets, and distinguish them from each other.

I am, dear Reader,
Thy obliged Friend,
R. SAUNDERS.

———

He that drinks his Cyder alone, let him catch his Horse alone.

Who is strong? He that can conquer his bad Habits. Who is rich? He that rejoices in his Portion.

He that has not got a Wife, is not yet a compleat Man.

What you would seem to be, be really.

If you'd lose a troublesome Visitor, lend him Money.

Tart Words make no Friends: a spoonful of honey will catch more flies than Gallon of Vinegar.

Make haste slowly.

Dine with little, sup with less:
Do better still; sleep supperless.

Industry, Perseverance, & Frugality, make Fortune yield.

I'll warrant ye, goes before *Rashness*; *Who'd-a-tho't it?* comes sneaking after.

Prayers and Provender hinder no Journey.

Hear *Reason*, or she'll make you feel her.

Give me yesterday's Bread, this Day's Flesh, and last Year's Cyder.

God heals, and the Doctor takes the Fees.

Sloth (like Rust) consumes faster than Labour wears: the used Key is always bright.

Light Gains heavy Purses.

Keep thou from the Opportunity, and God will keep thee from the Sin.

Where there's no Law, there's no Bread.

As Pride increases, Fortune declines.

Drive thy Business, or it will drive thee.

A full Belly is the Mother of all Evil.

The same man cannot be both Friend and Flatterer.

He who multiplies Riches multiplies Cares.

An old Man in a House is a good Sign.

Those who are fear'd, are hated.

The Things which hurt, instruct.

The Eye of a Master, will do more Work than his Hand.

A soft Tongue may strike hard.

If you'd be belov'd, make yourself amiable.

A true Friend is the best Possession.

Fear God, and your Enemies will fear you.

> *Epitaph on a Scolding Wife by her Husband.*
> Here my poor *Bridget*'s Corps doth lie,
> she is at rest,—and so am I.

Poor Richard, 1745

Courteous Reader,

For the Benefit of the Publick, and my own Profit, I have performed this my thirteenth annual Labour, which I hope will be as acceptable as the former.

The rising and setting of the Planets, and their Conjunctions with the Moon, I have continued; whereby those who are unacquainted with those heavenly Bodies, may soon learn to distinguish them from the fixed Stars, by observing the following Directions.

All those glittering Stars (except five) which we see in the

Firmament of Heaven, are called fixed Stars, because they keep the same Distance from one another, and from the Ecliptic; they rise and set on the same Points of the Horizon, and appear like so many lucid Points fixed to the celestial Firmament. The other five have a particular and different Motion, for which Reason they have not always the same Distance from one another; and therefore they have been called wandering Stars or Planets, *viz.* *Saturn* ♄, *Jupiter* ♃, *Mars* ♂, *Venus* ♀, and *Mercury* ☿, and these may be distinguished from the fixed Stars by their not twinkling. The brightest of the five is *Venus*, which appears the biggest; and when this glorious Star appears, and goes before the Sun, it is called *Phosphorus*, or the Morning-Star, and *Hesperus*, or the Evening-Star, when it follows the Sun. *Jupiter* appears almost as big as *Venus*, but not so bright. *Mars* may be easily known from the rest of the Planets, because it appears red like a hot Iron or burning Coal, and twinkles a little. *Saturn*, in Appearance, is less than *Mars*, and of a pale Colour, *Mercury* is so near the Sun, that it is seldom seen.

Against the 6th Day of *January* you may see ♂ rise 10 35, which signifies the Planet *Mars* rises 35 Minutes after 10 o' Clock at Night, when that Planet may be seen to appear in the East. Also against the 10th Day of *January* you will find ♀ sets 7 13, which shows *Venus* sets 13 Minutes after 7 o' Clock at Night. If you look towards the West that Evening, you may see that beautiful Star till the Time of its setting. Again, on the 18th Day of the same Month, you will find ♄ rise 9 18, which shews that *Saturn* rises 18 Minutes after 9 at Night.

Or the Planets may be known by observing them at the Time of their Conjunctions with the Moon, *viz.* against the 14 Day of *January* are inserted these Characters, ♂ ☽ ♄, which shews there will be a Conjunction of the Moon and *Saturn* on that Day. If you look out about 5 o' Clock in the Morning, you will see *Saturn* very near the Moon. The like is to be observed at any other time by the rising and setting of the Planets, and their Conjunctions with the Moon; by which Method they may be distinctly known from the fixed Stars.

I have nothing further to add at present, but my hearty

Wishes for your Welfare, both temporal and spiritual, and Thanks for all your past Favours, being,

Dear Reader,

Thy obliged Friend,

R. SAUNDERS.

———

Beware of little Expences, a small Leak will sink a great Ship.

Wars bring scars.

A light purse is a heavy Curse.

As often as we do good, we sacrifice.

> Help, Hands;
> For I have no Lands.

It's common for Men to give 6 pretended Reasons instead of one real one.

Vanity backbites more than *Malice*.

He's a Fool that cannot conceal his Wisdom.

Great spenders are bad lenders.

All blood is alike ancient.

You may talk too much on the best of subjects.

A Man without ceremony has need of great merit in its place.

No gains without pains.

Had I revenged wrong, I had not worn my skirts so long.

Graft good Fruit all, or graft not at all.

Idleness is the greatest Prodigality.

Old young and old long.

> Punch-coal, cut-candle, and set brand on end,
> is neither good house wife, nor good house-wife's friend.

> He who buys had need have 100 Eyes,
> but one's enough for him that sells the Stuff.

There are no fools so troublesome as those that have wit.

Many complain of their Memory, few of their Judgment.

One Man may be more cunning than another, but not more cunning than every body else.

To God we owe fear and love; to our neighbours justice and charity; to our selves prudence and sobriety.

Fools make feasts and wise men eat them.

Light-heel'd mothers make leaden-heel'd daughters.

> The good or ill hap of a good or ill life,
> is the good or ill choice of a good or ill wife.

'Tis easier to prevent bad habits than to break them.

Every Man has Assurance enough to boast of his honesty, few of their Understanding.

Interest which blinds some People, enlightens others.

> An ounce of wit that is bought,
> Is worth a pound that is taught.

He that resolves to mend hereafter, resolves not to mend now.

Poor Richard, 1746

PREFACE.

Who is *Poor Richard*? People oft enquire,
Where lives? What is he?—never yet the nigher.
Somewhat to ease your Curiositie,
Take these slight Sketches of my Dame and me.
    Thanks to kind Readers and a careful Wife,
With Plenty bless'd, I lead an easy Life;
My Business Writing; hers to drain the Mead,
Or crown the barren Hill with useful Shade;
In the smooth Glebe to see the Plowshare worn,
And fill the Granary with needful Corn.
Press nectarous Cyder from my loaded Trees,

Print the sweet Butter, turn the drying Cheese.
Some Books we read, tho' few there are that hit
The happy Point where Wisdom joins with Wit;
That set fair Virtue naked to our View,
And teach us what is *decent*, what is *true*.
The Friend sincere, and honest Man, with Joy
Treating or treated oft our Time employ.
Our Table neat, Meals temperate; and our Door
Op'ning spontaneous to the bashful Poor.
Free from the bitter Rage of Party Zeal,
All those we love who seek the publick Weal.
Nor blindly follow Superstition's Lore,
Which cheats deluded Mankind o'er and o'er.
Not over righteous, quite beyond the Rule,
Conscience perplext by every canting Tool.
Nor yet when Folly hides the dubious Line,
Where Good and Bad their blended Colours join;
Rush indiscreetly down the dangerous Steep,
And plunge uncertain in the darksome Deep.
Cautious, if right; if wrong resolv'd to part
The Inmate Snake that folds about the Heart.
Observe the *Mean*, the *Motive* and the *End*;
Mending our selves, or striving still to mend.
Our Souls sincere, our Purpose fair and free,
Without Vain Glory or Hypocrisy:
Thankful if well; if ill, we kiss the Rod;
Resign with Hope, and put our Trust in GOD.

————

When the Well's dry, we know the Worth of Water.

He that whines for Glass without G
Take away L and that's he.

A good Wife & Health,
is a Man's best Wealth.

A quarrelsome Man has no good Neighbours.

Wide will wear,
but Narrow will tear.

Silks and Sattins put out the Kitchen Fire.

Vice knows she's ugly, so puts on her Mask.

It's the easiest Thing in the World for a Man to deceive himself.

> Women & Wine, Game & Deceit,
> Make the Wealth small and the Wants great.

All Mankind are beholden to him that is kind to the Good.

A Plowman on his Legs is higher than a Gentleman on his Knees.

Virtue and Happiness are Mother and Daughter.

The generous Mind least regards money, and yet most feels the Want of it.

For one poor Man there are an hundred indigent.

Dost thou love Life? then do not squander Time; for that's the Stuff Life is made of.

Good Sense is a Thing all need, few have, and none think they want.

What's proper, is becoming: See the Blacksmith with his white Silk Apron!

The Tongue is ever turning to the aching Tooth.

Want of Care does us more Damage than Want of Knowledge.

Take Courage, Mortal; Death can't banish thee out of the Universe.

The Sting of a Reproach, is the Truth of it.

Do me the Favour to deny me at once.

The most exquisite Folly is made of Wisdom spun too fine.

A life of leisure, and a life of laziness, are two things.

Mad Kings and mad Bulls, are not to be held by treaties & packthread.

Changing Countries or Beds, cures neither a bad Manager, nor a Fever.

A true great Man will neither trample on a Worm, nor sneak to an Emperor.

Ni ffyddra llaw dyn, er gwneithr da idd ei hûn.

> *Tim* and his Handsaw are good in their Place,
> Tho' not fit for preaching or shaving a face.

Half-Hospitality opens his Doors and shuts up his Countenance.

Poor Richard, 1747

Courteous Reader,

This is the 15th Time I have entertain'd thee with my annual Productions; I hope to thy Profit as well as mine. For besides the astronomical Calculations, and other Things usually contain'd in Almanacks, which have their daily Use indeed while the Year continues, but then become of no Value, I have constantly interspers'd *moral* Sentences, *prudent* Maxims, and *wise* Sayings, many of them containing *much good Sense* in *very few* Words, and therefore apt to leave *strong* and *lasting* Impressions on the Memory of young Persons, whereby they may receive Benefit as long as they live, when both Almanack and Almanack-maker have been long thrown by and forgotten. If I now and then insert a Joke or two, that seem to have little in them, my Apology is, that such may have their Use, since perhaps for their Sake light airy Minds peruse the rest, and so are struck by somewhat of more Weight and Moment. The Verses on the Heads of the Months are also generally design'd to have the same Tendency. I need not tell thee that not many of them are of my own Making. If thou hast any Judgment in Poetry, thou wilt easily discern the Workman from the Bungler. I know as well as thee, that I am no *Poet born*; and it is a Trade I never learnt, nor indeed could learn. *If I make Verses, 'tis in Spight—Of Nature and my Stars, I write*. Why then should I give my Readers *bad Lines* of my own, when *good Ones* of other People's are so plenty? 'Tis methinks a poor Excuse for the bad Entertainment of Guests, that the Food we set before them, tho' coarse and ordinary, is *of one's own Raising, off one's own Plantation,* &c. when there is Plenty of what is ten times better, to be had in the Market.—On the contrary, I assure ye, my Friends, that I have procur'd the best I could for ye, and *much Good may't do ye.*

I cannot omit this Opportunity of making honourable Mention of the late deceased Ornament and Head of our Profession, Mr. JACOB TAYLOR, who for upwards of 40 Years (with some few Intermissions only) supply'd the good People of this and the neighbouring Colonies, with the most compleat Ephemeris and most accurate Calculations that have hitherto appear'd in *America*.—He was an ingenious Mathematician, as well as an expert and skilful Astronomer; and moreover, no mean Philosopher, but what is more than all, He was a PIOUS and an HONEST Man. *Requiescat in pace.*

I am thy poor Friend, to serve thee,

R. SAUNDERS.

———

Strive to be the *greatest* Man in your Country, and you may be disappointed; Strive to be the *best*, and you may succeed: He may well win the race that runs by himself.

'Tis a strange Forest that has no rotten Wood in't.
And a strange Kindred that all are good in't.

None know the unfortunate, and the fortunate do not know themselves.

There's a time to wink as well as to see.

Honest *Tom*! you may trust him with a house-full of untold Milstones.

There is no Man so bad, but he secretly respects the Good.

When there's more Malice shown than Matter:
On the Writer falls the satyr.

Courage would fight, but *Discretion* won't let him.

Delicate *Dick*! whisper'd the Proclamation.

Cornelius ought to be *Tacitus*.

Pride and the *Gout*,
are seldom cur'd throughout.

We are not so sensible of the greatest Health as of the least Sickness.

A good Example is the best sermon.

A Father's a Treasure; a Brother's a Comfort; a Friend is both.

Despair ruins some, Presumption many.

A quiet Conscience sleeps in Thunder,
but Rest and Guilt live far asunder.

He that won't be counsell'd, can't be help'd.

Craft must be at charge for clothes, but *Truth* can go naked.

Write Injuries in Dust, Benefits in Marble.

What is Serving God? 'Tis doing Good to Man.

What maintains one Vice would bring up two Children.

Many have been ruin'd by buying good pennyworths.

Better is a little with content than much with contention.

A Slip of the Foot you may soon recover:
But a Slip of the Tongue you may never get over.

What signifies your Patience, if you can't find it when you want it.

d. wise, *£* foolish.

Time enough, always proves *little enough.*

It is wise not to seek a Secret, and Honest not to reveal it.

A Mob's a Monster; Heads enough, but no Brains.

The Devil sweetens Poison with Honey.

He that cannot bear with other People's Passions, cannot govern his own.

He that by the Plow would thrive,
himself must either hold or drive.

Poor Richard Improved, *1748*

Kind Reader,

The favourable Reception my annual Labours have met
with from the Publick these 15 Years past, has engaged me in
Gratitude to endeavour some Improvement of my Almanack.
And since my Friend *Taylor* is no more, whose *Ephemerides*
so long and so agreeably serv'd and entertain'd these Provinces, I have taken the Liberty to imitate his well-known
Method, and give two Pages for each Month; which affords
me Room for several valuable Additions, as will best appear
on Inspection and Comparison with former Almanacks. Yet
I have not so far follow'd his Method, as not to continue
my own where I thought it preferable; and thus my Book is
increas'd to a Size beyond his, and contains much more
Matter.

Hail Night serene! thro' Thee where'er we turn
Our wond'ring Eyes, Heav'n's Lamps profusely burn;
And Stars unnumber'd all the Sky adorn.
    But lo!—what's that I see appear?
    It seems far off a pointed flame;
From Earthwards too the shining Meteor came:
    How swift it climbs th' etherial Space!
    And now it traverses each Sphere,
And seems some knowing Mind, familiar to the Place.
Dame, hand my Glass, the longest, strait prepare;—
'Tis He—'tis TAYLOR's Soul, that travels there.
O stay! thou happy Spirit, stay,
And lead me on thro' all th' unbeaten Wilds of Day;
Where Planets in pure Streams of Ether driven,
    Swim thro' the blue Expanse of Heav'n.
There let me, thy Companion, stray
    From Orb to Orb, and now behold
    Unnumber'd Suns, all Seas of molten Gold,
And trace each Comet's wandring Way.——

Souse down into Prose again, my Muse; for Poetry's no more thy Element, than Air is that of the Flying-Fish; whose Flights, like thine, are therefore always short and heavy.——

We complain sometimes of hard Winters in this Country; but our Winters will appear as Summers, when compar'd with those that some of our Countrymen undergo in the most Northern *British* Colony on this Continent, which is that upon *Churchill* River, in *Hudson's Bay*, Lat. 58d. 56m. Long. from *London* 94d. 50m. West. Captain *Middleton*, a Member of the *Royal Society*, who had made many Voyages thither, and winter'd there 1741–2, when he was in Search of the *North-West* Passage to the *South-Sea*, gives an Account of it to that Society, from which I have extracted these Particulars, *viz*.

The Hares, Rabbits, Foxes, and Partridges, in *September* and the Beginning of *October*, change their Colour to a snowy White, and continue white till the following Spring.

The Lakes and standing Waters, which are not above 10 or 12 Feet deep, are frozen to the Ground in Winter, and the Fishes therein all perish. Yet in Rivers near the Sea, and Lakes of a greater Depth than 10 or 12 Feet, Fishes are caught all the Winter, by cutting Holes thro' the Ice, and therein putting Lines and Hooks. As soon as the Fish are brought into the open Air, they instantly freeze stiff.

Beef, Pork, Mutton, and Venison, kill'd in the Beginning of the Winter, are preserved by the Frost for 6 or 7 Months, entirely free from Putrefaction. Likewise Geese, Partridges, and other Fowls, kill'd at the same Time, and kept with their Feathers on and Guts in, are preserv'd by the Frost, and prove good Eating. All Kinds of Fish are preserv'd in the same Manner.

In large Lakes and Rivers, the Ice is sometimes broken by imprison'd Vapours; and the Rocks, Trees, Joists, and Rafters of our Buildings, are burst with a Noise not less terrible than the firing of many Guns together. The Rocks which are split by the Frost, are heaved up in great Heaps, leaving large Cavities behind. If Beer or Water be left even in Copper Pots by the Bed-side, the Pots will be split before Morning. Bottles of strong Beer, Brandy, strong Brine, Spirits of Wine, set out in the open Air for 3 or 4 Hours, freeze to solid Ice. The Frost is never out of the Ground, how deep is not certain; but on digging 10 or 12 Feet down in the two Summer Months, it has been found hard frozen.

All the Water they use for Cooking, Brewing, &c. is melted Snow and Ice; no Spring is yet found free from freezing, tho' dug ever so deep down.—All Waters inland, are frozen fast by the Beginning of *October*, and continue so to the Middle of *May*.

The Walls of the Houses are of Stone, two Feet thick; the Windows very small, with thick wooden Shutters, which are close shut 18 Hours every Day in Winter. In the Cellars they put their Wines, Brandies, &c. Four large Fires are made every Day, in great Stoves to warm the Rooms: As soon as the Wood is burnt down to a Coal, the Tops of the Chimnies are close stopped, with an Iron Cover; this keeps the Heat in, but almost stifles the People. And notwithstanding this, in 4 or 5 Hours after the Fire is out, the Inside of the Walls and Bed-places will be 2 or 3 Inches thick with Ice, which is every Morning cut away with a Hatchet. Three or four Times a Day, Iron Shot, of 24 Pounds Weight, are made red hot, and hung up in the Windows of their Apartments, to moderate the Air that comes in at Crevices; yet this, with a Fire kept burning the greatest Part of 24 Hours, will not prevent Beer, Wine, Ink, &c. from Freezing.

For their Winter Dress, a Man makes use of three Pair of Socks, of coarse Blanketting, or Duffeld, for the Feet, with a Pair of Deerskin Shoes over them; two Pair of thick *English* Stockings, and a Pair of Cloth Stockings upon them; Breeches lined with Flannel; two or three *English* Jackets, and a Fur, or Leather Gown over them; a large Beaver Cap, double, to come over the Face and Shoulders, and a Cloth of Blanketting under the Chin; with Yarn Gloves, and a large Pair of Beaver Mittins, hanging down from the Shoulders before, to put the Hands in, reaching up as high as the Elbows. Yet notwithstanding this warm Clothing, those that stir Abroad when any Wind blows from the Northward, are sometimes dreadfully frozen; some have their Hands, Arms, and Face blistered and froze in a terrible Manner, the Skin coming off soon after they enter a warm House, and some lose their Toes. And keeping House, or lying-in for the Cure of these

Disorders, brings on the Scurvy, which many die of, and few are free from; nothing preventing it but Exercise and stirring Abroad.

The Fogs and Mists, brought by northerly Winds in Winter, appear visible to the naked Eye to be Icicles innumerable, as small as fine Hairs, and pointed as sharp as Needles. These Icicles lodge in their Clothes, and if their Faces and Hands are uncover'd, presently raise Blisters as white as a Linnen Cloth, and as hard as Horn. Yet if they immediately turn their Back to the Weather, and can bear a Hand out of the Mitten, and with it rub the blister'd Part for a small Time, they sometimes bring the Skin to its former State; if not, they make the best of their Way to a Fire, bathe the Part in hot Water, and thereby dissipate the Humours raised by the frozen Air; otherwise the Skin wou'd be off in a short Time, with much hot, serous, watry Matter, coming from under along with the Skin; and this happens to some almost every Time they go Abroad, for 5 or 6 Months in the Winter, so extreme cold is the Air, when the Wind blows any Thing strong.—Thus far Captain *Middleton.* And now, my tender Reader, thou that shudderest when the Wind blows a little at N-West, and criest, *'Tis extrrrrrream cohohold! 'Tis terrrrrrible cohold!* what dost thou think of removing to that delightful Country? Or dost thou not rather chuse to stay in *Pennsylvania,* thanking God that *He has caused thy Lines to fall in pleasant Places.*

> *I am,*
> *Thy Friend to serve thee,*
> R. SAUNDERS.

———

Robbers must exalted be,
Small ones on the Gallow-Tree,
While greater ones ascend to Thrones,
But what is that to thee or me?

Lost Time is never found again.

———

On the 19th of this Month, *Anno* 1493, was born the famous Astronomer *Copernicus,* to whom we owe the Invention, or rather the Revival (it being taught by *Pythagoras* near 2000 Years before) of that now generally receiv'd System of the World which bears his Name, and supposes the Sun in the Center, this Earth a Planet revolving round it in 365 Days, 6 Hours, &c. and that Day and Night are caused by the Turning of the Earth on its own Axis once round in 24 h. &c. The *Ptolomean* System, which prevail'd before *Copernicus*, suppos'd the Earth to be fix'd, and that the Sun went round it daily. Mr. *Whiston*, a modern Astronomer, says, the Sun is 230,000 times bigger than the Earth, and 81 Millions of Miles distant from it: That vast Body must then have mov'd more than 480 Millions of Miles in 24 h. A prodigious Journey round this little Spot! How much more natural is *Copernicus*'s Scheme!—*Ptolomy* is compar'd to a whimsical Cook, who, instead of Turning his Meat in Roasting, should fix That, and contrive to have his whole Fire, Kitchen and all, whirling continually round it.

———

> To lead a virtuous Life, my Friends, and get to Heaven
>   in Season,
> You've just so much more Need of *Faith*, as you have
>   less of *Reason*.

To avoid Pleurisies, &c. in cool Weather; Fevers, Fluxes, &c. in hot; beware of *Over-Eating* and *Over-Heating*.

The Heathens when they dy'd, went to Bed without a Candle.

> Knaves & Nettles are akin;
> stroak 'em kindly, yet they'll sting.

———

On the 20th of this month, 1727, died the prince of astronomers and philosophers, sir *Isaac Newton*, aged 85 years: Who, as *Thomson* expresses it, *Trac'd the boundless works of God, from laws sublimely simple*.

> What were his raptures then! how pure! how strong!
> And what the triumphs of old *Greece* and *Rome*,
> By his diminish'd, but the pride of boys
> In some small fray victorious! when instead
> Of shatter'd parcels of this earth usurp'd
> By violence unmanly, and sore deeds

Of cruelty and blood; *Nature* herself
Stood all-subdu'd by him, and open laid
Her every latent glory to his view.

Mr. *Pope*'s epitaph on sir *Isaac Newton*, is justly admired for its conciseness, strength, boldness, and sublimity:

Nature and nature's laws lay hid in night;
God said, *Let* NEWTON *be*, and all was light.

Life with Fools consists in Drinking;
With the wise Man Living's Thinking.

Eilen thut selten gut.

On the 25th of this month, *Anno* 1599, was OLIVER CROM-WELL born, the son of a private gentleman, but became the conqueror and protector (some say the tyrant) of three great kingdoms. His son *Richard* succeeded him, but being of an easy peaceable disposition, he soon descended from that lofty station, and became a private man, living, unmolested, to a good old age; for he died not till about the latter end of queen *Anne*'s reign, at his lodgings in *Lombard-street*, where he had lived many years unknown, and seen great changes in government, and violent struggles for that, which, by experience, he knew could afford no solid happiness.

Oliver was once about to remove to *New-England*, his goods being on shipboard; but somewhat alter'd his mind. There he would doubtless have risen to be a *Select Man*, perhaps a *Governor*; and then might have had 100 bushels of *Indian* corn *per Annum*, the salary of a governor of that then small colony in those days.

Sell-cheap kept Shop on *Goodwin Sands*, and yet had Store of Custom.

Liberality is not giving much but giving wisely.

Finikin *Dick*, curs'd with nice Taste,
Ne'er meets with good dinner, half starv'd at a feast.

Alas! that Heroes ever were made!
The *Plague*, and the *Hero*, are both of a Trade!
Yet the Plague spares our Goods which the Heroe does
    not;
So a Plague take such Heroes and let their Fames
    rot.   *Q. P. D.*

————

The 19th of this month, 1719, died the celebrated *Joseph Addison*, Esq; aged 47, whose writings have contributed more to the improvement of the minds of the *British* nation, and polishing their manners, than those of any other *English* pen whatever.

————

To Friend, Lawyer, Doctor, tell plain your whole Case;
Nor think on bad Matters to put a good Face:
How can they advise, if they see but a Part?
'Tis very ill driving black Hogs in the dark.

Suspicion may be no Fault, but shewing it may be a great
one.

He that's secure is not safe.

The second Vice is Lying; the first is Running in Debt.

The Muses love the Morning.

————

Muschitoes, or *Musketoes*, a little venomous fly, so light, that perhaps 50 of them, before they've fill'd their bellies, scarce weigh a grain, yet each has all the parts necessary to life, motion, digestion, generation, *&c.* as veins, arteries, muscles, *&c.* each has in his little body room for the five senses of seeing, hearing, feeling, smelling, tasting: How inconceivably small must their organs be! How inexpressibly fine the workmanship! And yet there are little animals discovered by the microscope, to whom a *Musketo* is an *Elephant*!—In a scarce summer any citizen may provide Musketoes sufficient for his own family, by leaving tubs of rain-water uncover'd in his yard; for in such water they lay their eggs, which when hatch'd, become first little fish, afterwards put forth legs and wings, leave the water, and fly into your windows. *Probatum est.*

Two Faults of one a Fool will make;
He half repairs, that owns & does forsake.

Harry Smatter,
has a Mouth for every Matter.

When you're good to others, you are best to yourself.

Half Wits talk much but say little.

If *Jack's* in love, he's no judge of *Jill*'s Beauty.

Most Fools think they are only ignorant.

———

On the 14th of this month, *Anno* 1644, was born WILLIAM PENN, the great founder of this Province; who prudently and benevolently sought success to himself by no other means, than securing the *liberty*, and endeavouring the *happiness* of his people. Let no envious mind grudge his posterity those advantages which arise to them from the wisdom and goodness of their ancestor; and to which their own merit, as well as the laws, give them an additional title.

———

On the 28th, *Anno* 1704, died the famous *John Locke*, Esq; the *Newton* of the *Microcosm*: For, as *Thomson* says,

> *He made the whole* internal world *his own*.

His book on the *Human Understanding*, shows it. *Microcosm*, honest reader, is a hard word, and, they say, signifies the *little world*, man being so called, as containing within himself the four elements of the *greater*, &c. &c. I here explain *Greek* to thee by *English*, which, I think, is rather a more intelligible way, than explaining *English* by *Greek*, as a certain writer does, who gravely tells us, *Man is rightly called* a little world, *because he is a* Microcosm.

———

On the 29th, *Anno* 1618, was the famous sir *Walter Rawleigh* beheaded; to the eternal shame of the attorney-general, who first prosecuted him, and of the king, who ratify'd the sentence.

———

How happy is he, who can satisfy his hunger with any

food, quench his thirst with any drink, please his ear with any musick, delight his eye with any painting, any sculpture, any architecture, and divert his mind with any book or any company! How many mortifications must he suffer, that cannot bear any thing but beauty, order, elegance & perfection! *Your man of* taste, *is nothing but a man of* distaste.

Pardoning the Bad, is injuring the Good.

He is not well-bred, that cannot bear Ill-Breeding in others.

> In Christmas feasting pray take care;
> Let not your table be a Snare;
> but with the Poor God's Bounty share.

Poor Richard Improved, 1749

Wealth and Content are not always Bed-fellows.

Wise Men learn by others harms; Fools by their own.

On the 7th of this month 1692 died *Robert Boyle*, Esq; one of the greatest philosophers the last age produced. He first brought the machine called an *Airpump*, into use; by which many of the surprizing properties of that wonderful element were discovered and demonstrated. His knowledge of natural history, and skill in chymistry, were very great and extensive; and his piety inferior to neither.

> ——BOYLE, *whose pious search*
> *Amid the dark recesses of his works*
> *The great* CREATOR *sought:*——Thomson.

is therefore an instance, that tho' *Ignorance* may in some be the *Mother of Devotion*, yet true learning and exalted piety are by no means inconsistent.

When we read in antient history of the speeches made by generals to very numerous armies, we sometimes wonder how they could be well heard; but supposing the men got together so close, that each took up no more ground than two foot in breadth, and one in depth, 45000 might stand in a space that was but 100 yards square, and 21780 on a single acre of ground. There are many voices that may be heard at 100 yards distance.

———

The end of Passion is the beginning of Repentance.

Words may shew a man's Wit, but *Actions* his Meaning.

———

On the 18th of this month, *anno* 1546 died that famous reformer, LUTHER: who struck the great blow to papal tyranny in *Europe*. He was remarkably *temperate* in meat and drink, sometimes fasting four days together; and at other times, for many days eating only a little bread and a herring. *Cicero* says, *There was never any* great *man who was not an* industrious *man*; to which may, perhaps, be added, *There was never any* industrious *man who was not a* temperate *man*: For intemperance in diet, abates the vigour and dulls the action both of mind and body.

———

Of SOUND.

Mr. *Flamstead*, Dr. *Halley* and Mr. *Derham*, agree that sound moves 1142 feet in a second, which is one *English* mile in 4 seconds and 5 8ths; that it moves in the same time in every different state of the atmosphere; that winds hardly make any difference in its velocity; that a languid or loud sound moves with the same velocity; and that different kinds of sounds, as of bells, guns, &c. have the same velocity, and are equally swift in the beginning as end of their motion.

———

'Tis a well spent penny that saves a groat.

Many Foxes grow grey, but few grow good.

Presumption first blinds a Man, then sets him a running.

———

The nose of a lady here, is not delighted with perfumes that she understands are in *Arabia*. Fine musick in *China* gives no pleasure to the nicest ear in *Pennsilvania*. Nor does the most exquisite dish serv'd up in *Japan*, regale a luxurious palate in any other country. But the benevolent mind of a virtuous man, is pleas'd, when it is inform'd of good and generous actions, in what part of the world soever they are done.

――――

A cold April,
The Barn will fill.

Content makes poor men rich; Discontent makes rich Men poor.

Too much plenty makes Mouth dainty.

――――

On the 7th of this month, 1626, died that *great little* man, Sir FRANCIS BACON; *great* in his prodigious genius, parts and learning; and *little*, in his servile compliances with a *little* court, and submissive flattery of a *little* prince. *Pope* characterises him thus, in one strong line;

> *If Parts allure thee, think how* BACON *shin'd,*
> *The wisest, brightest, meanest of mankind.*

He is justly esteem'd the father of the modern experimental philosophy. And another poet treats him more favourably, ascribing his blemishes to a wrong unfortunate choice of his way of Life;

> ―――BACON, hapless in his choice,
> Unfit to stand the civil storm of state,
> And thro' the smooth barbarity of courts,
> With firm, but pliant virtue, forward still
> To urge his course. Him for the studious shade
> Kind nature form'd, deep, comprehensive, clear,
> Exact, and elegant; in one rich soul,
> PLATO, the STAGYRITE, and TULLY join'd.
> The great deliverer he! who from the gloom
> Of cloister'd monks, and jargon-teaching schools,
> Led forth the true Philosophy, there long
> Held in the magic chain of words and forms,
> And definitions void: He led her forth,
> Daughter of HEAV'N! that slow ascending still,
> Investigating sure the chain of things,
> With radiant finger points to HEAV'N again.

If *Passion* drives, let *Reason* hold the Reins.

> Neither trust, nor contend, nor lay wagers, nor lend;
> And you'll have peace to your Lives end.

Drink does not drown *Care*, but waters it, and makes it grow faster.

Who dainties love, shall Beggars prove.

On the 27th, anno 1564, died at *Geneva* that famous reformer, Mr. *John Calvin*, A man of equal *temperance* and *sobriety* with *Luther*, and perhaps yet greater *industry*. His lectures were yearly 186, his sermons yearly 286; he published besides every year some great volume in folio; to which add his constant employments, in governing the church, answering letters from all parts of the reformed world, from pastors, concerning doubts, or asking counsel, *&c. &c.* He ate little meat, and slept but very little; and as his whole time was filled up with useful action, he may be said to have *lived* long, tho' he died at 55 years of age; since *sleep* and *sloth* can hardly be called *living*.

A Man has no more *Goods* than he gets Good by.

Welcome, Mischief, if thou comest alone.

Different Sects like different clocks, may be all near the matter, 'tho they don't quite agree.

On the 15th of this month, anno 1215, was *Magna Charta* sign'd by King *John*, for declaring and establishing *English Liberty*.

It was wise counsel given to a young man, *Pitch upon that course of life which is most excellent, and* CUSTOM *will make it the most delightful*. But many pitch on no course of life at all, nor form any scheme of living, by which to attain any valuable end; but wander perpetually from one thing to another.

> Hast thou not yet propos'd some certain end,
> To which thy life, thy every act may tend?

Hast thou no mark at which to bend thy bow?
Or like a boy pursu'st the carrion crow
With pellets and with stones, from tree to tree,
A fruitless toil, and liv'st *extempore*?
Watch the disease in time: For when, within
The dropsy rages, and extends the skin,
In vain for helebore the patient cries,
And sees the doctor, but too late is wise:
Too late for cure, he proffers half his wealth;
Ten thousand doctors cannot give him health.
   Learn, wretches, learn the motions of the mind,
Why you were mad, for what you were design'd,
And the great *moral end* of human kind.
Study thy self; what rank or what degree,
The wise creator has ordain'd for thee:
And all the offices of that estate,
Perform, and with thy prudence guide thy fate.

———

If your head is wax, don't walk in the Sun.

Pretty & *Witty*,
will wound if they hit ye.

Having been poor is no shame, but being ashamed of it, is.

'Tis a laudable Ambition, that aims at being better than his Neighbours.

The wise Man draws more Advantage from his Enemies, than the Fool from his Friends.

———

PRIDE is said to be the *last* vice the good man gets clear of. 'Tis a meer *Proteus*, and disguises itself under all manner of appearances, putting on sometimes even the mask of *humility*. If some are proud of neatness and propriety of dress; others are equally so of despising it, and acting the perpetual sloven.

———

All would live long, but none would be old.

Declaiming against Pride, is not always a Sign of Humility.

Neglect kills Injuries, Revenge increases them.

9 Men in 10 are suicides.

Doing an Injury puts you below your Enemy; *Revenging* one makes you but *even* with him; *Forgiving* it sets you *above* him.

Most of the Learning in use, is of no great Use.

Great Good-nature, without Prudence, is a great Misfortune.

> Keep Conscience· clear,
> Then never fear.

A Man in a Passion rides a mad Horse.

> Reader farewel, all Happiness attend thee;
> May each New-Year, better and richer find thee.

———

On the 25th of this month, *anno* 1642, was born the great Sir ISAAC NEWTON, prince of the modern astronomers and philosophers. But what is all our little boasted knowledge, compar'd with that of the angels? If they see our actions, and are acquainted with our affairs, our whole body of science must appear to them as little better than ignorance; and the common herd of our learned men, scarce worth their notice. Now and then one of our very great philosophers, an *Aristotle*, or a *Newton*, may, perhaps, by his most refined speculations, afford them a little entertainment, as it seems a mimicking of their own sublime amusements. Hence *Pope* says of the latter,

> *Superior beings, when of late they saw*
> *A mortal man unfold all nature's law,*
> *Admir'd such wisdom in a human shape,*
> *And shew'd a* Newton, *as we shew an ape.*

———

How to get RICHES.

The Art of getting Riches consists very much in THRIFT. All Men are not equally qualified for getting Money, but it is in the Power of every one alike to practise this Virtue.

He that would be beforehand in the World, must be beforehand with his Business: It is not only ill Management, but discovers a slothful Disposition, to do that in the Afternoon, which should have been done in the Morning.

Useful Attainments in your Minority will procure Riches in Maturity, of which Writing and Accounts are not the meanest.

Learning, whether Speculative or Practical, is, in Popular or Mixt Governments, the Natural Source of Wealth and Honour.

PRECEPT I.

In Things of moment, on thy self depend,
Nor trust too far thy Servant or thy Friend:
With private Views, thy Friend may promise fair,
And Servants very seldom prove sincere.

PRECEPT II.

What can be done, with Care perform to Day,
Dangers unthought-of will attend Delay;
Your distant Prospects all precarious are,
And Fortune is as fickle as she's fair.

PRECEPT III.

Nor trivial Loss, nor trivial Gain despise;
Molehills, if often heap'd, to Mountains rise:
Weigh every small Expence, and nothing waste,
Farthings long sav'd, amount to Pounds at last.

Poor Richard Improved, 1750

To the READER.

The Hope of acquiring lasting FAME, is, with many Authors, a most powerful Motive to Writing. Some, tho' few, have succeeded; and others, tho' perhaps fewer, may succeed here-after, and be as well known to Posterity by their Works, as the Antients are to us. We *Philomaths*, as ambitious of Fame as any other Writers whatever, after all our painful Watchings and laborious Calculations, have the constant Mortification to see our Works thrown by at the End of the Year, and treated as mere waste Paper. Our only Consolation is, that short-lived as they are, they out-live those of most of our Cotemporaries.

Yet, condemned to renew the *Sisyphean* Toil, we every Year heave another heavy Mass up the Muses Hill, which never can the Summit reach, and soon comes tumbling down again.

This, kind Reader, is my seventeenth Labour of the Kind. Thro' thy continued Good-will, they have procur'd me, if no *Bays*, at least *Pence*; and the latter is perhaps the better of the two; since 'tis not improbable that a Man may receive more solid Satisfaction from *Pudding*, while he is *living*, than from *Praise*, after he is *dead*.

In my last, a few Faults escap'd; some belong to the Author, but most to the Printer: Let each take his Share of the Blame, confess, and amend for the future. In the second Page of *August*, I mention'd 120 as the next perfect Number to 28; it was wrong, 120 being no perfect Number; the next to 28 I find to be 496. The first is 6; let the curious Reader, fond of mathematical Questions, find the fourth. In the 2d Page of *March*, in some Copies, the Earth's Circumference was said to be nigh 4000, instead of 24000 Miles, the Figure 2 being omitted at the Beginning. This was Mr. Printer's Fault; who being also somewhat niggardly of his Vowels, as well as profuse of his Consonants, put in one Place, among the Poetry, *mad*, instead of *made*, and in another *wrapp'd*, instead of *warp'd*; to the utter demolishing of all Sense in those Lines, leaving nothing standing but the Rhime. These, and some others, of the like kind, let the Readers forgive, or rebuke him for, as to their Wisdom and Goodness shall seem meet: For in such Cases the Loss and Damage is chiefly to the Reader, who, if he does not take my Sense at first Reading, 'tis odds he never gets it; for ten to one he does not read my Works a second Time.

Printers indeed should be very careful how they omit a Figure or a Letter: For by such Means sometimes a terrible Alteration is made in the Sense. I have heard, that once, in a new Edition of the *Common Prayer*, the following Sentence, *We shall all be changed in a Moment, in the Twinkling of an Eye*; by the Omission of a single Letter, became, *We shall all be hanged in a Moment*, &c. to the no small Surprize of the first Congregation it was read to.

May this Year prove a happy One to Thee and Thine, is the hearty Wish of, Kind Reader,

Thy obliged Friend,
R. SAUNDERS.

———

There are three Things extreamly hard, Steel, a Diamond and to know one's self.

Hunger is the best Pickle.

He is a Governor that governs his Passions, and he a Servant that serves them.

A Cypher and Humility make the other Figures & Virtues of ten-fold Value.

If it were not for the Belly, the Back might wear Gold.

Wouldst thou confound thine Enemy, be good thy self.

Pride is as loud a Beggar as *Want*, and a great deal more saucy.

Pay what you owe, and what you're worth you'll know.

Sorrow is good for nothing but Sin.

Many a Man thinks he is buying Pleasure, when he is really selling himself a Slave to it.

Graft good Fruit all,
Or graft not at all.

Tis hard (but glorious) to be poor and honest: An empty Sack can hardly stand upright; but if it does, 'tis a stout one!

He that can bear a Reproof, and mend by it, if he is not wise, is in a fair way of being so.

Beatus esse sine Virtute, nemo potest.

Sound, & sound Doctrine, may pass through a Ram's Horn, and a Preacher, without straitening the one, or amending the other.

Clean your Finger, before you point at my Spots.

He that spills the Rum, loses that only; He that drinks it, often loses both that and himself.

> That Ignorance makes devout, if right the Notion,
> 'Troth, *Rufus*, thou'rt a Man of great Devotion.

———

What an admirable Invention is Writing, by which a Man may communicate his Mind without opening his Mouth, and at 1000 Leagues Distance, and even to future Ages, only by the Help of 22 Letters, which may be joined 5852616738497664000 Ways, and will express all Things in a very narrow Compass. 'Tis a Pity this excellent Art has not preserved the Name and Memory of its Inventor.

———

Those that have much Business must have much Pardon.

Discontented Minds, and Fevers of the Body are not to be cured by changing Beds or Businesses.

> Little Strokes,
> Fell great Oaks.

You may be too cunning for One, but not for All.

Genius without Education is like Silver in the Mine.

Many would live by their Wits, but break for want of Stock.

Poor *Plain dealing*! dead without Issue!

You can bear your own Faults, and why not a Fault in your Wife.

Tho' Modesty is a Virtue, Bashfulness is a Vice.

> Hide not your Talents, they for Use were made.
> What's a Sun-Dial in the Shade!

What signifies knowing the Names, if you know not the Natures of Things.

Tim was so learned, that he could name a Horse in nine Languages; So ignorant, that he bought a Cow to ride on.

The Golden Age never was the present Age.

'Tis a Shame that your Family is an Honour to you! You ought to be an Honour to your Family.

Glass, China, and Reputation, are easily crack'd, and never well mended.

Poor Richard Improved, 1751

COURTEOUS READER,

Astrology is one of the most ancient Sciences, had in high Esteem of old, by the Wise and Great. Formerly, no Prince would make War or Peace, nor any General fight a Battle, in short, no important Affair was undertaken without first consulting an *Astrologer*, who examined the Aspects and Configurations of the heavenly Bodies, and mark'd the *lucky Hour*. Now the noble Art (more Shame to the Age we live in!) is dwindled into Contempt; the Great neglect us, Empires make Leagues, and Parliaments Laws, without advising with us; and scarce any other Use is made of our learned Labours, than to find the best Time of cutting Corns, or gelding Pigs.—This Mischief we owe in a great Measure to ourselves: The Ignorant Herd of Mankind, had they not been encourag'd to it by some of us, would never have dared to depreciate our sacred Dictates; but *Urania* has been betray'd by her own Sons; those whom she had favour'd with the greatest Skill in her divine Art, the most eminent Astronomers among the Moderns, the *Newtons*, *Halleys*, and *Whistons*, have wantonly contemn'd and abus'd her, contrary to the Light of their own Consciences. Of these, only the last nam'd, *Whiston*, has liv'd to repent, and speak his Mind honestly. In his former Works he had treated *Judiciary Astrology* as a Chimera, and asserted, That not only the fixed Stars, but the Planets (Sun and Moon excepted) were at so immense a Distance, as to be incapable of any Influence on this Earth, and consequently nothing could be foretold from their Positions: but now in the Memoirs of his Life, publish'd 1749, in the 82d Year of his Age, he foretels, Page 607, the sudden Destruction of the *Turkish* Empire, and of the House of *Austria*, *German* Emperors, *&c.* and *Popes* of *Rome*; the Restoration of the *Jews*, and Commencement of the *Millennium*; all by the Year 1766; and this not only from Scripture Prophecies; but (take his own Words)—"From the remarkable *astronomical* Signals that are to alarm Mankind of what is coming, *viz.* The *Northern Lights* since 1715; the six Comets at the Protestant Reformation in four Years, 1530, 1531, 1533, 1534, compar'd with the seven Comets already seen in these last eleven Years 1737, 1739, 1742, 1743, 1744, 1746, and 1748.—From the great Annular Eclipse of the Sun, *July* 14, 1748, whose Center pass'd through all the four Monarchies, from *Scotland* to the *East-Indies*.—From the Occultation of the *Pleiades* by the Moon each periodical Month, after the Eclipse last *July*, for above three Years, visible to the whole *Roman* Empire; as there was a like Occultation of the *Hyades* from *A.* 590, to *A.* 595, for six Years foretold by *Isaiah*.—From the Transit of *Mercury* over the *Sun*, *April* 25, 1753, which will be visible thro' that Empire.—From the Comet of *A. D.* 1456, 1531, 1607, and 1682, which will appear again about 1757 ending, or 1758 beginning, and will also be visible thro' that Empire.—From the Transit of *Venus* over the *Sun*, *May* 26, 1761, which will be visible over the same Empire: And lastly, from the annular Eclipse of the *Sun*, *March* 11, 1764, which will be visible over the same Empire."—From these *Astronomical Signs*, he foretels those great Events, That within 16 Years from this Time, "the *Millennium* or 1000 Years Reign of Christ shall begin, there shall be a *new Heavens*, and a *new Earth*; there shall be no more an Infidel in *Christendom*, Page 398, nor a Gaming-Table at *Tunbridge*!"—When these Predictions are accomplished, what glorious Proofs they will be of the Truth of our Art?—And if they happen to fail, there is no doubt but so profound an Astronomer as Mr. *Whiston*, will be able to see *other* Signs in the Heavens, foreshowing that the Conversion of Infidels was to be postponed, and the *Millennium* adjourn'd.—After these great Things can any Man doubt our being capable of predicting a little Rain or Sun-shine?— Reader, Farewell, and make the best Use of your Years and your Almanacks, for you see, that according to *Whiston*, you may have at most, but sixteen more of them.

R. SAUNDERS.

Patowmack, July 30, 1750.

Pray don't burn my House to roast your Eggs.

> Some *Worth* it argues, a Friend's *Worth* to know;
> *Virtue* to own the Virtue of a Foe.

Prosperity discovers Vice, Adversity Virtue.

———

The *Romans* were 477 Years, without so much as a Sun-dial to show the Time of Day: The first they had was brought from *Sicily*, by *Valerius Messala*: One hundred and eighteen Years afterwards, *Scipio Nasica*, produced to them an Invention for measuring the Hours in cloudy Weather, it was by the Dropping of Water out of one Vessel into another, somewhat like our Sand-Glasses. Clocks and Watches, to shew the Hour, are very modern Inventions. The Sub-dividing Hours into Minutes, and Minutes into Seconds, by those curious Machines, is not older than the Days of our Fathers, but now brought to a surprising Nicety.

Since our Time is reduced to a Standard, and the Bullion of the Day minted out into Hours, the Industrious know how to employ every Piece of Time to a real Advantage in their different Professions: And he that is prodigal of his Hours, is, in Effect, a Squanderer of Money. I remember a notable Woman, who was fully sensible of the intrinsic Value of *Time*. Her Husband was a Shoemaker, and an excellent Craftsman, but never minded how the Minutes passed. In vain did she inculcate to him, That *Time is Money*. He had too much Wit to apprehend her, and it prov'd his Ruin. When at the Alehouse among his idle Companions, if one remark'd that the Clock struck Eleven, *What is that, says he, among us all?* If she sent him Word by the Boy, that it had struck Twelve; *Tell her to be easy, it can never be more.* If, that it had struck One, *Bid her be comforted, for it can never be less.*

If we lose our Money, it gives us some Concern. If we are cheated or robb'd of it, we are angry: But Money lost may be found; what we are robb'd of may be restored: The Treasure of Time once lost, can never be recovered; yet we squander it as tho' 'twere nothing worth, or we had no Use for it.

> The Bell strikes *One*: We take no Note of Time,
> But from its Loss. To give it then a Tongue
> Is wise in Man. If heard aright

It is the Knell of our departed Hours;
Where are they? With the Years beyond the Flood:
It is the Signal that demands Dispatch;
How much is to be done?——
      Be wise To-day, 'tis Madness to defer;
Next day the fatal Precedent will plead;
Thus on, till Wisdom is push'd out of Life:
Procrastination is the Thief of Time,
Year after Year it steals till all are fled,
And to the Mercies of a Moment leaves
The vast Concerns of an eternal Scene.
If not so frequent, would not this be strange?
That 'tis so frequent, *This* is stranger still.

Many a Man would have been worse, if his Estate had been better.

We may give Advice, but we cannot give Conduct.

He that is conscious of a Stink in his Breeches, is jealous of every Wrinkle in another's Nose.

Love and *Tooth-ach* have many Cures, but none infallible, except *Possession* and *Dispossession*.

There are lazy Minds as well as lazy Bodies.

Most People return small Favours, acknowledge middling ones, and repay great ones with Ingratitude.

That admirable Instrument the MICROSCOPE has opened to us of these latter Ages, a World utterly unknown to the Ancients. There are very few Substances, in which it does not shew something curious and unexpected; but for the Sake of such Readers as are unacquainted with that Instrument, I shall set down some of the most remarkably entertaining Objects, upon which actual Observations have been made.

1. The Globules of the Blood, which are computed to be almost a two thousandth Part of an Inch in Diameter, each consisting of six small Globules, each of which again probably consists of six smaller, and so on. The Circulation of the Blood is to be seen very distinctly in the Tail of a small Fish,

the Web of the Foot of a Frog, &c. and the Globules to split
and divide, before they can enter the smallest Vessels.

2. The Bones of all Creatures, sliced extremely thin, afford
an entertaining Object for the Microscope, consisting of
innumerable Perforations, and Ramifications, disposed in an
endless Variety of Forms.

3. The Flesh of all Land and Sea Animals dried, and
cut into very thin Slices, gives a beautiful View of the various Fibres, and their Convolutions. The Brain, the spinal
Marrow, and even the Hairs of Animals, exhibit different
Curiosities.

4. The human Skin, by the Help of the Microscope, is
found to be covered over with an infinite Number of Scales
lying over one another, as in fishes; and it is probably the
same in other Animals. It has been computed that a Grain of
Sand will cover two hundred of these Scales.

5. All Sorts of Feathers, especially those of the Peacock, afford a surprizing View in the Microscope. It is supposed that
a single Feather contains no less than a Million of different
Parts.

6. Flies are found by the Microscope to be produced from
Eggs laid by the Mothers, from whence they are hatched in
the Form of Maggots, or small Worms, which are afterwards
transformed into Aurelias, and these into perfect Flies. This is
the Process most of the winged Insects go through in their
Production. They have a great Number of Eyes fixed to their
Heads, so that they see on all Sides around them, without
turning their Heads or Eyes. A common Fly is supposed to
have eight thousand, and a great Drone Fly no less than fourteen thousand Eyes, with a distinct optic Nerve to each; and
each Eye appears through the Microscope, tho' magnified
many hundred thousand Times, more exactly shaped, and
more curiously polished, than human Art could finish an Object as large as the whole Cluster, containing seven thousand
distinct ones. The Wings of Flies, especially of the Moth and
Butterfly Kind, are found to be contrived with admirable Art,
to answer their Use, and with inimitable Beauty and Ornament. The Dust, which sticks to the Fingers, when we handle
them, is found to be Feathers; each of which has its Quill and
vane Parts as compleat as that of a Fowl or a Goose, and are

inserted in the Film of the Wing, with the utmost Regularity of Arrangement. With the Microscope, the Stings of Moths and Bees appear to be Instruments finished to the highest Perfection; their Points, and saw-like Teeth, being perfectly polished and sharp; whereas the Edge of a Razor appears like that of a Butcher's Cleaver, and the Point of a Lancet like an iron Spike just come from the Anvil.

7. By the Help of the Microscope the innumerable and inconceivably minute Animalcules in various Fluids are discovered, of the Existence of which we have no Reason to suppose any Mortal had the least Suspicion, till last Century. In the Melt of a single Cod-fish ten Times more living Creatures are contained, than the Inhabitants of *Europe*, *Asia*, *Africa*, and *America*, taking it for granted, that all Parts of the World are as well peopled as *Holland*, which is very far from being the Case. Of a certain Species some are discovered so extremely minute, that it has been computed, three Millions of them, or three Times the Number of the Inhabitants of *London* and *Westminster*, would not equal the Bulk of a Grain of Sand. Of Animalcules, some Species resemble Tadpoles, Serpents or Eels, others are of a roundish or oval Form, others of very curiously turned and various Shapes; but in general they are extremely vigorous and lively, and almost constantly in Motion. Animalcules are to be found (besides those in the Bodies of Animals) in the Infusions of Pepper, Senna, Pinks, Roses, Jessamin, Tea, Rasberry Stalks, Fennel, Sage, Melons, sour Grapes, Wheat, Hay, Straw, and almost all vegetable Substances; in the Water, that is in the Shells of Oysters, Cockles, and other Shell-fish, in the Foulness upon our Teeth, and those of other Animals, in our Skins when affected with certain Diseases; in Vinegar, and Paste, and so on infinitely. In each of these Substances, when exposed to the Air some Time, Multitudes of living Creatures, beyond the Reach of Numbers, are discovered, of which many Hundreds of Species are already known, as different from one another as those of the largest Animals, and very probably there are many more yet unknown. As it is certain, that in the above mentioned Fluids few or no Animalcules are to be found, when covered from the Air, but when open to the Access of the Air, their Numbers are

beyond reckoning; it is hardly to be doubted, but that either the Air is replete with infinite Multitudes of living Creatures too small for Sight, which come and deposite their Eggs in Places proper for the Nutrition of the Young, or that their Eggs are floating every where in the Air, and falling promiscuously every where, only those are hatched, or come to Perfection, which fall upon Places fitted for them, and the others perish. However it is, the countless Numbers of those living Creatures, the Profusion of Life every where to be observed, is above Measure astonishing, and shews the Maker to be an infinite Being.

8. By the Help of the Microscope, we find that the Scales of almost every different Fish are different from those of others, in internal Texture; and that all of them are wrought with surprising Art and Beauty.

9. By Means of this noble Instrument we find, that the Seeds of almost all Manner of Vegetables contain in them the Stamina of the future Plant or Tree, and that their Production from the Seed, and their Growth to Maturity is only the Swelling and Enlarging of the Stamina by the Addition of nutritious Juices. It is probable the Manner of Production and Growth of Animals is analogous to this. The Fertility of some Plants is almost beyond Belief. One particularly is said by Naturalists to produce annually a Million of Seeds from one. The Farina of Flowers is found by the Help of the Microscope to be a regular organized Body, and not a meer Dust, as it appears to the naked Eye, and is reasonably supposed to be necessary to Fertility in Plants and Trees.

10. By the Microscope have been discovered many singular Properties of that most unaccountable of all Creatures the Polype, which is found at the Bottom of Ditches, and standing Waters; whose Manner of Production, Feeding and Digestion, are different from those of all other Animals. The young ones come out of the Sides of the old, like Buds and Branches from Trees, and at length drop off perfect Polypes. They do not seem to be of different Sexes. They take in Worms, and other Sustenance, by Means of a Sett of long Arms or *Antennæ*, which surround their Mouths, and after keeping them some Time in their Stomachs, throw them out again the same Way. The Animal's Body consists of a single

Cavity, like a Tube or Gut, and what is wonderful, and almost beyond Belief, is, that it will live and feed after it is turned inside out, and even when cut into a great many Pieces, each several Piece becomes a compleat Polype. They are infested with a Kind of Vermin, as are almost all Animals from the largest down to Bees and other Insects. These Vermin sometimes in a long Time will eat up the Head and Part of the Body of a Polype, after which, if it be cleared of them, it shall have the devoured Parts grow up again, and become as compleat as ever. Some Polypes have around their Mouths a Sort of Plume, which they whirl round, and making with it an Eddy in the Water, draw in their Prey, and devour it.

11. By the Microscope it is found, that neither the Wood, the Bark, the Root, the Leaves, the Fruit, nor even the Pith of the meanest Vegetable is a Mass of crude or indigested Matter; but that every different Species is different in its internal Structure, and all curiously and delicately wrought. A Bit of Cork, cut extremely thin, a Slice of Oak or Fir, or a Bit of Elder Pith, in the Microscope, are so many curious Pieces of *Mosaic* Work. Even a Bit of Charcoal or burnt Wood appears with the Microscope an admirable Object.

12. By this Instrument it is found, that what we call Mouldiness upon Flesh, Leather, or other Substances, is no other than a great Number of extremely small, but perfect Plants, having Stalks and Tops like Mushrooms, and sometimes an Appearance of Leaves. The Seeds of these minute Plants must, in all Probability, be diffused universally through the Air, and falling upon Substances fit for their Growth, spring up in astonishing Profusion. There is, in short, no End of microscopic Objects. A Sprig of Moss, with the Help of that Instrument, is found to be a regular Plant, consisting of a Root, a Stock, Branches, Leaves, *&c.* and Naturalists tell us, there are some Hundreds of different Species of it. A Bit of Spunge before the Microscope is a curious Piece of Net-work. Every different chymical Salt has its Parts differently figured. A Leaf of a common stinging Nettle, the Beard of a wild Oat, the Surfaces of some Pebble-stones, a Flake of Snow, a few Grains of Sand, or almost any natural Thing, with this Instrument, exhibit exquisite Beauties; while, on the contrary, the

most delicate Works of Art, can by no Means bear its Examination; but degenerate before it into Masses of Irregularity, and Deformity.

———

> Fond Pride of Dress is sure an empty Curse;
> E're *Fancy* you consult, consult your Purse.

Youth is pert and positive, *Age* modest and doubting: So Ears of Corn when young and light, stand bolt upright, but hang their Heads when weighty, full, and ripe.

'Tis easier to suppress the first Desire, than to satisfy all that follow it.

Don't judge of Mens Wealth or Piety, by their *Sunday* Appearances.

Friendship increases by visiting Friends, but by visiting seldom.

If your Riches are yours, why don't you take them with you to the t'other World?

What more valuable than Gold? Diamonds. Than Diamonds? Virtue.

To-day is Yesterday's Pupil.

If worldly Goods cannot save me from Death, they ought not to hinder me of eternal Life.

'Tis great Confidence in a Friend to tell him *your* Faults, greater to tell him *his*.

Talking against Religion is unchaining a Tyger; The Beast let loose may worry his Deliverer.

Ambition often spends foolishly what *Avarice* had wickedly collected.

Pillgarlic was in the *Accusative* Case, and bespoke a Lawyer in the *Vocative*, who could not understand him till he made use of the *Dative*.

> Great Estates may venture more;
> Little Boats must keep near Shore.

Nice Eaters seldom meet with a good Dinner.

Not to oversee Workmen, is to leave them your Purse open.

The Wise and Brave dares own that he was wrong.

Cunning proceeds from Want of Capacity.

———

It is an amusing Speculation to look back, and compute what Numbers of Men and Women among the Ancients, clubb'd their Endeavours to the Production of a single Modern. As you reckon backwards the Number encreases in the same Proportion as the Price of the Coat which was sold for a Half-penny a Button, continually doubled.

Thus, a present Nobleman (for Instance) is			1
His Father and Mother were			2
His Grandfathers and Grandmothers			4
His Great Grandfathers and Great Grandmothers,			8
And, supposing no Intermarriages among Relations,			
the next Predecessors will be			16
The next Ditto,	32	The next Ditto,	8192
The next Ditto,	64	The next Ditto,	16384
The next Ditto,	128	The next Ditto,	32768
The next Ditto,	256	The next Ditto,	65536
The next Ditto,	512	The next Ditto,	131072
The next Ditto,	1024	The next Ditto,	262144
The next Ditto,	2048	The next Ditto,	524288
The next Ditto,	4096	The next Do.	1048576

Here are only computed 21 Generations, which, allowing 3 Generations to 100 Years, carry us back no farther than the *Norman* Conquest, at which Time each present Nobleman, to exclude all ignoble Blood from his Veins, ought to have had One Million, Forty-eight Thousand, Five Hundred and Seventy-six noble Ancestors. Carry the Reckoning back 300 Years farther, and the Number amounts to above 500 Millions; which are more than exist at any one Time upon Earth, and shews the Impossibility of preserving Blood free from such Mixtures, and that the Pretension of such Purity of Blood in ancient Families is a mere Joke. Hence we see how it happens that every Nation has a kind of general Cast of Feature, by which it may be distinguished; continual Intermarriages for a

Course of Ages rendring all the People related by Blood, and, as it were, of one Family.

———

The Proud hate Pride—in others.

Who judges best of a Man, his Enemies or himself?

Drunkenness, that worst of Evils, makes some Men Fools, some Beasts, some Devils.

'Tis not a Holiday that's not kept holy.

Poor Richard Improved, 1752

KIND READER,

Since the King and Parliament have thought fit to alter our Year, by taking eleven Days out of *September*, 1752, and directing us to begin our Account for the future on the First of *January*, some Account of the Changes the Year hath heretofore undergone, and the Reasons of them, may a little gratify thy Curiosity.

The Vicissitude of *Seasons* seems to have given Occasion to the first Institution of the *Year*. Man naturally curious to know the Cause of that Diversity, soon found it was the Nearness and Distance of the Sun; and upon this, gave the Name *Year* to the Space of Time wherein that Luminary, performing his whole Course, returned to the same Point of his Orbit.

And hence, as it was on Account of the Seasons, in a great Measure, that the *Year* was instituted, their chief Regard and Attention was, that the same Parts of the *Year* should always correspond to the same Seasons; *i. e.* that the Beginning of the Year should always be when the Sun was in the same Point of his Orbit; and that they should keep Pace, come round, and end together.

This, different Nations aimed to attain by different Ways; making the *Year* to commence from different Points of the Zodiac; and even the Time of his Progress different. So that some of their Years were much more perfect than others, but none of them quite just; *i. e.* none of them but whose Parts shifted with Regard to the Parts of the Sun's Course.

It was the *Egyptians*, if we may credit *Herodotus*, that first formed the *Year*, making it to contain 360 Days, which they subdivided into twelve Months, of thirty Days each.

Mercury Trismegistus added five Days more to the Account.—And on this Footing *Thales* is said to have instituted the Year among the *Greeks.* Tho' that Form of the Year did not hold throughout all *Greece.* Add that the *Jewish, Syrian, Roman, Persian, Ethiopic, Arabic,* &c. Years, are all different.

In effect, considering the poor State of Astronomy in those Ages, it is no Wonder different People should disagree in the Calculus of the Sun's Course. We are even assured by *Diodorus Siculus, Plutarch,* and *Pliny,* that the *Egyptian Year* itself was at first very different from what it became afterwards.

According to our Account, the *Solar Year,* or the Interval of Time in which the Sun finishes his Course thro' the Zodiac, and returns to the same Point thereof from which he had departed, is 365 Days, 5 Hours, 49 Minutes; tho' some Astronomers make it a few Seconds, and some a whole Minute less; as *Kepler,* for Instance, who makes it 365 Days, 5 Hours, 48 Minutes, 57 Seconds, 39 Thirds. *Ricciolus,* 365 Days, 5 Hours, 48 Minutes. *Tycho Brahe,* 365 Days, 5 Hours, 48 Minutes.

The *Civil Year* is that Form of the *Year* which each Nation has contrived to compute Time by; or the *Civil* is the *Tropical Year,* considered as only consisting of a certain Number of whole Days; the odd Hours and Minutes being set aside, to render the Computation of Time in the common Occasions of Life more easy.

Hence as the *Tropical Year* is 365 Days, 5 Hours, 49 Minutes; the *Civil Year* is 365 Days. And hence also, as it is necessary to keep Pace with the Heavens, it is required that every fourth Year consist of 366 Days, which would for ever keep the Year exactly right, if the odd Hours of each Year were precisely 6.

The ancient *Roman Year,* as first settled by *Romulus,* consisted of ten Months only; *viz.* I. *March,* containing 31 Days. II. *April,* 30. III. *May,* 31. IV. *June* 30. V. *Quintilis,* 31. VI. *Sextilis,* 30. VII. *September,* 30. VIII. *October,* 31. IX. *November,*

30. X. *December*, 30; in all 304 Days; which came short of the *Solar Year*, by 61 Days.

Hence the Beginning of *Romulus's* Year was vague, and unfixed to any precise Season; which Inconvenience to remove, that Prince ordered so many Days to be added yearly, as would make the State of the Heavens correspond to the first Month, without incorporating these additional Days, or calling them by the Name of any Month.

Numa Pompilius corrected this irregular Constitution of the Year, and composed two new Months, *January* and *February*, of the Days that were used to be added to the former Year. Thus, *Numa's Year* consisted of twelve Months; *viz.* I. *January*, containing 29 Days. II. *February*, 28. III. *March*, 31. IV. *April*, 29. V. *May*, 31. VI. *June*, 29. VII. *Quintilis*, 31. VIII. *Sextilis*, 29. IX. *September*, 29. X. *October*, 31. XI. *November*, 29. XII. *December*, 29; in all 355 Days, which came short of the common Solar Year by ten Days; so that its Beginning was vague and unfixed.

Numa, however, desiring to have it fixed to the Winter Solstice, ordered 22 Days to be intercalated in *February* every second Year, 23 every fourth, 22 every sixth, and 23 every eighth Year.

But this Rule failing to keep Matters even, Recourse was had to a new Way of Intercalating; and instead of 23 Days every eighth Year, only 15 were added; and the Care of the whole committed to the *Pontifex Maximus*, or High Priest; who, neglecting the Trust, let Things run to the utmost Confusion. And thus the *Roman* Year stood till *Julius Cæsar* made a Reformation.

The *Julian Year*, is a Solar Year, containing commonly 365 Days; tho' every fourth Year, called *Bissextile*, contains 366.—The Names and Order of the Months of the *Julian Year*, and the Number of Days in each, are well known to us, having been long in Use.

The astronomical Quantity, therefore, of the *Julian Year*, is 365 Days, 6 Hours, which exceeds the true Solar Year by 11 Minutes; which Excess in 131 Years amounts to a whole Day.—And thus the *Roman Year* stood, till the Reformation made therein by Pope *Gregory*.

Julius Cæsar, in the Contrivance of his Form of the Year,

was assisted by *Sosigenes*, a famous Mathematician, called over from *Egypt* for this very Purpose; who, to supply the Defect of 67 Days which had been lost thro' the Fault of the High Priests, and to fix the Beginning of the Year to the Winter Solstice, made that Year to consist of 15 Months, or 445 Days; which for that Reason is used to be called *Annus Confusionis*, the *Year of Confusion*.

This Form of the Year was used by all Christian Nations, till the Middle of the 16th Century; and still continues to be so by several Nations; among the Rest, by the *Swedes*, *Danes*, &c. and by the *English* till the second of *September* next, when they are to assume the Use of the *Gregorian Year*.

The GREGORIAN YEAR is the *Julian Year* corrected by this Rule; that whereas on the common Footing, every Secular or Hundredth Year, is *Bissextile*; on the new Footing,' three of them are common Years, and only the fourth *Bissextile*.

The Error of eleven Minutes in the *Julian Year*, little as it was, yet, by being repeated over and over, at length became considerable; and from the Time when *Cæsar* made his Correction, was grown into 13 Days, by which the Equinoxes were greatly disturbed. To remedy this Irregularity, which was still a growing, Pope *Gregory* the XIII. called together the chief Astronomers of his Time, and concerted this Correction; and to restore the Equinoxes to their Place threw out the ten Days that had been got from the Council of *Nice*, and which had shifted the fifth of *October* to the 15th.

In the Year 1700, the Error of ten Days was grown to eleven; upon which the Protestant States of *Germany*, to prevent further Confusion, accepted the *Gregorian* Correction. And now in 1752, the *English* follow their Example.

Yet is the *Gregorian Year* far from being perfect, for we have shewn, that, in four Centuries, the *Julian Year* gains three Days, one Hour, twenty Minutes: But it is only the three Days are kept out in the *Gregorian Year*; so that here is still an Excess of one Hour, twenty Minutes, in four Centuries; which in 72 Centuries will amount to a whole Day.

As to the Commencement of the Year, the *legal Year* in *England* used to begin on the Day of the *Annunciation*; *i. e.* on the 25th of *March*; tho' the historical Year began on the Day of the *Circumcision*; *i. e.* the first of *January*, on which

Day the *Italian* and *German* Year also begins; and on which
Day ours is to begin from this Time forward, the first Day of
January being now by Act of Parliament declared the first
Day of the Year 1752.

At the Yearly Meeting of the People called *Quakers*, held in
London, since the Passing of this Act, it was agreed to recommend to their Friends a Conformity thereto, both in omitting the eleven Days of *September* thereby directed to be
omitted, and beginning the Year hereafter on the first Day of
the Month called *January*, which is henceforth to be by them
called and written, *The First Month*, and the rest likewise in
their Order, so that *September* will now be the *Ninth Month*,
December the *Twelfth*.

This *Act of Parliament*, as it contains many Matters of Importance, and extends expresly to all the *British Colonies*, I
shall for the Satisfaction of the Publick, give at full length:
Wishing withal, according to ancient Custom, that this *New
Year* (which is indeed a New Year, such an one as we never
saw before, and shall never see again) may be a happy Year to
all my kind Readers.

I am, Your faithful Servant,

R. SAUNDERS.

Observe old *Vellum*; he praises former Times, as if he'd a
mind to sell 'em.

Kings have long Arms, but Misfortune longer: Let none
think themselves out of her Reach.

For want of a Nail the Shoe is lost; for want of a Shoe, the
Horse is lost; for want of a Horse the Rider is lost.

The busy Man has few idle Visitors; to the boiling Pot the
Flies come not.

Calamity and Prosperity are the Touchstones of Integrity.

The Prodigal generally does more Injustice than the
Covetous.

Generous Minds are all of kin.

'Tis more noble to forgive, and more manly to despise, than
to revenge an Injury.

A Brother may not be a Friend, but a Friend will always be a Brother.

Meanness is the Parent of Insolence.

Mankind are very odd Creatures: One Half censure what they practise, the other half practise what they censure; the rest always say and do as they ought.

Severity is often Clemency; Clemency Severity.

Bis dat qui cito dat: He gives twice that gives soon; *i. e.* he will soon be called upon to give again.

A Temper to bear much, will have much to bear.

Pride dines upon Vanity, sups on Contempt.

Great Merit is coy, as well as great Pride.

An undutiful Daughter, will prove an unmanageable Wife.

Old Boys have their Playthings as well as young Ones; the Difference is only in the Price.

The too obliging Temper is evermore disobliging itself.

Hold your Council before Dinner; the full Belly hates Thinking as well as Acting.

The Brave and the Wise can both pity and excuse; when Cowards and Fools shew no Mercy.

Ceremony is not Civility; nor Civility Ceremony.

If Man could have Half his Wishes, he would double his Troubles.

It is ill Jesting with the Joiner's Tools, worse with the Doctor's.

Children and Princes will quarrel for Trifles.

Praise to the undeserving, is severe Satyr.

Success has ruin'd many a Man.

> Great Pride and Meanness sure are near ally'd;
> Or thin Partitions do their Bounds divide.

Poor Richard Improved, 1753

COURTEOUS READER,

This is the twentieth Time of my addressing thee in this Manner, and I have reason to flatter myself my Labours have not been unacceptable to the Publick. I am particularly pleas'd to understand that my *Predictions of the Weather* give such general Satisfaction; and indeed, such Care is taken in the Calculations, on which those Predictions are founded, that I could almost venture to say, there's not a single One of them, promising *Snow*, *Rain*, *Hail*, *Heat*, *Frost*, *Fogs*, *Wind*, or *Thunder*, but what comes to pass *punctually* and *precisely* on the very Day, in some Place or other on this little *diminutive* Globe of ours; (and when you consider the vast Distance of the Stars from whence we take our Aim, you must allow it no small Degree of Exactness to hit any Part of it) I say on this Globe; for tho' in other Matters I confine the Usefulness of my *Ephemeris* to the *Northern Colonies*, yet in that important Matter of the Weather, which is of such *general Concern*, I would have it more extensively useful, and therefore take in both Hemispheres, and all Latitudes from *Hudson's Bay* to *Cape Horn*.

You will find this Almanack in my former Method, only conformable to the *New-Stile* established by the Act of Parliament, which I gave you in my last at length; the new Act since made for Amendment of that first Act, not affecting us in the least, being intended only to regulate some Corporation Matters in *England*, before unprovided for. I have only added a Column in the second Page of each Month, containing the Days of the *Old Stile* opposite to their corresponding Days in the *New*, which may, in many Cases, be of Use; and so conclude (believing you will excuse a short Preface, when it is to make Room for something better)

Thy Friend and Servant,
R. SAUNDERS.

———

'Tis against some Mens Principle to pay Interest, and seems against others Interest to pay the Principal.

Philosophy as well as Foppery often changes Fashion.

Setting too good an Example is a Kind of Slander seldom forgiven; 'tis *Scandalum Magnatum.*

A great Talker may be no Fool, but he is one that relies on him.

When Reason preaches, if you won't hear her she'll box your Ears.

It is not Leisure that is not used.

The Good-will of the Governed will be starv'd, if not fed by the good Deeds of the Governors.

Paintings and Fightings are best seen at a distance.

> If you would reap Praise you must sow the Seeds,
> Gentle Words and useful Deeds.

Ignorance leads Men into a Party, and *Shame* keeps them from getting out again.

Haste makes Waste.

Many have quarrel'd about Religion, that never practis'd it.

Sudden Power is apt to be insolent, *Sudden Liberty* saucy; that behaves best which has grown gradually.

He that best understands the World, least likes it.

Anger is never without a Reason, but seldom with a good One.

He that is of Opinion Money will do every Thing, may well be suspected of doing every Thing for Money.

An ill Wound, but not an ill Name, may be healed.

When out of Favour, none know thee; when in, thou dost not know thyself.

A lean Award is better than a fat Judgment.

God, Parents, and *Instructors,* can never be requited.

He that builds before he counts the Cost, acts foolishly; and he that counts before he builds, finds he did not count wisely.

Patience in Market, is worth Pounds in a Year.

Danger is Sauce for Prayers.

If you have no Honey in your Pot, have some in your Mouth.

A Pair of good Ears will drain dry an hundred Tongues.

Serving God is Doing Good to Man, but Praying is thought an easier Service, and therefore more generally chosen.

Nothing humbler than *Ambition*, when it is about to climb.

The discontented Man finds no easy Chair.

Virtue and a Trade, are a Child's best Portion.

Gifts much expected, are *paid*, not *given*.

———

How to secure Houses, &c. *from* LIGHTNING.

It has pleased God in his Goodness to Mankind, at length to discover to them the Means of securing their Habitations and other Buildings from Mischief by Thunder and Lightning. The Method is this: Provide a small Iron Rod (it may be made of the Rod-iron used by the Nailers) but of such a Length, that one End being three or four Feet in the moist Ground, the other may be six or eight Feet above the highest Part of the Building. To the upper End of the Rod fasten about a Foot of Brass Wire, the Size of a common Knitting-needle, sharpened to a fine Point; the Rod may be secured to the House by a few small Staples. If the House or Barn be long, there may be a Rod and Point at each End, and a middling Wire along the Ridge from one to the other. A House thus furnished will not be damaged by Lightning, it being attracted by the Points, and passing thro the Metal into the Ground without hurting any Thing. Vessels also, having a sharp pointed Rod fix'd on the Top of their Masts, with a Wire from the Foot of the Rod reaching down, round one of the Shrouds, to the Water, will not be hurt by Lightning.

Poor Richard Improved, 1754

Kind READER,

I have now serv'd you three Apprenticeships, yet, old as I am, I have no Inclination to quit your Service, but should be glad to be able to continue in it three times three Apprenticeships longer.

The first *Astrologers* I think, were honest Husbandmen; and so it seems are the last; for my Brethren *Jerman* and *Moore*, and myself, the only remaining Almanack-makers of this Country, are all of that Class: Tho' in intermediate Times our Art has been cultivated in great Cities, and even in the Courts of Princes; witness History, from the Days of King NEBU-CHADNEZZAR I. of *Babylon*, to those of Queen JAMES I. of *England*.—But you will ask, perhaps, how I prove that the first Astrologers were Countrymen?—I own this is a Matter beyond the Memory of History, for Astrology was before Letters; but I prove it from the Book of the Heavens, from the Names of the twelve Signs, which were mostly given to remark some Circumstance relative to rural Affairs, in the several successive Months of the Year, and by that Means to supply the Want of Almanacks.—Thus, as the Year of the Ancients began most naturally with the Spring, *Aries* and *Taurus*, that is, the Ram and the Bull, represented the successive Addition to their Flocks of Sheep and Kine, by their Produce in that Season, Lambs and Calves.— *Gemini* were originally the Kids, but called the Twins, as Goats more commonly bring forth two than one: These follow'd the Calves.— *Cancer*, the Crab, came next, when that Kind of Fish were in Season.—Then follow'd *Leo*, the Lion, and *Virgo*, the Wench, to mark the Summer Months, and Dog-days, when those Creatures were most mischievous. In Autumn comes first *Libra*, the Ballance, to point out the Time for weighing and selling the Summer's Produce; or rather, a Time of Leisure for holding Courts of Justice in which they might plague themselves and Neighbours; I know some suppose this Sign to signify the equal Poise, at that Time, of Day and Night; but the other Signification is the truer, as plainly appears by the following Sign *Scorpio*, or the Scorpion, with the Sting in his Tail, which certainly denotes the Paying of Costs.—Then follows *Sagittary*, the Archer, to show the Season of Hunting; for now the Leaves being off the Trees and Bushes, the Game might be more easily seen and struck with their Arrows.—The *Goat* accompanies the short Days and long Nights of Winter, to shew the Season of Mirth, Feasting and Jollity; for what can *Capricorn* mean, but Dancing or Cutting of *Capers*?—At length comes *Aquarius*, or the Water-bearer, to show the Season of Snows, Rains and Floods; and lastly *Pisces*, or the two Shads, to denote the approaching Return of those Fish up the Rivers: Make your Wears, hawl your Seins; Catch 'em and pickle 'em, my Friends; they are excellent Relishers of old Cyder.—But if you can't get Shad, Mackrell may do better.

I know, gentle Readers, that many of you always expect a Preface, and think yourselves slighted if that's omitted. So here you have it, and much good may't do ye. As little as it is to the Purpose, there are many less so, now-a-days.—I have left out, you see, all the usual Stuff about the *Importunity of Friends*, and the like, or I might have made it much bigger. You think, however, that 'tis big enough o'Conscience, for any Matter of Good that's in it;—I think so too, if it fills the Page, which is the Needful at present, from

Your loving Friend to serve,
R. SAUNDERS.

———

The first Degree of Folly, is to conceit one's self wise; the second to profess it; the third to despise Counsel.

Take heed of the Vinegar of sweet Wine, and the Anger of Good-nature.

The Bell calls others to Church, but itself never minds the Sermon.

Cut the Wings of your Hens and Hopes, lest they lead you a weary Dance after them.

In Rivers & bad Governments, the lightest Things swim at top.

The Cat in Gloves catches no Mice.

If you'd know the Value of Money, go and borrow some.

The Horse thinks one thing, and he that saddles him another.

Love your Neighbour; yet don't pull down your Hedge.

When *Prosperity* was well mounted, she let go the Bridle, and soon came tumbling out of the Saddle.

Some make Conscience of wearing a Hat in the Church, who make none of robbing the Altar.

In the Affairs of this World Men are saved, not by Faith, but by the Want of it.

Friendship cannot live with *Ceremony*, nor without *Civility*.

Praise little, dispraise less.

The learned Fool writes his Nonsense in better Language than the unlearned; but still 'tis Nonsense.

A Child thinks 20 *Shillings* and 20 Years can scarce ever be spent.

Don't think so much of your own Cunning, as to forget other Mens: A cunning Man is overmatch'd by a cunning Man and a Half.

Willows are weak, but they bind the Faggot.

You may give a Man an Office, but you cannot give him Discretion.

He that doth what he should not, shall feel what he would not.

To be intimate with a foolish Friend, is like going to bed to a Razor.

Little Rogues easily become great Ones.

You may sometimes be much in the wrong, in owning your being in the right.

Friends are the true Sceptres of Princes.

Where Sense is wanting, every thing is wanting.

Many Princes sin with *David*, but few repent with him.

He that hath no *ill* Fortune will be troubled with *good*.

For Age and Want save while you may;
No Morning Sun lasts a whole Day.

Learning to the Studious; Riches to the Careful; Power to
the Bold; Heaven to the Virtuous.

Now glad the Poor with *Christmas* Cheer;
Thank God you're able so to end the Year.

Poor Richard Improved, 1755

Courteous READER,

It is a common Saying, that *One Half of the World does not
know how the other Half lives*. To add somewhat to your
Knowledge in that Particular, I gave you in a former Almanack, an Account of the Manner of living at *Hudson's-Bay*,
and the Effects produced by the excessive Cold of that Climate, which seem'd so strange to some of you, that it was
taken for a Romance, tho' really authentick.—In this, I shall
give you some Idea of a Country under the Torrid Zone,
which for the Variety of its Weather (where one would naturally expect the greatest Uniformity) is extreamly remarkable.
The Account is extracted from the Journal of Monsieur *Bouguer*, one of the *French* Academicians, sent by their King to
measure a Degree of Latitude under the Equinoctial, in order
to settle a Dispute between the *English* and *French* Philosophers concerning the Shape of the Earth, others being at the
same Time sent for the same Purpose to *Lapland*, under the
Polar Circle.—The Mountains in that Country are so lofty,
that the highest we have, being compared to them, are mere
Mole-hills. This Extract relates chiefly to the Country among
those Mountains.

The Method of this Almanack is the same I have observed
for some Years past; only in the third Column the Names of
some of the principal fixed Stars are put down against those
Days on which they come to the Meridian at nine a Clock in
the Evening, whereby those unacquainted, may learn to know
them. I am,

Your obliged Friend and Servant,
R. SAUNDERS.

A Man without a Wife, is but half a Man.

Speak little, do much.

He that would travel much, should eat little.

When the Wine enters, out goes the Truth.

If you would be loved, love and be loveable.

Ask and have, is sometimes dear buying.

The hasty Bitch brings forth blind Puppies.

Where there is Hunger, Law is not regarded; and where Law is not regarded, there will be Hunger.

Two dry Sticks will burn a green One.

The honest Man takes Pains, and then enjoys Pleasures; the Knave takes Pleasure, and then suffers Pains.

Think of three Things, whence you came, where you are going, and to whom you must account.

Necessity has no Law; Why? Because 'tis not to be had without Money.

There was never a good Knife made of bad Steel.

The Wolf sheds his Coat once a Year, his Disposition never.

> *Who is wise?* He that learns from every One.
> *Who is powerful?* He that governs his Passions.
> *Who is rich?* He that is content.
> *Who is that?* Nobody.

A full Belly brings forth every Evil.

The Day is short, the Work great, the Workmen lazy, the Wages high, the Master urgeth; Up, then, and be doing.

The Doors of Wisdom are never shut.

Much Virtue in Herbs, little in Men.

The Master's Eye will do more Work than both his Hands.

When you taste Honey, remember Gall.

Being ignorant is not so much a Shame, as being unwilling to learn.

God gives all Things to Industry.

An hundred Thieves cannot strip one naked Man, especially if his Skin's off.

Diligence overcomes Difficulties, Sloth makes them.

Neglect mending a small Fault, and 'twill soon be a great One.

Bad Gains are truly Losses.

A long Life may not be good enough, but a good Life is long enough.

Be at War with your Vices, at Peace with your Neighbours, and let every New-Year find you a better Man.

Poor Richard Improved, 1756

COURTEOUS READER,

I suppose my Almanack may be worth the Money thou hast paid for it, hadst thou no other Advantage from it, than to find the *Day of the Month*, the *remarkable Days*, the *Changes of the Moon*, the *Sun and Moon's Rising and Setting*, and to foreknow the *Tides* and the *Weather*; these, with other Astronomical Curiosities, I have yearly and constantly prepared for thy Use and Entertainment, during now near two Revolutions of the Planet *Jupiter*. But I hope this is not all the Advantage thou hast reaped; for with a View to the Improvement of thy *Mind* and thy *Estate*, I have constantly interspers'd in every little Vacancy, *Moral Hints*, *Wise Sayings*, and *Maxims of Thrift*, tending to impress the Benefits arising from *Honesty*, *Sobriety*, *Industry* and *Frugality*; which if thou hast duly observed, it is highly probable thou art *wiser* and *richer* many fold more than the Pence my Labours have cost thee. Howbeit, I shall not therefore raise my Price because thou art better able to pay; but being thankful for past Favours, shall endeavour to make my little Book more worthy thy Regard, by adding to those *Recipes* which were intended for the *Cure* of the *Mind*, some valuable Ones regarding the *Health* of the *Body*. They are recommended by the Skilful, and by successful Practice. I wish a Blessing may attend the Use of them, and to thee all Happiness, being

Thy obliged Friend,
R. SAUNDERS.

————

A Change of *Fortune* hurts a wise Man no more than a Change of the *Moon*.

Does Mischief, Misconduct, & Warrings displease ye; Think there's a Providence, 'twill make ye easy.

Mine is better than *Ours*.

Love your Enemies, for they tell you your Faults.

He that has a Trade, has an Office of Profit and Honour.

Be civil to *all*; serviceable to *many*; familiar with *few*; Friend to *one*; Enemy to *none*.

Vain-Glory flowereth, but beareth no Fruit.

————

As I spent some Weeks last Winter, in visiting my old Acquaintance in the *Jerseys*, great Complaints I heard for Want of Money, and that Leave to make more Paper Bills could not be obtained. *Friends and Countrymen*, my Advice on this Head shall cost you nothing, and if you will not be angry with me for giving it, I promise you not to be offended if you do not take it.

You spend yearly at least *Two Hundred Thousand Pounds*, 'tis said, in *European*, *East-Indian*, and *West-Indian* Commodities: Supposing one Half of this Expence to be in *Things absolutely necessary*, the other Half may be call'd *Superfluities*, or at best, Conveniences, which however you might live without for one little Year, and not suffer exceedingly. Now to save this Half, observe these few Directions.

1. When you incline to have new Cloaths, look first well over the old Ones, and see if you cannot shift with them another Year, either by Scouring, Mending, or even Patching if necessary. Remember a Patch on your Coat, and Money in your Pocket, is better and more creditable than a Writ on your Back, and no Money to take it off.

2. When you incline to buy China Ware, Chinces, *India* Silks, or any other of their flimsey slight Manufactures; I would not be so hard with you, as to insist on your absolutely *resolving against it*; all I advise, is, to *put it off* (as you do your Repentance) *till another Year*; and this, in some Respects, may prevent an Occasion of Repentance.

3. If you are now a Drinker of Punch, Wine or Tea, twice a Day; for the ensuing Year drink them but *once* a Day. If you now drink them but once a Day, do it but every other Day. If you do it now but once a Week, reduce the Practice to once a Fortnight. And if you do not exceed in Quantity as you lessen the Times, half your Expence in these Articles will be saved.

4thly and lastly, When you incline to drink Rum, fill the Glass *half* with Water.

Thus at the Year's End, there will be *An Hundred Thousand Pounds* more Money in your Country.

If Paper Money in ever so great a Quantity could be made, no Man could get any of it without giving something for it. But all he saves in this Way, will be *his own for nothing*; and his Country actually so much richer. Then the Merchants old and doubtful Debts may be honestly paid off, and Trading become surer thereafter, if not so extensive.

————

Laws *too gentle* are seldom *obeyed*; *too severe*, seldom *executed*.

Trouble springs from *Idleness*; *Toil* from *Ease*.

Love, and be *loved*.

A wise Man will desire no more, than what he may get justly, use soberly, distribute chearfully, and leave contentedly.

The diligent Spinner has a large Shift.

A false Friend and a Shadow, attend only while the Sun shines.

To-morrow, every Fault is to be amended; but that *To-morrow* never comes.

> Plough deep, while Sluggards sleep;
> And you shall have Corn, to sell and to keep.

He that sows Thorns, should never go barefoot.

Laziness travels so slowly, that *Poverty* soon overtakes him.

Sampson with his *strong Body*, had a *weak Head*, or he would not have laid it in a Harlot's Lap.

> When a Friend deals with a Friend
> Let the Bargain be clear and well penn'd,
> That they may continue Friends to the End.

He that never eats too much, will never be lazy.

To be *proud* of *Knowledge*, is to be *blind* with *Light*; to be *proud* of *Virtue*, is to *poison* yourself with the *Antidote*.

> Get what you can, and what you get, hold;
> 'Tis the *Stone* that will turn all your Lead into Gold.

An honest Man will receive neither *Money* nor *Praise*, that is not his Due.

———

Well, my Friend, thou art now just entering the last Month of another Year. If thou art a Man of Business, and of prudent Care, belike thou wilt now settle thy Accounts, to satisfy thyself whether thou hast gain'd or lost in the Year past, and how much of either, the better to regulate thy future Industry or thy common Expences. This is commendable.—But it is not all.—Wilt thou not examine also thy *moral* Accompts, and see what Improvements thou hast made in the Conduct of Life, what Vice subdued, what Virtue acquired; how much *better*, and how much *wiser*, as well as how much *richer* thou art grown? What shall it *profit* a Man, if he *gain* the whole World, and *lose* his own Soul? Without some Care in this Matter, tho' thou may'st come to count thy Thousands, thou wilt possibly still appear poor in the Eyes of the Discerning, even *here*, and be really so for ever *hereafter*.

Saying and *Doing*, have quarrel'd and parted.

Tell me my Faults, and mend your own.

Poor Richard Improved, 1757

COURTEOUS READER,

As no temporal Concern is of more Importance to us than *Health*, and that depends so much on the Air we every Moment breathe, the Choice of a good wholesome Situation to fix a Dwelling in, is a very serious Affair to every Countryman about to begin the World, and well worth his Consideration, especially as not only the *Comfort* of Living, but even the *Necessaries of Life*, depend in a great Measure upon it; since a Family frequently sick can rarely if ever thrive.—The following Extracts therefore from a late Medical Writer, Dr. *Pringle*, on that Subject, will, I hope, be acceptable and useful to some of my Readers.

I hear that some have already, to their great Advantage, put in Practice the Use of Oxen recommended in my last.—'Tis a Pleasure to me to be any way serviceable in communicating useful Hints to the Publick; and I shall be obliged to others for affording me the Opportunity of enjoying that Pleasure more frequently, by sending me from time to time such of their own Observations, as may be advantageous if published in the Almanack.

I am thy obliged Friend,
RICHARD SAUNDERS.

————

How to make a STRIKING SUNDIAL, *by which not only a Man's own Family, but all his Neighbours for ten Miles round, may know what o Clock it is, when the Sun shines, without seeing the Dial.*

Chuse an open Place in your Yard or Garden, on which the Sun may shine all Day without any Impediment from Trees or Buildings. On the Ground mark out your Hour Lines, as for a horizontal Dial, according to Art, taking Room enough for the Guns. On the Line for One o' Clock, place one Gun;

on the Two o' Clock Line two Guns, and so of the rest. The Guns must all be charged with Powder, but Ball is unnecessary. Your Gnomon or Style must have twelve burning Glasses annex'd to it, and be so placed as that the Sun shining through the Glasses, one after the other, shall cause the Focus or burning Spot to fall on the Hour Line of One, for Example, at one a Clock, and there kindle a Train of Gunpowder that shall fire one Gun. At Two a Clock, a Focus shall fall on the Hour Line of Two, and kindle another Train that shall discharge two Guns successively; and so of the rest.

Note, There must be 78 Guns in all. Thirty-two Pounders will be best for this Use; but 18 Pounders may do, and will cost less, as well as use less Powder, for nine Pounds of Powder will do for one Charge of each eighteen Pounder, whereas the Thirty-two Pounders would require for each Gun 16 Pounds.

Note also, That the chief Expence will be the Powder, for the Cannon once bought, will, with Care, last 100 Years.

Note moreover, That there will be a great Saving of Powder in cloudy Days.

Kind Reader, Methinks I hear thee say, *That it is indeed a good Thing to know how the Time passes, but this Kind of Dial, notwithstanding the mentioned Savings, would be very expensive; and the Cost greater than the Advantage.* Thou art wise, my Friend, to be so considerate beforehand; some Fools would not have found out so much, till they had made the Dial and try'd it.—Let all such learn that many a private and many a publick Project, are like this *Striking Dial*, great Cost for little Profit.

He that would rise at Court, must begin by Creeping.

Many a Man's own Tongue gives Evidence against his
    Understanding.

Nothing dries sooner than a Tear.

'Tis easier to build two Chimneys, than maintain one in Fuel.

Anger warms the Invention, but overheats the Oven.

It is Ill-Manners to silence a Fool, and Cruelty to let him
    go on.

Scarlet, Silk and Velvet, have put out the Kitchen Fire.

He that would catch Fish, must venture his Bait.

Men take more pains to mask than mend.

One *To-day* is worth two *To-morrows*.

———

Since Man is but of a very limited Power in his own Person, and consequently can effect no great Matter merely by his own personal Strength, but as he acts in Society and Conjunction with others; and since no Man can engage the active Assistance of others, without first engaging their Trust; And moreover, since Men will trust no further than they judge one, for his *Sincerity*, fit to be trusted; it follows, that a discovered Dissembler can atchieve nothing great or considerable. For not being able to gain Mens Trust, he cannot gain their Concurrence; and so is left alone to act singly and upon his own Bottom; and while that is the Sphere of his Activity, all that he can do must needs be contemptible.

> Sincerity has such resistless Charms,
> She oft the fiercest of our Foes disarms:
> No Art she knows, in native Whiteness dress'd,
> Her Thoughts all pure, and therefore all express'd:
> She takes from Error its Deformity;
> And without her all other Virtues die.
> Bright Source of Goodness! to my Aid descend,
> Watch o'er my Heart, and all my Words attend.

———

The way to be safe, is never to be secure.

Dally not with other Folks Women or Money.

Work as if you were to live 100 Years, Pray as if you were to die To-morrow.

———

It is generally agreed to be Folly, *to hazard the Loss of a Friend, rather than lose a Jest*. But few consider how easily a Friend may be thus lost. Depending on the known Regard their Friends have for them, Jesters take more Freedom with Friends than they would dare to do with others, little thinking how much deeper we are wounded by an Affront from one we love. But the strictest Intimacy can never warrant Freedoms of this Sort; and it is indeed preposterous to think they should; unless we can suppose Injuries are less Evils when they are done us by Friends, than when they come from other Hands.

> Excess of Wit may oftentimes beguile:
> Jests are not always pardon'd—by a Smile.
> Men may disguise their Malice at the Heart,
> And seem at Ease—tho' pain'd with inward Smart.
> Mistaken, we—think all such Wounds of course
> Reflection cures;—alas! it makes them worse.
> Like Scratches they with double Anguish seize,
> Rankle in time, and fester by Degrees.

But sarcastical Jests on a Man's Person or his Manners, tho' hard to bear, are perhaps more easily borne than those that touch his Religion. Men are generally warm in what regards their religious Tenets, either from Tenderness of Conscience, or a high Sense of their own Judgments. People of plain Parts and honest Dispositions, look on Salvation as too serious a Thing to be jested with; and Men of speculative Religion, who profess from the Conviction rather of their Heads than Hearts, are not a bit less vehement than the real Devotees. He who says a slight or a severe Thing of their Faith, seems to them to have thereby undervalued their Understandings, and will consequently incur their Aversion, which no Man of common Sense would hazard for a lively Expression; much less a Person of good Breeding, who should make it his chief Aim to be well with all.

> Like some grave Matron of a noble Line,
> With awful Beauty does Religion shine.
> Just Sense should teach us to revere the Dame,
> Nor, by imprudent Jests, to spot her Fame.
> In common Life you'll own this Reas'ning right,
> That none but Fools in gross Abuse delight:
> Then use it here—nor think the Caution vain;
> To be *polite*, Men need not be profane.

————

Pride breakfasted with *Plenty*, dined with *Poverty*, supped with *Infamy*.

Retirement does not always secure Virtue; *Lot* was upright
in the City, wicked in the Mountain.

Idleness is the Dead Sea, that swallows all Virtues: Be active
in Business, that *Temptation* may miss her Aim: The Bird
that sits, is easily shot.

Shame and the *Dry-belly-ach* were Diseases of the last Age;
this seems to be cured of them.

————

In studying Law or Physick, or any other Art or Science,
by which you propose to get your Livelihood, though you
find it at first hard, difficult and unpleasing, use *Diligence,
Patience* and *Perseverance*; the Irksomness of your Task will
thus diminish daily, and your Labour shall finally be crowned
with Success. You shall go beyond all your Competitors who
are careless, idle or superficial in their Acquisitions, and be at
the Head of your Profession. —*Ability* will command *Business, Business Wealth*; and *Wealth* an easy and honourable *Retirement* when Age shall require it.

> Near to the wide extended Coasts of *Spain*,
> Some Islands triumph o'er the raging Main;
> Where dwelt of old, as tuneful Poets say,
> *Slingers*, who bore from all the Prize away.
> While Infants yet, their feeble Nerves they try'd;
> Nor needful Food, till won by Art, supply'd.
> Fix'd was the Mark, the Youngster oft in vain,
> Whirl'd the misguided Stone with fruitless Pain:
> 'Till, by long Practice, to Perfection brought,
> With easy Sleight their former Task they wrought.
> Swift from their Arm th' unerring Pebble flew,
> And high in Air, the flutt'ring Victim slew.
> So in each Art Men rise but by Degrees,
> And Months of Labour lead to Years of Ease.

————

Tho' the Mastiff be gentle, yet bite him not by the Lip.

Great-Alms-giving, lessens no Man's Living.

The royal Crown cures not the Head-ach.

Act uprightly, and despise Calumny; Dirt may stick to a
Mud Wall, but not to polish'd Marble.

PARADOXES.

I. The *Christians* observe the *first* Day of the Week for their *Sunday*, the *Jews* the *Seventh* for their Sabbath, the *Turks* the *sixth* Day of the Week for the Time of their Worship; but there is a particular Place of the Globe, to which if a *Christian*, *Jew*, and *Turk* sail in one and the same Ship, they shall keep the Time for their Worship on different Days, as above, all the Time they are sailing to that particular Place; but when they arrive at that Place, and during the Time they remain at it, they shall all keep their Sabbath on one and the same Day; but when they depart from that Place, they shall all differ as before.

II. There is a certain Port, from which if three Ships depart at one and the same time, and sail on three particular different Courses, till they return to the Port they departed from; and if in one of these Ships be *Christians*, in the second *Jews*, and in the third *Turks*, when they return to the Port they departed from, they shall differ so with respect to real and apparent Time, that they all shall keep their Sabbath on one and the same Day of the Week, and yet each of them separately shall believe that he keeps his Sabbath on the Day of the Week his Religion requires.

————

The *Borrower* is a Slave to the *Lender*; the *Security* to *both.*

Singularity in the right, hath ruined many: Happy those who are convinced of the general Opinion.

Proportion your Charity to the Strength of your Estate, or God will proportion your Estate to the Weakness of your Charity.

The Tongue offends, and the Ears get the Cuffing.

————

Some antient Philosophers have said, that Happiness depends more on the inward Disposition of Mind than on outward Circumstances; and that he who cannot be happy in any State, can be so in no State. To be happy, they tell us we must be content. Right. But they do not teach how we may become content. *Poor Richard* shall give you a short good Rule for that. *To be content, look backward on those who possess less than yourself, not forward on those who possess more.* If this does not make you *content*, you don't deserve to be *happy*.

———

Sleep without Supping, and you'll rise without owing for it.

> When other Sins grow old by Time,
> Then Avarice is in its prime,
> Yet feed the Poor at *Christmas* time.

———

Learning is a valuable Thing in the Affairs of this Life, but of infinitely more Importance is *Godliness*, as it tends not only to make us happy here but hereafter. At the Day of Judgment, we shall not be asked, what Proficiency we have made in Languages or Philosophy; but whether we have liv'd virtuously and piously, as Men endued with Reason, guided by the Dictates of Religion. In that Hour it will more avail us, that we have thrown a Handful of Flour or Chaff in Charity to a Nest of contemptible Pismires, than that we could muster all the Hosts of Heaven, and call every Star by its proper Name. For then the Constellations themselves shall disappear, the Sun and Moon shall give no more Light, and all the Frame of Nature shall vanish. But our good or bad Works shall remain for ever, recorded in the Archives of Eternity.

> Unmov'd alone the *Virtuous* now appear,
> And in their Looks a calm Assurance wear.
> From East, from West, from North and South they come,
> To take from the most righteous Judge their Doom;
> Who thus, to them, with a serene Regard;
> (The Books of Life before him laid,
> And all the secret Records wide display'd)
> "According to your Works be your Reward:
> Possess immortal Kingdoms as your Due,
> Prepar'd from an eternal Date for you."

Poor Richard Improved, 1758

COURTEOUS READER,

I have heard that nothing gives an Author so great Pleasure, as to find his Works respectfully quoted by other learned

Authors. This Pleasure I have seldom enjoyed; for tho' I have been, if I may say it without Vanity, an *eminent Author* of Almanacks annually now a full Quarter of a Century, my Brother Authors in the same Way, for what Reason I know not, have ever been very sparing in their Applauses; and no other Author has taken the least Notice of me, so that did not my Writings produce me some solid *Pudding*, the great Deficiency of *Praise* would have quite discouraged me.

I concluded at length, that the People were the best Judges of my Merit; for they buy my Works; and besides, in my Rambles, where I am not personally known, I have frequently heard one or other of my Adages repeated, with, *as Poor Richard says*, at the End on't; this gave me some Satisfaction, as it showed not only that my Instructions were regarded, but discovered likewise some Respect for my Authority; and I own, that to encourage the Practice of remembering and repeating those wise Sentences, I have sometimes *quoted myself* with great Gravity.

Judge then how much I must have been gratified by an Incident I am going to relate to you. I stopt my Horse lately where a great Number of People were collected at a Vendue of Merchant Goods. The Hour of Sale not being come, they were conversing on the Badness of the Times, and one of the Company call'd to a plain clean old Man, with white Locks, *Pray, Father* Abraham, *what think you of the Times? Won't these heavy Taxes quite ruin the Country? How shall we be ever able to pay them? What would you advise us to?*—Father *Abraham* stood up, and reply'd, If you'd have my Advice, I'll give it you in short, for a *Word to the Wise is enough*, and *many Words won't fill a Bushel*, as *Poor Richard says*. They join'd in desiring him to speak his Mind, and gathering round him, he proceeded as follows;

"Friends, says he, and Neighbours, the Taxes are indeed very heavy, and if those laid on by the Government were the only Ones we had to pay, we might more easily discharge them; but we have many others, and much more grievous to some of us. We are taxed twice as much by our *Idleness*, three times as much by our *Pride*, and four times as much by our *Folly*, and from these Taxes the Commissioners cannot ease or deliver us by allowing an Abatement. However let us hearken to good Advice, and something may be done for us; *God helps them that help themselves*, as *Poor Richard* says, in his Almanack of 1733.

It would be thought a hard Government that should tax its People one tenth Part of their *Time*, to be employed in its Service. But *Idleness* taxes many of us much more, if we reckon all that is spent in absolute *Sloth*, or doing of nothing, with that which is spent in idle Employments or Amusements, that amount to nothing. *Sloth*, by bringing on Diseases, absolutely shortens Life. *Sloth, like Rust, consumes faster than Labour wears, while the used Key is always bright*, as *Poor Richard* says. But *dost thou love Life, then do not squa⹂ der Time, for that's the Stuff Life is made of*, as *Poor Richard* says.—How much more than is necessary do we spend in Sleep! forgetting that *The sleeping Fox catches no Poultry*, and that *there will be sleeping enough in the Grave*, as *Poor Richard* says. If Time be of all Things the most precious, *wasting Time* must be, as *Poor Richard* says, *the greatest Prodigality*, since, as he elsewhere tells us, *Lost Time is never found again*; and what we call *Time-enough, always proves little enough*: Let us then up and be doing, and doing to the Purpose; so by Diligence shall we do more with less Perplexity. *Sloth makes all Things difficult, but Industry all easy*, as *Poor Richard* says; and *He that riseth late, must trot all Day, and shall scarce overtake his Business at Night*. While *Laziness travels so slowly, that Poverty soon overtakes him*, as we read in *Poor Richard*, who adds, *Drive thy Business, let not that drive thee*; and *Early to Bed, and early to rise, makes a Man healthy, wealthy and wise*.

So what signifies *wishing* and *hoping* for better Times. We may make these Times better if we bestir ourselves. *Industry need not wish*, as *Poor Richard* says, and *He that lives upon Hope will die fasting. There are no Gains, without Pains*; then *Help Hands, for I have no Lands*, or if I have, they are smartly taxed. And, as *Poor Richard* likewise observes, *He that hath a Trade hath an Estate*, and *He that hath a Calling hath an Office of Profit and Honour*; but then the *Trade* must be worked at, and the *Calling* well followed, or neither the *Estate*, nor the *Office*, will enable us to pay our Taxes.—If we are industrious we shall never starve; for, as *Poor Richard* says, *At the working Man's House* Hunger *looks in, but dares not enter*. Nor will the

Bailiff or the Constable enter, for *Industry pays Debts, while Despair encreaseth them*, says *Poor Richard.*—What though you have found no Treasure, nor has any rich Relation left you a Legacy, *Diligence is the Mother of Good-luck*, as *Poor Richard* says, *and God gives all Things to Industry.* Then *plough deep, while Sluggards sleep, and you shall have Corn to sell and to keep*, says *Poor Dick.* Work while it is called To-day, for you know not how much you may be hindered To-morrow, which makes *Poor Richard* say, *One To-day is worth two To-morrows*; and farther, *Have you somewhat to do To-morrow, do it To-day.* If you were a Servant, would you not be ashamed that a good Master should catch you idle? Are you then your own Master, *be ashamed to catch yourself idle*, as *Poor Dick* says. When there is so much to be done for yourself, your Family, your Country, and your gracious King, be up by Peep of Day; *Let not the Sun look down and say, Inglorious here he lies.* Handle your Tools without Mittens; remember that *the Cat in Gloves catches no Mice*, as *Poor Richard* says. 'Tis true there is much to be done, and perhaps you are weak handed, but stick to it steadily, and you will see great Effects, for *constant Dropping wears away Stones*, and by *Diligence and Patience the Mouse ate in two the Cable*; and *little Strokes fell great Oaks*, as *Poor Richard* says in his Almanack, the Year I cannot just now remember.

Methinks I hear some of you say, *Must a Man afford himself no Leisure?*—I will tell thee, my Friend, what *Poor Richard* says, *Employ thy Time well if thou meanest to gain Leisure*; and, *since thou art not sure of a Minute, throw not away an Hour.* Leisure, is Time for doing something useful; this Leisure the diligent Man will obtain, but the lazy Man never; so that, as *Poor Richard* says, a *Life of Leisure and a Life of Laziness are two Things.* Do you imagine that Sloth will afford you more Comfort than Labour? No, for as *Poor Richard* says, *Trouble springs from Idleness, and grievous Toil from needless Ease. Many without Labour, would live by their* WITS *only, but they break for want of Stock.* Whereas Industry gives Comfort, and Plenty, and Respect: *Fly Pleasures, and they'll follow you. The diligent Spinner has a large Shift*; and *now I have a Sheep and a Cow, every Body bids me Good morrow*; all which is well said by *Poor Richard.*

But with our Industry, we must likewise be *steady, settled* and *careful*, and oversee our own Affairs *with our own Eyes*, and not trust too much to others; for, as *Poor Richard* says,

> *I never saw an oft removed Tree,*
> *Nor yet an oft removed Family,*
> *That throve so well as those that settled be.*

And again, *Three Removes is as bad as a Fire*; and again, *Keep thy Shop, and thy Shop will keep thee*; and again, *If you would have your Business done, go; If not, send*. And again,

> *He that by the Plough would thrive,*
> *Himself must either hold or drive.*

And again, *The Eye of a Master will do more Work than both his Hands*; and again, *Want of Care does us more Damage than Want of Knowledge*; and again, *Not to oversee Workmen, is to leave them your Purse open*. Trusting too much to others Care is the Ruin of many; for, as the *Almanack* says, *In the Affairs of this World, Men are saved, not by Faith, but by the Want of it*; but a Man's own Care is profitable; for, saith *Poor Dick, Learning is to the Studious*, and *Riches to the Careful*, as well as *Power to the Bold*, and *Heaven to the Virtuous*. And farther, *If you would have a faithful Servant, and one that you like, serve yourself*. And again, he adviseth to Circumspection and Care, even in the smallest Matters, because sometimes *a little Neglect may breed great Mischief*; adding, *For want of a Nail the Shoe was lost; for want of a Shoe the Horse was lost; and for want of a Horse the Rider was lost*, being overtaken and slain by the Enemy, all for want of Care about a Horse-shoe Nail.

So much for Industry, my Friends, and Attention to one's own Business; but to these we must add *Frugality*, if we would make our *Industry* more certainly successful. A Man may, if he knows not how to save as he gets, *keep his Nose all his Life to the Grindstone*, and die not worth a *Groat* at last. *A fat Kitchen makes a lean Will*, as *Poor Richard* says; and,

> *Many Estates are spent in the Getting,*
> *Since Women for Tea forsook Spinning and Knitting,*
> *And Men for Punch forsook Hewing and Splitting.*

If you would be wealthy, says he, in another Almanack, *think of Saving as well as of Getting: The* Indies *have not made* Spain *rich, because her* Outgoes *are greater than her* Incomes. Away then with your expensive Follies, and you will not have so much Cause to complain of hard Times, heavy Taxes, and chargeable Families; for, as *Poor Dick* says,

> *Women and Wine, Game and Deceit,*
> *Make the Wealth small, and the Wants great.*

And farther, *What maintains one Vice, would bring up two Children.* You may think perhaps, That a *little* Tea, or a *little* Punch now and then, Diet a *little* more costly, Clothes a *little* finer, and a *little* Entertainment now and then, can be no *great* Matter; but remember what *Poor Richard* says, *Many* a Little *makes a Mickle*; and farther, *Beware of* little *Expences*; *a small Leak will sink a great Ship*; and again, *Who Dainties love, shall Beggars prove*; and moreover, *Fools make Feasts, and wise Men eat them.*

Here you are all got together at this Vendue of *Fineries* and *Knicknacks.* You call them *Goods*, but if you do not take Care, they will prove *Evils* to some of you. You expect they will be sold *cheap*, and perhaps they may for less than they cost; but if you have no Occasion for them, they must be *dear* to you. Remember what *Poor Richard* says, *Buy what thou hast no Need of, and ere long thou shalt sell thy Necessaries.* And again, *At a great Pennyworth pause a while*: He means, that perhaps the Cheapness is *apparent* only, and not *real*; or the Bargain, by straitning thee in thy Business, may do thee more Harm than Good. For in another Place he says, *Many have been ruined by buying good Pennyworths.* Again, *Poor Richard* says, *'Tis foolish to lay out Money in a Purchase of Repentance*; and yet this Folly is practised every Day at Vendues, for want of minding the Almanack. *Wise Men*, as *Poor Dick* says, *learn by others Harms, Fools scarcely by their own*; but, *Felix quem faciunt aliena Pericula cautum.* Many a one, for the Sake of Finery on the Back, have gone with a hungry Belly, and half starved their Families; *Silks and Sattins, Scarlet and Velvets,* as *Poor Richard* says, *put out the Kitchen Fire.* These are not the *Necessaries* of Life; they can scarcely be called the *Conveniencies*, and yet only because they look pretty, how many *want* to *have* them. The *artificial* Wants of Mankind thus become more numerous than the *natural*; and, as *Poor Dick* says, *For one* poor *Person, there are an hundred* indigent. By these, and other Extravagancies, the Genteel are reduced to Poverty, and forced to borrow of those whom they formerly despised, but who through *Industry* and *Frugality* have maintained their Standing; in which Case it appears plainly, that a *Ploughman on his Legs is higher than a Gentleman on his Knees*, as *Poor Richard* says. Perhaps they have had a small Estate left them, which they knew not the Getting of; they think *'tis Day, and will never be Night*; that a little to be spent out of *so much*, is not worth minding; (*a Child and a Fool*, as *Poor Richard* says, *imagine* Twenty Shillings *and Twenty Years can never be spent*) but, *always taking out of the Meal-tub, and never putting in, soon comes to the Bottom*; then, as *Poor Dick* says, *When the Well's dry, they know the Worth of Water*. But this they might have known before, if they had taken his Advice; *If you would know the Value of Money, go and try to borrow some*; for, *he that goes a borrowing goes a sorrowing*; and indeed so does he that lends to such People, when he goes *to get it in again.* — *Poor Dick* farther advises, and says,

> *Fond* Pride of Dress, *is sure a very Curse;*
> *E'er* Fancy *you consult, consult your Purse.*

And again, *Pride is as loud a Beggar as Want, and a great deal more saucy.* When you have bought one fine Thing you must buy ten more, that your Appearance may be all of a Piece; but *Poor Dick* says, *'Tis easier to* suppress *the first Desire, than to* satisfy *all that follow it.* And 'tis as truly Folly for the Poor to ape the Rich, as for the Frog to swell, in order to equal the Ox.

> *Great Estates may venture more,*
> *But little Boats should keep near Shore.*

'Tis however a Folly soon punished; for *Pride that dines on Vanity sups on Contempt*, as *Poor Richard* says. And in another Place, *Pride breakfasted with Plenty, dined with Poverty, and supped with Infamy.* And after all, of what Use is this *Pride of Appearance*, for which so much is risked, so much is suffered? It cannot promote Health, or ease Pain; it makes no Increase of Merit in the Person, it creates Envy, it hastens Misfortune.

> *What is a Butterfly? At best*
> *He's but a Caterpillar drest.*
> *The gaudy Fop's his Picture just,*

as *Poor Richard* says.

But what Madness must it be to *run in Debt* for these

Superfluities! We are offered, by the Terms of this Vendue, *Six Months Credit*; and that perhaps has induced some of us to attend it, because we cannot spare the ready Money, and hope now to be fine without it. But, ah, think what you do when you run in Debt; *You give to another Power over your Liberty*. If you cannot pay at the Time, you will be ashamed to see your Creditor; you will be in Fear when you speak to him; you will make poor pitiful sneaking Excuses, and by Degrees come to lose your Veracity, and sink into base down-right lying; for, as *Poor Richard* says, *The second Vice is Lying, the first is running in Debt*. And again, to the same Purpose, *Lying rides upon Debt's Back*. Whereas a freeborn *Englishman* ought not to be ashamed or afraid to see or speak to any Man living. But Poverty often deprives a Man of all Spirit and Vir-tue: *'Tis hard for an empty Bag to stand upright*, as *Poor Rich-ard* truly says. What would you think of that Prince, or that Government, who should issue an Edict forbidding you to dress like a Gentleman or a Gentlewoman, on Pain of Impris-onment or Servitude? Would you not say, that you are free, have a Right to dress as you please, and that such an Edict would be a Breach of your Privileges, and such a Government tyrannical? And yet you are about to put yourself under that Tyranny when you run in Debt for such Dress! Your Creditor has Authority at his Pleasure to deprive you of your Liberty, by confining you in Goal for Life, or to sell you for a Servant, if you should not be able to pay him! When you have got your Bargain, you may, perhaps, think little of Payment; but *Creditors, Poor Richard* tells us, *have better Memories than Debtors*; and in another Place says, *Creditors are a superstitious Sect, great Observers of set Days and Times*. The Day comes round before you are aware, and the Demand is made before you are prepared to satisfy it. Or if you bear your Debt in Mind, the Term which at first seemed so long, will, as it less-ens, appear extreamly short. *Time* will seem to have added Wings to his Heels as well as Shoulders. *Those have a short Lent*, saith *Poor Richard, who owe Money to be paid at Easter*. Then since, as he says, *The Borrower is a Slave to the Lender, and the Debtor to the Creditor*, disdain the Chain, preserve your Freedom; and maintain your Independency: Be *indus-*

trious and *free*; be *frugal* and *free*. At present, perhaps, you may think yourself in thriving Circumstances, and that you can bear a little Extravagance without Injury; but,

> *For Age and Want, save while you may;*
> *No Morning Sun lasts a whole Day,*

as *Poor Richard* says.—Gain may be temporary and uncertain, but ever while you live, Expence is constant and certain; and *'tis easier to build two Chimnies than to keep one in Fuel*, as *Poor Richard* says. So *rather go to Bed supperless than rise in Debt.*

> *Get what you can, and what you get hold;*
> *'Tis the Stone that will turn all your Lead into Gold,*

as *Poor Richard* says. And when you have got the Philosopher's Stone, sure you will no longer complain of bad Times, or the Difficulty of paying Taxes.

This Doctrine, my Friends, is *Reason* and *Wisdom*; but after all, do not depend too much upon your own *Industry*, and *Frugality*, and *Prudence*, though excellent Things, for they may all be blasted without the Blessing of Heaven; and therefore ask that Blessing humbly, and be not uncharitable to those that at present seem to want it, but comfort and help them. Remember *Job* suffered, and was afterwards prosperous.

And now to conclude, *Experience keeps a dear School, but Fools will learn in no other, and scarce in that*; for it is true, *we may give Advice, but we cannot give Conduct*, as *Poor Richard* says: However, remember this, *They that won't be counselled, can't be helped*, as *Poor Richard* says: And farther, That *if you will not hear Reason, she'll surely rap your Knuckles.*"

Thus the old Gentleman ended his Harangue. The People heard it, and approved the Doctrine, and immediately practised the contrary, just as if it had been a common Sermon; for the Vendue opened, and they began to buy extravagantly, notwithstanding all his Cautions, and their own Fear of Taxes.—I found the good Man had thoroughly studied my Almanacks, and digested all I had dropt on those Topicks during the Course of Five-and-twenty Years. The frequent Mention he made of me must have tired any one else, but my Vanity was wonderfully delighted with it, though I was conscious that not a tenth Part of the Wisdom was my own which he ascribed to me, but rather the *Gleanings* I had made of the Sense of all Ages and Nations. However, I resolved to

be the better for the Echo of it; and though I had at first
determined to buy Stuff for a new Coat, I went away resolved
to wear my old One a little longer. *Reader*, if thou wilt do
the same, thy Profit will be as great as mine.

I am, as ever,

Thine to serve thee,

July 7, 1757.   RICHARD SAUNDERS.

———

One *Nestor* is worth two *Ajaxes*.

> When you're an Anvil, hold you still;
> When you're a Hammer, strike your Fill.

When Knaves betray each other, one can scarce be blamed,
or the other pitied.

He that carries a small Crime easily, will carry it on when it
comes to be an Ox.

Happy *Tom Crump*, ne'er sees his own Hump.

Fools need Advice most, but wise Men only are the better
for it.

Silence is not always a Sign of Wisdom, but Babbling is ever
a Mark of Folly.

Great Modesty often hides great Merit.

You may delay, but *Time* will not.

Virtue may not always make a Face handsome, but *Vice* will
certainly make it ugly.

Prodigality of *Time*, produces Poverty of Mind as well as of
Estate.

Content is the Philosopher's Stone, that turns all it touches
into Gold.

He that's content, hath enough; He that complains, has too
much.

Pride gets into the Coach, and *Shame* mounts behind.

The first Mistake in publick Business, is the going into it.

Half the Truth is often a great Lie.

The Way to see by *Faith*, is to shut the Eye of *Reason*: The Morning Daylight appears plainer when you put out your Candle.

A full Belly makes a dull Brain: The Muses starve in a Cook's Shop.

Spare and have is better than *spend and crave*.

Good-Will, like the Wind, floweth where it listeth.

The Honey is sweet, but the Bee has a Sting.

In a corrupt Age, the putting the World in order would breed Confusion; then e'en mind your own Business.

To serve the Publick faithfully, and at the same time please it entirely, is impracticable.

Proud Modern Learning despises the antient: *School-men* are now laught at by *School-boys*.

Men often *mistake* themselves, seldom *forget* themselves.

The idle Man is the Devil's Hireling; whose Livery is Rags, whose Diet and Wages are Famine and Diseases.

Rob not God, nor the Poor, lest thou ruin thyself; the Eagle snatcht a Coal from the Altar, but it fired her Nest.

With bounteous Cheer,
Conclude the Year.

THE AUTOBIOGRAPHY

Part One

Twyford, at the Bishop
of St Asaph's
1771.

Dear Son,

I have ever had a Pleasure in obtaining any little Anecdotes of my Ancestors. You may remember the Enquiries I made among the Remains of my Relations when you were with me in England; and the Journey I took for that purpose. Now imagining it may be equally agreable to you to know the Circumstances of *my* Life, many of which you are yet unacquainted with; and expecting a Weeks uninterrupted Leisure in my present Country Retirement, I sit down to write them for you. To which I have besides some other Inducements. Having emerg'd from the Poverty & Obscurity in which I was born & bred, to a State of Affluence & some Degree of Reputation in the World, and having gone so far thro' Life with a considerable Share of Felicity, the conducing Means I made use of, which, with the Blessing of God, so well succeeded, my Posterity may like to know, as they may find some of them suitable to their own Situations, & therefore fit to be imitated.—That Felicity, when I reflected on it, has induc'd me sometimes to say, that were it offer'd to my Choice, I should have no Objection to a Repetition of the same Life from its Beginning, only asking the Advantage Authors have in a second Edition to correct some Faults of the first. So would I if I might, besides corr^g the Faults, change some sinister Accidents & Events of it for others more favourable, but tho' this were deny'd, I should still accept the Offer. However, since such a Repetition is not to be expected, the Thing most like living one's Life over again, seems to be a *Recollection* of that Life; and to make that Recollection as durable as possible, the putting it down in Writing.—Hereby, too, I shall indulge the Inclination so natural in old Men, to be talking of themselves and their own past Actions, and I shall indulge it, without being troublesome to others who thro' respect to Age might think themselves oblig'd to give me a Hearing, since this may be read or not as any one pleases.

And lastly, (I may as well confess it, since my Denial of it will be believ'd by no body) perhaps I shall a good deal gratify my own *Vanity*. Indeed I scarce ever heard or saw the introductory Words, *Without Vanity I may say*, &c. but some vain thing immediately follow'd. Most People dislike Vanity in others whatever Share they have of it themselves, but I give it fair Quarter wherever I meet with it, being persuaded that it is often productive of Good to the Possessor & to others that are within his Sphere of Action: And therefore in many Cases it would not be quite absurd if a Man were to thank God for his Vanity among the other Comforts of Life.—

And now I speak of thanking God, I desire with all Humility to acknowledge, that I owe the mention'd Happiness of my past Life to his kind Providence, which led me to the Means I us'd & gave them Success.—My Belief of This, induces me to *hope*, tho' I must not *presume*, that the same Goodness will still be exercis'd towards me in continuing that Happiness, or in enabling me to bear a fatal Reverso, which I may experience as others have done, the Complexion of my future Fortune being known to him only: and in whose Power it is to bless to us even our Afflictions.

The Notes one of my Uncles (who had the same kind of Curiosity in collecting Family Anecdotes) once put into my Hands, furnish'd me with several Particulars, relating to our Ancestors. From those Notes I learnt that the Family had liv'd in the same Village, Ecton in Northamptonshire, for 300 Years, & how much longer he knew not, (perhaps from the Time when the Name *Franklin* that before was the Name of an Order of People, was assum'd by them for a Surname, when others took Surnames all over the Kingdom.—*) on a

---

*As a proof that FRANKLIN was anciently the common name of an order or rank in England, see Judge Fortescue, *De laudibus Legum Angliae*, written about the year 1412, in which is the following passage, to show that good juries might easily be formed in any part of England.

"Regio etiam illa, ita respersa refertaque est *possessoribus terrarum* et agrorum, quod in ea, villula tam parva reperiri non poterit, in qua non est *miles*, *armiger*, vel pater-familias, qualis ibidem *Franklin* vulgariter nuncupatur, magnis ditatus possessionibus, nec non libere tenentes et alii *valecti* plurimi, suis patrimoniis sufficientes ad faciendum juratam, in forma praenotata."

"Moreover, the same country is so filled and replenished with landed

Freehold of about 30 Acres, aided by the Smith's Business which had continued in the Family till his Time, the eldest Son being always bred to that Business. A Custom which he & my Father both followed as to their eldest Sons.—When I search'd the Register at Ecton, I found an Account of their Births, Marriages and Burials, from the Year 1555 only, there being no Register kept in that Parish at any time preceding.—By that Register I perceiv'd that I was the youngest Son of the youngest Son for 5 Generations back. My Grandfather Thomas, who was born in 1598, lived at Ecton till he grew too old to follow Business longer, when he went to live with his Son John, a Dyer at Banbury in Oxfordshire, with whom my Father serv'd an Apprenticeship. There my Grandfather died and lies buried. We saw his Gravestone in 1758. His eldest Son Thomas liv'd in the House at Ecton, and left it with the Land to his only Child, a Daughter, who with her Husband, one Fisher of Wellingborough sold it to Mr Isted, now Lord of the Manor there. My Grandfather had 4 Sons that grew up, viz. Thomas, John, Benjamin and Josiah. I will give you what Account I can of them at this distance from my Papers, and if those are not lost in my Absence, you will among them find many more Particulars. Thomas was bred a Smith under his Father, but being ingenious, and encourag'd in Learning (as all his Brothers like wise werre,) by an Esquire Palmer then the principal Gentleman in that Parish, he qualify'd himself for the Business of Scrivener, became a con-

---

menne, that therein so small a Thorpe cannot be found werein dweleth not a knight, an esquire, or such a householder, as is there commonly called a *Franklin*, enriched with great possessions; and also other freeholders and many yeomen able for their livelihoods to make a jury in form aforementioned."—(*Old Translation.*)

Chaucer too calls his Country Gentleman, a *Franklin*, and after describing his good housekeeping thus characterises him:

> "This worthy Franklin bore a purse of silk,
> Fix'd to his girdle, white as morning milk.
> Knight of the Shire, first Justice at th' Assize,
> To help the poor, the doubtful to advise.
> In all employments, generous, just, he proved;
> Renown'd for courtesy, by all beloved."

siderable Man in the County Affairs, was a chief Mover of all publick Spirited Undertakings, for the County or Town of Northampton & his own Village, of which many Instances were told us at Ecton and he was much taken Notice of and patroniz'd by the then Lord Halifax. He died in 1702 Jan. 6. old Stile, just 4 Years to a Day before I was born. The Account we receiv'd of his Life & Character from some old People at Ecton, I remember struck you as something extraordinary from its Similarity to what you knew of mine. Had he died on the same Day, you said one might have suppos'd a Transmigration.—John was bred a Dyer, I believe of Woollens. Benjamin, was bred a Silk Dyer, serving an Apprenticeship at London. He was an ingenious Man, I remember him well, for when I was a Boy he came over to my Father in Boston, and lived in the House with us some Years. He lived to a great Age. His Grandson Samuel Franklin now lives in Boston. He left behind him two Quarto Volumes, M.S. of his own Poetry, consisting of little occasional Pieces address'd to his Friends and Relations, of which the following sent to me, is a Specimen.

Sent to My Name upon a Report
of his Inclination to Martial affaires
7 July 1710

Beleeve me Ben. It is a Dangerous Trade
The Sword has Many Marr'd as well as Made
By it doe many fall Not Many Rise
Makes Many poor few Rich and fewer Wise
Fills Towns with Ruin, fields with blood beside
Tis Sloths Maintainer, And the Shield of pride
Fair Citties Rich to Day, in plenty flow
War fills with want, Tomorrow, & with woe
Ruin'd Estates, The Nurse of Vice, broke limbs & scarss
  Are the Effects of Desolating Warrs

Sent to B. F. in N. E. 15 July 1710

B   e to thy parents an Obedient Son
E   ach Day let Duty constantly be Done
N   ever give Way to sloth or lust or pride

I f free you'd be from Thousand Ills beside
A bove all Ills be sure Avoide the shelfe
M ans Danger lyes in Satan sin and selfe
I n vertue Learning Wisdome progress Make
N ere shrink at Suffering for thy saviours sake
F raud and all Falshood in thy Dealings Flee
R eligious Always in thy station be
A dore the Maker of thy Inward part
N ow's the Accepted time, Give him thy Heart
K eep a Good Consceince 'tis a constant Frind
L ike Judge and Witness This Thy Acts Attend
I n Heart with bended knee Alone Adore
N one but the Three in One Forevermore.

He had form'd a Shorthand of his own, which he taught me, but never practicing it I have now forgot it. I was nam'd after this Uncle, there being a particular Affection between him and my Father. He was very pious, a great Attender of Sermons of the best Preachers, which he took down in his Shorthand and had with him many Volumes of them. —He was also much of a Politician, too much perhaps for his Station. There fell lately into my Hands in London a Collection he had made of all the principal Pamphlets relating to Publick Affairs from 1641 to 1717. Many of the Volumes are wanting, as appears by the Numbering, but there still remains 8 Vols. Folio, and 24 in 4to & 8vo.—A Dealer in old Books met with them, and knowing me by my sometimes buying of him, he brought them to me. It seems my Uncle must have left them here when he went to America, which was above 50 Years since. There are many of his Notes in the Margins.—

This obscure Family of ours was early in the Reformation, and continu'd Protestants thro' the Reign of Queen Mary, when they were sometimes in Danger of Trouble on Account of their Zeal against Popery. They had got an English Bible, & to conceal & secure it, it was fastned open with Tapes under & within the Frame of a Joint Stool. When my Great Great Grandfather read in it to his Family, he turn'd up the

Joint Stool upon his Knees, turning over the Leaves then under the Tapes. One of the Children stood at the Door to give Notice if he saw the Apparitor coming, who was an Officer of the Spiritual Court. In that Case the Stool was turn'd down again upon its feet, when the Bible remain'd conceal'd under it as before. This Anecdote I had from my Uncle Benjamin.—The Family continu'd all of the Church of England till about the End of Charles the 2^{ds} Reign, when some of the Ministers that had been outed for Nonconformity, holding Conventicles in Northamptonshire, Benjamin & Josiah adher'd to them, and so continu'd all their Lives. The rest of the Family remain'd with the Episcopal Church.

Josiah, my Father, married young, and carried his Wife with three Children unto New England, about 1682. The Conventicles having been forbidden by Law, & frequently disturbed, induced some considerable Men of his Acquaintance to remove to that Country, and he was prevail'd with to accompany them thither, where they expected to enjoy their Mode of Religion with Freedom.—By the same Wife he had 4 Children more born there, and by a second Wife ten more, in all 17, of which I remember 13 sitting at one time at his Table, who all grew up to be Men & Women, and married;— I was the youngest Son and the youngest Child but two, & was born in Boston, N. England.

My Mother the 2^d Wife was Abiah Folger, a Daughter of Peter Folger, one of the first Settlers of New England, of whom honourable mention is made by Cotton Mather, in his Church History of that Country, (entitled Magnalia Christi Americana) as a *godly learned Englishman*, if I remember the Words rightly.—I have heard that he wrote sundry small occasional Pieces, but only one of them was printed which I saw now many Years since. It was written in 1675, in the homespun Verse of that Time & People, and address'd to those then concern'd in the Government there. It was in favour of Liberty of Conscience, & in behalf of the Baptists, Quakers, & other Sectaries, that had been under Persecution; ascribing the Indian Wars & other Distresses, that had befallen the Country to that Persecution, as so many Judgments of God, to punish so heinous an Offence; and exhorting a Repeal of those uncharitable Laws. The whole appear'd to me as written with a good deal of Decent Plainness & manly Freedom. The six last concluding Lines I remember, tho' I have forgotten the two first of the Stanza, but the Purport of them was that his Censures proceeded from *Goodwill*, & therefore he would be known as the Author,

> because to be a Libeller, (says he)
>   I hate it with my Heart.
> From *Sherburne Town where now I dwell,
>   My Name I do put here,
> Without Offence, your real Friend,
>   It is Peter Folgier.

*In the Island of Nantucket.

My elder Brothers were all put Apprentices to different Trades. I was put to the Grammar School at Eight Years of Age, my Father intending to devote me as the Tithe of his Sons to the Service of the Church. My early Readiness in learning to read (which must have been very early, as I do not remember when I could not read) and the Opinion of all his Friends that I should certainly make a good Scholar, encourag'd him in this Purpose of his. My Uncle Benjamin too approv'd of it, and propos'd to give me all his Shorthand Volumes of Sermons I suppose as a Stock to set up with, if I would learn his Character. I continu'd however at the Grammar School not quite one Year, tho' in that time I had risen gradually from the Middle of the Class of that Year to be the Head of it, and farther was remov'd into the next Class above it, in order to go with that into the third at the End of the Year. But my Father in the mean time, from a View of the Expence of a College Education which, having so large a Family, he could not well afford, and the mean Living many so educated were afterwards able to obtain, Reasons that he gave to his Friends in my Hearing, altered his first Intention, took me from the Grammar School, and sent me to a School for Writing & Arithmetic kept by a then famous Man, Mr Geo. Brownell, very successful in his Profession generally, and that by mild encouraging Methods. Under him I acquired fair Writing pretty soon, but I fail'd in the Arithmetic, & made no Progress in it.—At Ten Years old, I was taken home to

assist my Father in his Business, which was that of a Tallow
Chandler and Sope-Boiler. A Business he was not bred to,
but had assumed on his Arrival in New England & on finding
his Dying Trade would not maintain his Family, being in
little Request. Accordingly I was employed in cutting Wick for
the Candles, filling the Dipping Mold, & the Molds for cast
Candles, attending the Shop, going of Errands, &c.—I dislik'd the Trade and had a strong Inclination for the Sea; but
my Father declar'd against it; however, living near the Water,
I was much in and about it, learnt early to swim well, & to
manage Boats, and when in a Boat or Canoe with other Boys
I was commonly allow'd to govern, especially in any case of
Difficulty; and upon other Occasions I was generally a Leader
among the Boys, and sometimes led them into Scrapes, of
wch I will mention one Instance, as it shows an early projecting
public Spirit, tho' not then justly conducted. There was a Salt
Marsh that bounded part of the Mill Pond, on the Edge of
which at Highwater, we us'd to stand to fish for Minews. By
much Trampling, we had made it a mere Quagmire. My Proposal was to build a Wharf there fit for us to stand upon, and
I show'd my Comrades a large Heap of Stones which were
intended for a new House near the Marsh, and which would
very well suit our Purpose. Accordingly in the Evening when
the Workmen were gone, I assembled a Number of my Play-
fellows, and working with them diligently like so many Em-
mets, sometimes two or three to a Stone, we brought them
all away and built our little Wharff.— The next Morning the
Workmen were surpriz'd at Missing the Stones; which were
found in our Wharff; Enquiry was made after the Removers;
we were discovered & complain'd of; several of us were corrected by our Fathers; and tho' I pleaded the Usefulness of
the Work, mine convinc'd me that nothing was useful which
was not honest.—

I think you may like to know something of his Person &
Character. He had an excellent Constitution of Body, was of
middle Stature, but well set and very strong. He was ingenious, could draw prettily, was skill'd a little in Music and
had a clear pleasing Voice, so that when he play'd Psalm
Tunes on his Violin & sung withal as he some times did in
an Evening after the Business of the Day was over, it was

extreamly agreable to hear. He had a mechanical Genius too, and on occasion was very handy in the Use of other Tradesmen's Tools. But his great Excellence lay in a sound Understanding, and solid Judgment in prudential Matters, both in private & publick Affairs. In the latter indeed he was never employed, the numerous Family he had to educate & the Straitness of his Circumstances, keeping him close to his Trade, but I remember well his being frequently visited by leading People, who consulted him for his Opinion on Affairs of the Town or of the Church he belong'd to & show'd a good deal of Respect for his Judgment and Advice. He was also much consulted by private Persons about their Affairs when any Difficulty occur'd, & frequently chosen an Arbitrator between contending Parties.—At his Table he lik'd to have as often as he could, some sensible Friend or Neighbour, to converse with, and always took care to start some ingenious or useful Topic for Discourse, which might tend to improve the Minds of his Children. By this means he turn'd our Attention to what was good, just, & prudent in the Conduct of Life; and little or no Notice was ever taken of what related to the Victuals on the Table, whether it was well or ill drest, in or out of season, of good or bad flavour, preferable or inferior to this or that other thing of the kind; so that I was bro't up in such a perfect Inattention to those Matters as to be quite Indifferent what kind of Food was set before me; and so unobservant of it, that to this Day, if I am ask'd I can scarce tell, a few Hours after Dinner, what I din'd upon.— This has been a Convenience to me in travelling, where my Companions have been sometimes very unhappy for want of a suitable Gratification of their more delicate because better instructed Tastes and Appetites.—

My Mother had likewise an excellent Constitution. She suckled all her 10 Children. I never knew either my Father or Mother to have any Sickness but that of which they dy'd, he at 89 & she at 85 Years of age. They lie buried together at Boston, where I some Years since plac'd a Marble stone over their Grave with this Inscription

Josiah Franklin
And Abiah his Wife

Lie here interred.
They lived lovingly together in Wedlock
Fifty-five Years.—
Without an Estate or any gainful Employment,
By constant Labour and Industry,
With God's Blessing,
They maintained a large Family
Comfortably;
And brought up thirteen Children,
And seven Grandchildren
Reputably.
From this Instance, Reader,
Be encouraged to Diligence in thy Calling,
And distrust not Providence.
He was a pious & prudent Man,
She a discreet and virtuous Woman.
Their youngest Son,
In filial Regard to their Memory,
Places this Stone.
J. F. born 1655—Died 1744. Ætat 89
A. F. born 1667—died 1752——85

By my rambling Digressions I perceive my self to be grown old. I us'd to write more methodically.—But one does not dress for private Company as for a publick Ball. 'Tis perhaps only Negligence.—

To return. I continu'd thus employ'd in my Father's Business for two Years, that is till I was 12 Years old; and my Brother John, who was bred to that Business having left my Father, married and set up for himself at Rhodeisland, there was all Appearance that I was destin'd to supply his Place and be a Tallow Chandler. But my Dislike to the Trade continuing, my Father was under Apprehensions that if he did not find one for me more agreable, I should break away and get to Sea, as his Son Josiah had done to his great Vexation. He therefore sometimes took me to walk with him, and see Joiners, Bricklayers, Turners, Braziers, &c. at their Work, that he might observe my Inclination, & endeavour to fix it on some Trade or other on Land.—It has ever since been a Pleasure to me to see good Workmen handle their Tools; and it has been useful to me, having learnt so much by it, as to be able to do little Jobs my self in my House, when a Workman could not readily be got; & to construct little Machines for my Experiments while the Intention of making the Experiment was fresh & warm in my Mind. My Father at last fix'd upon the Cutler's Trade, and my Uncle Benjamin's Son Samuel who was bred to that Business in London being about that time establish'd in Boston, I was sent to be with him some time on liking. But his Expectations of a Fee with me displeasing my Father, I was taken home again.—

From a Child I was fond of Reading, and all the little Money that came into my Hands was ever laid out in Books. Pleas'd with the Pilgrim's Progress, my first Collection was of John Bunyan's Works, in separate little Volumes. I afterwards sold them to enable me to buy R. Burton's Historical Collections; they were small Chapmen's Books and cheap, 40 or 50 in all.—My Father's little Library consisted chiefly of Books in polemic Divinity, most of which I read, and have since often regretted, that at a time when I had such a Thirst for Knowledge, more proper Books had not fallen in my Way, since it was now resolv'd I should not be a Clergyman. Plutarch's Lives there was, in which I read abundantly, and I still think that time spent to great Advantage. There was also a Book of Defoe's called an Essay on Projects and another of Dr Mather's call'd Essays to do Good, which perhaps gave me a Turn of Thinking that had an Influence on some of the principal future Events of my Life.

This Bookish Inclination at length determin'd my Father to make me a Printer, tho' he had already one Son, (James) of that Profession. In 1717 my Brother James return'd from England with a Press & Letters to set up his Business in Boston. I lik'd it much better than that of my Father, but still had a Hankering for the Sea.—To prevent the apprehended Effect of such an Inclination, my Father was impatient to have me bound to my Brother. I stood out some time, but at last was persuaded and signed the Indentures, when I was yet but 12 Years old.—I was to serve as an Apprentice till I was 21 Years of Age, only I was to be allow'd Journeyman's Wages during the last Year. In a little time I made great Proficiency in the

Business, and became a useful Hand to my Brother. I now had Access to better Books. An Acquaintance with the Apprentices of Booksellers, enabled me sometimes to borrow a small one, which I was careful to return soon & clean. Often I sat up in my Room reading the greatest Part of the Night, when the Book was borrow'd in the Evening & to be return'd early in the Morning lest it should be miss'd or wanted.—And after some time an ingenious Tradesman* who had a pretty Collection of Books, & who frequented our Printing House, took Notice of me, invited me to his Library, & very kindly lent me such Books as I chose to read. I now took a Fancy to Poetry, and made some little Pieces. My Brother, thinking it might turn to account encourag'd me, & put me on composing two occasional Ballads. One was called the *Light House Tragedy*, & contain'd an Acc^t of the drowning of Capt. Worthilake with his Two Daughters; the other was a Sailor Song on the Taking of *Teach* or Blackbeard the Pirate. They were wretched Stuff, in the Grubstreet Ballad Stile, and when they were printed he sent me about the Town to sell them. The first sold wonderfully, the Event being recent, having made a great Noise. This flatter'd my Vanity. But my Father discourag'd me, by ridiculing my Performances, and telling me Verse-makers were generally Beggars; so I escap'd being a Poet, most probably a very bad one. But as Prose Writing has been a great Use to me in the Course of my Life, and was a principal Means of my Advancement, I shall tell you how in such a Situation I acquir'd what little Ability I have in that Way.

There was another Bookish Lad in the Town, John Collins by Name, with whom I was intimately acquainted. We sometimes disputed, and very fond we were of Argument, & very desirous of confuting one another. Which disputacious Turn, by the way, is apt to become a very bad Habit, making People often extreamly disagreable in Company, by the Contradiction that is necessary to bring it into Practice, & thence, besides souring & spoiling the Conversation, is productive of Disgusts & perhaps Enmities where you may have occasion for Friendship. I had caught it by reading my Father's Books

*Mr Matthew Adams

of Dispute about Religion. Persons of good Sense, I have
since observ'd, seldom fall into it, except Lawyers, University
Men, and Men of all Sorts that have been bred at Edin-
borough. A Question was once some how or other started
between Collins & me, of the Propriety of educating the Female Sex in Learning, & their Abilities for Study. He was of
Opinion that it was improper; & that they were naturally unequal to it. I took the contrary Side, perhaps a little for Dispute sake. He was naturally more eloquent, had a ready
Plenty of Words, and sometimes as I thought bore me down
more by his Fluency than by the Strength of his Reasons. As
we parted without settling the Point, & were not to see one
another again for some time, I sat down to put my Arguments in Writing, which I copied fair & sent to him. He
answer'd & I reply'd. Three or four Letters of a Side had
pass'd, when my Father happen'd to find my Papers, and read
them. Without entring into the Discussion, he took occasion
to talk to me about the Manner of my Writing, observ'd that
tho' I had the Advantage of my Antagonist in correct Spelling & pointing (which I ow'd to the Printing House) I fell
far short in elegance of Expression, in Method and in Perspicuity, of which he convinc'd me by several Instances. I saw
the Justice of his Remarks, & thence grew more attentive to
the *Manner* in Writing, and determin'd to endeavour at Improvement. —

About this time I met with an odd Volume of the Spectator. I had never before seen any of them. I bought it, read it
over and over, and was much delighted with it. I thought the
Writing excellent, & wish'd if possible to imitate it. With that
View, I took some of the Papers, & making short Hints of
the Sentiment in each Sentence, laid them by a few Days, and
then without looking at the Book, try'd to compleat the Papers again, by expressing each hinted Sentiment at length &
as fully as it had been express'd before, in any suitable Words
that should come to hand.

Then I compar'd my Spectator with the Original, discover'd some of my Faults & corrected them. But I found I
wanted a Stock of Words or a Readiness in recollecting &
using them, which I thought I should have acquir'd before
that time, if I had gone on making Verses, since the continual

Occasion for Words of the same Import but of different Length, to suit the Measure, or of different Sound for the Rhyme, would have laid me under a constant Necessity of searching for Variety, and also have tended to fix that Variety in my Mind, & make me Master of it. Therefore I took some of the Tales & turn'd them into Verse: And after a time, when I had pretty well forgotten the Prose, turn'd them back again. I also sometimes jumbled my Collections of Hints into Confusion, and after some Weeks, endeavour'd to reduce them into the best Order, before I began to form the full Sentences & compleat the Paper. This was to teach me Method in the Arrangement of Thoughts. By comparing my Work afterwards with the original, I discover'd many faults and amended them; but I sometimes had the Pleasure of Fancying that in certain Particulars of small Import, I had been lucky enough to improve the Method or the Language and this encourag'd me to think I might possibly in time come to be a tolerable English Writer, of which I was extreamly ambitious.

My Time for these Exercises & for Reading, was at Night after Work, or before Work began in the Morning; or on Sundays, when I contrived to be in the Printing House alone, evading as much as I could the common Attendance on publick Worship, which my Father used to exact of me when I was under his Care:—And which indeed I still thought a Duty; tho' I could not, as it seemed to me, afford the Time to practise it.

When about 16 Years of Age, I happen'd to meet with a Book written by one Tryon, recommending a Vegetable Diet. I determined to go into it. My Brother being yet unmarried, did not keep House, but boarded himself & his Apprentices in another Family. My refusing to eat Flesh occasioned an Inconveniency, and I was frequently chid for my Singularity. I made my self acquainted with Tryon's Manner of preparing some of his Dishes, such as Boiling Potatoes, or Rice, making Hasty Pudding, & a few others, and then propos'd to my Brother, that if he would give me Weekly half the Money he paid for my Board, I would board my self. He instantly agreed to it, and I presently found that I could save half what he paid me. This was an additional Fund for buying Books:

But I had another Advantage in it. My Brother and the rest
going from the Printing House to their Meals, I remain'd
there alone, and dispatching presently my light Repast,
(which often was no more than a Bisket or a Slice of Bread,
a Handful of Raisins or a Tart from the Pastry Cook's, and a
Glass of Water) had the rest of the Time till their Return, for
Study, in which I made the greater Progress from that greater
Clearness of Head & quicker Apprehension which usually at-
tend Temperance in Eating & Drinking. And now it was that
being on some Occasion made asham'd of my Ignorance in
Figures, which I had twice fail'd in learning when at School,
I took Cocker's Book of Arithmetick, & went thro' the whole
by my self with great Ease.—I also read Seller's & Sturmy's
Books of Navigation, & became acquainted with the little
Geometry they contain, but never proceeded far in that
Science.—And I read about this Time Locke on Human
Understanding and the Art of Thinking by Messrs du Port
Royal.

While I was intent on improving my Language, I met with
an English Grammar (I think it was Greenwood's) at the End
of which there were two little Sketches of the Arts of Rhetoric and Logic, the latter finishing with a Specimen of a Dispute in the Socratic Method. And soon after I procur'd
Xenophon's Memorable Things of Socrates, wherein there are
many Instances of the same Method. I was charm'd with it,
adopted it, dropt my abrupt Contradiction, and positive Argumentation, and put on the humble Enquirer & Doubter.
And being then, from reading Shaftsbury & Collins, become
a real Doubter in many Points of our Religious Doctrine, I
found this Method safest for my self & very embarassing to
those against whom I used it, therefore I took a Delight in it,
practis'd it continually & grew very artful & expert in drawing People even of superior Knowledge into Concessions the
Consequences of which they did not foresee, entangling them
in Difficulties out of which they could not extricate themselves, and so obtaining Victories that neither my self nor my
Cause always deserved.—I continu'd this Method some few
Years, but gradually left it, retaining only the Habit of expressing my self in Terms of modest Diffidence, never using
when I advance any thing that may possibly be disputed, the

Words, *Certainly*, *undoubtedly*, or any others that give the Air of Positiveness to an Opinion; but rather say, *I conceive*, or *I apprehend* a Thing to be so or so, *It appears to me*, or *I should think it so or so for such & such Reasons*, or *I imagine* it to be so, or *it is so* if *I am not mistaken.*—This Habit I believe has been of great Advantage to me, when I have had occasion to inculcate my Opinions & persuade Men into Measures that I have been from time to time engag'd in promoting.—And as the chief Ends of Conversation are to *inform*, or to be *informed*, to *please* or to *persuade*, I wish well meaning sensible Men would not lessen their Power of doing Good by a Positive assuming Manner that seldom fails to disgust, tends to create Opposition, and to defeat every one of those Purposes for which Speech was given us, to wit, giving or receiving Information, or Pleasure: For If you would *inform*, a positive dogmatical Manner in advancing your Sentiments, may provoke Contradiction & prevent a candid Attention. If you wish Information & Improvement from the Knowledge of others and yet at the same time express your self as firmly fix'd in your present Opinions, modest sensible Men, who do not love Disputation, will probably leave you undisturb'd in the Possession of your Error; and by such a Manner you can seldom hope to recommend your self in *pleasing* your Hearers, or to persuade those whose Concurrence you desire.—Pope says, judiciously,

> *Men should be taught as if you taught them not,*
> *And things unknown propos'd as things forgot,*—

farther recommending it to us,

> *To speak tho' sure, with seeming Diffidence.*

And he might have couple'd with this Line that which he has coupled with another, I think less properly,

> *For want of Modesty is want of Sense.*

If you ask why *less properly*, I must repeat the Lines;

> "Immodest Words admit of *no* Defence;
> "*For* Want of Modesty is Want of Sense."

Now is not *Want of Sense*, (where a Man is so unfortunate as to want it) some Apology for his *Want of Modesty*? and would not the Lines stand more justly thus?

> Immodest Words admit *but this* Defence,
> That Want of Modesty is Want of Sense.

This however I should submit to better Judgments.—

My Brother had in 1720 or 21, begun to print a Newspaper. It was the second that appear'd in America, & was called *The New England Courant*. The only one before it, was *the Boston News Letter*. I remember his being dissuaded by some of his Friends from the Undertaking, as not likely to succeed, one Newspaper being in their Judgment enough for America.— At this time 1771 there are not less than five & twenty.—He went on however with the Undertaking, and after having work'd in composing the Types & printing off the Sheets I was employ'd to carry the Papers thro' the Streets to the Customers.—He had some ingenious Men among his Friends who amus'd themselves by writing little Pieces for this Paper, which gain'd it Credit, & made it more in Demand; and these Gentlemen often visited us.—Hearing their Conversations, and their Accounts of the Approbation their Papers were receiv'd with, I was excited to try my Hand among them. But being still a Boy, & suspecting that my Brother would object to printing any Thing of mine in his Paper if he knew it to be mine, I contriv'd to disguise my Hand, & writing an anonymous Paper I put it in at Night under the Door of the Printing House. It was found in the Morning & communicated to his Writing Friends when they call'd in as Usual. They read it, commented on it in my Hearing, and I had the exquisite Pleasure, of finding it met with their Approbation, and that in their different Guesses at the Author none were named but Men of some Character among us for Learning & Ingenuity.—I suppose now that I was rather lucky in my Judges: And that perhaps they were not really so very good ones as I then esteem'd them. Encourag'd however by this, I wrote and convey'd in the same Way to the Press several more Papers, which were equally approv'd, and I kept my Secret till my small Fund of Sense for such Performances was pretty

well exhausted, & then I discovered it; when I began to be
considered a little more by my Brother's Acquaintance, and
in a manner that did not quite please him, as he thought,
probably with reason, that it tended to make me too vain.
And perhaps this might be one Occasion of the Differences
that we began to have about this Time. Tho' a Brother, he
considered himself as my Master, & me as his Apprentice;
and accordingly expected the same Services from me as he
would from another; while I thought he demean'd me too
much in some he requir'd of me, who from a Brother expected more Indulgence. Our Disputes were often brought
before our Father, and I fancy I was either generally in the
right, or else a better Pleader, because the Judgment was generally in my favour: But my Brother was passionate & had
often beaten me, which I took extreamly amiss; * and thinking my Apprenticeship very tedious, I was continually wishing for some Opportunity of shortening it, which at length
offered in a manner unexpected.

One of the Pieces in our News-Paper, on some political
Point which I have now forgotten, gave Offence to the Assembly. He was taken up, censur'd and imprison'd for a
Month by the Speaker's Warrant, I suppose because he would
not discover his Author. I too was taken up & examin'd before the Council; but tho' I did not give them any Satisfaction, they contented themselves with admonishing me, and
dismiss'd me; considering me perhaps as an Apprentice who
was bound to keep his Master's Secrets. During my Brother's
Confinement, which I resented a good deal, notwithstanding
our private Differences, I had the Management of the Paper,
and I made bold to give our Rulers some Rubs in it, which
my Brother took very kindly, while others began to consider
me in an unfavourable Light, as a young Genius that had a
Turn for Libelling & Satyr. My Brother's Discharge was accompany'd with an Order of the House, (a very odd one)
*that James Franklin should no longer print the Paper called the
New England Courant.* There was a Consultation held in our
Printing House among his Friends what he should do in this

*I fancy his harsh & tyrannical Treatment of me, might be a means of
impressing me with that Aversion to arbitrary Power that has stuck to me
thro' my whole Life.

Case. Some propos'd to evade the Order by changing the Name of the Paper; but my Brother seeing Inconveniences in that, it was finally concluded on as a better Way, to let it be printed for the future under the Name of *Benjamin Franklin*. And to avoid the Censure of the Assembly that might fall on him, as still printing it by his Apprentice, the Contrivance was, that my old Indenture should be return'd to me with a full Discharge on the Back of it, to be shown on Occasion; but to secure to him the Benefit of my Service I was to sign new Indentures for the Remainder of the Term, wch were to be kept private. A very flimsy Scheme it was, but however it was immediately executed, and the Paper went on accordingly under my Name for several Months. At length a fresh Difference arising between my Brother and me, I took upon me to assert my Freedom, presuming that he would not venture to produce the new Indentures. It was not fair in me to take this Advantage, and this I therefore reckon one of the first Errata of my Life: But the Unfairness of it weigh'd little with me, when under the Impressions of Resentment, for the Blows his Passion too often urg'd him to bestow upon me. Tho' He was otherwise not an ill-natur'd Man: Perhaps I was too saucy & provoking. —

When he found I would leave him, he took care to prevent my getting Employment in any other Printing-House of the Town, by going round & speaking to every Master, who accordingly refus'd to give me Work. I then thought of going to New York as the nearest Place where there was a Printer: and I was the rather inclin'd to leave Boston, when I reflected that I had already made my self a little obnoxious, to the governing Party; & from the arbitrary Proceedings of the Assembly in my Brother's Case it was likely I might if I stay'd soon bring my self into Scrapes; and farther that my indiscrete Disputations about Religion began to make me pointed at with Horror by good People, as an Infidel or Atheist; I determin'd on the Point: but my Father now siding with my Brother, I was sensible that if I attempted to go openly, Means would be used to prevent me. My Friend Collins therefore undertook to manage a little for me. He agreed with the Captain of a New York Sloop for my Passage, under the Notion of my being a young Acquaintance of his that had got a naughty

Girl with Child, whose Friends would compel me to marry her, and therefore I could not appear or come away publickly. So I sold some of my Books to raise a little Money, Was taken on board privately, and as we had a fair Wind, in three Days I found my self in New York near 300 Miles from home, a Boy of but 17, without the least Recommendation to or Knowledge of any Person in the Place, and with very little Money in my Pocket.—

My Inclinations for the Sea, were by this time worne out, or I might now have gratify'd them.—But having a Trade, & supposing my self a pretty good Workman, I offer'd my Service to the Printer of the Place, old Mr Wm Bradford.—He could give me no Employment, having little to do, and Help enough already: But, says he, my Son at Philadelphia has lately lost his principal Hand, Aquila Rose, by Death. If you go thither I believe he may employ you.—Philadelphia was 100 Miles farther. I set out, however, in a Boat for Amboy; leaving my Chest and Things to follow me round by Sea. In crossing the Bay we met with a Squall that tore our rotten Sails to pieces, prevented our getting into the Kill, and drove us upon Long Island. In our Way a drunken Dutchman, who was a Passenger too, fell over board; when he was sinking I reach'd thro' the Water to his shock Pate & drew him up so that we got him in again.—His Ducking sober'd him a little, & he went to sleep, taking first out of his Pocket a Book which he desir'd I would dry for him. It prov'd to be my old favourite Author Bunyan's Pilgrim's Progress in Dutch, finely printed on good Paper with copper Cuts, a Dress better than I had ever seen it wear in its own Language. I have since found that it has been translated into most of the Languages of Europe, and suppose it has been more generally read than any other Book except perhaps the Bible.—Honest John was the first that I know of who mix'd Narration & Dialogue, a Method of Writing very engaging to the Reader, who in the most interesting Parts finds himself as it were brought into the Company, & present at the Discourse. De foe in his Cruso, his Moll Flanders, Religious Courtship, Family Instructor, & other Pieces, has imitated it with Success. And Richardson has done the same in his Pamela, &c.—

When we drew near the Island we found it was at a Place

where there could be no Landing, there being a great Surff
on the stony Beach. So we dropt Anchor & swung round
towards the Shore. Some People came down to the Water
Edge & hallow'd to us, as we did to them. But the Wind was
so high & the Surff so loud, that we could not hear so as to
understand each other. There were Canoes on the Shore, &
we made Signs & hallow'd that they should fetch us, but they
either did not understand us, or thought it impracticable. So
they went away, and Night coming on, we had no Remedy
but to wait till the Wind should abate, and in the mean time
the Boatman & I concluded to sleep if we could, and so
crouded into the Scuttle with the Dutchman who was still
wet, and the Spray beating over the Head of our Boat, leak'd
thro' to us, so that we were soon almost as wet as he. In this
Manner we lay all Night with very little Rest. But the Wind
abating the next Day, we made a Shift to reach Amboy before
Night, having been 30 Hours on the Water without Victuals,
or any Drink but a Bottle of filthy Rum:—The Water we
sail'd on being salt.—

In the Evening I found my self very feverish, & went ill
to Bed. But having read somewhere that cold Water drank
plentifully was good for a Fever, I follow'd the Prescription,
sweat plentifully most of the Night, my Fever left me, and in
the Morning crossing the Ferry, proceeded on my Journey,
on foot, having 50 Miles to Burlington, where I was told I
should find Boats that would carry me the rest of the Way to
Philadelphia.

It rain'd very hard all the Day, I was thoroughly soak'd,
and by Noon a good deal tir'd, so I stopt at a poor Inn,
where I staid all Night, beginning now to wish I had never
left home. I cut so miserable a Figure too, that I found by
the Questions ask'd me I was suspected to be some runaway
Servant, and in danger of being taken up on that Suspicion.—However I proceeded the next Day, and got in the
Evening to an Inn within 8 or 10 Miles of Burlington, kept
by one Dr Brown.—

He entred into Conversation with me while I took some
Refreshment, and finding I had read a little, became very sociable and friendly. Our Acquaintance continu'd as long as he
liv'd. He had been, I imagine, an itinerant Doctor, for there

was no Town in England, or Country in Europe, of which
he could not give a very particular Account. He had some
Letters, & was ingenious, but much of an Unbeliever, &
wickedly undertook some Years after to travesty the Bible in
doggrel Verse as Cotton had done Virgil.—By this means he
set many of the Facts in a very ridiculous Light, & might have
hurt weak minds if his Work had been publish'd:—but it
never was.—At his House I lay that Night, and the next
Morning reach'd Burlington.—But had the Mortification to
find that the regular Boats were gone, a little before my coming, and no other expected to go till Tuesday, this being Saturday. Wherefore I return'd to an old Woman in the Town of
whom I had bought Gingerbread to eat on the Water, &
ask'd her Advice; she invited me to lodge at her House till a
Passage by Water should offer; & being tired with my foot
Travelling, I accepted the Invitation. She understanding I was
a Printer, would have had me stay at that Town & follow my
Business, being ignorant of the Stock necessary to begin with.
She was very hospitable, gave me a Dinner of Ox Cheek with
great Goodwill, accepting only of a Pot of Ale in return. And
I tho't my self fix'd till Tuesday should come. However walking in the Evening by the Side of the River a Boat came by,
which I found was going towards Philadelphia, with several
People in her. They took me in, and as there was no Wind,
we row'd all the Way; and about Midnight not having yet
seen the City, some of the Company were confident we must
have pass'd it, and would row no farther, the others knew not
where we were, so we put towards the Shore, got into a
Creek, landed near an old Fence with the Rails of which we
made a Fire, the Night being cold, in October, and there we
remain'd till Daylight. Then one of the Company knew the
Place to be Cooper's Creek a little above Philadelphia, which
we saw as soon as we got out of the Creek, and arriv'd there
about 8 or 9 a Clock, on the Sunday morning, and landed at
the Market street Wharff.—

I have been the more particular in this Description of my
Journey, & shall be so of my first Entry into that City, that
you may in your Mind compare such unlikely Beginning with
the Figure I have since made there. I was in my working
Dress, my best Cloaths being to come round by Sea. I was

dirty from my Journey; my Pockets were stuff'd out with
Shirts & Stockings; I knew no Soul, nor where to look for
Lodging. I was fatigu'd with Travelling, Rowing & Want of
Rest. I was very hungry, and my whole Stock of Cash consisted of a Dutch Dollar and about a Shilling in Copper. The
latter I gave the People of the Boat for my Passage, who at
first refus'd it on Acc^t of my Rowing; but I insisted on their
taking it, a Man being sometimes more generous when he has
but a little Money than when he has plenty, perhaps thro'
Fear of being thought to have but little. Then I walk'd up the
Street, gazing about, till near the Market House I met a Boy
with Bread. I had made many a Meal on Bread, & inquiring
where he got it, I went immediately to the Baker's he directed
me to in second Street; and ask'd for Bisket, intending such
as we had in Boston, but they it seems were not made in
Philadelphia, then I ask'd for a threepenny Loaf, and was told
they had none such: so not considering or knowing the Difference of Money & the greater Cheapness nor the Names of
his Bread, I bad him give me three pennyworth of any sort.
He gave me accordingly three great Puffy Rolls. I was surpriz'd at the Quantity, but took it, and having no Room in
my Pockets, walk'd off, with a Roll under each Arm, & eating
the other. Thus I went up Market Street as far as fourth
Street, passing by the Door of Mr Read, my future Wife's
Father, when she standing at the Door saw me, & thought I
made as I certainly did a most awkward ridiculous Appearance. Then I turn'd and went down Chestnut Street and part
of Walnut Street, eating my Roll all the Way, and coming
round found my self again at Market street Wharff, near the
Boat I came in, to which I went for a Draught of the River
Water, and being fill'd with one of my Rolls, gave the other
two to a Woman & her Child that came down the River in
the Boat with us and were waiting to go farther. Thus refresh'd I walk'd again up the Street, which by this time had
many clean dress'd People in it who were all walking the same
Way; I join'd them, and thereby was led into the great Meeting House of the Quakers near the Market. I sat down among
them, and after looking round a while & hearing nothing
said, being very drowzy thro' Labour & want of Rest the
preceding Night, I fell fast asleep, and continu'd so till the

Meeting broke up, when one was kind enough to rouse me. This was therefore the first House I was in or slept in, in Philadelphia.—

Walking again down towards the River, & looking in the Faces of People, I met a young Quaker Man whose Countenance I lik'd, and accosting him requested he would tell me where a Stranger could get Lodging. We were then near the Sign of the Three Mariners. Here, says he, is one Place that entertains Strangers, but it is not a reputable House; if thee wilt walk with me, I'll show thee a better. He brought me to the Crooked Billet in Water-Street. Here I got a Dinner. And while I was eating it, several sly Questions were ask'd me, as it seem'd to be suspected from my youth & Appearance, that I might be some Runaway. After Dinner my Sleepiness return'd: and being shown to a Bed, I lay down without undressing, and slept till Six in the Evening; was call'd to Supper; went to Bed again very early and slept soundly till the next Morning. Then I made my self as tidy as I could, and went to Andrew Bradford the Printer's.—I found in the Shop the old Man his Father, whom I had seen at New York, and who travelling on horse back had got to Philadelphia before me.—He introduc'd me to his Son, who receiv'd me civilly, gave me a Breakfast, but told me he did not at present want a Hand, being lately supply'd with one. But there was another Printer in town lately set up, one Keimer, who perhaps might employ me; if not, I should be welcome to lodge at his House, & he would give me a little Work to do now & then till fuller Business should offer.

The old Gentleman said, he would go with me to the new Printer: And when we found him, Neighbour, says Bradford, I have brought to see you a young Man of your Business, perhaps you may want such a One. He ask'd me a few Questions, put a Composing Stick in my Hand to see how I work'd, and then said he would employ me soon, tho' he had just then nothing for me to do. And taking old Bradford whom he had never seen before, to be one of the Towns People that had a Good Will for him, enter'd into a Conversation on his present Undertaking & Prospects; while Bradford not discovering that he was the other Printer's Father;

on Keimer's Saying he expected soon to get the greatest Part
of the Business into his own Hands, drew him on by artful
Questions and starting little Doubts, to explain all his Views,
what Interest he rely'd on, & in what manner he intended to
proceed.—I who stood by & heard all, saw immediately that
one of them was a crafty old Sophister, and the other a mere
Novice. Bradford left me with Keimer, who was greatly surpriz'd when I told him who the old Man was.

Keimer's Printing House I found, consisted of an old shat-
ter'd Press, and one small worn-out Fount of English, which
he was then using himself, composing in it an Elegy on
Aquila Rose before-mentioned, an ingenious young Man of
excellent Character much respected in the Town, Clerk of the
Assembly, & a pretty Poet. Keimer made Verses, too, but very
indifferently.—He could not be said to write them, for his
Manner was to compose them in the Types directly out of his
Head; so there being no Copy, but one Pair of Cases, and
the Elegy likely to require all the Letter, no one could help
him.—I endeavour'd to put his Press (which he had not yet
us'd, & of which he understood nothing) into Order fit to be
work'd with; & promising to come & print off his Elegy as
soon as he should have got it ready, I return'd to Bradford's
who gave me a little Job to do for the present, & there I
lodged & dieted. A few Days after Keimer sent for me to print
off the Elegy. And now he had got another Pair of Cases, and
a Pamphlet to reprint, on which he set me to work.—

These two Printers I found poorly qualified for their Business. Bradford had not been bred to it, & was very illiterate;
and Keimer tho' something of a Scholar, was a mere Compositor, knowing nothing of Presswork. He had been one of
the French Prophets and could act their enthusiastic Agita-
tions. At this time he did not profess any particular Religion,
but something of all on occasion; was very ignorant of the
World, & had, as I afterwards found, a good deal of the
Knave in his Composition. He did not like my Lodging at
Bradford's while I work'd with him. He had a House indeed,
but without Furniture, so he could not lodge me: But he got
me a Lodging at Mr Read's before-mentioned, who was the
Owner of his House. And my Chest & Clothes being come

by this time, I made rather a more respectable Appearance in the Eyes of Miss Read, than I had done when she first happen'd to see me eating my Roll in the Street. —

I began now to have some Acquaintance among the young People of the Town, that were Lovers of Reading with whom I spent my Evenings very pleasantly and gaining Money by my Industry & Frugality, I lived very agreably, forgetting Boston as much as I could, and not desiring that any there should know where I resided except my Friend Collins who was in my Secret, & kept it when I wrote to him. — At length an Incident happened that sent me back again much sooner than I had intended. —

I had a Brother-in-law, Robert Holmes, Master of a Sloop, that traded between Boston and Delaware. He being at New Castle 40 Miles below Philadelphia, heard there of me, and wrote me a Letter, mentioning the Concern of my Friends in Boston at my abrupt Departure, assuring me of their Goodwill to me, and that every thing would be accommodated to my Mind if I would return, to which he exhorted me very earnestly. — I wrote an Answer to his Letter, thank'd him for his Advice, but stated my Reasons for quitting Boston fully, & in such a Light as to convince him I was not so wrong as he had apprehended. — Sir William Keith Governor of the Province, was then at New Castle, and Capt. Holmes happening to be in Company with him when my Letter came to hand, spoke to him of me, and show'd him the Letter. The Governor read it, and seem'd surpriz'd when he was told my Age. He said I appear'd a young Man of promising Parts, and therefore should be encouraged: The Printers at Philadelphia were wretched ones, and if I would set up there, he made no doubt I should succeed; for his Part, he would procure me the publick Business, & do me every other Service in his Power. This my Brother-in-Law afterwards told me in Boston. But I knew as yet nothing of it; when one Day Keimer and I being at Work together near the Window, we saw the Governor and another Gentleman (which prov'd to be Col. French, of New Castle) finely dress'd, come directly across the Street to our House, & heard them at the Door. Keimer ran down immediately, thinking it a Visit to him. But the Governor enquir'd for me, came up, & with a Condescension &

Politeness I had been quite unus'd to, made me many Compliments, desired to be acquainted with me, blam'd me kindly for not having made my self known to him when I first came to the Place, and would have me away with him to the Tavern where he was going with Col. French to taste as he said some excellent Madeira. I was not a little surpriz'd, and Keimer star'd like a Pig poison'd. I went however with the Governor & Col. French, to a Tavern the Corner of Third Street, and over the Madeira he propos'd my Setting up my Business, laid beforre me the Probabilities of Success, & both he & Col French, assur'd me I should have their Interest & Influence in procuring the Publick Business of both Governments. On my doubting whether my Father would assist me in it, Sir William said he would give me a Letter to him, in which he would state the Advantages,—and he did not doubt of prevailing with him. So it was concluded I should return to Boston in the first Vessel with the Governor's Letter recommending me to my Father. In the mean time the Intention was to be kept secret, and I went on working with Keimer as usual, the Governor sending for me now & then to dine with him, a very great Honour I thought it, and conversing with me in the most affable, familiar, & friendly manner imaginable. About the End of April 1724. a little Vessel offer'd for Boston. I took Leave of Keimer as going to see my Friends. The Governor gave me an ample Letter, saying many flattering things of me to my Father, and strongly recommending the Project of my setting up at Philadelphia, as a Thing that must make my Fortune.—We struck on a Shoal in going down the Bay & sprung a Leak, we had a blustring time at Sea, and were oblig'd to pump almost continually, at which I took my Turn.—We arriv'd safe however at Boston in about a Fortnight.—I had been absent Seven Months and my Friends had heard nothing of me, for my Br. Holmes was not yet return'd; and had not written about me. My unexpected Appearance surpriz'd the Family; all were however very glad to see me and made me Welcome, except my Brother. I went to see him at his Printing-House: I was better dress'd than ever while in his Service, having a genteel new Suit from Head to foot, a Watch, and my Pockets lin'd with near Five Pounds Sterling in Silver. He receiv'd me not very frankly,

look'd me all over, and turn'd to his Work again. The Jour-
ney-Men were inquisitive where I had been, what sort of a
Country it was, and how I lik'd it? I prais'd it much, & the
happy Life I led in it; expressing strongly my Intention of
returning to it; and one of them asking what kind of Money
we had there, I produc'd a handful of Silver, and spread it
before them, which was a kind of Raree-Show they had not
been us'd to, Paper being the Money of Boston. Then I took
an Opportunity of letting them see my Watch: and lastly, (my
Brother still grum & sullen) I gave them a Piece of Eight to
drink & took my Leave.—This Visit of mine offended him
extreamly. For when my Mother some time after spoke to
him of a Reconciliation, & of her Wishes to see us on good
Terms together, & that we might live for the future as Brothers, he said, I had insulted him in such a Manner before his
People that he could never forget or forgive it.—In this however he was mistaken.—

My Father receiv'd the Governor's Letter with some apparent Surprize; but said little of it to me for some Days; when
Capt. Homes returning, he show'd it to him, ask'd if he knew
Keith, and what kind of a Man he was: Adding his Opinion
that he must be of small Discretion, to think of setting a Boy
up in Business who wanted yet 3 Years of being at Man's
Estate. Homes said what he could in favᶜ of the Project; but
my Father was clear in the Impropriety of it; and at last gave
a flat Denial to it. Then he wrote a civil Letter to Sir William
thanking him for the Patronage he had so kindly offered me,
but declining to assist me as yet in Setting up, I being in his
Opinion too young to be trusted with the Management of a
Business so important; & for which the Preparation must be
so expensive.—

My Friend & Companion Collins, who was a Clerk at the
Post-Office, pleas'd with the Account I gave him of my new
Country, determin'd to go thither also:—And while I waited
for my Fathers Determination, he set out before me by Land
to Rhodeisland, leaving his Books which were a pretty Collection of Mathematicks & Natural Philosophy, to come with
mine & me to New York where he propos'd to wait for me.
My Father, tho' he did not approve Sir William's Proposition
was yet pleas'd that I had been able to obtain so advantageous

a Character from a Person of such Note where I had resided, and that I had been so industrious & careful as to equip my self so handsomely in so short a time: therefore seeing no Prospect of an Accommodation between my Brother & me, he gave his Consent to my Returning again to Philadelphia, advis'd me to behave respectfully to the People there, endeavour to obtain the general Esteem, & avoid lampooning & libelling to which he thought I had too much Inclination;— telling me, that by steady Industry and a prudent Parsimony, I might save enough by the time I was One and Twenty to set me up, & that if I came near the Matter he would help me out with the Rest.—This was all I could obtain, except some small Gifts as Tokens of his & my Mother's Love, when I embark'd again for New-York, now with their Approbation & their Blessing.—

The Sloop putting in at Newport, Rhodeisland, I visited my Brother John, who had been married & settled there some Years. He received me very affectionately, for he always lov'd me.—A Friend of his, one Vernon, having some Money due to him in Pensilvania, about 35 Pounds Currency, desired I would receive it for him, and keep it till I had his Directions what to remit it in. Accordingly he gave me an Order.—This afterwards occasion'd me a good deal of Uneasiness.—At Newport we took in a Number of Passengers for New York: Among which were two young Women, Companions, and a grave, sensible Matron-like Quaker-Woman with her Attendants.—I had shown an obliging Readiness to do her some little Services which impress'd her I suppose with a degree of Good-will towards me.—Therefore when she saw a daily growing Familiarity between me & the two Young Women, which they appear'd to encourage, she took me aside & said, Young Man, I am concern'd for thee, as thou has no Friend with thee, and seems not to know much of the World, or of the Snares Youth is expos'd to; depend upon it those are very bad Women, I can see it in all their Actions, and if thee art not upon thy Guard, they will draw thee into some Danger: they are Strangers to thee,—and I advise thee in a friendly Concern for thy Welfare, to have no Acquaintance with them.—As I seem'd at first not to think so ill of them as she did, she mention'd some Things she had observ'd & heard

that had escap'd my Notice; but now convinc'd me she was
right. I thank'd her for her kind Advice, and promis'd to follow it.—When we arriv'd at New York, they told me where
they liv'd, & invited me to come and see them: but I avoided
it. And it was well I did: For the next Day, the Captain miss'd
a Silver Spoon & some other Things that had been taken out
of his Cabbin, and knowing that these were a Couple of
Strumpets, he got a Warrant to search their Lodgings, found
the stolen Goods, and had the Thieves punish'd.—So tho' we
had escap'd a sunken Rock which we scrap'd upon in the Passage, I thought this Escape of rather more Importance to me.
At New York I found my Friend Collins, who had arriv'd
there some Time before me. We had been intimate from Children, and had read the same Books together. But he had the
Advantage of more time for Reading, & Studying and a wonderful Genius for Mathematical Learning in which he far
outstript me. While I liv'd in Boston most of my Hours of
Leisure for Conversation were spent with him, & he continu'd a sober as well as an industrious Lad; was much respected for his Learning by several of the Clergy & other
Gentlemen, & seem'd to promise making a good Figure in
Life: but during my Absence he had acquir'd a Habit of Sotting with Brandy; and I found by his own Account & what I
heard from others, that he had been drunk every day since his
Arrival at New York, & behav'd very oddly. He had gam'd
too and lost his Money, so that I was oblig'd to discharge his
Lodgings, & defray his Expences to and at Philadelphia:
—Which prov'd extreamly inconvenient to me.—The then
Governor of N York, Burnet, Son of Bishop Burnet hearing
from the Captain that a young Man, one of his Passengers,
had a great many Books, desired he would bring me to see
him. I waited upon him accordingly, and should have taken
Collins with me but that he was not sober. The Gov.r treated
me with greet Civility, show'd me his Library, which was a
very large one, & we had a good deal of Conversation about
Books & Authors. This was the second Governor who had
done me the Honour to take Notice of me, which to a poor
Boy like me was very pleasing.—We proceeded to Philadelphia. I received on the Way Vernon's Money, without which
we could hardly have finish'd our Journey.—Collins wish'd

to be employ'd in some Counting House; but whether they discover'd his Dramming by his Breath, or by his Behaviour, tho' he had some Recommendations, he met with no Success in any Application, and continu'd Lodging & Boarding at the same House with me & at my Expence. Knowing I had that Money of Vernon's he was continually borrowing of me, still promising Repayment as soon as he should be in Business. At length he had got so much of it, that I was distress'd to think what I should do, in case of being call'd on to remit it.—His Drinking continu'd, about which we sometimes quarrel'd, for when a little intoxicated he was very fractious. Once in a Boat on the Delaware with some other young Men, he refused to row in his Turn: I will be row'd home, says he. We will not row you, says I. You must says he, or stay all Night on the Water, just as you please. The others said, Let us row; What signifies it? But my Mind being soured with his other Conduct, I continu'd to refuse. So he swore he would make me row, or throw me overboard; and coming along stepping on the Thwarts towards me, when he came up & struck at me, I clapt my Hand under his Crutch, and rising pitch'd him head-foremost into the River. I knew he was a good Swimmer, and so was under little Concern about him; but before he could get round to lay hold of the Boat, we had with a few Strokes pull'd her out of his Reach.—And ever when he drew near the Boat, we ask'd if he would row, striking a few Strokes to slide her away from him.—He was ready to die with Vexation, & obstinately would not promise to row; however seeing him at last beginning to tire, we lifted him in; and brought him home dripping wet in the Evening. We hardly exchang'd a civil Word afterwards; and a West India Captain who had a Commission to procure a Tutor for the Sons of a Gentleman at Barbadoes, happening to meet with him, agreed to carry him thither. He left me then, promising to remit me the first Money he should receive in order to discharge the Debt. But I never heard of him after.—The Breaking into this Money of Vernon's was one of the first great Errata of my Life. And this Affair show'd that my Father was not much out in his Judgment when he suppos'd me too Young to manage Business of Importance. But Sir William, on reading his Letter, said he was too prudent. There was great Difference in Persons, and Discretion did not always accompany Years, nor was Youth always without it. And since he will not set you up, says he, I will do it my self. Give me an Inventory of the Things necessary to be had from England, and I will send for them. You shall repay me when you are able; I am resolv'd to have a good Printer here, and I am sure you must succeed. This was spoken with such an Appearance of Cordiality, that I had not the least doubt of his meaning what he said.—I had hitherto kept the Proposition of my Setting up a Secret in Philadelphia, & I still kept it. Had it been known that I depended on the Governor, probably some Friend that knew him better would have advis'd me not to rely on him, as I afterwards heard it as his known Character to be liberal of Promises which he never meant to keep.—Yet unsolicited as he was by me, how could I think his generous Offers insincere? I believ'd him one of the best Men in the World.—

I presented him an Inventory of a little Print.ᵍ House, amounting by my Computation to about 100£ Sterling. He lik'd it, but ask'd me if my being on the Spot in England to chuse the Types & see that every thing was good of the kind, might not be of some Advantage. Then, says he, when there, you may make Acquaintances & establish Correspondencies in the Bookselling, & Stationary Way. I agreed that this might be advantageous. Then says he, get yourself ready to go with Annis; which was the annual Ship, and the only one at that Time usually passing between London and Philadelphia. But it would be some Months before Annis sail'd, so I continu'd working with Keimer, fretting about the Money Collins had got from me, and in daily Apprehensions of being call'd upon by Vernon, which however did not happen for some Years after.—

I believe I have omitted mentioning that in my first Voyage from Boston, being becalm'd off Block Island, our People set about catching Cod & hawl'd up a great many. Hitherto I had stuck to my Resolution of not eating animal Food; and on this Occasion, I consider'd with my Master Tryon, the taking every Fish as a kind of unprovok'd Murder, since none of them had or ever could do us any Injury that might justify the Slaughter.— All this seem'd very reasonable.—But I had formerly been a great Lover of Fish, & when this came hot out of the Frying Pan, it smelt admirably well. I balanc'd some time between Principle & Inclination: till I recollected, that when the Fish were opened, I saw smaller Fish taken out of their Stomachs:—Then, thought I, if you eat one another, I don't see why we mayn't eat you. So I din'd upon Cod very heartily and continu'd to eat with other People, returning only now & then occasionally to a vegetable Diet. So convenient a thing it is to be a *reasonable Creature*, since it enables one to find or make a Reason for every thing one has a mind to do.—

Keimer & I liv'd on a pretty good familiar Footing & agreed tolerably well: for he suspected nothing of my Setting up. He retain'd a great deal of his old Enthusiasms, and lov'd an Argumentation. We therefore had many Disputations. I us'd to work him so with my Socratic Method, and had trapann'd him so often by Questions apparently so distant from any Point we had in hand, and yet by degrees led to the Point, and brought him into Difficulties & Contradictions, that at last he grew ridiculously cautious, and would hardly answer me the most common Question, without asking first, *What do you intend to infer from that?* However it gave him so high an Opinion of my Abilities in the Confuting Way, that he seriously propos'd my being his Colleague in a Project he had of setting up a new Sect. He was to preach the Doctrines, and I was to confound all Opponents. When he came to explain with me upon the Doctrines, I found several Conundrums which I objected to, unless I might have my Way a little too, and introduce some of mine. Keimer wore his Beard at full Length, because somewhere in the Mosaic Law it is said, *thou shalt not mar the Corners of thy Beard*. He likewise kept the seventh day Sabbath; and these two Points were Essentials with him.—I dislik'd both, but agreed to admit them upon Condition of his adopting the Doctrine of using no animal Food. I doubt, says he, my Constitution will not bear that. I assur'd him it would, & that he would be the better for it. He was usually a great Glutton, and I promis'd my self some Diversion in half-starving him. He agreed to try the Practice if I would keep him Company. I did so and we held it for three Months. We had our Victuals dress'd and brought to us regularly by a Woman in the Neighbourhood, who had from me a List of 40 Dishes to be prepar'd for us at different times, in all which there was neither Fish Flesh nor Fowl, and the Whim suited me the better at this time from the Cheapness of it, not costing us above 18^d Sterling each, per Week.—I have since kept several Lents most strictly, Leaving the common Diet for that, and that for the common, abruptly, without the least Inconvenience: So that I think there is little in the Advice of making those Changes by easy Gradations.—I went on pleasantly, but Poor Keimer suffer'd grievously, tir'd of the Project, long'd for the Flesh Pots of Egypt, and order'd a roast Pig; He invited me & two Women Friends to dine with him, but it being brought too soon upon table, he could not resist the Temptation, and ate it all up before we came.—

I had made some Courtship during this time to Miss Read, I had a great Respect & Affection for her, and had some Reason to believe she had the same for me: but as I was about to take a long Voyage, and we were both very young, only a little above 18. it was thought most prudent by her Mother to prevent our going too far at present, as a Marriage if it was to take place would be more convenient after my Return, when I should be as I expected set up in my Business. Perhaps too she thought my Expectations not so well founded as I imagined them to be.—

My chief Acquaintances at this time were, Charles Osborne, Joseph Watson, & James Ralph; All Lovers of Reading. The two first were Clerks to an eminent Scrivener or Conveyancer in the Town, Charles Brogden; the other was Clerk to a Merchant. Watson was a pious sensible young Man, of great Integrity.—The others rather more lax in their Principles of Religion, particularly Ralph, who as well as Collins had been unsettled by me, for which they both made me suffer.—Osborne was sensible, candid, frank, sincere, and affectionate to his Friends; but in litterary Matters too fond of Criticising. Ralph, was ingenious, genteel in his Manners, & extreamly eloquent; I think I never knew a prettier Talker.—Both of them great Admirers of Poetry, and began to try their Hands in little Pieces. Many pleasant Walks we four had together, on Sundays into the Woods near Skuylkill, where we read to one another & conferr'd on what we read. Ralph was inclin'd to pursue the Study of Poetry, not doubting but he might become eminent in it and make his Fortune by it, alledging that the best Poets must when they first began to write, make as many Faults as he did.—Osborne dissuaded him, assur'd him he had no Genius for Poetry, & advis'd him to think of nothing beyond the Business he was bred to; that in the mercantile way tho' he had no Stock, he might by his Diligence & Punctuality recommend himself to Employment as a Factor, and in time acquire wherewith to trade on his own Account. I approv'd the amusing one's Self with Poetry now & then, so far as to improve one's Language, but no farther. On this it was propos'd that we should each of us at our next Meeting produce a Piece of our own Composing, in order to improve by our mutual Observations, Criticisms & Corrections. As Language & Expression was what we had in View, we excluded all Considerations of Invention, by agreeing that the Task should be a Version of the 18th Psalm, which describes the Descent of a Deity. When the Time of our Meeting drew nigh, Ralph call'd on me first, & let me know his Piece was ready. I told him I had been busy, & having little Inclination had done nothing.—He then show'd me his Piece for my Opinion; and I much approv'd it, as it appear'd to me to have great Merit. Now, says he, Osborne never will allow the least Merit in any thing of mine, but makes 1000 Criticisms out of mere Envy. He is not so jealous of you. I wish therefore you would take this Piece, & produce it as yours. I will pretend not to have had time, & so produce nothing: We shall then see what he will say to it.—It was agreed, and I immediately transcrib'd it that it might appear in my own hand. We met. Watson's Performance was read: there were some Beauties in it: but many Defects. Osborne's was read: It was much better. Ralph did it Justice, remark'd some Faults, but applauded the Beauties. He himself had nothing to produce. I was backward, seem'd desirous of being excus'd, had not had sufficient Time to correct; &c. but no Excuse could be admitted, produce I must. It was read and repeated; Watson and Osborne gave up the Contest; and join'd in applauding it immoderately. Ralph only made some Criticisms & propos'd some Amendments, but I defended my

Text. Osborne was against Ralph, & told him he was no better a Critic than Poet; so he dropt the Argument. As they two
went home together, Osborne express'd himself still more
strongly in favour of what he thought my Production, having
restrain'd himself before as he said, lest I should think it Flattery. But who would have imagin'd, says he, that Franklin
had been capable of such a Performance; such Painting, such
Force! such Fire! he has even improv'd the Original! In his
common Conversation, he seems to have no Choice of
Words; he hesitates and blunders; and yet, good God, how
he writes!—When we next met, Ralph discover'd the Trick
we had plaid him, and Osborne was a little laught at. This
Transaction fix'd Ralph in his Resolution of becoming a Poet.
I did all I could to dissuade him from it, but He continu'd
scribbling Verses, till *Pope* cur'd him.—He became however
a pretty good Prose Writer. More of him hereafter. But as I
may not have occasion again to mention the other two, I shall
just remark here, that Watson died in my Arms a few Years
after, much lamented, being the best of our Set. Osborne
went to the West Indies, where he became an eminent Lawyer
& made Money, but died young. He and I had made a serious Agreement, that the one who happen'd first to die,
should if possible make a friendly Visit to the other, and acquaint him how he found things in that separate State. But
he never fulfill'd his Promise.

The Governor, seeming to like my Company, had me
frequently to his House; & his Setting me up was always
mention'd as a fix'd thing. I was to take with me Letters
recommendatory to a Number of his Friends, besides the
Letter of Credit, to furnish me with the necessary Money for
purchasing the Press & Types, Paper, &c. For these Letters I
was appointed to call at different times, when they were to be
ready, but a future time was still named.—Thus we went on
till the Ship whose Departure too had been several times
postponed was on the Point of sailing. Then when I call'd to
take my Leave & receive the Letters, his Secretary, Dr Bard,
came out to me and said the Governor was extreamly busy,
in writing, but would be down at Newcastle before the Ship,
& there the Letters would be delivered to me.

Ralph, tho' married & having one Child, had determined

to accompany me in this Voyage. It was thought he intended to establish a Correspondence, & obtain Goods to sell on Commission. But I found afterwards, that thro' some Discontent with his Wifes Relations, he purposed to leave her on their Hands, & never return again.—Having taken leave of my Friends, & interchang'd some Promises with Miss Read, I left Philadelphia in the Ship, which anchor'd at Newcastle. The Governor was there. But when I went to his Lodging, the Secretary came to me from him with the civillest Message in the World, that he could not then see me being engag'd in Business of the utmost Importance, but should send the Letters to me on board, wish'd me heartily a good Voyage and a speedy Return, &c. I return'd on board, a little puzzled, but still not doubting.—

Mr Andrew Hamilton, a famous Lawyer of Philadelphia, had taken Passage in the same Ship for himself and Son: and with Mr Denham a Quaker Merchant, & Messrs Onion & Russel Masters of an Iron Work in Maryland, had engag'd the Great Cabin; so that Ralph and I were forc'd to take up with a Birth in the Steerage:—And none on board knowing us, were considered as ordinary Persons.—But Mr Hamilton & his Son (it was James, since Governor) return'd from New Castle to Philadelphia, the Father being recall'd by a great Fee to plead for a seized Ship.—And just before we sail'd Col. French coming on board, & showing me great Respect, I was more taken Notice of, and with my Friend Ralph invited by the other Gentlemen to come into the Cabin, there being now Room. Accordingly we remov'd thither.

Understanding that Col. French had brought on board the Governor's Dispatches, I ask'd the Captain for those Letters that were to be under my Care. He said all were put into the Bag together; and he could not then come at them; but before we landed in England, I should have an Opportunity of picking them out. So I was satisfy'd for the present, and we proceeded on our Voyage. We had a sociable Company in the Cabin, and lived uncommonly well, having the Addition of all Mr Hamilton's Stores, who had laid in plentifully. In this Passage Mr Denham contracted a Friendship for me that continued during his Life. The Voyage was otherwise not a pleasant one, as we had a great deal of bad Weather.—

When we came into the Channel, the Captain kept his Word with me, & gave me an Opportunity of examining the Bag for the Governor's Letters. I found none upon which my Name was put, as under my Care; I pick'd out 6 or 7 that by the Handwriting I thought might be the promis'd Letters, especially as one of them was directed to Basket the King's Printer, and another to some Stationer. We arriv'd in London the 24th of December, 1724.—I waited upon the Stationer who came first in my Way, delivering the Letter as from Gov. Keith. I don't know such a Person, says he: but opening the Letter, O, this is from Riddlesden; I have lately found him to be a compleat Rascal, and I will have nothing to do with him, nor receive any Letters from him. So putting the Letter into my Hand, he turn'd on his Heel & left me to serve some Customer.—I was surprized to find these were not the Governor's Letters. And after recollecting and comparing Circumstances, I began to doubt his Sincerity.—I found my Friend Denham, and opened the whole Affair to him. He let me into Keith's Character, told me there was not the least Probability that he had written any Letters for me, that no one who knew him had the smallest Dependance on him, and he laught at the Notion of the Governor's giving me a Letter of Credit, having as he said no Credit to give.—On my expressing some Concern about what I should do: He advis'd me to endeavour getting some Employment in the Way of my Business. Among the Printers here, says he, you will improve yourself; and when you return to America, you will set up to greater Advantage.—

We both of us happen'd to know, as well as the Stationer, that Riddlesden the Attorney, was a very Knave. He had half ruin'd Miss Read's Father by drawing him in to be bound for him. By his Letter it appear'd, there was a secret Scheme on foot to the Prejudice of Hamilton, (Suppos'd to be then coming over with us,) and that Keith was concern'd in it with Riddlesden. Denham, who was a Friend of Hamilton's, thought he ought to be acquainted with it. So when he arriv'd in England, which was soon after, partly from Resentment & Ill-Will to Keith & Riddlesden, & partly from Good Will to him: I waited on him, and gave him the Letter. He thank'd me cordially, the Information being of Importance to

him. And from that time he became my Friend, greatly to my
Advantage afterwards on many Occasions.

But what shall we think of a Governor's playing such pitiful Tricks, & imposing so grossly on a poor ignorant Boy! It
was a Habit he had acquired. He wish'd to please every body;
and having little to give, he gave Expectations.—He was otherwise an ingenious sensible Man, a pretty good Writer, & a
good Governor for the People, tho' not for his Constituents
the Proprietaries, whose Instructions he sometimes disregarded.—Several of our best Laws were of his Planning, and
pass'd during his Administration.—

Ralph and I were inseparable Companions. We took Lodgings together in Little Britain at 3/6 per Week, as much as we
could then afford.—He found some Relations, but they were
poor & unable to assist him. He now let me know his Intentions of remaining in London, and that he never meant to
return to Philad?—He had brought no Money with him, the
whole he could muster having been expended in paying his
Passage.—I had 15 Pistoles: So he borrowed occasionally of
me, to subsist while he was looking out for Business.—He
first endeavoured to get into the Playhouse, believing himself
qualify'd for an Actor; but Wilkes, to whom he apply'd, advis'd him candidly not to think of that Employment, as it was
impossible he should succeed in it.—Then he propos'd to
Roberts, a Publisher in Paternoster Row, to write for him a
Weekly Paper like the Spectator, on certain Conditions, which
Roberts did not approve. Then he endeavour'd to get Em-
ploym! as a Hackney Writer to copy for the Stationers &
Lawyers about the Temple: but could find no Vacancy.—

I immediately got into Work at Palmer's then a famous
Printing House in Bartholomew Close; and here I continu'd
near a Year. I was pretty diligent; but spent with Ralph a
good deal of my Earnings in going to Plays & other Places
of Amusement. We had together consum'd all my Pistoles,
and now just rubb'd on from hand to mouth. He seem'd
quite to forget his Wife & Child, and I by degrees my Engagements wth Miss Read, to whom I never wrote more than
one Letter, & that was to let her know I was not likely soon
to return. This was another of the great Errata of my Life,
which I should wish to correct if I were to live it over

again.—In fact, by our Expences, I was constantly kept unable to pay my Passage.

At Palmer's I was employ'd in Composing for the second Edition of Woollaston's Religion of Nature. Some of his Reasonings not appearing to me well-founded, I wrote a little metaphysical Piece, in which I made Remarks on them. It was entitled, *A Dissertation on Liberty & Necessity, Pleasure and Pain.*—I inscrib'd it to my Friend Ralph.—I printed a small Number. It occasion'd my being more consider'd by Mr Palmer, as a young Man of some Ingenuity, tho' he seriously expostulated with me upon the Principles of my Pamphlet which to him appear'd abominable. My printing this Pamphlet was another Erratum.

While I lodg'd in Little Britain I made an Acquaintance with one Wilcox a Bookseller, whose Shop was at the next Door. He had an immense Collection of second-hand Books. Circulating Libraries were not then in Use; but we agreed that on certain reasonable Terms which I have now forgotten, I might take, read & return any of his Books. This I esteem'd a great Advantage, & I made as much Use of it as I could.—

My Pamphlet by some means falling into the Hands of one Lyons, a Surgeon, Author of a Book intituled *The Infallibility of Human Judgment*, it occasioned an Acquaintance between us; he took great Notice of me, call'd on me often, to converse on these Subjects, carried me to the Horns a pale Ale-House in   Lane, Cheapside, and introduc'd me to Dr Mandevile, Author of the Fable of the Bees who had a Club there, of which he was the Soul, being a most facetious entertaining Companion. Lyons too introduc'd me to Dr Pemberton, at Batson's Coffee House, who promis'd to give me an Opportunity some time or other of seeing Sir Isaac Newton, of which I was extreamly desirous; but this never happened.

I had brought over a few Curiosities among which the principal was a Purse made of the Asbestos, which purifies by Fire. Sir Hans Sloane heard of it, came to see me, and invited me to his House in Bloomsbury Square; where he show'd me all his Curiosities, and persuaded me to let him add that to the Number, for which he paid me handsomely.—

In our House there lodg'd a young Woman; a Millener,

who I think had a Shop in the Cloisters. She had been gen-
teelly bred; was sensible & lively, and of most pleasing Conversation.—Ralph read Plays to her in the Evenings, they
grew intimate, she took another Lodging, and he follow'd
her. They liv'd together some time, but he being still out of
Business, & her Income not sufficient to maintain them with
her Child, he took a Resolution of going from London, to
try for a Country School, which he thought himself well qualify'd to undertake, as he wrote an excellent Hand, & was a
Master of Arithmetic & Accounts.—This however he deem'd
a Business below him, & confident of future better Fortune
when he should be unwilling to have it known that he once
was so meanly employ'd, he chang'd his Name, & did me the
Honour to assume mine.—For I soon after had a Letter from
him, acquainting me, that he was settled in a small Village in
Berkshire, I think it was, where he taught reading & writing
to 10 or a dozen Boys at 6 pence each per Week, recommending Mrs T. to my Care, and desiring me to write to him
directing for Mr Franklin Schoolmaster at such a Place. He
continu'd to write frequently, sending me large Specimens of
an Epic Poem, which he was then composing, and desiring
my Remarks & Corrections.—These I gave him from time to
time, but endeavour'd rather to discourage his Proceeding.
One of Young's Satires was then just publish'd. I copy'd &
sent him a great Part of it, which set in a strong Light the
Folly of pursuing the Muses with any Hope of Advancement
by them. All was in vain. Sheets of the Poem continu'd to
come by every Post. In the mean time Mrs T. having on his
Account lost her Friends & Business, was often in Distresses,
& us'd to send for me, and borrow what I could spare to help
her out of them. I grew fond of her Company, and being at
this time under no Religious Restraints, & presuming on my
Importance to her, I attempted Familiarities, (another Erratum) which she repuls'd with a proper Resentment, and
acquainted him with my Behaviour. This made a Breach
between us, & when he return'd again to London, he let me
know he thought I had cancel'd all the Obligations he had
been under to me.—So I found I was never to expect his
Repaying me what I lent to him or advanc'd for him. This
was however not then of much Consequence, as he was

totally unable.—And in the Loss of his Friendship I found my self reliev'd from a Burthen. I now began to think of getting a little Money beforehand; and expecting better Work, I left Palmer's to work at Watts's near Lincoln's Inn Fields, a still greater Printing House. Here I continu'd all the rest of my Stay in London.

At my first Admission into this Printing House, I took to working at Press, imagining I felt a Want of the Bodily Exercise I had been us'd to in America, where Presswork is mix'd with Composing. I drank only Water; the other Workmen, near 50 in Number, were great Guzzlers of Beer. On occasion I carried up & down Stairs a large Form of Types in each hand, when others carried but one in both Hands. They wonder'd to see from this & several Instances that the Water-American as they call'd me was *stronger* than themselves who drunk *strong* Beer. We had an Alehouse Boy who attended always in the House to supply the Workmen. My Companion at the Press, drank every day a Pint before Breakfast, a Pint at Breakfast with his Bread and Cheese; a Pint between Breakfast and Dinner; a Pint at Dinner; a Pint in the Afternoon about Six o'clock, and another when he had done his Day's-Work. I thought it a detestable Custom.—But it was necessary, he suppos'd, to drink *strong* Beer that he might be *strong* to labour. I endeavour'd to convince him that the Bodily Strength afforded by Beer could only be in proportion to the Grain or Flour of the Barley dissolved in the Water of which it was made; that there was more Flour in a Pennyworth of Bread, and therefore if he would eat that with a Pint of Water, it would give him more Strength than a Quart of Beer.—He drank on however, & had 4 or 5 Shillings to pay out of his Wages every Saturday Night for that muddling Liquor; an Expence I was free from.—And thus these poor Devils keep themselves always under.

Watts after some Weeks desiring to have me in the Composing-Room, I left the Pressmen. A new *Bienvenu* or Sum for Drink, being 5/, was demanded of me by the Compostors. I thought it an Imposition, as I had paid below. The Master thought so too, and forbad my Paying it. I stood out two or three Weeks, was accordingly considered as an Excommunicate, and had so many little Pieces of private Mischief done me, by mixing my Sorts, transposing my Pages, breaking my Matter, &c. &c. if I were ever so little out of the Room, & all ascrib'd to the Chapel Ghost, which they said ever haunted those not regularly admitted, that notwithstanding the Master's Protection, I found myself oblig'd to comply and pay the Money; convinc'd of the Folly of being on ill Terms with those one is to live with continually. I was now on a fair Footing with them, and soon acquir'd considerable Influence. I propos'd some reasonable Alterations in their * Chapel Laws, and carried them against all Opposition. From my Example a great Part of them, left their muddling Breakfast of Beer & Bread & Cheese, finding they could with me be supply'd from a neighbouring House with a large Porringer of hot Water-gruel, sprinkled with Pepper, crumb'd with Bread, & a Bit of Butter in it, for the Price of a Pint of Beer, viz, three halfpence. This was a more comfortable as well as cheaper Breakfast, & kept their Heads clearer.—Those who continu'd sotting with Beer all day, were often, by not paying, out of Credit at the Alehouse, and us'd to make Interest with me to get Beer, *their Light*, as they phras'd it, *being out*. I watch'd the Pay table on Saturday Night, & collected what I stood engag'd for them, having to pay some times near Thirty Shillings a Week on their Accounts.—This, and my being esteem'd a pretty good Riggite, that is a jocular verbal Satyrist, supported my Consequence in the Society.—My constant Attendance, (I never making a St. Monday), recommended me to the Master; and my uncommon Quickness at Composing, occasion'd my being put upon all Work of Dispatch which was generally better paid. So I went on now very agreably.—

My Lodging in Little Britain being too remote, I found another in Duke-street opposite to the Romish Chapel. It was two pair of Stairs backwards at an Italian Warehouse. A Widow Lady kept the House; she had a Daughter & a Maid Servant, and a Journey-man who attended the Warehouse, but lodg'd abroad.—After sending to enquire my Character at the House where I last lodg'd, she agreed to take me in at the same Rate 3/6 per Week, cheaper as she said from the Pro-

---

*A Printing House is always called a Chappel by the Workmen.—

tection she expected in having a Man lodge in the House. She was a Widow, an elderly Woman, had been bred a Protestant, being a Clergyman's Daughter, but was converted to the Catholic Religion by her Husband, whose Memory she much revered, had lived much among People of Distinction, and knew a 1000 Anecdotes of them as far back as the Times of Charles the second. She was lame in her Knees with the Gout, and therefore seldom stirr'd out of her Room, so sometimes wanted Company; and hers was so highly amusing to me; that I was sure to spend an Evening with her whenever she desired it. Our Supper was only half an Anchovy each, on a very little Strip of Bread & Butter, and half a Pint of Ale between us. — But the Entertainment was in her Conversation. My always keeping good Hours, and giving little Trouble in the Family, made her unwilling to part with me; so that when I talk'd of a Lodging I had heard of, nearer my Business, for 2/ a Week, which, intent as I now was on saving Money, made some Difference; she bid me not think of it, for she would abate me two Shillings a Week for the future, so I remain'd with her at 1/6 as long as I staid in London. —

In a Garret of her House there lived a Maiden Lady of 70 in the most retired Manner, of whom my Landlady gave me this Account, that she was a Roman-Catholic, had been sent abroad when young & lodg'd in a Nunnery with an Intent of becoming a Nun: but the Country not agreeing with her, she return'd to England, where there being no Nunnery, she had vow'd to lead the Life of a Nun as near as might be done in those Circumstances: Accordingly She had given all her Estate to charitable Uses, reserving only Twelve Pounds a Year to live on, and out of this Sum she still gave a great deal in Charity, living her self on Watergruel only, & using no Fire but to boil it. — She had lived many Years in that Garret, being permitted to remain there gratis by successive catholic Tenants of the House below, as they deem'd it a Blessing to have her there. A Priest visited her, to confess her every Day. I have ask'd her, says my Landlady, how she, as she liv'd, could possibly find so much Employment for a Confessor? O, says she, it is impossible to avoid *vain Thoughts*. I was permitted once to visit her: She was chearful & polite, & convers'd pleasantly. The Room was clean, but had no other

Furniture than a Matras, a Table with a Crucifix & Book, a Stool, which she gave me to sit on, and a Picture over the Chimney of St. *Veronica*, displaying her Handkerchief with the miraculous Figure of Christ's bleeding Face on it, which she explain'd to me with great Seriousness. She look'd pale, but was never sick, and I give it as another Instance on how small an Income Life & Health may be supported.—

At Watts's Printinghouse I contracted an Acquaintance with an ingenious young Man, one Wygate, who having wealthy Relations, had been better educated than most Printers, was a tolerable Latinist, spoke French, & lov'd Reading. I taught him, & a Friend of his, to swim, at twice going into the River, & they soon became good Swimmers. They introduc'd me to some Gentlemen from the Country who went to Chelsea by Water to see the College and Don Saltero's Curiosities. In our Return, at the Request of the Company, whose Curiosity Wygate had excited, I stript & leapt into the River, & swam from near Chelsea to Blackfryars, performing on the Way many Feats of Activity both upon & under Water, that surpriz'd & pleas'd those to whom they were Novelties.—I had from a Child been ever delighted with this Exercise, had studied & practis'd all Thevenot's Motions & Positions, added some of my own, aiming at the graceful & easy, as well as the Useful.—All these I took this Occasion of exhibiting to the Company, & was much flatter'd by their Admiration.—And Wygate, who was desirous of becoming a Master, grew more & more attach'd to me, on that account, as well as from the Similarity of our Studies. He at length propos'd to me travelling all over Europe together, supporting ourselves every where by working at our Business. I was once inclin'd to it. But mentioning it to my good Friend Mr Denham, with whom I often spent an Hour, when I had Leisure. He dissuaded me from it; advising me to think only of return^g to Pensilvania, which he was now about to do.—

I must record one Trait of this good Man's Character. He had formerly been in Business at Bristol, but fail'd in Debt to a Number of People, compounded and went to America. There, by a close Application to Business as a Merchant, he acquir'd a plentiful Fortune in a few Years. Returning to England in the Ship with me, He invited his old Creditors to an

Entertainment, at which he thank'd them for the easy Composition they had favour'd him with, & when they expected nothing but the Treat, every Man at the first Remove, found under his Plate an Order on a Banker for the full Amount of the unpaid Remainder with Interest.

He now told me he was about to return to Philadelphia, and should carry over a great Quantity of Goods in order to open a Store there: He propos'd to take me over as his Clerk, to keep his Books (in which he would instruct me) copy his Letters, and attend the Store. He added, that as soon as I should be acquainted with mercantile Business he would promote me by sending me with a Cargo of Flour & Bread &c to the West Indies, and procure me Commissions from others; which would be profitable, & if I manag'd well, would establish me handsomely. The Thing pleas'd me, for I was grown tired of London, remember'd with Pleasure the happy Months I had spent in Pennsylvania, and wish'd again to see it. Therefore I immediately agreed, on the Terms of Fifty Pounds a Year Pensylvania Money; less indeed than my then present Gettings as a Compostor, but affording a better Prospect. —

I now took Leave of Printing, as I thought for ever, and was daily employ'd in my new Business; going about with Mr Denham among the Tradesmen, to purchase various Articles, & see them pack'd up, doing Errands, calling upon Workmen to dispatch, &c. and when all was on board, I had a few Days Leisure. On one of these Days I was to my Surprize sent for by a great Man I knew only by Name, a Sir William Wyndham and I waited upon him. He had heard by some means or other of my Swimming from Chelsey to Blackfryars, and of my teaching Wygate and another young Man to swim in a few Hours. He had two Sons about to set out on their Travels; he wish'd to have them first taught Swimming; and propos'd to gratify me handsomely if I would teach them. — They were not yet come to Town and my Stay was uncertain, so I could not undertake it. But from this Incident I thought it likely, that if I were to remain in England and open a Swimming School, I might get a good deal of Money. — And it struck me so strongly, that had the Overture been sooner made me, probably I should not so

soon have returned to America.—After Many Years, you & I
had something of more Importance to do with one of these
Sons of Sir William Wyndham, become Earl of Egremont,
which I shall mention in its Place.—

Thus I spent about 18 Months in London. Most Part of the
Time, I work'd hard at my Business, & spent but little upon
my self except in seeing Plays, & in Books.—My Friend
Ralph had kept me poor. He owed me about 27 Pounds;
which I was now never likely to receive; a great Sum out of
my small Earnings. I lov'd him notwithstanding, for he had
many amiable Qualities.—tho' I had by no means improv'd
my Fortune.—But I had pick'd up some very ingenious Acquaintance whose Conversation was of great Advantage to
me, and I had read considerably.

We sail'd from Gravesend on the 23^d of July 1726.—For The
Incidents of the Voyage, I refer you to my Journal, where you
will find them all minutely related. Perhaps the most important Part of that Journal is the *Plan* to be found in it which I
formed at Sea, for regulating my future Conduct in Life. It is
the more remarkable, as being form'd when I was so young,
and yet being pretty faithfully adhered to quite thro' to old
Age.—We landed in Philadelphia the 11th of October, where
I found sundry Alterations. Keith was no longer Governor,
being superceded by Major Gordon: I met him walking the
Streets as a common Citizen. He seem'd a little asham'd at
seeing me, but pass'd without saying any thing. I should have
been as much asham'd at seeing Miss Read, had not her Fr.^{ds}
despairing with Reason of my Return, after the Receipt of
my Letter, persuaded her to marry another, one Rogers, a
Potter, which was done in my Absence. With him however
she was never happy, and soon parted from him, refusing to
cohabit with him, or bear his Name It being now said that
he had another Wife. He was a worthless Fellow tho' an excellent Workman which was the Temptation to her Friends.
He got into Debt, and ran away in 1727 or 28, went to the
West Indies, and died there. Keimer had got a better House,
a Shop well supply'd with Stationary, plenty of new Types, a
number of Hands tho' none good, and seem'd to have a great
deal of Business.

Mr Denham took a Store in Water Street, where we open'd

our Goods. I attended the Business diligently, studied Accounts, and grew in a little Time expert at selling.—We lodg'd and boarded together, he counsell'd me as a Father, having a sincere Regard for me: I respected & lov'd him: and we might have gone on together very happily: But in the Beginning of Feb.ʸ 172⁶₇ when I had just pass'd my 21ˢᵗ Year, we both were taken ill. My Distemper was a Pleurisy, which very nearly carried me off:—I suffered a good deal, gave up the Point in my own mind, & was rather disappointed when I found my self recovering; regretting in some degree that I must now sometime or other have all that disagreable Work to do over again.—I forget what his Distemper was. It held him a long time, and at length carried him off. He left me a small Legacy in a nuncupative Will, as a Token of his Kindness for me, and he left me once more to the wide World. For the Store was taken into the Care of his Executors, and my Employment under him ended:—My Brother-in-law Homes, being now at Philadelphia, advis'd my Return to my Business. And Keimer tempted me with an Offer of large Wages by the Year to come & take the Management of his Printing-House that he might better attend his Stationer's Shop.—I had heard a bad Character of him in London, from his Wife & her Friends, & was not fond of having any more to do with him. I try'd for farther Employment as a Merchant's Clerk; but not readily meeting with any, I clos'd again with Keimer.—

I found in *his* House these Hands; Hugh Meredith a Welsh-Pensilvanian, 30 Years of Age, bred to Country Work: honest, sensible, had a great deal of solid Observation, was something of a Reader, but given to drink:—Stephen Potts, a young Country Man of full Age, bred to the Same:—of uncommon natural Parts, & great Wit & Humour, but a little idle.—These he had agreed with at extream low Wages, per Week, to be rais'd a Shilling every 3 Months, as they would deserve by improving in their Business, & the Expectation of these high Wages to come on hereafter was what he had drawn them in with.—Meredith was to work at Press, Potts at Bookbinding, which he by Agreement, was to teach them, tho' he knew neither one nor t'other. John ——— a wild Irishman brought up to no Business, whose Service for 4

Years Keimer had purchas'd from the Captain of a Ship. He too was to be made a Pressman. George Webb, an Oxford Scholar, whose Time for 4 Years he had likewise bought, intending him for a Compositor: of whom more presently. And David Harry, a Country Boy, whom he had taken Apprentice. I soon perceiv'd that the Intention of engaging me at Wages so much higher than he had been us'd to give, was to have these raw cheap Hands form'd thro' me, and as soon as I had instructed them, then, they being all articled to him, he should be able to do without me.—I went on however, very chearfully; put his Printing House in Order, which had been in great Confusion, and brought his Hands by degrees to mind their Business and to do it better.

It was an odd Thing to find an Oxford Scholar in the Situation of a bought Servant. He was not more than 18 Years of Age, & gave me this Account of himself; that he was born in Gloucester, educated at a Grammar School there, had been distinguish'd among the Scholars for some apparent Superiority in performing his Part when they exhibited Plays; belong'd to the Witty Club there, and had written some Pieces in Prose & Verse which were printed in the Gloucester Newspapers.—Thence he was sent to Oxford; there he continu'd about a Year, but not well-satisfy'd, wishing of all things to see London & become a Player. At length receiving his Quarterly Allowance of 15 Guineas, instead of discharging his Debts, he walk'd out of Town, hid his Gown in a Furz Bush, and footed it to London, where having no Friend to advise him, he fell into bad Company, soon spent his Guineas, found no means of being introduc'd among the Players, grew necessitous, pawn'd his Cloaths & wanted Bread. Walking the Street very hungry, & not knowing what to do with himself, a Crimp's Bill was put into his Hand, offering immediate Entertainment & Encouragement to such as would bind themselves to serve in America. He went directly, sign'd the Indentures, was put into the Ship & came over; never writing a Line to acquaint his Friends what was become of him. He was lively, witty, good-natur'd and a pleasant Companion; but idle, thoughtless & imprudent to the last Degree.

John the Irishman soon ran away. With the rest I began to live very agreably; for they all respected me, the more as they

found Keimer incapable of instructing them, and that from
me they learnt something daily. We never work'd on a Saturday, that being Keimer's Sabbath. So I had two Days for
Reading. My Acquaintance with ingenious People in the
Town, increased. Keimer himself treated me with great Civility & apparent Regard; and nothing now made me uneasy
but my Debt to Vernon, which I was yet unable to pay being
hitherto but a poor Oeconomist.—He however kindly made
no Demand of it.

Our Printing-House often wanted Sorts, and there was no
Letter Founder in America. I had seen Types cast at James's
in London, but without much Attention to the Manner:
However I now contriv'd a Mould, made use of the Letters
we had, as Puncheons, struck the Matrices in Lead, and thus
supply'd in a pretty tolerable way all Deficiencies. I also en-
grav'd several Things on occasion. I made the Ink, I was
Warehouse-man & every thing, in short quite a Factotum.—

But however serviceable I might be, I found that my Services became every Day of less Importance, as the other
Hands improv'd in the Business. And when Keimer paid my
second Quarter's Wages, he let me know that he felt them
too heavy, and thought I should make an Abatement. He
grew by degrees less civil, put on more of the Master, frequently found Fault, was captious and seem'd ready for an
Out-breaking. I went on nevertheless with a good deal of
Patience, thinking that his incumber'd Circumstances were
partly the Cause. At length a Trifle snapt our Connexion. For
a great Noise happening near the Courthouse, I put my Head
out of the Window to see what was the Matter. Keimer being
in the Street look'd up & saw me, call'd out to me in a loud
Voice and angry Tone to mind my Business, adding some re-
proachful Words, that nettled me the more for their Publicity,
all the Neighbours who were looking out on the same Occasion being Witnesses how I was treated. He came up immediately into the Printing-House, continu'd the Quarrel, high
Words pass'd on both Sides, he gave me the Quarter's Warning we had stipulated, expressing a Wish that he had not been
oblig'd to so long a Warning: I told him his Wish was unnecessary for I would leave him that Instant; and so taking my
Hat walk'd out of Doors; desiring Meredith whom I saw

below to take care of some Things I left, & bring them to my Lodging.—

Meredith came accordingly in the Evening, when we talk'd my Affair over. He had conceiv'd a great Regard for me, & was very unwilling that I should leave the House while he remain'd in it. He dissuaded me from returning to my native Country which I began to think of. He reminded me that Keimer was in debt for all he possess'd, that his Creditors began to be uneasy, that he kept his Shop miserably, sold often without Profit for ready Money, and often trusted without keeping Account. That he must therefore fail; which would make a Vacancy I might profit of.—I objected my Want of Money. He then let me know, that his Father had a high Opinion of me, and from some Discourse that had pass'd between them, he was sure would advance Money to set us up, if I would enter into Partnership with him.—My Time, says he, will be out with Keimer in the Spring. By that time we may have our Press & Types in from London:—I am sensible I am no Workman. If you like it, Your Skill in the Business shall be set against the Stock I furnish; and we will share the Profits equally.—The Proposal was agreable, and I consented. His Father was in Town, and approv'd of it, the more as he saw I had great Influence with his Son, had prevail'd on him to abstain long from Dramdrinking, and he hop'd might break him of that wretched Habit entirely, when we came to be so closely connected. I gave an Inventory to the Father, who carry'd it to a Merchant; the Things were sent for; the Secret was to be kept till they should arrive, and in the mean time I was to get Work if I could at the other Printing House.—But I found no Vacancy there, and so remain'd idle a few Days, when Keimer, on a Prospect of being employ'd to print some Paper-money, in New Jersey, which would require Cuts & various Types that I only could supply, and apprehending Bradford might engage me & get the Jobb from him, sent me a very civil Message, that old Friends should not part for a few Words the Effect of sudden Passion, and wishing me to return. Meredith persuaded me to comply, as it would give more Opportunity for his Improvement under my daily Instructions.—So I return'd, and we went on more smoothly than for some time before.—The New Jersey Jobb was obtain'd. I contriv'd a Copper-Plate Press for it, the first that had been seen in the Country.—I cut several Ornaments and Checks for the Bills. We went together to Burlington, where I executed the Whole to Satisfaction, & he received so large a Sum for the Work, as to be enabled thereby to keep his Head much longer above Water.—

At Burlington I made an Acquaintance with many principal People of the Province. Several of them had been appointed by the Assembly a Committee to attend the Press, and take Care that no more Bills were printed than the Law directed. They were therefore by Turns constantly with us, and generally he who attended brought with him a Friend or two for Company. My Mind having been much more improv'd by Reading than Keimer's, I suppose it was for that Reason my Conversation seem'd to be more valu'd. They had me to their Houses, introduc'd me to their Friends and show'd me much Civility, while he, tho' the Master, was a little neglected. In truth he was an odd Fish, ignorant of common Life, fond of rudely opposing receiv'd Opinions, slovenly to extream dirtiness, enthusiastic in some Points of Religion, and a little Knavish withal. We continu'd there near 3 Months, and by that time I could reckon among my acquired Friends, Judge Allen, Samuel Bustill, the Secretary of the Province, Isaac Pearson, Joseph Cooper & several of the Smiths, Members of Assembly, and Isaac Decow the Surveyor General. The latter was a shrewd sagacious old Man, who told me that he began for himself when young by wheeling Clay for the Brickmakers, learnt to write after he was of Age, carry'd the Chain for Surveyors, who taught him Surveying, and he had now by his Industry acquir'd a good Estate; and says he, I foresee, that you will soon work this Man out of his Business & make a Fortune in it at Philadelphia. He had not then the least Intimation of my Intention to set up there or any where.— These Friends were afterwards of great Use to me, as I occasionally was to some of them.—They all continued their Regard for me as long as they lived.—

Before I enter upon my public Appearance in Business, it may be well to let you know the then State of my Mind, with regard to my Principles and Morals, that you may see how

far those influenc'd the future Events of my Life. My Parent's
had early given me religious Impressions, and brought me
through my Childhood piously in the Dissenting Way. But I
was scarce 15 when, after doubting by turns of several Points
as I found them disputed in the different Books I read, I began to doubt of Revelation it self. Some Books against Deism
fell into my Hands; they were said to be the Substance of
Sermons preached at Boyle's Lectures. It happened that they
wrought an Effect on me quite contrary to what was intended
by them: For the Arguments of the Deists which were quoted
to be refuted, appeared to me much Stronger than the Refu-
tations. In short I soon became a thorough Deist. My Arguments perverted some others, particularly Collins & Ralph:
but each of them having afterwards wrong'd me greatly without the least Compunction, and recollecting Keith's Conduct
towards me, (who was another Freethinker) and my own towards Vernon & Miss Read which at Times gave me great
Trouble, I began to suspect that this Doctrine tho' it might
be true, was not very useful.—My London Pamphlet, which
had for its Motto those Lines of Dryden

> ——Whatever is, is right
> Tho' purblind Man / Sees but a Part of
> The Chain, the nearest Link,
> His Eyes not carrying to the equal Beam,
> That poizes all, above.

And from the Attributes of God, his infinite Wisdom,
Goodness & Power concluded that nothing could possibly
be wrong in the World, & that Vice & Virtue were empty
Distinctions, no such Things existing: appear'd now not so
clever a Performance as I once thought it; and I doubted
whether some Error had not insinuated itself unperceiv'd,
into my Argument, so as to infect all that follow'd, as is common in metaphysical Reasonings.—I grew convinc'd that
Truth, Sincerity & *Integrity* in Dealings between Man & Man,
were of the utmost Importance to the Felicity of Life, and I
form'd written Resolutions, (w.ᶜʰ still remain in my Journal
Book) to practise them ever while I lived. Revelation had indeed no weight with me as such; but I entertain'd an Opinion, that tho' certain Actions might not be bad *because* they

were forbidden by it, or good *because* it commanded them; yet probably those Actions might be forbidden *because* they were bad for us, or commanded *because* they were beneficial to us, in their own Natures, all the Circumstances of things considered. And this Persuasion, with the kind hand of Providence, or some guardian Angel, or accidental favourable Circumstances & Situations, or all together, preserved me (thro' this dangerous Time of Youth & the hazardous Situations I was sometimes in among Strangers, remote from the Eye & Advice of my Father,) without any *wilful* gross Immorality or Injustice that might have been expected from my Want of Religion.—I say *wilful*, because the Instances I have mentioned, had something of *Necessity* in them, from my Youth, Inexperience, & the Knavery of others.—I had therefore a tolerable Character to begin the World with, I valued it properly, & determin'd to preserve it.—

We had not been long return'd to Philadelphia, before the New Types arriv'd from London.—We settled with Keimer, & left him by his Consent before he heard of it.—We found a House to hire near the Market, and took it. To lessen the Rent, (which was then but 24£ a Year tho' I have since known it let for 70) We took in Tho' Godfrey a Glazier, & his Family, who were to pay a considerable Part of it to us, and we to board with them. We had scarce opened our Letters & put our Press in Order, before George House, an Acquaintance of mine, brought a Countryman to us; whom he had met in the Street enquiring for a Printer. All our Cash was now expended in the Variety of Particulars we had been obliged to procure, & this Countryman's Five Shillings, being our First Fruits & coming so seasonably, gave me more Pleasure than any Crown I have since earn'd; and from the Gratitude I felt towards House, has made me often more ready than perhaps I should otherwise have been to assist young Beginners.—

There are Croakers in every Country always boding its Ruin. Such a one then lived in Philadelphia, a Person of Note, an elderly Man, with a wise Look and very grave Manner of Speaking. His Name was Samuel Mickle. This Gentleman, a Stranger to me, stopt one Day at my Door, and ask'd me if I was the young Man who had lately opened a new

Printing-house: Being answer'd in the Affirmative; He said he was sorry for me; because it was an expensive Undertaking, & the Expence would be lost, for Philadelphia was a sinking Place, the People already half Bankrupts or near being so; all Appearances of the contrary such as new Buildings & the Rise of Rents, being to his certain Knowledge fallacious, for they were in fact among the Things that would soon ruin us. And he gave me such a Detail of Misfortunes now existing or that were soon to exist, that he left me half-melancholy. Had I known him before I engag'd in this Business, probably I never should have done it.—This Man continu'd to live in this decaying Place, & to declaim in the same Strain, refusing for many Years to buy a House there, because all was going to Destruction, and at last I had the Pleasure of seeing him give five times as much for one as he might have bought it for when he first began his Croaking.—

I should have mention'd before, that in the Autumn of the preceding Year, I had form'd most of my ingenious Acquaintance into a Club, for mutual Improvement, which we call'd the Junto. We met on Friday Evenings. The Rules I drew up, requir'd that every Member in his Turn should produce one or more Queries on any Point of Morals, Politics or Natural Philosophy, to be discuss'd by the Company, and once in three Months produce and read an Essay of his own Writing on any Subject he pleased. Our Debates were to be under the Direction of a President, and to be conducted in the sincere Spirit of Enquiry after Truth, without fondness for Dispute, or Desire of Victory; and to prevent Warmth, all Expressions of Positiveness in Opinion, or of direct Contradiction, were after some time made contraband & prohibited under small pecuniary Penalties. The first Members were, Joseph Brientnal, a Copyer of Deeds for the Scriveners; a good-natur'd friendly middle-ag'd Man, a great Lover of Poetry, reading all he could meet with, & writing some that was tolerable; very ingenious in many little Nicknackeries, & of sensible Conversation. Thomas Godfrey, a self-taught Mathematician, great in his Way, & afterwards Inventor of what is now call'd Hadley's Quadrant. But he knew little out of his way, and was not a pleasing Companion, as like most Great Mathematicians I have met with, he expected unusual Precision in every thing said, or was forever denying or distinguishing upon Trifles, to the Disturbance of all Conversation.—He soon left us.— Nicholas Scull, a Surveyor, afterwards Surveyor-General, Who lov'd Books, & sometimes made a few Verses. William Parsons, bred a Shoemaker, but loving Reading, had acquir'd a considerable Share of Mathematics, which he first studied with a View to Astrology that he afterwards laught at. He also became Surveyor General.—William Maugridge, a Joiner, & a most exquisite Mechanic, & a solid sensible Man. Hugh Meredith, Stephen Potts, & George Webb, I have Characteris'd before. Robert Grace, a young Gentleman of some Fortune, generous, lively & witty, a Lover of Punning and of his Friends. And William Coleman, then a Merchant's Clerk, about my Age, who had the coolest clearest Head, the best Heart, and the exactest Morals, of almost any Man I ever met with. He became afterwards a Merchant of great Note, and one of our Provincial Judges: Our Friendship continued without Interruption to his Death, upwards of 40 Years. And the Club continu'd almost as long and was the best School of Philosophy, Morals & Politics that then existed in the Province; for our Queries which were read the Week preceding their Discussion, put us on reading with Attention upon the several Subjects, that we might speak more to the purpose: and here too we acquired better Habits of Conversation, every thing being studied in our Rules which might prevent our disgusting each other. From hence the long Continuance of the Club, which I shall have frequent Occasion to speak farther of hereafter; But my giving this Account of it here, is to show something of the Interest I had, every one of these exerting themselves in recommending Business to us.— Brientnal particularly procur'd us from the Quakers, the Printing 40 Sheets of their History, the rest being to be done by Keimer: and upon this we work'd exceeding hard, for the Price was low. It was a Folio, Pro Patria Size, in Pica with Long Primer Notes. I compos'd of it a Sheet a Day, and Meredith work'd it off at Press. It was often 11 at Night and sometimes later, before I had finish'd my Distribution for the next days Work: For the little Jobbs sent in by our other Friends now & then put us back. But so determin'd I was to continue doing a Sheet a Day of the Folio, that one Night when having impos'd my Forms, I thought my Days Work over, one of them by accident was broken and two Pages reduc'd to Pie, I immediately distributed & compos'd it over again before I went to bed. And this Industry visible to our Neighbours began to give us Character and Credit; particularly I was told, that mention being made of the new Printing Office at the Merchants Every-night-Club, the general Opinion was that it must fail, there being already two Printers in the Place, Keimer & Bradford; but Doctor Baird (whom you and I saw many Years after at his native Place, St. Andrews in Scotland) gave a contrary Opinion; for the Industry of that Franklin, says he, is superior to any thing I ever saw of the kind: I see him still at work when I go home from Club; and he is at Work again before his Neighbours are out of bed. This struck the rest, and we soon after had Offers from one of them to supply us with Stationary. But as yet we did not chuse to engage in Shop Business.

I mention this Industry the more particularly and the more freely, tho' it seems to be talking in my own Praise, that those of my Posterity who shall read it, may know the Use of that Virtue, when they see its Effects in my Favour throughout this Relation.—

George Webb, who had found a Friend that lent him wherewith to purchase his Time of Keimer, now came to offer himself as a Journeyman to us. We could not then imploy him, but I foolishly let him know, as a Secret, that I soon intended to begin a Newspaper, & might then have Work for him.—My Hopes of Success as I told him were founded on this, that the then only Newspaper, printed by Bradford was a paltry thing, wretchedly manag'd, no way entertaining; and yet was profitable to him.—I therefore thought a good Paper could scarcely fail of good Encouragem.' I requested Webb not to mention it, but he told it to Keimer, who immediately, to be beforehand with me, published Proposals for Printing one himself,—on which Webb was to be employ'd.—I resented this, and to counteract them, as I could not yet begin our Paper, I wrote several Pieces of Entertainm.' for Bradford's Paper, under the Title of the Busy Body which Breintnal continu'd some Months. By this means the Attention of the Publick was fix'd on that Paper, & Keimers Proposals which we

burlesqu'd & ridicul'd, were disregarded. He began his Paper
however, and after carrying it on three Quarters of a Year,
with at most only 90 Subscribers, he offer'd it to me for a
Trifle, & I having been ready some time to go on with it,
took it in hand directly and it prov'd in a few Years extreamly
profitable to me.—

I perceive that I am apt to speak in the singular Number,
though our Partnership still continu'd. The Reason may be,
that in fact the whole Management of the Business lay upon
me. Meredith was no Compostor, a poor Pressman, & seldom sober. My Friends lamented my Connection with him,
but I was to make the best of it.

Our first Papers made a quite different Appearance from
any before in the Province, a better Type & better printed:
but some spirited Remarks* of my Writing on the Dispute
then going on between Gov.ʳ Burnet and the Massachusetts
Assembly, struck the principal People, occasion'd the Paper &

*"His Excellency Governor *Burnet* died unexpectedly about two Days after
the Date of this Reply to his last Message: And it was thought the Dispute
would have ended with him, or at least have lain dormant till the Arrival of
a new Governor from *England*, who possibly might, or might not be inclin'd
to enter too rigorously into the Measures of his Predecessor. But our last
Advices by the Post acquaint us, that his Honour the Lieutenant Governour
(on whom the Government immediately devolves upon the Death and Absence of the Commander in Chief) has vigorously renew'd the Struggle on
his own Account; of which the Particulars will be seen in our Next.

"Perhaps some of our Readers may not fully understand the Original or
Ground of this warm Contest between the Governour and Assembly.—It
seems, that People have for these Hundred Years past, enjoyed the Privilege
of Rewarding the Governour for the Time being, according to *their Sense* of
his Merit and Services; and few or none of their Governors have hitherto
complain'd, or had Reason to complain, of a too scanty Allowance. But the
late Gov. *Burnet* brought with him Instructions to demand a *settled Salary* of
1000 *l. per Annum*, Sterling, on him and all his Successors, and the Assembly
were required to fix it immediately. He insisted on it strenuously to the last,
and they as constantly refused it. It appears by their Votes and Proceedings,
that they thought it an Imposition, contrary to their own Charter, and to
Magna Charta; and they judg'd that by the Dictates of Reason there should
be a mutual Dependence between the *Governor* and the *Governed*, and that to
make any Governour independent of his People, would be dangerous, and
destructive of their Liberties, and the ready Way to establish Tyranny: They
thought likewise, that the Province was not the less dependent on the Crown
of *Great-Britain*, by the Governour's depending immediately on them and
his own good Conduct for an ample Support, because all Acts and Laws

the Manager of it to be much talk'd of, & in a few Weeks brought them all to be our Subscribers. Their Example was follow'd by many, and our Number went on growing continually.—This was one of the first good Effects of my having learnt a little to scribble.—Another was, that the leading Men, seeing a News Paper now in the hands of one who could also handle a Pen, thought it convenient to oblige & encourage me.—Bradford still printed the Votes & Laws & other Publick Business. He had printed an Address of the House to the Governor in a coarse blundering manner; We reprinted it elegantly & correctly, and sent one to every Member. They were sensible of the Difference, it strengthen'd the Hands of our Friends in the House, and they voted us their Printers for the Year ensuing.

Among my Friends in the House I must not forget Mr Hamilton before mentioned, who was then returned from England & had a Seat in it. He interested himself for me strongly in that Instance, as he did in many others afterwards,

---

which he might be induc'd to pass, must nevertheless be constantly sent Home for Approbation in Order to continue in Force. Many other Reasons were given and Arguments us'd in the Course of the Controversy, needless to particularize here, because all the material Papers relating to it, have been inserted already in our Public News.

"Much deserved Praise has the deceas'd Governour receiv'd, for his steady Integrity in adhering to his Instructions, notwithstanding the great Difficulty and Opposition he met with, and the strong Temptations offer'd from time to time to induce him to give up the Point.—And yet perhaps something is due to the *Assembly* (as the Love and Zeal of that Country for the present Establishment is too well known to suffer any Suspicion of Want of Loyalty) who continue thus resolutely to Abide by what *they Think* their Right, and that of the People they represent, maugre all the Arts and Menaces of a Governour fam'd for his Cunning and Politicks, back'd with Instructions from Home, and powerfully aided by the great Advantage such an Officer always has of engaging the principal Men of a Place in his Party, by conferring where he pleases so many Posts of Profit and Honour. Their happy Mother Country will perhaps observe with Pleasure, that tho' her gallant Cocks and matchless Dogs abate their native Fire and Intrepidity when transported to a Foreign Clime (as the common Notion is) yet her SONS in the remotest Part of the Earth, and even to the third and fourth Descent, still retain that ardent Spirit of Liberty, and that undaunted Courage in the Defence of it, which has in every Age so gloriously distinguished BRITONS and ENGLISHMEN from all the Rest of Mankind."

continuing his Patronage till his Death.* Mr Vernon about this time put me in mind of the Debt I ow'd him:—but did not press me.—I wrote him an ingenuous Letter of Acknowledgments, crav'd his Forbearance a little longer which he allow'd me, & as soon as I was able I paid the Principal with Interest & many Thanks.—So that *Erratum* was in some degree corrected.—

But now another Difficulty came upon me, which I had never the least Reason to expect. Mr. Meredith's Father, who was to have paid for our Printing House according to the Expectations given me, was able to advance only one Hundred Pounds, Currency, which had been paid, & a Hundred more was due to the Merchant; who grew impatient & su'd us all. We gave Bail, but saw that if the Money could not be rais'd in time, the Suit must come to a Judgment & Execution, & our hopeful Prospects must with us be ruined, as the Press & Letters must be sold for Payment, perhaps at half-Price.—In this Distress two true Friends whose Kindness I have never forgotten nor ever shall forget while I can remember any thing, came to me separately unknown to each other, and without any Application from me, offering each of them to advance me all the Money that should be necessary to enable me to take the whole Business upon my self if that should be practicable, but they did not like my continuing the Partnership with Meredith, who as they said was often seen drunk in the Streets, & playing at low Games in Alehouses, much to our Discredit. These two Friends were *William Coleman* & *Robert Grace*. I told them I could not propose a Separation while any Prospect remain'd of the Merediths fulfilling their Part of our Agreement. Because I thought my self under great Obligations to them for what they had done & would do if they could. But if they finally fail'd in their Performance, & our Partnership must be dissolv'd, I should then think myself at Liberty to accept the Assistance of my Friends. Thus the matter rested for some time. When I said to my Partner, perhaps your Father is dissatisfied at the Part you have undertaken in this Affair of ours, and is unwilling to advance for you & me what he

*I got his Son once 500£.

would for you alone: If that is the Case, tell me, and I will resign the whole to you & go about my Business. No—says he, my Father has really been disappointed and is really unable; and I am unwilling to distress him farther. I see this is a Business I am not fit for. I was bred a Farmer, and it was a Folly in me to come to Town & put my self at 30 Years of Age an Apprentice to learn a new Trade. Many of our Welsh People are going to settle in North Carolina where Land is cheap: I am inclin'd to go with them, & follow my old Employment. You may find Friends to assist you. If you will take the Debts of the Company upon you, return to my Father the hundred Pound he has advanc'd, pay my little personal Debts, and give me Thirty Pounds & a new Saddle, I will relinquish the Partnership & leave the whole in your Hands. I agreed to this Proposal. It was drawn up in Writing, sign'd & seal'd immediately. I gave him what he demanded & he went soon after to Carolina; from whence he sent me next Year two long Letters, containing the best Account that had been given of that Country, the Climate, Soil, Husbandry, &c. for in those Matters he was very judicious. I printed them in the Papers, and they gave grate Satisfaction to the Publick.

As soon as he was gone, I recurr'd to my two Friends; and because I would not give an unkind Preference to either, I took half what each had offered & I wanted, of one, & half of the other; paid off the Company Debts, and went on with the Business in my own Name, advertising that the Partnership was dissolved. I think this was in or about the Year 1729.—

About this Time there was a Cry among the People for more Paper-Money, only 15,000£ being extant in the Province & that soon to be sunk. The wealthy Inhabitants oppos'd any Addition, being against all Paper Currency, from an Apprehension that it would depreciate as it had done in New England to the Prejudice of all Creditors.—We had discuss'd this Point in our Junto, where I was on the Side of an Addition, being persuaded that the first small Sum struck in 1723 had done much good, by increasing the Trade Employment, & Number of Inhabitants in the Province, since I now saw all the old Houses inhabited, & many new ones building, where as I remember'd well, that when I first walk'd about the Streets of Philadelphia, eating my Roll, I saw most of the Houses in Walnut street between Second & Front streets with Bills on their Doors, to be let; and many likewise in Chesnut Street, & other Streets; which made me then think the Inhabitants of the City were one after another deserting it.—Our Debates possess'd me so fully of the Subject, that I wrote and printed an anonymous Pamphlet on it, entituled, *The Nature & Necessity of a Paper Currency.* It was well receiv'd by the common People in general; but the Rich Men dislik'd it; for it increas'd and strengthen'd the Clamour for more Money; and they happening to have no Writers among them that were able to answer it, their Opposition slacken'd, & the Point was carried by a Majority in the House. My Friends there, who conceiv'd I had been of some Service, thought fit to reward me, by employing me in printing the Money, a very profitable Jobb, and a great Help to me.—This was another Advantage gain'd by my being able to write. The Utility of this Currency became by Time and Experience so evident, as never afterwards to be much disputed, so that it grew soon to 55000,£ and in 1739 to 80,000£ since which it arose during War to upwards of 350,000£. Trade, Building & Inhabitants all the while increasing. Tho' I now think there are Limits beyond which the Quantity may be hurtful.—

I soon after obtain'd, thro' my Friend Hamilton, the Printing of the NewCastle Paper Money, another profitable Jobb, as I then thought it; small Things appearing great to those in small Circumstances. And these to me were really great Advantages, as they were great Encouragements.—He procured me also the Printing of the Laws and Votes of that Government which continu'd in my Hands as long as I follow'd the Business.—

I now open'd a little Stationer's Shop. I had in it Blanks of all Sorts the correctest that ever appear'd among us, being assisted in that by my Friend Brientnal; I had also Paper, Parchment, Chapmen's Books, &c. One Whitemash a Compositor I had known in London, an excellent Workman now came to me & work'd with me constantly & diligently, and I took an Apprentice the Son of Aquila Rose. I began now gradually to pay off the Debt I was under for the Printing-

House.—In order to secure my Credit and Character as a Tradesmen, I took care not only to be in *Reality* Industrious & frugal, but to avoid all *Appearances* of the Contrary. I drest plainly; I was seen at no Places of idle Diversion; I never went out a-fishing or shooting; a Book, indeed, sometimes debauch'd me from my Work; but that was seldom, snug, & gave no Scandal: and to show that I was not above my Business, I sometimes brought home the Paper I purchas'd at the Stores, thro' the Streets on a Wheelbarrow. Thus being esteem'd an industrious thriving young Man, and paying duly for what I bought, the Merchants who imported Stationary solicited my Custom, others propos'd supplying me with Books, & I went on swimmingly.—In the mean time Keimer's Credit & Business declining daily, he was at last forc'd to sell his Printing-house to satisfy his Creditors. He went to Barbadoes, & there lived some Years, in very poor Circumstances.

His Apprentice David Harry, whom I had instructed while I work'd with him, set up in his Place at Philadelphia having bought his Materials. I was at first apprehensive of a powerful Rival in Harry, as his Friends were very able, & had a good deal of Interest. I therefore propos'd a Partnership to him; which he, fortunately for me, rejected with Scorn. He was very proud, dress'd like a Gentleman, liv'd expensively, took much Diversion & Pleasure abroad, ran in debt, & neglected his Business, upon which all Business left him; and finding nothing to do, he follow'd Keimer to Barbadoes; taking the Printinghouse with him. There this Apprentice employ'd his former Master as a Journeyman. They quarrel'd often. Harry went continually behind-hand, and at length was forc'd to sell his Types, and return to his Country Work in Pensilvania. The Person that bought them, employ'd Keimer to use them, but in a few years he died. There remain'd now no Competitor with me at Philadelphia, but the old one, Bradford, who was rich & easy, did a little Printing now & then by straggling Hands, but was not very anxious about the Business. However, as he kept the Post Office, it was imagined he had better Opportunities of obtaining News, his Paper was thought a better Distributer of Advertisements than mine, & therefore had many more, which was a profitable thing to him & a

Disadvantage to me. For tho' I did indeed receive & send
Papers by the Post, yet the publick Opinion was otherwise;
for what I did send was by Bribing the Riders who took them
privately: Bradford being unkind enough to forbid it: which
occasion'd some Resentment on my Part; and I thought so
meanly of him for it, that when I afterwards came into his
Situation, I took care never to imitate it.

I had hitherto continu'd to board with Godfrey who lived
in Part of my House with his Wife & Children, & had one
Side of the Shop for his Glazier's Business, tho' he work'd
little, being always absorb'd in his Mathematics.—Mrs Godfrey projected a Match for me with a Relation's Daughter,
took Opportunities of bringing us often together, till a serious Courtship on my Part ensu'd the Girl being in herself
very deserving. The old Folks encourag'd me by continual
Invitations to Supper, & by leaving us together, till at length
it was time to explain. Mrs Godfrey manag'd our little Treaty.
I let her know that I expected as much Money with their
Daughter as would pay off my Remaining Debt for the Printing-house, which I believe was not then above a Hundred
Pounds. She brought me Word they had no such Sum to
spare. I said they might mortgage their House in the Loan
Office.—The Answer to this after some Days was, that they
did not approve the Match; that on Enquiry of Bradford they
had been inform'd the Printing Business was not a profitable
one, the Types would soon be worn out & more wanted, that
S. Keimer & D. Harry had fail'd one after the other, and I
should probably soon follow them; and therefore I was forbidden the House, & the Daughter shut up.—Whether this
was a real Change of Sentiment, or only Artifice, on a Supposition of our being too far engag'd in Affection to retract,
& therefore that we should steal a Marriage, which would
leave them at Liberty to give or withold what they pleas'd, I
know not: But I suspected the latter, resented it, and went no
more. Mrs Godfrey brought me afterwards some more favourable Accounts of their Disposition, & would have drawn
me on again: But I declared absolutely my Resolution to have
nothing more to do with that Family. This was resented by
the Godfreys, we differ'd, and they removed, leaving me the
whole House, and I resolved to take no more Inmates. But

this Affair having turn'd my Thoughts to Marriage, I look'd round me, and made Overtures of Acquaintance in other Places; but soon found that the Business of a Printer being generally thought a poor one, I was not to expect Money with a Wife unless with such a one, as I should not otherwise think agreable. — In the mean time, that hard-to-be-govern'd Passion of Youth, had hurried me frequently into Intrigues with low Women that fell in my Way, which were attended with some Expence & great Inconvenience, besides a continual Risque to my Health by a Distemper which of all Things I dreaded, tho' by great good Luck I escaped it. —

A friendly Correspondence as Neighbours & old Acquaintances, had continued between me & Mrs Read's Family who all had a Regard for me from the time of my first Lodging in their House. I was often invited there and consulted in their Affairs, wherein I sometimes was of Service. — I pity'd poor Miss Read's unfortunate Situation, who was generally dejected, seldom chearful, and avoided Company. I consider'd my Giddiness & Inconstancy when in London as in a great degree the Cause of her Unhappiness; tho' the Mother was good enough to think the Fault more her own than mine, as she had prevented our Marrying before I went thither, and persuaded the other Match in my Absence. Our mutual Affection was revived, but there were now great Objections to our Union. That Match was indeed look'd upon as invalid, a preceding Wife being said to be living in England; but this could not easily be prov'd, because of the Distance &c. And tho' there was a Report of his Death, it was not certain. Then, tho' it should be true, he had left many Debts which his Successor might be call'd upon to pay. We ventured however, over all these Difficulties, and I took her to Wife Sept. 1. 1730. None of the Inconveniencies happened that we had apprehended, she prov'd a good & faithful Helpmate, assisted me much by attending the Shop, we throve together, and have ever mutually endeavour'd to make each other happy. — Thus I corrected that great *Erratum* as well as I could.

About this Time our Club meeting, not at a Tavern, but in a little Room of Mr Grace's set apart for that Purpose; a Proposition was made by me, that since our Books were often referr'd to in our Disquisitions upon the Queries, it might be

convenient to us to have them all together where we met, that
upon Occasion they might be consulted; and By thus club-
bing our Books to a common Library, we should, while we
lik'd to keep them together, have each of us the Advantage of
using the Books of all the other Members, which would be
nearly as beneficial as if each owned the whole. It was lik'd
and agreed to, & we fill'd one End of the Room with such
Books as we could best spare. The Number was not so great
as we expected; and tho' they had been of great Use, yet some
Inconveniencies occurring for want of due Care of them, the
Collection after about a Year was separated, & each took his
Books home again.

And now I set on foot my first Project of a public Nature,
that for a Subscription Library. I drew up the Proposals, got
them put into Form by our great Scrivener Brockden, and by
the help of my Friends in the Junto, procur'd Fifty Subscribers of 40/ each to begin with & 10/ a Year for 50 Years,
the Term our Company was to continue. We afterwards obtain'd a Charter, the Company being increas'd to 100. This
was the Mother of all the N American Subscription Libraries
now so numerous. It is become a great thing itself, & continually increasing.—These Libraries have improv'd the general
Conversation of the Americans, made the common Tradesmen & Farmers as intelligent as most Gentlemen from other
Countries, and perhaps have contributed in some degree to
the Stand so generally made throughout the Colonies in Defence of their Privileges.—

Mem?
Thus far was written with the Intention express'd in the
Beginning and therefore contains several little family Anecdotes of no Importance to others. What follows was written
many Years after in compliance with the Advice contain'd in
these Letters, and accordingly intended for the Publick. The
Affairs of the Revolution occasion'd the Interruption.

Part Two

Letter from Mr. Abel James, with Notes on my Life, (received in Paris.)

My dear & honored Friend.

I have often been desirous of writing to thee, but could not be reconciled to the Thought that the Letter might fall into the Hands of the British, lest some Printer or busy Body should publish some Part of the Contents & give our Friends Pain & myself Censure.

Some Time since there fell into my Hands to my great Joy about 23 Sheets in thy own hand-writing containing an Account of the Parentage & Life of thyself, directed to thy Son ending in the Year 1730 with which there were Notes likewise in thy writing, a Copy of which I inclose in Hopes it may be a means if thou continuedst it up to a later period, that the first & latter part may be put together; & if it is not yet continued, I hope thou wilt not delay it, Life is uncertain as the Preacher tells us, and what will the World say if kind, humane & benevolent Ben Franklin should leave his Friends & the World deprived of so pleasing & profitable a Work, a Work which would be useful & entertaining not only to a few, but to millions.

The Influence Writings under that Class have on the Minds of Youth is very great, and has no where appeared so plain as in our public Friends' Journals. It almost insensibly leads the Youth into the Resolution of endeavouring to become as good and as eminent as the Journalist. Should thine for Instance when published, and I think it could not fail of it, lead the Youth to equal the Industry & Temperance of thy early Youth, what a Blessing with that Class would such a Work be. I know of no Character living nor many of them put together, who has so much in his Power as Thyself to promote a greater Spirit of Industry & early Attention to Business, Frugality and Temperance with the American Youth. Not that I think the Work would have no other Merit & Use in the World, far from it, but the first is of such vast Importance, that I know nothing that can equal it.

———

The foregoing letter and the minutes accompanying it being shewn to a friend, I received from him the following:

LETTER FROM MR. BENJAMIN VAUGHAN.

Paris, January 31, 1783.

MY DEAREST SIR,

When I had read over your sheets of minutes of the principal incidents of your life, recovered for you by your Quaker acquaintance; I told you I would send you a letter expressing my reasons why I thought it would be useful to complete and publish it as he desired. Various concerns have for some time past prevented this letter being written, and I do not know whether it was worth any expectation: happening to be at leisure however at present, I shall by writing at least interest and instruct myself; but as the terms I am inclined to use may tend to offend a person of your manners, I shall only tell you how I would address any other person, who was as good and as great as yourself, but less diffident. I would say to him, Sir, I *solicit* the history of your life from the following motives.

Your history is so remarkable, that if you do not give it, somebody else will certainly give it; and perhaps so as nearly to do as much harm, as your own management of the thing might do good.

It will moreover present a table of the internal circumstances of your country, which will very much tend to invite to it settlers of virtuous and manly minds. And considering the eagerness with which such information is sought by them, and the extent of your reputation, I do not know of a more efficacious advertisement than your Biography would give.

All that has happened to you is also connected with the detail of the manners and situation of *a rising* people; and in this respect I do not think that the writings of Caesar and Tacitus can be more interesting to a true judge of human nature and society.

But these, Sir, are small reasons in my opinion, compared with the chance which your life will give for the forming of future great men; and in conjunction with your *Art of Virtue,* (which you design to publish) of improving the features of private character, and consequently of aiding all happiness both public and domestic.

The two works I allude to, Sir, will in particular give a noble rule and example of *self-education*. School and other education constantly proceed upon false principles, and shew a clumsy apparatus pointed at a false mark; but your apparatus is simple, and the mark a true one; and while parents and young persons are left destitute of other just means of estimating and becoming prepared for a reasonable course in life, your discovery that the thing is in many a man's private power, will be invaluable!

Influence upon the private character late in life, is not only an influence late in life, but a weak influence. It is in *youth* that we plant our chief habits and prejudices; it is in youth that we take our party as to profession, pursuits, and matrimony. In youth therefore the turn is given; in youth the education even of the next generation is given; in youth the private and public character is determined; and the term of life extending but from youth to age, life ought to begin well from youth; and more especially *before* we take our party as to our principal objects.

But your Biography will not merely teach self-education, but the education of *a wise man*; and the wisest man will receive lights and improve his progress, by seeing detailed the conduct of another wise man. And why are weaker men to be deprived of such helps, when we see our race has been blundering on in the dark, almost without a guide in this particular, from the farthest trace of time. Shew then, Sir, how much is to be done, *both to sons and fathers*; and invite all wise men to become like yourself; and other men to become wise.

When we see how cruel statesmen and warriors can be to the humble race, and how absurd distinguished men can be to their acquaintance, it will be instructive to observe the instances multiply of pacific acquiescing manners; and to find how compatible it is to be great and *domestic*; enviable and yet *good-humoured*.

The little private incidents which you will also have to relate, will have considerable use, as we want above all things, *rules of prudence in ordinary affairs*; and it will be curious to see how you have acted in these. It will be so far a sort of key to life, and explain many things that all men ought to have once explained to them, to give them a chance of becoming wise by foresight.

The nearest thing to having experience of one's own, is to have other people's affairs brought before us in a shape that is interesting; this is sure to happen from your pen. Your affairs and management will have an air of simplicity or importance that will not fail to strike; and I am convinced you have conducted them with as much originality as if you had been conducting discussions in politics or philosophy; and what more worthy of experiments and system, (its importance and its errors considered) than human life!

Some men have been virtuous blindly, others have speculated fantastically, and others have been shrewd to bad purposes; but you, Sir, I am sure, will give under your hand, nothing but what is at the same moment, wise, practical, and good.

Your account of yourself (for I suppose the parallel I am drawing for Dr. Franklin, will hold not only in point of character but of private history), will shew that you are ashamed of no origin; a thing the more important, as you prove how little necessary all origin is to happiness, virtue, or greatness.

As no end likewise happens without a means, so we shall find, Sir, that even you yourself framed a plan by which you became considerable; but at the same time we may see that though the event is flattering, the means are as simple as wisdom could make them; that is depending upon nature, virtue, thought, and habit.

Another thing demonstrated will be the propriety of every man's waiting for his time for appearing upon the stage of the world. Our sensations being very much fixed to the moment, we are apt to forget that more moments are to follow the first, and consequently that man should arrange his conduct so as to suit the *whole* of a life. Your attribution appears to have been applied to your *life*, and the passing moments of it have been enlivened with content and enjoyment, instead of being tormented with foolish impatience or regrets. Such a conduct is easy for those who make virtue and themselves their standard, and who try to keep themselves in countenance by examples of other truly great men, of whom patience is so often the characteristic.

Your Quaker correspondent, Sir, (for here again I will suppose the subject of my letter resembling Dr. Franklin,) praised your frugality, diligence, and temperance, which he considered as a pattern for all youth: but it is singular that he should have forgotten your modesty, and your disinterestedness, without which you never could have waited for your advancement, or found your situation in the mean time comfortable; which is a strong lesson to shew the poverty of glory, and the importance of regulating our minds.

If this correspondent had known the nature of your reputation as well as I do, he would have said; your former writings and measures would secure attention to your Biography, and Art of Virtue; and your Biography and Art of Virtue, in return, would secure attention to them. This is an advantage attendant upon a various character, and which brings all that belongs to it into greater play; and it is the more useful, as perhaps more persons are at a loss for the *means* of improving their minds and characters, than they are for the time or the inclination to do it.

But there is one concluding reflection, Sir, that will shew the use of your life as a mere piece of biography. This style of writing seems a little gone out of vogue, and yet it is a very useful one; and your specimen of it may be particularly serviceable, as it will make a subject of comparison with the lives of various public cut-throats and intriguers, and with absurd monastic self-tormentors, or vain literary triflers. If it encourages more writings of the same kind with your own, and induces more men to spend lives fit to be written; it will be worth all Plutarch's Lives put together.

But being tired of figuring to myself a character of which every feature suits only one man in the world, without giving him the praise of it; I shall end my letter, my dear Dr. Franklin, with a personal application to your proper self.

I am earnestly desirous then, my dear Sir, that you should let the world into the traits of your genuine character, as civil broils may otherwise tend to disguise or traduce it. Considering your great age, the caution of your character, and your peculiar style of thinking, it is not likely that any one besides yourself can be sufficiently master of the facts of your life, or the intentions of your mind.

Besides all this, the immense revolution of the present period, will necessarily turn our attention towards the author of it; and when virtuous principles have been pretended in it, it will be highly important to shew that such have really influenced; and, as your own character will be the principal one to receive a scrutiny, it is proper (even for its effects upon your vast and rising country, as well as upon England and upon Europe), that it should stand respectable and eternal. For the furtherance of human happiness, I have always maintained that it is necessary to prove that man is not even at present a vicious and detestable animal; and still more to prove that good management may greatly amend him; and it is for much the same reason, that I am anxious to see the opinion established, that there are fair characters existing among the individuals of the race; for the moment that all men, without exception, shall be conceived abandoned, good people will cease efforts deemed to be hopeless, and perhaps think of taking their share in the scramble of life, or at least of making it comfortable principally for themselves.

Take then, my dear Sir, this work most speedily into hand: shew yourself good as you are good, temperate as you are temperate; and above all things, prove yourself as one who from your infancy have loved justice, liberty, and concord, in a way that has made it natural and consistent for you to have acted, as we have seen you act in the last seventeen years of your life. Let Englishmen be made not only to respect, but even to love you. When they think well of individuals in your native country, they will go nearer to thinking well of your country; and when your countrymen see themselves well thought of by Englishmen, they will go nearer to thinking well of England. Extend your views even further; do not stop at those who speak the English tongue, but after having settled so many points in nature and politics, think of bettering the whole race of men.

As I have not read any part of the life in question, but know only the character that lived it, I write somewhat at hazard. I am sure however, that the life, and the treatise I allude to (on the *Art of Virtue*), will necessarily fulfil the chief of my expectations; and still more so if you take up the measure of suiting these performances to the several views above stated. Should they even prove unsuccessful in all that a sanguine admirer of yours hopes from them, you will at least have framed pieces to interest the human mind; and whoever gives a feeling of pleasure that is innocent to man, has added so much to the fair side of a life otherwise too much darkened by anxiety, and too much injured by pain.

In the hope therefore that you will listen to the prayer addressed to you in this letter, I beg to subscribe myself, my dearest Sir, &c. &c.

Signed   BENJ. VAUGHAN.

Continuation of the Account of my Life.
Begun at Passy 1784

It is some time since I receiv'd the above Letters, but I have been too busy till now to think of complying with the Request they contain. It might too be much better done if I were at home among my Papers, which would aid my Memory, & help to ascertain Dates. But my Return being uncertain, and having just now a little Leisure, I will endeavour to recollect & write what I can; If I live to get home, it may there be corrected and improv'd.

Not having any Copy here of what is already written, I know not whether an Account is given of the means I used to establish the Philadelphia publick Library, which from a small Beginning is now become so considerable, though I remember to have come down to near the Time of that Transaction, 1730. I will therefore begin here, with an Account of it, which may be struck out if found to have been already given.—

At the time I establish'd my self in Pensylvania, there was not a good Bookseller's Shop in any of the Colonies to the Southward of Boston. In New-York & Philadᵃ the Printers were indeed Stationers, they sold only Paper, &c. Almanacks, Ballads, and a few common School Books. Those who lov'd Reading were oblig'd to send for their Books from England.—The Members of the Junto had each a few. We had left the Alehouse where we first met, and hired a Room to hold our Club in. I propos'd that we should all of us bring our Books to that Room, where they would not only be ready to consult in our Conferences, but become a common

Benefit, each of us being at Liberty to borrow such as he
wish'd to read at home. This was accordingly done, and for
some time contented us. Finding the Advantage of this little
Collection, I propos'd to render the Benefit from Books more
common by commencing a Public Subscription Library. I
drew a Sketch of the Plan and Rules that would be necessary,
and got a skilful Conveyancer Mr Charles Brockden to put
the whole in Form of Articles of Agreement to be subscribed,
by which each Subscriber engag'd to pay a certain Sum down
for the first Purchase of Books and an annual Contribution
for encreasing them.—So few were the Readers at that time
in Philadelphia, and the Majority of us so poor, that I was
not able with great Industry to find more than Fifty Persons,
mostly young Tradesmen, willing to pay down for this purpose Forty shillings each, & Ten Shillings per Annum. On
this little Fund we began. The Books were imported. The
Library was open one Day in the Week for lending them to
the Subscribers, on their Promisory Notes to pay Double the
Value if not duly returned. The Institution soon manifested
its Utility, was imitated by other Towns and in other Provinces, the Librarys were augmented by Donations, Reading
became fashionable, and our People having no publick
Amusements to divert their Attention from Study became
better acquainted with Books, and in a few Years were
observ'd by Strangers to be better instructed & more intelligent than People of the same Rank generally are in other
Countries.—

When we were about to sign the above-mentioned Articles,
which were to be binding on us, our Heirs, &c for fifty Years,
Mr Brockden, the Scrivener, said to us, "You are young Men,
but it is scarce probable that any of you will live to see the
Expiration of the Term fix'd in this Instrument." A Number
of us, however, are yet living: But the Instrument was after a
few Years rendred null by a Charter that incorporated & gave
Perpetuity to the Company.—

The Objections, & Reluctances I met with in Soliciting the
Subscriptions, made me soon feel the Impropriety of presenting one's self as the Proposer of any useful Project that might
be suppos'd to raise one's Reputation in the smallest degree
above that of one's Neighbours, when one has need of their

Assistance to accomplish that Project. I therefore put my self as much as I could out of sight, and stated it as a Scheme of *a Number of Friends*, who had requested me to go about and propose it to such as they thought Lovers of Reading. In this way my Affair went on more smoothly, and I ever after practis'd it on such Occasions; and from my frequent Successes, can heartily recommend it. The present little Sacrifice of your Vanity will afterwards be amply repaid. If it remains a while uncertain to whom the Merit belongs, some one more vain than yourself will be encourag'd to claim it, and then even Envy will be dispos'd to do you Justice, by plucking those assum'd Feathers, & restoring them to their right Owner.

This Library afforded me the Means of Improvement by constant Study, for which I set apart an Hour or two each Day; and thus repair'd in some Degree the Loss of the Learned Education my Father once intended for me. Reading was the only Amusement I allow'd my self. I spent no time in Taverns, Games, or Frolicks of any kind. And my Industry in my Business continu'd as indefatigable as it was necessary. I was in debt for my Printing-house, I had a young Family coming on to be educated, and I had to contend with for Business two Printers who were establish'd in the Place before me. My Circumstances however grew daily easier: my original Habits of Frugality continuing. And My Father having among his Instructions to me when a Boy, frequently repeated a Proverb of Solomon, *"Seest thou a Man diligent in his Calling, he shall stand before Kings, he shall not stand before mean Men."* I from thence consider'd Industry as a Means of obtaining Wealth and Distinction, which encourag'd me; tho' I did not think that I should ever literally stand before Kings, which however has since happened.—for I have stood before five, & even had the honour of sitting down with one, the King of Denmark, to Dinner.

We have an English Proverb that says,

> He that would thrive
> Must ask his Wife;

it was lucky for me that I had one as much dispos'd to Industry & Frugality as my self. She assisted me chearfully in my Business, folding & stitching Pamphlets, tending Shop, purchasing old Linen Rags for the Paper-makers, &c &c. We kept no idle Servants, our Table was plain & simple, our Furniture of the cheapest. For instance my Breakfast was a long time Bread & Milk, (no Tea,) and I ate it out of a twopenny earthen Porringer with a Pewter Spoon. But mark how Luxury will enter Families, and make a Progress, in Spite of Principle. Being Call'd one Morning to Breakfast, I found it in a China Bowl with a Spoon of Silver. They had been bought for me without my Knowledge by my Wife, and had cost her the enormous Sum of three and twenty Shillings, for which she had no other Excuse or Apology to make, but that she thought *her* Husband deserv'd a Silver Spoon & China Bowl as well as any of his Neighbours. This was the first Appearance of Plate & China in our House, which afterwards in a Course of Years as our Wealth encreas'd, augmented gradually to several Hundred Pounds in Value.—

I had been religiously educated as a Presbyterian; and tho' some of the Dogmas of that Persuasion, such as the Eternal Decrees of God, Election, Reprobation, &c. appear'd to me unintelligible, others doubtful, & I early absented myself from the Public Assemblies of the Sect, Sunday being my Studying-Day, I never was without some religious Principles; I never doubted, for instance, the Existance of the Deity, that he made the World, & govern'd it by his Providence; that the most acceptable Service of God was the doing Good to Man; that our Souls are immortal; and that all Crime will be punished & Virtue rewarded either here or hereafter; these I esteem'd the Essentials of every Religion, and being to be found in all the Religions we had in our Country I respected them all, tho' with different degrees of Respect as I found them more or less mix'd with other Articles which without any Tendency to inspire, promote or confirm Morality, serv'd principally to divide us & make us unfriendly to one another.— This Respect to all, with an Opinion that the worst had some good Effects, induc'd me to avoid all Discourse that might tend to lessen the good Opinion another might have of his own Religion; and as our Province increas'd in People and new Places of worship were continually wanted, & generally erected by voluntary Contribution, my Mite for such purpose, whatever might be the Sect, was never refused.—

Tho' I seldom attended any Public Worship, I had still an Opinion of its Propriety, and of its Utility when rightly conducted, and I regularly paid my annual Subscription for the Support of the only Presbyterian Minister or Meeting we had in Philadelphia. He us'd to visit me sometimes as a Friend, and admonish me to attend his Administrations, and I was now and then prevail'd on to do so, once for five Sundays successively. Had he been, *in my Opinion*, a good Preacher perhaps I might have continued, notwithstanding the occasion I had for the Sunday's Leisure in my Course of Study: But his Discourses were chiefly either polemic Arguments, or Explications of the peculiar Doctrines of our Sect, and were all to me very dry, uninteresting and unedifying, since not a single moral Principle was inculcated or enforc'd, their Aim seeming to be rather to make us Presbyterians than good Citizens. At length he took for his Text that Verse of the 4th Chapter of Philippians, *Finally, Brethren, Whatsoever Things are true, honest, just, pure, lovely, or of good report, if there be any virtue, or any praise, think on these Things*; & I imagin'd in a Sermon on such a Text, we could not miss of having some Morality: But he confin'd himself to five Points only as meant by the Apostle, viz. 1. Keeping holy the Sabbath Day. 2. Being diligent in Reading the Holy Scriptures. 3. Attending duly the Publick Worship. 4. Partaking of the Sacrament. 5. Paying a due Respect to God's Ministers.—These might be all good Things, but as they were not the kind of good Things that I expected from that Text, I despaired of ever meeting with them from any other, was disgusted, and attended his Preaching no more.—I had some Years before compos'd a little Liturgy or Form of Prayer for my own private Use, viz, in 1728. entitled, *Articles of Belief & Acts of Religion*. I return'd to the Use of this, and went no more to the public Assemblies.—My Conduct might be blameable, but I leave it without attempting farther to excuse it, my present purpose being to relate Facts, and not to make Apologies for them.—

It was about this time that I conceiv'd the bold and arduous Project of arriving at moral Perfection. I wish'd to live without committing any Fault at any time; I would conquer all that either Natural Inclination, Custom, or Company might lead me into. As I knew, or thought I knew, what was right and wrong, I did not see why I might not *always* do the one and avoid the other. But I soon found I had undertaken a Task of more Difficulty than I had imagined: While my Care was employ'd in guarding against one Fault, I was often surpriz'd by another. Habit took the Advantage of Inattention. Inclination was sometimes too strong for Reason. I concluded at length, that the mere speculative Conviction that it was our Interest to be compleatly virtuous, was not sufficient to prevent our Slipping, and that the contrary Habits must be broken and good Ones acquired and established, before we can have any Dependance on a steady uniform Rectitude of Conduct. For this purpose I therefore contriv'd the following Method.—

In the various Enumerations of the moral Virtues I had met with in my Reading, I found the Catalogue more or less numerous, as different Writers included more or fewer Ideas under the same Name. Temperance, for Example, was by some confin'd to Eating & Drinking, while by others it was extended to mean the moderating every other Pleasure, Appetite, Inclination or Passion, bodily or mental, even to our Avarice & Ambition. I propos'd to myself, for the sake of Clearness, to use rather more Names with fewer Ideas annex'd to each, than a few Names with more Ideas; and I included under Thirteen Names of Virtues all that at that time occurr'd to me as necessary or desirable, and annex'd to each a short Precept, which fully express'd the Extent I gave to its Meaning.—

These Names of Virtues with their Precepts were

1. TEMPERANCE.

Eat not to Dulness

Drink not to Elevation.

2. SILENCE.

Speak not but what may benefit others or your self. Avoid trifling Conversation.

3. ORDER.

Let all your Things have their Places. Let each Part of your Business have its Time.

4. RESOLUTION.

Resolve to perform what you ought. Perform without fail what you resolve.

5. FRUGALITY.

Make no Expence but to do good to others or yourself: i.e. Waste nothing.

6. INDUSTRY.

Lose no Time.—Be always employ'd in something useful.—Cut off all unnecessary Actions.—

7. SINCERITY.

Use no hurtful Deceit.

Think innocently and justly; and, if you speak; speak accordingly.

8. JUSTICE.

Wrong none, by doing Injuries or omitting the Benefits that are your Duty.

9. MODERATION.

Avoid Extreams. Forbear resenting Injuries so much as you think they deserve.

10. CLEANLINESS

Tolerate no Uncleanness in Body, Cloaths or Habitation.—

11. TRANQUILITY

Be not disturbed at Trifles, or at Accidents common or unavoidable.

12. CHASTITY.

Rarely use Venery but for Health or Offspring; Never to Dulness, Weakness, or the Injury of your own or another's Peace or Reputation.—

13. HUMILITY.

Imitate Jesus and Socrates.—

My intention being to acquire the *Habitude* of all these Virtues, I judg'd it would be well not to distract my Attention by attempting the whole at once, but to fix it on one of them at a time, and when I should be Master of that, then to proceed to another, and so on till I should have gone thro' the thirteen. And as the previous Acquisition of some might facilitate the Acquisition of certain others, I arrang'd them with that View as they stand above. *Temperance* first, as it tends to procure that Coolness & Clearness of Head, which is so necessary where constant Vigilance was to be kept up, and Guard maintained, against the unremitting Attraction of ancient Habits, and the Force of perpetual Temptations. This being acquir'd & establish'd, *Silence* would be more easy, and my Desire being to gain Knowledge at the same time that I improv'd in Virtue, and considering that in Conversation it was obtain'd rather by the Use of the Ears than of the Tongue, & therefore wishing to break a Habit I was getting into of Prattling, Punning & Joking, which only made me acceptable to trifling Company, I gave *Silence* the second Place. This, and the next, *Order*, I expected would allow me more Time for attending to my Project and my Studies; RESOLUTION once become habitual, would keep me firm in my Endeavours to obtain all the subsequent Virtues; *Frugality* & *Industry*, by freeing me from my remaining Debt, & producing Affluence & Independance would make more easy the Practice of *Sincerity* and *Justice*, &c. &c.. Conceiving then that agreeable to the Advice of Pythagoras in his Golden Verses,* daily Examination would be necessary, I contriv'd the following Method for conducting that Examination.

I made a little Book in which I allotted a Page for each of the Virtues. I rul'd each Page with red Ink so as to have seven Columns, one for each Day of the Week, marking each Column with a Letter for the Day. I cross'd these Columns with thirteen red Lines, marking the Beginning of each Line with

*Let not the stealing God of Sleep surprize,
Nor creep in Slumbers on thy weary Eyes,
Ere ev'ry Action of the former Day,
Strictly *thou dost, and* righteously *survey.*
With Rev'rence at thy own Tribunal stand,
And answer justly to thy own Demand.
Where have I been? In what have I transgrest?
What Good or Ill has this Day's Life exprest?
Where have I fail'd in what I ought to do?
In what to GOD, to Man, or to myself I owe?
Inquire severe whate'er from first to last,
From Morning's Dawn till Ev'nings Gloom has past.
If Evil were thy Deeds, repenting mourn,
And let thy Soul with strong Remorse be torn:
If Good, the Good with Peace of Mind repay, ⎫
And to thy secret Self with Pleasure say, ⎬
Rejoice, my Heart, for all went well to Day. ⎭

the first Letter of one of the Virtues, on which Line & in its proper Column I might mark by a little black Spot every Fault I found upon Examination, to have been committed respecting that Virtue upon that Day.

Form of the Pages

	S	M	T	W	T	F	S
	TEMPERANCE.						
	Eat not to Dulness. *Drink not to Elevation.*						
T							
S	••	•		•		•	
O	•	•	•		•	•	•
R			•			•	
F		•			•		
I			•				
S							
J							
M							
Cl.							
T							
Ch							
H							

I determined to give a Week's strict Attention to each of the Virtues successively. Thus in the first Week my great Guard was to avoid every the least Offence against Temperance, leaving the other Virtues to their ordinary Chance, only marking every Evening the Faults of the Day. Thus if in the first Week I could keep my first Line marked T clear of Spots, I suppos'd the Habit of that Virtue so much strengthen'd and its opposite weaken'd, that I might venture extending my Attention to include the next, and for the following Week keep both Lines clear of Spots. Proceeding thus to the last, I could go thro' a Course compleat in Thirteen Weeks, and four Courses in a Year.—And like him who having a Garden to weed, does not attempt to eradicate all the bad Herbs at once, which would exceed his Reach and his Strength, but works on one of the Beds at a time, & having accomplish'd the first proceeds to a second; so I should have, (I hoped) the encouraging Pleasure of seeing on my Pages the Progress I made in Virtue, by clearing successively my Lines of their Spots, till in the End by a Number of Courses, I should be happy in viewing a clean Book after a thirteen Weeks daily Examination.

This my little Book had for its Motto these Lines from *Addison's Cato*;

> *Here will I hold: If there is a Pow'r above us,*
> *(And that there is, all Nature cries aloud*
> *Thro' all her Works) he must delight in Virtue,*
> *And that which he delights in must be happy.*

Another from *Cicero*.

> *O Vitæ Philosophia Dux! O Virtutum indagatrix, expultrixque vitiorum! Unus dies bene, & ex preceptis tuis actus, peccanti immortalitati est anteponendus.*

Another from the Proverbs of Solomon speaking of Wisdom or Virtue;

> Length of Days is in her right hand, and in her Left Hand Riches and Honours; Her Ways are Ways of Pleasantness, and all her Paths are Peace.   III, 16, 17.

And conceiving God to be the Fountain of Wisdom, I thought it right and necessary to solicit his Assistance for obtaining it; to this End I form'd the following little Prayer, which was prefix'd to my Tables of Examination; for daily Use.

> *O Powerful Goodness! bountiful Father! merciful Guide! Increase in me that Wisdom which discovers my truest Interests; Strengthen my Resolutions to perform what that Wisdom dictates. Accept my kind Offices to thy other Children, as the only Return in my Power for thy continual Favours to me.*

I us'd also sometimes a little Prayer which I took from *Thomson's* Poems. viz

> *Father of Light and Life, thou Good supreme,*
> *O teach me what is good, teach me thy self!*
> *Save me from Folly, Vanity and Vice,*
> *From every low Pursuit, and fill my Soul*
> *With Knowledge, conscious Peace, & Virtue pure,*
> *Sacred, substantial, neverfading Bliss!*

The Precept of *Order* requiring that *every Part of my Business should have its allotted Time*, one Page in my little Book contain'd the following Scheme of Employment for the Twenty-four Hours of a natural Day,

The Morning Question, What Good shall I do this Day?	5	Rise, wash, and address *Powerful Goodness;* contrive Day's Business and take the Resolution of the Day; prosecute the present Study: and breakfast.—
	6	
	7	
	8	
	9	Work.
	10	
	11	
	12	Read, or overlook my Accounts, and dine.
	1	
	2	Work.
	3	
	4	
	5	
	6	Put Things in their Places, Supper, Musick, or Diversion, or Conversation, Examination of the Day.
	7	
Evening Question, What Good have I done to day?	8	
	9	
	10	Sleep.—
	11	
	12	
	1	
	2	
	3	
	4	

I enter'd upon the Execution of this Plan for Self Examination, and continu'd it with occasional Intermissions for some time. I was surpriz'd to find myself so much fuller of Faults than I had imagined, but I had the Satisfaction of seeing them diminish. To avoid the Trouble of renewing now & then my little Book, which by scraping out the Marks on the Paper of old Faults to make room for new Ones in a new Course, became full of Holes: I transferr'd my Tables & Precepts to the Ivory Leaves of a Memorandum Book, on which the Lines were drawn with red Ink that made a durable Stain, and on those Lines I mark'd my Faults with a black Lead Pencil, which Marks I could easily wipe out with a wet Sponge. After a while I went thro' one Course only in a Year, and afterwards only one in several Years; till at length I omitted them entirely, being employ'd in Voyages & Business abroad with a Multiplicity of Affairs, that interfered. But I always carried my little Book with me. My Scheme of OR- DER, gave me the most Trouble, and I found, that tho' it might be practicable where a Man's Business was such as to leave him the Disposition of his Time, that of a Journey-man Printer for instance, it was not possible to be exactly observ'd by a Master, who must mix with the World, and often receive People of Business at their own Hours.— *Order* too, with re- gard to Places for Things, Papers, &c. I found extreamly dif- ficult to acquire. I had not been early accustomed to it, & having an exceeding good Memory, I was not so sensible of the Inconvenience attending Want of Method. This Article therefore cost me so much painful Attention & my Faults in it vex'd me so much, and I made so little Progress in Amend- ment, & had such frequent Relapses, that I was almost ready to give up the Attempt, and content my self with a faulty Character in that respect. Like the Man who in buying an Ax of a Smith my Neighbour, desired to have the whole of its Surface as bright as the Edge; the Smith consented to grind it bright for him if he would turn the Wheel. He turn'd while the Smith press'd the broad Face of the Ax hard & heavily on the Stone, which made the Turning of it very fatiguing. The Man came every now & then from the Wheel to see how the Work went on; and at length would take his Ax as it was without farther Grinding. No, says the Smith, Turn on, turn on; we shall have it bright by and by; as yet 'tis only speckled. Yes, says the Man; but— *I think I like a speckled Ax best.*— And I believe this may have been the Case with many who having for want of some such Means as I employ'd found the Difficulty of obtaining good, & breaking bad Habits, in other Points of Vice & Virtue, have given up the Struggle, & con- cluded that *a speckled Ax was best.* For something that pre- tended to be Reason was every now and then suggesting to me, that such extream Nicety as I exacted of my self might be a kind of Foppery in Morals, which if it were known would make me ridiculous; that a perfect Character might be at- tended with the Inconvenience of being envied and hated; and that a benevolent Man should allow a few Faults in him- self, to keep his Friends in Countenance. In Truth I found myself incorrigible with respect to *Order*; and now I am grown old, and my Memory bad, I feel very sensibly the want of it. But on the whole, tho' I never arrived at the Perfection I had been so ambitious of obtaining, but fell far short of it, yet I was by the Endeavour made a better and a happier Man than I otherwise should have been, if I had not attempted it; As those who aim at perfect Writing by imitating the engraved Copies, tho' they never reach the wish'd for Excellence of those Copies, their Hand is mended by the Endeavour, and is tolerable while it continues fair & legible.—

And it may be well my Posterity should be informed, that to this little Artifice, with the Blessing of God, their Ancestor ow'd the constant Felicity of his Life down to his 79th Year in which this is written. What Reverses may attend the Remainder is in the Hand of Providence: But if they arrive the Reflection on past Happiness enjoy'd ought to help his Bearing them with more Resignation. To *Temperance* he ascribes his long-continu'd Health, & what is still left to him of a good Constitution. To *Industry* and *Frugality* the early Easiness of his Circumstances, & Acquisition of his Fortune, with all that Knowledge which enabled him to be an useful Citizen, and obtain'd for him some Degree of Reputation among the Learned. To *Sincerity* & *Justice* the Confidence of his Country, and the honourable Employs it conferr'd upon him. And to the joint Influence of the whole Mass of the Virtues, even in their imperfect State he was able to acquire them, all that Evenness of Temper, & that Chearfulness in Conversation which makes his Company still sought for, & agreable even to his younger Acquaintance. I hope therefore that some of my Descendants may follow the Example & reap the Benefit.—

It will be remark'd that, tho' my Scheme was not wholly without Religion there was in it no Mark of any of the distinguishing Tenets of any particular Sect.—I had purposely avoided them; for being fully persuaded of the Utility and Excellency of my Method, and that it might be serviceable to People in all Religions, and intending some time or other to publish it, I would not have any thing in it that should prejudice any one of any Sect against it.—I purposed writing a little Comment on each Virtue, in which I would have shown the Advantages of possessing it, & the Mischiefs attending its opposite Vice; and I should have called my Book the ART *of Virtue*, because it would have shown the *Means & Manner* of obtaining Virtue; which would have distinguish'd it from the mere Exhortation to be good, that does not instruct & indicate the Means; but is like the Apostle's Man of verbal Charity, who only, without showing to the Naked & the Hungry *how* or where they might get Cloaths or Victuals, exhorted them to be fed & clothed. *James* II, 15, 16.—

But it so happened that my Intention of writing & publishing this Comment was never fulfilled. I did indeed, from time to time put down short Hints of the Sentiments, Reasonings, &c. to be made use of in it; some of which I have still by me: But the necessary close Attention to private Business in the earlier part of Life, and public Business since, have occasioned my postponing it. For it being connected in my Mind with a *great and extensive Project* that required the whole Man to execute, and which an unforeseen Succession of Employs prevented my attending to, it has hitherto remain'd unfinish'd.—

In this Piece it was my Design to explain and enforce this Doctrine, that vicious Actions are not hurtful because they are forbidden, but forbidden because they are hurtful, the Nature of Man alone consider'd: That it was therefore every ones Interest to be virtuous, who wish'd to be happy even in this World. And I should from this Circumstance, there being always in the World a Number of rich Merchants, Nobility, States and Princes, who have need of honest Instruments for the Management of their Affairs, and such being so rare, have endeavoured to convince young Persons, that no Qualities were so likely to make a poor Man's Fortune as those of Probity & Integrity.

My List of Virtues contain'd at first but twelve: But a Quaker Friend having kindly inform'd me that I was generally thought proud; that my Pride show'd itself frequently in Conversation; that I was not content with being in the right when discussing any Point, but was overbearing & rather insolent; of which he convinc'd me by mentioning several Instances;—I determined endeavouring to cure myself if I could of this Vice or Folly among the rest, and I added

Humility to my List, giving an extensive Meaning to the Word.—I cannot boast of much Success in acquiring the *Reality* of this Virtue; but I had a good deal with regard to the *Appearance* of it.—I made it a Rule to forbear all direct Contradiction to the Sentiments of others, and all positive Assertion of my own. I even forbid myself agreable to the old Laws of our Junto, the Use of every Word or Expression in the Language that imported a fix'd Opinion; such as *certainly*, *undoubtedly*, &c. and I adopted instead of them, *I conceive, I apprehend*, or *I imagine* a thing to be so or so, or it so appears to me at present.—When another asserted something that I thought an Error, I deny'd my self the Pleasure of contradicting him abruptly, and of showing immediately some Absurdity in his Proposition; and in answering I began by observing that in certain Cases or Circumstances his Opinion would be right, but that in the present case there *appear'd* or *seem'd* to me some Difference, &c. I soon found the Advantage of this Change in my Manners. The Conversations I engag'd in went on more pleasantly. The modest way in which I propos'd my Opinions, procur'd them a readier Reception and less Contradiction; I had less Mortification when I was found to be in the wrong, and I more easily prevail'd with others to give up their Mistakes & join with me when I happen'd to be in the right. And this Mode, which I at first put on, with some violence to natural Inclination, became at length so easy & so habitual to me, that perhaps for these Fifty Years past no one has ever. heard a dogmatical Expression escape me. And to this Habit (after my Character of Integrity) I think it principally owing, that I had early so much Weight with my Fellow Citizens, when I proposed new Institutions, or Alterations in the old; and so much Influence in public Councils when I became a Member. For I was but a bad Speaker, never eloquent, subject to much Hesitation in my choice of Words, hardly correct in Language, and yet I generally carried my Points.—

In reality there is perhaps no one of our natural Passions so hard to subdue as *Pride*. Disguise it, struggle with it, beat it down, stifle it, mortify it as much as one pleases, it is still alive, and will every now and then peep out and show itself.

You will see it perhaps often in this History. For even if I could conceive that I had compleatly overcome it, I should probably be proud of my Humility.—

Thus far written at Passy 1784

Part Three

I am now about to write at home, Augt 1788.—but cannot have the help expected from my Papers, many of them being lost in the War. I have however found the following.

Having mentioned *a great & extensive Project* which I had conceiv'd, it seems proper that some Account should be here given of that Project and its Object. Its first Rise in my Mind appears in the following little Paper, accidentally preserv'd, viz.

OBSERVATIONS on my Reading History in Library, May 9. 1731.

"That the great Affairs of the World, the Wars, Revolutions, &c. are carried on and effected by Parties.—

"That the View of these Parties is their present general Interest, or what they take to be such.—

"That the different Views of these different Parties, occasion all Confusion.

"That while a Party is carrying on a general Design, each Man has his particular private Interest in View.

"That as soon as a Party has gain'd its general Point, each Member becomes intent upon his particular Interest, which thwarting others, breaks that Party into Divisions, and occasions more Confusion.

"That few in Public Affairs act from a meer View of the Good of their Country, whatever they may pretend; and tho' their Actings bring real Good to their Country, yet Men primarily consider'd that their own and their Country's Interest was united, and did not act from a Principle of Benevolence.

"That fewer still in public Affairs act with a View to the Good of Mankind.

"There seems to me at present to be great Occasion for raising an united Party for Virtue, by forming the Virtuous and good Men of all Nations into a regular Body, to be govern'd by suitable good and wise Rules, which good and wise Men may probably be more unanimous in their Obedience to, than common People are to common Laws.

"I at present think, that whoever attempts this aright, and is well qualified, cannot fail of pleasing God, & of meeting with Success.— B F."—

Revolving this Project in my Mind, as to be undertaken hereafter when my Circumstances should afford me the necessary Leisure, I put down from time to time on Pieces of Paper such Thoughts as occur'd to me respecting it. Most of these are lost; but I find one purporting to be the Substance of an intended Creed, containing as I thought the Essentials of every known Religion, and being free of every thing that might shock the Professors of any Religion. It is express'd in these Words. viz.

"That there is one God who made all things.

"That he governs the World by his Providence.—

"That he ought to be worshipped by Adoration, Prayer & Thanksgiving.

"But that the most acceptable Service of God is doing Good to Man.

"That the Soul is immortal.

"And that God will certainly reward Virtue and punish Vice either here or hereafter."—

My Ideas at that time were, that the Sect should be begun & spread at first among young and single Men only; that each Person to be initiated should not only declare his Assent to such Creed, but should have exercis'd himself with the Thirteen Weeks Examination and Practice of the Virtues as in the before-mention'd Model; that the Existence of such a Society should be kept a Secret till it was become considerable, to prevent Solicitations for the Admission of improper Persons; but that the Members should each of them search among his Acquaintance for ingenuous well-disposed Youths, to whom with prudent Caution the Scheme should be gradually communicated: That the Members should engage to afford their Advice Assistance and Support to each other in promoting one another's Interest Business and Advancement in Life: That for Distinction we should be call'd the Society of the *Free and Easy*; Free, as being by the general Practice and Habit of the Virtues, free from the Dominion of Vice, and particularly by the Practice of Industry & Frugality, free from Debt, which exposes a Man to Confinement and a Species of Slavery to his Creditors. This is as much as I can now recollect of the Project, except that I communicated it in part to two young Men, who adopted it with some Enthusiasm. But my then narrow Circumstances, and the Necessity I was under of sticking close to my Business, occasion'd my Postponing the farther Prosecution of it at that time, and my multifarious Occupations public & private induc'd me to continue postponing, so that it has been omitted till I have no longer Strength or Activity left sufficient for such an Enterprize: Tho' I am still of Opinion that it was a practicable Scheme, and might have been very useful, by forming a great Number of good Citizens: And I was not discourag'd by the seeming Magnitude of the Undertaking, as I have always thought that one Man of tolerable Abilities may work great Changes, & accomplish great Affairs among Mankind, if he first forms a good Plan, and, cutting off all Amusements or other Employments that would divert his Attention, makes the Execution of that same Plan his sole Study and Business.—

In 1732 I first published my Almanack, under the Name of *Richard Saunders*; it was continu'd by me about 25 Years, commonly call'd *Poor Richard*'s Almanack. I endeavour'd to make it both entertaining and useful, and it accordingly came to be in such Demand that I reap'd considerable Profit from it, vending annually near ten Thousand. And observing that it was generally read, scarce any Neighbourhood in the Province being without it, I consider'd it as a proper Vehicle for conveying Instruction among the common People, who bought scarce any other Books. I therefore filled all the little Spaces that occurr'd between the Remarkable Days in the Calendar, with Proverbial Sentences, chiefly such as inculcated Industry and Frugality, as the Means of procuring Wealth and thereby securing Virtue, it being more difficult for a Man in Want to act always honestly, as (to use here one of those Proverbs) *it is hard for an empty Sack to stand upright*. These Proverbs, which contained the Wisdom of many Ages and Nations, I assembled and form'd into a connected Discourse prefix'd to the Almanack of 1757, as the Harangue of a wise old Man to the People attending an Auction. The bringing all these scatter'd Counsels thus into a Focus, enabled them to make greater Impression. The Piece being universally approv^ed was copied in all the Newspapers of the Continent, reprinted in Britain on a Broadside to be stuck up in Houses, two Translations were made of it in French, and great Numbers bought by the Clergy & Gentry to distribute gratis among their poor Parishioners and Tenants. In Pennsylvania, as it discouraged useless Expence in foreign Superfluities, some thought it had its share of Influence in producing that growing Plenty of Money which was observable for several Years after its Publication.—

I consider'd my Newspaper also as another Means of communicating Instruction, & in that View frequently reprinted in it Extracts from the Spectator and other moral Writers, and sometimes publish'd little Pieces of my own which had been first compos'd for Reading in our Junto. Of these are a Socratic Dialogue tending to prove, that, whatever might be his Parts and Abilities, a vicious Man could not properly be called a Man of Sense. And a Discourse on Self denial, showing that Virtue was not Secure, till its Practice became a Habitude, & was free from the Opposition of contrary Inclinations.—These may be found in the Papers about the beginning of 1735.—In the Conduct of my Newspaper I carefully excluded all Libelling and Personal Abuse, which is of late Years become so disgraceful to our Country. Whenever I was solicited to insert any thing of that kind, and the Writers pleaded as they generally did, the Liberty of the Press, and that a Newspaper was like a Stage Coach in which any one who would pay had a Right to a Place, my Answer was, that I would print the Piece separately if desired, and the Author might have as many Copies as he pleased to distribute himself, but that I would not take upon me to spread his Detraction, and that having contracted with my Subscribers to furnish them with what might be either useful or entertaining, I could not fill their Papers with private Altercation in which they had no Concern without doing them manifest Injustice. Now many of our Printers make no scruple of gratifying the Malice of Individuals by false Accusations of the fairest Characters among ourselves, augmenting Animosity even to the producing of Duels, and are moreover so indiscreet as to print scurrilous Reflections on the Government of neighbouring States, and even on the Conduct of our best national Allies, which may be attended with the most pernicious Consequences.— These Things I mention as a Caution to young Printers, &

that they may be encouraged not to pollute their Presses and disgrace their Profession by such infamous Practices, but refuse steadily; as they may see by my Example, that such a Course of Conduct will not on the whole be injurious to their Interests.—

In 1733, I sent one of my Journeymen to Charleston South Carolina where a Printer was wanting. I furnish'd him with a Press and Letters, on an Agreement of Partnership, by which I was to receive One Third of the Profits of the Business, paying One Third of the Expence. He was a Man of Learning and honest, but ignorant in Matters of Account; and tho' he sometimes made me Remittances, I could get no Account from him, nor any satisfactory State of our Partnership while he lived. On his Decease, the Business was continued by his Widow, who being born & bred in Holland, where as I have been inform'd the Knowledge of Accompts makes a Part of Female Education, she not only sent me as clear a State as she could find of the Transactions past, but continu'd to account with the greatest Regularity & Exactitude every Quarter afterwards; and manag'd the Business with such Success that she not only brought up reputably a Family of Children, but at the Expiration of the Term was able to purchase of me the Printing-House and establish her Son in it. I mention this Affair chiefly for the Sake of recommending that Branch of Education for our young Females, as likely to be of more Use to them & their Children in Case of Widowhood than either Music or Dancing, by preserving them from Losses by Imposition of crafty Men, and enabling them to continue perhaps a profitable mercantile House with establish'd Correspondence till a Son is grown up fit to undertake and go on with it, to the lasting Advantage and enriching of the Family.—

About the Year 1734. there arrived among us from Ireland, a young Presbyterian Preacher named Hemphill, who delivered with a good Voice, & apparently extempore, most excellent Discourses, which drew together considerable Numbers of different Persuasions, who join'd in admiring them. Among the rest I became one of his constant Hearers, his Sermons pleasing me as they had little of the dogmatical kind, but inculcated strongly the Practice of Virtue, or what in the

religious Stile are called Good Works. Those however, of our
Congregation, who considered themselves as orthodox Presbyterians, disapprov'd his Doctrine, and were join'd by most
of the old Clergy, who arraign'd him of Heterodoxy before
the Synod, in order to have him silenc'd. I became his zealous
Partisan, and contributed all I could to raise a Party in his
Favour; and we combated for him a while with some Hopes
of Success. There was much Scribbling pro & con upon the
Occasion; and finding that tho' an elegant Preacher he was
but a poor Writer, I lent him my Pen and wrote for him two
or three Pamphlets, and one Piece in the Gazette of April 1735.
Those Pamphlets, as is generally the Case with controversial
Writings, tho' eagerly read at the time, were soon out of
Vogue, and I question whether a single Copy of them now
exists. During the Contest an unlucky Occurrence hurt his
Cause exceedingly. One of our Adversaries having heard him
preach a Sermon that was much admired, thought he had
somewhere read that Sermon before, or at least a part of it.
On Search he found that Part quoted at length in one of the
British Reviews, from a Discourse of Dr Forster's. This De-
tection gave many of our Party Disgust, who accordingly
abandoned his Cause, and occasion'd our more speedy Dis-
comfiture in the Synod. I stuck by him, however, as I rather
approv'd his giving us good Sermons compos'd by others,
than bad ones of his own Manufacture; tho' the latter was the
Practice of our common Teachers. He afterwards acknowledg'd to me that none of those he preach'd were his own;
adding that his Memory was such as enabled him to retain
and repeat any Sermon after one Reading only.—On our Defeat he left us, in search elsewhere of better Fortune, and I
quitted the Congregation, never joining it after, tho' I continu'd many Years my Subscription for the Support of its
Ministers.—

I had begun in 1733 to study Languages. I soon made myself so much a Master of the French as to be able to read the
Books with Ease. I then undertook the Italian. An Acquaintance who was also learning it, us'd often to tempt me to play
Chess with him. Finding this took up too much of the Time
I had to spare for Study, I at length refus'd to play any more,
unless on this Condition, that the Victor in every Game,

should have a Right to impose a Task, either in Parts of the Grammar to be got by heart, or in Translation, &c. which Tasks the Vanquish'd was to perform upon Honour before our next Meeting. As we play'd pretty equally we thus beat one another into that Language.—I afterwards with a little Pains-taking acquir'd as much of the Spanish as to read their Books also. I have already mention'd that I had only one Years Instruction in a Latin School, and that when very young, after which I neglected that Language entirely.—But when I had attained an Acquaintance with the French, Italian and Spanish, I was surpriz'd to find, on looking over a Latin Testament, that I understood so much more of that Language than I had imagined; which encouraged me to apply my self again to the Study of it, & I met with the more Success, as those preceding Languages had greatly smooth'd my Way. From these Circumstances I have thought, that there is some Inconsistency in our common Mode of Teaching Languages. We are told that it is proper to begin first with the Latin, and having acquir'd that it will be more easy to attain those modern Languages which are deriv'd from it; and yet we do not begin with the Greek in order more easily to acquire the Latin. It is true, that if you can clamber & get to the Top of a Stair-Case without using the Steps, you will more easily gain them in descending: but certainly if you begin with the lowest you will with more Ease ascend to the Top. And I would therefore offer it to the Consideration of those who superintend the Educating of our Youth, whether, since many of those who begin with the Latin, quit the same after spending some Years, without having made any great Proficiency, and what they have learnt becomes almost useless, so that their time has been lost, it would not have been better to have begun them with the French, proceeding to the Italian &c. for tho' after spending the same time they should quit the Study of Languages, & never arrive at the Latin, they would however have acquir'd another Tongue or two that being in modern Use might be serviceable to them in common Life.

After ten Years Absence from Boston, and having become more easy in my Circumstances, I made a Journey thither to visit my Relations, which I could not sooner well afford. In returning I call'd at Newport, to see my Brother then settled there with his Printing-House. Our former Differences were forgotten, and our Meeting was very cordial and affectionate. He was fast declining in his Health, and requested of me that in case of his Death which he apprehended not far distant, I would take home his Son, then but 10 Years of Age, and bring him up to the Printing Business. This I accordingly perform'd, sending him a few Years to School before I took him into the Office. His Mother carry'd on the Business till he was grown up, when I assisted him with an Assortment of new Types, those of his Father being in a Manner worn out.—Thus it was that I made my Brother ample Amends for the Service I had depriv'd him of by leaving him so early.—

In 1736 I lost one of my Sons a fine Boy of 4 Years old, by the Small Pox taken in the common way. I long regretted bitterly & still regret that I had not given it to him by Inoculation; This I mention for the Sake of Parents, who omit that Operation on the Supposition that they should never forgive themselves if a Child died under it; my Example showing that the Regret may be the same either way, and that therefore the safer should be chosen.—

Our Club, the Junto, was found so useful, & afforded such Satisfaction to the Members, that several were desirous of introducing their Friends, which could not well be done without exceeding what we had settled as a convenient Number, viz. Twelve. We had from the Beginning made it a Rule to keep our Institution a Secret, which was pretty well observ'd. The Intention was, to avoid Applications of improper Persons for Admittance, some of whom perhaps we might find it difficult to refuse. I was one of those who were against any Addition to our Number, but instead of it made in Writing a Proposal, that every Member separately should endeavour to form a subordinate Club, with the same Rules respecting Queries, &c. and without informing them of the Connexion with the Junto. The Advantages propos'd were the Improvement of so many more young Citizens by the Use of our Institutions; Our better Acquaintance with the general Sentiments of the Inhabitants on any Occasion, as the Junto-Member might propose what Queries we should desire, and was to report to Junto what pass'd in his separate Club; the Promotion of our particular Interests in Business by more extensive Recommendations; and the Increase of our Influence in public Affairs & our Power of doing Good by spreading thro' the several Clubs the Sentiments of the Junto. The Project was approv'd, and every Member undertook to form his Club: but they did not all succeed. Five or six only were compleated, which were call'd by different Names, as the Vine, the Union, the Band, &c. they were useful to themselves, & afforded us a good deal of Amusement, Information & Instruction, besides answering in some considerable Degree our Views of influencing the public Opinion on particular Occasions, of which I shall give some Instances in course of time as they happened.—

My first Promotion was my being chosen in 1736 Clerk of the General Assembly. The Choice was made that Year without Opposition; but the Year following when I was again propos'd (the Choice, like that of the Members being annual) a new Member made a long Speech against me in order to favour some other Candidate. I was however chosen; which was the more agreable to me, as besides the Pay for immediate Service as Clerk, the Place gave me a better Opportunity of keeping up an Interest among the Members, which secur'd to me the Business of Printing the Votes, Laws, Paper Money, and other occasional Jobbs for the Public, that on the whole were very profitable. I therefore did not like the Opposition of this new Member, who was a Gentleman of Fortune, & Education, with Talents that were likely to give him in time great Influence in the House, which indeed afterwards happened. I did not however aim at gaining his Favour by paying any servile Respect to him, but after some time took this other Method. Having heard that he had in his Library a certain very scarce & curious Book, I wrote a Note to him expressing my Desire of perusing that Book, and requesting he would do me the Favour of lending it to me for a few Days. He sent it immediately; and I return'd it in about a Week, with another Note expressing strongly my Sense of the Favour. When we next met in the House he spoke to me, (which he had never done before) and with great Civility. And he ever afterwards manifested a Readiness to serve me on all Occasions, so that we became great Friends, & our Friendship continu'd to his Death. This is another Instance of the Truth of an old Maxim I had learnt, which says, *He that has once done you a Kindness will be more ready to do you another, than he whom you yourself have obliged.* And it shows how much more profitable it is prudently to remove, than to resent, return & continue inimical Proceedings.—

In 1737, Col. Spotswood, late Governor of Virginia, & then Post-master, General, being dissatisfied with the Conduct of his Deputy at Philadelphia, respecting some Negligence in rendering, & Inexactitude of his Accounts, took from him the Commission & offered it to me. I accepted it readily, and found it of great Advantage; for tho' the Salary was small, it facilitated the Correspondence that improv'd my Newspaper, encreas'd the Number demanded, as well as the Advertisements to be inserted, so that it came to afford me a very considerable Income. My old Competitor's Newspaper declin'd proportionably, and I was satisfy'd without retaliating his Refusal, while Postmaster, to permit my Papers being carried by the Riders. Thus He suffer'd greatly from his Neglect in due Accounting; and I mention it as a Lesson to those young Men who may be employ'd in managing Affairs for others that they should always render Accounts & make Remittances, with great Clearness and Punctuality.—The Character of observing Such a Conduct is the most powerful of all Recommendations to new Employments & Increase of Business.

I began now to turn my Thoughts a little to public Affairs, beginning however with small Matters. The City Watch was one of the first Things that I conceiv'd to want Regulation. It was managed by the Constables of the respective Wards in Turn. The Constable warn'd a Number of Housekeepers to attend him for the Night. Those who chose never to attend paid him Six Shillings a Year to be excus'd, which was suppos'd to be for hiring Substitutes; but was in Reality much more than was necessary for that purpose, and made the Constableship a Place of Profit. And the Constable for a little Drink often got such Ragamuffins about him as a Watch, that reputable Housekeepers did not chuse to mix with. Walking the Rounds too was often neglected, and most of the Night spent in Tippling. I thereupon wrote a Paper to be read in Junto, representing these Irregularities, but insisting more particularly on the Inequality of this Six Shilling Tax of the

Constables, respecting the Circumstances of those who paid
it, since a poor Widow Housekeeper, all whose Property to
be guarded by the Watch did not perhaps exceed the Value of
Fifty Pounds, paid as much as the wealthiest Merchant who
had Thousands of Pounds-worth of Goods in his Stores. On
the whole I proposed as a more effectual Watch, the Hiring
of proper Men to serve constantly in that Business; and as a
more equitable Way of supporting the Charge, the levying a
Tax that should be proportion'd to Property. This Idea being
approv'd by the Junto, was communicated to the other Clubs,
but as arising in each of them. And tho' the Plan was not
immediately carried into Execution, yet by preparing the
Minds of People for the Change, it paved the Way for the
Law obtain'd a few Years after, when the Members of our
Clubs were grown into more Influence.—

About this time I wrote a Paper, (first to be read in Junto
but it was afterwards publish'd) on the different Accidents
and Carelessnesses by which Houses were set on fire, with
Cautions against them, and Means proposed of avoiding
them. This was much spoken of as a useful Piece, and gave
rise to a Project, which soon followed it, of forming a Company for the more ready Extinguishing of Fires, and mutual
Assistance in Removing & Securing of Goods when in Danger. Associates in this Scheme were presently found amounting to Thirty. Our Articles of Agreement oblig'd every
Member to keep always in good Order and fit for Use, a certain Number of Leather Buckets, with strong Bags & Baskets
(for packing & transporting of Goods), which were to be
brought to every Fire; and we agreed to meet once a Month
& spend a social Evening together, in discoursing, and communicating such Ideas as occur'd to us upon the Subject of
Fires as might be useful in our Conduct on such Occasions.
The Utility of this Institution soon appeard, and many more
desiring to be admitted than we thought convenient for one
Company, they were advised to form another; which was accordingly done. And this went on, one new Company being
formed after another, till they became so numerous as to include most of the Inhabitants who were Men of Property;
and now at the time of my Writing this, tho' upwards of Fifty
Years since its Establishment, that which I first formed, called

the Union Fire Company, still subsists and flourishes, tho' the first Members are all deceas'd but myself & one who is older by a Year than I am.—The small Fines that have been paid by Members for Absence at the Monthly Meetings, have been apply'd to the Purchase of Fire Engines, Ladders, Firehooks, and other useful Implements for each Company, so that I question whether there is a City in the World better provided with the Means of putting a Stop to beginning Conflagrations; and in fact since these Institutions, the City has never lost by Fire more than one or two Houses at a time, and the Flames have often been extinguish'd before the House in which they began has been half-consumed.—

In 1739 arriv'd among us from England the Rev. Mr Whitefiel, who had made himself remarkable there as an itinerant Preacher. He was at first permitted to preach in some of our Churches; but the Clergy taking a Dislike to him, soon refus'd him their Pulpits and he was oblig'd to preach in the Fields. The Multitudes of all Sects and Denominations that attended his Sermons were enormous and it was matter of Speculation to me who was one of the Number, to observe the extraordinary Influence of his Oratory on his Hearers, and how much they admir'd & respected him, notwithstanding his common Abuse of them, by assuring them they were naturally *half Beasts and half Devils.* It was wonderful to see the Change soon made in the Manners of our Inhabitants; from being thoughtless or indifferent about Religion, it seem'd as if all the World were growing Religious; so that one could not walk thro' the Town in an Evening without Hearing Psalms sung in different Families of every Street. And it being found inconvenient to assemble in the open Air, subject to its Inclemencies, the Building of a House to meet-in was no sooner propos'd and Persons appointed to receive Contributions, but sufficient Sums were soon receiv'd to procure the Ground and erect the Building which was 100 feet long & 70 broad, about the Size of Westminster-hall; and the Work was carried on with such Spirit as to be finished in a much shorter time than could have been expected. Both House and Ground were vested in Trustees, expressly for the Use of any Preacher of any religious Persuasion who might desire to say something to the People of Philadelphia, the Design in building not being to accommodate any particular Sect, but the Inhabitants in general, so that even if the Mufti of Constantinople were to send a Missionary to preach Mahometanism to us, he would find a Pulpit at his Service.—

Mr Whitfield, in leaving us, went preaching all the Way thro' the Colonies to Georgia. The Settlement of that Province had lately been begun; but instead of being made with hardy industrious Husbandmen accustomed to Labour, the only People fit for such an Enterprise, it was with Families of broken Shopkeepers and other insolvent Debtors, many of indolent & idle habits, taken out of the Goals, who being set down in the Woods, unqualified for clearing Land, & unable to endure the Hardships of a new Settlement, perished in Numbers, leaving many helpless Children unprovided for. The Sight of their miserable Situation inspired the benevolent Heart of Mr Whitefield with the Idea of building an Orphan House there, in which they might be supported and educated. Returning northward he preach'd up this Charity, & made large Collections;—for his Eloquence had a wonderful Power over the Hearts & Purses of his Hearers, of which I myself was an Instance. I did not disapprove of the Design, but as Georgia was then destitute of Materials & Workmen, and it was propos'd to send them from Philadelphia at a great Expence, I thought it would have been better to have built the House here & brought the Children to it. This I advis'd, but he was resolute in his first Project, and rejected my Counsel, and I thereupon refus'd to contribute. I happened soon after to attend one of his Sermons, in the Course of which I perceived he intended to finish with a Collection, & I silently resolved he should get nothing from me. I had in my Pocket a Handful of Copper, Money, three or four silver Dollars, and five Pistoles in Gold. As he proceeded I began to soften, and concluded to give the Coppers. Another Stroke of his Oratory made me asham'd of that, and determin'd me to give the Silver; & he finish'd so admirably, that I empty'd my Pocket wholly into the Collector's Dish, Gold and all. At this Sermon there was also one of our Club, who being of my Sentiments respecting the Building in Georgia, and suspecting a Collection might be intended, had by Precaution emptied his Pockets before he came from home; towards the

Conclusion of the Discourse however, he felt a strong Desire to give, and apply'd to a Neighbour who stood near him to borrow some Money for the Purpose. The Application was unfortunately to perhaps the only Man in the Company who had the firmness not to be affected by the Preacher. His Answer was, *At any other time, Friend Hopkinson, I would lend to thee freely; but not now; for thee seems to be out of thy right Senses.*—

Some of Mr Whitfield's Enemies affected to suppose that he would apply these Collections to his own private Emolument; but I, who was intimately acquainted with him, (being employ'd in printing his Sermons and Journals, &c.) never had the least Suspicion of his Integrity, but am to this day decidedly of Opinion that he was in all his Conduct, a perfectly *honest Man*. And methinks my Testimony in his Favour ought to have the more Weight, as we had no religious Connection. He us'd indeed sometimes to pray for my Conversion, but never had the Satisfaction of believing that his Prayers were heard. Ours was a mere civil Friendship, sincere on both Sides, and lasted to his Death.

The following Instance will show something of the Terms on which we stood. Upon one of his Arrivals from England at Boston, he wrote to me that he should come soon to Philadelphia, but knew not where he could lodge when there, as he understood his old kind Host Mr Benezet was remov'd to Germantown. My Answer was; You know my House, if you can make shift with its scanty Accommodations you will be most heartily welcome. He reply'd, that if I made that kind Offer for Christ's sake, I should not miss of a Reward.—And I return'd, *Don't let me be mistaken; it was not for Christ's sake, but for your sake.* One of our common Acquaintance jocosely remark'd, that knowing it to be the Custom of the Saints, when they receiv'd any favour, to shift the Burthen of the Obligation from off their own Shoulders, and place it in Heaven, I had contriv'd to fix it on Earth.—

The last time I saw Mr Whitefield was in London, when he consulted me about his Orphan House Concern, and his Purpose of appropriating it to the Establishment of a College.

He had a loud and clear Voice, and articulated his Words & Sentences so perfectly that he might be heard and under-

stood at a great Distance, especially as his Auditories, however numerous, observ'd the most exact Silence. He preach'd
one Evening from the Top of the Court House Steps, which
are in the Middle of Market Street, and on the West Side of
Second Street which crosses it at right angles. Both Streets
were fill'd with his Hearers to a considerable Distance. Being
among the hindmost in Market Street, I had the Curiosity to
learn how far he could be heard, by retiring backwards down
the Street towards the River, and I found his Voice distinct
till I came near Front-Street, when some Noise in that Street,
obscur'd it. Imagining then a Semi-Circle, of which my Distance should be the Radius, and that it were fill'd with Auditors, to each of whom I allow'd two square feet, I computed
that he might well be heard by more than Thirty-Thousand.
This reconcil'd me to the Newspaper Accounts of his having
preach'd to 25000 People in the Fields, and to the antient
Histories of Generals haranguing whole Armies, of which I
had sometimes doubted.—

By hearing him often I came to distinguish easily between
Sermons newly compos'd, & those which he had often
preach'd in the Course of his Travels. His Delivery of the
latter was so improv'd by frequent Repetitions, that every
Accent, every Emphasis, every Modulation of Voice, was so
perfectly well turn'd and well plac'd, that without being
interested in the Subject, one could not help being pleas'd
with the Discourse, a Pleasure of much the same kind with
that receiv'd from an excellent Piece of Musick. This is an
Advantage itinerant Preachers have over those who are stationary: as the latter cannot well improve their Delivery of a
Sermon by so many Rehearsals.—

His Writing and Printing from time to time gave great
Advantage to his Enemies. Unguarded Expressions and even
erroneous Opinions del^d in Preaching might have been
afterwards explain'd, or qualify'd by supposing others that
might have accompany'd them; or they might have been
deny'd; But *litera scripta manet*. Critics attack'd his Writings
violently, and with so much Appearance of Reason as to diminish the Number of his Votaries, and prevent their Encrease: So that I am of Opinion, if he had never written any
thing he would have left behind him a much more numerous

and important Sect. And his Reputation might in that case have been still growing, even after his Death; as there being nothing of his Writing on which to found a Censure; and give him a lower Character, his Proselites would be left at Liberty to feign for him as great a Variety of Excellencies, as their enthusiastic Admiration might wish him to have possessed.

My Business was now continually augmenting, and my Circumstances growing daily easier, my Newspaper having become very profitable, as being for a time almost the only one in this and the neighbouring Provinces.—I experienc'd too the Truth of the Observation, that *after getting the first hundred Pound, it is more easy to get the second*: Money itself being of a prolific Nature: The Partnership at Carolina having succeeded, I was encourag'd to engage in others, and to promote several of my Workmen who had behaved well, by establishing them with Printing-Houses in different Colonies, on the same Terms with that in Carolina. Most of them did well, being enabled at the End of our Term, Six Years, to purchase the Types of me; and go on working for themselves, by which means several Families were raised. Partnerships often finish in Quarrels, but I was happy in this, that mine were all carry'd on and ended amicably; owing I think a good deal to the Precaution of having very explicitly settled in our Articles every thing to be done by or expected from each Partner, so that there was nothing to dispute, which Precaution I would therefore recommend to all who enter into Partnerships, for whatever Esteem Partners may have for & Confidence in each other at the time of the Contract, little Jealousies and Disgusts may arise, with Ideas of Inequality in the Care & Burthen of the Business, &c. which are attended often with Breach of Friendship & of the Connection, perhaps with Lawsuits and other disagreable Consequences.

I had on the whole abundant Reason to be satisfied with my being established in Pennsylvania. There were however two things that I regretted: There being no Provision for Defence, nor for a compleat Education of Youth. No Militia nor any College. I therefore in 1743, drew up a Proposal for establishing an Academy; & at that time thinking the Rev^d Mr Peters, who was out of Employ, a fit Person to superintend such an Institution, I communicated the Project to him. But he having more profitable Views in the Service of the Proprietor, which succeeded, declin'd the Undertaking. And not knowing another at that time suitable for such a Trust, I let the Scheme lie a while dormant.—I succeeded better the next Year, 1744, in proposing and establishing a Philosophical Society. The Paper I wrote for that purpose will be found among my Writings when collected.—

With respect to Defence, Spain having been several Years at War against Britain, and being at length join'd by France, which brought us into greater Danger; and the laboured & long-continued Endeavours of our Governor Thomas to prevail with our Quaker Assembly to pass a Militia Law, & make other Provisions for the Security of the Province having proved abortive, I determined to try what might be done by a voluntary Association of the People. To promote this I first wrote & published a Pamphlet, intitled, PLAIN TRUTH, in which I stated our defenceless Situation in strong Lights, with the Necessity of Union & Discipline for our Defence, and promis'd to propose in a few Days an Association to be generally signed for that purpose. The Pamphlet had a sudden & surprizing Effect. I was call'd upon for the Instrument of Association: And having settled the Draft of it with a few Friends, I appointed a Meeting of the Citizens in the large Building before mentioned. The House was pretty full. I had prepared a Number of printed Copies, and provided Pens and Ink dispers'd all over the Room. I harangu'd them a little on the Subject, read the Paper & explain'd it, and then distributed the Copies which were eagerly signed, not the least Objection being made. When the Company separated, & the Papers were collected we found above Twelve hundred Hands; and other Copies being dispers'd in the Country the Subscribers amounted at length to upwards of Ten Thousand. These all furnish'd themselves as soon as they could with Arms; form'd themselves into Companies, and Regiments, chose their own Officers, & met every Week to be instructed in the manual Exercise, and other Parts of military Discipline. The Women, by Subscriptions among themselves, provided Silk Colours, which they presented to the Companies, painted with different Devices and Motto's which I supplied. The

Officers of the Companies composing the Philadelphia Regiment, being met, chose me for their Colonel; but conceiving myself unfit, I declin'd that Station, & recommended Mr Lawrence, a fine Person and Man of Influence, who was accordingly appointed. I then propos'd a Lottery to defray the Expence of Building a Battery below the Town, and furnishing it with Cannon. It filled expeditiously and the Battery was soon erected, the Merlons being fram'd of Logs & fill'd with Earth. We bought some old Cannon from Boston, but these not being sufficient, we wrote to England for more, soliciting at the same Time our Proprietaries for some Assistance, tho' without much Expectation of obtaining it. Mean while Colonel Lawrence, William Allen, Abraham Taylor, Esquires, and myself were sent to New York by the Associators, commission'd to borrow some Cannon of Governor Clinton. He at first refus'd us peremptorily: but at a Dinner with his Council where there was great Drinking of Madeira Wine, as the Custom at that Place then was, he soften'd by degrees, and said he would lend us Six. After a few more Bumpers he advanc'd to Ten. And at length he very good-naturedly conceded Eighteen. They were fine Cannon, 18 pounders, with their Carriages, which we soon transported and mounted on our Battery, where the Associators kept a nightly Guard while the War lasted: And among the rest I regularly took my Turn of Duty there as a common Soldier.—

My Activity in these Operations was agreable to the Governor and Council; they took me into Confidence, & I was consulted by them in every Measure wherein their Concurrence was thought useful to the Association. Calling in the Aid of Religion, I propos'd to them the Proclaiming a Fast, to promote Reformation, & implore the Blessing of Heaven on our Undertaking. They embrac'd the Motion, but as it was the first Fast ever thought of in the Province, the Secretary had no Precedent from which to draw the Proclamation. My Education in New England, where a Fast is proclaim'd every Year, was here of some Advantage. I drew it in the accustomed Stile, it was translated into German, printed in both Languages and divulg'd thro' the Province. This gave the Clergy of the different Sects an Opportunity of Influencing their Congregations to join in the Association; and it would probably have been general among all but Quakers if the Peace had not soon interven'd.

It was thought by some of my Friends that by my Activity in these Affairs, I should offend that Sect, and thereby lose my Interest in the Assembly where they were a great Majority. A young Gentleman who had likewise some Friends in the House, and wish'd to succeed me as their Clerk, acquainted me that it was decided to displace me at the next Election, and he therefore in good Will advis'd me to resign, as more consistent with my Honour than being turn'd out. My Answer to him was, that I had read or heard of some Public Man, who made it a Rule never to ask for an Office, and never to refuse one when offer'd to him. I approve, says I, of his Rule, and will practise it with a small Addition; I shall never *ask*, never *refuse*, nor ever *resign* an Office. If they will have my Office of Clerk to dispose of to another, they shall take it from me. I will not by giving it up, lose my Right of some time or other making Reprisals on my Adversaries. I heard however no more of this. I was chosen again, unanimously as usual, at the next Election. Possibly as they dislik'd my late Intimacy with the Members of Council, who had join'd the Governors in all the Disputes about military Preparations with which the House had long been harass'd, they might have been pleas'd if I would voluntarily have left them; but they did not care to displace me on Account merely of my Zeal for the Association; and they could not well give another Reason.—Indeed I had some Cause to believe, that the Defence of the Country was not disagreeable to any of them, provided they were not requir'd to assist in it. And I found that a much greater Number of them than I could have imagined, tho' against offensive War, were clearly for the defensive. Many Pamphlets *pro & con.* were publish'd on the Subject, and some by good Quakers in favour of Defence, which I believe convinc'd most of their younger People. A Transaction in our Fire Company gave me some Insight into their prevailing Sentiments. It had been propos'd that we should encourage the Scheme for building a Battery by laying out the present Stock, then about Sixty Pounds, in Tickets of the Lottery. By our Rules no Money could be dispos'd of but at the next Meeting after the Proposal. The Company consisted of Thirty Members, of which Twenty-two were Quakers, & Eight only of other Persuasions. We eight punctually attended the Meeting; but tho' we thought that some of the Quakers would join us, we were by no means sure of a Majority. Only one Quaker, Mr James Morris, appear'd to oppose the Measure: He express'd much Sorrow that it had ever been propos'd, as he said *Friends* were all against it, and it would create such Discord as might break up the Company. We told him, that we saw no Reason for that; we were the Minority, and if *Friends* were against the Measure and outvoted us, we must and should, agreable to the Usage of all Societies, submit. When the Hour for Business arriv'd, it was mov'd to put the Vote. He allow'd we might then do it by the Rules, but as he could assure us that a Number of Members intended to be present for the purpose of opposing it, it would be but candid to allow a little time for their appearing. While we were disputing this, a Waiter came to tell me two Gentlemen below desir'd to speak with me. I went down, and found they were two of our Quaker Members. They told me there were eight of them assembled at a Tavern just by; that they were determin'd to come and vote with us if there should be occasion, which they hop'd would not be the Case; and desir'd we would not call for their Assistance if we could do without it, as their Voting for such a Measure might embroil them with their Elders & Friends; Being thus secure of a Majority, I went up, and after a little seeming Hesitation, agreed to a Delay of another Hour. This Mr Morris allow'd to be extreamly fair. Not one of his opposing Friends appear'd, at which he express'd great Surprize; and at the Expiration of the Hour, we carry'd the Resolution Eight to one; And as of the 22 Quakers, Eight were ready to vote with us and, Thirteen by their Absence manifested that they were not inclin'd to oppose the Measure, I afterwards estimated the Proportion of Quakers sincerely against Defence as one to twenty one only. For these were all regular Members, of that Society, and in good Reputation among them, and had due Notice of what was propos'd at that Meeting.

The honourable & learned Mr Logan, who had always been of that Sect, was one who wrote an Address to them, declaring his Approbation of defensive War, and supporting his Opinion by many strong Arguments: He put into my Hands Sixty Pounds, to be laid out in Lottery Tickets for the Battery, with Directions to apply what Prizes might be drawn wholly to that Service. He told me the following Anecdote of his old Master Wm Penn respecting Defence. He came over from England, when a young Man, with that Proprietary, and as his Secretary. It was War Time, and their Ship was chas'd by an armed Vessel suppos'd to be an Enemy. Their Captain prepar'd for Defence, but told Wm Penn and his Company of Quakers, that he did not expect their Assistance, and they might retire into the Cabin; which they did, except James Logan, who chose to stay upon Deck, and was quarter'd to a Gun. The suppos'd Enemy prov'd a Friend; so there was no Fighting. But when the Secretary went down to communicate the Intelligence, Wm Penn rebuk'd him severely for staying upon Deck and undertaking to assist in defending the Vessel, contrary to the Principles of *Friends*, especially as it had not been required by the Captain. This Reproof being before all the Company, piqu'd the Secretary, who answer'd, *I being thy Servant, why did thee not order me to come down: but thee was willing enough that I should stay and help to fight the Ship when thee thought there was Danger.*

My being many Years in the Assembly, the Majority of which were constantly Quakers, gave me frequent Opportunities of seeing the Embarassment given them by their Principle against War, whenever Application was made to them by Order of the Crown to grant Aids for military Purposes. They were unwilling to offend Government on the one hand, by a direct Refusal, and their Friends the Body of Quakers on the other, by a Compliance contrary to their Principles. Hence a Variety of Evasions to avoid Complying, and Modes of disguising the Compliance when it became unavoidable. The common Mode at last was to grant Money under the Phrase of its being *for the King's Use*, and never to enquire how it was applied. But if the Demand was not directly from the Crown, that Phrase was found not so proper, and some other was to be invented. As when Powder was wanting, (I think it was for the Garrison at Louisburg,) and the Government of New England solicited a Grant of some from Pensilvania, which was much urg'd on the House by Governor

Thomas, they could not grant Money to buy Powder, because that was an Ingredient of War, but they voted an Aid to New England, of Three Thousand Pounds, to be put into the hands of the Governor, and appropriated it for the Purchasing of Bread, Flour, Wheat, *or other Grain*. Some of the Council desirous of giving the House still farther Embarassment, advis'd the Governor not to accept Provision, as not being the Thing he had demanded. But he reply'd, "I shall take the Money, for I understand very well their Meaning; *Other Grain*, is Gunpowder;" which he accordingly bought; and they never objected to it. It was in Allusion to this Fact, that when in our Fire Company we feared the Success of our Proposal in favour of the Lottery, & I had said to my Friend Mr Syng, one of our Members, if we fail, let us move the Purchase of a Fire Engine with the Money; the Quakers can have no Objection to that: and then if you nominate me, and I you, as a Committee for that purpose, we will buy a great Gun, which is certainly a *Fire-Engine*: I see, says he, you have improv'd by being so long in the Assembly; your equivocal Project would be just a Match for their Wheat *or other Grain*.

These Embarassments that the Quakers suffer'd from having establish'd & published it as one of their Principles, that no kind of War was lawful, and which being once published, they could not afterwards, however they might change their minds, easily get rid of, reminds me of what I think a more prudent Conduct in another Sect among us; that of the Dunkers. I was acquainted with one of its Founders, Michael Welfare, soon after it appear'd.—He complain'd to me that they were grievously calumniated by the Zealots of other Persuasions, and charg'd with abominable Principles and Practices to which they were utter Strangers. I told him this had always been the case with new Sects; and that to put a Stop to such Abuse, I imagin'd it might be well to publish the Articles of their Belief and the Rules of their Discipline. He said that it had been propos'd among them, but not agreed to, for this Reason; "When we were first drawn together as a Society, says he, it had pleased God to inlighten our Minds so far, as to see that some Doctrines which we once esteemed Truths were Errors, & that others which we had esteemed Errors were real Truths. From time to time he has been pleased to afford us farther Light, and our Principles have been improving, & our Errors diminishing. Now we are not sure that we are arriv'd at the End of this Progression, and at the Perfection of Spiritual or Theological Knowledge; and we fear that if we should once print our Confession of Faith, we should feel ourselves as if bound & confin'd by it, and perhaps be unwilling to receive farther Improvement; and our Successors still more so, as conceiving what we their Elders & Founders had done, to be something sacred, never to be departed from."—This Modesty in a Sect is perhaps a singular Instance in the History of Mankind, every other Sect supposing itself in Possession of all Truth, and that those who differ are so far in the Wrong: Like a Man travelling in foggy Weather: Those at some Distance before him on the Road he sees wrapt up in the Fog, as well as those behind him, and also the People in the Fields on each side; but neer him all appears clear.—Tho' in truth he is as much in the Fog as any of them. To avoid this kind of Embarrassment the Quakers have of late Years been gradually declining the public Service in the Assembly & in the Magistracy. Chusing rather to quit their Power than their Principle.

In Order of Time I should have mentioned before, that having in 1742 invented an open Stove, for the better warming of Rooms and at the same time saving Fuel, as the fresh Air admitted was warmed in Entring, I made a Present of the Model to Mr Robert Grace, one of my early Friends, who having an Iron Furnace, found the Casting of the Plates for these Stoves a profitable Thing, as they were growing in Demand. To promote that Demand I wrote and published a Pamphlet Intitled, *An Account of the New-Invented* PENNSYLVANIA FIRE PLACES: *Wherein their Construction & manner of Operation is particularly explained; their Advantages above every other Method of warming Rooms demonstrated; and all Objections that have been raised against the Use of them answered & obviated, &c.* This Pamphlet had a good Effect, Gov.ʳ Thomas was so pleas'd with the Construction of this Stove, as describ'd in it that he offer'd to give me a Patent for the sole Vending of them for a Term of Years; but I declin'd it from a Principle which has ever weigh'd with me on such Occasions, viz. *That as we enjoy great Advantages from the Inventions of others, we should be glad of an Opportunity to serve others by any Invention of ours, and this we should do freely and generously.* An Ironmonger in London, however, after assuming a good deal of my Pamphlet & working it up into his own, and making some small Changes in the Machine, which rather hurt its Operation, got a Patent for it there, and made as I was told a little Fortune by it.—And this is not the only Instance of Patents taken out for my Inventions by others, tho' not always with the same Success:—which I never contested, as having no Desire of profiting by Patents my self, and hating Disputes.—The Use of these Fireplaces in very many Houses both of this and the neighbouring Colonies, has been and is a great Saving of Wood to the Inhabitants.—

Peace being concluded, and the Association Business therefore at an End, I turn'd my Thoughts again to the Affair of establishing an Academy. The first Step I took was to associate in the Design a Number of active Friends, of whom the Junto furnished a good Part; the next was to write and publish a Pamphlet intitled, *Proposals relating to the Education of Youth in Pennsylvania.*—This I distributed among the principal Inhabitants gratis; and as soon as I could suppose their Minds a little prepared by the Perusal of it, I set on foot a Subscription for Opening and Supporting an Academy; it was to be paid in Quotas yearly for Five Years; by so dividing it I judg'd the Subscription might be larger, and I believe it was so, amounting to no less (if I remember right) than Five thousand Pounds.—In the Introduction to these Proposals, I stated their Publication not as an Act of mine, but of some *publick-spirited Gentlemen*; avoiding as much as I could, according to my usual Rule, the presenting myself to the Publick as the Author of any Scheme for their Benefit.—

The Subscribers, to carry the Project into immediate Execution chose out of their Number Twenty-four Trustees, and appointed Mr Francis, then Attorney General, and myself, to draw up Constitutions for the Government of the Academy, which being done and signed, an House was hired, Masters engag'd and the Schools opened I think in the same Year 1749. The Scholars encreasing fast, the House was soon found too small, and we were looking out for a Piece of Ground properly situated, with Intention to build, when

Providence threw into our way a large House ready built, which with a few Alterations might well serve our purpose, this was the Building before mentioned erected by the Hearers of Mr Whitefield, and was obtain'd for us in the following Manner.

It is to be noted, that the Contributions to this Building being made by People of different Sects, Care was taken in the Nomination of Trustees, in whom the Building & Ground was to be vested, that a Predominancy should not be given to any Sect, lest in time that Predominancy might be a means of appropriating the whole to the Use of such Sect, contrary to the original Intention; it was therefore that one of each Sect was appointed, viz. one Church-of-England-man, one Presbyterian, one Baptist, one Moravian, &c. Those in case of Vacancy by Death were to fill it by Election from among the Contributors. The Moravian happen'd not to please his Colleagues, and on his Death, they resolved to have no other of that Sect. The Difficulty then was, how to avoid having two of some other Sect, by means of the new Choice. Several Persons were named and for that Reason not agreed to. At length one mention'd me, with the Observation that I was merely an honest Man, & of no Sect at all; which prevail'd with them to chuse me. The Enthusiasm which existed when the House was built, had long since abated, and its Trustees had not been able to procure fresh Contributions for paying the Ground Rent, and discharging some other Debts the Building had occasion'd, which embarrass'd them greatly. Being now a Member of both Sets of Trustees, that for the Building & that for the Academy, I had good Opportunity of negociating with both, & brought them finally to an Agreement, by which the Trustees for the Building were to cede it to those of the Academy, the latter undertaking to discharge the Debt, to keep forever open in the Building a large Hall for occasional Preachers according to the original Intention, and maintain a Free School for the Instruction of poor Children. Writings were accordingly drawn, and on paying the Debts the Trustees of the Academy were put in Possession of the Premises, and by dividing the great & lofty Hall into Stories, and different Rooms above & below for the several Schools, and purchasing some additional Ground, the whole was soon made fit for our purpose, and the Scholars remov'd into the Building. The Care and Trouble of agreeing with the Workmen, purchasing Materials, and superintending the Work fell upon me, and I went thro' it the more chearfully, as it did not then interfere with my private Business, having the Year before taken a very able, industrious & honest Partner, Mr David Hall, with whose Character I was well acquainted, as he had work'd for me four Years. He took off my Hands all Care of the Printing-Office, paying me punctually my Share of the Profits. This Partnership continued Eighteen Years, successfully for us both.—

The Trustees of the Academy after a while were incorporated by a Charter from the Governor; their Funds were increas'd by Contributions in Britain, and Grants of Land from the Proprietaries, to which the Assembly has since made considerable Addition, and thus was established the present University of Philadelphia. I have been continued one of its Trustees from the Beginning, now near forty Years, and have had the very great Pleasure of seeing a Number of the Youth who have receiv'd their Education in it, distinguish'd by their improv'd Abilities, serviceable in public Stations, and Ornaments to their Country.

When I disengag'd myself as above mentioned from private Business, I flatter'd myself that, by the sufficient tho' moderate Fortune I had acquir'd, I had secur'd Leisure during the rest of my Life, for Philosophical Studies and Amusements; I purchas'd all Dr Spence's Apparatus, who had come from England to lecture here; and I proceeded in my Electrical Experiments with great Alacrity; but the Publick now considering me as a Man of Leisure, laid hold of me for their Purposes; every Part of our Civil Government, and almost at the same time, imposing some Duty upon me. The Governor put me into the Commission of the Peace; the Corporation of the City chose me of the Common Council, and soon after an Alderman; and the Citizens at large chose me a Burgess to represent them in Assembly. This latter Station was the more agreable to me, as I was at length tired with sitting there to hear Debates in which as Clerk I could take no part, and which were often so unentertaining, that I was induc'd to amuse myself with making magic Squares, or Circles, or any

thing to avoid Weariness. And I conceiv'd my becoming a
Member would enlarge my Power of doing Good. I would
not however insinuate that my Ambition was not flatter'd by
all these Promotions. It certainly was. For considering my
low Beginning they were great Things to me. And they were
still more pleasing, as being so many spontaneous Testimonies
of the public's good Opinion, and by me entirely unsolicited.

The Office of Justice of the Peace I try'd a little, by attending a few Courts, and sitting on the Bench to hear Causes.
But finding that more Knowledge of the Common Law than
I possess'd, was necessary to act in that Station with Credit, I
gradually withdrew from it, excusing myself by my being
oblig'd to attend the higher Dutys of a Legislator in the
Assembly. My Election to this Trust was repeated every Year
for Ten Years, without my ever asking any Elector for his
Vote, or signifying either directly or indirectly any Desire
of being chosen.—On taking my Seat in the House, my Son
was appointed their Clerk.

The Year following, a Treaty being to be held with the Indians at Carlisle, the Governor sent a Message to the House,
proposing that they should nominate some of their Members
to be join'd with some Members of Council as Commissioners for that purpose. The House nam'd the Speaker (Mr Norris) and my self; and being commission'd we went to Carlisle,
and met the Indians accordingly.—As those People are extreamly apt to get drunk, and when so are very quarrelsome
& disorderly, we strictly forbad the selling any Liquor to
them; and when they complain'd of this Restriction, we told
them that if they would continue sober during the Treaty, we
would give them Plenty of Rum when Business was over.
They promis'd this; and they kept their Promise—because
they could get no Liquor—and the Treaty was conducted
very orderly, and concluded to mutual Satisfaction. They then
claim'd and receiv'd the Rum. This was in the Afternoon.
They were near 100 Men, Women & Children, and were
lodg'd in temporary Cabins built in the Form of a Square
just without the Town. In the Evening, hearing a great
Noise among them, the Commission.rs walk'd out to see
what was the Matter. We found they had made a great Bonfire in the Middle of the Square. They were all drunk Men

and Women, quarrelling and fighting. Their dark-colour'd
Bodies, half naked, seen only by the gloomy Light of the
Bonfire, running after and beating one another with Fire-
brands, accompanied by their horrid Yellings, form'd a Scene
the most resembling our Ideas of Hell that could well be imagin'd. There was no appeasing the Tumult, and we retired
to our Lodging. At Midnight a Number of them came thun-
dering at our Door, demanding more Rum; of which we
took no Notice. The next Day, sensible they had misbehav'd
in giving us that Disturbance, they sent three of their old
Counsellors to make their Apology. The Orator acknowledg'd the Fault, but laid it upon the Rum; and then endeavour'd to excuse the Rum, by saying, *"The great Spirit who
made all things made every thing for some Use, and whatever
Use he design'd any thing for, that Use it should always be put
to; Now, when he made Rum, he said,* LET THIS BE FOR IN-
DIANS TO GET DRUNK WITH. *And it must be so."*—And indeed if it be the Design of Providence to extirpate these
Savages in order to make room for Cultivators of the Earth,
it seems not improbable that Rum may be the appointed
Means. It has already annihilated all the Tribes who formerly
inhabited the Seacoast.—

In 1751. Dr Thomas Bond, a particular Friend of mine, conceiv'd the Idea of establishing a Hospital in Philadelphia for
the Reception and Cure of poor sick Persons, whether Inhabitants of the Province or Strangers. A very beneficent Design,
which has been ascrib'd to me, but was originally his. He was
zealous & active in endeavouring to procure Subscriptions for
it; but the Proposal being a Novelty in America, and at first
not well understood, he met with small Success. At length he
came to me, with the Compliment that he found there was
no such thing as carrying a public Spirited Project through,
without my being concern'd in it; "for, says he, I am often
ask'd by those to whom I propose Subscribing, Have you
consulted Franklin upon this Business? and what does he
think of it?—And when I tell them that I have not, (supposing it rather out of your Line,) they do not subscribe, but say
they will consider of it." I enquir'd into the Nature, & probable Utility of his Scheme, and receiving from him a very
satisfactory Explanation, I not only subscrib'd to it myself,

but engag'd heartily in the Design of Procuring Subscriptions from others. Previous however to the Solicitation, I endeavoured to prepare the Minds of the People by writing on the Subject in the Newspapers, which was my usual Custom in such Cases, but which he had omitted. The Subscriptions afterwards were more free and generous, but beginning to flag, I saw they would be insufficient without some Assistance from the Assembly, and therefore propos'd to petition for it, which was done. The Country Members did not at first relish the Project. They objected that it could only be serviceable to the City, and therefore the Citizens should alone be at the Expence of it; and they doubted whether the Citizens themselves generally approv'd of it: My Allegation on the contrary, that it met with such Approbation as to leave no doubt of our being able to raise 2000£ by voluntary Donations, they considered as a most extravagant Supposition, and utterly impossible. On this I form'd my Plan; and asking Leave to bring in a Bill, for incorporating the Contributors, according to the Prayers of their Petition, and granting them a blank Sum of Money, which Leave was obtain'd chiefly on the Consideration that the House could throw the Bill out if they did not like it, I drew it so as to make the important Clause a conditional One, viz. "And be it enacted by the Authority aforesaid That when the said Contributors shall have met and chosen their Managers and Treasurer, *and shall have raised by their Contributions a Capital Stock of 2000£ Value*, (the yearly Interest of which is to be applied to the Accommodating of the Sick Poor in the said Hospital, free of Charge for Diet, Attendance, Advice and Medicines) and *shall make the same appear to the Satisfaction of the Speaker of the Assembly* for the time being; that *then* it shall and may be lawful for the said Speaker, and he is hereby required to sign an Order on the Provincial Treasurer for the Payment of Two Thousand Pounds in two yearly Payments, to the Treasurer of the said Hospital, to be applied to the Founding, Building and Finishing of the same."—This Condition carried the Bill through; for the Members who had oppos'd the Grant, and now conceiv'd they might have the Credit of being charitable without the Expence, agreed to its Passage; And then in soliciting Subscriptions among the People we urg'd the conditional

Promise of the Law as an additional Motive to give, since every Man's Donation would be doubled. Thus the Clause work'd both ways. The Subscriptions accordingly soon exceeded the requisite Sum, and we claim'd and receiv'd the Public Gift, which enabled us to carry the Design into Execution. A convenient and handsome Building was soon erected, the Institution has by constant Experience been found useful, and flourishes to this Day.—And I do not remember any of my political Maneuvres, the Success of which gave me at the time more Pleasure. Or that in after-thinking of it, I more easily excus'd my-self for having made some Use of Cunning.—

It was about this time that another Projector, the Revd Gilbert Tennent, came to me, with a Request that I would assist him in procuring a Subscription for erecting a new Meeting-house. It was to be for the Use of a Congregation he had gathered among the Presbyterians who were originally Disciples of Mr Whitefield. Unwilling to make myself disagreable to my fellow Citizens, by too frequently soliciting their Contributions, I absolutely refus'd. He then desir'd I would furnish him with a List of the Names of Persons I knew by Experience to be generous and public-spirited. I thought it would be unbecoming in me, after their kind Compliance with my Solicitations, to mark them out to be worried by other Beggars, and therefore refus'd also to give such a List.—He then desir'd I would at least give him my Advice. That I will readily do, said I; and, in the first Place, I advise you to apply to all those whom you know will give something; next to those whom you are uncertain whether they will give any thing or not; and show them the List of those who have given: and lastly, do not neglect those who you are sure will give nothing; for in some of them you may be mistaken.—He laugh'd, and thank'd me, and said he would take my Advice. He did so, for he ask'd of *every body*; and he obtain'd a much larger Sum than he expected, with which he erected the capacious and very elegant Meeting-house that stands in Arch street.—

Our City, tho' laid out with a beautifull Regularity, the Streets large, strait, and crossing each other at right Angles, had the Disgrace of suffering those Streets to remain long unpav'd, and in wet Weather the Wheels of heavy Carriages plough'd them into a Quagmire, so that it was difficult to cross them. And in dry Weather the Dust was offensive. I had liv'd near what was call'd the Jersey Market, and saw with Pain the Inhabitants wading in Mud while purchasing their Provisions. A Strip of Ground down the middle of that Market was at length pav'd with Brick, so that being once in the Market they had firm Footing, but were often over Shoes in Dirt to get there.—By talking and writing on the Subject, I was at length instrumental in getting the Street pav'd with Stone between the Market and the brick'd Foot-Pavement that was on each Side next the Houses. This for some time gave an easy Access to the Market, dry-shod. But the rest of the Street not being pav'd, whenever a Carriage came out of the Mud upon this Pavement, it shook off and left its Dirt on it, and it was soon cover'd with Mire, which was not re-mov'd, the City as yet having no Scavengers.—After some Enquiry I found a poor industrious Man, who was willing to undertake keeping the Pavement clean, by sweeping it twice a week & carrying off the Dirt from before all the Neighbours Doors, for the Sum of Sixpence per Month, to be paid by each House. I then wrote and printed a Paper, setting forth the Advantages to the Neighbourhood that might be obtain'd by this small Expence; the greater Ease in keeping our Houses clean, so much Dirt not being brought in by People's Feet; the Benefit to the Shops by more Custom, as Buyers could more easily get at them, and by not having in windy Weather the Dust blown in upon their Goods, &c. &c. I sent one of these Papers to each House, and in a Day or two went round to see who would subscribe an Agreement to pay these Sixpences. It was unanimously sign'd, and for a time well ex-ecuted. All the Inhabitants of the City were delighted with the Cleanliness of the Pavement that surrounded the Market; it being a Convenience to all; and this rais'd a general Desire to have all the Streets paved; & made the People more willing to submit to a Tax for that purpose. After some time I drew a Bill for Paving the City, and brought it into the Assembly. It was just before I went to England in 1757. and did not pass till I was gone, and then with an Alteration in the Mode of Assessment, which I thought not for the better, but with an additional Provision for lighting as well as Paving the Streets, which was a great Improvement.—It was by a private Person, the late Mr John Clifton, his giving a Sample of the Utility of Lamps by placing one at his Door, that the People were first impress'd with the Idea of enlightning all the City. The Honour of this public Benefit has also been ascrib'd to me, but it belongs truly to that Gentleman. I did but follow his Example; and have only some Merit to claim respecting the Form of our Lamps as differing from the Globe Lamps we at first were supply'd with from London. Those we found inconvenient in these respects; they admitted no Air below, the Smoke therefore did not readily go out above, but circulated in the Globe, lodg'd on its Inside, and soon obstructed the Light they were intended to afford; giving, besides, the daily Trouble of wiping them clean: and an accidental Stroke on one of them would demolish it, & render it totally useless. I therefore suggested the composing them of four flat Panes, with a long Funnel above to draw up the Smoke, and Crevices admitting Air below, to facilitate the Ascent of the Smoke. By this means they were kept clean, and did not grow dark in a few Hours as the London Lamps do, but continu'd bright till Morning; and an accidental Stroke would generally break but a single Pane, easily repair'd. I have sometimes wonder'd that the Londoners did not, from the Effect Holes in the Bottom of the Globe Lamps us'd at Vauxhall, have in keeping them clean, learn to have such Holes in their Street Lamps. But those Holes being made for another purpose, viz. to communicate Flame more suddenly to the Wick, by a little Flax hanging down thro' them, the other Use of letting in Air seems not to have been thought of.—And therefore, after the Lamps have been lit a few Hours, the Streets of London are very poorly illuminated.—

The Mention of these Improvements puts me in mind of one I propos'd when in London, to Dr Fothergill, who was among the best Men I have known, and a great Promoter of useful Projects. I had observ'd that the Streets when dry were never swept and the light Dust carried away, but it was suffer'd to accumulate till wet Weather reduc'd it to Mud, and then after lying some Days so deep on the Pavement that there was no Crossing but in Paths kept clean by poor People with Brooms, it was with great Labour rak'd together & thrown up into Carts open above, the Sides of which suffer'd some of the Slush at every jolt on the Pavement to shake out and fall, some times to the Annoyance of Foot-Passengers. The Reason given for not sweeping the dusty Streets was, that the Dust would fly into the Windows of Shops and Houses. An accidental Occurrence had instructed me how much Sweeping might be done in a little Time. I found at my Door in Craven Street one Morning a poor Woman sweeping my Pavement with a birch Broom. She appeared very pale & feeble as just come out of a Fit of Sickness. I ask'd who employ'd her to sweep there. She said, "Nobody; but I am very poor and in Distress, and I sweeps before Gentlefolkeses Doors, and hopes they will give me something." I bid her sweep the whole Street clean and I would give her a Shilling. This was at 9 aClock. At 12 she came for the Shilling. From the Slowness I saw at first in her Working, I could scarce believe that the Work was done so soon, and sent my Servant to examine it, who reported that the whole Street was swept perfectly clean, and all the Dust plac'd in the Gutter which was in the Middle. And the next Rain wash'd it quite away, so that the Pavement & even the Kennel were perfectly clean.— I then judg'd that if that feeble Woman could sweep such a Street in 3 Hours, a strong active Man might have done it in half the time. And here let me remark the Convenience of having but one Gutter in such a narrow Street, running down its Middle, instead of two, one on each Side near the Footway. For Where all the Rain that falls on a Street runs from the Sides and meets in the middle, it forms there a Current strong enough to wash away all the Mud it meets with: But when divided into two Channels, it is often too weak to cleanse either, and only makes the Mud it finds more fluid, so that the Wheels of Carriages and Feet of Horses throw and dash it up on the Foot Pavement which is thereby rendred foul and slippery, and sometimes splash it upon those who are walking.—My Proposal communicated to the good Doctor, was as follows.

"For the more effectual cleaning and keeping clean the Streets of London and Westminster, it is proposed,

"That the several Watchmen be contracted with to have the

Dust swept up in dry Seasons, and the Mud rak'd up at other Times, each in the several Streets & Lanes of his Round.

"That they be furnish'd with Brooms and other proper Instruments for these purposes, to be kept at their respective Stands, ready to furnish the poor People they may employ in the Service.

"That in the dry Summer Months the Dust be all swept up into Heaps at proper Distances, before the Shops and Windows of Houses are usually opened: when the Scavengers with close-covered Carts shall also carry it all away.—

"That the Mud when rak'd up be not left in Heaps to be spread abroad again by the Wheels of Carriages & Trampling of Horses; but that the Scavengers be provided with Bodies of Carts, not plac'd high upon Wheels, but low upon Sliders; with Lattice Bottoms, which being cover'd with Straw, will retain the Mud thrown into them, and permit the Water to drain from it, whereby it will become much lighter, Water making the greatest Part of its Weight. These Bodies of Carts to be plac'd at convenient Distances, and the Mud brought to them in Wheelbarrows, they remaining where plac'd till the Mud is drain'd, and then Horses brought to draw them away."—

I have since had Doubts of the Practicability of the latter Part of this Proposal, on Account of the Narrowness of some Streets, and the Difficulty of placing the Draining Sleds so as not to encumber too much the Passage: But I am still of Opinion that the former, requiring the Dust, to be swept up & carry'd away before the Shops are open, is very practicable in the Summer, when the Days are long. For in walking thro' the Strand and Fleet street one Morning at 7 aClock I observ'd there was not one shop open tho' it had been Day-light & the Sun up above three Hours. The Inhabitants of London chusing voluntarily to live much by Candle Light, and sleep by Sunshine; and yet often complain a little absurdly, of the Duty on Candles and the high Price of Tallow.—

Some may think these trifling Matters not worth minding or relating: But when they consider, that tho' Dust blown into the Eyes of a single Person or into a single Shop on a windy Day, is but of small Importance, yet the great Number of the Instances in a populous City, and its frequent Repetitions give it Weight & Consequence; perhaps they will not censure very severely those who bestow some of Attention to Affairs of this seemingly low Nature. Human Felicity is pro- duc'd not so much by great Pieces of good Fortune that sel- dom happen, as by little Advantages that occur every Day. Thus if you teach a poor young Man to shave himself and keep his Razor in order, you may contribute more to the Happiness of his Life than in giving him a 1000 Guineas. The Money may be soon spent, and the Regret only remaining of having foolishly consum'd it. But in the other Case he escapes the frequent Vexation of waiting for Barbers, & of their sometimes, dirty Fingers, offensive Breaths and dull Razors. He shaves when most convenient to him, and enjoys daily the Pleasure of its being done with a good Instrument.—With these Sentiments I have hazarded the few preceding Pages, hoping they may afford Hints which some time or other may be useful to a City I love, having lived many Years in it very happily; and perhaps to some of our Towns in America.—

Having been for some time employed by the Postmaster General of America, as his Comptroller, in regulating the sev- eral Offices, and bringing the Officers to account, I was upon his Death in 1753 appointed jointly with Mr William Hunter to succeed him by a Commission from the Postmaster Gen- eral in England. The American Office had never hitherto paid any thing to that of Britain. We were to have 600£ a Year between us if we could make that Sum out of the Profits of the Office. To do this, a Variety of Improvements were nec- essary; some of these were inevitably at first expensive; so that in the first four Years the Office became above 900£ in debt to us.—But it soon after began to repay us, and before I was displac'd, by a Freak of the Minister's, of which I shall speak hereafter, we had brought it to yield *three times* as much clear Revenue to the Crown as the Post-Office of Ireland. Since that imprudent Transaction, they have receiv'd from it,—Not one Farthing.—

The Business of the Post-Office occasion'd my taking a Journey this Year to New England, where the College of Cambridge of their own Motion, presented me with the De- gree of Master of Arts. Yale College in Connecticut, had be- fore made me a similar Compliment. Thus without studying in any College I came to partake of their Honours. They were confer'd in Consideration of my Improvements & Discoveries in the electric Branch of Natural Philosophy.—

In 1754, War with France being again apprehended, a Congress of Commissioners from the different Colonies, was by an Order of the Lords of Trade, to be assembled at Albany, there to confer with the Chiefs of the Six Nations, concerning the Means of defending both their Country and ours. Governor Hamilton, having receiv'd this Order, acquainted the House with it, requesting they would furnish proper Presents for the Indians to be given on this Occasion; and naming the Speaker (Mr Norris) and my self, to join Mr Thomas Penn & Mr Secretary Peters, as Commissioners to act for Pennsylvania. The House approv'd the Nomination, and provided the Goods for the Present, tho' they did not much like treating out of the Province, and we met the other Commissioners and met at Albany about the Middle of June. In our Way thither, I projected and drew up a Plan for the Union of all the Colonies, under one Government so far as might be necessary for Defence, and other important general Purposes. As we pass'd thro' New York, I had there shown my Project to Mr James Alexander & Mr Kennedy, two Gentlemen of great Knowledge in public Affairs, and being fortified by their Approbation I ventur'd to lay it before the Congress. It then appear'd that several of the Commissioners had form'd Plans of the same kind. A previous Question was first taken whether a Union should be established, which pass'd in the Affirmative unanimously. A Committee was then appointed. One Member from each Colony, to consider the several Plans and report. Mine happen'd to be prefer'd, and with a few Amendments was accordingly reported. By this Plan, the general Government was to be administred by a President General appointed and supported by the Crown, and a Grand Council to be chosen by the Representatives of the People of the several Colonies met in their respective Assemblies. The Debates upon it in Congress went on daily hand in hand with the Indian Business. Many Objections and Difficulties were started, but at length they were all overcome, and the Plan was unanimously agreed to, and Copies ordered to be transmitted to the Board of Trade and to the Assemblies of the several Provinces. Its Fate was singular. The Assemblies did not adopt it, as they all thought there was too much *Prerogative* in it; and in England it was judg'd to have too much of the *Democratic*: The Board of Trade therefore did not approve of it; nor recommend it for the Approbation of his Majesty; but another Scheme was form'd (suppos'd better to answer the same Purpose) whereby the Governors of the Provinces with some Members of their respective Councils were to meet and order the raising of Troops, building of Forts, &c. &c to draw on the Treasury of Great Britain for the Expence, which was afterwards to be refunded by an Act of Parliament laying a Tax on America. My Plan, with my Reasons in support of it, is to be found among my political Papers that are printed. Being the Winter following in Boston, I had much Conversation with Govr Shirley upon both the Plans. Part of what pass'd between us on the Occasion may also be seen among those Papers.—The different & contrary Reasons of dislike to my Plan, makes me suspect that it was really the true Medium; & I am still of Opinion it would have been happy for both Sides the Water if it had been adopted. The Colonies so united would have been sufficiently strong to have defended themselves; there would then have been no need of Troops from England; of course the subsequent Pretence for Taxing America, and the bloody Contest it occasioned, would have been avoided. But such Mistakes are not new; History is full of the Errors of States & Princes.

> *"Look round the habitable World, how few*
> *Know their own Good, or knowing it pursue."*

Those who govern, having much Business on their hands, do not generally like to take the Trouble of considering and carrying into Execution new Projects. The best public Measures are therefore seldom *adopted from previous Wisdom*, but *forc'd by the Occasion*.

The Governor of Pennsylvania in sending it down to the Assembly, express'd his Approbation of the Plan "as appearing to him to be drawn up with great Clearness & Strength of Judgment, and therefore recommended it as well worthy their closest & most serious Attention." The House however, by the Managem^t of a certain Member, took it up when I happen'd to be absent, which I thought not very fair, and reprobated it without paying any Attention to it at all, to my no small Mortification.

In my Journey to Boston this Year I met at New York with our new Governor, Mr Morris, just arriv'd there from England, with whom I had been before intimately acquainted. He brought a Commission to supersede Mr Hamilton, who, tir'd with the Disputes his Proprietary Instructions subjected him to, had resigned. Mr Morris ask'd me, if I thought he must expect as uncomfortable an Administration. I said, No; you may on the contrary have a very comfortable one, if you will only take care not to enter into any Dispute with the Assembly; "My dear Friend, says he, pleasantly, how can you advise my avoiding Disputes. You know I love Disputing; it is one of my greatest Pleasures: However, to show the Regard I have for your Counsel, I promise you I will if possible avoid them." He had some Reason for loving to dispute, being eloquent, an acute Sophister, and therefore generally successful in argumentative Conversation. He had been brought up to it from a Boy, his Father (as I have heard) accustoming his Children to dispute with one another for his Diversion while sitting at Table after Dinner. But I think the Practice was not wise, for in the Course of my Observation, these disputing, contradicting & confuting People are generally unfortunate in their Affairs. They get Victory sometimes, but they never get Good Will, which would be of more use to them. We parted, he going to Philadelphia, and I to Boston. In returning, I met at New York with the Votes of the Assembly, by which it appear'd that notwithstanding his Promise to me, he and the House were already in high Contention, and it was a continual Battle between them, as long as he retain'd the Government. I had my Share of it; for as soon as I got back to my Seat in the Assembly, I was put on every Committee for answering his Speeches and Messages, and by the Committees always desired to make the Drafts. Our Answers as well as his Messages were often tart, and sometimes indecently abusive. And as he knew I wrote for the Assembly, one might have imagined that when we met we could hardly avoid cutting Throats. But he was so good-natur'd a Man, that no personal Difference between him and me was occasion'd by the Contest, and we often din'd together. One Afternoon in the height of this public Quarrel, we met in the Street. "Franklin, says he, you must go home with me and spend the Evening. I am to have some Company that you will like;" and taking me by the Arm he led me to his House. In gay Conversation over our Wine after Supper he told us Jokingly that he much admir'd the Idea of Sancho Panza, who when it was propos'd to give him a Government, requested it might be a Government of *Blacks*, as then, if he could not agree with his People he might sell them. One of his Friends who sat next me, says, "Franklin, why do you continue to side with these damn'd Quakers? had not you better sell them? the Proprietor would give you a good Price." The Governor, says I, has not yet *black'd* them enough. He had indeed labour'd hard to blacken the Assembly in all his Messages, but they wip'd off his Colouring as fast as he laid it on, and plac'd it in return thick upon his own Face; so that finding he was likely to be negrify'd himself, he as well as Mr Hamilton, grew tir'd of the Contest, and quitted the Government.

These public Quarrels were all at bottom owing to the Proprietaries, our hereditary Governors; who when any Expence was to be incurr'd for the Defence of their Province, with incredible Meanness instructed their Deputies to pass no Act for levying the necessary Taxes, unless their vast Estates were in the same Act expresly excused; and they had even taken Bonds of those Deputies to observe such Instructions. The Assemblies for three Years held out against this Injustice, Tho' constrain'd to bend at last. At length Capt. Denny, who was Governor Morris's Successor, ventur'd to disobey those Instructions; how that was brought about I shall show hereafter.

But I am got forward too fast with my Story; there are still some Transactions to be mentioned that happened during the Administration of Governor Morris.—

War being, in a manner, commenced with France, the Government of Massachusets Bay projected an Attack upon Crown Point, and sent Mr Quincy to Pennsylvania, and Mr Pownall, afterwards Govr Pownall, to N. York to sollicit Assistance. As I was in the Assembly, knew its Temper, & was Mr Quincy's Countryman, he apply'd to me for my Influence & Assistance. I dictated his Address to them which was well receiv'd. They voted an Aid of Ten Thousand Pounds, to be laid out in Provisions. But the Governor refusing his Assent to their Bill, (which included this with other Sums granted for the Use of the Crown) unless a Clause were inserted exempting the Proprietary Estate from bearing any Part of the Tax that would be necessary, the Assembly, tho' very desirous of making their Grant to New England effectual, were at a Loss how to accomplish it. Mr Quincy laboured hard with the Governor to obtain his Assent, but he was obstinate. I then suggested a Method of doing the Business without the Governor, by Orders on the Trustees of the Loan-Office, which by Law the Assembly had the Right of Drawing. There was indeed little or no Money at that time in the Office, and therefor I propos'd that the Orders should be payable in a Year and to bear an Interest of Five percent. With these Orders I suppos'd the Provisions might easily be purchas'd. The Assembly with very little Hesitation adopted the Proposal. The Orders were immediately printed, and I was one of the Committee directed to sign and dispose of them. The Fund for Paying them was the Interest of all the Paper Currency then extant in the Province upon Loan, together with the Revenue arising from the Excise which being known to be more than sufficient, they obtain'd instant Credit, and were not only receiv'd in Payment for the Provisions, but many money'd People who had Cash lying by them, vested it in those Orders, which they found advantageous, as they bore Interest while upon hand, and might on any Occasion be used as Money: So that they were eagerly all bought up, and in a few Weeks none of them were to be seen. Thus this important Affair was by my means compleated, Mr Quincy return'd Thanks to the Assembly in a handsome Memorial, went home highly pleas'd with the Success of his Embassy, and ever after bore for me the most cordial and affectionate Friendship.—

The British Government not chusing to permit the Union of the Colonies, as propos'd at Albany, and to trust that Union with their Defence, lest they should thereby grow too military, and feel their own Strength, Suspicions & Jealousies at this time being entertain'd of them; sent over General Braddock with two Regiments of Regular English Troops for that purpose. He landed at Alexandria in Virginia, and thence march'd to Frederic Town in Maryland, where he halted for Carriages. Our Assembly apprehending, from some Information, that he had conceived violent Prejudices against them, as averse to the Service, wish'd me to wait upon him, not as from them, but as Postmaster General, under the guise of proposing to settle with him the Mode of conducting with most Celerity and Certainty the Dispatches between him and the Governors of the several Provinces, with whom he must necessarily have continual Correspondence, and of which they propos'd to pay the Expence. My Son accompanied me on this Journey. We found the General at Frederic Town, waiting impatiently for the Return of those he had sent thro' the back Parts of Maryland & Virginia to collect Waggons. I staid with him several Days, Din'd with him daily, and had full Opportunity of removing all his Prejudices, by the Information of what the Assembly had before his Arrival actually done and were still willing to do to facilitate his Operations. When I was about to depart, the Returns of Waggons to be obtain'd were brought in, by which it appear'd that they amounted only to twenty-five, and not all of those were in serviceable Condition. The General and all the Officers were surpriz'd, declar'd the Expedition was then at an End, being impossible, and exclaim'd against the Ministers for ignorantly landing them in a Country destitute of the Means of conveying their Stores, Baggage, &c. not less than 150 Waggons being necessary. I happen'd to say, I thought it was pity they had not been landed rather in Pennsylvania, as in that Country almost every Farmer had his Waggon. The General eagerly laid hold of my Words, and said, "Then you, Sir, who are a Man of Interest there, can probably procure them for us; and I beg you will undertake it." I ask'd what Terms were to be offer'd the Owners of the Waggons; and I was desir'd to put on Paper the Terms that appear'd to me necessary. This I did, and they were agreed to, and a Commission and Instructions accordingly prepar'd immediately. What those Terms were will appear in the Advertisement I publish'd as soon as I arriv'd at Lancaster; which being, from the great and sudden

Effect it produc'd, a Piece of some Curiosity, I shall insert at length, as follows.

ADVERTISEMENT.

Lancaster, April 26, 1755.

WHEREAS 150 Waggons, with 4 Horses to each Waggon, and 1500 Saddle or Pack-Horses are wanted for the Service of his Majesty's Forces now about to rendezvous at *Wills's* Creek; and his Excellency General *Braddock* hath been pleased to impower me to contract for the Hire of the same; I hereby give Notice, that I shall attend for that Purpose at *Lancaster* from this Time till next *Wednesday* Evening; and at *York* from next *Thursday* Morning 'till *Friday* Evening; where I shall be ready to agree for Waggons and Teams, or single Horses, on the following Terms, *viz.*

1*st.* That there shall be paid for each Waggon with 4 good Horses and a Driver, *Fifteen Shillings* per *Diem*: And for each able Horse with a Pack-Saddle or other Saddle and Furniture, *Two Shillings* per *Diem*. And for each able Horse without a Saddle, *Eighteen Pence* per *Diem*.

2*dly*, That the Pay commence from the Time of their joining the Forces at *Wills's* Creek (which must be on or before the twentieth of *May* ensuing) and that a reasonable Allowance be made over and above for the Time necessary for their travelling to *Wills's* Creek and home again after their Discharge.

3*dly*, Each Waggon and Team, and every Saddle or Pack Horse is to be valued by indifferent Persons, chosen between me and the Owner, and in Case of the Loss of any Waggon, Team or other Horse in the Service, the Price according to such Valuation, is to be allowed and paid.

4*thly*, Seven Days Pay is to be advanced and paid in hand by me to the Owner of each Waggon and Team, or Horse, at the Time of contracting, if required; and the Remainder to be paid by General *Braddock*, or by the Paymaster of the Army, at the Time of their Discharge, or from time to time as it shall be demanded.

5*thly*, No Drivers of Waggons, or Persons taking care of the hired Horses, are on any Account to be called upon to do the Duty of Soldiers, or be otherwise employ'd than in conducting or taking Care of their Carriages and Horses.

6*thly*, All Oats, Indian Corn or other Forage, that Waggons or Horses bring to the Camp more than is necessary for the Subsistence of the Horses, is to be taken for the Use of the Army, and a reasonable Price paid for it.

Note. My Son *William Franklin*, is impowered to enter into like Contracts with any Person in *Cumberland* County.

B. FRANKLIN.

To the Inhabitants of the Counties of
Lancaster, York, *and* Cumberland.
Friends and Countrymen,

BEING occasionally at the Camp at *Frederic* a few Days since, I found the General and Officers of the Army extreamly exasperated, on Account of their not being supply'd with Horses and Carriages, which had been expected from this Province as most able to furnish them; but thro' the Dissensions between our Governor and Assembly, Money had not been provided nor any Steps taken for that Purpose.

It was proposed to send an armed Force immediately into these Counties, to seize as many of the best Carriages and Horses as should be wanted, and compel as many Persons into the Service as would be necessary to drive and take care of them.

I apprehended that the Progress of a Body of Soldiers thro' these Counties on such an Occasion, especially considering the Temper they are in, and their Resentment against us, would be attended with many and great Inconveniencies to the Inhabitants; and therefore more willingly undertook the Trouble of trying first what might be done by fair and equitable Means.

The People of these back Counties have lately complained to the Assembly that a sufficient Currency was wanting; you have now an Opportunity of receiving and dividing among you a very considerable Sum; for if the Service of this Expedition should continue (as it's more than probable it will) for 120 Days, the Hire of these Waggons and Horses will amount to upwards of *Thirty thousand Pounds*, which will be paid you in Silver and Gold of the King's Money.

The Service will be light and easy, for the Army will scarce march above 12 Miles per Day, and the Waggons and Baggage

Horses, as they carry those Things that are absolutely necessary to the Welfare of the Army, must march with the Army and no faster, and are, for the Army's sake, always plac'd where they can be most secure, whether on a March or in Camp.

If you are really, as I believe you are, good and loyal Subjects to His Majesty, you may now do a most acceptable Service, and make it easy to yourselves; for three or four of such as cannot separately spare from the Business of their Plantations a Waggon and four Horses and a Driver, may do it together, one furnishing the Waggon, another one or two Horses, and another the Driver, and divide the Pay proportionably between you. But if you do not this Service to your King and Country voluntarily, when such good Pay and reasonable Terms are offered you, your Loyalty will be strongly suspected; the King's Business must be done; so many brave Troops, come so far for your Defence, must not stand idle, thro' your backwardness to do what may be reasonably expected from you; Waggons and Horses must be had; violent Measures will probably be used; and you will be to seek for a Recompence where you can find it, and your Case perhaps be little pitied or regarded.

I have no particular Interest in this Affair; as (except the Satisfaction of endeavouring to do Good and prevent Mischief) I shall have only my Labour for my Pains. If this Method of obtaining the Waggons and Horses is not like to succeed, I am oblig'd to send Word to the General in fourteen Days; and I suppose Sir *John St. Clair* the Hussar, with a Body of Soldiers, will immediately enter the Province, for the Purpose aforesaid, of which I shall be sorry to hear, because

I am,   *very sincerely and truly*
              your Friend and Well-wisher,

                                B. FRANKLIN

I receiv'd of the General about 800£ to be disburs'd in Advance-money to the Waggon-Owners &c: but that Sum being insufficient, I advanc'd upwards of 200£ more, and in two Weeks, the 150 Waggons with 259 carrying Horses were on their March for the Camp.—The Advertisement promised Payment according to the Valuation, in case any Waggon or

Horse should be lost. The Owners however, alledging they did not know General Braddock, or what Dependance might be had on his Promise, insisted on my Bond for the Performance, which I accordingly gave them.

While I was at the Camp, supping one Evening with the Officers of Col. Dunbar's Regiment, he represented to me his Concern for the Subalterns, who he said were generally not in Affluence, and could ill afford in this dear Country to lay in the Stores that might be necessary in so long a March thro' a Wilderness where nothing was to be purchas'd. I commisserated their Case, and resolved to endeavour procuring them some Relief. I said nothing however to him of my Intention, but wrote the next Morning to the Committee of Assembly, who had the Disposition of some public Money, warmly recommending the Case of these Officers to their Consideration, and proposing that a Present should be sent them of Necessaries & Refreshments. My Son, who had had some Experience of a Camp Life, and of its Wants, drew up a List for me, which I inclos'd in my Letter. The Committee approv'd, and used such Diligence, that conducted by my Son, the Stores arrived at the Camp as soon as the Waggons. They consisted of 20 Parcels, each containing

6 lb Loaf Sugar
6 lb good Muscovado D°—
1 lb good Green Tea
1 lb good Bohea D°
6 lb good ground Coffee
6 lb Chocolate
1/2 C.wt best white Biscuit
1/2 lb Pepper
1 Quart best white Wine Vinegar
1 Gloucester Cheese
1 Kegg cont.g 20 lb good Butter
2 Doz. old Madeira Wine
2 Gallons Jamaica Spirits
1 Bottle Flour of Mustard
2 well-cur'd Hams
1/2 Doz dry'd Tongues
6 lb Rice
6 lb Raisins.

These 20 Parcels well pack'd were plac'd on as many Horses, each Parcel with the Horse, being intended as a Present for one Officer. They were very thankfully receiv'd, and the Kindness acknowledg'd by Letters to me from the Colonels of both Regiments in the most grateful Terms. The General too was highly satisfied with my Conduct in procuring him the Waggons, &c. and readily paid my Acc^t of Disbursements; thanking me repeatedly and requesting my farther Assistance in sending Provisions after him. I undertook this also, and was busily employ'd in it till we heard of his Defeat, advancing, for the Service, of my own Money, upwards of 1000£ Sterling, of which I sent him an Account. It came to his Hands luckily for me a few Days before the Battle, and he return'd me immediately an Order on the Paymaster for the round Sum of 1000£ leaving the Remainder to the next Account. I consider this Payment as good Luck; having never been able to obtain that Remainder; of which more hereafter.

This General was I think a brave Man, and might probably have made a Figure as a good Officer in some European War. But he had too much self-confidence, too high an Opinion of the Validity of Regular Troops, and too mean a One of both Americans and Indians. George Croghan, our Indian Interpreter, join'd him on his March with 100 of those People, who might have been of great Use to his Army as Guides, Scouts, &c. if he had treated them kindly;—but he slighted & neglected them, and they gradually left him. In Conversation with him one day, he was giving me some Account of his intended Progress. "After taking Fort Du Quesne, says he, I am to proceed to Niagara; and having taken that, to Frontenac, if the Season will allow time; and I suppose it will; for Duquesne can hardly detain me above three or four Days; and then I see nothing that can obstruct my March to Niagara."—Having before revolv'd in my Mind the long Line his Army must make in their March, by a very narrow Road to be cut for them thro' the Woods & Bushes; & also what I had read of a former Defeat of 1500 French who invaded the Iroquois Country, I had conceiv'd some Doubts,— & some Fears for the Event of the Campaign. But I ventur'd only to say, To be sure, Sir, if you arrive well before Duquesne, with these fine Troops so well provided with Artillery, that Place, not yet compleatly fortified, and as we hear with no very strong Garrison, can probably make but a short Resistance. The only Danger I apprehend of Obstruction to your March, is from Ambuscades of Indians, who by constant Practice are dextrous in laying & executing them. And the slender Line near four Miles long, which your Army must make, may expose it to be attack'd by Surprize in its Flanks, and to be cut like a Thread into several Pieces, which from their Distance cannot come up in time to support each other. He smil'd at my Ignorance, & reply'd, "These Savages may indeed be a formidable Enemy to your raw American Militia; but, upon the King's regular & disciplin'd Troops, Sir, it is impossible they should make any Impression." I was conscious of an Impropriety in my Disputing with a military Man in Matters of his Profession, and said no more.—The Enemy however did not take the Advantage of his Army which I apprehended its long Line of March expos'd it to, but let it advance without Interruption till within 9 Miles of the Place; and then when more in a Body, (for it had just pass'd a River, where the Front had halted till all were come over) & in a more open Part of the Woods than any it had pass'd, attack'd its advanc'd Guard, by a heavy Fire from behind Trees & Bushes; which was the first Intelligence the General had of an Enemy's being near him. This Guard being disordered, the General hurried the Troops up to their Assistance, which was done in great Confusion thro' Waggons, Baggage and Cattle; and presently the Fire came upon their Flank; the Officers being on Horseback were more easily distinguish'd, pick'd out as Marks, and fell very fast; and the Soldiers were crowded together in a Huddle, having or hearing no Orders, and standing to be shot at till two thirds of them were killed, and then being seiz'd with a Pannick the whole fled with Precipitation. The Waggoners took each a Horse out of his Team, and scamper'd; their Example was immediately follow'd by others, so that all the Waggons, Provisions, Artillery and Stores were left to the Enemy. The General being wounded was brought off with Difficulty, his Secretary Mr Shirley was killed by his Side, and out of 86 Officers 63 were killed or wounded, and 714 Men killed out of 1100. These 1100 had been picked Men, from the whole Army, the Rest had been left behind with

Col. Dunbar, who was to follow with the heavier Part of the Stores, Provisions and Baggage. The Flyers, not being pursu'd, arriv'd at Dunbar's Camp, and the Pannick they brought with them instantly seiz'd him and all his People. And tho' he had now above 1000 Men, and the Enemy who had beaten Braddock did not at most exceed 400, Indians and French together; instead of Proceeding and endeavouring to recover some of the lost Honour, he order'd all the Stores Ammunition, &c to be destroy'd, that he might have more Horses to assist his Flight towards the Settlements and less Lumber to remove. He was there met with Requests from the Governor's of Virginia, Maryland and Pennsylvania, that he would post his Troops on the Frontiers so as to afford some Protection to the Inhabitants; but he continu'd his hasty March thro' all the Country, not thinking himself safe till he arriv'd at Philadelphia, where the Inhabitants could protect him. This whole Transaction gave us Americans the first Suspicion that our exalted Ideas of the Prowess of British Regulars had not been well founded.—

In their first March too, from their Landing till they got beyond the Settlements, they had plundered and stript the Inhabitants, totally ruining some poor Families, besides insulting, abusing & confining the People if they remonstrated. —This was enough to put us out of Conceit of such Defenders if we had really wanted any. How different was the Conduct of our French Friends in 1781, who during a March thro' the most inhabited Part of our Country, from Rhodeisland to Virginia, near 700 Miles, occasion'd not the smallest Complaint, for the Loss of a Pig, a Chicken, or even an Apple!

Capt. Orme, who was one of the General's Aid de Camps, and being grievously wounded was brought off with him, and continu'd with him to his Death, which happen'd in a few Days, told me, that he was totally silent, all the first Day, and at Night only said, *Who'd have thought it?* that he was silent again the following Days, only saying at last, *We shall better know how to deal with them another time*; and dy'd a few Minutes after.

The Secretary's Papers with all the General's Orders, Instructions and Correspondence falling into the Enemy's Hands, they selected and translated into French a Number of the Articles, which they printed to prove the hostile Intentions of the British Court before the Declaration of War. Among these I saw some Letters of the General to the Ministry speaking highly of the great Service I had rendred the Army, & recommending me to their Notice. David Hume too, who was some Years after Secretary to Lord Harcourt when Minister in France, and afterwards to Gen! Conway when Secretary of State, told me he had seen among the Papers in that Office Letters from Braddock highly recommending me. But the Expedition having been unfortunate, my Service it seems was not thought of much Value, for those Recommendations were never of any Use to me.—

As to Rewards from himself, I ask'd only one, which was, that he would give Orders to his Officers not to enlist any more of our bought Servants, and that he would discharge such as had been already enlisted. This he readily granted, and several were accordingly return'd to their Masters on my Application.—Dunbar, when the Command devolv'd on him, was not so generous. He Being at Philadelphia on his Retreat, or rather Flight, I apply'd to him for the Discharge of the Servants of three poor Farmers of Lancaster County that he had inlisted, reminding him of the late General's Orders on that head. He promis'd me, that if the Masters would come to him at Trenton, where he should be in a few Days on his March to New York, he would there deliver their Men to them. They accordingly were at the Expence & Trouble of going to Trenton,—and there he refus'd to perform his Promise, to their great Loss & Disappointment.—

As soon as the Loss of the Waggons and Horses was generally known, all the Owners came upon me for the Valuation wch I had given Bond to pay. Their Demands gave me a great deal of Trouble, my acquainting them that the Money was ready in the Paymaster's Hands, but that Orders for pay^g it must first be obtained from General Shirley, and my assuring them that I had apply'd to that General by Letter, but he being at a Distance an Answer could not soon be receiv'd, and they must have Patience; all this was not sufficient to satisfy, and some began to sue me. General Shirley at length reliev'd me from this terrible Situation, by appointing Commissioners to examine the Claims and ordering Payment.

They amounted to near twenty Thousand Pound, which to pay would have ruined me.

Before we had the News of this Defeat, the two Doctors Bond came to me with a Subscription Paper, for raising Money to defray the Expence of a grand Fire Work, which it was intended to exhibit at a Rejoicing on receipt of the News of our Taking Fort Duquesne. I looked grave and said, "it would, I thought, be time enough to prepare for the Rejoicing when we knew we should have occasion to rejoice."— They seem'd surpriz'd that I did not immediately comply with their Proposal. "Why, the D——l, says one of them, you surely don't suppose that the Fort will not be taken?" "I don't know that it will not be taken; but I know that the Events of War are subject to great Uncertainty."—I gave them the Reasons of my doubting. The Subscription was dropt, and the Projectors thereby miss'd that Mortification they would have undergone if the Firework had been prepared.—Dr Bond on some other Occasions afterwards said, that he did not like Franklin's forebodings.—

Governor Morris who had continually worried the Assembly wth. Message after Message before the Defeat of Braddock, to beat them into the making of Acts to raise Money for the Defence of the Province without Taxing among others the Proprietary Estates, and had rejected all their Bills for not having such an exempting Clause, now redoubled his Attacks, with more hope of Success, the Danger & Necessity being greater. The Assembly however continu'd firm, believing they had Justice on their side, and that it would be giving up an essential Right, if they suffered the Governor to amend their Money-Bills. In one of the last, indeed, which was for granting 50,000£ his propos'd Amendment was only of a single Word; the Bill express'd that all Estates real and personal were to be taxed, those of the Proprietaries *not* excepted. His Amendment was; For *not* read *only*. A small but very material Alteration!—However, when the News of this Disaster reach'd England, our Friends there whom we had taken care to furnish with all the Assembly's Answers to the Governor's Messages, rais'd a Clamour against the Proprietaries for their Meanness & Injustice in giving their Governor such Instructions, some going so far as to say that by obstructing the

Defence of their Province, they forfeited their Right to it. They were intimidated by this, and sent Orders to their Receiver General to add 5000£ of their Money to whatever Sum might be given by the Assembly, for such Purpose. This being notified to the House, was accepted in Lieu of their Share of a general Tax, and a new Bill was form'd with an exempting Clause which pass'd accordingly. By this Act I was appointed one of the Commissioners for disposing of the Money, 60,000£. I had been active in modelling it, and procuring its Passage: and had at the same time drawn a Bill for establishing and disciplining a voluntary Militia, which I carried thro' the House without much Difficulty, as Care was taken in it, to leave the Quakers at their Liberty. To promote the Association necessary to form the Militia, I wrote a Dialogue,* stating and answering all the Objections I could think of to such a Militia, which was printed & had as I thought great Effect. While the several Companies in the City & Country were forming and learning their Exercise, the Governor prevail'd with me to take Charge of our Northwestern Frontier, which was infested by the Enemy, and provide for the Defence of the Inhabitants by raising Troops, & building a Line of Forts. I undertook this military Business, tho' I did not conceive myself well-qualified for it. He gave me a Commission with full Powers and a Parcel of blank Commissions for Officers to be given to whom I thought fit. I had but little Difficulty in raising Men, having soon 560 under my Command. My Son who had in the preceding War been an Officer in the Army rais'd against Canada, was my Aid de Camp, and of great Use to me. The Indians had burnt Gnadenhut, a Village settled by the Moravians, and massacred the Inhabitants, but the Place was thought a good Situation for one of the Forts. In order to march thither, I assembled the Companies at Bethlehem, the chief Establishment of those People. I was surprized to find it in so good a Posture of Defence. The Destruction of Gnadenhut had made them apprehend Danger. The principal Buildings were defended by a Stockade: They had purchased a Quantity of Arms & Ammunition from New York, and had even plac'd Quantities of small Paving

*This Dialogue and the Militia Act, are in the Gent Magazine for Feb^y & March 1756—

Stones between the Windows of their high Stone Houses, for
their Women to throw down upon the Heads of any Indians
that should attempt to force into them. The armed Bretheren
too, kept Watch, and reliev'd as methodically as in any Garrison Town. In Conversation with Bishop Spangenberg, I mention'd this my Surprize; for knowing they had obtain'd an Act
of Parliament exempting them from military Duties in the
Colonies, I had suppos'd they were conscienciously scrupulous of bearing Arms. He answer'd me, "That it was not one
of their establish'd Principles; but that at the time of their
obtaining that Act, it was thought to be a Principle with
many of their People. On this Occasion, however, they to
their Surprize found it adopted by but a few." It seems they
were either deceiv'd in themselves, or deceiv'd the Parliament.
But Common Sense aided by present Danger, will sometimes
be too strong for whimsicall Opinions.

It was the Beginning of January when we set out upon this
Business of Building Forts. I sent one Detachment towards
the Minisinks, with Instructions to erect one for the Security
of that upper Part of the Country; and another to the lower
Part, with similar Instructions. And I concluded to go myself
with the rest of my Force to Gnadenhut, where a Fort was
tho't more immediately necessary. The Moravians procur'd
me five Waggons for our Tools, Stores, Baggage, &c. Just before we left Bethlehem, Eleven Farmers who had been driven
from their Plantations by the Indians, came to me, requesting
a supply of Fire Arms, that they might go back and fetch off
their Cattle. I gave them each a Gun with suitable Ammunition. We had not march'd many Miles before it began to rain,
and it continu'd raining all Day. There were no Habitations
on the Road, to shelter us, till we arriv'd near Night, at the
House of a German, where and in his Barn we were all hud-
dled together as wet as Water could make us. It was well we
were not attack'd in our March, for Our Arms were of the
most ordinary Sort, and our Men could not keep their Gun-
locks dry. The Indians are dextrous in Contrivances for that
purpose, which we had not. They met that Day the eleven
poor Farmers above-mentioned & kill'd Ten of them. The one
who escap'd inform'd that his & his Companions Guns
would not go off, the Priming being wet with the Rain. The

next Day being fair, we continu'd our March and arriv'd at
the desolated Gnadenhut. There was a Saw Mill near, round
which were left several Piles of Boards, with which we soon
hutted ourselves; an Operation the more necessary at that inclement Season, as we had no Tents. Our first Work was to
bury more effectually the Dead we found there, who had
been half interr'd by the Country People. The next Morning
our Fort was plann'd and mark'd out, the Circumference
measuring 455 feet, which would require as many Palisades to
be made of Trees one with another of a Foot Diameter each.
Our Axes, of which we had 70 were immediately set to work,
to cut down Trees; and our Men being dextrous in the Use
of them, great Dispatch was made. Seeing the Trees fall so
fast, I had the Curiosity to look at my Watch when two Men
began to cut at a Pine. In 6 Minutes they had it upon the
Ground; and I found it of 14 Inches Diameter. Each Pine
made three Palisades of 18 Feet long, pointed at one End.
While these were preparing, our other Men, dug a Trench all
round of three feet deep in which the Palisades were to be
planted, and our Waggons, the Body being taken off, and the
fore and hind Wheels separated by taking out the Pin which
united the two Parts of the Perch, we had 10 Carriages with
two Horses each, to bring the Palisades from the Woods to
the Spot. When they were set up, our Carpenters built a
Stage of Boards all round within, about 6 Feet high, for the
Men to stand on when to fire thro' the Loopholes. We had
one swivel Gun which we mounted on one of the Angles;
and fired it as soon as fix'd, to let the Indians know, if any
were within hearing, that we had such Pieces. And thus our
Fort, (if such a magnificent Name may be given to so miserable a Stockade) was finished in a Week, tho' it rain'd so hard
every other Day that the Men could not work.

This gave me occasion to observe, that when Men are employ'd they are best contented. For on the Days they work'd
they were good-natur'd and chearful; and with the consciousness of having done a good Days work they spent the Evenings jollily; but on the idle Days they were mutinous and
quarrelsome, finding fault with their Pork, the Bread, &c. and
in continual ill-humour: which put me in mind of a Sea-
Captain, whose Rule it was to keep his Men constantly at

Work; and when his Mate once told him that they'had done every thing, and there was nothing farther to employ them about; O, says he, *make them scour the Anchor*.

This kind of Fort, however contemptible, is a sufficient Defence against Indians who have no Cannon. Finding our selves now posted securely, and having a Place to retreat to on Occasion, we ventur'd out in Parties to scour the adjacent Country. We met with no Indians, but we found the Places on the neighbouring Hills where they had lain to watch our Proceedings. There was an Art in their Contrivance of these Places that seems worth mention. It being Winter, a Fire was necessary for them. But a common Fire on the Surface of the Ground would by its Light have discover'd their Position at a Distance. They had therefore dug Holes in the Ground about three feet Diameter, and some what deeper. We saw where they had with their Hatchets cut off the Charcoal from the Sides of burnt Logs lying in the Woods. With these Coals they had made small Fires in the Bottom of the Holes, and we observ'd among the Weeds & Grass the Prints of their Bodies made by their laying all round with their Legs hanging down in the Holes to keep their Feet warm, which with them is an essential Point. This kind of Fire, so manag'd, could not discover them either by its Light, Flame; Sparks or even Smoke. It appear'd that their Number was not great, and it seems they saw we were too many to be attack'd by them with Prospect of Advantage.

We had for our Chaplain a zealous Presbyterian Minister, Mr Beatty, who complain'd to me that the Men did not generally attend his Prayers & Exhortations. When they enlisted, they were promis'd, besides Pay & Provisions, a Gill of Rum a Day, which was punctually serv'd out to them half in the Morning and the other half in the Evening, and I observ'd they were as punctual in attending to receive it. Upon which I said to Mr. Beatty, "It is perhaps below the Dignity of your Profession to act as Steward of the Rum. But if you were to deal it out, and only just after Prayers, you would have them all about you." He lik'd the Thought, undertook the Office, and with the help of a few hands to measure out the Liquor executed it to Satisfaction; and never were Prayers more generally & more punctually attended. So that I thought this

Method preferable to the Punishments inflicted by some military Laws for Non-Attendance on Divine Service.

I had hardly finish'd this Business, and got my Fort well stor'd with Provisions, when I receiv'd a Letter from the Governor, acquainting me that he had called the Assembly, and wish'd my Attendance there, if the Posture of Affairs on the Frontiers was such that my remaining there was no longer necessary. My Friends too of the Assembly pressing me by their Letters to be if possible at the Meeting, and my three intended Forts being now compleated, and the Inhabitants contented to remain on their Farms under that Protection, I resolved to return. The more willingly as a New England Officer, Col. Clapham, experienc'd in Indian War, being on a Visit to our Establishment, consented to accept the Command. I gave him a Commission, and parading the Garrison had it read before them, and introduc'd him to them as an Officer who from his Skill in Military Affairs, was much more fit to command them than myself; and giving them a little Exhortation took my Leave. I was escorted as far as Bethlehem, where I rested a few Days, to recover from the Fatigue I had undergone. The first Night being in a good Bed, I could hardly sleep, it was so different from my hard Lodging on the Floor of our Hut at Gnaden, wrapt only in a Blanket or two.—

While at Bethlehem, I enquir'd a little into the Practices of the Moravians. Some of them had accompanied me, and all were very kind to me. I found they work'd for a common Stock, eat at common Tables, and slept in common Dormitorys, great Numbers together. In the Dormitories I observ'd Loopholes at certain Distances all along just under the Cieling, which I thought judiciously plac'd for Change of Air. I was at their Church, where I was entertain'd with good Musick, the Organ being accompanied with Violins, Hautboys, Flutes, Clarinets, &c. I understood that their Sermons were not usually preached to mix'd Congregations; of Men Women and Children, as is our common Practice; but that they assembled sometimes the married Men, at other times their Wives, then the Young Men, the young Women, and the little Children, each Division by itself. The Sermon I heard was to the latter, who came in and were plac'd in Rows on Benches, the Boys under the Conduct of a young Man their Tutor, and the Girls conducted by a young Woman. The Discourse seem'd well adapted to their Capacities, and was delivered in a pleasing familiar Manner, coaxing them as it were to be good. They behav'd very orderly, but look'd pale and un-healthy, which made me suspect they were kept too much within-doors, or not allow'd sufficient Exercise. I enquir'd concerning the Moravian Marriages, whether the Report was true that they were by Lot? I was told that Lots were us'd only in particular Cases. That generally when a young Man found himself dispos'd to marry, he inform'd the Elders of his Class, who consulted the Elder Ladies that govern'd the young Women. As these Elders of the different Sexes were well acquainted with the Tempers & Dispositions of their re-spective Pupils, they could best judge what Matches were suitable, and their Judgments were generally acquiesc'd in. But if for example it should happen that two or three young Women were found to be *equally* proper for the young Man, the Lot was then recurr'd to. I objected, If the Matches are not made by the mutual Choice of the Parties, some of them may chance to be very unhappy. And so they may, answer'd my Informer, if you let the Parties chuse for themselves.—Which indeed I could not deny.

Being return'd to Philadelphia, I found the Association went on swimmingly, the Inhabitants that were not Quakers having pretty generally come into it, form'd themselves into Companies, and chosen their Captains, Lieutenants and En-signs according to the new Law. Dr B. visited me, and gave me an Account of the Pains he had taken to spread a general good Liking to the Law, and ascrib'd much to those En-deavours. I had had the Vanity to ascribe all to my Dialogue; However, not knowing but that he might be in the right, I let him enjoy his Opinion, which I take to be generally the best way in such Cases.—The Officers meeting chose me to be Colonel of the Regiment;—which I this time accepted. I forget how many Companies we had, but We paraded about 1200 well-looking Men, with a Company of Artillery who had been furnish'd with 6 brass Field Pieces, which they had become so expert in the Use of as to fire twelve times in a Minute. The first Time I review'd my Regiment, they accompanied me to my House, and would salute me with some Rounds fired before my Door, which shook down and broke several Glasses of my Electrical Apparatus. And my new Honour prov'd not much less brittle; for all our Commissions were soon after broke by a Repeal of the Law in England.—

During the short time of my Colonelship, being about to set out on a Journey to Virginia, the Officers of my Regiment took it into their heads that it would be proper for them to escort me out of town as far as the Lower Ferry. Just as I was getting on Horseback, they came to my door, between 30 & 40, mounted, and all in their Uniforms. I had not been previously acquainted with the Project, or I should have prevented it, being naturally averse to the assuming of State on any Occasion, & I was a good deal chagrin'd at their Appearance, as I could not avoid their accompanying me. What made it worse, was, that as soon as we began to move, they drew their Swords, and rode with them naked all the way. Somebody wrote an Account of this to our Proprietor, and it gave him great Offence. No such Honour had been paid him when in the Province; nor to any of his Governors; and he said it was only proper to Princes of the Blood Royal; which may be true for aught I know, who was, and still am, ignorant of the Etiquette, in such Cases. This silly Affair, however greatly increas'd his Rancour against me, which was before considerable, not a little, on account of my Conduct in the Assembly, respecting the Exemption of his Estate from Taxation, which I had always oppos'd very warmly, & not without severe Reflections on his Meanness & Injustice in contending for it. He accus'd me to the Ministry as being the great Obstacle to the King's Service, preventing by my Influence in the House the proper Forming of the Bills for raising Money; and he instanc'd this Parade with my Officers as a Proof of my having an Intention to take the Government of the Province out of his Hands by Force. He also apply'd to Sir Everard Fauckener, then Post Master General, to deprive me of my Office. But this had no other Effect, than to procure from Sir Everard a gentle Admonition.

Notwithstanding the continual Wrangle between the Governor and the House, in which I as a Member had so large a

Share, there still subsisted a civil Intercourse between that Gentleman & myself, and we never had any personal Difference. I have sometimes since thought that his little or no Resentment against me for the Answers it was known I drew up to his Messages, might be the Effect of professional Habit, and that, being bred a Lawyer, he might consider us both as merely Advocates for contending Clients in a Suit, he for the Proprietaries & I for the Assembly, He would therefore sometimes call in a friendly way to advise with me on difficult Points, and sometimes, tho' not often, take my Advice. We acted in Concert to supply Braddock's Army with Provisions, and When the shocking News arriv'd of his Defeat, the Govern.ʳ sent in haste for me, to consult with him on Measures for preventing the Desertion of the back Counties. I forget now the Advice I gave, but I think it was, that Dunbar should be written to and prevail'd with if possible to post his Troops on the Frontiers for their Protection, till by Reinforcements from the Colonies he might be able to proceed on the Expedition.—And after my Return from the Frontier, he would have had me undertake the Conduct of such an Expedition with Provincial Troops, for the Reduction of Fort Duquesne, Dunbar & his Men being otherwise employ'd; and he propos'd to commission me as General. I had not so good an Opinion of my military Abilities as he profess'd to have; and I believe his Professions must have exceeded his real Sentiments: but probably he might think that my Popularity would facilitate the Raising of the Men, and my Influence in Assembly the Grant of Money to pay them;—and that perhaps without taxing the Proprietary Estate. Finding me not so forward to engage as he expected, the Project was dropt: and he soon after left the Government, being superseded by Capt. Denny.—

Before I proceed in relating the Part I had in public Affairs under this new Governor's Administration, it may not be amiss here to give some Account of the Rise & Progress of my Philosophical Reputation.—

In 1746 being at Boston, I met there with a Dr Spence, who was lately arrived from Scotland, and show'd me some electric Experiments. They were imperfectly perform'd, as he was not very expert; but being on a Subject quite new to me, they equally surpriz'd and pleas'd me. Soon after my Return to Philadelphia, our Library Company receiv'd from Mr Peter Colinson, F.R.S. of London a Present of a Glass Tube, with some Account of the Use of it in making such Experiments. I eagerly seiz'd the Opportunity of repeating what I had seen at Boston, and by much Practice acquir'd great Readiness in performing those also which we had an Account of from England, adding a Number of new Ones.—I say much Practice, for my House was continually full for some time, with People who came to see these new Wonders. To divide a little this Incumbrance among my Friends, I caused a Number of similar Tubes to be blown at our Glass-House, with which they furnish'd themselves, so that we had at length several Performers. Among these the principal was Mr Kinnersley, an ingenious Neighbour, who being out of Business, I encouraged to undertake showing the Experiments for Money, and drew up for him two Lectures, in which the Experiments were rang'd in such Order and accompanied with Explanations, in such Method, as that the foregoing should assist in Comprehending the following. He procur'd an elegant Apparatus for the purpose, in which all the little Machines that I had roughly made for myself, were nicely form'd by Instrument-makers. His Lectures were well attended and gave great Satisfaction; and after some time he went thro' the Colonies exhibiting them in every capital Town, and pick'd up some Money. In the West India Islands indeed it was with Difficulty the Experim.^{ts} could be made, from the general Moisture of the Air.

Oblig'd as we were to Mr Colinson for his Present of the Tube, &c. I thought it right he should be inform'd of our Success in using it, and wrote him several Letters containing Accounts of our Experiments. He got them read in the Royal Society, where they were not at first thought worth so much Notice as to be printed in their Transactions. One Paper which I wrote for Mr. Kinnersley, on the Sameness of Lightning with Electricity, I sent to Dr. Mitchel, an Acquaintance of mine, and one of the Members also of that Society; who wrote me word that it had been read but was laught at by the Connoisseurs: The Papers however being shown to Dr Fothergill, he thought them of too much value to be stifled, and advis'd the Printing of them. Mr Collinson then gave them to *Cave* for publication in his Gentleman's Magazine; but he chose to print them separately in a Pamphlet, and Dr Fothergill wrote the Preface. *Cave* it seems judg'd rightly for his Profit; for by the Additions that arriv'd afterwards they swell'd to a Quarto Volume, which has had five Editions, and cost him nothing for Copy-money.

It was however some time before those Papers were much taken Notice of in England. A Copy of them happening to fall into the Hands of the Count de Buffon, a Philosopher deservedly of great Reputation in France, and indeed all over Europe he prevail'd with M. Dalibard to translate them into French; and they were printed at Paris. The Publication offended the Abbé Nollet, Preceptor in Natural Philosophy to the Royal Family, and an able Experimenter, who had form'd and publish'd a Theory of Electricity, which then had the general Vogue. He could not at first believe that such a Work came from America, & said it must have been fabricated by his Enemies at Paris, to decry his System. Afterwards having been assur'd that there really existed such a Person as Franklin of Philadelphia, which he had doubted, he wrote and published a Volume of Letters, chiefly address'd to me, defending his Theory, & denying the Verity of my Experiments and of the Positions deduc'd from them. I once purpos'd answering the Abbé, and actually began the Answer. But on Consideration that my Writings contain'd only a Description of Experiments, which any one might repeat & verify, and if not to be verify'd could not be defended; or of Observations, offer'd as Conjectures, & not deliverd dogmatically, therefore not laying me under any Obligation to defend them; and reflecting that a Dispute between two Persons writing in different Languages might be lengthend greatly by mis-translations, and thence misconceptions of one anothers Meaning, much of one of the Abbe's Letters being founded on an Error in the Translation; I concluded to let my Papers shift for themselves; believing it was better to spend what time I could spare from public Business in making new Experiments, than in Disputing about those already made. I therefore never answer'd M. Nollet; and the Event gave me no Cause to repent my Silence; for my friend M. le Roy of the Royal Academy of Sciences took up my Cause & refuted him, my Book was translated into the Italian, German and Latin Languages, and the Doctrine it contain'd was by degrees universally adopted by the Philosophers of Europe in preference to that of the Abbé, so that he liv'd to see himself the last of his Sect: except Mr B—— his Eleve & immediate Disciple.

What gave my Book the more sudden and general Celebrity, was the Success of one of its propos'd Experiments, made by Messrs Dalibard & Delor, at Marly; for drawing Lightning from the Clouds. This engag'd the public Attention every where. M. Delor, who had an Apparatus for experimental Philosophy, and lectur'd in that Branch of Science, undertook to repeat what he call'd the *Philadelphia Experiments*, and after they were performed before the King & Court, all the Curious of Paris flock'd to see them. I will not swell this Narrative with an Account of that capital Experiment, nor of the infinite Pleasure I receiv'd in the Success of a similar one I made soon after with a Kite at Philadelphia, as both are to be found in the Histories of Electricity.—Dr Wright, an English Physician then at Paris, wrote to a Friend who was of the Royal Society an Account of the high Esteem my Experiments were in among the Learned abroad, and of their Wonder that my Writings had been so little noticed in England. The Society on this resum'd the Consideration of the Letters that had been read to them, and the celebrated Dr Watson drew up a summary Acc^t of them, & of all I had afterwards sent to England on the Subject, which he accompanied with some Praise of the Writer. This Summary was then printed in their Transactions: And some Members of the Society in London, particularly the very ingenious Mr Canton, having verified the Experiment of procuring Lightnin from the Clouds by a Pointed Rod, and acquainting them with the Success, they soon made me more than Amends for the Slight with which they had before treated me. Without my having made any Application for that Honour, they chose me a Member, and voted that I should be excus'd the customary Payments, which would have amounted to twenty-five Guineas, and ever since have given me their Transactions gratis.—They also presented me with the Gold Medal of Sir Godfrey Copley for the Year 1753, the Delivery of which was accompanied by a very handsome Speech of the President Lord Macclesfield, wherein I was highly honoured.—

Our new Governor, Capt. Denny, brought over for me the before mentioned Medal from the Royal Society, which he presented to me at an Entertainment given him by the City. He accompanied it with very polite Expressions of his Esteem for me, having, as he said been long acquainted with my Character. After Dinner, when the Company as was customary at that time, were engag'd in Drinking, he took me aside into another Room, and acquainted me that he had been advis'd by his Friends in England to cultivate a Friendship with me, as one who was capable of giving him the best Advice, & of contributing most effectually to the making his Administration easy. That he therefore desired of all things to have a good Understanding with me; and he begg'd me to be assur'd of his Readiness on all Occasions to render me every Service that might be in his Power. He said much to me also of the Proprietor's good Dispositions towards the Province, and of the Advantage it might be to us all, and to me in particular, if the Opposition that had been so long continu'd to his Measures, were dropt, and Harmony restor'd between him and the People, in effecting which it was thought no one could be more serviceable than my self, and I might depend on adequate Acknowledgements & Recompences, &c. &c. The Drinkers finding we did not return immediately to the Table, sent us a Decanter of Madeira, which the Governor made liberal Use of, and in proportion became more profuse of his Solicitations and Promises. My Answers were to this purpose, that my Circumstances, Thanks to God, were such as to make Proprietary Favours unnecessary to me; and that being a Member of the Assembly I could not possibly accept of any; that however I had no personal Enmity to the Proprietary, and that whenever the public Measures he propos'd should appear to be for the Good of the People, no one should espouse and forward them more zealously than myself, my past Opposition having been founded on this, that the Measures which had been urg'd were evidently intended to serve the Proprietary Interest with great Prejudice to that of the People. That I was much obliged to him (the Governor) for his Professions of Regard to me, and that he might rely on every thing in my Power to make his Administration as easy to him as possible, hoping at the same time that he had not brought with him the same unfortunate Instructions his Predecessor had been hamper'd with. On this he did not then explain himself. But when he afterwards came to do Business with the Assembly they appear'd again, the Disputes were renewed, and I was as active as ever in the Opposition, being the Penman first of the Request to have a Communication of the Instructions, and then of the Remarks upon them, which may be found in the Votes of the Time, and in the Historical Review I afterwards publish'd; but between us personally no Enmity arose; we were often together, he was a Man of Letters, had seen much of the World, and was very entertaining & pleasing in Conversation. He gave me the first Information that my old Friend Jaˢ Ralph was still alive, that he was esteem'd one of the best political Writers in England, had been employ'd in the Dispute between Prince Frederic and the King, and had obtain'd a Pension of Three Hundred a Year; that his Reputation was indeed small as a Poet, *Pope* having damn'd his Poetry in the Dunciad, but his Prose was thought as good as any Man's.—

The Assembly finally, finding the Proprietaries obstinately persisted in manacling their Deputies with Instructions inconsistent not only with the Privileges of the People, but with the Service of the Crown, resolv'd to petition the King against them, and appointed me their Agent to go over to England to present & support the Petition. The House had sent up a Bill to the Governor granting a Sum of Sixty Thousand Pounds for the King's Use, (10,000£ of which was subjected to the Orders of the then General Lord Loudon,) which the Governor absolutely refus'd to pass in Compliance with his Instructions. I had agreed with Captain Morris of the Packet at New York for my Passage, and my Stores were put on board, when Lord Loudon arriv'd at Philadelphia, expresly, as he told me to endeavour an Accomodation between the Governor and Assembly, that his Majesty's Service might not be obstructed by their Dissensions: Accordingly he desir'd the Governor & myself to meet him, that he might hear what was to be said on both sides. We met and discuss'd the Business. In behalf of the Assembly I urg'd all the Arguments that may be found in the publick Papers of that Time, which were of my Writing, and are printed with the Minutes of the Assembly & the Governor pleaded his Instructions, the Bond he had given to observ them, and his Ruin if he disobey'd: Yet seem'd not unwilling to hazard himself if Lord Loudon would advise it. This his Lordship did not chuse to do, tho' I once thought I had nearly prevail'd with him to do it; but finally he rather chose to urge the Compliance of the Assembly; and he intreated me to use my Endeavours with them for that purpose; declaring he could spare none of the King's Troops for the Defence of our Frontiers, and that if we did not continue to provide for that Defence ourselves they must remain expos'd to the Enemy. I acquainted the House with what had pass'd, and presenting them with a Set of Resolutions I had drawn up, declaring our Rights, & that we did not relinquish our Claim to those Rights but only suspended the Exercise of them on this Occasion thro' *Force*, against which we protested, they at length agreed to drop that Bill and frame another conformable to the Proprietary Instructions. This of course the Governor pass'd, and I was then at Liberty to proceed on my Voyage: but in the meantime the Pacquet had sail'd with my Sea-Stores, which was some Loss to me, and my only Recompence was his Lordship's Thanks for my Service, all the Credit of obtaining the Accommodation falling to his Share.

He set out for New York before me; and as the Time for dispatching the Pacquet Boats, was in his Disposition, and there were two then remaining there, one of which he said was to sail very soon, I requested to know the precise time, that I might not miss her by any Delay of mine. His Answer was, I have given out that she is to sail on Saturday next, but I may let you know *entre nous*, that if you are there by Monday morning you will be in time, but do not delay longer. By some Accidental Hindrance at a Ferry, it was Monday Noon before I arrived, and I was much afraid she might have sailed as the Wind was fair, but I was soon made easy by the Information that she was still in the Harbour, and would not move till the next Day.—

One would imagine that I was now on the very point of Departing for Europe. I thought so; but I was not then so well acquainted with his Lordship's Character, of which *In-decision* was one of the Strongest Features. I shall give some Instances. It was about the Beginning of April that I came to New York, and I think it was near the End of June before we sail'd. There were then two of the Pacquet Boats which had been long in Port, but were detain'd for the General's Letters, which were always to be ready to-morrow. Another Pacquet arriv'd, and she too was detain'd, and before we sail'd a fourth was expected. Ours was the first to be dispatch'd, as having been there longest. Passengers were engag'd in all, & some extreamly impatient to be gone, and the Merchants uneasy about their Letters, & the Orders they had given for Insur-ance (it being War-time) & for Fall Goods, But their Anxiety avail'd nothing; his Lordships Letters were not ready. And yet whoever waited on him found him always at his Desk, Pen in hand, and concluded he must needs write abundantly. Going my self one Morning to pay my Respects, I found in his Antechamber one Innis, a Messenger of Philadelphia, who had come from thence express, with a Pacquet from Governor Denny for the General. He deliver'd to me some Letters from my Friends there, which occasion'd my enquiring when he was to return & where he lodg'd, that I might send some Letters by him. He told me he was order'd to call to-morrow at nine for the General's Answer to the Governor, and should set off immediately. I put my Letters into his Hands the same Day. A Fortnight after I met him again in the same Place. So you are soon return'd, Innis! *Return'd*; No, I am not *gone* yet.—How so?—I have call'd here by Order every Morning these two Weeks past for his Lordship's Letter, and it is not yet ready.—Is it possible, when he is so great a Writer, for I see him constantly at his Scritore. Yes, says Innis, but he is like St. George on the Signs, *always on horseback, and never rides on*. This Observation of the Messenger was it seems well founded; for when in England, I understood that Mr Pitt gave it as one Reason for Removing this General, and send-ing Amherst & Wolf, *that the Ministers never heard from him, and could not know what he was doing*.

This daily Expectation of Sailing, and all the three Packets going down Sandy hook, to join the Fleet there the Passen-gers, thought it best to be on board, lest by a sudden Order

the Ships should sail, and they be left behind. There if I remember right we were about Six Weeks, consuming our Sea
Stores, and oblig'd to procure more. At length the Fleet
sail'd, the General and all his Army on board, bound to
Lewisburg with Intent to besiege and take that Fortress; all
the Packet-Boats in Company, ordered to attend the General's
Ship, ready to receive his Dispatches when those should be
ready. We were out 5 Days before we got a Letter with Leave
to part; and then our Ship quitted the Fleet and steered for
England. The other two Packets he still detain'd, carry'd them
with him to Halifax, where he staid some time to exercise the
Men in sham Attacks upon sham Forts, then alter'd his Mind
as to besieging Louisburg, and return'd to New York with all
his Troops, together with the two Packets abovementioned
and all their Passengers. During his Absence the French and
Savages had taken Fort George on the Frontier of that Province, and the Savages had massacred many of the Garrison
after Capitulation. I saw afterwards in London, Capt. Bonnell, who commanded one of those Packets. He told me, that
when he had been detain'd a Month, he acquainted his Lordship that his Ship was grown foul, to a degree that must necessarily hinder her fast Sailing, a Point of consequence for a
Packet Boat, and requested an Allowance of Time to heave
her down and clean her Bottom. He was ask'd how long time
that would require. He answer'd Three Days. The General
reply'd, If you can do it in one Day, I give leave; otherwise
not; for you must certainly sail the Day after to-morrow. So
he never obtain'd leave tho' detain'd afterwards from day to
day during full three Months. I saw also in London one of
Bonell's Passengers, who was so enrag'd against his Lordship
for deceiving and detaining him so long at New-York, and
then carrying him to Halifax, and back again, that he swore
he would sue him for Damages. Whether he did or not I
never heard; but as he represented the Injury to his Affairs it
was very considerable. On the whole I then wonder'd much,
how such a Man came to be entrusted with so important a
Business as the Conduct of a great Army: but having since
seen more of the great World, and the means of obtaining &
Motives for giving Places, & Employments my Wonder is diminished. General Shirley, on whom the Command of the

Army devolved upon the Death of Braddock, would in my Opinion if continued in Place, have made a much better Campaign than that of Loudon in 1757, which was frivolous, expensive and disgraceful to our Nation beyond Conception: For tho' Shirley was not a bred Soldier, he was sensible and sagacious in himself, and attentive to good Advice from others, capable of forming judicious Plans, quick and active in carrying them into Execution. Loudon, instead of defending the Colonies with his great Army, left them totally expos'd while he paraded it idly at Halifax, by which means Fort George was lost;—besides he derang'd all our mercantile Operations, & distress'd our Trade by a long Embargo on the Exportation of Provisions, on pretence of keeping Supplies from being obtain'd by the Enemy, but in Reality for beating down their Price in Favour of the Contractors, in whose Profits it was said, perhaps from Suspicion only, he had a Share. And when at length the Embargo was taken off, by neglecting to send Notice of it to Charlestown, the Carolina Fleet was detain'd near three Months longer, whereby their Bottoms were so much damag'd by the Worm, that a great Part of them founder'd in the Passage home. Shirley was I believe sincerely glad of being reliev'd from so burthensom a Charge as the Conduct of an Army must be to a Man unacquainted with military Business. I was at the Entertainment given by the City of New York, to Lord Loudon on his taking upon him the Command. Shirley, tho' thereby superseded, was present also. There was a great Company of Officers, Citizens and Strangers, and some Chairs having been borrowed in the Neighbourhood, there was one among them very low which fell to the Lot of Mr Shirley. Perceiving it as I sat by him, I said, they have given you, Sir, too low a Seat.—No Matter, says he; Mr Franklin; I find *a low Seat* the easiest!

While I was, as aforemention'd, detain'd at New York, I receiv'd all the Accounts of the Provisions, &c. that I had furnish'd to Braddock, some of which Acc^ts could not sooner be obtain'd from the different Persons I had employ'd to assist in the Business. I presented them to Lord Loudon, desiring to be paid the Ballance. He caus'd them to be regularly examin'd by the proper Officer, who, after comparing every Article with its Voucher, certified them to be right, and the

Ballance due, for which his Lordship promis'd to give me an Order on the Paymaster. This, however, was put off from time to time, and tho' I called often for it by Appointment, I did not get it. At length, just before my Departure, he told me he had on better Consideration concluded not to mix his Accounts with those of his Predecessors. And you, says he, when in England, have only to exhibit your Accounts at the Treasury, and you will be paid immediately. I mention'd, but without Effect, the great & unexpected Expence I had been put to by being detain'd so long at N York, as a Reason for my desiring to be presently paid; and On my observing that it was not right I should be put to any farther Trouble or Delay in obtaining the Money I had advanc'd, as I charg'd no Commissions for my Service. O, Sir, says he, you must not think of persuading us that you are no Gainer. We understand better those Affairs, and know that every one concern'd in supplying the Army finds means in the doing it to fill his own Pockets. I assur'd him that was not my Case, and that I had not pocketed a Farthing: but he appear'd clearly not to believe me; and indeed I have since learnt that immense Fortunes are often made in such Employments.—As to my Ballance, I am not paid it to this Day, of which more hereafter.—

Our Captain of the Pacquet had boasted much before we sail'd, of the Swiftness of his Ship. Unfortunately when we came to Sea, she proved the dullest of 96 Sail, to his no small Mortification. After many Conjectures respecting the Cause, when we were near another Ship almost as dull as ours, which however gain'd upon us, the Captain order'd all hands to come aft and stand as near the Ensign Staff as possible. We were, Passengers included, about forty Persons. While we stood there the Ship mended her Pace, and soon left our Neighbour far behind, which prov'd clearly what our Captain suspected, that she was loaded too much by the Head. The Casks of Water it seems had been all plac'd forward. These he therefore order'd to be remov'd farther aft; on which the Ship recover'd her Character, and prov'd the best Sailer in the Fleet. The Captain said she had once gone at the Rate of 13 Knots, which is accounted 13 Miles per hour. We had on board as a Passenger Captain Kennedy of the Navy, who contended that it was impossible, that no Ship ever sailed so fast, and that there must have been some Error in the Division of the Log-Line, or some Mistake in heaving the Log. A Wager ensu'd between the two Captains, to be decided when there should be sufficient Wind. Kennedy thereupon examin'd rigorously the Log-line, and being satisfy'd with that, he determin'd to throw the Log himself. Accordingly some Days after when the Wind blew very fair & fresh, and the Captain of the Packet (Lutwidge) said he believ'd she then went at the Rate of 13 Knots, Kennedy made the Experiment, and own'd his Wager lost. The above Fact I give for the sake of the following Observation. It has been remark'd as an Imperfection in the Art of Ship-building, that it can never be known 'till she is try'd, whether a new Ship will or will not be a good Sailer; for that the Model of a good sailing Ship has been exactly follow'd in a new One, which has prov'd on the contrary remarkably dull. I apprehend this may be partly occasion'd by the different Opinions of Seamen respecting the Modes of lading, rigging & sailing of a Ship. Each has his System. And the same Vessel laden by the Judgment & Orders of one Captain shall sail better or worse than when by the Orders of another. Besides, it scarce ever happens that a Ship is form'd, fitted for the Sea, & sail'd by the same Person. One Man builds the Hull, another riggs her, a third lades and sails her. No one of these has the Advantage of knowing all the Ideas & Experience of the others, & therefore cannot draw just Conclusions from a Combination of the whole. Even in the simple Operation of Sailing when at Sea, I have often observ'd different Judgments in the Officers who commanded the successive Watches, the Wind being the same, One would have the Sails trimm'd sharper or flatter than another, so that they seem'd to have no certain Rule to govern by. Yet I think a Set of Experiments might be instituted, first to determine the most proper Form of the Hull for swift sailing; next the best Dimensions & properest Place for the Masts; then the Form & Quantity of Sail, and their Position as the Winds may be; and lastly the Disposition of her Lading. This is the Age of Experiments; and such a Set accurately made & combin'd would be of great Use. I am therefore persuaded that ere long some ingenious Philosopher will undertake it:—to whom I wish Success—

We were several times chas'd on our Passage, but outsail'd every thing, and in thirty Days had Soundings. We had a good Observation, and the Captain judg'd himself so near our Port, (Falmouth) that if we made a good Run in the Night we might be off the Mouth of that Harbour in the Morning, and by running in the Night might escape the Notice of the Enemy's Privateers, who often cruis'd near the Entrance of the Channel. Accordingly all the Sail was set that we could possibly make, and the Wind being very fresh & fair, we went right before it, & made great Way. The Captain after his Observation, shap'd his Course as he thought so as to pass wide of the Scilly Isles: but it seems there is sometimes a strong Indraught setting up St. George's Channel which deceives Seamen, and caus'd the Loss of Sir Cloudsley Shovel's Squadron. This Indraught was probably the Cause of what happen'd to us. We had a Watchman plac'd in the Bow to whom they often call'd, *Look well out befor'e, there*; and he as often answer'd *Aye, Aye!* But perhaps had his Eyes shut, and was half asleep at the time: they sometimes answering as is said mechanically: For he did not see a Light just before us, which had been hid by the Studding Sails from the Man at Helm & from the rest of the Watch; but by an accidental Yaw of the Ship was discover'd, & occasion'd a great Alarm, we being very near it, the light appearing to me as big as a Cart Wheel. It was Midnight, & Our Captain fast asleep. But Capt. Kennedy jumping upon Deck, & seeing the Danger, ordered the Ship to wear round, all Sails standing. An Operation dangerous to the Masts, but it carried us clear, and we escap'd Shipwreck, for we were running right upon the Rocks on which the Lighthouse was erected. This Deliverance impress'd me strongly with the Utility of Lighthouses, and made me resolve to encourage the building more of them in America, if I should live to return there.—

In the Morning it was found by the Soundings, &c. that we were near our Port, but a thick fog hid the Land from our Sight. About 9 aClock the Fog began to rise, and seem'd to be lifted up from the Water like the Curtain at a Play-house, discovering underneath the Town of Falmouth, the Vessels in its Harbour, & the Fields that surrounded it. A most pleasing Spectacle to those who had been so long without any other

Prospects, than the uniform View of a vacant Ocean!—And it gave us the more Pleasure, as we were now freed from the Anxieties which the State of War occasion'd.—

I set out immediately wth my Son for London, and we only stopt a little by the Way to view Stonehenge on Salisbury Plain, and Lord Pembroke's House and Gardens, with his very curious Antiquities at Wilton.

We arriv'd in London the 27th of July 1757. As soon as I was settled in a Lodging Mr Charles had provided for me, I went to visit Dr Fothergill, to whom I was strongly recommended, and whose Counsel respecting my Proceedings I was advis'd to obtain. He was against an immediate Complaint to Governm^t, and thought the Proprietaries should first be personally apply'd to, who might possibly be induc'd by the Interposition & Persuasion of some private Friends to accommodate Matters amicably. I then waited on my old Friend and Correspondent Mr Peter Collinson, who told me that John Hanbury, the great Virginia Merchant, had requested to be informed when I should arrive, that he might carry me to Lord Granville's, who was then President of the Council, and wish'd to see me as soon as possible. I agreed to go with him the next Morning. Accordingly Mr Hanbury called for me and took me in his Carriage to that Nobleman's, who receiv'd me with great Civility; and after some Questions respecting the present State of Affairs in America, & Discourse thereupon, he said to me, "You Americans have wrong Ideas of the Nature of your Constitution; you contend that the King's Instructions to his Governors are not Laws, and think yourselves at Liberty to regard or disregard them at your own Discretion. But those Instructions are not like the Pocket Instructions given to a Minister going abroad, for regulating his Conduct in some trifling Point of Ceremony. They are first drawn up by Judges learned in the Laws; they are then considered, debated & perhaps amended in Council, after which they are signed by the King. They are then so far as relates to you, the *Law of the Land*; for THE KING IS THE LEGISLATOR OF THE COLONIES." I told his Lordship this was new Doctrine to me. I had always understood from our Charters, that our Laws were to be made by our Assemblies, to be presented indeed to the King for his Royal Assent, but that being once given the King could not repeal or alter them. And as the Assemblies could not make permanent Laws without his Assent, so neither could he make a Law for them without theirs. He assur'd me I was totally mistaken. I did not think so however. And his Lordship's Conversation having a little alarm'd me as to what might be the Sentiments of the Court concerning us, I wrote it down as soon as I return'd to my Lodgings.—I recollected that about 20 Years before, a Clause in a Bill brought into Parliament by the Ministry, had propos'd to make the King's Instructions Laws in the Colonies; but the Clause was thrown out by the Commons, for which we ador'd them as our Friends & Friends of Liberty, till by their Conduct towards us in 1765, it seem'd that they had refus'd that Point of Sovereignty to the King, only that they might reserve it for themselves.

After some Days, Dr Fothergill having spoken to the Proprietaries, they agreed to a Meeting with me at Mr J. Penn's House in Spring Garden. The Conversation at first consisted of mutual Declarations of Disposition to reasonable Accommodation; but I suppose each Party had its own Ideas of what should be meant by *reasonable*. We then went into Consideration of our several Points of Complaint which I enumerated. The Proprietaries justify'd their Conduct as well as they could, and I the Assembly's. We now appeared very wide, and so far from each other in our Opinions, as to discourage all Hope of Agreement. However, it was concluded that I should give them the Heads of our Complaints in Writing, and they promis'd then to consider them.—I did so soon after; but they put the Paper into the Hands of their Solicitor Ferdinando John Paris, who manag'd for them all their Law Business in their great Suit with the neighbouring Proprietary of Maryland, Lord Baltimore, which had subsisted 70 Years, and wrote for them all their Papers & Messages in their Dispute with the Assembly. He was a proud angry Man; and as I had occasionally in the Answers of the Assembly treated his Papers with some Severity, they being really weak in point of Argument, and haughty in Expression, he had conceiv'd a mortal Enmity to me, which discovering itself whenever we met, I declin'd the Proprietary's Proposal that he and I should discuss the Heads of Complaint between our two selves, and refus'd treating with any one but them. They then by his Advice put the Paper into the Hands of the Attorney and Solicitor General for their Opinion and Counsel upon it, where it lay unanswered a Year wanting eight Days, during which time I made frequent Demands of an Answer from the Proprietaries but without obtaining any other than that they had not yet receiv'd the Opinion of the Attorney & Solicitor General: What it was when they did receive it I never learnt, for they did not communicate it to me, but sent a long Message to the Assembly drawn & signed by Paris reciting my Paper, complaining of its want of Formality as a Rudeness on my part, and giving a flimsey Justification of their Conduct, adding that they should be willing to accomodate Matters, if the Assembly would send over *some Person of Candour* to treat with them for that purpose, intimating thereby that I was not such. The want of Formality or Rudeness, was probably my not having address'd the Paper to them with their assum'd Titles of true and absolute Proprietaries of the Province of Pensilvania, wch I omitted as not thinking it necessary in a Paper the Intention of which was only to reduce to a Certainty by writing what in Conversation I had delivered *vivâ voce*. But during this Delay, the Assembly having prevail'd with Govr Denny to pass an Act taxing the Proprietary Estate in common with the Estates of the People, which was the grand Point in Dispute, they omitted answering the Message.

When this Act however came over, the Proprietaries counsell'd by Paris determin'd to oppose its receiving the Royal Assent. Accordingly they petition'd the King in Council, and a Hearing was appointed, in which two Lawyers were employ'd by them against the Act, and two by me in Support of it. They alledg'd that the Act was intended to load the Proprietary Estate in order to spare those of the People, and that if it were suffer'd to continue in force, & the Proprietaries who were in Odium with the People, left to their Mercy in proportioning the Taxes, they would inevitably be ruined. We reply'd that the Act had no such Intention and would have no such Effect. That the Assessors were honest & discreet Men, under an Oath to assess fairly & equitably, & that any Advantage each of them might expect in lessening his own

THE AUTOBIOGRAPHY

Tax by augmenting that of the Proprietaries was too trifling to induce them to perjure themselves. This is the purport of what I remember as urg'd by both Sides, except that we insisted strongly on the mischievous Consequences that must attend a Repeal; for that the Money, 100,000£, being printed and given to the King's Use, expended in his Service, & now spread among the People, the Repeal would strike it dead in their Hands to the Ruin of many, & the total Discouragement of future Grants, and the Selfishness of the Proprietors in soliciting such a general Catastrophe, merely from a groundless Fear of their Estate being taxed too highly, was insisted on in the strongest Terms. On this Lord Mansfield, one of the Council rose, & beckoning to me, took me into the Clerk's Chamber, while the Lawyers were pleading, and ask'd me if I was really of Opinion that no Injury would be done the Proprietary Estate in the Execution of the Act. I said, Certainly. Then says he, you can have little Objection to enter into an Engagement to assure that Point. I answer'd None, at all. He then call'd in Paris, and after som Discourse his Lordship's Proposition was accepted on both Sides; a Paper to the purpose was drawn up by the Clerk of the Council, which I sign'd with Mr Charles, who was also an Agent of the Province for their ordinary Affairs; when Lord Mansfield return'd to the Council Chamber where finally the Law was allowed to pass. Some Changes were however recommended and we also engag'd they should be made by a subsequent Law; but the Assembly did not think them necessary, For one Year's Tax having been levied by the Act before the Order of Council arrived, they appointed a Committee to examine the Percedings of the Assessors, & On this Committee they put several particular Friends of the Proprietaries. After a full Enquiry they unanimously sign'd a Report that they found the Tax had been assess'd with perfect Equity. The Assembly look'd on my entring into the first Part of the Engagement as an essential Service to the Province, since it secur'd the Credit of the Paper Money then spread over all the Country; and they gave me their Thanks in form when I return'd.—But the Proprietaries were enrag'd at Governor Denny for having pass'd the Act, & turn'd him out, with Threats of suing him for Breach of Instructions which he had given Bond to observe. He however having done it the Instance of the General & for his Majesty's Service, and having some powerful Interest at Court, despis'd the Threats, and they were never put in Execution

Chronology

1706   Born January 17 (Jan. 6, 1705, Old Style) in Milk Street, Boston, opposite Old South Church, where he was baptized Benjamin; youngest son and fifteenth child of Josiah Franklin, tallow chandler and soap boiler who had emigrated from England in 1683 to practice his Puritan faith freely. Eleven brothers and sisters are then living: five of Josiah's seven children by first wife (Elizabeth, b. 1678; Samuel, b. 1681; Hannah, b. 1683; Josiah, b. 1685; Anne, b. 1687) and six of seven so far born to second wife, Abiah Folger Franklin, who came from family of Nantucket Puritans (John, b. 1690; Peter, b. 1692; Mary, b. 1694; James, b. 1697; Sarah, b. 1699; Thomas, b. 1703). Two sisters, Lydia (b. 1708) and Jane (b. 1712) followed.

1714–16   Studies at Boston Grammar School (now Boston Latin) 1714–15, but because of expense, is withdrawn by father at end of school year. Father's widowed brother, Benjamin, comes from England in 1715 and joins household. Attends George Brownell's English school, which follows non-classical curriculum, for second and final year of formal study (1715–16).

1716–17   Works with father making candles and soap, but dislikes it; tries cutler's trade briefly, but returns to father's shop. Older brother James returns from London, March 1717, and sets up printing business in Boston.

1718–20   Apprenticed to James. Writes broadside ballads "The Lighthouse Tragedy," 1718, and "On the Taking of *Teach* or Blackbeard the Pirate," 1719 (neither extant). December 1719, James hired to print *The Boston Gazette*, second American newspaper; loses contract August 1, 1720. Franklin borrows books to read—among them Bunyan, Defoe, Locke, Xenophon, various histories and religious polemics, as well as such contemporary freethinkers as Shaftesbury and Collins—and improves writing by imitating London *Spectator* essays of Addison and Steele.

1721   Continues working for James when he starts his own newspaper, lively and irreverent *New-England Courant*, August 7, first American newspaper to feature humorous essays and other literary content.

1722   Becomes vegetarian, saving money for books. April to Oc-
            tober, writes fourteen "Silence Dogood" essays for *Cou-
            rant*, submitting them anonymously, believing his brother
            will not print them otherwise. Manages paper while James
            is imprisoned by Massachusetts Assembly (June 12–July 7)
            for suggesting collusion between pirates and local officials.

1723   After *Courant* satirizes ministers and local officials, James
            is forbidden by Massachusetts Assembly to print news-
            paper without prior censorship. James defies order, prints
            Courant, then goes into hiding, leaving Franklin again in
            charge (Jan. 24–Feb. 12). *Courant* hereafter lists Benjamin
            Franklin as editor. Unhappy with James's "harsh & tyran-
            nical" treatment ("Tho' a Brother, he considered himself
            as my Master"), sails secretly September 25 for New York,
            breaking indentures, but fails to find work. Sails for Phil-
            adelphia October 1, encounters squall and spends thirty
            hours on the water; arrives at Perth Amboy, New Jersey,
            next evening with fever. Walks two days across New Jersey
            to Bordentown, then to Burlington; arrives in Philadel-
            phia October 6 with only a Dutch dollar and a few copper
            pence. Finds work the next day with Samuel Keimer as
            journeyman printer. Takes lodging with John Read (father
            of future wife, Deborah) next door to Keimer's shop in
            Market Street.

1724   Encouraged by Pennsylvania Governor William Keith,
            who has sought his acquaintance, to open his own print-
            ing shop; Keith promises to get him public printing. Re-
            turns to Boston near end of April to ask father for money
            to set up business, but Josiah gives him only small pres-
            ents and good wishes. Visits brother James, who takes
            offense at Franklin's display of prosperity. Calls on Cotton
            Mather. Returns to Philadelphia early June, where Keith
            offers to lend money to set up printing shop and suggests
            he go to London to buy materials and arrange for supplies
            from stationers, booksellers, and printers. John Read dies
            July 3. During the fall, Franklin reveals to Deborah Read
            his plan to sail to London; her mother discourages their
            courtship. Sails for London November 5 with friend James
            Ralph and merchant Thomas Denham, relying on letters
            of credit promised by Governor Keith to obtain printing
            equipment. Arrives Christmas Eve and finds that Keith,
            with "no credit to give," had duped him, and sent no

letters; finds employment before January at Samuel Palmer's printing office. Lodges with Ralph in Little Britain section of inner London, next door to bookseller John Wilcox, from whom he borrows books to continue education.

1725   After setting in type William Wollaston's *The Religion of Nature Delineated*, writes and prints rejoinder, *A Dissertation on Liberty and Necessity, Pleasure and Pain*, arguing against free will. William Lyons, surgeon, admires pamphlet and introduces him to Bernard Mandeville and Henry Pemberton, another physician, who promises introduction to Isaac Newton (never fulfilled). Deborah Read marries John Rogers August 5 in Philadelphia; Rogers abandons her in December and is never heard from again. Franklin leaves Palmer's printing shop in fall for larger establishment of John Watts. Moves to Duke Street.

1726   Sails for home July 21 with Thomas Denham, who has hired him as clerk. Keeps journal of voyage July 22–October 11. Following arrival, works for Denham as shopkeeper and bookkeeper.

1727   Denham falls severely ill (dies July 4, 1728); March and April, Franklin critically ill with pleurisy. Returns to printing with Keimer in June. Forms Junto, self-improvement and mutual aid society for ambitious young men of his acquaintance, which meets on Friday evenings; members include three others from Keimer's shop (Hugh Meredith, Stephen Potts, George Webb) along with Joseph Breintnall, Thomas Godfrey, Nicholas Scull, William Parsons, William Maugridge, Robert Grace, Philip Syng, Hugh Roberts, and William Coleman, young men of various occupations and similar interests.

1728   Prints paper currency with Keimer at Burlington, New Jersey, February to May; quits in June and forms printing partnership with friend Hugh Meredith, whose father loans them money to start. Keimer, learning of Franklin's plans for newspaper, hurries into print, October 1, proposal for paper to be called *The Pennsylvania Gazette* (first issue appears Dec. 24). Observing objectionable conduct of freethinkers among his acquaintance, formulates private creed and worship service (*Articles of Belief and Acts of Religion*) November 20, outlining mixture of deistic and polytheistic tenets.

1729   Begins "Busy-Body" essay series February 4 in *The American Weekly Mercury*, Philadelphia newspaper published by Andrew Bradford, hoping to divert readership from Keimer's *Gazette*. Writes *A Modest Enquiry into the Nature and Necessity of a Paper Currency*, published April 10, first of many proposals to stimulate economy by increasing money supply. Buys failing *Pennsylvania Gazette* from Keimer September 25; October 2 issue is first to bear his name. During next decade, it becomes the most widely read newspaper in colonies. About 1729 or 1730, son William is born, out of wedlock, to an unidentified mother.

1730   Named official printer for Pennsylvania January 30. Borrows money from two friends, William Coleman and Robert Grace, to buy out Meredith, who wants to return to farming. Unable to marry Deborah (Read) Rogers in legal ceremony (because Rogers was not known to have died and Franklin, in any case, didn't want to be liable for his debts), forms common-law union with her, September 1; son William is taken into household. Begins to study French and German.

1731   Joins Freemasons in January, beginning lifelong involvement; June, elected junior warden of St. John's Lodge (the first of many Masonic offices he will hold in America and Europe). Drafts "Instrument of Association" for Library Company of Philadelphia, first American subscription library, July 1. Sponsors his journeyman Thomas Whitemarsh as printing partner in South Carolina, advancing necessary equipment and materials in return for one-third of profits, for six-year term (first of several financial sponsorships that will gradually increase his wealth).

1732   Publishes America's first German-language newspaper, *Philadelphische Zeitung*, May 6; it soon fails. Son Francis Folger Franklin born October 20 (baptized in Christ Church, Sept. 16, 1733). Publishes first *Poor Richard's Almanack* December 19 (continued annually by Franklin until he goes to England in 1757). Occasional attendance at Presbyterian services comes to an end.

1733   Conceives "the bold and arduous Project of arriving at moral Perfection"; July 1, begins keeping ledger, systematically recording personal faults. In fall, visits family in Boston and brother James in Newport, Rhode Island. November, sponsors another journeyman, Louis Timothée, as South Carolina printing partner succeeding Whitemarsh. Studies Italian, Spanish, and Latin.

1734   Elected grand master of Masons of Pennsylvania June 24.

1735   Brother James dies February 4 in Newport. Franklin proposes fire protection society in *Pennsylvania Gazette*. Resumes church attendance during winter and spring to hear sermons of Rev. Samuel Hemphill, who emphasizes practical morals. After Hemphill is denounced by ministerial colleagues as unorthodox in April, Franklin writes pamphlets in his defense; when Hemphill is suspended by Presbyterian Synod in September, leaves congregation permanently, but continues to contribute money. Suffers second pleurisy attack in early summer, with left lung suppurating. Proposes system of paid night watchmen for Philadelphia (adopted in 1752).

1736   Prints New Jersey's paper currency in Burlington, July to September; to hinder forgeries, devises new nature-printing technique (reproducing images of tree leaves). Appointed clerk of Pennsylvania Assembly October 15. Son Francis, age four, dies of smallpox November 21 and is buried in Christ Church burial ground. Organizes Union Fire Company, Philadelphia's first, December 7.

1737   Begins duties as postmaster of Philadelphia October 5. Increasingly bored with Assembly proceedings, amuses himself by contriving mathematical puzzles.

1738   Accused in *American Weekly Mercury* (Feb. 14) of participation in mock Masonic initiation in 1737 which resulted in fatal burning of young apprentice. Denies responsibility in trial testimony and in *Gazette* account.

1739   Befriends evangelist George Whitefield, English Methodist preacher, who arrives in Philadelphia November 2 urging religious revival in addresses to large outdoor crowds.

Franklin solicits subscriptions to print Whitefield's journals and sermons.

1740   *American Weekly Mercury* (Feb. 12) criticizes Franklin for favoring the popular anti-Proprietary party in his reporting. (Proprietors were descendants of Pennsylvania's founder, William Penn, who lived in England and were privileged by charter to appoint and instruct governor of the colony.) Becomes official printer for New Jersey (appointment continues to 1744). Announces in *Gazette* (Nov. 13) forthcoming *General Magazine*; accuses Andrew Bradford and John Webbe of stealing his plan for first American magazine; Franklin's price (9 *d.* per issue) undercuts Bradford's proposed magazine (announced at 12 *s.* per year).

1741   Designs Pennsylvania fireplace (Franklin stove) during winter of 1740–41; early version advertised for sale to the public February 5. Publishes first issue of *The General Magazine and Historical Chronicle* February 16; it fails after six issues.

1742   Sponsors employee James Parker as printing partner in New York. Organizes and publicizes, March 17, a project to sponsor Philadelphia botanist John Bartram's collecting trips.

1743   Publishes *A Proposal for Promoting Useful Knowledge* May 14, founding document of American Philosophical Society (first scientific society in America). Journeys to New England in late spring, meeting Cadwallader Colden in Connecticut and attending Archibald Spencer's lectures on electricity in Boston. Begins business correspondence with William Strahan that will develop into lifelong friendship; encourages David Hall, young journeyman printer in Strahan's London shop, to emigrate to America, suggesting that he will sponsor Hall in another colony. Daughter Sarah ("Sally") born August 31; baptized in Christ Church October 27.

1744   David Hall arrives in Philadelphia, June 20, and lodges with Franklin. Publishes *An Account of the New Invented Pennsylvanian Fire-Places*.

1745   Drafts presentment of the Grand Jury against public houses and other nuisances, January 3. Father dies January 16, aged eighty-seven. Peter Collinson, member of Royal Society of London, sends pamphlet about recent German experiments in electricity to Library Company in April, together with glass tube, stimulating Franklin to begin electrical experimentation. Publishes woodcut of the "Plan of the Town and Harbour of Louisburgh" June 6, first illustrated news event in *The Pennsylvania Gazette*.

1746   "Immersed in electrical experiments" during the summer. Visits New England in fall and winter.

1747   Sends, May 25, first account of electrical experiments to Peter Collinson, who shows it to members of the Royal Society. November, publishes pamphlet *Plain Truth*, containing America's first political cartoon and warning of Pennsylvania's vulnerability to French and Spanish privateer raids on the Delaware River. Organizes voluntary militia for defense.

1748   Refuses position as colonel in militia, January 1, avowing military inexperience, and serves instead as common soldier. Forms printing partnership with David Hall, January 1, placing shop in Hall's hands in return for half the profits, and retires as printer; hereafter devotes himself mainly to scientific research and civic affairs. (Annual income from printing partnerships, real estate investments, and postmastership will amount to almost two thousand pounds in coming years, as much as the salary of Pennsylvania's governor.) Moves to new house away from shop, and acquires first of several black slaves. April, sponsors Thomas Smith, another of his journeymen, as printing partner in Antigua. Elected to Common Council of Philadelphia October 4.

1749   Writes "new Hypothesis for explaining . . . Thundergusts" for Ebenezer Kinnersley, April 29. Kinnersley, lecturing in Annapolis, Maryland, on electricity, first publishes and demonstrates (in miniature) Franklin's lightning rod experiments, May 10. Named Justice of the Peace for Philadelphia, June 30. Appointed provincial grand master of Masons of Pennsylvania, July 10. Writes *Proposals Relating to the Education of Youth in Pensilvania* by October 23, resulting in establishment of Philadelphia Academy, now University of Pennsylvania (formally opens Jan. 7, 1751). November 7, notes similarities between lightning and electricity in his journal of experiments, and calls for experiment to prove their identity.

1750   Has first attack of gout in February. Proposes use of lightning rods to protect houses in March 2 letter to Collinson. July 29, devises experiment involving sentry-box with pointed rod on its roof, to be erected on hilltop or in church steeple, with rod attached to Leyden jar which would collect the electrical charge, and thus prove lightning to be a form of electricity. Revises lightning rod proposal to include provision for grounding. Severely shocked, December 23, while electrocuting a turkey.

1751   Pennsylvania Assembly passes Franklin's innovative bill, providing public funds to match private contributions, to found Pennsylvania Hospital, February 7. Collection of scientific letters, *Experiments and Observations on Electricity*, edited by Dr. John Fothergill, published in London in April. Elected May 9 and takes seat in Pennsylvania Assembly August 13 (reelected annually until 1764); son William succeeds him as clerk. Initiates proposal to merge city's fire companies into insurance company July 26; representatives of different companies meet on September 7 and organize Philadelphia Contributionship. Elected alderman of Philadelphia, October 1.

1752   Pennsylvania Hospital opens February 6. Mother dies in Boston, May 8, aged eighty-four. June, devises and performs kite experiment proving lightning is electrical. August, sponsors nephew Benjamin Mecom as partner in printing office in West Indies. September, equips his house with lightning rod, connecting it to bells that ring when rod is electrified. *Pennsylvania Gazette* of October 19 explains how to perform kite experiment; writes for *Poor Richard* of 1753 instructions for installing lightning rods. Designs a flexible catheter for brother John, who suffers from bladder stone, December 8.

1753   Abbé Nollet publishes *Lettres sur l'Electricité* in January, disputing Franklin's electrical theories. Second set of electrical experiments (*Supplemental Experiments and Observa-*

tions) published in London in March. Sponsors former journeyman Samuel Holland as printing partner in Lancaster, Pennsylvania, June 14. Travels through New England from mid-June to September, receiving honorary Master of Arts degrees from Harvard (July 25) and Yale (Sept. 12). Appointed joint deputy postmaster general of North America August 10, having solicited appointment from England. September 26–October 4, negotiates treaty at Carlisle, Pennsylvania, with Ohio Indians; prints resulting treaty in November. Awarded Copley Medal of Royal Society of London, November 30, for work in electricity.

1754   Disturbed by increasing French pressure along western frontier, devises and prints cartoon of snake cut into sections, over heading "Join or Die," in *Gazette* May 9— America's first symbol of the united colonies. Attends Albany Congress as commissioner from Pennsylvania, June–July; meeting brings together representatives from seven colonies to restore alliance with Iroquois and arrange common defense of frontier against the French. July 2, conference votes to form colonial union; Franklin proposes plan, which is approved July 10 and sent to colonies for ratification. Pennsylvania Assembly rejects Albany Plan August 17, as do other colonies and British government. Third set of electrical experiments (*New Experiments and Observations on Electricity*) published in September in London, along with second edition of first two parts. Writes series of letters to Massachusetts Governor William Shirley in December protesting taxation without representation and claiming American right to self-government.

1755   Sets up postal communications for Major-General Edward Braddock, commander of British forces in North America; confers with Braddock at Frederick, Maryland, April 22–23, undertaking to supply Braddock's forces with wagons for their march against French at Fort Duquesne. Requisitions wagons at Lancaster and York, Pennsylvania, April 26–May 11. Writes biblical hoaxes "A Parable Against Persecution" and "A Parable on Brotherly Love" by summer. August, joins forces with Quaker party to demand that landholdings of Proprietors be taxed, along with other property, to raise money for defense of frontier. Chosen colonel in October by regiment of foot raised in Philadelphia. Assembly passes Franklin's militia bill, November 25, and approves £60,000 for defense, November 27. Travels to frontier to build forts and organize defenses, December 18 to February 5, with son William as aide.

1756   Unanimously elected to membership in Royal Society of London, April 29, and admitted with waiver of customary fees. Pennsylvania Assembly passes Franklin's bill providing night watchmen and street lighting for Philadelphia on March 9. Meets George Washington, March 21, on way to Virginia on post office business. Receives honorary Master's degree from William and Mary College April 20. Elected corresponding member of Royal Society of Arts, September 1. Undertakes military inspection tour to Carlisle, Harris's Ferry, and New York, October 2–14. Along with other commissioners, confers with Delaware Indians at Easton, Pennsylvania, November 5–18.

1757   Accepts nomination by Pennsylvania Assembly to serve as agent to England, to negotiate long-standing dispute with Proprietors, February 3. Meets with Lord Loudoun, commander-in-chief of British forces in America, March 14–22, presenting Assembly's position favoring bill to raise taxes for military supplies. Loudoun persuades Pennsylvania Governor Denny to waive instructions of Proprietors (who refused to have their estates taxed) and pass bill. Travels to New York with son William April 4 en route to England; delayed until June 23 waiting for Loudoun to give permission to sail. While at sea, completes preface for *Poor Richard* for 1758, "Father Abraham's Speech" (later known as "The Way to Wealth"), the last of series of almanacs written by Franklin. Arrives in London July 26 and stays with Peter Collinson; sees Lord Granville, president of Privy Council, who alarms Franklin with his claim that King is supreme legislator of colonies. Takes lodgings on July 30 at No. 7 Craven Street with Mrs. Margaret Stevenson, widow with whom he thereafter makes his home in England. Meets with Proprietors Richard and Thomas Penn in August, giving them list of grievances. Late September to early November, ill with severe cold, headaches, and dizziness. Resumes conferences with Thomas Penn November 14.

1758   Establishes routine of club attendance that lasts throughout years in England. On Mondays often dines at George and Vulture with group of scientists, philanthropists, and explorers, including John Ellicot and, occasionally, Captain James Cook. Thursdays, usually dines with favorite group, Club of Honest Whigs, at St. Paul's Coffeehouse; members include John Canton, Richard Price, Joseph Priestley, James Burgh, William Rose, Andrew Kippis, and, occasionally, James Boswell. Sundays, frequently dines with Sir John Pringle, who gradually displaces printer William Strahan as closest friend in England; Alexander Small and David Hume are often guests. January to May, confers with Penns and defends Pennsylvania at Board of Trade; finally, November 27, Penns concede limited taxation, but they write the next day to Pennsylvania Assembly averring that Franklin lacks candor. Spends week at Cambridge in late May performing evaporation experiments with John Hadley, professor of chemistry. Visits ancestral homes at Ecton and Banbury in July with son William, collecting genealogical information. Invents damper for stoves or chimneys, December 2.

1759   Receives honorary degree of Doctor of Laws in absentia from University of St. Andrews in Scotland, February 12; hereafter referred to as "Dr. Franklin." Reports to Joseph Galloway April 7 that Richard Jackson, Englishman who later served as agent of Pennsylvania Assembly in London and then became friend of America in Parliament, proposed to get him elected to Parliament, "but I am too old to think of changing Countries." Takes extensive tour of northern England and Scotland, August 8–November 2, meeting Adam Smith, William Robertson, and Lord Kames.

1760   Third edition of *Experiments and Observations on Electricity* published (reprinted 1762 and 1764). Writes *The Interest of Great Britain Considered* ("The Canada Pamphlet"), published April 17, arguing economic and strategic importance of Canada to colonies and Britain. Meets Dr. Samuel Johnson on May 1 at the Associates of Dr. Bray, a philanthropic organization (of which Franklin had been elected chairman on March 6) that sponsors charity schools for blacks in Philadelphia, New York, Rhode Island, and Williamsburg, Virginia. Board of Trade rejects seven of nineteen acts passed by Pennsylvania Assembly, including taxes on Penn estates, June 24; August, Franklin appeals to Privy Council, which overrules Board of Trade and allows taxation of Penn estates.

1761   Has emerged as active and influential member of Society of Arts (which mainly sponsors farming methods and introduces new crops), of Royal Society of London (premier scientific society of the day), and of Associates of Dr. Bray. Tours Austrian Netherlands and Dutch Republic with son William and Richard Jackson, August–September. Upon return to England, witnesses coronation of George III September 22.

1762   Receives honorary degree of Doctor of Civil Law from Oxford, April 30. Sends Giambatista Beccaria, Italian scientist who disseminated Franklin's electrical theories, a description on July 13 of recently invented musical instrument, glass armonica, which he had been working on since 1761; Mozart and Beethoven later compose for it. Leaves London in August for Portsmouth to embark for Pennsylvania; arrives in Philadelphia November 1. Son William marries Elizabeth Downes September 4 in London, and is commissioned royal governor of New Jersey September 9.

1763   Tours New Jersey, New York, and New England inspecting post offices June 7 to November 5. Visits charity school sponsored by Associates of Dr. Bray in Philadelphia, and reports December 17 that he has "conceived a higher Opinion of the natural Capacities of the black Race, than I had ever before entertained."

1764   Angered by massacre of friendly Christian Indians in Lancaster County by frontier mob ("Paxton Boys"), drafts bill providing for trial of capital offenses between whites and Indians, January 4; bill arouses intense opposition and Assembly quickly kills it. Publishes *A Narrative of the Late Massacres* January 30, denouncing Paxton Boys; they march on Philadelphia, February 5–8. Franklin organizes defense, then meets with leaders of rioters and persuades them to present grievances and disperse. Writes *Cool Thoughts* (April 12), supporting Assembly's recent resolutions in favor of royal charter. Elected speaker of Assembly, May 26; drafts petition to King for change of government, and signs it as speaker after Assembly adopts it. Massachusetts House of Representatives writes Franklin as speaker urging other colonies to oppose Stamp Act, Parliamentary measure to raise revenue by taxing printed matter in colonies; September 12, Franklin lays proposal before Assembly, which instructs its London agent, Richard Jackson, to oppose passage of proposed Stamp Act, to seek modifications of Sugar Act (enacted April 5), and to argue that only the Pennsylvania legislature has the right to impose taxes in Pennsylvania; Franklin signs instructions. August and September, election campaign for Assembly features vicious attacks on Franklin's character (it is alleged that he favored royal government because he coveted governorship; that he had drawn large income from public monies while Assembly agent in England; that he had been careless with public funds given to his supervision; that William's mother was his maidservant Barbara, and that he had buried her in an unmarked grave; in addition, an old ethnic slur—Franklin had called German immigrants "Palatine Boors" in 1751—was brought up), and he is defeated October 1. His party retains a majority and appoints him October 26 to join Jackson as Assembly's agent in London. Minority members impugn Franklin, who defends his integrity November 5 in *Remarks on a Late Protest*. Leaves Philadelphia November 7; wife, Deborah, again refusing to sail overseas, remains in Philadelphia. Arrives at Isle of Wight December 9; reaches London the next day and takes up residence at old lodgings with Mrs. Stevenson.

1765   With other colonial agents, holds interview February 2 with First Minister George Grenville to protest laying of stamp duties in America. Grenville introduces annual budget in Parliament containing proposal for Stamp Act. Franklin and Thomas Pownall, former colonial governor who favored stronger ties between colonies and Great Britain, meet Grenville February 12 and offer an alternative proposal to raise revenue in America by issuing paper money at interest, but are ignored. Stamp Act passes House of Commons February 27, receives royal assent March 22, and is scheduled to take effect November 1. At Grenville's request, Franklin nominates his friend John Hughes as Pennsylvania stamp distributor, leading to rumors that Franklin actually supports the Stamp Act.

Franklin and Pownall succeed in April in getting Quartering Bill amended to eliminate forcible quartering of British troops in private dwellings in America; amended act passes May 3. Burlesques foolish news reports about America in English newspapers by publishing tall tales, May 3, concluding, "The Grand Leap of the Whale in that Chace up the Fall of Niagara is esteemed by all who have seen it, as one of the finest Spectacles in Nature!" Stamp Act protests spread throughout colonies during summer; in Philadelphia, mobs attack stamp distributors, and Franklin's house is threatened, September 16–17; Deborah arms herself, refusing to flee. Mob is dissuaded by readiness of 800 Franklin supporters to combat them. November 1, Stamp Act fails to go into effect as courts refuse to convene and administration of government in colonies breaks down. Franklin presents Privy Council with Pennsylvania petition for change to royal government, but consideration is postponed. Winter, writes newspaper articles defending the colonies and agitating for repeal of Stamp Act.

1766   Designs anti-Stamp Act cartoon and sends messages during early 1766 on cards bearing design. Partnership with David Hall expires January 21, and Hall buys the shop according to terms of 1748 partnership agreement. Examined by Committee of the Whole of House of Commons February 13 concerning the Stamp Act; Franklin's defense of American position contributes to repeal of act February 22, and establishes him as preeminent representative of American colonies. Travels to Germany with Sir John Pringle, June 15–August 16; elected at Göttingen to Royal Academy of Sciences.

1767   Continues to campaign against Parliamentary taxation of colonies in letters to London newspapers. Charles Townshend, Chancellor of the Exchequer, proposes duties in House of Commons, May 13; passed July 2, they intensify the crisis in the colonies. Franklin and Pringle visit Paris, August 28–October 8, where Horace Walpole calls on them (Sept. 13), and they are presented to Louis XV at Versailles. Daughter Sarah marries Richard Bache, Philadelphia merchant, October 29.

1768   Reviews history of relations between Britain and Ameri-
        can colonies in *Causes of the American Discontents
        before 1768*, January 7. Appointed agent of Georgia
        Assembly April 11 (serves until May 2, 1774). Writes Mary
        Stevenson July 20 using phonetic alphabet of his own de-
        vising. Fall, has maps printed showing the course of the
        Gulf Stream.

1769   Supervises publication of corrected and enlarged fourth
        edition of *Experiments and Observations on Electricity*.
        Elected president of American Philosophical Society in
        Philadelphia January 2, and reelected annually until his
        death. Winter, Deborah Franklin suffers stroke, which im-
        pairs her memory and understanding; her health deterio-
        rates thereafter. Joins organizers of land company to seek
        grants in Ohio Valley from King, hoping to sell parcels to
        settlers. Grandson Benjamin Franklin Bache born August
        12. Appointed agent by New Jersey House of Representa-
        tives, November 8 (serves until March 1775). November
        29, writes Strahan a major statement of American position
        intended for private circulation to Cabinet and selected
        members of Parliament.

1770   Elected agent of Massachusetts House of Representatives
        October 24 (retaining position until leaving England in
        March 1775), making him agent for four colonies (Penn-
        sylvania, Georgia, New Jersey, and Massachusetts).

1771   Presents credentials as Massachusetts agent on January 16
        to Lord Hillsborough, secretary of state for the colonies,
        who refuses to accept them because Franklin had been ap-
        pointed by Assembly without governor's concurrence.
        Elected to Batavian Society of Experimental Science, Rot-
        terdam, June 11. June 17–24, and again July 30–August 13,
        visits Bishop Jonathan Shipley at Twyford, where, on lat-
        ter visit, writes first part of autobiography. Tours Ireland
        and Scotland with Richard Jackson from August 25 to No-
        vember 30; attends opening of Irish Parliament, October
        8; stays with David Hume in Edinburgh, and with Lord
        Kames at Blair-Drummond. At end of trip, visits mother
        and sister of son-in-law Richard Bache at Preston in
        Lancashire, meets Richard for first time, and returns to
        London with him.

1772   After Board of Trade rejects land company plans, April 29, appeals to Privy Council on June 5, which approves the grant on July 1, but territory is never officially conveyed. Has come to believe that slavery is inherently evil and unjust (1758 will provided for manumission of two slaves he owned, and he evidently freed them sometime during 1760s); first writes against the institution of slavery in "The Sommersett Case and the Slave Trade," June 20. Elected foreign associate of Académie Royale des Sciences, Paris, August 16. October, Mrs. Stevenson moves to No. 10 Craven Street, and Franklin moves with her. Clandestinely obtains correspondence of Massachusetts Governor Thomas Hutchinson and Lieutenant Governor Andrew Oliver with English authorities, finds that it advocates repressive measures, and sends it to Massachusetts Speaker Thomas Cushing.

1773   Hutchinson letters are laid before Massachusetts House June 2; House resolves that they were intended to subvert constitution and appoints committee to petition crown for Hutchinson's and Oliver's removal. Hutchinson surreptitiously obtains copy of July 7 letter from Franklin to Massachusetts Speaker Cushing and sends it to Lord Dartmouth, colonial secretary, who judges it treasonable and asks General Thomas Gage, commander-in-chief in America, to obtain original so Franklin can be prosecuted; Gage fails to obtain it (Cushing may have destroyed the original after copying to protect Franklin). Franklin forwards to Lord Dartmouth petition for removal of Hutchinson and Oliver. Publishes satires "Rules by Which a Great Empire May Be Reduced to a Small One" and "Edict by the King of Prussia" in September. Experiments with use of oil to calm waters of Spithead in October.

1774   January, attends preliminary hearing on petition to remove Hutchinson and Oliver. News of Boston Tea Party reaches London January 20. Accused of stealing the Hutchinson letters, is excoriated and denounced as thief by Solicitor General Alexander Wedderburn before Privy Council during hearing on petition from Massachusetts House; refuses to respond to Wedderburn's accusations. Dismissed as deputy postmaster general for North America January 31. Unsuccessfully petitions House of Commons against Boston Port Bill; March 31 it becomes law, closing port. Attends opening of Theophilus Lindsey's Essex House Chapel, April 17, first enduring Unitarian congregation in England, contributing five guineas for its construction. Effigies of Wedderburn and Hutchinson carted through Philadelphia May 3, hanged, and burned by electricity. First Continental Congress opens in Philadelphia and adopts Continental Association September 5; petitions King through Franklin and other agents. Franklin becomes involved in two series of negotiations to restore calm between Britain and America: one, evidently authorized by Dartmouth, with merchant David Barclay and physician John Fothergill; the other with Lord Howe, secretly meeting at Howe's sister's, under pretense of playing chess. Drafts "Hints for a Durable Union Between England and America" at request of Barclay and Fothergill; forwarded to Dartmouth's office, it is considered and rejected. December 25, asked by Lord Howe to prepare another set of terms for conciliation; these too are not accepted. Deborah Franklin, who had not seen her husband in ten years, suffers a stroke on December 14 and dies in Philadelphia December 19, aged sixty-six; buried at Christ Church.

1775   Confers several times in late January with William Pitt, Earl of Chatham, on Chatham's unsuccessful conciliatory plan. Address to King, adopted by both Houses of Parliament February 9, declares Massachusetts to be in rebellion. Leaves London for Portsmouth March 20 to embark for America. During voyage, begins writing account of peace negotiations; speculates about why sailing from Europe to America takes longer than reverse crossing; measures temperature of air and water, proving that Gulf Stream is warmer than sea on either side of it. Lands in Philadelphia May 5 and next day is unanimously chosen delegate to Second Continental Congress by Pennsylvania Assembly. Active on various committees of Congress, among them one on paper currency, for which he designs devices and mottoes to be used on Continental money. Drafts Articles of Confederation in July, asserting America's political sovereignty, but Congress is unwilling to take such bold action. Submits resolutions proposing free trade, with no duties whatever; resolution is shelved until April 6, 1776, when it is finally adopted with proviso that individual colonies might impose their own import duties.

August 23, King proclaims colonies in rebellion. Congress reconvenes September 13, and Franklin is again active on various committees. Leaves Philadelphia October 4 with committee to confer with George Washington at his Massachusetts headquarters; returns November 9, bringing sister Jane Mecom, who had fled occupied Boston. Reappointed to several committees and offices of Pennsylvania Assembly, and reappointed delegate to Congress November 4. Congress creates standing committee of secret correspondence November 29 to deal with foreign affairs and appoints Franklin to it; committee meets secretly with agent of French court in December. Writes essays, song, and mock epitaph encouraging American war effort; epitaph, published December 14, concludes with words Jefferson adopts as his personal motto: "Rebellion to Tyrants is Obedience to God."

1776   New Jersey militia, acting on resolution of Congress, deprives William Franklin of official functions as royal governor of New Jersey in January; confined to his home in Perth Amboy, he is arrested in June and sent under guard to Connecticut to be imprisoned. Franklin, in Congress, declines to intercede for his son. Argues for "Instrument of Confederation" January 16 in Congress but is defeated. Urges four New England governments to enter into confederation and invite other colonies then to accede to it, February 19. Congress orders new designs for fractional dollars, and Franklin creates device of thirteen linked circles and "Fugio" design (later used on first United States coin, Fugio cent of 1787). Resigns from Pennsylvania Assembly February 26 to devote himself to Congressional duties. Appointed commissioner to Canada by Congress; March 26–May 30, on mission to Montreal, suffering from large boils, swollen legs, and dizziness. Appointed by Congress to committee to draft declaration of independence, June 1; Thomas Jefferson composes draft of declaration. Votes in favor of Richard Henry Lee's motion for independence, July 2. Congress adopts Declaration of Independence, July 4. Elected delegate from Philadelphia to Pennsylvania state convention, July 8; chosen president of Pennsylvania convention July 16; named by convention as Congressional delegate July 20. Asks for and receives Congress's permission to answer personal letter from Lord Howe; writes, July 20: "Long did I endeavour with unfeigned and unwearied Zeal, to preserve from breaking, that fine and noble China Vase the British Empire." Revises draft of Declaration of Rights before August 15, suggesting radical note (rejected by Pennsylvania convention) that claims the state has the right to discourage large concentrations of property as a danger to the happiness of mankind. During Congressional debates on Articles of Confederation, July 30—August 1, unsuccessfully advocates proportional, rather than equal, representation of states in Congress. Appointed by Congress to meet with Lord Howe, September 11, on Staten Island; they are unable to conciliate English and American differences. September, elected by Congress commissioner to France with Silas Deane and Arthur Lee, and is instructed to negotiate treaty. Drafts "Sketch of Propositions for a peace" in fall, suggesting Britain cede Canada to United States. Leaves Philadelphia and sails for France October 27, taking grandsons William Temple Franklin (William's illegitimate son) and Benjamin Franklin Bache (eldest of Sarah's children). Lands at Auray December 3 and proceeds to Paris; meets secretly on December 28 with Comte de Vergennes, French foreign minister.

1777   Commissioners formally request French aid, January 5; Louis XVI approves response to commissioners January 9, and January 13 they receive verbal promise of two million livres. Moves to Paris suburb of Passy about February 27, where he remains during French mission. Elected to Royal Medical Society of Paris, June 17. Combats reports of British victories spread by English Ambassador Lord Stormont by making his name a laughingstock: asked in August if it was true that six battalions in Washington's army had surrendered, Franklin replies, "No, Monsieur, it is not true; it is only a Stormont." Downplays the significance of Sir William Howe's taking of Philadelphia by commenting "it was not he who had taken Philadelphia, but instead Philadelphia had taken him." August 25, orders fifty pounds of type, evidently intending to set up small printing press at home; quantity of type indicates he was planning to print only small notes, forms, and documents. (Purchases additional type in 1778 and 1779, and occasionally employs printers from 1779 to 1783 to work on larger documents, pamphlets, and books. Probably

prints small pieces, including the bagatelles, himself.)
News of British defeat at Saratoga in October arrives December 4, and spurs negotiations leading to French alliance. Establishes several circles of friends in Passy area,
including Louis Le Veillard, Madame Brillon de Jouy (to
whom he writes flirtatious letters and bagatelles), La
Comtesse d'Houdetot (Jean Jacques Rousseau's mistress),
and especially the widow Madame Helvétius, whose salon
includes Anne Robert Jacques Turgot, France's finance
minister, and other notable French intellectuals.

1778   Commissioners report to Congress, January 28, French
            grant of six million livres for year. Treaties of "alliance for
            mutual defense" and of amity and commerce signed with
            France February 6; symbolically, Franklin wears to the
            signing ceremony same brown velvet suit he had worn
            January 29, 1774, when accused by Wedderburn before
            Privy Council. American commissioners formally pre-
            sented to Louis XVI March 20. Assists at initiation of Vol-
            taire in Masonic Lodge of the Nine Sisters, April 7.
            Embraces Voltaire at request of audience at meeting of
            French Academy of Sciences, which recognizes them as
            leading intellectual exemplars of their nations. In London,
            Boswell quotes Franklin's definition of man as "a tool-
            making animal" to Dr. Johnson, April 7. Joined by John
            Adams, appointed as fellow commissioner to France to
            replace Silas Deane. France goes to war with Britain, June
            17. Replies scornfully July 1 to offer of official rewards in
            return for aid in scheme of reconciliation proposed by se-
            cret English agent. Elected sole minister plenipotentiary to
            France September 14. Officiates at Masonic funeral ser-
            vices for Voltaire, November 28.

1779   Spain declares war on Britain June 21. Obtains another
            three million livres from France. December, Benjamin
            Vaughan publishes *Political, Miscellaneous, and Philsophical
            Pieces* in London, first general compilation of Franklin's
            nonscientific writings.

1780   Reports to Congress August 9 that John Adams, now
            commissioner to negotiate peace with Britain, has given
            offense to French court by repeated insults in letters to
            Vergennes, copies of which Franklin sends to Congress at
            Vergennes's request. Adams is thereafter bitterly hostile to

French and to Franklin. Rejects, October 2, surrendering American claims to the Mississippi as price for Spanish aid: "A Neighbour might as well ask me to sell my Street Door."

1781   Writes Vergennes February 13 of America's financial and military necessities, explaining failure of Spanish mission to date, saying " we can rely on France alone." June 4 and 10, again asks Vergennes for money to pay bills of Congress, as well as those of Adams (who is now in Holland) and John Jay in Spain. Congress appoints Franklin, Jay, Henry Laurens, and Thomas Jefferson to join Adams as commissioners to negotiate peace; new instructions require them to act only with knowledge and concurrence of France. General Charles Cornwallis surrenders to Washington at Yorktown, Virginia, October 19.

1782   Continues to request money from France to pay bills presented by Jay and Adams. Edmund Burke writes him as "the friend of mankind," February 28. Holds informal peace negotiations with British emissaries, March–June; suggests on April 18 to negotiator Richard Oswald that Britain should cede Canada to United States. July 10, Franklin suggests to Oswald "necessary" terms for peace without previously communicating them to Vergennes as his instructions from Congress require. July to October, Jay insists on prior recognition of American independence as condition for formal negotiation; Oswald's new commission from Britain, September 21, effectively recognizes United States. Draft articles for treaty prepared and sent to England without consulting Vergennes. August to October, Franklin has severe attack of gout, succeeded by passing gravel in urine. Adams arrives in Paris October 26 and joins negotiations. Oswald and American commissioners sign preliminary articles of peace November 30; when Vergennes complains in December of American failure to consult French, Franklin diplomatically admits impropriety, expresses gratitude to France, and asks for another loan. Vergennes assures Franklin of further six million livres.

1783   Attends signing of Anglo-French and Anglo-Spanish preliminary articles with Adams at Versailles, January 20; commissioners declare armistice. Requests another six million livres from France January 25, bringing total to twenty million. Crowned with laurel and myrtle March 6 at Musée de Paris celebration of successful conclusion of war. Requests permission from Vergennes to print French translations of American state constitutions together with Articles of Confederation and treaty with France; presents copies, translated by Duc de La Rochefoucauld, to all foreign ministers. Signs treaty of amity and commerce with Sweden April 3. Consulted by papal Nuncio in Paris, July 1783–July 1784, about organizing Roman Catholic Church in United States; suggests John Carroll (who accompanied him on 1776 mission to Canada) as its head (Carroll receives appointment as superior of Catholic clergy in America July 1784, and bishopric shortly thereafter). Fascinated by early experimental balloon ascensions, reports on them to Sir Joseph Banks, president of Royal Society; witnesses two of the first manned flights, November 21 and December 1. When asked by scoffing observer, "What use is it?" replies with defense of pure research: "What use is a new-born baby?" Definitive treaty of peace between Great Britain and United States signed September 3 by David Hartley for the British and by Adams, Franklin, and Jay for United States. Elected honorary fellow of Royal Society of Edinburgh.

1784   Mocks aristocratic pretensions of Society of the Cincinnati (organization of veteran officers of American Revolution) and eagle as symbol of the United States in January 26 letter to daughter Sarah; facetiously proposes native American turkey as better symbol. March, appointed by Louis XVI to investigate F. A. Mesmer's theories of animal magnetism; *Rapport* of August 11 and *Exposé*, read to Academy of Sciences September 4, conclude animal magnetism does not exist. May 12, formal ratification of peace treaty with Great Britain exchanged; Franklin requests on following day to be relieved from post to return home. Writes second part of autobiography, probably during late spring. Congress names Adams, Franklin, and Jefferson joint commissioners to negotiate treaties with European nations and Barbary States; they begin work August 30. Elected member of Royal Academy of History of Madrid.

1785   Receives word May 2 that Congress has given long-awaited permission to come home and has appointed Jefferson his successor as minister plenipotentiary to France. Describes invention of bifocal glasses May 23. Signs treaty with Prussia July 9, embodying idealistic views on neutrality, privateering, and exemption of private property from capture at sea. Leaves Passy July 12; because bladder stone makes coach travel painful, is furnished with one of Queen Marie Antoinette's litters, borne by Spanish mules. Sails from Havre July 22; arrives at Southampton, England, July 24, and is visited by son William (with whom he reconciled the previous year), Bishop and Mrs. Shipley and daughter Catherine, and by other friends. Sails July 28 for Philadelphia. On voyage, writes "Maritime Observations," containing notes on best form of rigging to improve swiftness of vessels; further observations on course, velocity, and temperature of Gulf Stream; and design of sea anchor for holding ship in wind during rough weather. Lands at Philadelphia September 14, met by cannon salutes, pealing bells, and cheering crowds. Elected to Supreme Executive Council of Pennsylvania for three-year term, October 11; elected its president October 18, and unanimously reelected the next two years. Donates salary to charity.

1786   Designs instrument for taking down books from high shelves, January. Finding Market Street house (now occupied by daughter Sarah Bache, her husband, and six children) too cramped, builds addition, including large dining room and library to house more than 4,000 volumes.

1787   February, helps found Society for Political Enquiries, dedicated to improvement of knowledge of government; elected first president. Named president of reorganized Pennsylvania Society for Promoting the Abolition of Slavery, April 23; devotes much of remaining time and energy to abolition. Serves May 28–September 17 as Pennsylvania delegate to Federal Constitutional Convention. Opposes salaries for highest executive positions. Argues June 11 that representation to Congress should be proportional to population. Moves June 28 that sessions of Convention be opened with prayer; motion, proving controversial, is dropped. July 3, proposes "Great Compromise" on representation, making representation proportional to population in House and equal by state in Senate; approved by

Grand Committee, and enacted by Convention July 16. Argues August 7 and 10 for extending right to vote as widely as possible; condemns property qualification for franchise and for officeholding as unnecessary. James Wilson reads Franklin's closing speech at convention September 17, urging every member to "doubt a little of his own Infallibility," put aside specific reservations, and vote unanimously for approval of Constitution.

1788   Writes last will and testament, July 17, leaving bulk of estate to daughter Sarah and her family; makes smaller bequests to grandsons William Temple Franklin and Benjamin Bache; citing "the part he acted against me in the late war," leaves son William almost nothing (adds codicil, June 23, 1789, making bequests to Boston and Philadelphia). Begins writing third part of autobiography in August. Ends service as president of Supreme Executive Council of Pennsylvania October 14, terminating career in public office.

1789   As president of the Pennsylvania Society for Promoting the Abolition of Slavery, writes and signs first remonstrance against slavery addressed to American Congress, February 12; after debate, committee reports March 5 that Congress has no authority to interfere in internal affairs of states. Congratulates Washington on September 16 on the success of new government under his administration and expresses satisfaction that he has lived to see present situation of United States. Sends copies of first three parts of autobiography to friends in England and France November 2 and 13. Observes to Jean Baptiste Le Roy November 13, "In this world, nothing can be said to be certain except death and taxes." Elected member of Russian Imperial Academy of Sciences, St. Petersburg.

1790   Petitions Congress February 3 as president of Pennsylvania Abolition Society against slavery and slave trade. Restates religious beliefs March 9 in letter to Ezra Stiles, expressing faith in benevolent deity. Last public writing, March 23, satirizes a defense of slavery. In last letter and final public service, April 8, replies to Secretary of State Jefferson's query on northeast boundary as settled at Paris by peace commissioners; sends his copy of Mitchell map used there.

Dies quietly at home, the evening of April 17. Although painfully afflicted in last years by bladder stone, dies of pleurisy, accompanied by suppurated lungs. Buried April 21 beside wife, Deborah, and son Francis in Christ Church burial ground, Philadelphia.

Note on the Texts

The present volume contains a broad selection of Benjamin Franklin's writings, both published and private. Included are pamphlets and broadsides published separately in Philadelphia and elsewhere, contributions to books and periodicals, a selection of letters, the complete prefaces and maxims from the "Poor Richard" almanacs, and a newly prepared edition of the *Autobiography*.

Many of Franklin's writings were published in some form in his lifetime, often under his own supervision as editor, printer, and sometimes typesetter. For these writings, the texts printed here are those of that first publication (newspaper, broadside, pamphlet, or book). For Franklin's published writings while in England, the texts are those of the original newspapers (except in a few cases where the particular issue is not known to be extant). The texts of works published separately are those of the original pamphlet editions.

For many of the remaining pieces (including most of the letters), the texts have been taken from the scholarly edition in progress at Yale University, *The Papers of Benjamin Franklin*, ed. Leonard W. Labaree, William B. Willcox et al. (New Haven, 1959–), co-sponsored by Yale and the American Philosophical Society, both major repositories of Franklin materials. This edition is the preferred source for writings edited from manuscript. For manuscript pieces dating from 1778 and later, texts have been taken in most cases from *The Writings of Benjamin Franklin*, ed. Albert H. Smyth (10 vols., New York, 1905–07). Where no manuscript of a piece is known to survive, the present volume reprints the text of the best earlier printed source. The order of preference for choosing this source is the following: Franklin's own collection of scientific writings (*Experiments and Observations on Electricity*, London, 1769); the collection of Franklin's writings edited by his friend Benjamin Vaughan (London, 1779); the collection edited by Franklin's grandson William Temple Franklin (London, 1817–18); William Duane's collection (Philadelphia, 1808–18); Jared Sparks's collection (Boston, 1836–40). The few exceptions to this order of preference are detailed in the list of sources below.

Titles of individual pieces in most cases are the customary titles by which the pieces have become known, and are usually derived from the editions that are the sources of the texts. Titles that were given during Franklin's lifetime are indicated by a dagger in the tables of contents of the various sections. Writings are ordered chronologically according to date of composition (if known), or by a date in the text (if given), otherwise by date of publication or by date inferred from external evidence, recorded in datelines added at the end of individual pieces.

The most common sources are indicated by these abbreviations:

Amacher   *Franklin's Wit & Folly: The Bagatelles.* Ed. Richard E. Amacher. New Brunswick, New Jersey: Rutgers University Press. 1953. Copyright 1953 by the Trustees of Rutgers College in New Jersey.

Bagatelles   *The Bagatelles from Passy.* New York: The Eakins Press, 1967. Copyright 1967 The Eakins Press Foundation.

Duane   *The Works of Dr. Benjamin Franklin, published from the originals by his grandson William Temple Franklin.* 6 vols. Philadelphia: William Duane. 1808–18.

E&O   Benjamin Franklin. *Experiments and Observations on Electricity.* London: David Henry & Francis Newberry, 1769.

Papers   *The Papers of Benjamin Franklin.* Ed. Leonard W. Labaree, William B. Willcox et al. New Haven: Yale University Press, 1959–.

Passy   Printed by Franklin on his press at Passy, France.

Smyth   *The Writings of Benjamin Franklin.* Ed. Albert Henry Smyth. 10 vols. New York: The Macmillan Company, 1905–07.

Sparks   *The Works of Benjamin Franklin.* Ed. Jared Sparks. 10 vols. Boston: Hilliard, Gray, and Company, 1836–40.

Vaughan   Benjamin Franklin. *Political, Miscellaneous, and Philo-*
            sophical Pieces. Ed. Benjamin Vaughan. London: J. John-
            son, 1779.

WTF   *Memoirs of the Life and Writings of Benjamin Franklin,*
            . . . Ed. William Temple Franklin. 3 vols. London: H.
            Colburn, 1817–18.

SOURCES

Letters from London, 1757–1775

———, December 13, 1757. *Papers,* VII, 294–95.

John Pringle, December 21, 1757. *Papers,* VII, 298–300.

John Pringle, January 6, 1758. *E&O,* 362.

John Lining, June 17, 1758. *E&O,* 363–68.

Jane Mecom, September 16, 1758. *Papers,* VIII, 152–55.

Hugh Roberts, September 16, 1758. *Papers,* VIII, 159–61.

Lord Kames, January 3, 1760. *Papers,* IX, 5–10.

Jane Mecom, January 9, 1760. *Papers,* IX, 17–19.

Lord Kames, May 3, 1760. *Papers,* IX, 103–06.

Peter Franklin, May 7, 1760. *E&O,* 379–80.

Mary Stevenson, June 11, 1760. *Papers,* IX, 119–22.

Mary Stevenson, September 13, 1760. *Papers,* IX, 212–17. Illustration
    reproduced with permission of the Library of Congress (restored).

David Hume, September 27, 1760. *Papers,* IX, 227–30.

Mary Stevenson, [November? 1760]. *Papers,* IX, 247–52.

John Baskerville, [1760?]. *General Evening Post,* August 11, 1763.

Peter Franklin, [c. 1761]. *E&O,* 473–78. Music reproduced with permission
    of The Library Company of Philadelphia.

David Hume, May 19, 1762. *Papers,* X, 82–84.

Giambatista Beccaria, July 13, 1762. *E&O,* 427–33. Illustration reproduced
    with permission of The Library Company of Philadelphia.

Oliver Neave, July 20, 1762. *E&O,* 435–37.

John Pringle, December 1, 1762. *E&O,* 438–40.

Jared Ingersoll, December 11, 1762. *Papers,* X, 174–76.

Mary Stevenson, March 25, 1763. *Papers,* X, 231–35.

John Waring, December 17, 1763. *Papers,* X, 395–96.

William Strahan, December 19, 1763. *Papers,* X, 406–08.

John Fothergill, March 14, 1764. *Papers,* XI, 101–04.

Peter Collinson, April 30, 1764. *Papers,* XI, 180–83.

Sarah Franklin, November 8, 1764. *Papers,* XI, 448–50.

Lord Kames, June 2, 1765. *Papers,* XII, 158–65.

Charles Thomson, July 11, 1765. *Papers,* XII, 206–08.

Jane Mecom, March 1, 1766. *Papers,* XIII, 187–89. Illustration reproduced
    with permission of The Library Company of Philadelphia (restored).

Deborah Franklin, April 6, 1766. *Papers,* XIII, 233–34.

Cadwalader Evans, May 9, 1766. *Hazard's Register of Pennsylvania* XVI, 5 (August 1, 1835), 65.

Joseph Galloway, November 8, 1766. *Papers*, XIII, 487–88.

Mary Stevenson, September 14, 1767. *Papers*, XIV, 250–55.

Margaret Stevenson, November 3, [1767]. *Papers*, XIV, 299–300.

Jane Mecom, December 24, 1767. *Papers*, XIV, 344–45.

William Franklin, January 9, 1768. *WTF*, II, 151.

Jean Chappe d'Auteroche, January 31, 1768. *Papers*, XV, 33–34.

John Pringle, May 10, 1768. *E&O*, 492–96.

Jacques Barbeu-Dubourg, July 28, 1768. *The American Museum*, VIII (July, 1790), 120. Misdated July 21 in *American Museum*.

John Alleyne, [August 9, 1768]. *Papers*, XV, 183–85.

Mary Stevenson, October 28, 1768. *Papers*, XV, 244–45.

————, November 28, 1768. *WTF*, II, 169–70.

Oliver Neave, [before 1769]. *E&O*, 463–68.

John Bartram, July 9, 1769. *Papers*, XVI, 172–73.

George Whitefield, [before September 2, 1769]. Joseph Belcher, *George Whitefield* (New York, 1857), 414–15.

Mary Stevenson, September 2, 1769. *Papers*, XVI, 193–94.

Timothy Folger, September 29, 1769. *Papers*, XVI, 207–10.

William Strahan, November 29, 1769. *Papers*, XVI, 243–49.

[Charles Thomson], March 18, 1770. *Papers*, XVII, 111–13.

Mary Stevenson, May 31, 1770. *Papers*, XVII, 152–53.

Samuel Cooper, June 8, 1770. *Papers*, XVII, 161–65.

Mary Stevenson Hewson, July 18, 1770. *Papers*, XVII, 194–95.

Deborah Franklin, October 3, 1770. *Papers*, XVII, 239–40.

Jane Mecom, December 30, 1770. *Papers*, XVII, 313–16.

Thomas Percival, [June? 1771]. *Memoirs of the Literary and Philosophical Society of Manchester*, II (1785), 110–13.

Jane Mecom, July 17, 1771. *Papers*, XVIII, 184–87.

Anna Mordaunt Shipley, August 13, 1771. *Papers*, XVIII, 199–202. Misdated August 12 in manuscript, according to *Papers*.

Joshua Babcock, January 13, 1772. *Papers*, XIX, 6–7.

Ezra Stiles, January 13, 1772. *Papers*, XIX, 30–31.

Anthony Benezet, August 22, 1772. *Papers*, XIX, 269.

Samuel Rhoads, August 22, 1772. *Papers*, XIX, 278–79.

Joseph Priestley, September 19, 1772. *Papers*, XIX, 299–300.

Georgiana Shipley, September 26, 1772. *Papers*, XIX, 301–03.

William Marshall, February 14, 1773. *Papers*, XX, 71–72.

Samuel Mather, July 7, 1773. *Papers*, XX, 286–89.

Benjamin Rush, July 14, 1773. *Papers*, XX, 314–16.

William Franklin, October 6, 1773. *Duane*, VI, 332–34.

Peter P. Burdett, November 3, 1773. *Papers*, XX, 459–60.

William Brownrigg, November 7, 1773. *Papers*, XX, 463–74.

Josiah Tucker, February 12, 1774. *Papers*, XXI, 83–85.

Josiah Tucker, February 26, 1774. *Papers*, XXI, 125–28.

Joseph Priestley, April 10, 1774. Joseph Priestley, *Experiments and Observations on Different Kinds of Air*, 3 vols. (London: J. Johnson, 1774–77), I, 321–23.

William Strahan, July 5, 1775. *Papers*, XXII, 85.

[Joseph Priestley], July 7, 1775. *Vaughan*, 552–54.

David Hartley, October 3, 1775. *Vaughan*, 555–56.

PARIS, 1776–1785

The Sale of the Hessians, February 18, 1777. *Smyth*, VII, 27–29.

Model of a Letter of Recommendation, April 2, 1777. *Papers*, XXIII, 549–50.

The Twelve Commandments, March 10, 1778. *Smyth*, X, 437–38.

Petition of the Letter Z, [c. August, 1778]. *The Letters of Benjamin Franklin & Jane Mecom*, ed. Carl Van Doren (Princeton: Princeton University Press, 1950), 256–57.

The Ephemera, September 20, 1778. Gilbert Chinard, "Random Notes on Two 'Bagatelles,' " *Publications of the American Philosophical Society*, 103 (1959), 741, 744.

The Elysian Fields (M. Franklin to Madame Helvétius), December 7, 1778. *Amacher*, 54–56. Copyright 1953 by the Trustees of Rutgers College in New Jersey.

Bilked for Breakfast (Mr. Franklin to Madame la Freté), [c. 1778]. *Bagatelles*, 12–13. Trans. Willard Trask. Copyright 1967 The Eakins Press Foundation.

Passport for Captain Cook, March 10, 1779. *Smyth*, VII, 242–43.

The Morals of Chess, June, 1779. *Smyth*, VII, 357–62.

The Whistle, November 10, 1779. *Passy*.

The Levée, [1779?]. *Smyth*, VII, 430–32.

Proposed New Version of the Bible, [1779?]. *Smyth*, VII, 432–33.

Drinking Song (To the Abbé de La Roche, at Auteuil), [1779?]. *WTF*, III, 345–47.

A Tale, [1779?]. *Bagatelles*, 27. Trans. Willard Trask. Copyright 1967 The Eakins Press Foundation.

On Wine (From the Abbé Franklin to the Abbé Morellet), [1779?]. *Bagatelles*, 54–59. Trans. Willard Trask. Copyright 1967 The Eakins Press Foundation. Drawings reproduced from the *Mémoires inédits* of the Abbé Morellet with permission of The Library Company of Philadelphia.

Dialogue Between the Gout and Mr. Franklin, October 22, 1780. *Bagatelles*, 34–45. Trans. Willard Trask. Copyright 1967 The Eakins Press Foundation.

The Handsome and the Deformed Leg, November, 1780. *Amacher*, 100–02. Copyright 1953 by the Trustees of Rutgers College in New Jersey.

To the Royal Academy of *****, [c. 1781]. *Passy*.

Notes for Conversation, April 18, 1782. *Smyth*, VIII, 471–72.

Supplement to the Boston Independent Chronicle, April, 1782. *Supplement to the Boston Independent Chronicle*, 2d ed., printed by Franklin on his press at Passy, France.

Articles for a Treaty of Peace with Madame Brillon, July 27, 1782. *Benjamin Franklin's Autobiographical Writings*, ed. Carl Van Doren (New York: Viking Press, 1945), 584–86. Copyright 1945 Carl Van Doren. Reprinted by permission of Viking Penguin Inc.

Apologue, [c. November, 1782]. *Smyth*, VIII, 650–51.

Remarks Concerning the Savages of North-America, 1783. *Passy.*

Information to Those Who Would Remove to America, February, 1784. *Passy.*

An Economical Project, April 26, 1784. *Smyth*, IX, 183–89. Printed in the *Journal de Paris*, April 26, 1784.

Loose Thoughts on a Universal Fluid, June 25, 1784. *Smyth*, IX, 227–30.

The Flies (To Madame Helvétius), [1784?]. *Bagatelles*, 14–15. Trans. Willard Trask. Copyright 1967 The Eakins Press Foundation.

LETTERS

Lord Howe, July 20, 1776. *Papers*, XXII, 519–21.

Emma Thompson, February 8, 1777. *Papers*, XXIII, 297–99.

—— Lith, April 6, 1777. *Papers*, XXIII, 557–59.

[Lebègue de Presle], October 4, 1777. *Papers*, XXV, 25–26.

Arthur Lee, April 3, 1778. *Smyth*, VII, 132.

Charles de Weissenstein, July 1, 1778. *Smyth*, VII, 166–72.

David Hartley, February 3, 1779. *Smyth*, VII, 226–29.

Sarah Bache, June 3, 1779. *Smyth*, VII, 346–50

Edward Bridgen, October 2, 1779. *Smyth*, VII, 381–82.

Elizabeth Partridge, October 11, 1779. *Smyth*, VII, 393–94.

John Paul Jones, October 15, 1779. *Smyth*, VII, 395–96.

Benjamin Vaughan, November 9, 1779. *Smyth*, VII, 410–13.

Joseph Priestley, February 8, 1780. *Smyth*, VIII, 9–12.

George Washington, March 5, 1780. *Smyth*, VIII, 27–79.

Thomas Bond, March 16, 1780. *Smyth*, VIII, 37–38.

William Carmichael, June 17, 1780. *Smyth*, VIII, 98–100.

Samuel Huntington, August 9, 1780. *Smyth*, VIII, 124–30.

John Jay, October 2, 1780. William Jay, *The Life of John Jay: with Selections from his Correspondence and Miscellaneous Papers*, 2 vols. (New York: J. & J. Harper, 1833), II, 62–64.

Richard Price, October 9, 1780. *Smyth*, VIII, 153–54.

Benjamin Waterhouse, January 18, 1781. *Smyth*, VIII, 194–95.

John Adams, February 22, 1781. *Smyth*, VIII, 211–12.

Court de Gebelin, May 7, 1781. *Smyth*, VIII, 246–48.

Comte de Vergennes, June 10, 1781. *Smyth*, VIII, 263–66.

William Jackson, July 10, 1781. *Smyth*, VIII, 281–84.

William Nixon, September 5, 1781. *Smyth*, VIII, 298–99.

William Strahan, December 4, 1781. *Smyth*, VIII, 335–36.

John Adams, December 17, 1781. *Smyth*, VIII, 347–48.

Robert R. Livingston, March 4, 1782. *Smyth*, VIII, 388–94.

John Adams, April 22, 1782. *Smyth*, VIII, 432–33.

Joseph Priestley, June 7, 1782. *Smyth*, VIII, 451–53.

Richard Price, June 13, 1782. *Smyth*, VIII, 457–58.

Miss Alexander, June 24, 1782. *Smyth*, VIII, 458–59.

James Hutton, July 7, 1782. *Smyth*, VIII, 561–63.

Robert R. Livingston, August 12, 1782. *Smyth*, VIII, 576–80.

The Marquis de Lafayette, September 17, 1782. *Smyth*, VIII, 595–96.

The Abbé Soulavie, September 22, 1782. *Transactions of the American Philosophical Society*, III (Philadelphia, 1793), 1–5.

Comte de Vergennes, December 17, 1782. *Smyth*, VIII, 642–43.

Mary Hewson, January 27, 1783. *Smyth*, IX, 11–13.

Robert R. Livingston, July 22, 1783. *Smyth*, IX, 59–73.

Sir Joseph Banks, July 27, 1783. *Smyth*, IX, 73–75.

Sir Joseph Banks, August 30, 1783. *Smyth*, IX, 79–85.

John Jay, September 10, 1783. *The Diplomatic Correspondence of the American Revolution*, ed. Jared Sparks (Boston: N. Hale and Gray & Bowen, 1829–30), IV, 163–64.

Robert Morris, December 25, 1783. *Smyth*, IX, 135–40.

———, [January, 1784?]. *Smyth*, IX, 149–50.

Sarah Bache, January 26, 1784. *Smyth*, IX, 161–68.

William Strahan, February 16, 1784. *Smyth*, IX, 171–73.

La Sabliere de la Condamine, March 19, 1784. *Smyth*, IX, 181–83.

Samuel Mather, May 12, 1784. *Smyth*, IX, 208–10.

Charles Thomson, May 13, 1784. *Smyth*, IX, 212–14.

Mason Locke Weems and Edward Gant, July 18, 1784. *Smyth*, IX, 238–40.

William Franklin, August 16, 1784. *Smyth*, IX, 252–54.

William Strahan, August 19, 1784. *Smyth*, IX, 259–64.

Joseph Priestley, August 21, 1784. *Smyth*, IX, 266–67.

Richard Price, March 18, 1785. *Smyth*, IX, 300–01.

George Whatley, May 23, 1785. *Smyth*, IX, 331–39. Illustration, from Franklin's manuscript, reproduced with permission of the Library of Congress.

PHILADELPHIA, 1785–1790

A Petition of the Left Hand, 1785. *Smyth*, X, 125–26.

Description of an Instrument for Taking Down Books from High Shelves, January, 1786. *Smyth*, VI, 552. Illustration from *Sparks*, VI, 562, reproduced with permission of The Library Company of Philadelphia.

The Art of Procuring Pleasant Dreams, May 2, 1786. *Smyth*, X, 131–37.

The Retort Courteous, 1786. *Smyth*, X, 105–16.

Speech in the Convention on the Subject of Salaries, June 2, 1787. *Smyth*, IX, 590–95.

Speech in a Committee of the Convention on the Proportion of Representation and Votes, June 11, 1787. *Smyth*, IX, 595–99.

Motion for Prayers in the Convention, June 28, 1787. *Smyth*, IX, 600–01.

Speech in the Convention at the Conclusion of its Deliberations, September

17, 1787. *The Documentary History of the Constitution*, ed. John P.
Kaminski and Gaspare J. Salidino (Madison: State Historical Society of
Wisconsin, 1981), XIII, 213–214.

On Sending Felons to America, 1787. *Smyth*, IX, 628–30.

A Comparison of the Conduct of the Ancient Jews and of the Anti-
Federalists in the United States of America, [c. 1788]. *Smyth*, IX, 698–703,
from the manuscript in the Library of Congress. Printed in *The Federal
Gazette* (Philadelphia), April 8, 1788.

On the Abuse of the Press, [after March 30, 1788]. *Smyth*, IX, 639–42.

An Account of the Supremest Court of Judicature in Pennsylvania, viz.
The Court of the Press, September 12, 1789. *The Federal Gazette*
(Philadelphia), September 12, 1789.

An Address to the Public from the Pennsylvania Society for Promoting the
Abolition of Slavery, and the Relief of Free Negroes Unlawfully Held in
Bondage, November 9, 1789. *Smyth*, X, 66–68.

Plan for Improving the Condition of the Free Blacks, [1789?]. *Smyth*, X, 127–29.

Sidi Mehemet Ibrahim on the Slave Trade, March 23, 1790. *Smyth*, X, 87–91,
from the manuscript in the Library of Congress. Printed in *The Federal
Gazette* (Philadelphia), March 25, 1790.

LETTERS

Jonathan Shipley, February 24, 1786. *Smyth*, IX, 488–91.

Benjamin Vaughan, July 31, 1786. *Smyth*, IX, 530–33.

Rev. John Lathrop, May 31, 1788. *Smyth*, IX, 649–52.

Benjamin Vaughan, October 24, 1788. *WTF*, II, 113–14.

John Langdon, 1788. Lewis J. Carey, *Franklin's Economic Views* (Garden
City, New York: Doubleday, Doran & Company, 1928), 87–88. Used by
permission of Doubleday & Company, Inc.

Jane Mecom, August 3, 1789. *The Letters of Benjamin Franklin & Jane
Mecom*, ed. Carl Van Doren (Princeton: Princeton University Press, 1950),
327–28.

John Wright, November 4, 1789. *Smyth*, X, 60–63.

Noah Webster, December 26, 1789. *Smyth*, X, 75–82.

Ezra Stiles, March 9, 1790. *Smyth*, X, 83–86.

The present volume reprints the prefaces, maxims, and a
selection of short items thought to have been written by
Franklin from the original *Poor Richard's Almanack* printed
in Philadelphia by Franklin from 1733 to 1758. The calendars,
meteorological data, and other contents have been omitted.
The maxims, printed in italics in the originals to distinguish
them from the surrounding material in which they were em-
bedded, are printed in roman type here (with styling accordingly reversed).

The text of the *Autobiography* presented here is a newly prepared clear text, derived from the genetic text edited by J. A. Leo Lemay and P. M. Zall, which was prepared from the manuscript in the Huntington Library in San Marino, California (*The Autobiography of Benjamin Franklin: A Genetic Text*. Ed. J. A. Leo Lemay and P. M. Zall. Knoxville: Univ. of Tennessee Press, 1981). The genetic text prints Franklin's cancellations and revisions, using a system of typographical sigla to indicate interlinear interpolations, marginal interpolations, superscriptions, etc. The cancellations are omitted here (along with the related editorial sigla), as are punctuation marks associated with cancellations but left uncanceled themselves. (A few of the more interesting canceled phrases and passages are reproduced in the notes to the present volume.) Franklin's revisions are printed here without the editorial sigla indicating interlinear interpolations, marginal insertions, and canceled words or phrases. Conjectural readings of undecipherable words, printed within square brackets in the genetic text, are accepted here, and printed without brackets.

Some emendations have been necessary in the preparation of this clear text, due to the unfinished nature of Franklin's manuscript. In a number of places, extra punctuation has been omitted. In some cases, the extraneous punctuation occurs where Franklin evidently finished a sentence, then continued it without canceling his previous mark of punctuation. In other cases, punctuation associated with a canceled phrase was left uncanceled itself, or punctuation was rendered superfluous or redundant when Franklin revised a passage, but didn't cancel the superseded punctuation. Where a sentence plainly ends, but Franklin did not punctuate it, a period has been added; no period has been added, however, after the last word of the *Autobiography*. And where Franklin added a word to an italicized passage (or inserted it in a context where parallel words were italicized) but did not italicize the added word, the present text italicizes it. Finally, Franklin's notes, queries, and reminders to himself in the manuscript (e.g., indicating the placement of texts to be added) have been omitted.

Certain other emendations have also been made and are

recorded below. In a few places the sense of a passage demanded that a mark of punctuation be added, altered, or omitted for the sake of intelligibility. Spelling, if plainly incorrect (or a slip of the pen), is emended. In six places, Franklin inadvertently repeated a word, and in ten places redundancies indicate that he was considering alternative phrasings but neglected to cancel one of them; the present text emends accordingly (choosing in most cases his second alternative as the more likely), and records the emendation. In the following list, the word or words preceding the bracket are those of the present text, and the words after the bracket are those of the genetic text edition: 569.39, beloved."] beloved.; 599.39, if] if if; 600.30, Watson] Watson Watson; 601.18, Task] Task Task; 604.36, ought to] should ought to; 605.23, that] that,; 607.39, advanc'd] advan'd; 610.2, Woman,] Woman; 610.5, revered,] revered; 611.9, Wygate,] Wygate.; 613.26, seeing] see^{g}ing; 613.35, 28,] 28.; 613.37, Stationary,] Stationary; 614.28, Work:] Work; 623.25, Journeyman] Joureyman; 625.16, then] now then; 631.17, Situation,] Situation; 631.25, invalid,] invalid; 639.24, considerable,] considerable.; 644.6–7, Care was employ'd] *Attention was taken up* Care was employ'd; 650.2, But] but; 650.7, exactly] exastly; 650.11, it] *Method* it; 651.17, *Temperance*] *Temperance.*; 651.40, which] whch; 652.28, rare,] rare; 654.3, be] by; 655.31, the] the the; 655.33, wise] wiss; 655.38, BF."—] BF.—; 657.4, Occupations] Occupapations; 661.27, Educating] Eduting; 682.17, *so.*"—] *so.*—; 682.28, for] towards for; 684.26, least] leas; 686.13, obstructed the] obstructed the the; 686.17, flat] flatt flat; 691.28, *pursue.*"] *pursue.*; 695.22, brought] brought,; 695.28, Baggage,] Baggage.; 704.11, you] "you; 704.12, taken?"] taken?; 704.14, Uncertainty."—] Uncertainty.—; 706.16, whimsicall] whimsicll; 707.29, And] Qu and; 708.17, the Sides] th Sides; 708.24, even] evon; 708.31, punctually] puctually; 710.33, Opinion,] Opinion.; 714.19, decry] oppose decry; 718.14, presenting] presenteding; 718.19, conformable;] agreable conformable; 719.8, detain'd,] detain'd.; 719.38, the] thr; 721.6–7, others,] others.; 721.24, Business.] Business,; 725.3, occasion'd] accosion'd; 726.15, they] the; 726.39, me,] me.; 727.18, Paper] Pager.

The genetic text edition inadvertently omits four of the black "Spots" from the illustration of a page of the "Book"

766 NOTE ON THE TEXTS

in which Franklin recorded his daily offenses against virtue
(page 647 in the present volume). One of the missing spots
is on the line corresponding to the second virtue, "Silence,"
in the column under "Friday"; two are under "Tuesday," on
the lines corresponding to the fourth and sixth virtues, "Resolution" and "Industry"; and the fourth is on the line corresponding to the fifth virtue, "Frugality," in the column
under "Thursday." In addition, a question mark was omitted
and a period substituted after the word "breakfast" in the
diagram of the "Scheme of Employment" (page 649 in the
present volume). These have been corrected here.

Franklin never completed his writing and revision of the
Autobiography, and the text as we have it manifests its unfinished character in various ways. The dashes that appear
throughout the manuscript have been retained, even though
they may be a manuscript convention that Franklin would not
have printed; likewise, manuscript conventions preserved in
the genetic text such as ampersands, abbreviations, and superscript characters are printed here as they appeared in the
manuscript. Spelling has been neither modernized nor regu-
larized, and original spellings have been retained. Thus the
Reverend George Whitefield, for example, appears here vari-
ously as *Whitefiel*, *Whitfield*, and *Whitefield*. Ordinary eighteenth-century spellings such as *deny'd*, *publick*, *learnt*,
agreable, *compleat*, *surpriz'd*, *Cloaths*, *intituled* (or *entituled*),
and *chuse*—as well as unusual spellings (some of which are
possibly, but not certainly, slips of the pen) such as *werre*,
Sope, *Wharff*, *Surff*, *beforre*, *Compostors*, *Matras*, *Risque*, *ren-
derd*, *deliverd*, *lenthend*, *Lightnin*, *observ*, *som*, and *Percedings*—have been left unaltered. Some of these spellings have
a "phonetic" character and may reflect Franklin's interest in
spelling reform. Italics and large and small capitals indicated
by Franklin in the manuscript are followed here. The several
supplemental texts that Franklin wished to insert in his
manuscript (i.e., the note on the name Franklin, his uncle
Benjamin's poems, the *Pennsylvania Gazette* editorial of October 9, 1759, the letters from Abel James and Benjamin
Vaughan, the Golden Verses of Pythagoras, and the wagon
advertisement) have been printed within the text where

Franklin indicated; the texts are from the appendices to the genetic text edition. The title, which is customary ("The Autobiography"), has been added by the editor, although it is not in the manuscript and Franklin usually referred to his manuscript as "Memoirs"; the part titles (e.g., "Part One") are also customary and have been added by the editor.

Throughout this volume, conventional features of eighteenth-century writing (spelling and punctuation) and printing, such as italics for proper names and place names and large and small capitals, have been preserved, since Franklin can be presumed to have authorized them. Only obvious typographical and orthographical errors have been corrected, and these corrections are listed below. The long "s" has been printed as the modern short "s" throughout, and ligatures (except æ and œ digraphs) have been printed as separate letters. Footnote symbols have been reordered to correspond, where necessary, to new pagination. In eighteenth-century printing, quotation marks were placed at the beginning of every line of an extended quotation, but in the present volume only the opening quotation mark has been retained (and a closing quotation mark added where needed).

The *Papers* and *Writings*, as well as the William Temple Franklin, Sparks, and Vaughan editions, modernize and regularize Franklin's orthography in various ways. The *Papers*, for instance, omits some dashes and commas, disregards the italicization of proper nouns, expands contractions, spells out abbreviations, brings superscript letters down to the line, and prints "and" for the ampersand. In pieces reprinted from the *Papers* and other editions, the present volume eliminates editorial comment from the text. For instance, where the editors of the *Papers* print "[illegible]" to indicate that the manuscript they are transcribing cannot be read, the present volume simply indicates an indecipherable word or words by brackets—i.e., "[   ]"—and prints Franklin's interlinear revisions without the word or words canceled in the process (if any) and without brackets. The present volume also accepts the conjectural readings of words (faded or otherwise obscured in the manuscript) that are supplied in a few places

by the editors of the *Papers* and the other editions. Usually
printed in brackets and sometimes in italics in those editions,
they are given without brackets and in roman type here. Editorial comments such as "(*sic*)" have been omitted. Franklin's
name at the end of letters has also been omitted. Finally, in a
few places, long verse or prose extracts (or other extended
passages) printed in italics in the original texts have been
printed in roman type in the present volume; styling has accordingly been reversed in these passages, with roman type
being set in italics.

This volume is concerned with presenting the texts of the
selections included; it does not attempt to reproduce features
of their typographic design, such as the display capitalization
of chapter and paragraph openings. It does, however, reproduce capital letters for substantives, italic and boldface type,
superscript letters, large and small capitals, and other typographical features, where the original texts have preserved
them. In a letter to Noah Webster, December 26, 1789 (pp.
433–38 in the present volume), Franklin decried the disuse of
these typographical conventions, and explained what he took
to be their functions. To the extent that modern typesetting
will allow, therefore, this volume preserves those features. The
following is a list of the typographical errors corrected, cited
by page and line number: 37.37, who; 53.29, the the; 122.23,
any any; 182.34, Music; 183.28, our; 240.31, being; 240.31, oy;
240.32, an; 241.2, sey; 241.4, wil; 241.15, to; 399.4, it"; 426.20,
if, it; 428.6, —"Having; 445.16, desire; 446.27, effect effect;
446.30, rainy.; 447.12, head; 447.16, fleas; 447.25, preach;
448.7, spurs,; 448.28, afte; 451.4, things; 454.4, can; 454.12,
him; 456.13, behind; 457.6, deny; 457.21, milk; 457.30, 2;
461.20, people; 463.38, & and; 463.39, 5 s; 464.32, cats; 465.12,
said; 466.17, t'other; 466.19, for for; 468.9, you; 468.12, himself; 468.20, ou; 469.5, hour; 469.9, on; 469.15, Lead; 469.24,
error; 470.15, Ingnorant; 470.21, Mouth; 471.1, J—m n; 473.18,
tongue; 477.15, immortal; 478.24, ti; 479.17, cheek by-jole;
480.11, she'as; 489.4, beware,; 489.25, nine:; 490.18, so It is
so;; 492.10, complea; 493.6, Cares; 494.17, *Sa urn*; 495.7,
scars; 495.17, ancient; 497.26, Thanful; 498.22, Knowledge;
501.6, sermon; 501.17, pennyworths; 503.24, stiff; 507.32, feast;
508.31, uncoinver'd; 514.5, dise se; 514.25, Friends; 515.25, fear;

516.23, sav'd; 519.27, Natur s; 519.29, Languages; 526.31-32, standing;; 529.32, upon upon; 545.33, exceedingly; 546.1, fi st; 546.7, Ware; 546.15, then; 546.15, o her; 548.10, on y; 551.16, general y; 551.18, heir; 551.22, eal; 551.36, profane; 553.33, te l; 561.21, wo ld; 562.27, *Knuckles.*; 563.8, *Ajaxes.*

Notes

In the notes below, the reference numbers denote page and line of the present volume (the line count includes titles). No note is made for material included in a standard desk-reference book. Footnotes in the text are Franklin's own. Translations of classical authors in the notes below are from volumes of the Loeb Classical Library unless otherwise indicated; citations from James Thomson's *The Seasons* are to the line counts in the edition by James Sambrook (Oxford: At the Clarendon Press, 1981). For further biographical information than is provided in the Chronology, see James Parton, *Life and Times of Benjamin Franklin*, 2 vols. (Boston: Ticknor & Fields, 1864), Carl Van Doren, *Benjamin Franklin* (New York: The Viking Press, 1938), Claude-Anne Lopez and Eugenia W. Herbert, *The Private Franklin: The Man and His Family* (New York: W. W. Norton & Company, 1975), and Esmond Wright, *Franklin of Philadelphia* (Cambridge, Massachusetts: The Belknap Press of Harvard Univ. Press, 1986). For historical information on many of the pieces printed in the present volume, see the headnotes and annotations in relevant volumes of *The Papers of Benjamin Franklin*, ed. Leonard W. Labaree, William B. Willcox et al. (New Haven: Yale Univ. Press, 1959–). The scholarship of the *Papers* has been an essential aid in preparation of the present volume. See also the annotations, background materials, and bibliography in the Norton Critical Edition of Franklin's *Autobiography*, ed. J. A. Leo Lemay and P. M. Zall (New York: W. W. Norton & Company, 1986).

LETTERS FROM LONDON, 1757–1775

11.34   Mr. *Mitchell's*] The paper by Rev. John Michell (1724–93) is probably "Conjectures concerning the Cause, and Observations upon the Phaenomena of Earthquakes . . . ," printed in the *Philosophical Transactions* LI, 2 (1760), pp. 566–634.

12.26   Dr. *Hadley*] Dr. John Hadley (1731–64). See Chronology, 1758.

14.9   *June* 1750] Actually, June 18, 1749.

17.1   *None but Christ*] Clement Cotton, *None but Christ* (1723).

19.17   Potts and Parsons] Stephen Potts (1704–58) and William Parsons (1701–57), the former a Quaker bookbinder (mentioned in the *Autobiography*, pp. 614, 622), the latter a shoemaker who became surveyor-general (see *Autobiography*, p. 622).

20.19–20   PRE SENCE . . . ALL ENgag'd]   Franklin puns on the name of William Allen, leader of the Proprietary party.

24.3   Book]   [Richard Jackson, comp.], *An Historical Review of . . . Pennsylvania* (1759).

25.31   Mr. Bailey]   Rev. Jacob Bailey (1731–1818), who became a Tory, fled to Nova Scotia during the Revolution, and satirized Franklin in his poetry.

26.28   Chapter]   Franklin's "Parable Against Persecution" pretended to be a chapter from Genesis.

26.33   *The Art of Virtue*]   Franklin never published his "Art of Virtue" as a separate work; when Benjamin Vaughan reminded him of his intention to do so in 1783 (see p. 634 in the present volume), Franklin responded by incorporating the elements of his scheme into Part Two of the *Autobiography* under the guise of his "bold and arduous Project of arriving at moral Perfection" (p. 643).

31.21–24   Nicholas . . . Satyrist.]   Thomas Shadwell ridiculed Nicholas Gimcrack in his play *The Virtuoso* (1676), and Joseph Addison added to the satire in *The Tatler*, Nos. 216 and 221 (Aug. 26 and Sept. 7, 1710).

32.17   Selden tells us]   John Selden, *Table Talk* (1689), p. 50.

44.31   *The additional . . .* Maccabeus]   "Wise men flatt'ring may deceive us" in Handel's *Judas Maccabeus* (1747), Act 2.

46.10–12   *the Monster . . . Galatea*]   Handel's chorus "Wretched Lovers!" in *Acis and Galatea* (1718), Act 2.

48.11   *a Case in Point*]   Franklin probably created the anecdote.

48.30–32   We are . . . Street.]   2 Chronicles 1:16.

50.3   Mr. *Puckeridge*]   Richard Pockrich, musician (d. 1759).

50.10   Mr. *E. Delaval*]   Franklin had nominated Edward H. Duval (1729–1814) for membership in the Royal Society in 1759.

57.22   *Old Tenor*]   Connecticut money bills infamous for their rapid depreciation.

59.33–60.3   Full . . . too.]   From William Whitehead's *A Charge to the Poets* (1762).

63.10   Ad Exemplum Regis, &c.]   Probably an echo of Claudian *Panegyricus de Quarto Consulatu Honorii Augusti* 299–300: "componitur orbis regis ad exemplum" ("the world shapes itself after its ruler's pattern").

82.10–15   Friar . . . Ears.]   Franklin adapts a legend concerning the theologian Roger Bacon (1214–94?), a heterodox Franciscan; he may have known it from Robert Greene's play, *The Honorable Historie of Frier Bacon, and Frier Bongay* (1594).

85.31 this:] Franklin's words in the drawing, clockwise from upper right: "Mad. Sophie," "Mad. Adelaide," "The King," "The Queen," "Mad. Victoire," "Mad. Louise," "Waiters."

90.28 last Piece] Franklin refers to a piece printed in *The London Chronicle*, November 24, 1767, in which he decried the evasion of taxes by smugglers, and insisted that the receiver of smuggled goods was as culpable as the smuggler.

91.25 one paper] "Causes of the American Discontents Before 1768."

95.30 *July* 28] Dated July 21 in the copy-text for the present printing, but corrected to July 28, as in its first printing (in French).

124.18–19 great . . . *them.*] Sir William Temple, *Miscellanea: The Second Part* (1690), "Essay II. Upon the Gardens of Epicurus, or of Gardening in the Year 1685," p. 5.

125.40 Discourse] Franklin reprinted an advertisement for it, with Samuel Keimer's comments, from Keimer's *Barbadoes Gazette* in *The Pennsylvania Gazette*, February 20, 1733/34.

126.26 Touchwood] Wood, or another substance easily ignited, used for tinder; hence, a person who is easily incensed.

132.5 13] Franklin wrote "August 12," but since he stayed at the Shipleys' through the 12th, he must have written this letter the next day.

132.7–8 my Charge] Franklin's "Charge" was Catherine (Kitty) Shipley, about eleven years old, the daughter of Bishop Jonathan and Anna Mordaunt Shipley.

137.10 This . . . Chronicle] "The Sommersett Case and the Slave Trade."

138.35 Affair . . . you] Priestley was considering leaving Leeds to become the librarian of Lord Shelburne.

139.34 1772] Franklin wrote "1773" originally, but since he enclosed a draft of this letter to Georgiana Shipley in his letter to Deborah Franklin of February 14, 1773, he must have written it in 1772.

140.3 Skuggs] In a letter to Deborah Franklin (February 14, 1773) Franklin explained, "Skugg, you must know is a common Name by which all Squirrels are called here, as all Cats are called *Puss.*"

140.26 Ranger] The dog that killed Georgiana's squirrel.

142.4 fugitive Piece] "Toleration in Old and New England."

142.16 1723] Franklin ran away from Boston in September, 1723.

142.36–37 Argument . . . Ancients] Samuel Mather, *An Attempt to Shew, that America Must be Known to the Ancients* (1773).

143.1   Tubalcain] See Genesis 4:22.

143.4   Professor Kalm] Pehr Kalm (1716–79), the Swedish botanist sent by Linnaeus to America to collect specimens.

143.15   Krantz] David Cranz, *The History of Greenland*, 2 vols. (1767), I, 241–79.

144.24   Version of the Prayer] "A New Version of the Lord's Prayer."

146.11   Friend's] Rev. Thomas Coombe, Jr. (1747–1822), a young friend of Franklin's who at one time lodged in the Craven Street house.

149.17   *Moral Virtue delineated*] Marin le Roy de Gomberville, *Moral Virtue Delineated* (1726).

156.33–157.9   Extrait . . . chapitre.] "Extract of a Letter from Mr. Tengnagel to Mr. le Comte de Bentinck, written from Batavia January 15, 1770. Near St. Paul and Amsterdam Islands we endured a storm, which hadn't anything particular about it to be noticed, except that our Captain felt himself obliged in turning leeward, to pour out some oil on the high seas, in order to prevent the waves from breaking against the ship, which succeeded in saving us and had a very good effect: as he had poured only a small quantity altogether, the Company perhaps owes its vessel to six demi-ahms of olive oil: I was present when this happened, and I would not have informed you of that circumstance, if we hadn't found the people here so skeptical of the experience, that neither the officers on shore nor myself raised any objections to giving an assurance of the truth of the matter."

160.1   new Book] Josiah Tucker, *Four Tracts* (1774).

165.8   *To William Strahan*] Franklin did not send this angry letter to his friend Strahan.

168.8   *last* petition] The Olive Branch Petition of July 8, 1775.

PARIS, 1776–1785

179.22   MADAME BRILLON] Mme. d'Hardancourt Brillon de Jouy (1744–1824), a favorite among Franklin's female friends in France, a talented musician, handsome and lively.

181.1   *Petition of the Letter Z*] Franklin herein satirizes Ralph Izard (1742–1804), one of his fellow American commissioners in Paris in 1778. His notes in the left column explain the allegory.

181.3   ISAAC BICKERSTAFF] A character invented by Jonathan Swift, in his parody of an almanac maker's predictions (see note 445.20); Richard Steele adopted the name for the pretended author of his *Tatler*, of which the present "Petition" pretends to be an issue.

182.11   my dear Friend] Mme. Brillon.

183.27–28   *what . . . Morals.*] Horace *Odes* 3. 24. 35.

183.31   *Art . . . short!*] Hippocrates *Aphorisms* 1. 1.

183.33–34   *lived . . . Glory*] Cicero *Pro M. Marcello* 25.

184.5   BRILLANTE] "Diamond." Also a reference to Mme. Brillon.

184.6   *The Elysian Fields*] This bagatelle, among others, was printed by
Franklin only in French; the present text is a translation. The other French
bagatelles are "Bilked for Breakfast" (p. 185 in the present volume), "A Tale"
(p. 198), "On Wine" (p. 199), "Dialogue Between the Gout and Mr.
Franklin" (p. 203), "The Handsome and the Deformed Leg" (p. 210), and
"The Flies" (p. 250). The translators are identified in the list of sources in the
Note on the Texts.

184.7   MADAME HELVÉTIUS] Mme. Ligniville de Helvétius, wealthy
widow of the Baron Claude Adrian de Helvétius, a writer and philosopher;
she conducted a salon that attracted many notable French intellectuals. In her
sixties when Franklin met her, she was strong-minded and unconventional.
She turned down Franklin's proposal of marriage (perhaps tendered half-
seriously), as is evident from the text.

184.16   H——] Baron Claude Adrian de Helvétius (1715–1771). See note
184.7.

185.5–6   Abbé de la R——] Martin Lefèbvre de la Roche (d. 1806), a
former Benedictine; friend and literary executor of Helvétius, translator of
Horace and editor of Montesquieu, and one of Franklin's Passy friends.

185.6   Abbé M——] Abbé André Morellet (1727–1819), another of Franklin's Passy associates, and a frequent visitor to Mme. Helvétius's salon. He
translated Thomas Jefferson's *Notes on the State of Virginia*.

185.29   MADAME LA FRETÉ] Mme. Martinville de la Freté, another of
Franklin's female friends, of whom little is known. Her husband had business
dealings with the colonies.

191.22   my dear Friend's] Mme. Brillon's.

191.28   M. B.] M. Brillon, the husband of Mme. Brillon (to whom this
bagatelle was written); twenty-four years her senior, theirs was a marriage of
convenience.

201–02   Drawings] These drawings, the work of one of Franklin's grandsons, were printed in the *Memoires inédits* (1822) of the Abbé Morellet.

212.14   *****] "Brusselles" is written after the title in the original
manuscript.

212.18–20   *"Une figure . . . donnée"*] "Given any single figure, one is
asked to inscribe therein as many times as possible another smaller figure, also
given."

212.21–23   *"l'Académie . . . UTILITÉ"*]   "The Academy has judged that this discovery, by widening the boundaries of our knowledge, will not be without UTILITY."

215.5   *Notes for Conversation*]   Franklin used these notes on April 18, 1782, in discussions with Richard Oswald, at the beginning of the peace negotiations between England and the United States.

216.28–29   *Supplement . . . Chronicle*]   This "Supplement" was printed by Franklin on his press at Passy. The number "705" was the real number of an issue of the *Boston Independent Chronicle* for March.

223.35   *"Nerone Neronior"*]   "More Nero than Nero himself." From John Milton, *Pro Populo Anglicano Defensia* (1651), ch. 1.

237.39–40   *There . . . WATTS.*]   The Latin in the text is from Horace *Epistles* 1. 2. 27. Watts's paraphrase was: "There are a Number of us creep / Into this World, to eat and sleep; / And know no Reason why they're born, / But merely to consume the Corn." Watts, *Miscellaneous Thoughts* (1734), p. 61.

246.30   *Nil desperandum*]   "Never despair." Horace *Odes* 1. 7. 27.

247.14   *ce n'est . . . coûte*]   "It's only the first time that it costs" (i.e., "the first step is the hardest").

256.39   *un peu dérangées*]   "A little deranged."

257.33   *"avec Sureté"*]   "With safety."

257.36   *"sans . . . Dépenses,"*]   "Without too great expenses."

268.8–9   *"d'etre . . . convenable"*]   "To be received in an agreeable manner."

259.29   *To Arthur Lee*]   Franklin did not send this letter; instead, the next day, he wrote again, patiently replying to all of Lee's accusations.

260.14   *Weissenstein*]   "Weissenstein" was evidently the assumed name of a British secret agent.

262.36   *Arcana Imperii*]   Mark Zuirius Boxhorn, *Arcana imperii detecta; or, divers select cases in Government* (1701).

267.1–2   *God-send or The Wreckers*]   Franklin probably created the title and the scene.

273.27   *Serapis*]   On September 23, 1779, Jones, in his ship the *Bonhomme Richard*, took the English ship the *Serapis*, even though the heavily damaged *Bonhomme Richard* sank the next day.

275.22   *Chapter*]   "A Parable Against Persecution."

276.19   piece]   "On the Providence of God in the Government of the World."

277.33   Situation . . . Person] Priestley was unhappy in his position as Lord Shelburne's librarian and requested Franklin's advice about leaving the post.

282.3   little piece] "The Ephemera."

282.27–28   little piece] An essay called "On Human Vanity" reprinted by Franklin in *The Pennsylvania Gazette*, December 4, 1735, from the *Free-thinker*, April 24, 1719.

289.2   *tante de gagne*] "So much gained."

290.15   excellent Pamphlet] *Essay on the Population of England* (2d ed., 1780).

291.14   the *London*] The London Coffee House, where Franklin's favorite Club of Honest Whigs had been meeting since March, 1772.

294.9   Account] By Cotton Mather. *Philosophical Transactions*, 29 (1714), pp. 70–71, with illustration Fig. 8.

294.10   Remarks] Court de Gebelin judged the petroglyphs on Dighton Rock to be Phoenician. *Monde Primitif* (1781), VIII, 561–68.

299.34   little Book] *Prosody Made Easy* (1781).

300.25   "Tully . . . Age,"] James Logan's translation of Cicero's *Cato Major* (1744). This was among Franklin's finest examples of printing.

300.32   M. Didot] François-Ambroise Didot (1730–1804), to whom Franklin's grandson Benjamin Bache was briefly apprenticed.

301.1   "Salust" . . . Madrid] The Spanish printer Joachim de Ibarra published his edition of *Don Quixote* in 1771 and Sallust in 1772.

304.26   a medal] Franklin later had the medal, *Libertas Americana*, struck by the engraver Augustin Dupré.

307.5   a paper] "Supplement to the Boston Independent Chronicle" (pp. 216–24 in the present volume).

309.25   Club] Franklin's Club of Honest Whigs met on Thursdays at St. Paul's (later the London) Coffee House.

310.28   Papa] William Alexander, Franklin's neighbor in France, a tobacco merchant of Scots birth who later emigrated to Virginia. His daughter Mariamne married Franklin's grandnephew Jonathan Williams, Jr.; this letter is to another daughter.

310.35   *plus de Chaleur*] "Much heat."

311.6   *Ménagère*] "Manager" (i.e., housekeeper).

314.17   monument] The monument in memory of General Richard Montgomery. It was placed in the portico of St. Paul's Church in New York City.

315.35–316.1   Children . . . State.] Lafayette had named his newborn daughter "Virginia."

320.4   *To Comte de Vergennes*] As Vergennes complained to Franklin in a letter of December 15, the American peace commissioners had concluded preliminary articles of peace with Britain without communicating with France, despite instructions from Congress "that nothing shall be done without the participation of the King." This letter is Franklin's apology on behalf of the peace commissioners.

320.34   *bienséance*] "Propriety" or "decorum."

321.23   dearest Friend] Margaret Stevenson died on January 1, 1783.

324.10–11   one of my Colleagues] John Adams.

325.5   Shakespear . . . Air,"] *Othello*, III, iii, 322–24: "Trifles light as air / Are to the jealous, confirmations strong / As proof is of Holy Writ."

339.4   respectable person] Dr. Samuel Cooper (1725–83) of Boston wrote to Franklin warning him of the allegations being made against him in America, presumably by John Adams.

340.4   Public Person] John Adams.

340.29–30   *Caisse d'Escompte*] According to Franklin, "an institution similar to the Bank of England" (letter to Elias Boudinot, Nov. 1, 1783).

348.40   *"Virtutis Premium,"*] "Reward of virtue."

349.1   *"Esto perpetua"*] "Let her be eternal."

349.8   *omnia reliquit*] "He left all behind."

349.22   OMNIA VANITAS] "All is vanity."

352.12   *"Essays to do Good"*] Cotton Mather's *Bonifacius* (1710) was also known by its running title, "Essays to Do Good."

353.10   *Esto perpetua*] See note 349.1.

356.10   Seymour] Edward Seymour (1633–1708) was one of the Lords of Treasury who opposed James Blair's attempt to secure quitrent money for the salary of Virginia's clergy. John Somers (1651–1716), not Seymour, was attorney general.

356.11–12   College . . . Province] The College of William and Mary.

362.31–32   General Melvill] Robert Melville (1723–1809).

363.28   honest Minister] Theophilus Lindsey (1723–1808). See Chronology, 1774.

364.30   *bavarder*] To "chat" or "gossip."

364.31   Saying of Alphonsus] King Alphonsus wished to have old friends, old books, old wine, and old wood.

365.23   *The Old Man's Wish*]   Dr. Walter Pope evidently wrote the song in 1684.

365.5–6   *"Car . . . tetons."*]   " 'Because,' he said, 'they don't have any breasts at all.' "

367.18   *Enfans Trouvés*]   "Foundlings" (i.e., orphanage).

367.34–35   *pour . . . Nourrice*]   "For the nurse's monthly salary" (i.e., for not paying it).

369.17   Mr. Dollond's]   Peter Dollond (1730–1820), optician.

369.28   thus,]   Franklin's words in the drawing: top left: "least convex for distant Objects"; bottom left: "most convex for Reading"; top right: "least convex"; bottom right: "most convex."

PHILADELPHIA, 1785–1790

396.9   43]   Smyth prints this as "41 [sic]" (here and also at 396.11); in Madison's notes of the debates, the correct sum of 43 is given.

399.3–4   "except . . . it."]   Psalms 127:1.

399.35–400.4   Steele . . . *Wrong.*]   The mock dedication to Pope Clement XI of Urbano Cerri, *An Account of the state of the Roman Catholic Religion* (1715), though attributed to Richard Steele, was actually by Bishop Benjamin Hoadley. The quotation is: "You are Infallible, and We always in the Right," p. ii.

400.14–15   if well administred]   Alluding to Alexander Pope, *An Essay on Man* (1733–34), Epistle III, ll. 303–04: "For Forms of Government let fools / contest; Whate'er is best administered is best."

402.21   Petition to Parliament]   This is Franklin's own "Mock Petition to Parliament." Drawn up when the House of Commons was considering extending to Scotland the system of transportation of felons to the American colonies, it was never presented formally, but only shown to some members by Richard Jackson ("it occasion'd some Laughing," Franklin reported).

412.29–34   *"There . . .* DRYDEN.]   Stephen Hervey's translation of Juvenal's ninth satire, ll. 193–96, published in *The Satires of Decimus Junius Juvenalis. Translated into English Verse. By Mr. Dryden, And several Other Eminent Hands . . . (1693).*

417.27   Mr. Jackson]   James Jackson (1757–1806), a representative from Georgia in the first Congress, 1789–91.

420.25   Mr. Brown]   Andrew Brown (c. 1744–1797), publisher of *The Federal Gazette.*

421.23   *Burton on Melancholly*]   Robert Burton, *The Anatomy of Melancholy* (1621).

422.4   little Piece]   Probably "The Retort Courteous" (pp. 382–90 in the present volume).

428.31   little piece]   Probably "A Comparison of the Conduct of the Ancient Jews and the Anti-Federalists" (pp. 404–08 in the present volume).

440.11   Copy . . . enclosed]   To Joseph Huey, June 6, 1753.

440.15   Copy . . . Letter]   To ——, [Dec. 13, 1757] (pp. 9–10 in the present volume).

POOR RICHARD'S ALMANACK, 1733–1758

445.20   Mr. *Titan Leeds*]   Titan Leeds (1699–1738) wrote the best-selling almanac of the Middle Colonies—until Poor Richard appeared. Franklin's prediction of Leeds' death echoes Jonathan Swift's Bickerstaff hoax, as well as Thomas Fleet's imitation of Swift in *The New-England Courant*, February 12, 1721/2.

450.31   Principiis obsta.]   "Meet the first beginnings" (i.e., "Nip it in the bud").

454.30–31   *ingratum . . . dixeris*]   "If you say he is ungrateful, you say everything."

455.15–16   *Sapiens . . . astris*]   "The wise man will be governed by the stars."

455.28   *ex ore . . . est*]   "He is condemned out of his own mouth."

456.24   Dyrro . . . ddoethach.]   "Give drink to a wise man [and] he will be wiser."

463.2   *J——n*]   John Jerman (1684–1769), who produced a rival almanac.

464.35   Felix quem, *&c.*]   See note 490.21.

466.23   Nec sibi . . . mundo.]   Cato's rule of life, according to Lucan's *Civil War* 2. 383: "To believe that one is born not for himself, but for the whole world."

471.1   Brother *J—m–n*]   See note 463.2.

472.12–13   Doll . . . look.]   The two Latin phrases were mnemonic tags used in Latin grammars of the time to familiarize students with noun genders and declensions. The whole saying, incorporating the Latin, may be translated as follows: "Doll, learning without book [i.e., from experience] the particular attribute of men, looks like the image of generative increasing [i.e., pregnant]."

472.29   *Probatum est*]   "It is proved."

475.33   *J. J——n*]   See note 463.2.

475.37   *W. B——t*]   William Birkett, a rival almanac maker.

478.25   *Poor Richard, 1741*]   "Instead of a trifling Preface that this Page uses to be fill'd with," Franklin wrote, "accept the following Chronological Account of MEMORABLE EVENTS Since the Revolution in 1688," and a list of events followed.

483.4   Bis . . . dat.]   See 535.8–9.

483.17   Reniego . . . d'oro.]   "Despise chains, though they be of gold."

484.7   Heb . . . digon.]   "Without God, without anything; with God, with enough."

484.12–13   Fient . . . jugement.]   "Dog's dung and silver mark will all be one on Judgment Day."

488.34   Le sage . . . mot.]   "The wise man understands a hint."

489.13   A achwyno . . . iddo.]   "Let him who complains without cause, be given cause to complain."

489.16   Borgen . . . sorgen.]   "He that goes borrowing, goes sorrowing."

489.26   A noddo . . . noddir.]   "What will be protected by God will be protected completely."

489.30–31   Na funno . . . ûn.]   "Let no man do to another what he would not wish for himself."

490.10   Tugend . . . vergehet.]   "Virtue stays when all else goes."

490.14–15   Con todo . . . Ingalatierra.]   "War with all the world, and peace with England."

490.21   Felix . . . cautum.]   "Happy is he whom others' experiences make cautious."

499.5   Ni ffyddra . . . hûn.]   "Man's hand alone, without God's help, cannot do himself good."

500.11   JACOB TAYLOR]   Taylor (1670–1746), formerly surveyor-general of Pennsylvania, was a schoolteacher, poet, and sometime printer.

500.18   *Requiescat in pace.*]   "Rest in peace."

502.18–36   Hail . . . Way.]   Adapted from John Hughes, *The Ecstasy* (1720).

505.24   this Month]   January.

506.26   this month]   March.

506.28–29   *Thomson . . . simple.*] Adapted from James Thomson, *The Seasons*, "Summer," ll. 1560–62.

506.30–507.3   What were . . . view.] James Thomson, *A Poem Sacred to the Memory of Sir Isaac Newton* (1727), ll. 30–38.

507.6–7   Nature . . . light.] Alexander Pope, Epitaph XII in his collected works.

507.10   Eilen . . . gut.] "Hurry seldom does well."

507.11   this month] April.

508.7   this month] June.

509.9   this month] October.

509.17   28th] Of October.

509.19   *He made . . . own.*] James Thomson, *The Seasons*, "Summer," l. 1559.

509.28   29th] Of October.

510.12   *Poor Richard Improved, 1749*] The Preface for 1749, omitted here, was by John Bartram.

510.15   this month] January.

510.22–24   BOYLE . . . *sought*.] James Thomson, *The Seasons*, "Summer," ll. 1556–58.

511.9   this month] February.

512.10   this month] April.

512.15–16   *If Parts . . . mankind.*] Alexander Pope, *An Essay on Man* (1733–34), Epistle IV, ll. 281–82.

512.21–36   BACON . . . again.] James Thomson, *The Seasons*, "Summer," ll. 1535–50.

513.7   27th] Of May.

513.23   this month] June.

514.12   mad] As Poor Richard explained in the 1750 almanac, this was a typographical error (see p. 517 of the present volume).

515.12   this month] December.

515.24–27   *Superior . . . ape.*] Alexander Pope, *An Essay on Man* (1733–34), Epistle II, ll. 31–34.

517.24–25   *wrapp'd, . . . warp'd]* This refers to a poem under May in the 1749 almanac, not reprinted in the present volume.

518.27   Beatus . . . potest.] "Beauty without virtue is powerless."

522.36–523.13   The Bell . . . still.] Edward Young, *The Complaint: Or, Night Thoughts on Life, Death, and Immortality* (1742–45), I, 54–56, 57–61, 389–97.

537.2   *Scandalum Magnatum*] "The scandal of the peerage." The name given to a statute of Richard II by which punishment was to be inflicted for any scandal or wrong offered to or uttered against a noble personage.

542.19–20   Journal . . . *Bouguer*] A translation (not reprinted here) of Pierre Bouguer, "Relation Abrégée du Voyage Fait au Pérou," *Histoire de L'Académie Royale des Sciences* (1744), pp. 249–73.

548.13   following Extracts] The extracts from John Pringle, *Observations on Diseases of the Army* (1752), are not reprinted here.

548.17   recommended in my last] The piece called "*Remarks, on the Advantages that may arise from a more general* Use of Oxen *for* Draft *in the Province of* Pennsylvania," submitted by a "Correspondent" and printed in the 1756 almanac, is not included in the present volume.

550.17–24   Sincerity . . . attend.] Benjamin Stillingfleet, *Essay on Conversation* (1737), ll. 400–07, reprinted in Robert Dodsley, *A Collection of Poems* (1748).

THE AUTOBIOGRAPHY

567.2   Twyford] Bishop Jonathan Shipley's country home, fifty miles north of London, where Franklin stayed while writing Part One of the *Autobiography*, between July 30 and August 13, 1771.

567.5   Son] William Franklin had been governor of New Jersey since 1762.

567.17   Reputation] Franklin's autograph manuscript, in the Huntington Library in San Marino, California, shows that he revised his text extensively. For instance, here Franklin first wrote "Fame," then changed it to "Reputation." Other examples of revisions are given in notes at 574.9, 579.8–9, 579.26–27, 579.38, 599.37, 615.7, 620.11–12, 623.23, 624.7, 632.30, 641.11–12, 644.11, and 679.1 below.

570.6   old Stile] England did not adopt the Gregorian calendar until September 13, 1752. Under the old (Julian) calendar, the new year began on March 25, and the old calendar was, by the eighteenth century, eleven days behind the new. Thus Franklin was born January 6, 1705, "old style," or January 17, 1706, "new style." The Preface to *Poor Richard Improved, 1752*, is an essay on the history of the calendar (pp. 530–34 in the present volume).

572.31   one . . . printed] Peter Folger's *A Looking Glass for the Times*, though written in 1676, was not printed until 1725.

573.23   his Character]   His shorthand method.

574.9   against it;]   Franklin first wrote here, "and so it seem'd that I was destin'd for a Tallow Chandler," then canceled the clause.

576.22   By my rambling Digressions]   It may have been at this point, after writing eight pages of his manuscript, that Franklin felt the need of an outline for his work. Several versions of the outline are extant. The version closest to Franklin's original working outline is a copy in the Pierpont Morgan Library in New York City, printed in the Lemay–Zall genetic text, and reproduced here with the genetic text's sigla included. These symbols, used throughout the genetic text, are omitted in the clear text of the *Autobiography* in the present volume; they are retained in the following outline as a sample of the genetic text's format.

↑ ↓   single arrows enclose interlinear additions.
< >   angle brackets enclose cancellations.
{ }   braces enclose matter written over by the following matter.
[p. o]   page numbers within brackets indicate the pagination of the original manuscript.

Copie d'un {Autographe} Projet très curieux de Bn. Franklin.—1ere. Esquisse memorandum de ses mémoires. Les additions à l'encre rouge sont de la main de Franklin.

My writing. Mrs.. Dogoods Letters—Differences arise between my Brother and me (his temper and mine) their Cause in general. His News Paper. The Prosecution he suffered. My Examination. Vote of Assembly. His Manner of evading it. Whereby I became free. My Attempt to get employ with other Printers. He prevents me. Our frequent pleadings before our Father. The final Breach. My Inducements to quit Boston. Manner of coming to a Resolution. My leaving him & going to New York. (return to eating Flesh.) thence to Pennsylvania, The Journey, and its Events on the Bay, at Amboy, the Road, meet with Dr. Brown. his Character. his great work. At Burlington. The Good Woman. On the River. My Arrival at Philada... First Meal and first Sleep. Money left. Employment. Lodging. First Acquaintance with my Afterwards Wife. with J. Ralph. with Keimer. their Characters. Osborne. Watson. The Governor takes Notice of me. the Occasion and Manner. his Character. Offers to set me up. My return to Boston. <y> Voyage and Accidents. Reception. My Father dislikes the proposal. I return to New York and Philada... Governor Burnet. J. Collins. the Money for Vernon. The Governors Deceit. Collins not finding Employment goes to Barbados much in my Debt. Ralph and I go to England. Disappointment of Governors Letters. Col. French his Friend. Cornwallis's Letters. Cabbin. Denham. Hamilton, Arrival in England. Get Employment. Ralph not. He is an Expence to me. Adventures in England. Write a Pamphlet and print 100. Schemes. Lyons. Dr Pemberton. My Diligence and yet poor thro Ralph. My Landlady. her Character. Wygate. Wilkes. Cibber. Plays. Books I borrowed. Preachers I heard. Redmayne. At Watts's— Tem-

NOTES

perance. Ghost,. Conduct and Influence among the Men, persuaded by Mr
Denham to return with him to Philada.. & be his Clerk. Our Voyage. and
Arrival. My resolutions in Writing. My Sickness. His Death. Found D. R mar-
ried. Go to work again with Keimer. Terms. His ill Usage of me. My Re-
sentment. Saying of Decow. My Friends at Burlington. Agreement with H
Meredith to set up in Partnership. Do so. Success with the Assembly. Ham-
iltons Friendship. Sewells History. Gazette. Paper Money. Webb. Writing
Busy Body. Breintnal. Godfrey. his Character. Suit against us. Offer of my
Friends Coleman and Grace. continue the Business and M. goes to Carolina.
Pamphlet on Paper Money. Gazette from Keimer. Junto erected, its plan.
Marry. Library erected. Manner of conducting the Project. Its plan and Util-
ity. Children. Almanack. the Use I made of it. Great Industry. Constant Study.
Fathers Remark and Advice upon Diligence. Carolina Partnership. Learn
French and German. Journey to Boston after 10 years. Affection of my
Brother. His Death and leaving me [p. 2] his Son. Art of Virtue. Occasion.
City Watch. amended. Post Office. Spotswood. Bradfords Behaviour. Clerk
of Assembly. Lose one of my Sons. Project of subordinate Junto's. Write
occasionally in the papers. Success in Business. Fire Companys. Engines. Go
again to Boston in 1743. See Dr Spence. Whitefield. My Connection with him.
His Generosity to me. my returns. Church Differences. My part in them.
Propose a College. not then prosecuted. Propose and establish a Philosophical
Society. War. Electricity. my first knowledge of it. Partnership with D Hall
&c. Dispute in Assembly upon Defence. Project for it. Plain Truth. its Success.
10.000 Men raised and Disciplined. Lotteries. Battery built. New Castle. My
Influence in the Council. Colours, Devices and Motto's.— Ladies. Military
Watch. Quakers. chosen of the common council. Put in the Commission of
the Peace. Logan fond of me. his Library. Appointed post Master General.
Chosen Assembly Man. Commissioner to treat with Indians at Carlisle. ↑and
at Easton.↓ Project and establish Academy. Pamphlet on it. Journey to Boston. At Albany. Plan of Union of the Colonies. Copy of it. Remarks upon it.
It fails and how. (Journey to Boston in 1754.) Disputes about it in our Assembly. My part in them. New Governor. Disputes with him. His Character and
Sayings to me. Chosen Alderman. Project of Hospital my Share in it. Its
Success. Boxes. Made a Commissioner of the treasury My Commission to
defend the Frontier Counties. Raise Men & build Forts. Militia Law of my
drawing. Made Colonel. Parade of my Officers. Offence to Proprietor. Assistance to Boston Ambassadors— Journey with Shirley &c.. Meet with Braddock. Assistance to him. To the Officers of his Army. Furnish him with
Forage. His Concessions to me and Character of me. Success of my Electrical
Experiments. Medal sent me per Royal Society and Speech of President. Den-
nys Arrival & Courtship to me. his Character. My Service to the Army in the
Affair of Quarters. Disputes about the Proprietors Taxes continued. Project
for paving the City. I am sent to England.] Negociation there. Canada delenda
est. My Pamphlet. Its reception and Effect. Projects drawn from me concerning the Conquest. Acquaintance made and their Services to me. Mrs.. S.., Mr
Small. Sir John P. Mr. Wood. Sargent Strahan and others. their Characters.

Doctorate from Edinburg ↑St. Andrews↓ <F——d-> [p. 3] Doctorate from
Oxford. Journey to Scotland. Lord Leicester. Mr. Prat.— DeGrey. Jackson.
State of Affairs in England. Delays. Event. Journey into Holland and Flanders.
Agency from Maryland. Sons Appointment. My Return. Allowance and
thanks. Journey to Boston. John Penn Governor. My Conduct towards him.
The Paxton Murders. My Pamphlet Rioters march to Philada... Governor retires to my House. My Conduct, <towards him. The Paxton Murders.> Sent
out to the Insurgents—Turn them back. Little Thanks. Disputes revived. Resolutions against continuing under Proprietary Government. Another Pamphlet. Cool Thoughts. Sent again to England with Petition. Negociation
there. Lord H. his Character. Agencies from New Jersey, Georgia, Massachusets. Journey into Germany 1766. Civilities received there. Gottingen Observations. Ditto into France in 1767. Ditto in 1769. Entertainment there at the
Academy. Introduced to the King and the Mesdames. Mad. Victoria and Mrs.
Lamagnon. Duc de Chaulnes, M Beaumont. Le Roy. Dali{t}bard. Nollet. See
Journals. Holland. Reprint my papers and add many. Books presented to me
<by> ↑from↓ many Authors. My Book translated into French. Lightning
Kite. various Discoveries. My Manner of prosecuting that Study. King of Den-
mark invites me to Dinner. Recollect my Fathers Proverb. Stamp Act. My
Opposition to it. Recommendation of J. Hughes. Amendment of it. Exami-
nation in Parliament. Reputation it gave me. Caress'd by Ministry. Charles
Townsends Act. Opposition to it. Stoves and Chimney plates. ↑Armonica.↓
Accquaintance with Ambassadors. Russian Intimation. Writing in Newspapers.
Glasses from Germany. Grant of Land in Nova Scotia. Sicknesses. Letters to
America returned hither. the Consequences. Insurance Office. My Character.
Costs me nothing to be civil to inferiors, a good deal to be submissive to
superiors &c &c..

Farce of perpetl. Motion
Writing for Jersey Assembly.   verte
[p. 4] Hutchinson's Letters. Temple. Suit in Chancery, Abuse before the Privy
Council.—Lord Hillsborough's Character. & Conduct. Lord Dartmouth. Negotiation to prevent the War.—Return to America. Bishop of St Asaph. Congress, Assembly. Committee of Safety. Chevaux de Frize.—Sent to Boston, to
the Camp. To Canada. to <Gu> Lord Howe.— To France, Treaty, &c

Source: *The Autobiography of Benjamin Franklin: A Genetic Text*, ed. J. A.
Leo Lemay and P. M. Zall (Knoxville: University of Tennessee Press, 1981),
pp. 202–05. The headnote in French translates as follows: "Copy of a {Au-
tograph} very curious Project of Bn. Franklin.—1st. Outline memorandum of
his memoirs. The additions in red ink are in the hand of Franklin."

579.8–9   a little . . . sake.]   Franklin first wrote, "because he left me no
Choice," then canceled the phrase and substituted this one.

579.26–27   Spectator.]   A canceled phrase following here indicates that "It
was the Third."

579.38   Stock of Words] Franklin first wrote "Copia Verborum," then changed to the English phrase.

582.26–27   *Men . . . forgot*] Alexander Pope, *An Essay on Criticism* (1711), ll. 574–75, substituting "should" for "must."

582.29   *To speak . . . Diffidence*] Pope, *An Essay on Criticism*, l. 567, substituting "To" for "And."

582.30–31   "Immodest . . . Sense."] Wentworth Dillon, Earl of Roscommon, *An Essay on Translated Verse* (1684), ll. 113–14, substituting "Modesty" for "Decency."

583.9–10   The Boston News Letter] *The Boston News-Letter* began publication in 1704; *The Boston Gazette* in 1719; *The American Weekly Mercury* (Philadelphia) later in 1719; and *The New-England Courant* in 1721.

583.25–26   anonymous Paper] The first "Silence Dogood" essay.

584.23   Author] James Franklin twice had serious troubles with the authorities. The first time he was imprisoned for nearly a month, June 12 to July 7, 1722; the second time he hid from the sheriff from January 24 to February 12, 1722/3.

584.35–36   *that . . . Courant*] On January 16, 1722/3, the General Court resolved that James Franklin be forbidden to publish the *Courant* "except it be first supervised by the Secretary of the Province." The *Courant* first appeared under Benjamin Franklin's name on February 12, 1722/3. Franklin gave the "Rulers some Rubs" in his "Rules for *The New-England Courant*" and "To 'your Honour'."

588.34   Sunday morning] October 6, 1723.

591.31   French Prophets] The Camisards, Protestant peasants of the Cévennes region of France, famous for their emotionalism.

594.25   Impropriety of it;] Franklin first continued here, "and said he had advanc'd too much already to my Brother James," then canceled the clause.

599.37   Glutton] Franklin first called Keimer a "Gormandizer," then changed it to "Glutton."

602.15   *Pope* cur'd him] Alexander Pope included unfavorable references to Ralph in *The Dunciad* (1728).

606.39   handsomely] Franklin offered to sell Sir Hans Sloane the purse in a letter of June 2, 1725.

607.24   Young's Satires] Probably Edward Young's *The Universal Passion* (1725–28).

609.1–2   mixing . . . Matter] By mixing his types, putting the manuscript pages in the wrong order, and breaking up the type he had already set.

611.18   Chelsea to Blackfryars]   Over three miles.

611.22   Thevenot's . . . Positions]   Melchisédec Thévenot, *The Art of Swimming* (1699).

613.18   *Plan*]   "Plan of Conduct."

614.13   carried him off]   After a long illness, Denham died on July 4, 1728.

614.14   small Legacy]   In an oral will, Denham forgave Franklin the £10 Franklin owed him for the return from London.

615.7   Wages]   Franklin first wrote "80 Pounds a Year," then canceled the phrase and wrote instead, "Wages so much higher . . . "

619.8   Boyle's Lectures]   The English scientist Robert Boyle (1627–91) endowed a lecture series against "notorious Infidels."

619.21–25 *Whatever . . . above.*]   John Dryden, *Oedipus* (1679), III, i, 244–48, though the first line is taken from Alexander Pope, *An Essay on Man* (1733–34), Epistle I, l. 294.

620.11–12 Religion.—]   Franklin first continued here, "some foolish Intrigues with low Women excepted, which from the Expence were rather more inconvenient to me than to them." After changing "inconvenient" to "prejudicial," he canceled the clause entirely, but returned to the subject later (see p. 631 in the present volume).

621.17–18 Autumn . . . Year]   In the fall of 1727.

622.37   Distribution]   Putting the letters back into their cases after the printing had been done.

623.23   Friend]   Franklin added "She Female" before "Friend," then canceled his revision.

623.38   Busy Body]   "The Busy-Body" appeared in Bradford's *American Weekly Mercury* from February 4, 1728, through September 25, 1729.

624.7   singular Number]   Franklin had written "my Paper" at 623.36–37, then changed it to "our Paper."

624.15   spirited Remarks*]   Franklin's "Remarks" appeared in *The Pennsylvania Gazette*, October 9, 1729, the second issue of the paper after he bought it from Keimer. He did not include the text of this essay in his manuscript. It is reprinted here from the Lemay–Zall *Genetic Text* (pp. 179–81, with the quotation marks added to correspond to Franklin's practice in a similar footnote at 568.36 in the present volume).

627.18   two long Letters]   In *The Pennsylvania Gazette*, May 6 and 13, 1731.

627.28–29 the Year 1729.]   The partnership was officially disbanded on July 4, 1730.

632.14   Subscription Library]   The Library Company of Philadelphia was founded on July 1, 1731.

632.30   Beginning]   Franklin first wrote here, "of gratifying the suppos'd Curiosity of my Son; what follows being . . . " After adding "and others of Posterity" after "Son," he canceled the entire clause.

633.1   *Part Two*]   Franklin wrote the second section of the *Autobiography* in 1784 at Passy, France (as indicated on pp. 639 and 654 of the present volume).

635.2   *Notes*]   The "Notes" consisted of a copy of the outline of topics that Franklin had made in 1771 for the *Autobiography*. See note 576.22.

634.5–639.10   MY . . . VAUGHAN.]   Quotation marks around this letter, presumably added by William Temple Franklin (it is from his edition that the text of this letter derives), have been omitted.

634.36   *Art of Virtue*]   See note 26.33.

641.11–12   plucking . . . Owner.]   Franklin first wrote "returning the Reputation thus assumed to its right owner," then rewrote the clause.

641.26–28   "*Seest . . . Men.*"]   Proverbs 22:29.

642.17   Presbyterian]   Franklin was raised as a member of Boston's Congregational Old South Church, but Presbyterianism was more similar to Congregationalism than were most religious denominations.

644.11   our Interest]   Franklin first wrote "my Interest," and, in the next line, "my Slipping."

647.5   *Form of the Pages.*]   In Franklin's manuscript, the lines of the chart are drawn in red ink; the words, letters, and dots are in black ink.

648.8–11   *Here . . . happy.*]   Joseph Addison, *Cato* (1713), V, i, 15–18.

648.13–15   *O Vitæ . . . anteponendus.*]   *Tusculan Disputations* 5. 2. 5 (several lines omitted). "O, Philosophy, guide of life! O teacher of virtue and corrector of vice. One day of virtue is better than an eternity of vice."

648.33–38   *Father . . . Bliss!*]   James Thomson, *The Seasons*, "Winter," ll. 217–22.

649   Chart]   In Franklin's manuscript, the lines of the chart are drawn in red ink; the words, numbers, and braces are in black ink.

655.1   *Part Three*]   Franklin began to write this third part of the *Autobiography* in 1788 at home in Philadelphia, and continued it at intervals between then and May, 1789.

657.34–35   connected Discourse]   "The Way to Wealth" (a title supplied by later editors) is printed in the present volume, pp. 554–63.

658.12–15   Socratic . . . Sense.]   "A Man of Sense."

658.15   Discourse . . . denial]   "Self-Denial Not the Essence of Virtue."

665.16   Paper]   "On Protection of Towns from Fire."

665.25   Articles of Agreement]   Drawn up on December 7, 1736.

669.36   *litera . . . manet*]   The full proverb is *Vox audita perit, littera scripta manet.* "The spoken word passes away, the written word remains."

671.7   Paper]   "A Proposal for Promoting Useful Knowledge Among the British Plantations in America."

676.5   *or other Grain*]   The Assembly so voted on July 25, 1745, although the amount was 4,000 rather than 3,000.

679.1   Providence]   Franklin first wrote "Fortune," then changed it to "Providence."

680.27   Dr Spence's]   Archibald Spencer.

683.3–4   writing . . . Newspapers]   "Appeal for the Hospital."

683.23–26   "And be . . . same."]   Franklin presented the bill to the Assembly on January 23, 1750/1.

689.31   displac'd]   Franklin was fired on January 30, 1774, for his pro-American writings and actions, and especially for surreptitiously obtaining the letters of Massachusetts Governor Thomas Hutchinson and sending them back to America. Since he did not bring the *Autobiography* down to 1774, the topic does not recur.

689.38–40   Degree . . . Compliment.]   The Harvard degree, July 27, 1753, was first; the Yale degree was September 12; these were the highest degrees Harvard and Yale then awarded.

690.18   Plan]   "The Albany Plan of Union."

691.27–28   *"Look . . . pursue."*]   John Dryden's translation of Juvenal's tenth satire, ll. 1–2, in *The Satires of Decimus Junius Juvenalis. Translated into English Verse. By Mr. Dryden, And several other Eminent Hands . . .* (1693).

693.7–8   Idea of Sancho Panza]   Cervantes, *Don Quixote* (Part 1, chapter 29). Sancho Panza grieves at the idea of governing blacks until he realizes that he can sell them.

699.24   D°]   "Ditto."

699.29   C.ʷᵗ]   "Hundredweight."

705.14–15   Dialogue]   "Dialogue Between X, Y, and Z, Concerning the Present State of Affairs in Philadelphia."

712.37   Dr Spence]   See note 680.27.

713.17   two Lectures]   "Course of Experiments."

714.3   print . . . Pamphlet]   *Experiments and Observations on Electricity* (1751).

725.8   1757.]   Franklin interrupted his writing at this point and began again sometime after November 13, 1789, with "As soon . . . "

726.9   Clause in a Bill]   The bill containing this clause died when Parliament adjourned in 1744 without passing it.

726.13–16   Conduct . . . themselves.]   The Declaration Act of 1766 asserted Parliament's right to legislate for the colonies.

729.4   Execution]   Franklin stopped writing here, probably shortly before his death on April 17.

Index

Contents of this volume are shown in capitals and small capitals.

Aaron, 405–06.

Abbeville, France, 84.

Abolition of slavery (see Slavery).

Academy of Philadelphia, proposal for establishment, 670–71; founding, 678–79; BF made trustee, 679; receives charter, 680.

Academy of Sciences (Academy Royale des Sciences), Lavoisier experiment at, 309; balloon flight, 336.

Account of the New-Invented Pennsylvanian Fire-Places, sent to Kames, 21; BF writes, 677.

ACCOUNT OF THE SUPREMEST COURT OF JUDICATURE IN PENNSYLVANIA, VIZ. THE COURT OF THE PRESS, AN, 410–14.

ADAMS, John, letters to, 292–93, 301, 306–07; offends French, 284–85; seeks aid from Holland, 285; congressional funds exhausted, 286; and Dutch loan, 295–96; advice, 298; distrusts France, 324; BF protests calumnies of, 339.

Adams, Matthew, lends BF books, 578.

Addison, Joseph, *Cato* quoted, 648; tribute to, 508.

ADDRESS TO THE PUBLIC FROM THE PENNSYLVANIA SOCIETY FOR PROMOTING THE ABOLITION OF SLAVERY, AN, 414–15.

Africa, 384.

Air, baths in, 95–96; unhealthiness of confined, 145, 379.

Airpump, invented by Boyle, 510.

Albany, army idle at, 37.

Albany Congress, BF commissioner to, 690.

Albany Plan of Union, The, BF proposes, comments on, 690–92; Britain prevents, 694.

ALEXANDER, Miss, letter to, 310–11.

Alexander, James, and Plan of Union, 690.

Alexander, Robert, 49, 70.

Alexander, William, 343.

Alexander & Williams, French tobacco contract, 342.

Alexander the Great, 221; and Bucephalus, 452.

Algiers, and piracy, 332, 417–18.

Allegheny Mountains, as American boundary, 315.

Allemand, Jean, and oil on water experiment, 154.

Allen, Judge John, 618.

Allen, William, 672.

ALLEYNE, John, letter to, 96–98.

Alliance (ship), problems on board, 283; and prize money, 329–31.

Almanacs, 463, 536. (See also POOR RICHARD'S ALMANACK.)

Alphabet, 519.

Alphonsus, 364.

Amazon River, 38.

America, first discoverers of, 142–43; nature of inhabitants, 235–36; plentifulness of land in, 238–39; conditions of apprentices in, 241–42; discovery by Phoenicians, 294.

American Philosophical Society, honors M. Gerard, 280; establishment, 401.

Amherst, Sir Jeffrey, 719.

Amontons, Guillaume, 317.

Amsterdam, 273.

Animal magnetism (see Mesmerism).

Annapolis, Maryland, 40.

Annis, Thomas, captains London packet, 598.

ANONYMOUS, letters to, 9–10, 100–01, 343–44.

Anti-Federalists, 404–09.

APOLOGUE, 227–28.

Apprenticeship, of James, Jr., conditions in America, 241–42; of father, 569; of uncle Benjamin, 570; of brothers, 573; BF to chandler, 573–74; BF to printer, 577–78; under Keimer, 614–16.

Arabs, 234.

Arcana imperii (see Boxham, Mark Zuirius).

Ariel (ship), John Paul Jones sails to America, 283.

Aristotle, 214.

Arithmetic and accounts, for women, 659.

Arlond, Miss, 58.

Armed neutrality, proposed by Russia, 286–87.

Armonica, 49–53, 60.

Army, unconstitutionality of standing, 119; no necessity for standing in United States, 261. (See also Militia.)

Army, British, takes Charleston, S.C., 287; burns American towns, 386; officers receive gifts from Pennsylvania Assembly, 699; behavior toward civilians, 702.

Army, Continental, and Mrs. Barrow, 255; hindered by French delay, 295–96.

Army, French, 702.

Arnauld, Antoine, *Logic: or the Art of Thinking*, 581.

Arnold, Benedict, in England, 305, 387.

ARTICLES FOR A TREATY OF PEACE WITH MADAME BRILLON, 224–26.

"Articles of Belief and Acts of Religion," BF writes, 643.

Articles of Confederation, printed, 239; disapprove of hereditary titles, 344.

ART OF PROCURING PLEASANT DREAMS, THE, 378–82.

Asia, H.M.S., New Yorkers take refuge on, 255.

Association (for defense), formed against rioters, 72; BF organizes, 671–72; BF refuses colonelship, 672; defense, 705; BF elected colonel, 710–11. (See also Militia.)

Astrology, 455, 470–71, 520–21; rural origins, 539–41.

Astronomy, 493–94.

Atheism, 243.

Aurora Borealis, BF paper on, 277.

Austria, seeks trade agreements with United States, 331–32.

AUTEROCHE, Jean Chappe d', letter to, 92–93.

Auteuil, 204, 206.

AUTOBIOGRAPHY, THE, 565–729; Part One, 567–632; Part Two, 633–54; Part Three, 655–725; Part Four, 725–29; composition, 428.

Baal, 482, 491.

BABCOCK, Joshua, letter to, 134–36.

Babel, Tower of, 399, 400.

Bache, Benjamin Franklin, education, 269; religion, 269, 322.

Bache, Sarah Franklin (see FRANKLIN, Sarah).

Bache, William, 269.

Bacon, Sir Francis, 214, 357; quoted, 433; commemorated, 512.

Bacon, Roger, and the brazen wall, 82.

Bailey, Jacob, carries mail, 25.

Baird, Patrick, 602; praises BF, 623.

Baker, Polly (see Pseudonyms).

Balloon flight, of M. Charles, 334–36, 338; proposed by Montgolfier, 336–37.

Baltimore, Charles Calvert, 3d Baron of, 726.

Bank of North America, 368.

BANKS, Sir Joseph, letters to, 333–34, 334–38; botanical engravings, 149–50; and oil on water experiment, 159.

Banks, 340.

Barbary States, piracy connived at by Britain, 332; BF suggests friendship with, 332.

BARBEU-DUBOURG, Jacques, letter to, 95–96; translates BF, 145.

Barclay, Thomas, 314; and *Bonhomme Richard*, 329, 341.

Bard, Patrick (see Baird, Patrick).

Barney, Captain Joshua, 323, 344.

Barometer, 30.

Barrow, Thomas, takes refuge on H.M.S. *Asia*, 255.

Barrow, Mrs. Thomas, and American army, 255.

BARTRAM, John, letter to, 104–05; mentioned, 66.

BASKERVILLE, John, letter to, 42–43.

Baths, in cold air, 95–96.

Bavaria, seeks trade agreement with United States, 331.

Beatty, Rev. Charles, 708–09.

Beaumarchais, Pierre Augustin Caron de, repayment of, 286.

BECCARIA, Giovanni Battista (Giambatista), letter to, 49–53.
Beckett, Thomas, 300.
Beckwith, Major John, reports from Prussia, 62.
Bedford, John Russell, 4th Duke of, supports Canada expedition, 36.
Bedford Party, in cabinet, 91; opposes colonial appeasement, 116.
BENEZET, Anthony, letter to, 137.
Bentinck, Captain John Albert, and oil on water experiment, 156, 157, 159.
Bergen, Norway, and John Paul Jones's prizes, 274.
Bernard (Barnard), Sir Francis, opposes Stamp Act, 78; misinforms Parliament, 116; unfriendly to colonies, 143–44.
Bernier, François, Histoire de la Derniere Revolution, 13.
Bertin, Henri-Leonard-Jean-Baptiste, 311.
Bertram (see Bartram).
Bethlehem, Pennsylvania, and Moravians, 709.
Bevan, Sylvanus, sculpts bust of Penn, 22–23.
Bible, Eliot's translation, 293–94; faithful history, 404; travestied by Dr. Brown, 587–88. (See also Old Testament.)
Bickerstaff, Isaac, 181.
Bifocals (see Spectacles)
BILKED FOR BREAKFAST, 185–86.
Birkett, William, 475.
Birmingham, England, Baskerville type from, 42; silverplate, 130.
Blackbeard (see Teach, Edward).
Blackstone, Sir William, 357.
Blagden, Dr. Charles, and oil on water experiment, 159, 333–34.
Blair, James, and William and Mary College, 356.
Blake, Francis, 21.
Blunt, Catherine, 100.
Board of Trade, 691.
Bois du Boulogne, Paris, 207.
Boldsworth, Jonathan, 382.
BOND, Thomas, letter to, 280; and inoculation, 280; and hospital subscription, 682; and Phineas Bond, 704.

Bonhomme Richard (ship), and prize money, 313, 329–30.
Bonnell, John, 720.
Boston, resolutions, 91; danger of troops in, 105–06; troops resented in, 114; Gage's treachery to, 166; Lafayette arrives in, 281; BF's nostalgia for, 353, 427; blockaded, 384; BF leaves, 585; young BF returns to, 593.
Boston Weekly News-Letter, quoted, 583.
Botany Bay, Australia, 404.
Bouguer, Pierre, reports on tropics, 542.
Boulogne, France, 84.
Boxham, Mark Zuirius, Arcana imperii detecta, 262.
Boyd, James, conveys scalps to British, 217.
Boyle, Sir Robert, commemorated, 510.
Boyle Lectures, 619.
Braddock, General Edward, 699; begins campaign, 695–96; empowers BF, 696; lack of foresight, 700–01, 704; defeat and death of, 701–02; governor's reaction to defeat, 712; payment for provisioning denied BF, 721.
Bradford, Andrew, 590, 617; BF writes "Busy-Body" for, 623; work inferior to BF's, 625; restrains circulation of Gazette, 628–30, 629; deprived of post office, 664.
Bradford, William, advises BF to go to Philadelphia, 586; introduces BF to Keimer, 590–91.
Brahe, Tycho, and calendar, 531.
Breintnall, Joseph, characterized, 621; recommends BF to Quakers, 622; continues "Busy-Body," 623; in BF's shop, 628.
BRIGDEN, Edward, letter to, 271–72.
Brightland, John, A Grammar of the English Tongue, 581.
Brillon de Jouy, M., 207–09.
Brillon de Jouy, Anne-Louise Boivin d'Hardancourt, 179, 224–26, 282.
British Empire, importance of America, 21.
Brockden, Charles, 600, 632; and Library Company, 640.
Browne, Dr. John, travesties Bible, 587–88.

Brownell, George, teaches BF, 573.

BROWNRIGG, William, letter to, 150–59.

Brownrigg, Mrs. William, 150.

Brown, Andrew, editor of *The Federal Gazette*, 420.

Brutus, letters discovered, 281.

Buffon, Georges-Louis Leclerc, Comte de, arranges translation of BF's papers, 714.

Bunker Hill, battle of, 166.

Bunyan, John, *Pilgrim's Progress*, 577; in Dutch, 586.

BURDETT, Peter B., letter to, 148–50.

Burgh, James, 309.

Burlington, New Jersey, 587–88.

Burnet, Gilbert, 596.

Burnet, William, receives BF, 596; in BF's editorial, 624–25; quarrels with Assembly, 624–25.

Burton, R. (see Crouch, Nathaniel).

Burton, Robert, *Anatomy of Melancholy*, 421.

Bustill, Samuel, 618.

Busy-Body, BF writes for Bradford, 623.

Bute, John Stuart, 3d Earl of, exonerated of Stamp Act, 81.

Button-mold Bay, 68.

Caesar, Julius, cited, 183; in *Poor Richard*, 468; and calendar, 532.

Calais, France, BF arrives at, 84.

Calcutta, Black Hole of, 379.

Calendar, changes, 530–34; history of, 531–34.

Calvin, John, commemorated, 513.

Cambridge, England, experiments at, 12.

Cambridge, Massachusetts, 167.

Canaanites, 407.

Canada, threat to New England, restoration to France, 21–22; frontier with United States, 215; and Revolutionary War, 216.

Canals, ship velocity in, 93–95; superior to rivers, 137–38.

Canassetego, and Christian worship, 233–34.

Canterbury, Archbishop of, refuses to ordain Americans, 355.

Canton, John, verifies BF's lightning experiment, 715.

Carleton, Sir Guy, Congress refuses to treat with, 313; and escaped slaves, 388.

Carlisle, Pennsylvania, Indian treaty of, 681.

CARMICHAEL, William, letter to, 281–82; mentioned, 289.

Carnac, General John, and oil on water experiment, 159.

Carolinas, land, 343; and debts to British slavers, 386–87. (See also North Carolina.)

Caslon, William, typeface, 42–43.

Castration, solution for colonial problem, 360.

Catholic Church (see Roman Catholic Church).

"Causes of the American Discontents Before 1768," BF sends to William Franklin, 91.

Cave, Edward, prints BF's electrical papers, 714.

Cavendish, Lord Charles, and raindrop experiment, 127.

Chandler, Samuel, 164.

Charles I, of England, Hambden's lawsuit, 222; and Nero, 223.

Charles II, of England, 572.

Charles IX, of France, 348.

Charles, Jacques Alexandre Cesar, and balloon flight, 334.

Charles, Robert, 725.

Charleston, South Carolina, false rumor of relief, 281; British seize, 287; trade embargo on, 386.

Charlottesville, Virginia, 287.

Chaucer, Geoffrey, quoted, 569.

Chaulnes, Marie Joseph Louis D'ailly, Duc de, 276.

Chaumont, Donatien LeRay, Comte de, misunderstanding with John Paul Jones, 274; ship delayed, 295; agent for Jones, 313; and prize money negotiations, 329–31.

Cheap, Andrew, 255.

Chesapeake Bay, 39.

Chess, didactic merits of, 187–89; etiquette in, 189–91; BF plays, 660.

Chester, Pennsylvania, 69

Chesterfield, Philip Dormer Stanhope, 4th Earl of, 437.

"Chevy Chace" (song), 43.

"Children in the Wood" (song), 43.

China, 294; chess in, 187; honors in, 344.

Christianity, Indian response to, 231–34.

Chronicles, 48.

Churchill River, Newfoundland, living conditions, 503–05.

Church of England, 400; in fable, 198; ordination, in United States, 355.

Cicero, M. Tullius, quoted, 183, 648; "On Old Age," 300.

Cincinnati, Society of the, 344–49; unpopularity of, 368.

Clapham, William, succeeds BF in militia command, 709.

Clapham Common, Mount Pond, England, and oil on water experiment, 150.

Clarke, General Thomas, and castration of American rebels, 360.

Clarkson, Thomas, *Essay on the Slavery and Commerce of the Human Species*, 430.

Clifton, John, and street lighting, 686.

Cliftons, Misses, 268.

Clinton, George, provides cannon for militia, 672.

Clinton, Sir Henry, false rumor of death, 281, 295.

Cobham, Richard Temple, Viscount, and bust of Penn, 22–23.

Cocker, Edward, *Arithmetic*, 581.

Coinage, designs for, 271–72.

Coke, Sir Edward, 357.

Cold (common), 145–46.

Coleman, William, books for, 80; Junto member, 622; funds BF, 626–27.

Collins, Anthony, 581.

Collins, John, boyhood correspondent of BF, 578–79; helps BF leave Boston, 585, 592; sets out for Philadelphia, 594; borrows Vernon's money, 596; goes to Barbados, 596–97; becomes drunkard, 596, 598, 619.

Collinson, Michael, 105.

COLLINSON, Peter, letter to, 66–68; Beccaria praises Franklin to, 49; pre-

sents apparatus to Library Company and submits BF's papers to Royal Society, 713; BF visits, 725.

Colonies, arts in, 58–59; marriage customs, 97; not constitutionally subordinate to Parliament, 110–12; dispute with Parliament explained, 110–15; seek restoration of status quo, 111–14; charters and constitutions, 120; compared to Ireland, 135; determined to be independent, 261–62; nature of constitutions, 724–25. (See also Albany Plan of Union, Massachusetts, Pennsylvania, etc., United States.)

Colors, 40–42.

Columbus, 143, 294.

Commercial Article, in Treaty of Paris, 325.

Commodities, 545–46.

COMPARISON OF THE CONDUCT OF THE ANCIENT JEWS AND OF THE ANTI-FEDERALISTS IN THE UNITED STATES OF AMERICA, A, 404–08; BF sends to Vaughan, 428.

Comus, 351.

Conejogatchie, letter to British, 218–19.

Congress, BF attends, 166; in session, 168; passage for Captain Cook, 186–87; and printing of constitutions of states, 239; refuses incentives for immigration, 239–41; Lith seeks recommendation to, 258; commissioners to treat with, 264; and appointment of overseas officers, 283; writes to Luzerne, 285; and fisheries, 285–86; European finances, 286, 292, 294–97, 340–41; Spanish loans, 288; BF warns against unsecured credit, 289; funds exhausted, 295; and French debts, 312–13; refuses to treat with Carleton, 313; account of negotiations, 320; and peace commissioners, 323; and Provisional Treaty, 323; treaty with Portugal, 326; BF requests dismissal from service, 329; right to impose taxes, 342; delays recalling BF, 354, 357–58; advantages over Parliament, 359; compensation for members disapproved, 359; representation in, 368, 394–98; supplies by voluntary contribution, 397–98; first session of, 431.

Connecticut, religion, 57; British reprisals, 272.

Constitution, United States, BF opposes religious clause, 363; superior to British, 368–69; BF's speech on salaries, 391–94; BF's speech on representation, 394–98; BF's motion for prayers in convention, 398–99; BF's speech at conclusion of convention, 399–401; BF's support for, 400.

Constitutions, of American states, 239.

Convicts (see Transportation of convicts).

Conway, Henry Seymour, 703; resigns, 91.

Cook, Captain James, passport for, 186–87.

Cooper, Joseph, 618.

COOPER, Samuel, letter to, 119–22.

Copernicus, 505–06.

Copley Medal, awarded to BF, 715–16.

Copperplate, engraving on earthenware, 149.

Corah, 405.

Corn (see Indian corn).

Cornwallis, Charles, 1st Marquis, 305, 387.

Cotton, Charles, Scarronides, 588.

Cotton, Clement, None but Christ, 17.

Courier of Europe, 302.

Courtanvaux, François Cesar le Tellier, Marquis de, 92.

COURT DE GEBELIN, Antoine, letter to, 293–95; mentioned, 199; and Indian orthography, 293.

Couteulx & Co, 340.

Cranz, David, 143.

Craufurd, James, letter accompanying scalps, 217–19.

Crawford, Adair, 276.

Creutz, Count Gustav Philip, Swedish ambassador, 330.

Crèvecoeur, Hector St. John de, Letters from an American Farmer, 343.

Croft, Richard, prisoner of war, 287.

Croghan, George, Indian interpreter, 700.

Cromwell, Oliver, commemorated, 507.

Cromwell, Richard, 507.

Crouch, Nathaniel, Historical Collections, 577.

Crown, rule preferable to Proprietors, 66; differentiated from Parliament, 112–13; Parliament usurps rights, 120; forfeits sovereignty, 262.

Crumerus, Dr., 178.

Crusades, harmful consequences of, 253.

Cullen, Dr. William, Synopsis nosologiae methodicae, 145.

Cumberland County, Pennsylvania, wagons collected in, 697.

Cuthbert, Thomas, 80.

Dagge, James, 351.

Dalibard, Thomas-François, translates BF's papers, 714; repeats BF's experiments, 715.

Dalrymple, Sir John, 281.

Dana, Francis, 290.

Danes (see Vikings).

David, in Poor Richard, 473.

Deane, Silas, delays commission accounts, 284; disaffection of, 305–06; and power held from Congress, 326.

Decow, Isaac, 618.

Defense, association formed against rioters, 72.

Defoe, Daniel, Essay upon Projects, 577; Religious Courtship, 586; Moll Flanders, Robinson Crusoe, and Family Instructor, 586.

De Grasse (see Grasse).

Deism, 619.

Delaval (see Duval, Edward H.).

Delaware, 396.

Delaware Indians, orthography of, 293.

Delaware River, 33, 278.

Delor, ——, repeats BF's experiments, 715.

Denham, Mr., 363.

Denham, Thomas, 603; exposes Keith, 604; befriends BF, 611–12; death of, 613–14.

Denmark, surrenders American prizes to British, 284; route to America, 294; complaints of, 314; and prize money negotiations, 327–28; seeks relations with United States, 327, 330–31.

Denny, William, obstructs supply bill, 717–18; disobeys Proprietors' instructions, 693; appointed governor, 712; and Proprietary interests, 716–17; presents medal to BF, 716; agrees to pass taxation on Proprietory estate, 727; dismissed, 728.

Derbyshire, England, geological formations of, 316, 425.

Derham, William, *Physico-Theology*, 511.

Derry, bishop of, and American ordination, 355.

Descartes, René, 214.

DESCRIPTION OF AN INSTRUMENT FOR TAKING DOWN BOOKS FROM HIGH SHELVES, 376–78.

Deux-Ponts, Charles August Christian, Duc de, 331.

DIALOGUE BETWEEN THE GOUT AND MR. FRANKLIN, 203–10.

"Dialogue Between X, Y, and Z, Concerning the Present State of Affairs in Pennsylvania, A," BF comments on, 705.

Dick, Sir Alexander, 49.

Didot, François, 300–01.

Diodorus Siculus, and calendar, 531.

Dissenters, favor colonists, 117.

"Dissertation on Liberty and Necessity, Pleasure and Pain, A," BF comments upon, 275–76, 606.

Dolland, Peter, 369.

Don Quixote, 301, 693.

Douse, Elizabeth (Franklin), 18.

Dover, England, 84.

Drinking, 199–02; London printers, 608–09.

DRINKING SONG, 196–98.

Dryden, John, quoted, 275–76, 412, 619.

Dublin Journal, 437.

Dunbar, Thomas, and penurious officers, 699–700; retreat of, 702; and indentured servants, 703, and Morris, 712.

Dunkers, religious sect, 676–77.

Duns Scotus, 185.

Dupont de Nemours, Pierre Samuel, *Table Economique*, 276.

Duportail (see Le Bégue Duportail).

Duval, Edward H., 50.

Earth, strata, 11–12; convulsions of, 12; formation, 316–20; magnetic properties, 318–19.

East Indies, BF's brother returns from, 25.

ECONOMICAL PROJECT, AN, 244–48.

Economistes, les, 277.

Ecton, England, Franklin family from, 568–69.

"Edict by the King of Prussia, An," success of, 145–46.

Education, of blacks, 60–61; and Indians, 229–31; of Benjamin Bache, 269; of William Temple Franklin, 357; and left hand, 375–76; of freed slaves, 415, 416; of BF, 573. (See also Harvard College.)

Egremont, Sir Charles Wyndham, 2d Earl of, and swimming, 613.

Egypt, 405, 407.

Electricity, use in medicine, 10–11, 351; experiments, 680, 712–13, 715.

Elements of Criticism (see Kames).

Eliot, John, translation of Bible, 294.

Elphinston, James, 358.

ELYSIAN FIELDS, THE, 184–85.

Emigration, advice on, 237–41; increases population, 362; foolishness of British opposition, 370.

England, and Union with Scotland, 395; commencement of legal year, 533–34. (See also Great Britain.)

English language, BF defends use of, 37–38; advantage of neologisms, 37–38; spread, 435–36.

Ennis (Innis), James, 719.

EPHEMERA, THE, 182–84; sent to Carmichael, 282.

Epictetus, 359.

Episcopalianism (see Church of England).

Errata, in *Poor Richard*, 517; BF's, 597, 605, 607.

Escurial Library, Dalrymple's discoveries in, 281.

EVANS, Cadwalader, letter to, 81–82.

Evaporation, cooling effects, 12–16; of rivers, 39–40.

Exercise, 203–10; and digestion, 378–79.

Exodus, 406.

Experiments, and cooling bodies, 12;

with sun and colors, 40; with oil and water, 55–56; ship velocity in canals, 93–95; on size of raindrops, 127–28; oil on water, 151–59; marsh gas, 163–65.

Fables, Montresor and the priest, 198; the lion and the dogs, 227–28; the speckled axe, 650.

Falmouth, England, BF lands at, 724.

Farish, James, and oil on water experiment, 159.

"Father Abraham's Speech" ("The Way to Wealth"), in *Poor Richard*, 555–62; mentioned in *Autobiography*, 657.

Faujas de Saint Fond, M., and balloon experiment, 338.

Faulkner, George, Dublin printer, 437.

Fawkener, Sir Everard, admonishes BF, 711.

Federalists, and excesses of press, 409.

Feutry, Aime Ambrose Joseph, 280.

Fier Rodrique (ship), 284.

Finley, Samuel, experiments with marsh gas, 164–65.

Firefighting, volunteer, 665–66.

Fisher, Mary Franklin, 569; sells ancestral property, 77–78.

Fisher, Richard, 569.

Fisheries, and Congressional instructions, 286; and peace treaty, 323, 339.

Fitzgerald, Lieutenant, in scalp hoax, 219–20.

Fitzherbert, Alleyne, 315.

Fizeaux & Grand, Messrs., 298, 306.

Flamsteed, John, on sound, 511.

Flanders, religion in, 57.

Flatulence, 212–15.

Fleury, François Louis Teissedre, Marquis de, medal for, 286.

FLIES, THE, 250–51.

Folger, Abiah (see Franklin, Abiah Folger).

Folger, Peter, Mather mentions, 572; verse by, 573.

FOLGER, Timothy, letter to, 107–08; mentioned, 430.

Foster, James, Hemphill plagiarizes, 660.

Fort Detroit, 63.

Fort Duquesne, 92; Braddock's campaign, 700–01, 704; BF proposed to lead attack on, 712.

Fortescue, John, *De laudibus Legum Angliae* cited, 568.

Fort Frontenac, and Braddock's campaign, 700.

Fort George, French capture, 720.

Forton prison, Americans imprisoned in, 332.

Fossils, discoveries in America, 92–93.

FOTHERGILL, Dr. John, letter to, 63–66; mentioned, 105; death, 291, 321; and street-cleaning proposal, 686–87; and BF's electrical papers, 713–14; BF visits, 725; and Proprietors, 726.

Foundling Hospital of Paris, 366.

Fouquet, M., gunpowder expert, 286.

Foxcroft, Thomas, 80, 105.

France, danger of restoring Canada to, 21–22; invades Portugal, 71; BF's tour of, 83–88; women described, 84–85, 272; politeness of inhabitants, 87; friendship to United States, 261, 303; refusal to renounce alliance with, 265–66; printing in, 273; pledges funds to Congress, 288; difficulty of paying, 292; delays reinforcements for American army, 295; opinion of trade, 303; not to be excluded from treaty, 320–21; reaction to Provisional Treaty, 323; honorable conduct toward America, 324; distrusted by Adams, 324; expectations of trade, 326; union with United States threatened, 340; floats new loan, 342–43; importance of alliance with, 353; child rearing in, 367; and official salaries, 393; slavery in, 419; war with, 693. (See also French language.)

Francis, Tench, and Philadelphia Academy, 678.

Franklin, Abiah Folger (mother), marries Josiah Franklin, 572; described, 575–76.

Franklin, Benjamin (uncle), letter from quoted, 16; acrostic by, 17–18; relations with brother, 129; trade, 130; gives BF family history, 568–70; character and verse acrostic by, 570–71;

devises shorthand, 571; book collection, 571; piety, 571; and BF's education, 573.

Franklin, Benjamin, elected to Assembly in absentia, 71; Assembly votes compensation to, 71; inspects colonial post offices, 71–72; forms association against rioters, 72; appointed commissioner for militia funds, 72; ousted from Assembly, 72–73; reappointed agent for colonies, 73; impartiality suspected by both sides, 100–01; defends conduct in post office, 124–25; accused of inciting the people, 146; denies application to stamp office, 160; questioned in Parliament, 162; self-description, 256; image on medallions, 268–69; solicits funds from France, 288; diplomatic powers of, 326; requests dismissal from congressional service, 329; protests calumnies of Adams, 339; Congress delays recall, 354; political works published, 357; statement for abolition society, 414–15; presents book to Yale, 439.

FRANKLIN, Deborah Read (wife), letters to, 79–81, 122–23; mentioned, 60, 185; first sees BF, 589, 592; BF courts, 600; BF forgets, 605; marries Rogers, 613, 619; becomes wife of BF, 631; virtues of, 641–42.

Franklin, Francis Folger (son), death of, 662.

Franklin, James (brother), 580–81; arrested by order of Assembly, 584; BF apprenticed to, 577–78; starts New-England Courant, 583; irritated by BF's visit, 593–95; BF visits, 662.

Franklin, James, Jr. (nephew), apprenticed to BF, 662.

Franklin, Jane (cousin) (see Page, Jane Franklin).

Franklin, John (brother), leaves father for Rhode Island, 576.

Franklin, John (uncle), 16; trade of, 130, 569–70; Josiah apprenticed to, 569.

Franklin, Josiah (brother), 25, 576.

Franklin, Josiah (father), birthplace, 16; wisdom of, 129; apprenticeship of, 569; religion and emigration of, 572;

character, 574–75; epitaph, 575–76; refuses to set BF up in business, 594, 597; quotes Solomon, 641.

FRANKLIN, Peter (brother), letters to, 28–29, 43–47; illness, 80.

Franklin, Samuel (cousin), 570, 577.

FRANKLIN, Sarah (Sally) (daughter), letter to, 69–70; mentioned, 60, 268–71, 344–49; gifts for, 80.

Franklin, Sarah (cousin), genealogy, 130.

Franklin, Thomas (grandfather), grave of, 130, 569.

Franklin, Thomas (uncle), 77; occupation and career, 569–70.

FRANKLIN, William (son), letters to, 91–92, 146–48, 356–58; marriage, 71; reconciled with BF, 356–58; Autobiography addressed to, 567; accompanies BF to Braddock, 695, 697; and penurious officers, 699.

Franklin, William Temple (grandson), 363; BF's affection for, 269; recommended for foreign service, 330; BF seeks employment for, 354; joins father in England, 357; to study law, 357; recommended to Strahan, 358; becomes gentleman farmer, 422–23.

Franklin, town of, books for library, 364.

Franklin family, genealogy, 130–31; origin of name, 568–69; religion of, 572.

Franklin stove (see Pennsylvania fireplace).

Frederick II, of Prussia, abilities praised, 62.

Frederick Augustus III, Elector of Saxony, seeks trade relations with United States, 328.

Frederick Louis, Prince of Wales, and Ralph, 719.

Frederick, Maryland, Braddock encamps at, 695.

Freeman, Captain James, 78, 90.

French, Colonel John, 592–93, 603.

French language, constitutions to be translated into, 331; universality, 435; BF studies, 660–61.

Gage, General Thomas, behavior censured, 165; seizes Boston merchandise, 385.

GALLOWAY, Joseph, letter to, 82–83; mentioned, 69, 357.

GANT, Edward, letter to, 354–56.

Gazettes (see Newspapers).

Genealogy, of Franklin family, 130, 569; mocked, 529.

Genesis, 427.

Geneva, Switzerland, Benjamin Bache educated at, 269.

Gentleman's Magazine, The, 437; and BF's electrical papers, 714.

George I, of England, in *Poor Richard*, 473.

George II, of England, 436.

George III, of England, as Muley Ishmael, 220, 307; and Nero, 223–24; desolation of America, 260; on coins, 271; obstinate in war, 303; war crimes of, 311–12; petitioned by Pennsylvania Assembly, 717.

George (BF's servant), 80.

George, Saint, 469.

Georgia, Whitefield in, 667.

Gerard, Conrad-Alexandre, honored by American Philosophical Society, 280.

German language, 37; and English typography, 436–37.

Germany, electric cures, 10.

Gibraltar, 306.

Gillon, Alexander, transaction with Laurens, 294–95, 298.

Gladwin, Major Henry, grants Indian truce, 63.

Gluck, Christophe Willibald, and musical dispute, 282.

Gnadenhut, Pennsylvania, burned by Indians, 705; BF occupies, 706–07.

God, in Job, 193–96; and economy of creation, 366.

Godfrey, Thomas, BF's tenant, 620; and Hadley's Quadrant, 621; wife arranges match for BF, 630.

Gomberville, Marin Le Roy de, *Moral Virtue Delineated*, 149.

Gordon, Lord George, riots, 281–82; committed to Tower, 282.

Gordon, Patrick, 613.

Gout, in dialogue, 203–10.

Gouvion, Jean Baptiste de, 302.

Gower, Granville Leveson-Gower, 2d Earl of, President of Privy Council, 91.

Grace, Robert, 631; Junto member, 622; loan to BF, 626–27; and Franklin stove, 677.

Grafton, Augustus Henry Fitzroy, Duke of, favors appeasement, 116.

Grand, Ferdinand, 289, 340–42, 358.

Grand, Sir George, returns promissory notes, 292.

Granville, John Carteret, 1st Earl of, on colonial constitutions, 725.

Grasse, François Joseph Paul, Comte de, 308.

Gravesend, England, and river tides, 34.

Great Britain, desires world trade monopoly, 68; opens hostilities against colonists, 165–66; conditions for peace with colonies, 215–16; and Canada, 216; American scalps to be sent to, 217–20; rapacity, 221; BF censures behavior, 252–54; American prisoners in, 304–05; releases American prisoners, 314, 332; underestimates Americans, 359–60; contempt for Yankees, 360; overpopulation of, 370; and American debtors, 383; interrupts American trade, 384–86; counterfeits American money, 387; placeholders in government, 391; slavery in, 419; prevents Albany Plan of Union, 694. (See also England, Scotland, Ireland, Constitution, Army.)

Great Commoner (see Pitt, William).

Greece, hospitality, 234; philosophers, 477.

Greenland, 143, 369; route to America, 294.

Gregory XIII, and calendar reform, 532–33.

Grenville, George, stamp office offer to BF, 161–62; BF's opposition, 161; questions BF in Parliament, 162.

Grenville, Thomas, 315.

Guichen, Luc Urbain du Bouexic, Comte de, 304.

Hadley, John, and evaporation experiment, 12.

Hadley's Quadrant, invented by Godfrey, 621.

Haldimand, Sir Frederick, 216.

Halifax, Charles Montagu, 1st Earl of, 570.

Hall, David, becomes partner to BF, 680.

Halley, Edmond, on sound, 511, 520.

Hamburg, Germany, American trade, 384.

Hamilton, Andrew, 603, 623–24; and Riddlesden, 604; BF's patron, 628.

Hamilton, James, 603; and Albany congress, 690; approves Plan of Union, 691; resigns, 692.

Hampden, John, 222.

Hanbury, John, presents BF to Lord Granville, 725.

Handel, George Frederick, *Judas Maccabeus* and *Acis and Galatea* reproved, 44–46.

HANDSOME AND THE DEFORMED LEG, THE, 210–12.

Hanover (see George I, George II, George III).

Hanson, Hans, Indian trader, 233.

Happiness, 78.

Harcourt (see Hertford).

Harp, 75.

Harpsichord, advantage over harp, 75.

Harry, David, apprentice, 615; leaves business for Barbados, 628–30.

HARTLEY, David, letters to, 167–68, 265–68; and Definitive Treaty, 353.

Harvard College, grants BF honorary M.A., 689.

Harvelay, M. de, 296.

Hawkesworth, Dr. John and Mrs., 58, 100.

Health, and electricity, 10–11, 19; and divine punishment, 64; and gout, 203–10; and old age, 365; and perspiration, 380; lead poisoning, 423–26, 548; rules for, 484–85; inoculation, 662. (See also Hospitals.)

Heat, effect on colors, 40–42; speculations on, 248–50; and structure of earth, 319.

Heathcott, Mrs., 256.

Heberden, Dr. William, and raindrop experiment, 127.

Helvétius, Anne-Catherine, 184–85, 250–51; natural philosophy of, 206.

Helvétius, Claude-Adrien, Baron de, 184, 196, 198.

Hemphill, Samuel, controversy around, 659–60.

Henckell, Miss, 100.

Henley, William, death of, 277.

Hercules, 270, 302.

Heretics, honesty of, 429.

Herodotus, 531.

Hertford, Francis Seymour Conway, Marquis of, 703.

Hessians, satire on, 177–79.

Hewson, Mary Stevenson (see STEVENSON, Mary).

Hewson, William, marriage to Mary Stevenson, 122.

Hilliard, Timothy, 426.

Hillsborough, Wills Hill, 1st Earl and 2d Viscount of, secretary of state for colonies, 91.

Hindustan, Bernier's travels, 13.

Hippocrates, cited, 183.

History of the Academy of Sciences, 368.

Hohendorf, Baron (fictional), 177.

Holland, colony in Abbeville, 84; canals in, 93; and John Paul Jones letter, 220; difficulty of paying, 292; and congressional funds, 295; American credit in, 298; separate peace with England, 307; loan guaranteed by Louis XVI, 313; American trade, 384.

Homer, 294; in *Poor Richard*, 474.

Homes (Holmes), Robert (brother-in-law), 592, 594, 614.

Honest Whigs Club, 309.

Hopkinson, Thomas, and Franklin medallion, 268.

Horace, quoted, 183, 237, 246; and moral prints, 149.

Hospitals, BF raises funds for, 682–83; in Paris, 425–26.

Hottentots, 9.

House, George, 620.

House of Commons, compared to Indian councils, 231; Scottish representation, 395. (See also Parliament.)

House of Lords, 333; Scottish representation, 395.

HOWE, Richard, Viscount, letter to, 252–54.
Huck (Huck-Saunders), Dr. Richard, 255.
Hudibras, cited, 455.
Hudson Bay, Canada, 503.
Hughes, John, BF proposes for stamp office, 161.
Hughes, John, *The Ecstasy* quoted, 502.
Humane Society, 426.
HUME, David, letters to, 36–38, 47–49; *Jealousy of Trade*, 37; tells BF Braddock's opinion of him, 703.
Hungary, products, 332.
Hunter, William, joint postmaster general, 689.
HUNTINGTON, Samuel, letter to, 282–87.
Hutchinson, Thomas, 147–48; accuses BF of inciting the people, 146; death of, 281.
HUTTON, James, letter to, 311–12.
"Hymn to the Creator" (see Milton, John).

Ilive, Elizabeth, cosmological theory of, 125–26.
Illinois, 63.
Immigration, advice on, 235–43; and land values, 343–44.
India, Anquetil-Duperon's travels in, 136; chess, 188.
Indian corn, mythical origins, 232; United States compared to, 279.
Indians, sue for peace, 63; and Quakers, 64; English allies, 215; send American scalps to England, 217–20; customs of, 229–34; rules of order, 230–31; languages, 293–94; massacre of Moravian, 311–12; and rum, 681–82; treaty with, 681–82; attack Gnadenhut, 705; siegecraft, 708. (See also Iroquois, etc.)
Indienne (ship), 295.
Indies, 490. (See also East Indies, West Indies.)
INFORMATION TO THOSE WHO WOULD REMOVE TO AMERICA, 235–43.
Ingenhousz, Jan, 280.

INGERSOLL, Jared, letter to, 56–57.
Inoculation, and Thomas Bond, 280; BF omits son's, 662.
Insects, 30, 508.
Inventions, armonica, 49–53; bifocals, 369–71; instrument for reaching books, 376–78; progress as result of, 427; Franklin stove, 677–78.
Ireland, 50, 117; condition of poor, 135; and colonial union, 82; voluntary taxation, 397.
Iroquois (Six Nations), and education, 229; pact with Virginia, 229; negotiations with, 690.
Isaiah, 521.
Isted, Ambrose, 569.
Italian, BF studies, 660–61.
Italy, electric cures, 10; slavery in, 419; courtiers, 477.
Izard, Ralph, BF satirizes, 181–82.

Jackson, James, Georgia congressman, 417.
Jackson, Richard, 57.
JACKSON, William, letter to, 297–99.
Jael, 363.
James I, of England, 539.
James III (see Pretender).
James, Abel, 69; letter from in *Autobiography*, 633.
James, Charles, 60.
James, Philip, 432.
James, Thomas, 424; type foundry, 616.
James, Saint, 652.
James River, 40.
Jansenists, 259.
JAY, John, letters to, 287–90, 339; congressional funds exhausted, 286; and Spanish loan, 295–96, 301, 315; and proposed Moroccan treaty, 332; BF protests about Adams to, 339; and peace treaty, 353.
Jay, Sarah Livingston, 290.
Jerman, John, almanac maker, 471, 475, 482, 491, 539.
Jerusalem, 409.
Jessop, William, and oil on water experiment, 153.
Jesuits (see Society of Jesus).

Jesus, 291, 645; faith in not necessary for virtue, 27; BF doubts divinity of, 439.

Jews, ancient, 407; in Anti-Federalist allegory, 404–08.

Job, BF modernizes, 193–96.

John I, of England, apples of, 193; and Magna Carta, 513.

John, BF's servant, writes letter for BF, 77.

John, printer's apprentice, 614–15.

Johnson, Samuel, *Taxation No Tyranny*, 386.

Johnston, Thomas, 305.

Jones, Griffith, editor of *Chronicle*, 91.

Jones, John, mentions Richard Price on toleration, 290.

JONES, John Paul, letter to, 273–74; BF fakes letter from, 220–24; quarrels with Landais, 283; pretended letter, 307.

Joseph, 188.

Josephus, 405.

Journal, of voyage to America, composition of, 613.

Julian year, 532–33.

Junto, death of members, 19; formed, first members, 621–22; and paper currency, 627; and Library Company, 637, 639; rule against fixed opinions, 653; essays composed for, 658; additions to, 662–63; and volunteer firemen, 665; and reform of nightwatch, 665.

Juvenal, in Hervey's translation, 412; in Dryden's translation, 691.

Kalm, Pehr, 143.

Kames, Lady Agatha, 21, 23, 28, 75.

KAMES, Lord (Henry Home), letters to, 20–24, 26–28, 70–76; mentioned, 49; *Principles of Equity*, 26; *Elements of Criticism*, 73; death, 321.

Keimer, Samuel, BF employed by, 590–93, 598; proposes new sect, 599–600; BF returns to work for, 614; quarrels with BF, 616; prints paper money, 618–19; BF leaves, 620, 622, 623; leaves for Barbados, 629–31.

Keith, George, and slave trade, 432.

Keith, Sir William, befriends BF 592–93,

594; proposes BF go to England, 597–98; and letters of credit, 602–03; character of, 604, 605, 613, 619.

Kennedy, Archibald, and Albany Plan of Union, 690.

Kennedy, Archibald, Jr., and ship's speed, 722–23; saves ship, 724.

Kepler, Johannes, and calendar, 531.

Kingston-on-Thames, London, 41.

Kinnersley, Ebenezer, BF writes paper for, 713.

Kite experiment, 715.

Labor, scarcity in America, 240.

Lacedæmonians, 178.

La Charité Hospital, and lead poisoning, 425.

LA CONDAMINE, La Sabliere de, letter to, 351.

LAFAYETTE, Marquis de, letter to, 315–16; recommended to BF, 279; arrives at Boston, 281; honored, 302; in France, 314; commerce negotiations, 342.

La Freté, Mme. Martinville de, note to, 185.

La Marck, Mme. de, 310.

Lancaster, Treaty of, 229–30.

Lancaster County, Pennsylvania, massacre of Indians at, 72; wagons collected at, 696–97.

Land, plentifulness in America, 238–39.

Landais, Captain Pierre, court-martial proposed, 374; quarrels with John Paul Jones, 283.

LANGDON, John, letter to, 429–30.

Lange, M., lamp of, 244.

Language, Indian, 293–94; English increased by emigration, 362; Spanish most extensive, 362; and neologisms, 434; BF studies, 660–61. (See also English, French, German, Italian, Latin.)

Lapland, 542.

La Roche (see Lefèbvre de la Roche).

La Rochefoucauld, d'Enville, Duc de, 309, promises to translate constitutions into French, 331.

LATHROP, Rev. John, letter to, 426–28.

Latin, and neologism, 37; of Cincinnatus faulted, 347–49; neglect of, 435; BF studies, 661.

Laurens, Henry, and congressional debts, 286, 289, 315; and Adams' calumnies, 340.

Laurens, Colonel John, and congressional supplies, 294–96; appointed envoy extraordinary, 293, 298, 301.

Lavoisier, Antoine-Laurent, experiments on heat, 309.

Lawrence, Thomas, 672.

Lay, Benjamin, and abolition, 432.

Lead poisoning, causes and effects, 424–26.

LEBÈGUE DE PRESLE, Achille-Guillaume, letter to, 258–59.

Le Bégue Duportail, Louis, 302.

LEE, Arthur, letter to, 259–60; congressional powers, 326.

Le Despencer, Francis Dashwood, Baron, and BF's "Edict," 146; death of, 321.

Lefèbvre de la Roche, Martin, 185; song for, 196.

Leonidas, 178.

Le Roy, Jean-Baptiste, defends BF's theories, 714–16.

LEVÈE, THE, 193–95.

Lexington, Massachusetts, British defeat at, 166.

Library Company of Philadelphia, 263; grows out of Junto, 632; organized, benefits of, 639–41; receives electrical apparatus, 713.

Light, as fluid, 248–50.

"Light House Tragedy," ballad by BF, 578.

Lightning rods, grounding of, 47–48; controversy with Wilson, 258–59; instructions for, 538.

LINING, John, letter to, 12–16.

Linnaeus, Carl, aids king of Sweden, 30–31.

Lisbon, Portugal, 152.

LITH, ——, letter to, 257–58.

LIVINGSTON, Robert R., letters to, 302–06, 312–15, 322–33.

Loan office, used to circumvent proprietory restrictions, 694.

Locke, John, commemorated, 509;

Essay concerning Human Understanding, 581.

Logan, James, contributes for defense, 674–75; and William Penn, 675.

London, London Bridge and river tides, 34; and Gordon riots, 281–82; merchants of, 383; inferior lighting of, 686; BF arrives at, 725.

London Chronicle, The, 116.

LOOSE THOUGHTS ON A UNIVERSAL FLUID, 248–50.

Lord's Prayer, sends own version to Mather, 144. (See also Prayer.)

Loudoun, John Campbell, 4th Earl of, and supply bill, 717–18; character of, 718–19; Louisbourg campaign, 720–21; defers payment of debt to BF, 721–22.

Louis XIV, 142.

Louis XV, BF presented to, 85–86; and BF's experiments, 715.

Louis XVI, assists United States, 285; and American aid, 288; guarantees Holland loan, 313; respected by Americans, 320–21; presents books to Yale, 440.

Louis XVII (Dauphin), birth, 313.

Louisbourg, failure of attack on, 68, 151, 675; Loudoun's campaign, 720.

Lovell, James, BF complains to about Adams, 284–85.

Loyalists, and peace treaty, 323–24, 389. (See also APOLOGUE.)

Lucan, quoted, 466.

Lucifer, in song, 197.

Luther, Martin, 513; commemorated, 511.

Lutherans, 355.

Lutwidge, Walter, and ship's speed, 722–23.

Luzerne, Anne César, Chevalier de la, Congress writes to, 285, 304.

Lyons, William, *The Infallibility, Dignity, and Excellence of Humane Judgment*, 606.

Macclesfield, George Parker, 2d Earl of, honors BF, 716.

Maddison, John, armonica for, 60.

Madeira, 70; experiment at, 55.

Madrid, Spain, 282; printing, 300.

Magelhaens (Magellans), Jean Hyacinthe de, 259.

Magic square, 680.

Magna Carta, 143, 513, 624.

Magnetism, and stability of the earth, 318–19.

Mahomet, 418, 479.

Mahometans, 24.

Maize (see Indian corn).

Malta, St. Paul on, 234; medal presented to Grand Master, 332.

Manchester, George Montagu, 4th Duke of, 333.

Mandeville, Bernard, BF introduced to, 606.

"Man of Sense, A," mentioned in *Autobiography*, 658.

Mansfield, William Murray, Baron, praises BF's "Edict," 147; house burned in riots, 281; arbitrates in Proprietary dispute, 728.

Manufactures, British, colonial dependence on, 67; effect of non-importation agreements on, 117.

Manufactures, colonial, advantages over British, 109; in America, 239–41. (See also Commodities.)

Marbois, François de, 323.

Marchant, Henry, 134; sends *Zend-Avesta*, 136.

Marie Lesczinska, queen of France, BF sees, 85–86.

Marischal, George Keith, 10th Earl, anecdote for, 48.

Marly, France, BF's experiments repeated at, 715.

Marriage, advantages of early, 96–97; BF advises Mary Stevenson on, 118; conversation on, 132–33; BF's own, 630–31.

MARSHALL, William, letter to, 141.

Marsh gas, experiments with 163–65.

Maryland, 356.

Mary I, of England, Franklins persecuted under, 571–72.

Mary II, of England, 356.

Massachusetts, Folger land claim, 108; constitution, 290; lead poisoning,

424; Assembly imprisons James Franklin, 584; Assembly's quarrel with Burnet, 624–25; requests military aid, 693.

Mathematics, 131. (See also Arithmetic and accounts, Magic square.)

Mather, Cotton, anecdotes of, 142, 352–53; *Memorable Providences*, 434; *Magnalia Christi Americana*, 572; *Bonifacius*, 352, 577.

Mather, Increase, anecdote of, 142.

MATHER, Samuel, letters to, 141–44, 352–53.

Maugridge, William, Junto member, 622.

Maundorff, Major, 178.

Mawhood, William John, prisoner of war, 287.

Mechanic arts, respected in America, 237.

Mecom, Benjamin, advances legacy to Jane Mecom, 24–25; business fails, 61–63.

MECOM, Jane, letters to, 16–18, 24–25, 77–79, 89–90, 123–26, 128–32, 430–31; mentioned by uncle, 16–18.

Mecom family, genealogy of, 131.

Medals, BF on, 268–69; for United States victories, 302, 314; presented to Grand Master of Malta, 332.

Melville, General Robert, 362.

Mercantilism, 383–84. (See also Colonies, Great Britain.)

Merchants, American, BF defends, 382–90; British accuse of defaulting on debts, 383.

Merchants, British, petition against penalizing colonists, 117; and slave trade, 386; and Act on Recovering Debts, 388–89.

Mercury Trismegistus, and calendar, 531.

Meredith, Hugh, apprentice, 614; proposes partnership to BF 617; Junto member, 622; unsatisfactory as partner, 624, 626; dissolves partnership, 627.

Meredith, Simon, reneges on funds, 626–27.

Mesmer, F. A., 351.

Mesmerism, scepticism about, 351.

Methusalah, 379.

Michell, John, on strata of the earth, 11–12.

Mickle, Samuel, 620.

Microscope, 508, 523–28.

Middleton, Christopher, account of Churchill River expedition, 503–05.

Militia, colonial, effectiveness, 261; Assembly fails to set up, 671; BF commissioned in, 705.

Militia Act, colonial, 65; Assembly passes, 705.

Millennium, foretold, 521.

Milton, John, quoted 734; compares Charles I to Nero, 223.

Minerva, 302.

Mississippi River, 38; refusal to sell rights to Spain, 289; as American boundary, 315.

Mitchell, Dr. John, earthenware printing, 149; submits BF's papers to Royal Society, 713.

"Mock Petition to the House of Commons, A," BF later comments on, 402.

MODEL OF A LETTER OF RECOMMENDATION, 179.

Mohawk Indians, and orthography, 293.

Molini, Jean Claude, 92.

Molinists, 259.

Money, advice on, 463–64. (See also Paper Currency, Labor.)

Monro, Alexander, 38.

Montgolfier, Jacques Etienne and Joseph Michel, and balloon flight, 334, 336–38.

Montmartre, Paris, 204.

Moore, astrologer, 539.

Moore, conveys Indian letter, 218.

Morality, method of moral algebra, 139, 277; BF's project for moral perfection, 643.

MORALS OF CHESS, THE, 187–91.

Moravian Indians, massacre of, 311–12, 315.

Moravians, 369; massacred by Indians, 705; supply BF, 706; customs of, 709–10.

Morellet, Abbé André, letter to on wine, 199–202.

Morocco, emperor of, BF suggests friendship with, 332.

Morris, James, pacificism of, 674.

Morris, Luke, 280.

MORRIS, Robert, letter to, 339–43; mentioned, 304, 313, 329.

Morris, Robert Hunter, disputes with Assembly, 692; vetoes aid for Massachusetts, 694; loan office circumvents veto, 694; and Proprietary taxation, 704; BF's relations with, 711–12.

Morris, William, ship captain, 717.

Moses, 404–07; and Pentateuch, 136.

Mosquitoes, 508.

MOTION FOR PRAYERS IN THE CONVENTION, 398–99.

Moulin Joli, in "Ephemera," 182–83; described, 282.

Muette, jardin de la, 207.

Muley Ishmael (see George III).

Mungo the squirrel, epitaph for, 140.

Music, natural and unnatural, 43–47; Italian, 49; harmony and melody in, 73–75; superiority of Scottish, 74–75.

Nantucket, 573.

"Narrative of the Late Massacres in Lancaster County, of a Number of Indians, Friends of this Province, by Persons Unknown," sent to Kames, 72.

Navy, British, raids American coast, 385.

NEAVE, Oliver, letters to, 53–55, 101–04.

Nebuchadnezzar, 543.

Negroes, effects of climate on, 15; education, 60–61; plan for improving conditions of, 416–17.

Nero, and English tyranny, 223.

Netherlands (see Holland).

Neufville, Messrs. de, 301; and congressional debts, 286.

Newcastle, Thomas Pelham-Hollis, Duke of, procrastination of, 37.

Newcastle, England, 69.

New England, 57; route to America, 294.

New-England Courant, The, James Franklin starts, 583; BF edits, 584–85.

Newfoundland, route to America, 294.

New Jersey, 64; marsh gas, 163; scalps of inhabitants, 217; redivision, 396.

Newport, Rhode Island, and oil on water experiment, 154; BF visits brother in, 595, 661–63.

Newspapers, attack Quakers, 67; abuse of America in, 115; mendacity of, 167; and libel, 658. (See also Press, Printing.)

Newspapers, British, attack United States 350; oppugn American honesty, 383. (See also Press, Printing.)

Newton, Sir Isaac, 43, 214, 506–07, 515, 520, 606.

"New Version of the Lord's Prayer, A," sends to Samuel Mather, 144.

New York, scalps of inhabitants, 217; army at, 295; trade embargo on, 386; evacuation, 388.

Niagara, and Braddock's campaign, 700.

NIXON, William, letter to, 299–300.

Noah, 199.

Nollet, Abbé Jean-Antoine, attacks BF's theories, 714.

Non-Importation agreements, effectiveness, 108–09; effect on Britain, 117.

Nord, Comte de (Paul I, of Russia), 309.

Norris, Isaac, and Indian treaty, 681; and Albany Congress, 690.

North, Lord Frederick, 177, 266; favors appeasement, 116; supports repeal of Townshend Act, 119.

North Carolina, lead poisoning, 424; considers accepting Constitution, 431. (See also Carolinas.)

Northington, Lord, resigns, 91.

Northwest Passage, 503.

Norway, and discovery of America, 143; receives prize from John Paul Jones, 274; route to America, 294.

Norwich, England, salt mines, 29.

NOTES FOR CONVERSATION, 215–16.

Notre Dame de Paris, 87; proposed for secret meeting, 263.

Nova Scotia, route to America, 294.

Numa Pompilius, and calendar, 532.

Numbers, 405.

"Observations Concerning the Increase of Mankind, Peopling of Countries, &c.," sent to Kames, 21.

Observations on my Reading History in Library, notes for a society of the virtuous, 655.

Odyssey (see Homer).

Ogden, Colonel Mathias, 323.

Oil, effects on water, 55–56, 151–59.

Old Bailey, sessions paper cited, 382.

"Old Man's Wish" (song), cited, 365.

Old Testament, 363.

Onion, Stephen, 603.

Onondaga, New York, council at, 233.

"On Protection of Towns from Fire," mentioned in *Autobiography,* 665.

ON SENDING FELONS TO AMERICA, 402–04.

ON THE ABUSE OF THE PRESS, 408–10.

"On the Providence of God in the Government of the World," mentions to Vaughan, 276.

ON WINE, 199–202.

Order of St. Louis, 347.

Order of the Bath, 347.

Order of the Garter, 347.

Order of the Thistle, 347.

Ordination, for American ministers, 355–56.

Orinoco River, 38.

Orme, Robert, reports Braddock's death, 702.

Orthography, and Indian languages, 293.

Osborne, Charles, and poetry contest, 600–02; moves to West Indies, 602.

Oswald, James, musical skill commended, 75.

Oswald, Richard, and peace commission, 315.

Oswegatchie, New York, expedition to, 216.

Oxly, John, 382.

Page, Jane Franklin, death, 16.

Page, Robert, 16.

Palfrey, Colonel William, consul general, 293.

Palmer, John, 569.

Palmer, Samuel, employs BF, 424, 605–06; BF leaves, 608.

Paper currency, 545–46; Britain counterfeits American, 387; controversy over, 627–28; BF prints, 628; BF writes on, 628.

"Parable Against Persecution, A," BF sends to Kames, 26; sends to Vaughan, 275.

Paris, Ferdinand John, Proprietors' solicitor, 726–27.

Paris, France, 204, 279, 285; described, 86–87; and printing of constitutions of states, 239; opera, 282; printing, 300; booksellers, 435.

Parker, James, in debt to Strahan, 61.

Parliament, represented on Congressional currency, 67; representation of colonies considered, 81–82; lacks authority without consent, 110–12; Long Parliament and colonies, 111; differentiated from crown, 112–13; misinformed about America, 114–15; usurps crown rights, 120; sovereignty denied, 120, 147; threat of sovereignty to religious freedom, 143; BF questioned in, 162; debates on reconciliation, 215; desolation of America, 260; lacks sovereignty, 262; suggested reforms, 290; need for reform, 350; contempt for Americans, 360; passes act blockading Boston, 384; forbids inquiry into naval piracy, 385; petition against transportation, 402; and calendar reform, 534; rejects instructions to governors' clause, 726. (See also House of Commons, House of Lords.)

Parmesan cheese, 105, 150.

Parsons, William, death and character of, 19–20; Junto member, 622.

PARTRIDGE, Elizabeth, letter to, 272–73.

PASSPORT FOR CAPTAIN COOK, 186–87.

Passy, France, 204, 206, 654.

Paul, Saint, 27; advises Timothy on wine, 200; shipwrecked, 234; in *Poor Richard*, 471; Philippians, 643.

Payne, Mrs., 256.

Peace Commission, necessity for open negotiations, 263–64; Deane delays accounts, 284; and Congress, 323.

Pearson, Isaac, 618.

Peerages, BF's contempt for, 264–65.

Pemberton, Ebenezer, 142.

Pemberton, Henry, BF meets, 606.

Pemberton, James, 291.

Pembroke, Earl of, BF visits domain, 725.

Penn, John, appointed governor, 65; relations with Assembly, 65–66; measures against Lancaster rioters, 72; ousts Franklin from Assembly, 72–73; meeting with Proprietors, 726.

Penn, Thomas, and Albany Congress, 690.

Penn, William, portrait of, 22–23; commemorated, 509; pacifism, 675.

Pennsylvania, climate, 14; scalps of inhabitants, 217; constitution cited, 236; redivision, 396; newspapers, 410; BF becomes president of state government, 421.

Pennsylvania Assembly, and John Penn as governor, 65–66; votes compensation to BF, 71; BF elected to in absentia, 71; BF ousted from, 72–73; clashes with governor, 72; petitions crown, 73; reappoints BF agent, 73; oath-taking 141; dominated by Scotch-Irish, 362; act on recovering debts, 388–90; votes BF printer, 625; passes money bill, 628; BF elected clerk of, 663; and Militia Bill, 671, 705; BF elected to, 680; votes matching funds for hospital, 683; bill for paving and lighting streets, 685–86; rejects Plan of Union, 691–92; disputes with governors, 692–93; votes aid for Massachusetts, 693; sends gifts to Braddock's officers, 699; and Proprietary taxation, 704–05; BF appointed London agent for, 717; governor vetoes supply bill, 717; taxes Proprietary estates, 727.

Pennsylvania fireplace, 21; BF invents, 677–78.

Pennsylvania Gazette, The, BF praises for restraint, 408; BF founds, 623–25; in *Autobiography*, 658; and Hemphill controversy, 660; success of, 670.

Pennsylvania Society for Promoting the Abolition of Slavery, 414–15, 429.

PERCIVAL, Thomas, letter to, 126–28.

Persia, chess, 187.

Peter, Saint, in fable, 198.

Peters, Richard, offered position at Academy, 670; and Albany Congress, 690.

PETITION OF THE LEFT HAND, A, 375–76.

PETITION OF THE LETTER Z, 181–82.

Pharaoh, 392, 406.

Philadelphia, seat of philosophical society, 671; and river tides, 33; mobs in, 64; BF returns after six years, 71; BF represents in Assembly, 71; trade embargo on, 386; newspapers of, 409; BF sets out for, 586; BF first arrives at, 588; young BF returns to, 613; reform of city watch, 664–65.

Philippians, quoted, 643.

Phillips, General William, 387.

Philosophical Society (Hume), 47.

Philosophical Transactions, and Phoenician inscription, 294.

Phoenicians, inscription and discovery of America, 294.

Phonetic Alphabet (see Language).

Piccini, Niccolo, and musical dispute, 282.

Pilatre de Rozier, Jean François, balloon ascent, 336–37.

Pilgrim's Progress (see Bunyan, John).

Pitt, Miss, 31, 60; leaves England, 58.

Pitt, William, colonists favored by friends of, 116; removes Loudoun, 719.

Plain Truth, BF publishes, 671.

PLAN FOR IMPROVING THE CONDITION OF THE FREE BLACKS, 416–17.

"Plan of Conduct," composition of, 613.

Pliny, and oil on water experiment, 150, 156; and calendar, 531.

Plutarch, and calendar, 531; *Lives*, 577.

Pockrich, Richard, performer on musical glasses, 50.

Poetry, BF dissuaded from, 578; of James Ralph, 600–03.

Poissonière, Pierre Isaac, 145.

Political, Miscellaneous and Philosophical Pieces, Vaughan publishes, 275.

Poor Richard, quoted, 186, 208.

POOR RICHARD'S ALMANACK, *1733*, 445–46; *1734*, 449–54; *1735*, 454–58; *1736*, 459–63; *1737*, 462–66; *1738*, 466–70; *1739*, 470–74; *1740*, 474–78; *1741*, 478–81; *1742*, 481–86; *1743*, 486–90; *1744*, 490–93; *1745*, 493–96; *1746*, 496–99; *1747*, 499–02; in *Autobiography*, 657.

POOR RICHARD IMPROVED, *1748*, 502–10; *1749*, 510–15; *1750*, 516–20; *1751*, 520–30; *1752*, 530–35; *1753*, 536–38; *1754*, 539–42; *1755*, 542–44; *1756*, 544–48; *1757*, 548–54; *1758*, 554–64.

Pope, Alexander, quoted, 582–83; on Newton, 507, 515; on Bacon, 512; lampoons Ralph, 602, 717.

Port Mahon, Minorca, fall of, 306.

Port Royal, Messrs. du (see Arnauld, Antoine).

Portsmouth, England, oil on water experiment, 157–59.

Portugal, British ally, 71; complains of American navy, 302; seeks relations with United States 326; American trade, 384; slavery in, 419.

Post office, BF inspects, 71–72; BF allocates, 80; Sandwich appointed to, 91; BF's conduct in, 124–25; BF appointed Philadelphia postmaster, 664; BF made postmaster general, 689.

Potomac River, 40.

Potts, Stephen, death and character of, 19; apprentice, 614; Junto member, 622.

Pownall, Thomas, amicable to colonists, 121; emissary from Massachusetts, 693.

Prayer, BF writes his own 643, 648; motion in Constitutional Convention on, 398–99.

Presbyterianism, 355; self-righteousness, 24; hated by king, 266; and Benjamin

Bache, 269; BF educated in, 642; BF withdraws from, 643; and Hemphill controversy, 660.

Press, liberty endangered by excess, 408–10; advantages, 409–11; satire on excesses, 410–14.

Pretender (James Francis Edward Stuart), in *Poor Richard*, 473.

PRICE, Richard, letters to, 290–91, 309–10, 364; mentioned, 429.

PRIESTLEY, Joseph, letters to, 138–39, 163–65, 165–67, 277–78, 307–09, 362–64; and *A Dissertation*, 275; considers emigration to America, 363; mentioned, 429.

PRINGLE, Sir John, letters to, 10–11, 11–12, 55–56, 93–95; tours France with BF, 83, 86, 425; and oil on water experiment, 154; death of, 321; mentioned, 360, 548.

Printing, quality in Boston and Paris, 273; rivalry between Paris and Madrid, 300–01; metaphor for government, 350; success of BF and Strahan, 361; American publishing, 361–62; in France, 435; Spanish commended, 438; illegibility of recent, 438; BF apprenticed in, 577–78; venture in Charleston, South Carolina, 659; BF trains printers for different colonies, 670. (See also Typography.)

Prisoners of war, American, in England, 304–05; released 312, 332.

Privateers, supplies from, 296.

Progress, through science, 277; and war, 333–35; rapidity of, 427.

Property, and convention, 341–42.

"Proposals Relating to the Education of Youth in Pensilvania," BF distributes, 678.

PROPOSED NEW VERSION OF THE BIBLE, 195–96.

Proprietors, seek BF's aid, 65; false report of letters from, 76; and Academy of Philadelphia, 680; dissensions caused by, 692–94; taxation dispute with Assembly, 694, 727–28; exemption and defense funds, 704–05; angry at honor to BF, 711; and supply bill, 717–18; meet and disagree with BF, 726–27. (See also Penn, John.)

Proteus, 514.

Proverbs, 641.

Providentia (ship), and Admiralty Courts, 328.

Prussia, seeks trade relations with United States, 328.

Psalms, 399.

Pseudonyms, Fart-Hing, 215; A Good Conscience, 382; Historicus, 420; The Left Hand, 376; Samuel Gerrish, Capt., 216, 220; Sidi Mehemet Ibrahim, 417; Silence Dogood, 583.

Ptolemy, 506.

Puritans, and Maypole, 48.

Pythagoras, 505; "Golden Verses," 646.

Quakers, 291; and portraiture, 22–23; accused of Indian sympathies, 64; in fable, 198; unsalaried officials among, 393–94; and calendar reform, 534; BF prints history for, 622; position of Assembly members toward defense, 673–77; and Militia Act, 705.

Quebec, Canada, fleet, 296.

Quincy, Josiah, emissary from Massachusetts, 693–94.

Quinquet, M., lamp of, 244.

Quintus Curtius, 221.

Radcliff, Mr., 363.

Raindrops, experiment on size of, 127–28.

Raleigh, Sir Walter, commemorated, 509.

Ralph, James, 59; dedicatee of *A Dissertation*, 276, 606; and poetry contest, 600–02; accompanies BF to England, 602–03; Pope lampoons, 602, 603; job hunting in London, 605; takes BF's name, 607; owes BF money, 613, 619; career of, 717.

Rappahannock River, 40.

Read, Deborah (see FRANKLIN, Deborah Read).

Read, John, 589; BF lodges with, 591; deceived by Riddlesden, 604.

Read, Sarah White, 631.

Reading, BF's fondness for, 577.

Reformation, and comets, 521.

Religion, as aid to virtue, 9–10; enthusiasm, 107; revelation, 126, 619–20; threatened by Parliamentary sovereignty, 143; in America, 243; and religious tests, 291; BF's beliefs, 439–40, 642–43, 656.

Religious tests, 290–91.

REMARKS CONCERNING THE SAVAGES OF NORTH-AMERICA, 229–34.

Representation, in Congress, 368, 394–98.

RETORT COURTEOUS, THE, 382–90; BF sends to Shipley, 422.

Revenue Act, BF assists in repealing, 124.

RHOADS, Samuel, letter to, 137–38; mentioned, 280.

Rhode Island, trade embargo on, 386; considers accepting Constitution, 431; John Franklin removes to, 576.

Riccioli, Giovanni Battista, and calendar, 531.

Richardson, Samuel, *Pamela*, 586.

Riddlesden, William, roguery of, 604.

Riot act, 65.

Rivers, courses discussed, 38–40; control, 137–38.

Robert, M., and balloon experiment, 338.

ROBERTS, Hugh, letter to, 19–20; mentioned, 280.

Roberts, James, Ralph solicits, 605.

Robin Hood, model for robbery, 221.

Roche, Pierre Louis Lefèbvre de la (see Lefèbvre de la Roche).

Rochefocaut (see La Rochefoucauld).

Rockingham, Charles Watson-Wentworth, Marquis of, favors colonists, 116.

Rodney, Admiral George, 308.

Rogers, John, marries and leaves Deborah Read, 613.

Roman Catholic Church, 355, 400, 482, 491; Papists, 24; in fable, 198.

Rome, calendar of, 531–32.

Romulus, and calendar, 531.

Rooke, Mrs., 60.

Rose, Aquila, death of, 586; elegy for, 591; BF takes son as apprentice, 628.

Rose, Joseph, 628.

Rosencrone, M., Danish prime minister, 330.

Ross, Dr., 349.

Ross, John, purchases cloth, 283.

Rousseau, Jean Jacques, and rights of children, 367.

Royalists (see Loyalists).

Royal Society of London, 50, 334, 503; informed of marsh gas experiments, 164; laughs at BF's theories, 713; prints account of BF's experiments, 715; BF elected to, 715; presents BF with Copley Medal, 715–16.

Rufane, Lieutenant General, as marriage prospect, 131.

"Rules by Which a Great Empire May Be Reduced to a Small One," BF's comments on, 145.

Rum, and lead poisoning, 424. (See also Drinking.)

RUSH, Benjamin, letter to, 144–46.

Russell, James, 49; improves lightning rod, 47.

Russia, proposes Armed Neutrality, 286; Comte de Nord (Paul I), 309; war with Turkey, 428.

Sabbath, observance paradox, 553.

St. Asaph, bishop of (see SHIPLEY, Jonathan).

St. Clair, Sir John, and wagons, 698.

St. John, Hector (see Crèvecoeur).

Salaries, congressional, BF's speech against, 391–94.

SALE OF THE HESSIANS, THE, 177–79.

Sallust, 301.

Salt, origins of, 28–29; in estuary waters, 40.

Samaritans, book on coins of presented to Yale, 439.

Sampson, in *Poor Richard*, 480.

Sandwich, John Montagu, 4th Earl of, postmaster general, 91; rumor of resignation, 303.

Sandyford, Ralph, and abolition, 432.

Sanoy, 204.

Saracens, hospitality, 234.

Saratoga, battle of, commemorative medal for, 314.

Sartine, Antoine Gabriel de, suggests censure of Landais, 274, 330.

Satan, in Job, 193–96.

Saunders, Bridget (fictional), 454; preface by, 466–67.

Saunders, Richard (see Poor Richard).

Savannah, Georgia, trade embargo on, 386.

Saxony (see Frederick Augustus III).

Scalps, BF's hoax, 217–20.

Schaumbergh, Count de (fictional), 177.

Schuylkill River, difficulties of navigation, 138.

Science, progress of, 277. (See also Experiments, Inventions, Mathematics.)

Scipio Nascia, and timekeeping, 522.

Scotland, agreeableness of, 23; superiority of music, 74–75; union with England, 121, 395; and poor, 135; herring fishery, 154; and American ordination, 355; and transportation, 403.

Scull, Nicholas, Junto member, 622.

Scythians, hospitality, 234.

Searle, James, 288, 289, 305.

Selden, John, *Table Talk*, 32.

"Self-Denial Not the Essence of Virtue," mentioned in *Autobiography*, 658.

Seller, John, *Practical Navigation*, 581.

Seneca, writings newly discovered, 281.

Seneca Indians, collect American scalps for British, 217.

Serapis, and John Paul Jones, 273–74.

Seymour, Charles, Duke of Somerset, and William and Mary College, 356.

Shaftesbury, Anthony Ashley Cooper, Earl of, causes doubts in BF, 581.

Shakespeare, William, quoted, 325.

Sheffield, England, 130.

Shelburne, Sir William Petty, 2d Earl of, 116; resigns, 91; and fossils, 92.

Shipbuilding, necessity of scientific approach to, 723.

Shipley, Anna Maria, 133.

SHIPLEY, Anna Mordaunt, letter to, 132–34.

Shipley, Betsy, 132–34.

Shipley, Catherine, trip with BF, 132–34; dreams, 378.

Shipley, Emily, 132–33.

SHIPLEY, Georgiana, letter to, 139–41; mentioned 132–34.

SHIPLEY, Jonathan (Bishop of St. Asaph), letter to, 421–23; BF writes *Autobiography* at home of, 567.

Ships, speed in canals, 93–95; determination of speed, 723–24.

Shirley, William, and Plan of Union, 691; settles with wagon owners, 703; abilities of, 720–21.

Shirley, William, Jr., dies with Braddock, 701.

Shovel, Sir Cloudsley, disaster of, 724.

SIDI MEHEMET IBRAHIM ON THE SLAVE TRADE, 417–20.

Silence Dogood, BF submits letters to *Courant*, 583.

Six Nations (see Iroquois).

Slavery, antipathy to in America, 137; and British creditors, 386–87; abolition, 414–15, 432; satirized, 417–20.

Slaves, Samuel Johnson incites to rebellion, 386; Britain protects escaped, 388; education necessary for freed, 415.

Slave trade, 432; British hypocrisy in, 137; BF asks Senate president to restrict, 429–30.

Sleep, advice on, 378–82.

Sloane, Sir Hans, buys asbestos purse, 606.

Smallpox, 95; BF accuses Britain of using in war, 387; death of BF's son, 662.

Smeaton, John, and Irish canal problems, 138; and oil on water experiment, 153.

Smith, Mary, 80.

Smith, William, hostility of, 59.

Smuggling, article on sent to Jane Mecom, 90; morality of, 106–07.

Soap, Franklin family business, 574; recipe for, 131.

Society of Jesus, 348.

Society of the Free and Easy, project for founding, 656.

Socrates, quoted, 184, 581, 645.

Solander, Daniel, and oil on water experiment, 159.

Solomon, 48, 271, 409; BF fulfills prophecy of, 641; quoted, 648.

"Sommersett Case and the Slave Trade, The," mentions to Benezet, 137.

Sosigenes, and calendar reform, 533.

SOULAVIE, Abbé Jean Louis Giraud, letter to, 316–20.

Sound, queries for experiments on, 53–55; speed of, 511.

Southampton, England, 423.

Spain, invades Portugal, 71; territorial exchange with opposed, 288–89; difficulty of paying, 292; loan to United States, 295–96; wishes to restrict American expansion, 315; noblesse of, 345; American trade, 384; slavery in, 419; Indies, 490.

Spangenburg, Augustus, and Moravian pacifism, 706.

Spaniards, bring chess to America, 188.

Spanish language, extent of, 362; BF studies, 661.

Spanish Inquisition, press compared to, 411.

"Spanish Lady" (song), 43.

Spectacles, advice on, 130; bifocals, 369–70.

Spectator, The, 658; BF learns writing from, 579–80.

SPEECH IN A COMMITTEE OF THE CONVENTION ON THE PROPORTION OF REPRESENTATION AND VOTES, 394–398.

SPEECH IN THE CONVENTION AT THE CONCLUSION OF ITS DELIBERATIONS, 399–401.

SPEECH IN THE CONVENTION ON THE SUBJECT OF SALARIES, 391–94.

Spencer (Spence), Archibald, BF buys electical apparatus from, 680; BF observes experiments, 712.

Spotswood, Alexander, appoints BF postmaster, 664.

Stamp Act, impossibility of preventing passage of, 77; repeal of, 78–79; opposed by Bernard, 78; Bute exonerated of, 81; BF denies support of, 82; situation before, 112.

Stamp office, BF denies applying to, 160; BF explains rumor of his application, 161–62.

Stanley, John, music admired, 58–59; tutor of Josiah Williams, 123.

Steele, Sir Richard, cited, 400.

Stennet, Samuel, *Discourses on Personal Religion,* 364.

STEVENSON, Margaret, letter to, 88–89; mentioned, 80, 90, 108, 130; death of, 323.

STEVENSON, Mary (Polly), letters to, 29–31, 31–36, 38–42, 57–60, 83–88, 98–100, 106–07, 118–19, 122, 321–22; marriage of, 122; mentioned, 130.

STILES, Ezra, letters to, 136, 438–40.

Stillingfleet, Benjamin, quoted, 550.

Stonehenge, BF views, 725.

Stony Point, New York, 287.

Stove, Franklin (see Pennsylvania fireplace).

Strahan, Margaret Penelope, 63.

STRAHAN, William, letters to, 61–63, 110–15, 165, 300–01, 349–51, 358–62; solicits BF's views, 119–20.

Strange, Isabella, 300.

Streets, paving, 684–85; lighting, 686; cleaning, 686–88.

Stuart, Archibald, medal for, 286.

Stuart, Charles (see Charles I).

Stuart, House of (see James I, Charles I, Charles II, Pretender, Mary II.)

Sturgeon, William, and Negro school, 60.

Sturmy, Samuel, *Mariner's Magazine,* 581.

Sundial, mock instructions for, 548–49.

SUPPLEMENT TO THE BOSTON INDEPENDENT CHRONICLE, 216–24; sends to Adams, 307.

Susquehanna Indians, reply to missionaries, 231–32.

Susquehanna River, 40.

Sweden, seeks relations with United States, 326; and Russo-Turk war, 428.

Swimming, instructions for, 101–04; colds not due to, 146; BF demonstrates, 611.

Switzerland, friendship with France, 261.

Syng, John, death of, 20.

Syng, Philip, 280, 676.

T., Mrs., courted by Ralph and BF, 607.

Tacitus, writings discovered, 281.

TALE, A, 198.

Talmud, 405.

Taxation, diminishes trade revenue, 67–68; right of Congress to impose, 342; assessed on Proprietary estates, 727; equity of on Proprietors, 728.

Taylor, Abraham, 672.

Taylor, Jacob, tribute to, 500; *Ephemerides*, 502.

Tea, resistance to principle of duties, 111; duties not repealed, 119.

Teach, Edward, inspires ballad by BF, 578.

Temple, Sir William, paraphrased, 124.

Ten Commandments, 180.

Tengnagel, Mr., letter on effects of oil on water, 156–57.

Tennent, Gilbert, and subscriptions, 684.

Thales, and calendar, 531.

Thames River, 39–40.

Thermopylæ, 180.

Thévenot, Melchisédech, *Art of Swimming*, 611.

Thomas Aquinas, Saint, 187.

Thomas, George, 671, 676, 677.

THOMPSON, Emma, letter to, 254–57.

THOMSON, Charles, letters to, 76–77, 116–17, 353–54; authenticates financial statement, 329.

Thomson, James, *Seasons*, quoted, 506, 648; poem on Newton quoted, 506; on Locke, 509; on Boyle, 510; on Bacon, 512.

Thomson, Ruth Mather, 77.

Tickell, Mary, 60; Mary Stevenson's difficulties with, 98–99, 107.

Tides, in rivers and canals, 32–36.

Timothy, counseled on wine, 200.

Titan Leeds, astrology hoax, 445, 449–50, 455, 474–76, 481.

Tobacco, mythical origins, 232; and French contract, 342.

"Toleration in Old and New England," BF sends to Samuel Mather, 142.

To the ROYAL ACADEMY OF *****, 212–15.

Townshend Acts, objections to, 111; partial repeal of opposed, 111; tea duties and preamble not repealed, 119.

Tracey, N., Congress indebted to, 292.

Trade, revenue from diminished by taxes, 67–68; colonists accept restrictions on, 110, 113; French opinion of, 303; advantages of free trade, 325–26; various powers seek agreements with United States, 331.

Transportation of convicts, BF proposes to send felons back to Britain, 402–04.

Treasury Board, 107.

Treaty of Paris, ratification of definitive version, 353–54; and payment of creditors, 388.

Trenton, battle of, 179.

Trieste, Italy, and Hungarian commerce, 331–32.

Tryon, Thomas, *Way to Health*, 580, 598.

Tryon, Governor William, takes refuge on H.M.S. *Asia*, 255.

Tubalcain, 143.

TUCKER, Josiah, letters to, 159–60, 160–63; false conclusions about BF, 162.

Tully (see Cicero).

Turin, Italy, 49.

Turkey, war with Russia, 428.

Turkey (bird), as American emblem, 348.

TWELVE COMMANDMENTS, THE, 178–79.

Typesetting, and lead poisoning, 424.

Typography, changes deplored, 42–43, 273, 436–37.

Ulysses, 294.

United Provinces (see Holland).

United States, chess, 188; conditions for peace with Britain, 215–16; frontier with Canada, 215; opportunities in, 236–43; universities in, 236; skilled labor admired in, 237, 239–41; religion in, 243; friendship of France for, 303; importance of friendship with France, 253; and publishing, 361–62; trade interrupted by Britain, 384–86; excesses of press in, 408–10. (See also America, Colonies.)

University of Pennsylvania, grows from Academy, 680.

Valerius Messala, and timekeeping, 522.

VAUGHAN, Benjamin, letters to, 275–77, 423–26, 428–29; publishes *Miscellaneous Pieces*, 275; publishes *Political Works* of BF, 357; paid, 433; letter from, in *Autobiography*, 634–39.

Vaughan, William, 433.

Vegetarianism, BF adopts, 580–81; BF relaxes, 598–99.

Venus, in song, 196.

VERGENNES, Charles Gravier, Comte de, letters to, 294–97, 320–21; Adams fears plots of, 325; and Escurial discoveries, 281; Adams offends, 284–85; letters from, 302; delay of ratification of money contract, 329; opinion of grandson, 330.

Vernon, Samuel, commissions BF to collect debt, 595, 619; BF loans money to Collins, 596–98; BF delays repaying, 616; BF repays, 626.

Versailles, France, BF visits, 85–86.

Vikings, and discovery of America, 294.

Viner, Charles, 357.

Virgil, travestied by Cotton, 588.

Virginia, 57, 284; scalps of inhabitants, 217; pact with Indians, 229; language of Indians, 293–94; land in, 343; William and Mary College, 356; and debts to British slavers, 386–87.

Virtue, aided by religion, 9–10; guide to acquiring, 26–27; and revelation, 619–21; BF's catalogue of, 644–45; method for improving, 646–47; applicable to all religions, 651.

Voltaire, François Marie Arouet, *Treatise on Toleration*, 435.

Wadsworth, James, 305.

Wagons, BF collects for Braddock, 695–99; BF loses money on, 700; BF liable for loss of, 703.

Walker family, genealogy of, 131.

Walterstorff, M., Danish commissioner, 330.

War, satirized, 308; retards progress, 333–34; inferior to commerce, 429.

WARING, John, letter to, 60–61.

WASHINGTON, George, letter to, 279–80; letter of address to desired, 258; military operations approved, 270; title in Cincinnatus medal, 348; success of, 360.

Washington (ship), 320.

Water, effects of oil on, 55–56, 151–59.

WATERHOUSE, Benjamin, letter to, 291–92.

Watson, Joseph, and poetry contest, 600–01; death of, 602.

Watts, Isaac, quoted, 237, 422.

Watts, John, hires BF, 608.

Wayne, Brigadier General Anthony, medal for, 286.

"Way to Wealth, The" (see "Father Abraham's Speech").

Wealth, acquiring, 515–16.

Weather, forecasting in almanacs, 463, 536.

Webb, George, apprentice, 615; Junto member, 622; betrays BF to Keimer, 623.

WEBSTER, Noah, letter to, 433–38; *Dissertation on the English Language*, 433; *Spelling Book*, 438.

WEEMS, Mason Locke, letter to, 354–56; and ordination difficulties, 355–56.

Weiser, Conrad, Indian interpreter, 233.

WEISSENSTEIN, Charles de, letter to, 260–05.

Welfare, Michael, founder of Dunkers, 676.

West, Benjamin, Mr. and Mrs., 88–89, 146.

West Indies, 67; American commerce, 328, 384.

Weymouth, Thomas Thynne, Viscount, secretary for Northern Department, 91.

INDEX

Wharton, Joseph, borrows money from BF, 81.

Wharton, Thomas, 69.

Whately, John, questions BF in Parliament, 162.

Whately, Thomas, Grenville's secretary, 161.

WHATLEY, George, letter to, 364–70.

Whigs, principles forgotten in Britain, 222–23; hated by king, 266.

WHISTLE, THE, 191–93.

Whiston, William, 506; astrological absurdities of, 520.

WHITEFIELD, George, letter to, 105–06; mentioned, 147; building for, 666–67; Georgia orphanage, 667; as speaker and writer, 668–70; relations with BF, 668; meeting house used for Academy, 679, 684.

Whitehaven, England, coal mines, 316.

Whitehead, Paul, author of "Manners," 148.

Whitehead, William, quoted, 59–60.

Wilcox, John, lends BF books, 606.

Wilkes, Israel and Elizabeth, 255.

Wilks, Robert, disparages Ralph's acting, 605.

William and Mary, College of, and education of Iroquois, 229–30; founding, 356.

Williams, Mr., 364.

Williams, John, 77.

Williams, Jonathan, 78, 124, 131, 430.

Williams, Jonathan, Jr., purchases cloth, 283.

Williams, Josiah, tuition of, 123–24, 131.

Williams family, genealogy of, 131.

Williamsburg College (see William and Mary, College of).

Willinck & Co., 340.

Willis, Nathaniel, editor of *Boston Independent Chronicle*, 115, 220.

Wilson, Benjamin, and controversy about lightning rods, 258–59.

Wilton House, BF visits, 725.

Windsor, England, 40.

Wine, St. Paul on, 200; directions for making, 486–88. (See also Drinking.)

Winthrop, John, 167.

Wolfe, General James, 719.

Wollaston, William, *Religion of Nature Delineated*, 606.

Worthylake, George, inspires ballad by BF, 578.

"Wreckers," playlet, 267–68.

Wren, Dr. Thomas, kindness to American prisoners, 332.

Wright, Edward, and BF's experiments, 715.

WRIGHT, John, letter to, 431–33.

Writing, invention of, 519; BF teaches himself, 579–80.

Wygate, John, and swimming, 611.

Wyndham, Charles (see Egremont).

Wyndham, Sir William, and swimming school, 612–13.

Xenophon, *Memorabilia*, 581.

Yale, Elihu, 438.

Yale College, 439; grants BF honorary M.A., 689.

Yankees, British contempt for, 360.

Yates, Mr., 80.

York, Sir Joseph, recipient of John Paul Jones letter, 220; sycophancy of, 224.

York County, Pennsylvania, wagons collected in, 697.

York River, 40.

Yorktown, commemorative medal for battle, 314.

Young, Edward, quoted, 522–23; *Satires*, 607.

Yranda, Marquis d', and payment of Madrid bills, 289.

Zend-Avesta, translation by Anquetil-Duperron, 136.

Zoroaster, and translation of *Zend-Avesta*, 136.

LIBRARY OF CONGRESS CATALOGING-IN-PUBLICATION DATA

Franklin, Benjamin, 1706–1790.
  [Selections. 1997]
  Autobiography, Poor Richard, and later writings, 1757–1790 / Benjamin
Franklin.
      p.   cm.
  Other title information: London, 1757–1775, Paris, 1776–1785,
Philadelphia, 1785–1790, Poor Richard's almanack, 1733–1758, The
autobiography.
  "J. A. Leo Lemay wrote the notes and selected the texts for this
volume"—P. facing verso t.p.
  Includes index.
  ISBN 1–883011–53–1
  1. United States—Politics and government—To 1775.   2. United
States—Politics and government—1775–1783.   3. Franklin, Benjamin,
1706–1790.   4. Statesmen—United States—Biography.   I. Lemay,
J. A. Leo (Joseph A. Leo), 1935–   .   II. Title.   III. Title:
Autobiography   IV. Title: Poor Richard's almanack.
  E302.F82   1997   97–21611
  973.2—dc21   CIP

THE LIBRARY OF AMERICA SERIES

The Library of America fosters appreciation and pride in America's literary heritage by publishing, and keeping permanently in print, authoritative editions of America's best and most significant writing. An independent nonprofit organization, it was founded in 1979 with seed funding from the National Endowment for the Humanities and the Ford Foundation.

1. Herman Melville: *Typee, Omoo, Mardi*
2. Nathaniel Hawthorne: *Tales and Sketches*
3. Walt Whitman: *Poetry and Prose*
4. Harriet Beecher Stowe: *Three Novels*
5. Mark Twain: *Mississippi Writings*
6. Jack London: *Novels and Stories*
7. Jack London: *Novels and Social Writings*
8. William Dean Howells: *Novels 1875–1886*
9. Herman Melville: *Redburn, White-Jacket, Moby-Dick*
10. Nathaniel Hawthorne: *Collected Novels*
11. Francis Parkman: *France and England in North America*, Vol. I
12. Francis Parkman: *France and England in North America*, Vol. II
13. Henry James: *Novels 1871–1880*
14. Henry Adams: *Novels, Mont Saint Michel, The Education*
15. Ralph Waldo Emerson: *Essays and Lectures*
16. Washington Irving: *History, Tales and Sketches*
17. Thomas Jefferson: *Writings*
18. Stephen Crane: *Prose and Poetry*
19. Edgar Allan Poe: *Poetry and Tales*
20. Edgar Allan Poe: *Essays and Reviews*
21. Mark Twain: *The Innocents Abroad, Roughing It*
22. Henry James: *Literary Criticism: Essays, American & English Writers*
23. Henry James: *Literary Criticism: European Writers & The Prefaces*
24. Herman Melville: *Pierre, Israel Potter, The Confidence-Man, Tales & Billy Budd*
25. William Faulkner: *Novels 1930–1935*
26. James Fenimore Cooper: *The Leatherstocking Tales*, Vol. I
27. James Fenimore Cooper: *The Leatherstocking Tales*, Vol. II
28. Henry David Thoreau: *A Week, Walden, The Maine Woods, Cape Cod*
29. Henry James: *Novels 1881–1886*
30. Edith Wharton: *Novels*
31. Henry Adams: *History of the U.S. during the Administrations of Jefferson*
32. Henry Adams: *History of the U.S. during the Administrations of Madison*
33. Frank Norris: *Novels and Essays*
34. W.E.B. Du Bois: *Writings*
35. Willa Cather: *Early Novels and Stories*
36. Theodore Dreiser: *Sister Carrie, Jennie Gerhardt, Twelve Men*
37a. Benjamin Franklin: *Silence Dogood, The Busy-Body, & Early Writings*
37b. Benjamin Franklin: *Autobiography, Poor Richard, & Later Writings*
38. William James: *Writings 1902–1910*
39. Flannery O'Connor: *Collected Works*
40. Eugene O'Neill: *Complete Plays 1913–1920*
41. Eugene O'Neill: *Complete Plays 1920–1931*
42. Eugene O'Neill: *Complete Plays 1932–1943*
43. Henry James: *Novels 1886–1890*
44. William Dean Howells: *Novels 1886–1888*
45. Abraham Lincoln: *Speeches and Writings 1832–1858*
46. Abraham Lincoln: *Speeches and Writings 1859–1865*
47. Edith Wharton: *Novellas and Other Writings*
48. William Faulkner: *Novels 1936–1940*
49. Willa Cather: *Later Novels*
50. Ulysses S. Grant: *Memoirs and Selected Letters*
51. William Tecumseh Sherman: *Memoirs*
52. Washington Irving: *Bracebridge Hall, Tales of a Traveller, The Alhambra*
53. Francis Parkman: *The Oregon Trail, The Conspiracy of Pontiac*
54. James Fenimore Cooper: *Sea Tales: The Pilot, The Red Rover*
55. Richard Wright: *Early Works*
56. Richard Wright: *Later Works*
57. Willa Cather: *Stories, Poems, and Other Writings*
58. William James: *Writings 1878–1899*
59. Sinclair Lewis: *Main Street & Babbitt*
60. Mark Twain: *Collected Tales, Sketches, Speeches, & Essays 1852–1890*
61. Mark Twain: *Collected Tales, Sketches, Speeches, & Essays 1891–1910*
62. *The Debate on the Constitution: Part One*
63. *The Debate on the Constitution: Part Two*
64. Henry James: *Collected Travel Writings: Great Britain & America*
65. Henry James: *Collected Travel Writings: The Continent*

66. *American Poetry: The Nineteenth Century*, Vol. 1
67. *American Poetry: The Nineteenth Century*, Vol. 2
68. Frederick Douglass: *Autobiographies*
69. Sarah Orne Jewett: *Novels and Stories*
70. Ralph Waldo Emerson: *Collected Poems and Translations*
71. Mark Twain: *Historical Romances*
72. John Steinbeck: *Novels and Stories 1932–1937*
73. William Faulkner: *Novels 1942–1954*
74. Zora Neale Hurston: *Novels and Stories*
75. Zora Neale Hurston: *Folklore, Memoirs, and Other Writings*
76. Thomas Paine: *Collected Writings*
77. *Reporting World War II: American Journalism 1938–1944*
78. *Reporting World War II: American Journalism 1944–1946*
79. Raymond Chandler: *Stories and Early Novels*
80. Raymond Chandler: *Later Novels and Other Writings*
81. Robert Frost: *Collected Poems, Prose, & Plays*
82. Henry James: *Complete Stories 1892–1898*
83. Henry James: *Complete Stories 1898–1910*
84. William Bartram: *Travels and Other Writings*
85. John Dos Passos: *U.S.A.*
86. John Steinbeck: *The Grapes of Wrath and Other Writings 1936–1941*
87. Vladimir Nabokov: *Novels and Memoirs 1941–1951*
88. Vladimir Nabokov: *Novels 1955–1962*
89. Vladimir Nabokov: *Novels 1969–1974*
90. James Thurber: *Writings and Drawings*
91. George Washington: *Writings*
92. John Muir: *Nature Writings*
93. Nathanael West: *Novels and Other Writings*
94. *Crime Novels: American Noir of the 1930s and 40s*
95. *Crime Novels: American Noir of the 1950s*
96. Wallace Stevens: *Collected Poetry and Prose*
97. James Baldwin: *Early Novels and Stories*
98. James Baldwin: *Collected Essays*
99. Gertrude Stein: *Writings 1903–1932*
100. Gertrude Stein: *Writings 1932–1946*
101. Eudora Welty: *Complete Novels*
102. Eudora Welty: *Stories, Essays, & Memoir*
103. Charles Brockden Brown: *Three Gothic Novels*
104. *Reporting Vietnam: American Journalism 1959–1969*
105. *Reporting Vietnam: American Journalism 1969–1975*
106. Henry James: *Complete Stories 1874–1884*
107. Henry James: *Complete Stories 1884–1891*
108. *American Sermons: The Pilgrims to Martin Luther King Jr.*
109. James Madison: *Writings*
110. Dashiell Hammett: *Complete Novels*
111. Henry James: *Complete Stories 1864–1874*
112. William Faulkner: *Novels 1957–1962*
113. John James Audubon: *Writings & Drawings*
114. *Slave Narratives*
115. *American Poetry: The Twentieth Century*, Vol. 1
116. *American Poetry: The Twentieth Century*, Vol. 2
117. F. Scott Fitzgerald: *Novels and Stories 1920–1922*
118. Henry Wadsworth Longfellow: *Poems and Other Writings*
119. Tennessee Williams: *Plays 1937–1955*
120. Tennessee Williams: *Plays 1957–1980*
121. Edith Wharton: *Collected Stories 1891–1910*
122. Edith Wharton: *Collected Stories 1911–1937*
123. *The American Revolution: Writings from the War of Independence*
124. Henry David Thoreau: *Collected Essays and Poems*
125. Dashiell Hammett: *Crime Stories and Other Writings*
126. Dawn Powell: *Novels 1930–1942*
127. Dawn Powell: *Novels 1944–1962*
128. Carson McCullers: *Complete Novels*
129. Alexander Hamilton: *Writings*
130. Mark Twain: *The Gilded Age and Later Novels*
131. Charles W. Chesnutt: *Stories, Novels, and Essays*
132. John Steinbeck: *Novels 1942–1952*
133. Sinclair Lewis: *Arrowsmith, Elmer Gantry, Dodsworth*
134. Paul Bowles: *The Sheltering Sky, Let It Come Down, The Spider's House*
135. Paul Bowles: *Collected Stories & Later Writings*
136. Kate Chopin: *Complete Novels & Stories*
137. *Reporting Civil Rights: American Journalism 1941–1963*
138. *Reporting Civil Rights: American Journalism 1963–1973*
139. Henry James: *Novels 1896–1899*
140. Theodore Dreiser: *An American Tragedy*
141. Saul Bellow: *Novels 1944–1953*
142. John Dos Passos: *Novels 1920–1925*

143. John Dos Passos: *Travel Books and Other Writings*
144. Ezra Pound: *Poems and Translations*
145. James Weldon Johnson: *Writings*
146. Washington Irving: *Three Western Narratives*
147. Alexis de Tocqueville: *Democracy in America*
148. James T. Farrell: *Studs Lonigan: A Trilogy*
149. Isaac Bashevis Singer: *Collected Stories I*
150. Isaac Bashevis Singer: *Collected Stories II*
151. Isaac Bashevis Singer: *Collected Stories III*
152. Kaufman & Co.: *Broadway Comedies*
153. Theodore Roosevelt: *The Rough Riders, An Autobiography*
154. Theodore Roosevelt: *Letters and Speeches*
155. H. P. Lovecraft: *Tales*
156. Louisa May Alcott: *Little Women, Little Men, Jo's Boys*
157. Philip Roth: *Novels & Stories 1959–1962*
158. Philip Roth: *Novels 1967–1972*
159. James Agee: *Let Us Now Praise Famous Men, A Death in the Family*
160. James Agee: *Film Writing & Selected Journalism*
161. Richard Henry Dana Jr.: *Two Years Before the Mast & Other Voyages*
162. Henry James: *Novels 1901–1902*
163. Arthur Miller: *Collected Plays 1944–1961*
164. William Faulkner: *Novels 1926–1929*
165. Philip Roth: *Novels 1973–1977*
166. *American Speeches: Part One*
167. *American Speeches: Part Two*
168. Hart Crane: *Complete Poems & Selected Letters*
169. Saul Bellow: *Novels 1956–1964*
170. John Steinbeck: *Travels with Charley and Later Novels*
171. Capt. John Smith: *Writings with Other Narratives*
172. Thornton Wilder: *Collected Plays & Writings on Theater*
173. Philip K. Dick: *Four Novels of the 1960s*
174. Jack Kerouac: *Road Novels 1957–1960*
175. Philip Roth: *Zuckerman Bound*
176. Edmund Wilson: *Literary Essays & Reviews of the 1920s & 30s*
177. Edmund Wilson: *Literary Essays & Reviews of the 1930s & 40s*
178. *American Poetry: The 17th & 18th Centuries*
179. William Maxwell: *Early Novels & Stories*
180. Elizabeth Bishop: *Poems, Prose, & Letters*
181. A. J. Liebling: *World War II Writings*
182s. *American Earth: Environmental Writing Since Thoreau*
183. Philip K. Dick: *Five Novels of the 1960s & 70s*
184. William Maxwell: *Later Novels & Stories*
185. Philip Roth: *Novels & Other Narratives 1986–1991*
186. Katherine Anne Porter: *Collected Stories & Other Writings*
187. John Ashbery: *Collected Poems 1956–1987*
188. John Cheever: *Collected Stories & Other Writings*
189. John Cheever: *Complete Novels*
190. Lafcadio Hearn: *American Writings*
191. A. J. Liebling: *The Sweet Science & Other Writings*
192s. *The Lincoln Anthology: Great Writers on His Life and Legacy from 1860 to Now*
193. Philip K. Dick: *VALIS & Later Novels*
194. Thornton Wilder: *The Bridge of San Luis Rey and Other Novels 1926–1948*
195. Raymond Carver: *Collected Stories*
196. *American Fantastic Tales: Terror and the Uncanny from Poe to the Pulps*
197. *American Fantastic Tales: Terror and the Uncanny from the 1940s to Now*
198. John Marshall: *Writings*
199s. *The Mark Twain Anthology: Great Writers on His Life and Works*
200. Mark Twain: *A Tramp Abroad, Following the Equator, Other Travels*
201. Ralph Waldo Emerson: *Selected Journals 1820–1842*
202. Ralph Waldo Emerson: *Selected Journals 1841–1877*
203. *The American Stage: Writing on Theater from Washington Irving to Tony Kushner*
204. Shirley Jackson: *Novels & Stories*
205. Philip Roth: *Novels 1993–1995*
206. H. L. Mencken: *Prejudices: First, Second, and Third Series*
207. H. L. Mencken: *Prejudices: Fourth, Fifth, and Sixth Series*
208. John Kenneth Galbraith: *The Affluent Society and Other Writings 1952–1967*
209. Saul Bellow: *Novels 1970–1982*
210. Lynd Ward: *Gods' Man, Madman's Drum, Wild Pilgrimage*
211. Lynd Ward: *Prelude to a Million Years, Song Without Words, Vertigo*
212. *The Civil War: The First Year Told by Those Who Lived It*
213. John Adams: *Revolutionary Writings 1755–1775*
214. John Adams: *Revolutionary Writings 1775–1783*
215. Henry James: *Novels 1903–1911*
216. Kurt Vonnegut: *Novels & Stories 1963–1973*

217. *Harlem Renaissance: Five Novels of the 1920s*

218. *Harlem Renaissance: Four Novels of the 1930s*

219. Ambrose Bierce: *The Devil's Dictionary, Tales, & Memoirs*

220. Philip Roth: *The American Trilogy 1997–2000*

221. *The Civil War: The Second Year Told by Those Who Lived It*

222. Barbara W. Tuchman: *The Guns of August & The Proud Tower*

223. Arthur Miller: *Collected Plays 1964–1982*

224. Thornton Wilder: *The Eighth Day, Theophilus North, Autobiographical Writings*

225. David Goodis: *Five Noir Novels of the 1940s & 50s*

226. Kurt Vonnegut: *Novels & Stories 1950–1962*

227. *American Science Fiction: Four Classic Novels 1953–1956*

228. *American Science Fiction: Five Classic Novels 1956–1958*

229. Laura Ingalls Wilder: *The Little House Books, Volume One*

230. Laura Ingalls Wilder: *The Little House Books, Volume Two*

231. Jack Kerouac: *Collected Poems*

232. *The War of 1812: Writings from America's Second War of Independence*

233. *American Antislavery Writings: Colonial Beginnings to Emancipation*

234. *The Civil War: The Third Year Told by Those Who Lived It*

235. Sherwood Anderson: *Collected Stories*

236. Philip Roth: *Novels 2001–2007*

237. Philip Roth: *Nemeses*

238. Aldo Leopold: *A Sand County Almanac & Other Writings on Ecology and Conservation*

239. May Swenson: *Collected Poems*

240. W. S. Merwin: *Collected Poems 1952–1993*

241. W. S. Merwin: *Collected Poems 1996–2011*

242. John Updike: *Collected Early Stories*

243. John Updike: *Collected Later Stories*

244. Ring Lardner: *Stories & Other Writings*

245. Jonathan Edwards: *Writings from the Great Awakening*

246. Susan Sontag: *Essays of the 1960s & 70s*

247. William Wells Brown: *Clotel & Other Writings*

248. Bernard Malamud: *Novels and Stories of the 1940s & 50s*

249. Bernard Malamud: *Novels and Stories of the 1960s*

250. *The Civil War: The Final Year Told by Those Who Lived It*

251. *Shakespeare in America: An Anthology from the Revolution to Now*

252. Kurt Vonnegut: *Novels 1976–1985*

253. *American Musicals 1927–1949: The Complete Books & Lyrics of Eight Broadway Classics*

254. *American Musicals 1950–1969: The Complete Books & Lyrics of Eight Broadway Classics*

255. Elmore Leonard: *Four Novels of the 1970s*

256. Louisa May Alcott: *Work, Eight Cousins, Rose in Bloom, Stories & Other Writings*

257. H. L. Mencken: *The Days Trilogy, Expanded Edition*

258. Virgil Thomson: *Music Chronicles 1940–1954*

259. *Art in America 1945–1970: Writings from the Age of Abstract Expressionism, Pop Art, and Minimalism*

260. Saul Bellow: *Novels 1984–2000*

261. Arthur Miller: *Collected Plays 1987–2004*

262. Jack Kerouac: *Visions of Cody, Visions of Gerard, Big Sur*

263. Reinhold Niebuhr: *Major Works on Religion and Politics*

264. Ross Macdonald: *Four Novels of the 1950s*

265. *The American Revolution: Writings from the Pamphlet Debate, Volume I, 1764–1772*

266. *The American Revolution: Writings from the Pamphlet Debate, Volume II, 1773–1776*

267. Elmore Leonard: *Four Novels of the 1980s*

268. *Women Crime Writers: Four Suspense Novels of the 1940s*

269. *Women Crime Writers: Four Suspense Novels of the 1950s*

270. Frederick Law Olmsted: *Writings on Landscape, Culture, and Society*

271. Edith Wharton: *Four Novels of the 1920s*

272. James Baldwin: *Later Novels*

To subscribe to the series or to order individual copies, please visit www.loa.org or call (800) 964-5778.

This book is set in 10 point Linotron Galliard,
a face designed for photocomposition by Matthew Carter
and based on the sixteenth-century face Granjon. The paper
is acid-free lightweight opaque and meets the requirements
for permanence of the American National Standards Institute.
The binding material is Brillianta, a woven rayon cloth made
by Van Heek–Scholco Textielfabrieken, Holland. Composition
by The Clarinda Company. Printing and binding
by Edwards Brothers Malloy, Ann Arbor.
Designed by Bruce Campbell.

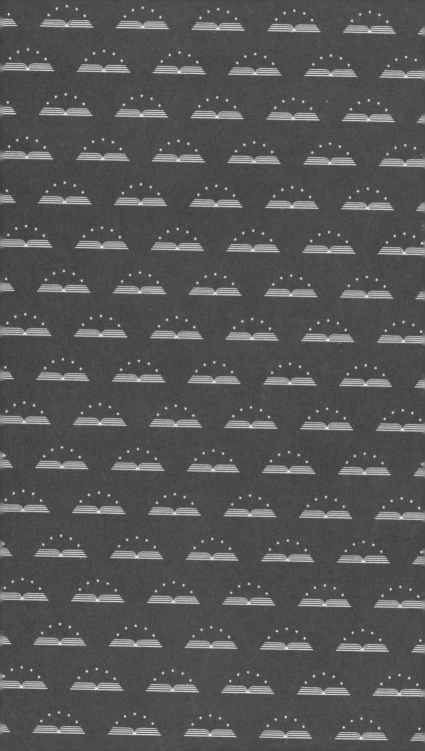